LEGAL, MORAL, AND METAPHYSICAL TRUTHS

Legal, Moral, and Metaphysical Truths

The Philosophy of Michael S. Moore

Edited by
KIMBERLY KESSLER FERZAN
University of Virginia
STEPHEN J. MORSE
University of Pennsylvania

OXFORD
UNIVERSITY PRESS

OXFORD
UNIVERSITY PRESS

Great Clarendon Street, Oxford, OX2 6DP,
United Kingdom

Oxford University Press is a department of the University of Oxford.
It furthers the University's objective of excellence in research, scholarship,
and education by publishing worldwide. Oxford is a registered trade mark of
Oxford University Press in the UK and in certain other countries

First Edition published in 2016

Impression: 1

Published in the United States of America by Oxford University Press
198 Madison Avenue, New York, NY 10016, United States of America

British Library Cataloguing in Publication Data
Data available

Library of Congress Control Number: 2015951309

ISBN 978–0–19–870324–2

Printed and bound by
CPI Group (UK) Ltd, Croydon, CR0 4YY

For my parents—K. K. F.
For Elisabeth A. Morse—S. J. M.

Table of Contents

List of Contributors

Larry Alexander is Warren Distinguished Professor of Law and Co-Director of the Institute for Law and Philosophy at the University of San Diego.

Mitchell N. Berman is the Leon Meltzer Professor of Law, Professor of Philosophy, and Co-Director of the Institute for Law and Philosophy at the University of Pennsylvania.

Brian H. Bix is the Frederick W. Thomas Professor of Law and Philosophy at the University of Minnesota.

R. A. Duff is Professor of Philosophy Emeritus at Stirling University.

Kimberly Kessler Ferzan is Harrison Robertson Professor of Law and Caddell and Chapman Professor of Law at the University of Virginia.

Richard Fumerton is F. Wendell Miller Professor of Philosophy at the University of Iowa.

Leslie Green is the Professor of the Philosophy of Law at the University of Oxford, and a Fellow of Balliol College. He is also Professor of Law and Distinguished University Fellow at Queen's University in Canada.

Heidi M. Hurd is David C. Baum Professor and former Dean of the College of Law, Professor of Philosophy, and Co-Director of the Program in Law and Philosophy at the University of Illinois at Urbana-Champaign.

Douglas Husak is Distinguished Professor of Philosophy at Rutgers University and Co-Director of the Institute for Law and Philosophy at Rutgers University.

Leo Katz is Frank Carano Professor of Law at the University of Pennsylvania.

Phillip Montague is Professor of Philosophy Emeritus at Western Washington University.

Michael S. Moore is Charles R. Walgreen University Chair at the University of Illinois. He is also Professor of Law, Professor of Philosophy, Professor of the Center for Advanced Studies, and Co-Director of the Program in Law and Philosophy at the University of Illinois at Urbana-Champaign.

Stephen J. Morse is Ferdinand Wakeman Hubbell Professor of Law, Professor of Psychology and Law in Psychiatry, and Associate Director of the Center for Neuroscience and Society at the University of Pennsylvania.

John Oberdiek is Acting Co-Dean and Professor at the Rutgers Law School, and Co-Director of the Institute for Law and Philosophy at Rutgers University.

Michael H. Shapiro is Dorothy W. Nelson Professor of Law at the University of Southern California.

Kenneth W. Simons is Chancellor's Professor of Law, University of California, Irvine School of Law.

Horacio Spector is Professor of Law and former Dean and former Provost at the Universidad Torcuato Di Tella in Buenos Aires. He is also Professor of Law at the University of San Diego.

Victor Tadros is Professor of Law at Warwick University.

Jeremy Waldron is University Professor, Professor of Philosophy, and Professor of Law at New York University.

Peter Westen is Frank G. Millard Professor of Law Emeritus at the University of Michigan, Ann Arbor.

Richard W. Wright is University Distinguished Professor and Professor of Law at the Illinois Institute of Technology Chicago-Kent College of Law.

Gideon Yaffe is Professor of Law, Professor of Philosophy, and Professor of Psychology at Yale.

1

Editors' Introduction

Kimberly Kessler Ferzan and *Stephen J. Morse*

Ordinarily, the editors' introduction to a festschrift would both systematize the honoree's work and taxonomize the contributions. But anyone who knows the dynamic duo of Heidi Hurd and Michael Moore will fully understand that both of them have beaten us to the punch. Heidi's contribution, "Living with Genius," details Michael's life's work, setting forth not only his arguments, but also their causal antecedents. It is an unadorned and unabashed look at the man behind this monumental body of work, full of both triumphs and sadness. To explore not only what Michael has written but who he is, we refer you to her contribution.

Our other duty would have been to cast the remaining contributions in order. Of course, Michael has done this in his reply. So, we shall only restate, without taking any credit for his systemization. After Heidi's contribution, this volume engages with Michael's work in criminal law. Michael, famous for his retributivism, is taken to task by three friendly critics, who seek to elucidate retributivism's value in a theory of punishment, and to unpack its dimensions (Mitchell Berman, "Modest Retributivism"; Douglas Husak, "What Do Criminals Deserve?"; Peter Westen, "Retributive Desert as Fair Play"). From here, the contributions turn to Michael's theory of criminalization, asking whether and in what form the fact that an action is morally wrong can appropriately serve as the reason why the conduct ought to be prohibited by the criminal law (Victor Tadros, "The Wrong and the Free"; Antony Duff, "Legal Moralism and Public Wrongs").

Next, the volume addresses Michael's work in the various aspects of the general part of the criminal law. Chapters consider Michael's position on how to understand criminal acts for double jeopardy purposes; Michael's claim that accomplice liability is superfluous; and Michael's views about the culpability of negligence and the relationship between that view and proximate causation (Gideon Yaffe, "Moore in Jeopardy, Again"; Leo Katz, "Do We Need a Doctrine of Complicity?"; Kenneth Simons, "Reluctant Pluralist: Moore on Negligence"; John Oberdiek, "Putting (and Keeping) Proximate Cause in its Place"). Three further contributions press Michael on his claims with respect to the metaphysics of causation (Richard Wright, "Causation: Metaphysics or Intuition?"; Horacio Spector, "The Moral Asymmetry Between Acts and Omissions"; Richard Fumerton, "Moore and the Metaphysics of Causation").

Michael has also greatly contributed to our understanding of justifications and excuses. Continuing the engagement with the general part, one of the volume editors presses him for more details about self-defense, the other questions conclusions reached within Michael's vast work at the intersection of psychiatry, cognitive neuroscience, and criminal law (Kimberly Kessler Ferzan, "Self-Defense: Tell Me Moore"; Stephen J. Morse, "Moore on the Mind").

As though conquering act, mind, causation, and justifications and excuses were not sufficient for his life's work, Michael has also elucidated the deontological theory that his theories presuppose. Two further contributors take on delineating the nature of this deontological morality. (Larry Alexander, "The Means Principle"; Phillip Montague, "Moral Dilemmas and Moral Theory: Toward a Viable Deontology"). Leaving no stone unturned, Moore also has meta-ethical views about these moral positions, which are challenged in a further contribution (Jeremy Waldron, "Just No Damned Good").

As is readily apparent, Michael does not conquer a topic unless he conquers all aspects of that topic. Hence, this already impressive body of work would cover (1) a meta-ethical view; (2) a position on the content of moral obligations; (3) a stance on the implications of that content for the criminal law, both in terms of what to punish and why; (4) a theory of mental states fully informed by the cognitive sciences; (5) a view on voluntary actions, backed by action theory; and (6) claims about the nature of causation, contextualized within a full metaphysical theory. But that would leave us without the role of the criminal law in a system of *laws*, and Michael's expansive reach includes contributions to general jurisprudence as well. Hence, the final group of contributions concludes with Moore's view about statutory interpretation and the role of a judge (Michael Shapiro, "Conceptual Breakage and Reconstruction: Michael S. Moore's Natural-Law Theory of Interpretation"; Brian Bix, "Metaphysical Realism and Legal Reasoning"; Leslie Green, "Law and the Role of a Judge").

We've also granted Michael the last word (Michael S. Moore, "Responses and Appreciations").

But we shall take the first last words here.

Kim: No one who witnessed the first few interactions I had with Michael would ever think that I would play a role in this festschrift. Michael first spoke to me when Heidi had a potluck dinner for her Torts students at their home in October 1992. As I was placing my cheesecake on the table, Michael came up to me and said, "Hi, I'm Michael." I (ever fearful of grown-ups), smiled, nodded, and (hopefully gracefully) walked away. Our second and third interactions were in the spring of 1993, when I took Michael's class, "Legal Personhood." During or after class, our two interactions were (1) my musing as to whether animals have mental states because my cat at the time clearly dreamed, and (2) my querying what Michael thought about the view that we could just be brains in a vat (blame my dad, he raised it when I was ten, and I have never fully gotten over it). All I can say is that I wish Michael had just smiled, nodded, and gracefully walked away. I am sure he was surprised when I did well in that class.

But taking Legal Personhood at the same time I was taking Criminal Law with Stephen was momentous and life-changing for me. My love of all things criminal law, and all things philosophy, is directly attributable to the joy I found in those puzzles that semester. Had I not taken those two classes, I would never have found this path.

On this path, Michael is my lodestar. For him, there is no puzzle too deep, no query too wide, no discipline too tall that they should not be conquered. And, the reason is simple. He seeks truth.

Over the years, one truth I have had to face is that part of the reason that he manages the taxonomizing, systemizing, and other discipline-resolving that he does is that he is just smarter than many of us mere mortals. Anyone who has attended a conference with him has witnessed with awe that moment when Michael deftly summarizes what appeared to be an hour of scattered discussion. I used to think that was just what senior scholars did until another senior scholar remarked to me how tremendous it was that Michael can do this because he is so absurdly smart. So, maybe I'll never leap tall disciplines in a single bound, as he does. Though, I maintain, we should all try …

Most of all, I am just grateful that the distributor of eye-rolling in Legal Personhood turned to mentor for my student note, evolved to colleague, and ultimately became a good friend. Whether he's teasing me about an incident in Death Valley (it's a long story) or I'm smack talking him during a game of poker or pool, it's just been tremendous fun to know the person beyond the work.

Stephen: I second everything Kim said about Michael, who has been my good friend and colleague for four decades (where have the years gone?). It is always intellectually and personally invaluable to spend time with Michael, whether we are at a conference, hiking the Grand Canyon rim to rim, running the San Francisco Marathon, or just hanging out to watch USC football. As Kim says, his intellect is simply extraordinary, but he is also a great bon vivant, as the contributors to this volume know. Michael is no unidimensional brain in a skull.

Here's a recent anecdote that sums Michael up. It will surprise no one who knows him or has ever seen Michael in action. A few years ago, a philosopher in Aachen, Germany organized at the local university a conference to celebrate Michael's causation book. The invited speakers were luminaries from Germany, England, and other places. The format was for each speaker to present their papers, which Michael had not seen previously, for about 45 minutes, followed by Michael's response and then some general discussion. Most of the papers were technical and difficult. There were probably six or seven papers the first day. Recall that Michael was hearing these presentations for the first time. The generic Moorean response went as follows. "[Polite thank you.] Your paper makes three major arguments, each of which has three sub-arguments. Let's take them in turn." Then, in perfect sentences and paragraphs, with no misspeaking or empty interjections, Michael would dissect the paper, after having offered the presenter a better organization and argument structure than the presenter realized he had. This was true of Michael's response to every paper. At the end of the day, the obviously bedazzled organizer came up to me and asked, "Is Michael always this good?" I mused for a second and responded straightfaced, that no, he's usually much better but he's jet-lagged after the long flight from Australia. The poor organizer had no idea whether I was kidding or serious. By the end of the two-and-a-half days of exactly the same extraordinary level of Moorean performance, the organizer knew that I had been dead serious. And at the conclusion of the conference, rather than collapsing, Michael suggested that we repair to the finest, ritziest restaurant in Aachen, located in a luxurious, imperial-style hotel. We ate a most satisfying, one might even say extravagant, dinner, accompanied by an exquisite Bordeaux that Michael had chosen.

Michael's exceptional organizing talents deserve special mention. He, and also our mutual friend, Larry Alexander, have organized numerous criminal law theory conferences that have been the most intellectually stimulating meetings I have ever attended. Michael knows how to structure a conference as well as a general conversation. Michael has been the unofficial leader of a group of scholars who think of themselves primarily as criminal law theorists and many of the contributors to this volume have benefitted enormously from frequent attendance and interaction with Michael. We are all in his debt.

Let us both conclude with some general thanks. We owe a great debt to our co-conspirator, Heidi Hurd, with whom we consulted from the beginning. We were particularly delighted that she organized a conference for Michael's 70th birthday, where the agenda for the day was—what else?—a somewhat less formal conference devoted to his work. Although Michael knew the topic, little did he know that the papers presented were intended for this festschrift in his honor. Our birthday present to Michael was to surprise him with this volume, which had recently been accepted by Oxford. We could not have done it without Heidi's masterful ingenuity.

Finally, we share Michael's belief that people ought to get what they deserve. So, celebrating Michael's work is not gratuitous; it is simply the right thing to do. We are delighted that the book has come to such fine fruition and warmly thank the scholars who have contributed. It is a fitting tribute to our friend, Michael Moore. We can think of no one more deserving.

2

Living with Genius

The Life and Work of Michael S. Moore

*Heidi M. Hurd**

I. Introduction

During my many years with Michael Moore—years that reached from my first semester in law school at the University of Southern California (USC) where he was my first-year Torts professor, through years of marriage, co-parenthood, co-authorship, and colleagueship—I have enjoyed countless, indeed daily, spirited debates. We have argued about such things as the nature of causation, the possibility of free will, the coherence of compatibilism, the demands of retributivism, the scope of legitimate consequentialist reasoning, the morality of mercy, and the question that is always good for a round or two over a glass of wine: whether angels are angelic because they do the good in the face of being tempted by the bad, or because they are not tempted by the bad at all. Quite frankly, I'm exhausted. If I were to pick some new philosophical fight with Michael, I would have to dedicate the next six months of breakfasts, lunches, dinners, and dates to defending my views on the topic—and, more onerously, to listening to his views, all of which would come in enumerated parts, with multiple sections and subsections—to the exclusion of hearing about our children's school days, discussing the latest necessary home repair, or gossiping about our colleagues. I simply don't have it in me.

So, instead, I have chosen to do something with which Michael cannot argue. In this introductory contribution, I will synthesize Michael's lifetime of work, organizing the topics and restating the theses that he has defended within the diverse fields he has explored, and extracting from these theses a number of common themes. Along the way, I will draw on personal experiences in Michael's life that may have influenced his scholarly choices. On pain of committing the genetic fallacy against which Michael has often warned,[1] one cannot think that explaining beliefs in terms of their causal antecedents goes any distance towards either bolstering or debunking them. Still, the causal antecedents of beliefs can be interesting for their own sake. So my project is to provide a systematic and comprehensive taxonomy of Michael's work and to salt it with biographical events, relationships, triumphs, and tragedies that illuminate how personal the ideas that have defined his extraordinary academic legacy have been.[2]

* I have enjoyed a great deal of help from Michael in writing this piece. I have also put up with a lot of back-talk. I am grateful for the former. I am also grateful to Caitlyn McCutcheon (Illinois Class of 2014) for her extensive research assistance—which was provided without nearly as much back-talk.

1 Moore, 1982a; Moore, 1984a; Moore, 1997b, ch. 3; Moore, 2004c, ch. 1.

2 Some of the experiences I will relate are from my own knowledge, having shared Michael's life all these years; others I have explicitly solicited from him in conversations recorded in recent months.

II. Topics Raised and Theses Defended in the Scholarship of Michael Moore

It is no small task to get one's arms around the work of a career that has spanned forty-nine years and produced 138 publications covering a dizzying array of issues. Fortunately, some years ago Michael himself provided something of a roadmap to his own work when paying tribute to his thirteen years on the faculty of the USC Law School.[3] At the risk of costing our family a month of dinners spent debating the merits of so doing, I have taken the liberty of reorganizing Michael's own taxonomy, altering the number and content of the categories to which his writings can be assigned, and updating the references to accommodate the fourteen years of work that Michael has done since writing his Southern California "remembrance."

A. The metaphysics of mind, action, and causation

Although Michael often presents his work on the metaphysics of human action, mental states, and causation as if his interests in these areas were entirely motivated by the role such states, events, and relations play in ascribing responsibility, in fact his interest in metaphysics is as much free-standing as it is dependent upon his moral and legal interests. He regards acts and other events, mental states like intention and belief, and relations such as causation, as presenting puzzles worthy of attention in their own right. I have thus separated Michael's work in pure metaphysics from his application of that work to responsibility issues (which I deal with below as his fourth area of scholarly interest).[4]

Michael's main preoccupation in the metaphysics of mind, action, and causation has been to naturalize phenomena often seen as recalcitrant to ordinary scientific description and explanation. These phenomena have included: the Intentionality of mental states and of some actions;[5] the supposed mystery of human agency and the actions through which that agency is expressed; causation (both *of* human choice and *by* human choice) as a natural relation; the entities causation relates as natural entities; causal laws as framed in terms of induction about such natural entities and relations; and counterfactual dependence as a natural relation in this, the actual world (despite counterfactuals having on their face seemingly "otherwordly" qualities).

Michael has long been fascinated by what many regard as the hardest problem in the philosophy of mind, namely how content is to be ascribed to Intentional mental

[3] Moore, 2000d.

[4] Some commentators on Michael's work treat it as a contribution to metaphysics independent of its implications for legal and moral responsibility. For example, Stephen Mumford wrote: "Moore's book [*Causation and Responsibility*] is an outstanding contribution not just to the philosophy of law but also to the metaphysics of causation." Stephen Mumford, "Causes for Laws," 4 *Jurisprudence* 109 (2013), 114.

[5] "Intentionality" or "Intentional states" are technical terms referring to representational states that have content. These terms are capitalized to distinguish them from the more idiomatic use of the term "intentional" which refers to just one kind of Intentional state, namely intentions. Beliefs and desires are Intentional states because they have content, despite, of course, not being intentions. This usage of "Intentional" was revived by Roderick Chisholm in *Perceiving* (Ithaca, NY: Cornell University Press, 1959).

states.[6] Early in his career, he explored Quinean skepticism about such content.[7] He then tentatively proposed the very non-Quinean solution that propositions (rather than events or sentences) form the content of what Russell dubbed the "propositional attitudes."[8] These explorations in the content of Intentional states have been, as he would admit, tentative. His only certainty has been that *some* answer must be given to the question of content,[9] both for purposes of assessing moral responsibility and for purposes of keeping the psychology of Intentional states scientifically respectable.[10]

Human actions also come in for their share of non-natural or "otherworldly" analyses. To forestall the need to resort to the mysterious, Michael has consistently sought to analyze human actions as events are analyzed generally, which (in the Davidsonian tradition at least) is as spatio-temporally located particulars. More specifically, Michael has analyzed each human action as a complex event consisting of both a volition (or willing) and a bodily movement where the bodily movement is both the effect and the object of the willing—in short, as a willed bodily movement.[11] This analysis places human actions squarely within the causal-explanatory nature of the world, and does so for two reasons. First, the peculiarities in action descriptions (that tempt some philosophers to become mysterious) are conceived as just that, namely peculiarities in *descriptions* of actions rather than in actions themselves. And second, such an analysis is a species of what is generically called the causal theory of action (or "CTA"), which importantly asserts that human agency is not irreducible or mysterious, but rather is fully explicable as a form of mental state causation. This is a conclusion Michael explicitly draws from his own version of the CTA.[12]

Such agency does have further aspects to it, however, beyond those required by the CTA. Michael's work describes two such important attributes, both involving causation. The first is that human beings often cause the existence of the objects of their willings, wants, and intendings. Michael argues that this causal capacity is fundamental to the agency of persons, and he defends the existence of this capacity against the challenge of recent neuroscientific findings that purport to show that willings are merely epiphenomenal with the actions willed, rather than causes of such actions.[13] The second aspect of human agency which Michael defends is that the causation of intendings, wantings, choosings, and willings by factors outside the control of an actor does not impact upon an actor's agency.[14] All that is needed for such agency is the capacity to have chosen otherwise,[15] which according to Michael is a capacity which persons possess despite their causings being caused.

[6] Michael tells me that Judith Thomson once advised him (when both were teaching at Berkeley in the early '80s) not to even try to solve this problem; that so doing would be "crazy" in light of the numerous philosophical lances that had already been broken on this tournament field.

[7] Moore, 1993a; Moore, 1997b, ch. 8.

[8] Moore, 1987c; Moore, 1997b, ch. 11.

[9] It has been gratifying to Michael to observe younger scholars whom he is proud to have influenced tackle some of the complexities here. See particularly Kimberly Ferzan, "Beyond Intention," 29 *Cardozo Law Review* 1147 (2008); Kimberly Ferzan, "Intention," in Dennis Patterson (ed.), *A Companion to Philosophy of Law and Legal Theory*, 2nd edn. (Oxford: Blackwell, 2010); Gideon Yaffe, *Attempts* (New York: Oxford University Press, 2010), discussed at length by Michael (Moore, 2013c, 150–77).

[10] Moore, 2011b; Moore, 2013c.

[11] Moore, 1993c; Moore, 1994c; Moore, 1997b, ch. 6.

[12] Moore, 2010.

[13] Moore, 2011a.

[14] Moore, 1985c; Moore, 1997b, ch. 12; Moore, 2014b; Moore, 2014e.

[15] Moore, 2014d.

As Michael insists, causation is basic to our understanding of human agency. But then, causation is basic to our scientific understanding of the universe. Michael has accordingly devoted substantial energies to pinpointing the nature of causation within the natural world.[16] He identifies causation as a relation naturally existing between states of affairs, and only constructively between events and facts as derivative causal relata. Such states of affairs do not include omissions or other absences, and the causal relation is singularist and not to be identified as probabilistic chance-raising, nomic sufficiency, or counterfactual necessity. Michael seems to think such singular causal relations may be either physicalist in nature, or *sui generis* ("primitive"); in either case, the singular relation is scalar, not bivalent. Causal laws are derived from such singular relations, and not the other way around; such laws are sometimes at least to be seen as giving sufficient conditions; and every singular causal relation presupposes the existence of some causal law(s). Importantly, Michael rigorously distinguishes counterfactual dependence from the causal relation, yet nonetheless finds counterfactual dependence to be a real relation as well.[17] Such counterfactual dependence relates absences as well as presences, and it too is scalar, but in ways that differ from causation.[18]

The biographical antecedents of Michael's metaphysical apparatus appear to reach all the way back to his college days. Having found the US Naval Academy shockingly anxious to enforce rules of order and decorum against an Oregon kid who mostly liked to ski, Michael survived as a midshipman for only three months, twenty-two days, and ten hours. Having turned down the chance to study mathematics at MIT for the prospect of giving orders on the bridge of a destroyer, Michael's departure from Annapolis left him with little choice but to return to his home in Eugene. There, however (while living in the fraternity next door to the iconic wreck used in the movie *Animal House*), he entered the newly founded Honors College at the University of Oregon where he found ample intellectual nourishment during his undergraduate years (1961–4). Honors College graduates had to take year-long core courses and comprehensive year-end exams in US history, economics, calculus, chemistry, physics, English literature, philosophy, and a foreign language. Students could petition to waive one such core course and Michael promptly petitioned to waive philosophy, on the stated ground that he was "an empiricist for whom knowledge consisted of testable facts, whereas philosophy was just moving concepts around (and around and around) so that no progress was possible and no new knowledge gained."[19] Remarkably, his petition was granted (presumably by a member of the science faculty!).

Michael's interest in and respect for empirical science has thus been long standing. Indeed, he has always had a mathematics/hard science bias, regarding the standards of those disciplines as the standards of rational thought. (He was always proud of the fact that when his high school math teacher, Mr. Oscar Schaaf, heard that Michael had headed to Harvard Law School, his comment to Michael's father was, "What a waste!")

[16] Moore, 1987b; Moore, 1997b, ch. 7; Moore, 1998d; Moore, 2000b; Moore, 2002d; Moore, 2003b; Moore, 2005a; Moore, 2009a; Moore, 2009d; Moore, 2011c; Moore, 2011f; Moore, 2012a; Moore, 2012d; Moore, 2013a; Moore, 2013b.

[17] Moore, 1987b; Moore, 1997b, ch. 7; Moore, 2003b; Moore, 2007e; Moore, 2009b; Moore, 2009d; Moore, 2012d.

[18] Moore, 2012d.

[19] From a recorded conversation, December 2013.

What Michael didn't appreciate at the time was that his interest in science was the philosopher's interest, not the scientist's interest. He liked, as he has put it, "theories, overviews, knowledge about the world in large clumps" and, unsurprisingly, he thus found that he did as poorly in lab courses as he did well in lecture courses (earning three As in Chemistry, and a C, D, and W (in lieu of an expected F) in Chemistry Lab). And so, after disdaining philosophy for the sciences, Michael found his way to metaphysics, which for Michael is literally that; namely physics (and science generally) at a higher (or "meta") level of abstraction. But his interest in the discoveries of the empirical sciences continues to the present time, and when he isn't reading the latest work in neuroscience, he is indulging the bedtime hobby of exploring the history of physics, from Maxwell's equations to string theory.

B. The philosophy of science applied to the psychological sciences

One of the earliest areas of scholarship which Michael undertook was the application of the philosophy of science to academic psychology. Although interdisciplinary, his work in this arena was not concerned with his primary discipline of law, but rather with the disciplines of philosophy and psychology. More specifically, Michael applied the philosophy of science to psychological science (that is, psychoanalysis, psychiatry, behaviorism, cognitive psychology, and neuroscience).

Three theoretical aspects of psychoanalytic science drew Michael's attention early in his career: the psychoanalytic understanding of dreams, the claimed existence of a dynamic unconscious, and the subdivisions of self posited by the five metapsychological viewpoints of Freud's version of psychoanalytic theory. Michael cautiously conceded that in various senses of the word, *unconscious* mental processes existed.[20] He sought, however, to decouple that thesis from Freud's more specific and more animistic conclusions. In the theory of dreams, for example, Michael reconstrued each of the three levels of explanation of Freudian dream theory so as to dispense with Freud's animistic reliance on the notion of unconsciously motivated actions.[21] For example, Michael urged that instead of thinking of dreams as satisfying a motive or wish to sleep, as Freud hypothesized, we should think of dreams as fulfilling the function of sustaining sleep. Similarly, Michael sought to de-animize Freud's putatively motivational explanations of parapraxes (such as slips of the tongue) and neurotic symptoms. And finally, he sought to defuse the supposedly radical disunities that stemmed from Freud's division of the self along the three lines of experienced conflicts, consciousness versus unconsciousness, and differential functional roles. Michael concluded that these three divisions of self did not evidence any fracturing of the agency that marks each of us as but one person, nor did the three divide personality in congruent ways.[22]

By de-animizing psychoanalytic theory, Michael left open the question of how much of the theory (so reconstrued) could be taken seriously as an attempt by Freud to state an ontologically respectable, functionalist theory of mind. Michael's answer came as a divided verdict: some parts of the theory, such as the dream-work, Michael took to be a

[20] Moore, 1984d, ch. 7. [21] Moore, 1983e; Moore, 1984d, chs. 1, 8.
[22] Moore, 1983d; Moore, 1984d, ch. 11.

genuine attempt at functionally specifying sub-personal states that underlie the ordinary mental processes of whole persons; other aspects of the theory, such as the structural metaphysychology (ego, id, superego), Michael saw as less successful. The ego, for example, Michael took to be a "far too smart general" to serve as a vehicle for gradually reducing the intelligent to the mechanical via the strategy known as "homuncular functionalism."[23] In general Michael evinced skepticism that the conflicts persons experience in dreams, neurotic symptoms, or everyday slips of the tongue or movement could give rise to useful starting points for the general functional subdivision of mind that should be part of a truly general psychology.[24]

Apart from reconstructing psychoanalytic theory in a more scientifically respectable way, Michael's other early topic in this area was psychiatry's conceptualization of mental illness. There were, as Michael saw it, two errors to be avoided within psychiatry. One was the error of thinking that mental illness "was a myth," as was the conclusion of Thomas Szasz, R. D. Laing, and other members of the radical psychiatric movement of the 1960s and 1970s in the US and the UK. The opposite error was to "medicalize morals" in the expansive way that Karl Menninger (Michael's supervisor during his time as a lecturer at the Menninger Foundation in the early 1970s) and those like him were wont to do. Michael avoided the first error by showing how the claims of "myth" were based on inadequate philosophies of mind and science.[25] He sought to channel psychiatry away from the second error by cabining the criteria that were used by the psychiatric profession for a "mental disorder" so as to avoid its equation with socially deviant behavior or attitudes.[26] Michael did this with the express purpose of keeping psychiatry within the bounds of concern for the aberrational and exceptional phenomena commonly thought of as mental illness, and with an eye to discrediting any claimed psychiatric expertise about the ethics of the good and virtuous life.

Given his interest in science, it is no surprise that some of Michael's earliest work was in the philosophy of science.[27] In the late 1960s, he would arrive at his law firm in San Francisco (then Howard, Prim, Smith, Rice, & Downs; but now Arnold & Porter) by 6:00 a.m., typically a good two hours before anyone else, in order to work on his first paper on dream theory. As he describes it, it had a kind of "mad scientist" feel to it, given the disjunction between his early morning theoretical work and the practicalities of the typical workday.

His general interest in science explains some such activity; but why the philosophy of science as applied to psychology, psychiatry, and psychoanalysis? One of his specific interests within psychology/psychiatry is perhaps easily explained; the interest in how mental illness should be conceptualized. Such an interest was somewhat forced on Michael by the fact that many of those who were closest to him suffered from serious mental diseases, ranging from classic paranoid schizophrenia to clinical depression and bipolar disease. His mother lost custody of Michael (for a period of about six years)

23 Moore, 1988b; Moore, 1997b, ch. 10.

24 Moore, 1988b; Moore, 1997b, ch. 10.

25 Moore, 1975a; Moore, 1975b; Moore, 1984d, ch. 4.

26 Moore, 1978a; Moore, 1984d, ch. 5; Moore, 2014f.

27 In the 1970s, Michael became friends with the three leading philosophers of science in America, Carl (or "Peter," as he was known to friends like Michael) Hempel, Adolf Grunbaum, and Ernst Nagel, and all three were quite encouraging of his work.

when he was only seven, partly because she was a lesbian and was thus thought to possess a mental disease in the psychiatry of early 1950s Oregon. As if it weren't enough to lose his mother to a period of involuntary commitment in the state mental instituton for this "deviance," others very near and dear to Michael, both during his childhood and in the formative years of early adulthood, battled textbook conditions that proved tragic. He spent years seeing those he loved go in and out of mental hospitals, and he remembers quite desperately seeking to unravel the delusions symptomatic of their psychotic disorders and working fruitlessly to lighten the burdens of severe depression. He grappled with five instances of attempted suicide by five people to whom he was deeply bonded, two of which were heart-breakingly successful.

Given those experiences, it is no surprise that one of Michael's earliest efforts in this area was to refute those radical psychiatrists who loudly proclaimed that mental illness was a myth. In Michael's experience, mental illness was a cruel reality that robbed children of parents, parents of children, brothers of sisters, and lovers and friends of kindred spirits. But it is also no surprise that Michael worked to limit expansive psychiatric conceptions of mental disease. He was affronted by the idea that life choices considered "abnormal" by a majority could be designated as "deviant" by a profession such as psychiatry. Given his experience with his mother and her life partner by whom he was eventually jointly raised, Michael applauded the self-described feminists who disrupted the annual meeting of the American Psychiatric Association in San Francisco in 1970 to protest what they took to be a dishonest medicalizing of mere (conventional) morals.

Tracing the origins of Michael's interest in theory-construction vis-à-vis psychoanalysis particularly is a little less easy. Bored out of his mind by the standard Harvard Law School courses offered in the mid 1960s, Michael wandered into a then-new class offered by Alan Stone and Alan Dershowitz, "Psychoanalysis and Law." He quickly discovered that the "and Law" part taught by Dershowitz interested him very little, so Michael began attending only Stone's half of the lectures. Stone's detailed analysis of psychoanalytic theory fascinated Michael, both for its promise of personal wisdom and for its wildly speculative nature as a theory of human behavior. Michael's final paper in the course, entitled "The Wish to Bleed," was a send-up of Freud's run-away anthropomorphization of human phenomena. Facetiously positing that we bleed when cut because we unconsciously want to bleed, this intended *reductio* was the direct antecedent of the de-animization of Freudian theory that characterized Michael's later published papers.

Psychoanalysts often say that people become psychoanalysts because of a morbid fascination with their own psychology. I don't think this is true in Michael's case: I think he has never thought that there are any particularly interesting recesses in his psyche that merit either his attention or anyone else's. Instead, when asked, Michael will trace his interest in psychoanalysis to growing up with a father and three strong women—his mother, her life partner, and his sister—amongst whom interpretations of hidden motives abounded. Here is Michael's account in his own words:

> I recall some examples of free-of-charge, intra-familial interpretations by my mother. On my casual mode of dress: "You just think you are so much better than everyone else that you don't have to dress well." And on my choice of slim women as romantic

partners: "Are you sure you wouldn't really prefer boys?" But even my less overtly interpretive father could deliver up some zingers on all aspects of my choices, from cars to careers to women. Some of them were quite good, as when he said of the woman for whom I left my first wife: "Ah, you are seeking your mother then?" Between the four of them I developed a taste for the kind of interpretation of human behavior that is the meat and potatoes of the psychoanalytic enterprise.[28]

C. The challenges of academic psychology to the folk psychology on which personhood and responsibility is based

Michael's interest in psychiatry, psychoanalysis, behaviorism, cognitive psychology, and neuroscience has not only been to keep such theories respectable as psychological sciences. He has also had an interest in defending the folk psychology of persons (and the doctrines of responsibility that are built on such folk psychology) from the attacks of Freud, James, Skinner, and other academic psychologies. So this I shall count as the third area of his scholarship.

He has recently taxonomized six challenges to folk psychology that have inspired his response: (1) the hard determinist challenge that all of our actions and choices are caused by factors that we do not control; (2) the epiphenomenal challenge that our choices do not cause the actions chosen but only accompany such choices as psychological side-shows; (3) the eliminative materialist challenge that there is no place for folk psychological entities like intentions or beliefs in the best explanations of human behavior (explanations which are rightly framed in terms of brain states, if eliminative materialists are right); (4) the reductionist challenge that persons are nothing but mechanisms, their actions and mental states no more than dumb clockwork-like robotics; (5) the epistemic challenge that persons are often in error and have no privileged access to the mental states that cause their behavior; and (6) the consequentialist challenge that the greater predictability of human behavior made possible by advances in the psychological sciences will lead to the replacement of responsibility assessments in law and morals by legal strategies and social philosophies that pursue preventative rather than punitive regimes.[29] Although psychoanalytic and behavioral psychologies have in the past mounted most of these six challenges at one time or another, it is neuroscience today that is seen as the most threatening harbinger of change in who we conceive ourselves to be. Michael has accordingly focused his recent work there, charting in detail these challenges as they are presented by contemporary neuroscience.[30]

As part of his work in this area, Michael has mapped the salient aspects of folk psychology that are challenged in these ways by various academic psychologies. Throughout his work Michael has described persons as free, rational, autonomous, emotional, Intentional, unified, reasons-responsive, character-possessing creatures—in short, as possessing the defining characteristics assigned to persons by folk psychology[31] —and he has dealt in detail with some of these folk-psychological attributes of persons and the challenges presented to them by certain academic psychologies. Early in his career he examined the challenges presented by the existence of unconscious mental states, as

[28] From a recorded conversation on the topic, December 2013.
[29] Moore, 2014e. [30] Moore, 2012g.
[31] Moore, 1997b, ch. 15; Moore, 2011b; Moore, 2012g; Moore, 2014c; Moore, 2014f.

these were conceived in psychoanalytic theory.[32] Certain Freudian interpretations of such states threatened both to diminish personal responsibility to the vanishing point, because we were made mere puppets in the control of the unconscious puppeteer, and to enlarge responsibility to alarming levels, because *we* became as much puppeteers as puppets, our agency identified as much with our unconscious as with our conscious mental states.

Michael's work in the philosophy of science that de-animized the unconscious was part of his answer to these specifically Freudian challenges. More recently, Michael has sought to defuse a more contemporary version of the epistemic challenge—the version issuing from such explorers of the "new unconscious" as psychologists John Barge and Daniel Wegner.[33] Michael concedes to these psychologies a greater scientific respectability than that accorded their psychoanalytic predecessors. Still, he defends the view that the weak privileged access that folk psychology attributes to persons is in fact untouched by these more contemporary psychologists of the unconscious.

Apart from addressing different versions of the epistemic challenge to the folk psychology of persons and responsibility, Michael has also gone after the epiphenomenal challenge. Here he has defended autonomy (the capacity to cause the objects of one's willings) against recent challenges of neuroscientists like the late Benjamin Libet, concluding that their epiphenomenalist views are based on a faulty philosophy of mind.[34] Michael urges, first, that a better philosophy of mind would reveal that our willings (properly conceived) do cause the bodily movements that are the objects of such willings, just as folk psychology postulates; and second, that sometimes, when this isn't true, we are responsible nonetheless for some real-world harms that counterfactually depend on our willings, even when we achieve such harms other than by causing them through willed bodily movements. (This second point constitutes a kind of compatibilism between responsibility and epiphenomenalism.)

The third challenge with which Michael has dealt at length is that of the hard determinist.[35] Early in his career Michael sought to show how the established excuses (the ones commonly accepted in both law and morality) are not in fact based on the supposition that causation of choice or action is an excuse.[36] More recently, Michael has undertaken a more general defense of the compatibilist view.[37] Michael's conclusion is that being responsible for some choice or action is fully compatible with that choice or action being sufficiently caused by factors not within the control of the actor. Michael distinguishes a variety of compatibilisms within philosophy, and defends what is usually called "classical compatibilism"—the view that we were able to choose and do other than we did even if our choices and actions were fully caused by factors over which we had no control.

Michael has also focused on two more particular sorts of excuses as a means of shedding light on the folk-psychological attributes that persons must generally have in order

[32] Moore, 1979b; Moore, 1980b; Moore, 1984d, chs. 9–10.
[33] Moore, 2012g.
[34] Moore, 2011a.
[35] When I first met Michael he was preoccupied with this issue, and we devoted our first lunch in 1985 to the debate about free will and determinism. For the record, I was and remain a committed incompatibilist, despite, or perhaps because of, listening to almost thirty years of argument-lite dogmatism from Michael, the assertions of which tellingly lack parts and subparts.
[36] Moore, 1985c; Moore, 1997b, ch. 12.
[37] Moore, 2014b; Moore, 2014e.

to be responsible. First, he has used the excuse of insanity to plumb the contours of the kind of rationality a creature must possess in order to be a person and a moral agent.[38] Second, he has drawn on the family of excuses that fall under the rubric of "compulsions"—duress, natural necessity, addiction, provocation, and the like—in order to map the kinds of freedom a creature must have to be a person and a moral agent.[39]

D. Moral responsibility and its role within criminal law

Michael's fourth broad area of work leaves the psychological sciences and their challenges to responsibility to focus on responsibility itself. In a very considerable body of work, Michael has pressed the questions: "When and for what is a person responsible and blamable?" Given what Michael has always seen as a close tie between moral responsibility and the defensible conditions of punishment within Anglo-American criminal law, Michael's work in this area is as much substantive criminal law scholarship as it is moral philosophy.

Michael bases his work in this area on two major suppositions: first, that absent moral blameworthiness, no one should be liable to punishment; and second, that moral blameworthiness (or responsibility) itself exists only if certain natural properties and relations exist, such as acting, intending, causing, etc.[40] Michael's contributions in this area thus both blend moral philosophy and criminal law analysis, and appeal to the scientific insights about the nature of actions, intentions, causation, etc., that Michael achieved in earlier work.[41]

Michael divides his work on responsibility into three parts: the "theory of responsibility proper"; the theories of the "nature of the elements of responsibility"; and the theory of the subjects of responsibility, or "a theory of personhood."[42] He has pursued the first of these in assessing the "conditions of fair fault ascription" that are reflected in "the general part of the criminal law."[43] He urges that one can be responsible for some harm H if: one caused H; one failed to prevent H when one had a duty to do so; one aided another to cause H; one procured another to cause H; one tried to cause H; one consciously and unreasonably risked causing H; or one agreed with another that she would cause H.[44] With some overlap and combination, these possibilities yield the four "theories of liability" within Anglo-American criminal law: principal liability; accomplice liability; inchoate liability; and conspiracy liability.

Michael has sought to refine criminal law's four-part general structure by demonstrating, for example, that accomplice liability is superfluous given the other bases for liability;[45] that inchoate liability consists of two very different bases—trying and risking;[46] and that principal liability is in fact predicated on two quite distinct relations—causation and counterfactual dependence.[47] But despite these recommended emendations, Michael is by-and-large both appreciative of, and an

[38] Moore, 1975c; Moore, 1979a; Moore, 1984d, ch. 6; Moore, 1997b, ch. 14; Moore, 2014f.
[39] Moore, 2014d. [40] Moore, 2009d, vii. [41] Moore, 2009d.
[42] Moore, 1997b, 35. [43] Moore, 1990b; Moore, 1997b, ch. 1; Moore, 2012f.
[44] Moore, 2012f. [45] Moore, 2007c; Moore, 2009d, ch. 13. [46] Moore, 2013c.
[47] Moore, 2009b; Moore, 2009d, ch. 18.

uncommon defender of, the coherence and systematicity of Anglo-American criminal law and its underlying morality.[48]

Much of Michael's work on responsibility has concerned the second part mentioned above—the nature of the discrete natural properties on which the moral property of responsibility supervenes. One of the most basic requirements for responsibility is that one must *act*,[49] and Michael has thus employed his work in the philosophy of action to chart the relation between action and responsibility.[50] In Michael's theory of action (that every action is a willed bodily movement), one's responsibility for a harm begins with one's willing an act. Following Bentham and Austin, Michael argues that two sorts of elements—circumstance elements and consequence elements—combine with such simple acts to comprise the more complex act types that law and morality more typically care about, act-types like burning, killing, disfiguring, etc.[51]

The consequential complexity of actions has led naturally to Michael's second discrete enquiry, which is into the causal relations between an act and a harm that render such a harm a "consequence-element" of some (criminal or moral) wrong. Causation being the labyrinth that it is, Michael spends considerable effort mastering and mapping its metaphysical complexities and its relation to responsibility.[52] Michael carefully isolates the jurisdiction of causation as a determinant of an agent's responsibility for a harm. Distinguishing counterfactual dependence as a desert-determinant independent of causation, Michael finds that it is this relation, not causation, that grounds both moral responsibility and legal liability for omissions, preventions, allowings, double-preventions, and *de minimusly* caused remote harms.[53] He further distinguishes the "matching" aspect of the culpability requirement from the causation requirement; the matching condition being the requirement that the harm that actually occurs match the type of harm intended, foreseen, or consciously risked.[54] Such a culpability requirement is often treated as a causation requirement, but the two, Michael urges, are distinct, and liability as a principal for a completed crime requires culpability in addition to causal or counterfactual relations.[55]

Michael has also charted in detail the role of causation in marking the boundaries of permissible consequentialist justifications.[56] In so doing, he assigns causation a quite different moral role than it typically plays when increasing an agent's blameworthiness, for, in his argument, it is the absence (or at least the weakness) of the causal connection in the enabling, accelerating, redirecting, omitting, and allowing cases that makes such cases eligible for consequentialist justifications.

Michael's major effort in explicating legal (or "proximate") causation is made in his compelling critique of the three leading tests of proximate causation in

[48] Moore, 2012f.

[49] Michael does allow for omission liability on an exceptional basis, where omissions are conceived of as absences of certain types of action. Moore, 1993c, chs. 2–3; Moore, 1994c; Moore, 1997b, ch. 4; Moore, 2009b; Moore, 2009d, ch. 18; Moore, 2013b.

[50] Moore, 1993c; Moore, 1994c; Moore, 1997b, ch. 4; Moore, 2010.

[51] Moore, 1993c, ch. 8.

[52] Moore, 1987b; Moore, 1993a; Moore, 1994b; Moore, 1997b, chs. 5, 7–8; Moore, 1998d; Moore, 2000b; Moore, 2002d; Moore, 2005a; Moore, 2007e; Moore, 2009b; Moore, 2009d; Moore, 2011e; Moore, 2011f; Moore, 2012a; Moore, 2012d; Moore, 2013a; Moore, 2013b.

[53] Moore, 2009b; Moore, 2009d, ch. 18.

[54] Moore and Hurd, 2002a.

[55] Moore, 2011f; Moore, 2012d.

[56] Moore, 2008a; Moore, 2009d, ch. 3.

Anglo-American criminal law: foreseeability,[57] harm within the risk,[58] and direct causation.[59] Michael advances, instead, a quantitative test based on the substantiality of a factor's (or agent's) causal contribution; a test that depends, of course, on the success with which Michael vindicates a scalar understanding of the metaphysics of the causal relation.

In addition to the core conditions of action and causation, the third discrete element of responsibility that Michael has examined is culpability. Michael distinguishes intending from foreseeing and from predictively believing,[60] and urges that intending reflects greater culpability than does foresight.[61] He has joined me in distinguishing intentions from motivations and in urging that bias, prejudice, hate, ill feeling, and other such unfortunate motivations have no place in determining criminal culpability.[62] And together, we have examined whether the inadvertent creation of an unreasonable risk (negligence) can be a further basis for culpability, reluctantly (and quite counterintuitively, given our common experience with our teenage children Aidan and Gillian) concluding that inadvertence, even when unreasonable, generates no moral blame, and thus provides no basis for punishment when the risks to which the actor was inadvertent materialize.[63]

Action, causation, and culpability together make up what criminal law professors call the prima facie case of criminal liability. But there are also the defenses to be considered before a prima facie liable defendant is *actually* liable to criminal punishment. Such defenses are usually divided between justifications and excuses, and Michael so groups them for separate treatment.

Michael's work on the justificatory defenses has focused on the most general "balance of evils" defense, so called because it seemingly provides that one can do any act prohibited by a criminal code so long as the evil of the act is less than the evil it prevents. The central problem with the balance of evils defense is to determine how it avoids licensing morally appalling actions such as rape, pillage, and murder whenever a net balance of good consequences will ensue—a result most (except the most die-hard of utilitarians) find morally outrageous. Michael attempts to cabin the use of good consequences in the justification of prima facie evil actions, allowing only three opportunities for consequentialist justifications: (1) where there is an exception to the norm that prohibits the evil act done, as self-defense is an exception to the prohibition on killing; (2) where the consequentially justified act lies outside the jurisdiction of a norm (as is the case, for example, when the bad consequences of the act (by virtue of which the act is prima facie prohibited) are merely forseen, but not intended); and (3) where the consequences of not doing the prima facie wrongful act are so awful that they place the act beyond the "threshold" that determines when categorical obligations apply.[64]

Despite their heteronomous appearance, Michael has insisted that it must be possible to give a general theory of the excuses. He distinguishes the causal theory of

[57] Moore, 1993a; Moore, 1997b, ch. 8. [58] Moore and Hurd, 2002a; Moore, 2009d, chs. 7–10.
[59] Moore, 2000b; Moore, 2009d, chs. 11–12. [60] Moore, 1987e; Moore, 1997b, ch. 11.
[61] Moore, 1995b; Moore, 1997b, ch. 9; Moore, 2011b; Moore, 2013c.
[62] Hurd and Moore, 2004b. [63] Moore and Hurd, 2011d; Hurd and Moore, 2011e.
[64] Moore, 1989h; Moore, 1997b, ch. 17; Moore and Alexander, 2007d; Moore, 2008a; Moore, 2009d, ch. 3; Moore and Alexander, 2012e.

excuse[65] from the character and choice theories, and throws his intellectual weight behind the last of these three,[66] advocating that the touchstone of excuse is to be found in the lack of opportunity[67] or the lack of capacity to have chosen other than one did.[68]

This "alternate possibilities" view of excuses is later applied to the compulsion excuses such as duress, necessity, addiction, and provocation.[69] Michael urges that an actor *could* have done other than he did when he *would* have done otherwise in certain close possible worlds, namely worlds where he either tried very hard to do otherwise, or where he wanted very much to choose to do otherwise.[70] Significantly, Michael does not think that insanity fits this theory of excuse,[71] because he does not think that insanity is a true excuse. Rather, insanity is a status exemption like that provided for infants.[72] As Michael concludes, we excuse the mentally ill not because their choices to do what is right are too difficult for them, but rather because they lack the status of being moral agents to start with.

Early in his career when he was writing a series of papers on discrete topics within responsibility, Michael's Harvard mentor, Alan Stone, commented that in his seemingly disparate papers Michael was implicitly working out a general theory of the person. Michael has since been quite explicit about the need for a sub-theory of personhood within the theory of responsibility. (This is the "third part" of his theory of responsibility earlier distinguished.) His own view of persons is that persons must be rational, autonomous, emotional, character-possessing agents. What is not required is that persons stand outside the natural causal order so as to be contra-causally free in their choices. When possessed of the properties described, persons, while of the natural order, can rightly be praised or blamed in morality, rewarded or punished in law.

Michael's extended investigation into responsibility and the conditions of its ascription probably wears its motivation and genesis on its face. As his friend Sally Salter once said of him, he has a very strong sense of being in control of his life in all of its phases; professional, financial, and personal. With the strong sense that he controls his destiny comes a strong sense of responsibility. On pain of elitism, he takes others to be as responsible for their choices, and the consequences of those choices, as is he, even if they lack a similarly strong *sense* that they are in control of their fate. But if this sounds harsh, it should also be understood that he is the first to make excuses for his children; he is shockingly generous in forgiving the transgressions of his friends and family; and he carries very few grudges, allowing people to reinvent themselves with him even when a good retributivist would consider them quite undeserving of ready forgiveness. So all of his tough talk about responsibility masks a remarkable facility for indulging the weaknesses of others!

E. **Political philosophy**

The fifth area in which Michael has devoted considerable scholarly energy is in the field of political philosophy, and specifically, the political philosophy that undergirds the

[65] Moore, 1985c; Moore, 1997b, ch. 12. [66] Moore, 1990a; Moore, 1997b, ch. 13.
[67] Michael seems to have changed his mind on the opportunity branch of this. See Moore, 2014d.
[68] Moore, 1985c; Moore, 1990a; Moore, 1997b, chs. 12–13. [69] Moore, 1989c; Moore, 2014d.
[70] Moore, 2014d; Moore, 2014e. [71] Moore, 2014f.
[72] Moore, 1975b; Moore, 1975e; Moore, 1979a; Moore, 1984d, ch. 6; Moore, 2014f.

substantive criminal law. Michael has written extensively in the two areas of political philosophy of greatest relevance to criminal law, namely the theory of punishment and the theory of the justified scope and limits of legitimate criminal legislation within a democracy.

As to the first of these, Michael has famously defended a retributive account according to which we should impose punishment because and only because an offender deserves it.[73] Such a theory contrasts sharply with utilitarian theories according to which punishment, even of those who deserve it, is an evil that can be justified only by its contribution to some greater good such as crime prevention. Such a theory also contrasts sharply with rehabilitative and mixed theories of punishment. As Joel Feinberg admiringly described Michael's retributivism:

> It is marked not only by profundity and subtlety but also clarity. This work . . . deserves to become a classic . . . [and] is all the more valuable in being uncompromising. He knows very well what rehabilitation is, and he rejects it. He knows what vengeance is, and he rejects it. He knows what mixed theories are, and he rejects them. He is the pure retributivist . . ., a person who will not back away from the sufficiency thesis.[74]

Michael's main argument for retributivism has come to be called "the experiential argument," for it is intuitionistic and emotion-based. Rejecting what he calls the "tired metaphors" of "paying a debt to society" or "restoring some moral balance," Michael premises his defense of retributivism on the feeling of guilt that virtuous people feel when they have culpably done wrong. In Michael's view, the judgment to which such virtuous feelings lead is a judgment of deserved suffering. Not only is the imposition of such suffering on those who deserve it an intrinsic good, it is also the good uniquely served by criminal law, and it should thus be thought to define the proper function of such law.[75]

Michael's "experiential argument" for retributivism is explicitly built on the guilt feelings virtuous people feel when they have culpably done wrong. As Michael says in his most recently published work about this form of argument: "Anyone who wants to live the academic moral philosophy they write about, and who has felt the compelling power of deep guilt feelings for harms caused, will brush such arguments [about the irrelevance of guilt feelings] aside."[76, 77] Michael's friend and mentor Herb Morris also built his "moral education" defense of retributivism on feelings of guilt, shame, and remorse (although in a quite different way from Michael).[78] That led many to speculate about the events in Herb's life that made him so deferential to these emotions. No doubt some might indulge similar speculations about what in Michael's past so convinced him

[73] Moore, 1982e; Moore, 1987e; Moore, 1993b; Moore, 1997b, chs. 2–4; Moore, 2002c.

[74] Joel Feinberg and Jules Coleman, *Philosophy of Law*, 6th edn. (Belmont: Wadsworth, 2000), 685.

[75] Moore, 1990b; Moore, 1997b, ch. 1.

[76] Moore, 2009d, 30–31.

[77] He has been pleased that others (such as John Gardner in his review of Michael's experiential argument) have joined him in thinking that personal experience of guilt compels judgment. John Gardner, "Wrongdoing by Results: Moore's Experiential Argument," 18 *Legal Theory* 459 (2012).

[78] Herbert Morris, "A Paternalist Theory of Punishment," 18 *American Philosophical Quarterly* 263 (1981).

that feelings of guilt have "compelling power." And so I asked him. Here is his quite touching confession:

> I have felt guilty about many small experiences of hurting, or at least, not helping others. But the big ones? Here are some real possibilities—take your pick: One was on the occasion of leaving my first wife, Leslie, and two young daughters, to pursue a kind of romantic relationship that I had long desired but never had. Sitting in my children's bedroom, the scene of many of their happy early childhood memories, I was hit with overwhelming guilt that left me at rock-bottom on the depression scale. Another was undertaking to help, but not carrying through in a meaningful way, with the mental health problems of the woman, Janean, for whom I left Leslie. Seeing that she was suicidal I had arranged for therapy with the best psychiatrist I knew, Alan Stone, but he had graciously agreed to do it only with the admonition that this had to be really important to me because what I was asking took extraordinary effort on his part. I released Alan from his agreement, and Janean left my apartment in Cambridge to go to her parents in Kansas to seek therapy at the Menninger Foundation. Knowing that homes we have left are dangerous places in such circumstances, I called Janean after about a month to say that I was coming for her, but she urged me not to come. That was the night before she shot herself with her father's pistol. Janean's suicide also left me at ground-zero on the depression scale. Another occasion was when I undertook to help my mother a few years later after her own serious suicide attempt, also due to mental health problems. I was also not very successful in this effort, in part due to my own perceived inability at that point in my career (when I was in the midst of a visit at Stanford) to devote the kind of time needed to help my mother fill her days in Palo Alto.
>
> I actually do not think that it matters much what one's experiences might be. Anyone who has lived anything but an extraordinarily benign life—and anyone not so benighted that he doesn't notice the havoc he has sometimes sown—will have some such experiences, and some such corresponding judgments. As Dick Hare once said, moral wisdom requires moral experience, and if you don't have enough yet, just wait a little.[79]

Michael's retributivism is of a piece with his deontological view of morality and his moral realist view of meta-ethics. These same ethical and meta-ethical views motivate similar justice theories of other areas of law, such as a corrective justice theory of torts (and also of contracts), natural rights theories of property and constitutional law, etc. In Michael's view, such justice theories compete in many areas of law (not just in criminal law) both with utilitarian and with egalitarian theories. Michael's extended defense of retributive justice is only the best known of his justice-based accounts of an area of law. Less well known (because less well developed in print) are Michael's corrective justice and natural rights views of torts, contracts, property, and constitutional law. Inasmuch as Michael teaches all of these subjects within the first-year law school curriculum on a rotating basis, his students get what they would think of as very well-defended accounts of the justice behind correcting wrongs, enforcing promises, protecting property, and

[79] From a recorded conversation, December 2013. Michael's reference to Hare was to Richard Hare, *Freedom and Reason* (Oxford: Clarendon Press, 1963), where, in the Introduction, Hare urges those of his readers who have not faced a serious moral problem in their lives to come back to his book when they have gained more moral experience.

constitutionally enshrining rights to privacy, speech, association, etc. One suspects that if Michael's classroom-tested views were fully worked out in print, they would be the pure, uncompromising justice views of these core areas of law that comprise his retributivist view of the criminal law.[80]

The second kind of political philosophy in which Michael has engaged has been what is sometimes called the theory of criminalization. The central questions in this arena are those of John Stuart Mill: In a democracy, are there any principled limits to what can be prohibited within a just and rational criminal code, beyond the requirement of democratic promulgation, and if so, what are those limits? Michael's answers to Mill's questions are carefully layered.[81] First, contrary to majoritarians like J. F. Stephen and Robert Bork, there are substantive and principled limits to the criminal law that even democratic majorities should respect. This follows for Michael from his "bully pulpit" view of democratic leadership, according to which democracy is best practiced by leaders who lead by their own principles rather than by attempting to represent the principles held by a majority of their constituents. Second, there are values that generally counsel restraint in the use of criminal sanctions, values that Michael believes justify a presumption in favor of negative liberty (and thus against the criminalization of behavior). The minor good that derives from punishing minor wrongdoers is insufficient, Michael argues, to overcome this presumption. Third, citizens have what Michael calls a "derived right of liberty." This right is derivative of a more basic duty on the part of legislators to aim at some things and not others as they pass criminal legislation. Echoing Mill, Michael singles out for particular condemnation criminal legislation that is paternalistically motivated. Fourth, citizens also enjoy what Michael calls, the "basic" (or sometimes "strong") right to liberty. This is a right protecting self-defining choices from state coercion for any but the most compelling of reasons.[82]

Michael thus defends a broadly libertarian view of the limits of criminal legislation. Such libertarianism is part and parcel of his retributive theory of punishment. And both his libertarianism and his retributivism are related to the good that Michael assigns to personal autonomy, even when it is badly deployed. Both depend on the sense that we are in control of much (even if not all) of what matters in our lives. Such control not only generates a sense of guilt and of responsibility at the root of retributivism, but also

[80] The exception for Michael appears to be the law of contracts; see Moore, 2007b. For Michael shares my view (Heidi M. Hurd, "Promises, Schmomises," unpublished manuscript) that the obligation to keep one's promises (if such an obligation exists at all) is far too weak to ground an entire area of law such as contracts. Even here, however, he eschews utilitarian defenses. Instead, he follows me in finding that promises (and their legal expressions in contracts) merit enforcement when they have generated reliance interests that would leave promisors deserving of corrective justice if breached.

[81] Moore, 1984e; Moore, 1989d; Moore, 1989i; Moore, 1997b, chs. 16, 18; Moore, 1998a; Moore, 1998b; Moore, 2005b; Moore, 2007b; Moore, 2009c; Moore, 2014c.

[82] These four aspects of Michael's liberty-protecting views motivated his first public foray into this area of political philosophy, a newspaper debate with Senator John Briggs on Proposition 8 on the 1978 California ballot (Moore, 1978b). This Proposition would have banned gays from teaching in the California public school system. Michael was outraged that his mother, a schoolteacher during the Depression before becoming an accountant, would have been prevented from teaching by this kind of law. The problem, as he saw it, was not the Millian objection that Briggs was using the wrong kind of argument in support of the law—namely an argument that appealed to notions of immorality. The problem was with the kind of morality that Briggs brought to the debate.

supports a right to be left alone to decide who we will be and how we will act to the greatest extent possible consistent with our obligations to others.

These three views—retributivism, responsibility, and the right to liberty—combine in a philosophy that has a distinctive "carry-your-own water" flavor to it. The general view is that persons generally deserve the fruits of their labors, both good and bad, and that because each *can* do the good and avoid the bad, there are limited duties of beneficence that are owed by those who succeed to those who do not. On such a largely libertarian view, need often loses out to accomplishment as a desert-base for social redistribution.[83]

F. Meta-ethics

The sixth area in which Michael has written extensively is meta-ethics, which (as the name implies) concerns itself with study of such "external" moral questions as whether moral qualities exist, whether moral propositions are capable of being true or false, and what meanings there might be for moral statements. Michael began in this area by charting nine tempting routes to skepticism.[84] He then applied what he called the "parallel argument," which drew parallels between such moral skepticisms and more general cognitive skepticisms.[85] He urged that, given the parallel vulnerabilities of science and morals to such skepticisms, if such skeptical considerations did not erode one's realism about scientific truths, they should not erode one's realism about moral truths either.

Ten years later, Michael expanded his defense of moral realism beyond the conditional defense provided by his "parallel argument." He argued more positively, on inference-to-the-best-explanation grounds, that moral qualities and entities had the kind of mind-independent existence distinctive of metaphysical realism in all domains of knowledge.[86] He then turned his naturalist realism to instrumental goods, and specifically, to those particular instrumental goods constituting (as Michael saw it) most legal properties.[87] By pressing the multiple realizability of moral qualities by natural properties, of legal properties by moral and natural properties, and of mental properties by physical properties, Michael defended a kind of supervenient, yet still reductivist, analysis in all three fields of ethics, law, and psychology.

From the start, Michael recognized that his moral (as well as scientific) realism was related to the kind of semantics that he had independently defended in his work on interpretation (See section II.H. below). This is often called "K–P semantics," after its two most famous purveyors in philosophy, Saul Kripke and Michael's early teacher in the philosophy of language, Hilary Putnam. On this semantics, the meaning of a word is not to be given by a Lockean concept (definition, Fregean "sense"), that is, a set of

83 That said, nothing appalls Michael more than to be mistaken for a Republican! For, despite his deontic libertarianism, Michael has ample capacity to make room in his moral psychology, his ethical ontology, and his personal life for a set of aretaic obligations that, if satisfied, will compel the development of personal virtues that will be expressed in considerable generosity on the part of those who have to those who do not. In his view, deontic duties have substantial limits, and inasmuch as the law should respect those limits, it is not entitled to make us as good as we should be. But on aesthetic grounds alone he finds it unseemly to join the political ranks of those who are positively proud of the vices that the law cannot touch and the inequalities in wealth and opportunity that those vices permit.

84 Moore, 2004c, "Introduction".

85 Moore, 1982a; Moore, 2004c, ch. 1.

86 Moore, 1992b; Moore, 2004c, ch. 2.

87 Moore, 2002b; Moore, 2004c, ch. 6.

properties analytically necessary for proper usage of the word; rather, the meaning of a word is given by the essential nature of the thing(s) to which it directly refers. Michael used such a semantics not to argue for the truth of realism (in ethics or anywhere else),[88] but, rather, as a helpful handmaiden to realism defended on other, non-semantic grounds.[89]

While I was born a Platonist, and was thus inclined toward moral realism from an early age (so as to find Michael's contentious objectivism perfectly sensible upon our first dinner over the subject),[90] Michael entered the academy as a committed Glauconian skeptic, and was thus youthfully dubious of claims about the objectivity of things that could not be quantified and tested. Michael's favorite slogan as an undergraduate, which he often proclaimed in his classes, was "Morality is expediency!" His political theory professor, puzzled about why Michael was such a skeptic, asked him what he had read. "Nothing! I figured it out for myself!" was his brazen reply. Jim Klonoski, Michael's undergraduate Political Science Department advisor, had a firm view of the objectivity of morality (and Klonoski had a far easier time convincing Lee Bollinger, also a student in the UO's Political Science Department a few years later, of the objective goodness of affirmative action than he had of convincing Michael of anything at all). Klonoski was so disgusted with Michael's skepticism that he said, "If you ever get committed to some normative ideal, you let me know; send me a telegram!"

Klonoski's words came home to roost, for Michael eventually found that "such skepticism doesn't live very well."[91] With increasing philosophical sophistication, such skepticism seemed less compelling, and eventually, unsustainable. But Michael's mode of investigating the plausibility of moral objectivity was clearly influenced by the heavy dose of moral skepticism that he had injected into his thinking at an early age. His first article for the meta-ethics series in 1982, "Moral Reality," spends most of its time trying to separate out the various strands of skepticism before it uses the parallel argument to answer them. What he was doing, of course, was simply systematizing his own earlier skepticism, the better to answer it.

In the 1990s Michael took a rather surprising detour into theology, spending the summer of 1994 steeped in the literature of religious ethics. His self-assigned task was to investigate the relationship between theism and moral realism. One can guess at his conclusions. He decided, first, that theism did no work in defending objectivity in ethics, and second, that theists typically betrayed a skeptical cast of mind about morality by accepting what are usually skepticism-producing tenets. Such "inchoate skeptics" are saved, Michael concluded, only by one last desperate maneuver in metaphysics—namely the positing of a personalized god.[92]

It would be easy to assume that Michael would have reached these judgments without spending the summer meticulously poring over dusty texts in theological ethics. After all, despite being the great-grandson of a well-known American theologian, he has been a lifelong atheist, and an arrogant one at that! At the age of four he was warned

[88] Moore, 2007a. [89] Moore, 2014a.

[90] As Stephen Morse declared at our wedding in 1987, ours was "a marriage forged in metaphysics," for, rather than either of us influencing the other to the view, our attraction was in part a product of our mutual commitment to "crazy realism."

[91] Moore, 2004c, ix. [92] Moore, 1995a; Moore, 2004c, ch. 3.

not to lean over the rail at the mill race in Eugene, Oregon, and when his sister Sharon declared, "Don't worry, Jesus will save him," Michael retorted: "Naw, he'd just fall in too." This motivated some hasty home-schooling by his conventionally religious mother, who he then frustrated with the usual questions that a curious child asks: "Where does God live?" "If He created everything, who created Him?" Her inability to squelch these inquiries won him enrollment in an evening Bible study class, in which he humiliated both himself and her. The children were lined up along one wall and asked questions that tested their mastery of a particular biblical text. When they gave correct answers, they crossed to the other wall. Every week, when Michael's mother came to collect him, there he was, standing alone, his back pressed to the original wall, defiantly insisting, as an example, that he didn't know who built the Ark. And he didn't.

Still, while Michael did not delve into theology in adulthood to satisfy any sense of spiritual hunger, he did so with genuine meta-ethical honesty. His was not a quest for footnote fodder for a paper already written in his head. It was a genuine search for an argument that might provide some surprising insight into how objectivist ethics might be alternatively motivated for those with the luxury of a metaphysical trump card in their Sunday pockets. I think it surprised him to find real moral skepticism among those who needed God in order to be confident in their morals, for only by considering moral maxims true relative to someone's beliefs (in this case, God's) could they imagine them being true in any sense at all.

G. Substantive ethics

Side by side with his work in meta-ethics, Michael has also worked in substantive ethics in both the aretaic and deontic arenas. His work in aretaic ethics has been limited to conceptualizing the categories of aretaic evaluation, such as the supererogatory, the suberogatory, the quasi-erogatory, and the aretaically indifferent. Proposing the revision of Aristotle's square of opposition, Michael has advanced a considerably more complicated set of aretaic relations.[93]

Michael's work in deontic ethics has been more extensive and more ambitious, focusing on how best to demarcate the divide between legitimate consequentialist (or "agent-neutral") and deontological (or "agent-relative") moral decision-making. Michael began his work in this area by focusing on a particular problem in ethics: the use of torture by Israeli intelligence services during the period of 1967–84.[94],[95] Despite finding the norm against torture to be as categorical, as "absolute," as any in morality, Michael followed his best arguments to the conclusion that there are three instances in which torture might nonetheless be justified by its good consequences. One is when a certain threshold of terrible consequences will be reached if torture is not inflicted. A second is when exceptions (such as self-defense) are plausibly thought to be part of more complete statements of applicable moral norms. And the third is when one or more of what

[93] Moore, 1998b. [94] Moore, 1989h; Moore, 1997b, ch. 17.

[95] He came to this topic by virtue of a seminar in 1989 that he and Joseph Raz co-taught on deontological ethics. Upon hearing of their inquiries, a group of Israeli civil rights groups asked Michael to assess the then recently released Landau Report on the use of "pressure" (the Israeli euphemism for torture) during custodial interrogation.

Michael calls "scope-limitations" apply—that is, those general attributes about the content of moral norms that determine their applicability to particular situations.

I was present at the initial public presentation at USC of Michael's paper on "Torture and the Balance of Evils." My own dissertation advisor, Barbara Herman, was the commentator on the paper, and she was prescient when she warned that although Michael thought he was engaged in an academic exercise of applied ethics, he would be taken by those beyond the ivory tower to be making a political statement about a matter of great controversy. Her prediction was correct. Michael's paper drew an immediate, very critical response from Amnesty International, which invited him to its annual meeting in New York to defend "this rubbish." Some of the members of the civil rights groups in Israel that had invited the paper adamantly disavowed it (Michael's friend, Ruth Gavison, telling him, for example, that his paper would "hang in every torture chamber in the Middle East"). And Michael subsequently received invitations to speak on the topic at universities and bar association meetings in Israel, Argentina, Germany, Switzerland, Ukraine, Canada, the UK, and China, as well as throughout the US. Some of these fora proved quite hostile, so much so that after a vigorous exchange at the annual meeting of the German Bar Association in Dresden, Michael had to ask in all seriousness whether he was still going to get lunch. Even the American CIA took an interest in the paper, inviting Michael to address the then newly formed Joint Task Force on Terrorism, several weeks after September 11, 2001.[96]

Out of this rather colorful beginning, Michael developed his well-known, partially agent-relative, partially agent-neutral, conception of deontic morality.[97] Michael now presents his conception as a "three-layer cake."[98] The first layer is a mix of consequentialist reasons given by good and bad states of affairs. The second layer consists of two kinds of overrides of the consequentialist calculations constituting the first layer; these overrides consist of agent-relative prerogatives and of agent-relative obligations. The latter have both exceptions and scope limitations that are drawn in terms of the act/omission, doing/allowing, intending/foreseeing, and other such distinctions.[99] The third layer is the override of both agent-relative prerogatives and agent-relative obligations which may be accomplished by there being over-the-threshold amounts of good or bad consequences that would follow from actions that, absent these consequences, would violate these rights and duties. As Jeffrey Brand-Ballard has declared, this "three-layer cake" view of the mixed consequentialist and deontological structure of morality is "as internally consistent and plausible as any deontological position with which I am familiar."[100]

[96] Since I had begged him not to lend his reputation to the CIA on this matter, I was relieved when the invitation was withdrawn the day before his scheduled address because the US Senate Judiciary Committee began issuing subpoenas to anyone thought to know about CIA practices of custodial interrogation.

[97] Moore and Alexander, 2007d; Moore, 2008a; Moore, 2009d, ch. 3; Moore and Alexander, 2012e.

[98] Moore, 2009d, ch. 3.

[99] The agent-centered (versus patient-centered or rights-based) nature of Michael's view is particularly revealed in the limitations that define the scope of deontological obligations (limitations that reveal the significance of the distinctions between acts and omissions, intent and foresight, doing and allowing, etc.). It is just this agent-centered focus that caused Michael's co-author, Larry Alexander, to insert his own patient-centered view for contrast in their jointly authored entry on "Deontological Ethics" for the *Stanford Encyclopedia of Philosophy*. Alexander and Moore, 2007d; Alexander and Moore, 2012e.

[100] Jeffrey Brand-Ballard, "Moral Emotions and the Culpability for Resultant Harm," 42 *Rutgers Law Journal* 315 (2011), 317.

On the strength of this more general work in ethics, Michael had recent occasion to return to particular moral dilemmas, applying his general view of deontic morality to an assessment of the current American and Israeli practices of "targeted killings," finding some (but limited) room for justified assassination within his three-layered view of ethics.[101]

One distinctive feature of Michael's view is that his deontology is conjoined with the naturalist-realism in meta-ethics described earlier. While deontologists are not untypically moral realists in their meta-ethics, they are less typically naturalists; for maximizing welfare or some other natural state of affairs comes more easily than does deontology to those with a naturalist meta-ethics. Michael here is an exception.

Michael would deny that his essentially deontological moral views have any deep psychological or experiential roots. Religion is probably a natural source of deontology for many, because the agent-relative nature of moral norms (the hallmark of deontology) fits nicely with the view that those norms are commands by God directed to each of us personally that tell us to keep our own moral houses in order without regard to maximizing the moral cleanliness, or minimizing the moral filth, of others' houses. But inasmuch as Michael is a thoroughgoing non-believer, his deontology is rather an honest attempt to capture the subtleties and tensions of intuitive moral thought.[102] It isn't very "pure," as John Dreher noted at USC in 1988, because it allows for lots of consequentialist calculations. Still, as Michael has said, "it is what I think we think, messy as it is." And in Michael's hands it isn't messy at all; it's just complex.

H. Interpretation in the hermeneutic disciplines

The eighth area of Michael's scholarship centers on the practice of interpretation. Michael has had both a parochial (in the sense of discipline-specific) and non-parochial (in the sense of interdisciplinary) interest in interpretation. His parochial interest is that of a lawyer interested in the interpretation of legal texts. His non-parochial interest is in the broad claims that remain in current intellectual fashion—claims that purport to debunk objectivity in fields as diverse as aesthetics, literary interpretation, psychoanalysis, history, psychology, and even physics. The "truths" discovered by these disciplines, so it is often claimed, amount to no more than some observer's "interpretation."

Michael's parochial interest in interpretation is part and parcel of his general interest in how judges both do and should reason in deciding disputed law cases (see section II.I. below). Interpretation in this context, as Michael sees it, is a means by which judges connect general legal texts to the facts of specific cases in order to render decisions.[103] A theory of legal interpretation is thus a necessary part of any judge's tool kit, joining logic, a theory of law, an understanding of the facts of a case, and applicable values to form an overall theory of adjudication.[104]

101 Moore, 2012b.

102 This contradicts the kind of "closet religiosity" that Stephen Morse has long attributed to Michael because of Michael's deontological and realist ethical views. Michael does allow, however, that Stephen's accusation here did partly motivate Michael's one foray into religion (Moore, 1995a). As Michael puts it, "I had vowed at some point to answer [Stephen's] charge of theism." Moore, 2000d, 246.

103 Moore, 1981; Moore, 1985b.

104 Moore, 1995e.

The right theory of interpretation in law, as Michael sees it, consists of, first, a theory of semantics (of what words used in legal texts mean in a natural language such as English); second, an understanding of speakers'-meaning (what a speaker means to say as opposed to what she actually said) to the extent necessary to secure a determinate reference for the words used (what Michael calls "essential context"); third, a theory of precedent for prior, authoritative interpretations of the same legal text; fourth, the value, purpose, or function served by the rule or principle in which the word appears; and fifth, a "safety-valve" question of general common sense and justice.[105] Values can enter into all five parts of this interpretive recipe, and the main criterion of good judging, as Michael sees it, is for a judge not to inject too many[106] or too few[107] of her values in her own assessment of these five ingredients.[108] Michael reminds us that a secondary feature of good judging, of course, lies in a judge having the right values with which to inject her judging.[109]

A salient feature of Michael's general theory of legal interpretation is his advocacy of the use of K–P semantics to provide the content of the first part of the five-part theory.[110] Michael has repeatedly applied this aspect of his general theory of legal interpretation to the special case of American constitutional interpretation.[111] Here Michael insists that we should interpret the rights-conferring clauses of the US Constitution as those clauses were understood by their natural rights-subscribing authors, Madison and Hamilton; that is, such clauses should be seen not as creating rights, but as referring to pre-existing moral rights whose nature gives the meaning of the words that refer to them.

Michael's non-parochial interests in interpretation were made evident by his critical survey of what he calls "the interpretive turn" in modern theory.[112] Michael surveyed the view that all knowing is a kind of interpretation (Heidegger, Rorty, Fish, Gadamer, etc.); the idea that the sciences of human understanding (the geisteswissenschaften) are interpretive even if the natural sciences (the naturwissenschaften) are not; and the idea that particular activities within certain disciplines like psychoanalysis and law can credibly lay claim to being interpretive. His final word on interpretation appears to be his general theory of when an activity in any field or discipline is usefully thought to be *interpretive* (as opposed to descriptive, explanatory, or predictive).[113] Working through what he calls the "four hermeneutic disciplines" of psychoanalysis, law, theology, and literary criticism, Michael advances the thesis that interpretation is an activity we do when we have some reason to treat something as a text, interpretations of which are capable of generating content-independent reasons either for belief or for action.

Michael maintains that his parochial interest in specifically *legal* interpretation stemmed from the accidents of teaching assignments early in his teaching career. As he finished his Senior Fellowship at Harvard in 1977, and with it his stewardship of Harvard's Law and Humanities Program, he was hired at USC to revise the (still-) required first-year course "Law, Language and Ethics" (LL&E) which had been inaugurated by

[105] Moore, 1981; Moore, 1985b. [106] Moore, 1985d; Moore, 1985e; Moore, 1985f; Moore, 1986a.
[107] Moore, 1983b; Moore, 1987f; Moore, 1988c; Moore, 1989d. [108] Moore, 1986d; Moore, 1987g.
[109] Moore, 1991b. [110] Moore, 1981; Moore, 1985b.
[111] Moore, 1989b; Moore, 1989g; Moore, 2001b; Moore, 2001e; Moore, 2008b.
[112] Moore, 1989f; Moore, 2000a, ch. 10. [113] Moore, 1994a; Moore, 2000a, ch. 11.

Bill Bishin and Chris Stone in the 1960s.[114] He packed up his motorcycle and embarked on a pilgrimage that was designed to put behind him the demise of his first marriage to Leslie and Janean's ensuing suicide, and to give himself a sense of a fresh start. He left Cambridge on his 750cc Honda, rode through the Deep South, up the backbone of the Rockies to Alaska, down the Inland Passage to Vancouver, and on to Los Angeles. His odyssey took all summer, during which time his only reading material was the LL&E course book by Bishin and Stone. As he warmly recalls, he "couldn't make hide or hair of its organization." Herb Morris had told him a year earlier that he had gotten so frustrated with the book that he "threw it across the room and left it there."[115] The one thing that stood out for Michael as a centrally important lesson was the need to master the amorphous set of factors that appropriately went into the interpretation of legal texts. So his substantially revised course materials (which he never published) and his early writings[116] reflected that early jurisprudential focus.

Once launched into the peculiarly fashionable interpretation debate of the 1980s, Michael combined his earlier interest in interpretation within psychoanalysis with his even earlier work in Continental philosophy (Nietzsche, Heidegger, Sartre, Kierkegaard, Husserl, etc.)[117] to broaden his work on interpretation into its cross-disciplinary, non-parochial form. This was motivated by his sense that in the 1980s "interpretation" was becoming the new refuge for sloppy, relativistic, or skeptical thought. As he put it:

> Like the "form of life" and "paradigm" pattern that Wittgenstein and Kuhn visited upon earlier decades, our "interpretive" patter does very little work in discovering or justifying any conclusion .... "It is only your interpretation" has descended to the level of cocktail conversation as our preferred way of expressing metaphysical or epistemological skepticism about anything, but it rarely does any work in justifying such skepticism.[118]

As with theological ethics, Michael dug deep into the writings of Gadamer, Barth, Habermas, Ricoeur, Foucault, and the like, piling their books about his desk until it took acrobatic feats to reach his chair. While reasonably sure that he would disagree with their fundamental tenets, he wanted his criticisms to be well-informed and fair to their subjects, so he persisted in weeks of reading that was far from being to his adult philosophical tastes (even as the study reminded him of his more youthful appetite for Continental philosophy years before).[119] He then road-tested his critique by, for example, debating Stanley Fish on numerous occasions and within numerous venues; engaging

[114] This course culminated in their book, William Bishin and Christopher Stone, *Law, Language, and Ethics* (Mineola: Foundation Press, 1972).

[115] Only when he arrived at USC did then-Dean Dorothy Nelson explain that to get the book finished she had intervened to assign Bishin and Stone alternating chapters. So it is no surprise that the overall organization of the book was opaque.

[116] Moore, 1981; Moore, 1985b.

[117] Michael's "Continental phase," as he calls it, began in law school where in his second year he read all of Nietzsche's collected works and then talked his skeptical law dean, Erwin Griswold, into letting him take Stanley Cavell's course on Heidegerrean metaphysics; the phase continued at UC Berkeley where he took courses with Bert Dreyfus and Phillipa Foot on existentialism, phenomenology, and French literature.

[118] Moore, 1994a, 1; Moore, 2000a, 424.

[119] The one exception (as he himself hints at in Moore, 1989f, 872) was the Critical Legal Studies literature of the 1980s, which he couldn't bring himself to "wade through," relying instead on the research of his assistant at Berkeley, (now Professor) Linda Helyar.

in a semester-long seminar on interpretation at the Humanities Research Institute at UC Irvine with the likes of Jacque Derrida, J. Hillis Miller, Geoffrey Hartman, Fish, and others; accepting Richard Rorty's invitation to defend his own natural law theory of legal interpretation at a day-long, university-wide faculty seminar at the University of Virginia, at which Rorty, A.J. Simmons, Christine Korsgaard, and others gave comments; and by fielding critical questions about his theory at a seminar on interpretation on Heidegger's home turf at Albert-Ludwigs University in Freiburg, Germany.

I. Jurisprudence and philosophy of law

Michael's ninth area of scholarship is one on which virtually all philosophers of law sharpen their teeth. (Michael calls this the "compulsory figures part of his skating program.") This is the field of jurisprudence, consisting both of general jurisprudence (which asks the question of what law is generally) and particular jurisprudence (which asks the more particular question of what law is within a particular legal culture such as that of the US or the UK). Michael recognizes this traditional way of dividing up the jurisprudential pie, but urges that such a distinction is not congruent with a distinction that interests him more, namely the distinction between the theory of law proper and the theory of adjudication. Michael thus resists classifying his work in the theory of adjudication as being exclusively either general or particular.[120]

Although he rarely classifies other legal philosophers besides himself by use of the general/particular jurisprudence distinction, Michael has critically worked through "the usual suspects" in both camps. Thus, he summarized H. L. A. Hart's legal positivism in general jurisprudence;[121] examined in detail the functionalist natural law theories of Lon Fuller, John Finnis, and Ronald Dworkin, all of which were written in reaction to Hart;[122] took a "hard look" (as Neil MacCormick once called it)[123] at the central notion of Joseph Raz's legal positivism, the notion of second-order, exclusionary reasons;[124] engaged one of the central implications of Ronald Dworkin's theory of adjudication, the right answer thesis;[125] and examined and rejected the skepticism about law that is the hallmark of the Legal Realists and their latter-day descendants, the "critical this-and-thats," as Michael calls them.[126]

In addition to assessing the jurisprudential thoughts of others—what Michael (borrowing a line from Hegel) calls, "educating oneself in public"[127]—Michael more positively engaged in a detailed analysis of three concepts of rules as they relate to law;[128] gave a similarly detailed analysis of legal principles;[129] and worked through his own theory of the force and content of precedent.[130] In the latter essay Michael indulged his familiar penchant for reaching beyond the law to place precedent in the context of more general concerns, namely those about universalizability and generalization in science and ethics as well as in law.

[120] Moore, 1998c; Moore, 2000a, ch. 3. [121] Moore, 1990c; Moore, 2009a, ch. 3.
[122] Moore, 1992a; Moore, 2000a, ch. 9.
[123] Neil MacCormick, "Preface," 62 *Southern California Law Review* 743 (1989), 745.
[124] Moore, 1989c; Moore, 2000a, ch. 5; Moore, 2003a; Moore, 2004c, ch. 5.
[125] Moore, 1987a; Moore, 2000a, ch. 8.
[126] Moore, 1984b; Moore, 2000a, ch. 6; Moore, 2003a; Moore, 2004c, ch. 5.
[127] Moore, 2000a. [128] Moore, 1991a; Moore, 2000a, ch. 4.
[129] Moore, 1997a; Moore, 2000a, ch. 7. [130] Moore, 1987d.

Michael has also lavished considerable attention on the jurisprudential question concerning the relationship between law and morality.[131] In Michael's view, morality necessarily enters into the reasoning of judges, and thus into the truth conditions of those singular propositions of law decisive of disputed law cases. Morality also necessarily enters into the truth conditions of certain general propositions of law, namely those propositions expressed in common law rules and legal principles.

Finally, Michael has taken some pains to apply his jurisprudential views to the judicial reasoning of particular judges and nominees for judicial office.[132] Having never thought of his theory as belonging to the ivory tower, he has both taught it to sitting judges in innumerable judicial education sessions and used it for purposes of judging such judges' performance.

Freud once wrote that the only things deeply satisfying in adult life are those things which satisfy either an actual or a sublimated desire of childhood. I doubt that jurisprudence is one of those things for very many people, no matter how rarified the sublimation. It is simply too dry, too bloodless, a subject. Such was Michael's early reaction to the general jurisprudence of John Austin, Jeremy Bentham, and Herbert Hart. It seemed neither difficult nor important. And the older natural law writers that he had read during his undergraduate days in international law (such as Grotius, Pfuffendorf, and Lauterpacht) he thought even worse. So Michael resolved early on to do philosophy *and* law—that is, philosophy applied to discrete legal concepts and problems such as action, intention, causation, and responsibility—and to leave philosophy *of* law—that is, jurisprudence—to others.

Two things combined to change his mind. First, Michael overlapped at Harvard in 1976–7 with Ronald Dworkin, where they had a formal public exchange about Dworkin's new book, *Taking Rights Seriously*. It was friendly, if competitive, and Dworkin was a good enough philosopher to make Michael reconsider whether philosophy *of* law might not be worth pursuing. The second was teaching "Law, Language and Ethics" at USC, starting in the fall of 1977, which persuaded him that the theory of adjudication—the theory of how judges should reason in particular cases—was at least neither dull nor academic (in the pejorative sense of the word).

Michael's interest in the theory of adjudication had a long run, but it too eventually waned. As he described his loss of interest in the subject, the issues and arguments simply ceased to be sufficiently difficult to be sustaining. After giving a paper in the philosophy of science at the Third Annual Meeting of the Union of the History and the Philosophy of Science in Montreal in 1980, Michael was stung by a comment made to him by a distinguished philosopher of science: "Why do you ever waste your time and obvious talents in the philosophy of law? Why don't you get a lab and get down to serious work?" And so Michael eventually skated off from the compulsory figures of jurisprudence to work on his philosophical triple Lutz and quadruple Salchow.

[131] Moore, 1981; Moore, 1985b; Moore, 1987d; Moore, 1989g; Moore, 1992a; Moore, 2001a; Moore, 2001b; Moore, 2001c; Moore, 2004c, ch. 4; Moore, 2007b; Moore, 2008b; Moore, 2012c.

[132] Moore, 1985d; Moore, 1985e; Moore, 1985f; Moore, 1986a; Moore, 1986d; Moore, 1986e; Moore, 1987f; Moore, 1987g; Moore, 1989d; Moore, 1991b.

III. General Themes in the Life and Work of Michael Moore

Michael's voluminous portfolio of scholarship and his life-long enthusiasm for debate and discussion exhibit a number of general themes, both methodological and substantive. While the teachings of his work across the above nine fields of inquiry cannot be overlooked by those who work in those fields, these larger themes are the lessons of his career as a whole. None of us own our legacies, for like our reputations, which exist in the minds of others, our legacies reside in the lessons that others take from our work. Still, if Michael could choose his own intellectual legacy, it would be comprised of the following commitments.

1. *An enthusiasm for the life of the mind.* Michael's favorite form of social interaction is the joint pursuit of ideas. For him, ordinary conversation typically pales in comparison to what he calls "chasing rabbits around the room." This is because ideas animate Michael in a way few other things do. As Colin Diver, our much-admired dean at the University of Pennsylvania Law School once put it, "Michael Moore has a ... prodigious appetite for knowledge."[133]

2. *A faith in the power of reason and of good argument.* A self-declared son of the Enlightenment, Michael values careful and precise argumentation not just for its own sake, but because he believes that only in this way can one discover and verify the truth about anything. As David Richards emphasized in characterizing Michael's early work, "There is no stridency here, no sterile self-promotion, no confusion of academic prestige with good argument, no debasement of academic standards. There is, simply, the quiet voice of a reasonable person working through problems and subjecting himself, as the humility of learning requires, to the highest standards of good argument observed anywhere today."[134]

3. *The conviction that knowledge is statable.* Michael's faith, like that of the logical positivists, is that what can be known can be said, difficult as it may be sometimes to find the right words. This is true for Michael even for areas of knowledge that seem to resist clear statement, such as the vagueness of expression, the emotional life of persons, or the meaning of life. As Michael puts it at one point, "there is no necessity that one speak vaguely even when discussing vagueness."[135] Michael's ideal here seems close to that of another of his early teachers, Paul Grice, who famously enjoined speakers to take on his "maxim of manner:" try to be clear and brief, and as orderly as one can in what one says, and avoid obscurity or ambiguity.

4. *A disdain for academic mush.* Relatedly, Michael has little tolerance for what he pejoratively calls "mush"—academic writing that is unclear, confused, obfuscating, disorganized, vague in reference, and/or pretentious. One of his favorite quotations is by John Searle about the work of Derrida: "This stuff is in danger of giving bullshit a bad

[133] Colin Diver, Dean Emeritus of the University of Pennsylvania Law School and President Emeritus of Reed College, quoted with permission at Michael's investiture in the University Walgreen Chair at the University of Illinois.

[134] David A. J. Richards, "Law, Psychiatry, and Philosophical Analysis: Review of *Law and Psychiatry: Rethinking the Relationship* by Michael S. Moore," 73 *California Law Review* 1659 (1985), 1669.

[135] Moore, 1985b.

name."[136] As Michael himself says about the mantras of the day, "Intellectual fashions are like metaphors ... Although they may begin life fresh and full of promise, they eventually become the tired counters in a patter that prevents insight rather than conveys it."[137]

5. *A devotion to the systematicity of ideas.* Michael further believes in the interrelatedness of all knowledge. Ideas for him are not isolated data points; they share relationships that require systematicity in one's thought if one is to capture their interconnectedness. Thus Michael casts his nets widely, relating common law reasoning from precedents, for example, both to generalization in ethics and inductive reasoning in science;[138] or finding parallels between the one-box solution to the Newcomb paradox and certain solutions to the epiphenomenalist challenge to responsibility issued by some neuroscientists.[139] As Jeffrey Brand-Ballard summed it up, Michael "is a major system builder for our time."[140]

6. *The necessity of logical organization.* Because Michael is always seeking to capture the systematicity with which ideas are related, organization is a crucial feature of his writing. Some have likened his work to a kind of "poetry in logic" because of its careful attention to logical organization. Michael typically gives each paper numerous oral presentations because, as he says, if the organization is not right, "the paper won't talk" (i.e., it cannot be given orally without notes). The result of Michael's attention to organizational tightness is a body of work that has won high praise for the rigor with which it accommodates "both the metaphysical implications of legal doctrines and the theoretical standards of intelligibility, coherence and stringency called for in philosophical analysis."[141]

7. *The need to cross disciplinary boundaries.* Michael believes that often issues and the arguments needed to resolve them refuse to honor the boundaries by which we separate the various academic disciplines. The result is that scholars cannot help but pursue interdisciplinary scholarship if they are successfully to engage such topics.

Michael's standard for good interdisciplinary scholarship is a high one. As he recently stated that standard: "Good interdisciplinary scholarship cannot be dilettant ish on either side of the equation; to be good at it, one needs sufficient expertise to be able to advance the cutting edge of understanding in each discipline."[142] Capturing Michael's success in living up to this standard, the famous sociologist Jean Floud wrote that Michael's professional pedigree is "happily unclear," for as a "true interdisciplinarian, he works comfortably in all three areas" of law, philosophy, and psychiatry.[143]

The interdisciplinary nature of Michael's scholarship is of a piece with the interdisciplinary nature of his intellectual entrepreneurship within the academy. As the Senior

[136] John Searle, "The Word Turned Upside Down," 30 *New York Review of Books* 74 (1983), 78 n. 3. Quoted in Moore, 1989f, at p. 871.

[137] Moore, 1994a, 1; Moore, 2000a, 424. [138] Moore, 1987d. [139] Moore, 2011a.

[140] Jeffrey Brand-Ballard, "Moral Emotions," 315.

[141] Dieter Birnbacher and David Hommen, "Omissions as Causes—Genuine, Quasi, or Not at All?," in Benedikt Kahmen and Markus Stepanians (eds.), *Critical Essays on Causation and Responsibility* (Berlin: De Gruyter, 2013), 133.

[142] Moore, 2013c, 137.

[143] Jean Floud, "Pleading Insanity," *The Times Higher Education Supplement*, July 13, 1984, 18. For a very similar assessment, see Gerard Casey, "Review of Moore, *Law and Psychiatry*," 39 *Review of Metaphysics* 576 (1986).

Fellow in charge of the Harvard Law and Humanities Program, he marshalled the considerable resources of the Harvard/MIT community to educate law professors about how their teaching and scholarship could be enriched with the insights of the arts and social sciences. He continued this work ten years later at UC Berkeley as co-chair (with Jeremy Waldron) of the jurisprudence component of the Jurisprudence and Social Policy Program, which is devoted to training legal academics in philosophy, politics, economics, sociology, and anthropology. He has, over the years, also joined several multi-disciplinary think tanks, such as the Humanities Research Institute for the University of California system, located on UC Irvine's campus, and the Research School for Social Sciences of the Australian National University.

This career-long dedication to high-level interdisciplinary work has garnered Michael some of his highest praise. David Richards, for example, lauded Michael for revealing "the power of interdisciplinary legal scholarship when it holds itself to uncompromising standards of rigor, precision, and clarity of argument."[144] Douglas Husak wrote that the details of Michael's application of philosophy of action to law "are bound to baffle readers who specialize in one discipline but only dabble in the other. Only the handful of theorists who possess a genuine expertise in both areas are in a position to appreciate the outstanding quality of Moore's important contribution."[145] Marcelo Ferrante declared that "[w]ith a remarkable combination of genius and erudition, he establishes profound connections between legal and philosophical discussions."[146] And other admirers concluded that "[on]e would be hard pressed to find another contemporary thinker with a comparable grasp of the problems and an equally sovereign command of the relevant literature in jurisprudence, action theory, moral theory, philosophy of language, ontology and metaphysics."[147]

8. *Metaphysical realism.* Michael's long-time friend and colleague Simon Blackburn once introduced his son to Michael, saying, "Now here is a real realist, not a half-baked job like myself."[148] Blackburn was right: Michael is a realist about quite a few things—not just natural kinds, but also moral kinds, human-made artifacts, legal kinds, law itself, etc. And of course, as Blackburn himself makes clear, Michael is a realist about causation: "[Moore's] work pulsates with arguments and examples, all in the service of an integrated picture of the interactions between law, morals, the philosophy of mind, and the metaphysics of causation. Moore's uncompromising realism brings a remarkable unity to his argument ...".[149]

Michael's substantive commitment to realism about various classes of entities seems to be consistent with his methodological distaste for "mush." He is fairly convinced that the various forms of relativism and skepticism are all-too-common refuges for those

[144] David A. J. Richards, "*Law, Psychiatry, and Philosophical Analysis,*" 1659.

[145] Douglas Husak, "The Relevance of the Concept of Action to the Criminal Law," 6 *Criminal Law Forum* 327 (1995), 327.

[146] Marcelo Ferrante, "Book Review of Michael S. Moore's *Causation and Responsibility,*" 14 *New Criminal Law Review*162 (2011), 162.

[147] Benedikt Kahmen and Markus Stepanians (eds.), "Introduction," *Critical Essays on Causation and Responsibility* (Berlin: De Gruyter, 2013), 1.

[148] Simon Blackburn is a well-known, self-proclaimed "quasi-realist" about moral qualities. See e.g., Simon Blackburn, *Essays in Quasi-Realism* (Oxford: Oxford University Press, 1993).

[149] Blackburn, book cover of Michael S. Moore, *Causation and Responsibility* (Oxford: Oxford University Press, 2010).

"too lazy or too ill-disposed to work through difficult terrain."[150] However, Michael is not a realist about everything, of course; no sensible person is. He is specifically skeptical about the existence of religious entities, for example, and he isn't even slightly amused by persistent town gossip that our house is haunted by a woman wearing a long white gauzy dress who many townsfolk claim to have seen floating in our upper bedrooms. I sometimes think he is just too lazy or ill-disposed to work through the spectral complexities of such residential metaphysics!

9. *Monistic naturalism.* Michael is both a monist and a naturalist about minds, morals, causation, events, actions, and law. He is, as he himself puts it, a "one-worlder," and that one world is the natural world studied by the sciences. Thus, he rejects G. E. Moore's non-naturalist realism about moral qualities; he rejects any form of Cartesian or Kantian dualism about minds and persons; he rejects any form of causal dualism that proclaims that causation by persons is a different kind of causation (e.g., Chisholm's "agent-causation") from the causation between natural entities; and he rejects any view that makes disciplines such as law autonomous in their ontological posits, as if each discipline could construct a world according to its own unique needs (e.g., that legal subjects are free in their choices if legal responsibility demands that they be free). Everything that allegedly exists, for Michael, has to be shown to exist by occupying a place in the best explanations we have of our experience. This is true for moral qualities like goodness as much as for natural properties like temperature.

10. *Reductionism.* Given the seemingly disparate kinds of things there are in the world, anyone with Michael's "one-worlder" view has to be some kind of reductionist. That is, in order to get everything into one natural world, one must endorse some scheme for reducing apparently non-natural entities to natural ones. Thus, Michael explicitly endorses a reduction of law to a blend of moral and social facts, a reduction of social and other mental facts to physical facts, and a reduction of moral facts to natural facts. Such reductions, however, are of the multiple-realizability kind, such that one supervening property can be realized by different base properties in different contexts.

11. *Non-foundationalist epistemology and emotional knowledge.* Throughout his career, Michael has relied on a non-foundationalist, coherence mode of justification. This is a style of justification that eschews there being any natural starting points for argumentation; for if they existed, such starting points would be some unquestionably foundational (or "self-evident") beliefs from which the truth of other beliefs could be inferred. While Michael confesses that he too "share[s] the wish that [he] had proofs anyone with a lick of understanding could not resist," he knows that this is precluded by the coherentist epistemenology that he adopts. Still, "a satisfying certainty in philosophy is possible despite the lack of such proofs."[151]

In his adoption of a non-foundationalist mode of argument, Michael was pretty plainly influenced by one of his early teachers in ethics, John Rawls. Still, Michael's style of justification differs from Rawls's in at least two significant respects. One is the metaphysical realism about morals that Michael, but not Rawls, marries to the coherence style of justification. How one extracts realism in metaphysics from a coherentist mode

[150] From a recorded conversation, December 2013. [151] Moore, 2004c, xiv.

of justification in epistemology is a well-known conundrum in philosophy,[152] but one which Michael has only glancingly addressed. Michael's other difference with Rawls lies in Michael's greater reliance on emotions. In his "experiential argument" for retribution, for moral luck, and for other moral phenomena, Michael allows the emotions a justificatory role that finds no analogue in Rawls's "considered judgments" about morality. Joel Feinberg, for one, thought that this was one of the great strengths of Michael's approach to moral epistemology:

> [Moore] treats us to one of the most thorough and sensitive discussions of the relations between moral judgment and the emotions since Aristotle proclaimed that the realm of moral philosophy concerns not only our dispositions to act . . . but also our dispositions to have the *feelings* that are appropriate.[153]

IV. Conclusion

So what will Michael do next? Having written book-length treatments of two of the three prima facie elements of criminal responsibility (action and causation), there is no question that those who teach and write in the area of criminal law expect him to finish the trilogy with a book on the mental states that define criminal culpability. But beyond this tall order, it is hard to predict what will spark Michael's fancy so as to inspire him to surround his desk with haphazardly stacked piles of new books. As others enter their seventies with aspirations to play golf and enjoy their grandchildren, Michael accepts professional commitments at a rate that requires him to work hours that would challenge the most ambitious of young law associates. Ever the master at advancing his written projects within the small cracks of each day, Michael scribbles paragraphs on restaurant napkins, on the backs of train tickets, and within frayed novels that he is still reading while trekking through remote regions in the Himalayas. Inasmuch as the trajectory of his insatiable curiosity remains as unbounded as his energy, one can only predict that as he watches his four beloved children emulate his own commitment to living a purposeful life, Michael will continue to seek out new mountains of the mind.

[152] See Lawrence Bonjour, *The Structure of Empirical Knowledge* (Cambridge: Harvard University Press, 1985).

[153] Feinberg and Coleman, *Philosophy of Law*, 685.

3

Modest Retributivism

*Mitchell N. Berman**

I. Introduction

Michael Moore is a giant of legal philosophy. Over the course of an academic career that already spans more than four decades yet shows no signs of abating, Moore has made profound contributions to our collective understanding of such diverse matters as moral realism and its implications for law, the relationship between law and psychiatry, the theory of action that undergirds Anglo-American criminal jurisprudence, the nature of legal interpretation, and, most recently, the metaphysics of causation. Very probably, though, Moore has achieved his greatest fame and influence as a theorist and proponent of a retributivist justification for criminal punishment.

When Moore's first papers in punishment theory appeared in the early 1980s, retributivism was only starting to recover from what had become, by mid-century, its near-total repudiation in respectable philosophical circles. Within a generation of Moore's arrival, however, scholars were widely contending—albeit more in horror than satisfaction—that retributivism had re-emerged as the dominant account of the moral justifiability of the infliction of criminal punishment.[1] Regardless of whether that is an accurate description of the state of theory in the early twenty-first century (and I confess to some skepticism), that retributivism has enjoyed a remarkable revival cannot reasonably be questioned. Nor can it be seriously doubted that Moore himself bears greater responsibility for the retributivist renaissance than does any other scholar. Moore is the foremost living retributivist among Anglophone moral theorists and philosophers of law.

My goal in this chapter is to critically assess the form of retributivism that Moore has advocated with rigor and acuity, and to great success. Plausibly, and only to a first approximation, the core retributivist claim—the claim that distinguishes retributivist views from their non-retributivist alternatives—holds that it is intrinsically valuable or right to furnish wrongdoers with the negative consequences that they deserve. But Moore claims much more for a wrongdoer's negative desert than this. That is, he

* A distant predecessor to this paper was presented at the Colloquium on Moral versus Political Perspectives on the Criminal Law, held at Berkeley Law in October, 2013. I am very grateful to the organizers and participants at that event for helpful reactions, and especially wish to acknowledge debts to Antony Duff, Alon Harel, Leora Katz, Chris Kutz, Sandra Marshall, Seana Shiffrin, Victor Tadros, and Arthur Yates. I am indebted as well to: David Dolinko for excellent written comments on a draft; the editors of this volume, Kim Ferzan and Stephen Morse, for inviting me to contribute; and our honoree, Michael Moore, for all that he has taught me. I feel deeply privileged to hold the Chair at Penn Law that Michael previously held and to which he brought great honor and distinction.

[1] See, e.g., Mirko Bagaric and Kumar Amarasekara, "The Errors of Retributivism," 24 *Melbourne University Law Review* 124 (2000), 126.

attributes significantly greater normative force to the noninstrumental value or rightness of furnishing a wrongdoer with his negative desert than is necessary for a view to qualify as retributivist. I will call Moore's retributivism "robust retributivism." An account that resides at nearly the opposite pole of retributivist logical space may be labeled "modest retributivism." In this chapter, I sketch robust and modest retributivism and aim to make the latter more eligible, principally by raising doubts about Moore's arguments for each of the components that jointly comprise the former. My ambition is neither to defend modest retributivism nor to defeat robust retributivism. It is to establish that retributivism embraces a greater diversity of possible and even plausible views than Moore himself allows—including views that, in a fairly straightforward sense, are considerably more moderate than the version that Moore has defended.

II. The Core of Retributivism

Any simple definition of retributivism will be contestable. That acknowledged, it is widely agreed that, for a justification of punishment to qualify as retributivist, a wrongdoer's negative desert must play some significant role in the justificatory account.[2] Very probably, little can be said about the particular nature of desert's role, or about how it figures in the logic of the justificatory argument, without taking sides in intra-retributivist disagreements. Accordingly, if any claim can be fairly identified as core or central to retributivism, let alone definitional of it, that claim must be formulated in quite general or vague terms.

Commentators reflect this point when describing retributivism as the theory, say, that punishment must be justified "in terms of" a wrongdoer's negative desert.[3] Yet that is perhaps a little *too* general or vague. Consider the most commonly espoused version of a "mixed theory"—the view (to a first approximation) that punishment is justified if and only if it produces net good consequences and is not inflicted on persons who lack negative desert.[4] Such a view justifies punishment by reference, in part, to an offender's negative desert and therefore would count as retributivist if mere reference to desert were sufficient to render a justification of punishment retributivist. And, sure enough, John Mackie's name for this view—"negative retributivism"[5]—held for a number of years. Increasingly, however, philosophers of punishment find it more accurate or illuminating to locate this position outside of retributivism, many preferring Antony Duff's apt label for this view: "side-constrained consequentialism."[6]

[2] Doug Husak makes the same observation in his contribution to this volume. See Douglas Husak, "What Do Criminals Deserve?" (this volume).

[3] C. L. Ten, *Crime, Guilt, and Punishment* (New York: Clarendon, 1987), 46.

[4] I say this is only a first approximation of the view because those who reject wholly objective conceptions of moral justification would likely add some sort of epistemic qualifiers, possibly at two places. A partially subjectivized variant of this version of the mixed theory might maintain, for example, that punishment is justified if and only if it is *reasonably expected* to produce net good consequences and is not *knowingly* inflicted on persons who lack negative desert, or is inflicted only on persons whom the punishing authorities *believe in good faith* to deserve it, or something along these lines.

[5] J. L. Mackie, "Morality and the Retributive Emotions," 1 *Criminal Justice Ethics* 3 (1982), 3.

[6] R. A. Duff, *Punishment, Communication, and Community* (New York: Oxford, 2001), 11.

Here, then, is a stab (subject to refinement) at the core retributivist thesis:

> (R) The goodness or rightness of satisfying a wrongdoer's negative desert morally justifies the infliction of criminal punishment, without regard for any further good consequences that might be realized as a contingent result of satisfying the wrongdoer's desert.[7]

I do not claim that acceptance of (R) is definitional of any thesis properly denominated "retributivist." Still, it is highly likely that (R) is accepted by the overwhelming majority of extant views about punishment that are considered retributivist by their adherents and critics alike. Importantly, (R) takes no position on such contested matters within the retributivist camp as what a wrongdoer's negative desert consists in (e.g., suffering, or being punished),[8] or whether the logical structure of the justification that a wrongdoer's negative desert provides is consequentialist or deontological.

III. Moorean Retributivism

In a well-known portion of his 1984 book, *Law and Psychiatry: Rethinking the Relationship*, reprinted and revised as "Closet Retributivism" thirteen years later in his *Placing Blame: A General Theory of the Criminal Law*, Moore explains what retributivism is, and is not. It is not, says Moore, any of several views with which it has frequently been confused. For example, it is not *lex talionis*, for retributivists as such need not endorse any single view of the proper measure of punishment. It is also not "negative retributivism," for while retributivists will endorse this position, one need not be a retributivist to do so. "The distinctive aspect of retributivism is that the moral desert of an offender is a *sufficient* reason to punish him," and not only, as negative retributivism maintains, that it is a necessary condition.[9] Similarly, retributivism is not a denunciatory theory of punishment, "should not be confused with a theory of formal justice (the treating of like cases alike)," and is not the view "that punishment of offenders satisfies the desires for vengeance of their victims, . . . [or] that the preferences of all citizens (not just crime victims) should be satisfied, . . . [or] that punishment is justified because without it vengeful citizens would take the law into their own hands."[10]

[7] (R) should not be taken to claim that the goodness or rightness of satisfying a wrongdoer's negative desert justifies the infliction of punishment "conclusively" or "all things considered," without regard for other considerations. The form of moral justification at issue in (R) is what I call "tailored." I elaborate on the distinction in section IV.B.

[8] On Feinberg's influential triadic analysis of desert, an agent, A, deserves some treatment or state of affairs, O, on account of some action or property, B. Feinberg called that which grounds a deserved treatment the "desert basis" (B, in the statement above). Joel Feinberg, *Doing and Deserving: Essays in the Theory of Responsibility* (Princeton, NJ: Princeton University Press, 1970). I call that which is deserved (O, in the statement above) the "desert object." To suffer and to be punished are different desert objects if, as is widely accepted, punishment itself is defined in partly functional or intentional terms, say as a treatment intended to be experienced as disagreeable by the subject upon whom it is imposed. See, e.g., H. L. A. Hart, *Punishment and Responsibility: Essays in the Philosophy of Law* (New York: Oxford, 1968), 4–5. If what a wrongdoer deserves is *to suffer*, then his negative desert can be realized even if he is not *punished*. What about the converse? Is it punishment if the person subjected to it does not suffer? Or, better, must punishment be designed to inflict suffering (or something close to it)? People hold different views about this.

[9] Moore, 1997b, 88. For simplicity, all citations to Moore's work will be to *Placing Blame* alone, and not also to predecessor books and articles.

[10] Moore, 1997b, 88–90.

Retributivism is none of these things. Instead, it

> is a very straightforward theory of punishment: We are justified in punishing because and only because offenders deserve it. Moral responsibility ("desert") in such a view is not only necessary for justified punishment, it is also sufficient. Such sufficiency of justification gives society more than merely a *right* to punish culpable offenders. It does this, making it not unfair to punish them, but retributivism justifies more than this. For a retributivist, the moral responsibility of an offender also gives society the *duty* to punish. Retributivism, in other words, is truly a theory of justice such that, if it is true, we have an obligation to set up institutions so that retribution is achieved.[11]

I accept each and every contention in Moore's list of "nots." None of the views from which Moore withholds the retributivist label is equivalent to, entails, or is entailed by, (R). But nor does the rejection of these several views entail the theory that Moore ends up advancing as the definition of retributivism. Three features of Moore's definition of retributivism warrant isolation and attention in particular.

First, for Moore, the goodness or rightness of giving wrongdoers what they deserve does not justify criminal punishment only in the sense that it renders the infliction of punishment morally permissible. Rather, the goodness or rightness of giving wrongdoers what they deserve grounds a moral *obligation* to inflict criminal punishment. In a footnote that follows the fourth sentence in the passage quoted above, Moore specifically cites K. G. Armstrong for the proposition that retributivism "only giv[es] the state the *right* to punish but not the *duty* to do so," but dismisses this view as yet another "mischaracterization of retributivism."[12] As he puts it elsewhere, while "[t]he desert of offenders certainly gives [state] officials *permission* to punish offenders, ... retributivism goes further. As a theory of a kind of justice, it *obligates* us to seek retribution through the punishment of the guilty."[13]

Second, the goodness or rightness of giving wrongdoers what they deserve does not merely justify (by making obligatory) the infliction of punishment in an individual case. Rather, it grounds an obligation to establish and maintain *institutions* devoted to the imposition of criminal punishment. The obligation to inflict retributivist punishment, says Moore, "means that officials have a duty to punish deserving offenders and that citizens have a duty to set up and support institutions that achieve such punishments."[14]

Third, it is not merely the case that the goodness or rightness of giving wrongdoers what they deserve, without regard for any further good consequences of doing so, is sufficient to justify the infliction of criminal punishment. Rather, Moorean retributivism maintains that effectuating just deserts is the *only* goal, consideration, or rationale that can justify criminal punishment. It is "only because" offenders deserve punishment that we are justified in inflicting it.

Each of the foregoing three features stakes a position on a distinct dimension on which different accounts of the justifiability of punishment could plausibly vary. Call

[11] Moore, 1997b, 91 (emphases in original; citation omitted).

[12] More precisely, Moore calls Armstrong's conception "perhaps an eighth mischaracterization of retributivism." Moore, 1997b, 91 n.17 (citing K. G. Armstrong, "The Retributivist Hits Back," in H. B. Acton (ed.), *The Philosophy of Punishment* (London: Macmillan, 1969)). It is hard to know what sense to make of that (uncharacteristically) fudgy "perhaps."

[13] Moore, 1997b, 154 (emphases in original).

[14] Moore, 1997b, 154.

these the dimensions, respectively, of *force*, *scope*, and *exclusivity*. With respect to *force*, Moore maintains that not only does the goodness or rightness of inflicting negative desert provide a reason to inflict punishment that is sometimes adequate to justify it, all things considered, but it grounds a duty to do so as well. With respect to *scope*, he contends that a wrongdoer's negative desert provides an obligation, not only to impose criminal punishment in individual cases, but to establish and maintain institutions of criminal punishment as well. And with regard to *exclusivity*, Moore claims that furnishing negative consequences because they are deserved is the only morally acceptable justification for the infliction of criminal punishment.

Let us call this package of views "robust retributivism." It is a stipulated term of art. David Dolinko termed a version of retributivism that is strong on the dimension of force alone (i.e., that views the satisfying of negative desert not only as permissible but as obligatory) "bold" retributivism.[15] Robust retributivism is triply bold.

A retributivist package of views that represents a polar alternative to robust retributivism would differ on all three of these dimensions. It would maintain that the value or rightness of realizing negative desert provides reason to punish but does not ground an obligation to punish; that considerations other than desert must be relied upon to justify the creation and maintenance of an institution of criminal punishment; and that proper recognition of the moral significance of negative desert does not foreclose the possibility that the act or institution of punishment could be justified on the strength of other values or reasons. Call this package "modest retributivism." The two positions are summarized in the following table.

	Robust retributivism	**Modest retributivism**
Scope	Negative desert justifies the institution of punishment as well as individual instances.	Negative desert justifies the infliction of punishment on wrongdoers, but does not by itself justify creation and maintenance of the institution of criminal punishment.
Force	Negative desert grounds not only a reason to punish but a duty to punish as well.	Negative desert grounds only a reason to punish, and not also a duty.
Exclusivity	Negative desert grounds the only morally acceptable justification for the infliction of criminal punishment.	Although negative desert can justify the infliction of criminal punishment, punishment is at least potentially justifiable on other grounds as well.

There are possible views intermediate between robust and modest retributivism. For example, one could maintain that negative desert justifies the institution of punishment but is not the only potentially available ground for a satisfactory justification. In focusing on the especially minimal account that I am calling modest retributivism, I do not intend to deny or disparage this or any other intermediate options. Similarly, the dimensions of force, scope, and exclusivity are not the only dimensions on which versions of retributivism could differ. I do not even claim that they are the most significant ones. I claim only that they are significant enough to warrant our attention.

[15] David Dolinko, "Some Thoughts About Retributivism," 101 *Ethics* 537 (1991), 542.

IV. Less than Moore

To reiterate a point made earlier, I am not setting out to show that Moorean robust retributivism is wrong or defective. I aim only to show that several of the elements that comprise it are optional from a retributivist perspective. Moore himself equates his version of retributivism (what I'm terming "robust retributivism") with retributivism, *simpliciter*. It is my impression that many people view things just that way. My aim here is to raise doubts about that equation and thus to make more apparent other retributivist possibilities, in particular possibilities that require negative desert to do significantly less work than Moore demands of it.

A. Force

In his 1993 article, *Justifying Retributivism*, Moore acknowledged (for the first time in print, as far as I'm aware) that retributivism could be a consequentialist approach to justifying punishment. "One can, of course, *define* retributivism so that a retributivist must be a deontologist," he remarked. But that would be a mistake. The "distinctively retributivist" thesis, he insisted—broadly in accord with (R)—is "that the guilty receiving their just deserts is an intrinsic good."[16]

Yet, as we have seen, Moore also contends that we have a duty or obligation both to inflict punishment on wrongdoers and to establish institutions whose purpose or function is to mete out retributive punishment. It seems plain on the face of things that these claims go far beyond (R) or the view that Moore has described as "distinctively retributivist." Not plain, in my estimation, are the arguments that Moore advances for this bolder position.

Let us start with the dimension of force. The usual arguments for retributivism, including those advanced by Moore, depend heavily upon thought experiments.[17] Common are two-world hypotheticals: Worlds A and B are identical in all respects except that, in A, some vicious wrongdoer suffers or is punished on account of his wrongs, whereas in B he lives happily ever after. If we stipulate that the punishment or suffering of the wrongdoer in World A does not generate any downstream consequences that further distinguish the two worlds, and if we think that World A is nonetheless better, then we have grounds to accept something like (R). And, as Moore has further observed, your attachment to (R) might be strengthened by imagining that you are the wrongdoer and by then reflecting both on the guilt that you would yourself experience, and the judgment that you might reach that you too should be punished.[18] If we believe that there is value in the satisfaction of negative desert, and if we further believe that, presumptively, we have some reason to bring about valuable states of affairs, then we should conclude that we have reason to promote the satisfaction of negative desert.

Notice that I have spoken so far only in terms of value and reason. I have said nothing about duties, obligations, or justice, for the simple reason that nothing about

[16] Moore, 1997b, 157.
[17] See, e.g., John Kleinig, *Punishment and Desert* (The Hague: Martinus Nijhoff, 1973), 67.
[18] Moore, 1997b, 145–9.

hypotheticals of this kind naturally invites conclusions formulated in such terms. Moore, however, maintains that we have a "duty" or "obligation" to satisfy negative deserts, and that such a duty or obligation is one of "justice."

Frankly, I am uncertain precisely what Moore means by these terms or what their normative upshot is. I assume only (thanks in part to the frequent use of italics) that Moore understands and intends to signal a normative escalation. On most accounts, duties and obligations are not only moral reasons but reasons that are particularly weighty or have second-order exclusionary characteristics, or are in other respects especially stringent (even if not "absolute" or "conclusive"). I therefore interpret the move from normative concepts like "reason," "right," "permissible," and "justified" to "duty," "obligation," and "justice" to raise the stakes, so to speak. Yet I do not see what about the thought experiments themselves warrants any normative escalation from claims about value and reason to claims about duties of justice, nor am I aware of distinct arguments that Moore provides for this move. We must be careful not to start by assuming that the justification for which we search will necessarily supply obligations and not merely reasons and permissions, or even that retributivism is a form of justice. That would be to put the rabbit in the hat.

To be sure, Moore could maintain, perhaps following Aristotle, that duty and justice are built into the very concept of desert. According to one such view, for example, it is a conceptual entailment of the proposition that A deserves O that justice demands that A get O, and we are all under a standing obligation to advance justice. There are difficulties with this account of desert, for it is common, and not clearly mistaken, to assert in some contexts both that some A deserves φ, and that nobody is obligated to see that A gets φ.[19] But even if the contention that justice and obligation are built into the concept of desert can be successfully defended, it would remain for Moore to establish that the reactions that the retributivists' two-world hypotheticals frequently pump go beyond judgments that it is good or right that the blameworthy wrongdoers at issue "suffer" (or "are punished"), and really amount to judgments that the wrongdoers "deserve" to suffer (or to be punished) in the particular sense of *desert* that entails that others are obligated to furnish such suffering (or punishment).[20] This cannot be taken for granted.

B. Scope

So much for my doubts about the robust retributivist position on the dimension of force. Suppose, however, that this aspect of robust retributivism is correct even if not

[19] For elaboration, see Mitchell N. Berman, "Rehabilitating Retributivism," 32 *Law and Philosophy* 83 (2013), 90–3.

[20] This is an appropriate place to register my own tentative sense that prevailing views regarding the sort of thing that desert is might be mistaken. Husak describes desert as a "reason-giving property." Husak, "What Do Criminals Deserve?" (Chapter 4 ms. at 7). Moore often says similar things (see Moore, 1997b, 168 n. 25, 178, 180), though elsewhere he describes desert as a "principle" (Moore, 1997b, 170, 171). I am disposed to doubt that desert is best conceived as a property belonging to individuals. But because this is not the place to elaborate on my doubts, I have tried in this chapter to speak of desert in terms that square with common understandings and usage. Some things I say in this chapter—possibly including my formulation of (R)—could require restatement to accord with the conception of desert (negative or otherwise) that I might ultimately favor.

definitional of retributivism: we, or some of us, have a duty to inflict deserved suffering or deserved punishment on wrongdoers. Does it follow that we have a duty to establish and maintain institutions of criminal punishment (still assuming that duties are especially stringent in some fashion yet to be fully elucidated)? Again, it is hard to know for sure without knowing what such a duty amounts to. But it is important to note that the thought experiments upon which retributivists rely do not require that conclusion: they are generally about individual cases.

More significantly, the focus on individual cases appears non-accidental once we reflect on what retributivist theories of punishment are (or at least can be) designed or offered to do. Some commentators, perhaps influenced by Hart's insistence on distinguishing between the "general justifying aim" of punishment and principles of distribution, assume that theories of punishment must be designed to justify the institution of criminal punishment and not just individual inflictions of punishment. I think this is a consequentialist bias, and that the argumentative dialectic concerning the justification of punishment does not require retributivists to have been arguing that the institution of punishment can be justified by reference to the goodness or rightness of furnishing deserved suffering.

I have argued elsewhere that it is useful to distinguish two types of justification: "all-things-considered" and "tailored."[21] An all-things-considered justification of an act or practice is just what it sounds like: it purports to establish that the act or practice is morally permitted in light of all considerations. A tailored justification aims to establish the permissibility of the act or practice at issue against one or more grounds for doubt, what I have termed "demand bases." It shows that the particular grounds explicitly invoked or implicitly relied upon for thinking the act or practice unjustifiable are chimerical or overridden.

In my view, the dominant strand within punishment theory has involved the effort to provide tailored justifications against the particularly salient and forceful complaint that it is wrongful to intentionally cause people to suffer. (R) is a promising response to this demand basis. As such, it can be sensibly advanced to justify punishment in the individual case. The argument can be construed thus: assuming that there already exists an institution with lawful authority to inflict punishments (or that the instant case can, for whatever reason, be treated as a one-off that does not require a preexisting institution dedicated to the infliction of criminal punishment),[22] then the fact that a person has done grave wrong provides a fully sufficient reason to inflict punishment, regardless of whether punishment in this case would serve any of the values that the institution was created to serve.

When we turn our attention to the entire institution of punishment, however, other objections—additional demand bases—become salient, indeed inescapable. Here are two: the institution of punishment consumes substantial social resources that could be put to other uses, and invariably results in the infliction of suffering on wholly innocent persons. If I am right that these objections are squarely on the table in the institutional case but not necessarily in the individual case, then the contention that we have an

[21] Mitchell N. Berman, "Punishment and Justification," 118 *Ethics* 258 (2008), 262–6.

[22] Think of a Nuremberg-like situation, or a domestic equivalent.

obligation to establish institutions of criminal punishment solely on the strength of the value of realizing negative deserts seems both doubtful and unnecessary to attribute to retributivists, even though modest retributivists should surely believe that the noninstrumental value of satisfying negative deserts *contributes* to a successful justification of the institution.

Some readers may feel that the account I have just offered regarding why a successful retributivist justification for instances of criminal punishment need not extend to or entail a successful retributivist justification for the institution of criminal punishment depends too heavily on a particular contestable account of the dialectical logic of justification. I think, in contrast, that it accurately captures the truth that distinct questions are sometimes in play. Very frequently, we ask the "what justifies punishment?" question when we have in mind some particular case of actual or contemplated punishment. Especially when the familiar consequentialist justifications for punishment strike us as significantly attenuated (as when the offense charged is sufficiently unusual as to weaken the apparent need for general deterrence, and when the offender is sufficiently old as to weaken the need for specific deterrence or incapacitation), the question is posed "what reason have we to punish *him*?" In such cases, the retributivist response is: "because he deserves it." That can be an acceptable answer to the question on the table (if perhaps a little telegraphic) even if it is not an acceptable answer to the broader question: "what justifies the creation and maintenance of a system of criminal punishment?"[23]

C. Exclusivity

According to Moore, retributivism maintains that negative desert is a necessary and sufficient condition for infliction of punishment and that, equivalently, "punishment is justified if and only if the person or persons receiving it deserve it." [24] Thus, he says, "retributivism asserts that punishment is properly inflicted because, and only because, the person deserves it."[25] I believe this is doubly mistaken.

Perhaps the most obvious objection would be that an offender's negative desert does not constitute a sufficient condition for the justified infliction of punishment. It is always imaginable that some individual act of punishment would produce horrendous consequences overall and it seems implausible that, even if we have moral reason, or even obligation, to inflict deserved punishment, such reasons or obligation are so stringent as to require that we do so regardless of the consequences. This, however, is one

[23] Husak has recognized that these are different questions and has agreed that negative desert alone goes farther toward answering the former than the latter. See Douglas Husak, "Holistic Retributivism," 88 *California Law Review* 991 (2000), 995. But he seems also to believe that the latter question—concerning a "complete justification for creating an institution of punishment," ("Holistic Retributivism," at 996)—is, in some meaningful sense, the real question, and therefore that retributivism gains greater plausibility than it genuinely warrants "only if we *artificially narrow* our conception of the nature" of the problem that we are called upon to resolve ("Holistic Retributivism,"at 993) (emphasis added). Samuel Sheffler has taken issue with this suggestion of Husak's, insisting on the independent significance of "the question of whether and when society's punishment of an individual is compatible with just treatment of that individual." Samuel Sheffler, "Justice and Desert in Liberal Theory," 88 *California Law Review* 965 (2000), 987 n. 73. I'm with Sheffler on this point.

[24] Moore, 1997b, 92. [25] Moore, 1997b, 92.

objection I waive, for Moore has made clear, in response to Dolinko's leveling of this very charge, that his invocation of sufficiency is intended to be context-sensitive:

> [W]hen we say that one condition was sufficient for another—as in the counterfactual statement that a particular fire was sufficient to burn down someone's house—we mean that within some limited set of conditions this one by itself was sufficient. Other conditions outside that set—such as the presence of oxygen in my fire example—are invariably *necessary* even while we idiomatically describe a condition within that set as 'sufficient'.
>
> The retributivist's usage of 'sufficiency' is to be so construed. *Within the set of conditions constituting intelligible reasons to punish,* the retributivist asserts, desert is sufficient, i.e., no other *of these* conditions is necessary.[26]

Given this helpful clarification about Moore's sufficiency claim, my two objections are these. First, embracing (R) does not entail that desert is a necessary condition for the infliction of punishment. Second, even if negative desert is both a necessary and sufficient condition for the justified infliction of punishment (so long as sufficiency is construed in the somewhat loose manner just described), that does not establish that punishment may be inflicted "because and only because" the person punished deserves it, on the most common construal of that expression.

1. Retributivism need not be committed to the proposition that negative desert furnishes a necessary condition for the justified infliction of punishment. Let me say more about the argumentative dialectic that births not only retributivism but consequentialism, too. We hold out for consideration an actual or hypothetical act of criminal punishment and raise a moral objection: *this*, we say, is deeply morally problematic. It is ordinarily profoundly wrongful to treat people in this way. Therefore, if we are to continue to do such things, we need to explain how it can be morally justified. Our theories of punishment are efforts to meet this demand. One tradition says, in effect, we can justify doing such things by reference to the fact that wrongdoers deserve it. Another tradition offers a different account: we can justify doing such things by the good net consequences thereby produced. Abolitionists believe that both positions are wrong, and that there are no other better options waiting in the wings. But just as both accounts could be wrong, both could be right. More significantly, there is no reason why it must be part of either of these proposed answers to reject the other. To be sure, one who accepts one of the justificatory theories could, at the same time, reject the other. A retributivist could be an anti-consequentialist about punishment, and a consequentialist could be an anti-retributivist. My point is only that both types of theory are, by the nature of what they are asked to do, accounts about what does or can justify punishment; they are not accounts about what does not or cannot justify it. Therefore, the rejection of consequentialist justifications is no integral part of retributivism, and the rejection of retributivist justifications is no integral part of consequentialism.[27] If this is right, Moore is

[26] Moore, 1997b, 173 (emphasis in original).

[27] I am speaking here of consequentialism as a justification of punishment, not as a comprehensive moral theory. As a comprehensive moral theory, consequentialism does deny deontological retributivism, but because we have already seen that consequentialist retributivism is a real possibility, it is not even true that consequentialism as a comprehensive moral theory entails the falsity of all varieties of retributivism.

simply mistaken to define retributivism as the view that "punishment is justified if and only if the person or persons receiving it deserve it."[28]

Of course, even if I am right that Moore's "necessary condition" claim attributes more content to retributivism *simpliciter* than is warranted, it could still be true that punishment is justified only when deserved.[29] Most criminal law theorists espouse that view, and they could well be correct. If they are correct, however, it is on the strength of a substantive moral judgment to the effect that (to a first approximation) it is unjust or otherwise wrongful to inflict punishment on somebody who doesn't deserve it—or, in a more subjectivist spirit, without a bona fide belief that the person is guilty and blameworthy. Call that substantive moral claim (Q). But just as consequentialists about punishment may help themselves to (Q) (witness "side-constrained consequentialism"), retributivists—i.e., those who accept (R)—are free to eschew it. (R) does not entail (Q).

2. Retributivism need not be committed to the proposition that punishment is justified only when inflicted "because" the person punished deserves it. Now let us suppose, arguendo, that (R) and (Q) are both true. If so, we might fairly conclude that negative desert constitutes both a sufficient and a necessary condition for the justified infliction of punishment (so long as sufficiency is construed in an adequately contextual or pragmatic way), which is also to say that punishment is justified if and only if the person punished deserves it. Nonetheless, it would not follow that persons may be punished "because and only because" they deserve it, if that locution means that punishment is justified only when inflicted *for the reason* that the person punished deserves it. Conditions need not be reasons, for the absence of a fact that, if present, would render some action φ impermissible, is a necessary condition for the permissibility of φing, but not itself a reason to φ.[30] That you have not promised not to quack like a duck might be a necessary condition for you to be justified in quacking but is not itself a reason for you to quack. And if you do quack, it would be unnatural to say that you did so "because of" the fact that you had not promised not to.

So the fact, if true, that a person's negative desert constitutes both a necessary condition and a sufficient condition for punishing him does not itself entail that we are justified in punishing somebody because and only because he has negative desert. But, of course, the latter claim could nonetheless be true. Are there any reasons for a retributivist (i.e., somebody who endorses (R)) to resist Moore's contention that punishment is justified only when inflicted "because" the punishee deserves it?

Here are two. First, one might believe, in a Kantian vein, that the value of an action depends upon the actor's motivations or explanatory reasons. Indeed, I think that Moore himself believes this.[31] Adding this view to Moore's claim that, in order for

[28] Moore, 1997b, 91. See also Moore, 1997b, 92.

[29] Or, only when inflicted in the good faith belief that it is deserved, or something similar. See note 4 above.

[30] I think that the distinction between conditions and reasons lies close to the heart of the difference between what Dolinko calls "rational" and "moral" justification; see David Dolinko, "Retributivism, Consequentialism, and the Intrinsic Goodness of Punishment," 16 *Law and Philosophy* 507 (1997), 518, and what Michael Lessnoff termed "teleological" and "entitling" justification; Michael Lessnoff, "Two Justifications of Punishment," 21 *Philosophical Quarterly* 141 (1971). The distinction is also fundamental to rights-forfeiture theories of punishment. See, e.g., Christopher Heath Wellman, "The Rights Forfeiture Theory of Punishment," 122 *Ethics* 371 (2012).

[31] At one point, Moore comments on the "tension that exists between crime-prevention and retributive goals … due to retributivism's inability to share the stage with any other punishment goal. To achieve

punishment of a wrongdoer to be morally justified, the offender's negative desert must supply the reason that punishment is inflicted, yields a conclusion that a retributivist might not want to own. Take the standard imagined case of punishment in which the person punished deserves it and the punishment would promote net good consequences (even putting aside any supposed value of realizing negative desert). If we follow Moore (as I construe him) in believing that, in order for punishment in such a case to be morally justified, the offender's negative desert must supply the reason for punishment, then the value—and possibly the justifiability—of punishment will depend upon the reasons that move the punishing authorities. A retributivist could avoid this conclusion by refusing to join Moore in traveling from "if and only if" to "because and only because."

Second, there is a cost to contending that punishment is justified only if imposed because—i.e., for the reason that—wrongdoers deserve it. Such a claim implies that if, contrary to what the retributivist believes, (R) is false, then punishment is not morally justifiable: if the only reason that supposedly favors punishment turns out to be no reason at all, then there are no morally cognizable reasons to punish. This is a steep price to pay for membership in the retributivist camp. For myself, I am more confident that morally justified systems, and instances, of criminal punishment are possible than I am that (R) is true.

V. Retributivism from the Back Door, Again

In his well-known "argument for retributivism from the back door," excerpted in several editions of the highly regarded Kadish and Schulhofer casebook,[32] Moore defends the correctness of retributivism precisely by purporting to have shown that the only "theories of punishment truly competitive with retributivism, namely, the pure utilitarian theory, and the mixed theory, are each unacceptable to us."[33] But if retributivism

retributive justice, the punishment must be inflicted because the offender did the offense. To the extent that someone is punished for reasons other than that he deserves to be punished, retributive justice is not achieved." If "part of the reason motivating those who punish [a wrongdoer] is that his punishment will serve as an example to others," he says, then "the criminal justice system is not achieving retributive justice." Moore, 1997b, 28.

Elsewhere, however, Moore writes that "the only difference" between the two most plausible versions of mixed theory—desert-constrained consequentialism and consequences-constrained retributivism—"is in the *motivations* of those who hold them. And while that may make a difference in our moral judgements of those who hold the different branches of the mixed theory of punishment, it does not make a difference in terms of the actual social institutions and judgements such theories will justify." (Moore, 1997b, 94 emphasis in original). These passages strike me as inconsistent insofar as the second appears to convert a consideration that the first treats as bearing on act evaluations into a matter relevant only to actor evaluations. Still, I would not be so foolhardy as to rule out that Moore has in mind a basis for reconciling these passages that eludes me.

[32] See, for example, Sanford H. Kadish and Stephen J. Schulhofer, *Criminal Law and Its Processes: Cases and Materials*, 5th edn. (Boston: Little, Brown, 1989), 142–4.

[33] Moore, 1997b, 103. Some philosophers of punishment will reject the starting assumption that consequentialist, retributivist, and mixed theories exhaust the possible justifications of punishment. Additional possibilities would be deontological accounts that do not assume, and might even deny, that the suffering that a wrongdoer experiences is either good or right. Duff's communicative theory is plausibly one such view, as is the view that we act rightfully in (temporarily or permanently) removing wrongdoers from law-abiding society. With many others, I am skeptical that the non-retributivist deontological positions on offer

supplies the only acceptable justification of criminal punishment, what does it maintain? I have argued that retributivism is properly understood as committed to something very close to (R), and that the version of retributivism that Moore himself embraces goes significantly beyond this minimal content, on at least three discrete dimensions of variability.

Have I, at the same time, done anything to bolster the prospects for retributivism of any form? Not directly, for I offer no new arguments for (R) itself. Perhaps, though, my effort to identify respects in which Moorean retributivism goes beyond minimal retributivist commitments can serve as an indirect argument for modest retributivism, or something in its vicinity. Readers who had been disposed against Moorean robust retributivism, but had not appreciated the availability of accounts that claim much less for negative desert, might now be moved to reconsider their resistance to retributivism *tout court*. This argument, then, like Moore's, proceeds through the back door.

But is it a back door to the same house? Because modest retributivism is so unbold—perhaps even timid or pallid?—one might wonder whether it fairly qualifies as a version of retributivism at all.[34] It is impossible to address this concern fully without wading deeply into methodological debates concerning the demarcation and analysis of concepts. In concluding that what I am terming modest retributivism is indeed a version of retributivism, I rely heavily on my impressions of the criteria that criminal law theorists seem to invoke or have in mind when characterizing their own views, or even themselves, as retributivist or anti-retributivist. As a descriptive matter, it appears to me that the line between avowed retributivists and their avowed critics is most faithfully drawn between those who believe and those who deny that a wrongdoer morally deserves to suffer (or to experience hardship or deprivation, or the like) in any sense of desert that would provide some others, including the state, with reasons—nontrivial reasons, or reasons that can at least sometimes make a difference—to provide that suffering or deprivation.[35]

(R) aims to capture the proposition that self-described retributivists overwhelmingly accept and that their self-described opponents overwhelmingly reject. But the pith of retributivism could perhaps be put in simpler and more colloquial terms: *Ceteris paribus*, the world goes better when wrongdoers receive their comeuppance.

have the resources to justify treatment that rightly qualifies as punishment; see my "The Justification of Punishment," in Andrei Marmor (ed.), *The Routledge Companion to Philosophy of Law* (New York: Routledge, 2012), 141—but we can safely table that question for the limited purposes of this essay.

[34] Duff describes "the core retributivist thought" differently than I do. The core thought, in his view, is "that what gives criminal punishment its meaning and the core of its normative justification is its relationship, not to any contingent future benefits that it might bring, but to the past crime for which it is imposed." R. A. Duff, "Retrieving Retributivism," in Mark D. White (ed.), *Retributivism: Essays on Theory and Policy* (New York: Oxford, 2011), 3. I do not think that an account need view desert as supplying the "core normative justification" for punishment for it to qualify as retributivist.

[35] Moore once opined that "[t]he true worry that most people have about retributivism" is that retributivist emotions, urges, and judgments are always pathological. Moore, 1997b, 119. I take this to be offered as an explanation for many people's rejection of the central retributivist thesis. My experience jibes with Moore's observation.

4

What Do Criminals Deserve?

*Douglas Husak**

I. Introduction: Moore on Deserved Punishment

Michael Moore is famous (inter alia) for formulating (and then for defending) the particular version of retributivism quoted most frequently by contemporary philosophers of law. According to Moore, retributivism

> is the view that punishment is justified by the desert of the offender. The good that is achieved by punishing, on this view, has nothing to do with future states of affairs, such as the prevention of crime or the maintenance of social cohesion. Rather, the good that punishment achieves is that someone who deserves it gets it. Punishment of the guilty is thus for the retributivist an *intrinsic* good, not merely the *instrumental* good that it may be to the utilitarian.[1]

He concludes, "the distinctive aspect of retributivism is that the moral desert of an offender is a *sufficient* reason to punish him or her."[2] This particular account of a retributive theory of punishment has probably been attacked more often than it has been defended. In the absence of further clarification, it is an easy target. Despite his stature as the most influential philosopher of criminal law in the United States and the most well-known retributivist anywhere, Moore's work may have had the perverse effect of making retributivism *less* popular than it should be. Critics of this tradition borrow the above definition and suppose that all retributivists believe desert is sufficient to justify punishment. By showing that desert cannot possibly have this function, these critics conclude that retributivism itself must be rejected. If desert need not play the role Moore assigns it in a retributive penal philosophy, these objections miss their target.

Critics are correct to respond that desert cannot *suffice* to justify punishment. In response, Moore claims to have been misunderstood. He replies: "'Sufficiency' is like 'qualitatively identical' in that we almost never use such words or phrases literally. When we say that one condition was sufficient for another... we mean that within some limited set of conditions that one by itself was sufficient. Other conditions outside that set... are invariably *necessary* even while we idiomatically describe a condition within that set as 'sufficient.'" He continues: "It would be a crude caricature of the retributivist to make him monomaniacally focused on the achievement of retributive

* Special thanks to Mitchell Berman, Kenworthy Bilz, John Jeffries, and to members of the University of Illinois Roundtable for Law and Philosophy for helpful comments and suggestions.

1 Moore, 1997b, 87–8 (italics in original). *Criminals,* as used here, refer to persons who culpably commit morally wrongful acts without justification or excuse.

2 Moore, 1997b, 88 (italics in original).

justice. The retributivist like anyone else can admit that there are other intrinsic goods . . . The retributivist can also admit that sometimes some of these [other] rights will trump the achieving of retributive justice."[3] Without further clarification, this remark obfuscates as much as it illuminates. We now know that Moore denies that desert *literally* suffices to justify punishment. Desert is sufficient only "within some limited set of conditions." We do *not* know, however, *what* these conditions encompass. Are they trivial and satisfied almost *everywhere* in the real world? Or are they stringent and never actually satisfied *anywhere*? More to the point, are they satisfied throughout the United States in the twenty-first century?

More generally, what *is* the exact role of desert in a justification of punishment? In this chapter I propose to explore some of the complexities in answering this question. A large part of my project is to separate the easy problems from the hard problems, as well as to identify the blind alleys that are likely to impede progress. Although my account will diverge in several respects from Moore's, I hasten to add that we proceed squarely within the same tradition. Our relatively minor differences should not conceal the fact that we concur much more than we disagree. Most significantly, we are united in seeking a justification of punishment that rejects the possibility of a wholly consequentialist defense. We agree that desert is an indispensable element of an adequate justification of punishment.

Philosophers of punishment tend to gravitate to extreme positions. According to some thinkers, desert plays no role in a theory of justified punishment. According to others, desert plays a central role. I doubt, however, that desert can occupy either position. It is essential but not decisive in justifying punishment. I hope the following distinction helps to make this point plausible. I have argued elsewhere that it is imperative to distinguish between the following two questions: (1) What do criminals deserve?; and (2) Should the state actually treat criminals as they deserve?[4] Part of my project here is to clarify this distinction and to show how it is important to a justification of punishment.

In my view, desert may be all that is needed to justify punishment in a divine realm, but it provides an extraordinarily weak reason to create earthly institutions that treat persons as they deserve. Systems of penal justice in the real world are notoriously problematic: they are astronomically expensive, prone to error and mistake, and subject to enormous abuse by the officials they empower. Citizen-taxpayers need much better reasons to create such institutions than that they treat offenders as they deserve. What additional reasons should citizens demand? Systems of criminal justice promote several worthy objectives,[5] but the protection of society through deterrence—both general and special—is the most important of these purposes. Thus I contend that penal institutions should not be created simply on grounds of desert; we must also have reason to believe they will protect rights by reducing crime. Here, then, is the legitimate place of crime reduction in a theory of justified punishment: it provides the most important

[3] Moore, 1997b, 172–3.

[4] Douglas Husak, "Why Punish the Deserving?," in Douglas Husak (ed.), *The Philosophy of Criminal Law* (Oxford: Oxford University Press, 2010), 339.

[5] Joel Feinberg, "The Expressive Function of Punishment," in Joel Feinberg (ed.), *Doing and Deserving* (Princeton: Princeton University Press, 1970), 95.

rationale for creating institutions that treat persons as they deserve. I am unsure whether Moore agrees. He explicitly says the value of treating wrongdoers as they deserve provides "*strong* reason to set up institutions to achieve such retributive justice" and that the good "achieved by punishing . . . has *nothing to do* with future states of affairs, such as the prevention of crime."[6] Yet he might plausibly include deterrence among the set of (unidentified) conditions that must be satisfied before desert literally suffices to justify punishment. In any event, I *hope* Moore agrees. It is hard (for me) to believe that a punitive system could be justified *without* reducing crime even though it treats offenders as they deserve.

I can scarcely exaggerate the importance of contrasting the two questions I have asked about punishment. In what follows, however, I focus as far as possible entirely on question (1): "what do criminals deserve?" I will discuss (2): "should we actually treat criminals as they deserve?" only for a very limited purpose. As we will see, it is not always easy to decide whether a given consideration that clearly is relevant in deciding whether punishment is justified should be conceptualized as material to question (1) or to question (2). In other words, we might be unsure whether a given factor is relevant to what persons deserve or to whether we should actually treat persons as they deserve. The main source of this uncertainty is that part of *what* persons deserve is that they *receive* given kinds of treatment, not simply that others have specified *reactions* to them. The difficulty of keeping these questions distinct contributes to the complexity in identifying the role desert plays in a theory of punishment.

Our justificatory endeavor must begin by specifying what punishment *is*. That is, we must be able to recognize when given treatments are instances of punishment. Unless we say what punishment is, we may fail to recognize what it is *about* punishment that requires a justification. In my view, a response amounts to a punishment when it deliberately expresses condemnation and imposes a deprivation or hardship. Each of these components is crucial. A treatment is not punitive because it happens to deprive and condemn. The very *purpose* of a response must be to deprive and to condemn for it to qualify as a punishment. That is, punishments *intentionally* impose condemnation and deprivation. Armed with this definition, we can clarify the exact question to be addressed. The question of why the state is justified in punishing criminals is identical to the question of why the state is justified in deliberately condemning and imposing a deprivation on persons who commit crimes.

This definition has the virtue of allowing us to focus on what I will allege (in section III) to be the single most important difficulty in providing a justification of punishment that awards a prominent role to desert. This difficulty was identified roughly fifty years ago in a seminal contribution by Joel Feinberg. After noticing that "both the 'hard treatment' aspect of punishment and its reprobative function must be part of the *definition* of legal punishment," Feinberg observed that "each of these aspects raises its own kind of question about the *justification* of legal punishment as a general practice."[7] The depth and complexity of the task of specifying the role of desert in punishment cannot be grasped unless we heed Feinberg's insight. Most theorists agree that desert plays a more obvious role in justifying the condemnatory than the deprivation ingredient. They are

[6] Moore, 1997b, 50, 87 (emphasis added).

[7] Feinberg, "Expressive," 98 (italics in original).

correct. As we will see, however, even the condemnatory component of punishment is not easily rationalized solely in terms of desert.

II. Easy Questions and Red Herrings

Here, as in many other contexts, among the most difficult methodological problems is to advance the inquiry without straying into topics that need not be addressed at all or are quagmires that probably cannot be resolved to anyone's satisfaction. To this end, I make a number of assumptions that some philosophers are bound to reject. I hope that most theorists would recognize that a defense of these assumptions—if they are possible to defend at all—would take my project too far afield. Of course, others will disagree; they will protest that I beg questions and insist that we cannot make headway without presenting and evaluating arguments on these very issues. Fully aware that my list is controversial, I suggest that legal philosophers *not* dwell on the topics I mention here if they hope to further our understanding of the role desert plays in a theory of punishment.

In the first place, we should not spin our wheels attempting to define retributivism itself. As I construe it, retributivism is not the name of a theory, but rather the name of a *kind* or *type* of theory. It is no easier to specify what all theories of this type share in common than, for example, to identify the defining characteristics of liberalism. Perhaps all we can say is that all such theories award a prominent place to desert in their justifications of punishment.[8] I tend to categorize my own position as a version of retributivism, but others may disagree. Fortunately, we need not resolve this issue. Although labels are important for any number of purposes, I fear that philosophers are too often distracted by definitions generally and by the definition of retributivism in particular. As I have indicated, such distraction may be more pervasive among those who purport to attack retributivism than to defend it. In any event, we should not agonize too much about what retributivism *is* or whether Moore's definition captures it adequately. Surely the more important question is whether and how a theory of punishment is justified—whatever it may be called.

What about desert? Does it really exist? I also believe this question should be avoided if we hope to make progress. This question should be avoided not because it is an unimportant distraction from the project at hand, but because it is exceedingly difficult if not impossible to provide good arguments on one side or the other. In what follows, I will assume without argument that desert is sensible despite requiring explication and analysis. Like obligation and responsibility, desert is part of the moral furniture of the world. This latter claim, like many comparable claims about moral concepts, is notoriously difficult to defend.[9] I confess that I find myself unable to persuade or to produce non-question-begging arguments against nihilists who deny the intelligibility of *all*

[8] "Retributivism without *desert* . . . is like *Hamlet* without the Prince of Denmark." Hugo Bedau, "Retribution and the Theory of Punishment," 75 *Journal of Philosophy* 601 (1978), 608 (emphasis in original).

[9] For empirical evidence that "the bare retributive norm is a basic, independent part of our moral worldview" and is among those "norms [that] retain normative legitimacy even if they have no independent justification," see Shaun Nichols, "Brute Retributivism," in Thomas A. Nadelhoffer (ed.), *The Future of Punishment* (Oxford: Oxford University Press, 2013), 25, 32, and 43.

moral discourse.[10] I am also at a loss to convince skeptics who are perfectly willing to countenance, say, the good and the right, but reject talk of rights or duties. Unfortunately, I am in the same position when philosophers accept moral discourse generally but reject desert in particular.

How could we possibly show that desert exists? One strategy would be to provide one or more examples in which our intuitive response requires a commitment to desert. Unfortunately, I am unaware of any such example. In this context, intuitive responses to particular examples diverge widely. But even when our intuitions about particular cases coincide, it is uncertain whether they require a commitment to desert. Consider an example which Shelly Kagan assumes without argument to raise a question about desert. He asks us to imagine that Amos and Boris have both been harmed by an explosion in a factory, and a bystander has the resources to rescue one but not both. Suppose further that Amos is entirely faultless but Boris deliberately caused the explosion. Kagan assigns the name *fault forfeits first* to the position that "it is better to aid innocent Amos than it is to aid culpable Boris."[11] And *this* position, Kagan believes, is most naturally expressed by saying that Amos and Boris differ in their *desert*. But many other possibilities might explain why rescue efforts should give priority to Amos. We might say (1) Boris is culpable for the harm to Amos, which undermines his complaint when he is not rescued; or (2) we have stronger reasons to prevent homicide than to prevent death—if Amos is rescued, no homicide will have been committed; or (3) Boris is responsible for his own death if he dies, which diminishes our responsibility for it;[12] and so on. My point is that it is remarkably difficult to find an example in which it is clear that desert is needed to explain our intuitions—even when our intuitions converge. At any rate, I make no effort to do so here. I concur with a remark Kagan directs to philosophers who devise clever metaphysical arguments to show desert does not exist: "I find myself far more confident of the claim that some people are more morally deserving than others than I am of any particular philosophical theses concerning the supposed metaphysical preconditions of desert."[13]

Even if we are convinced of the existence of desert, I fear too much attention has been paid to another question: whether the condemnation and deprivation inherent in punishment are *intrinsically good* when they are deserved. The central problem is to understand how such states as condemnation and hardship *can possibly* be intrinsically good. I am inclined to think that some small intrinsic good probably is achieved when persons are treated in accordance with their desert—as it is when persons who are equal in morally relevant respects are treated equally. Still, it is extraordinarily difficult to defend this position—or indeed, *any* position about intrinsic value. This difficulty is compounded when we introduce *impersonal* goods into our calculus—as we must.[14] No one knows how to balance these impersonal goods against what is good *for* persons. Nonetheless, philosophers persist in trying to assess retributivism by reference to its

[10] See, for example, Richard T. Garner, *Beyond Morality* (Philadelphia: Temple University Press, 1994).

[11] Shelly Kagan, *The Geometry of Desert* (Oxford: Oxford University Press, 2012), 24.

[12] I am indebted to Victor Tadros for pointing out some of the many ways the substantive conclusion in Kagan's example might be accepted without invoking desert.

[13] Kagan, *Geometry*, 13.

[14] For an argument to the contrary, see Richard Kraut, *Against Absolute Goodness* (Oxford: Oxford University Press, 2011).

supposed commitments about intrinsic value. Intuitions about hypothetical cases are routinely solicited to support (and to challenge) these alleged commitments. Most of these cases are hard to imagine, so we should lack confidence in whatever intuitions we report.[15] And even if we are confident about our intuitive response, we may be hard-pressed to decide that whatever value we think is achieved is intrinsic or merely instrumental.

We find ourselves in this predicament when we are asked whether more intrinsic goodness would be created in the kinds of cases with which philosophers of punishment have long been forced to wrestle. Suppose a monstrous villain—call him Hitler—has evaded capture, has never paid for his crimes, and is found to be living a happy and tranquil life on some island paradise. It is stipulated that nothing done or not done to Hitler will ever be known to outsiders and thus will not deter future wrongdoing or promote any other instrumental benefits. Is intrinsic value produced by punishing him? I do not believe we should have any certainty in our answer. Among other difficulties, the facts we are given are too meager to allow us to respond. Are we to suppose that punishment is imposed by a state or by private parties? Is Hitler to be tried and afforded due process? What jurisdiction would have the authority to call this villain to answer for his crimes on the island where he is found? How can we guarantee that detection is avoided? In any real case, punishing such a notorious character would reap tremendous instrumental benefits. Can we be sure our intuitions are not contaminated by the unrealistic stipulation that no instrumental value will be achieved? Whether or not any intrinsic goodness is achieved, wouldn't it be even better to add the enormous instrumental value that would follow from publicizing his capture? If so, why not do so? Answers to these questions would either undermine the point of the example or move it even further from anything familiar in the real world.

Perhaps we can escape this morass. In light of the difficulties we philosophers encounter when addressing these hypothetical cases, it would be preferable if we did not need to resolve disputes about intrinsic value at all. Hopefully, we only need believe that desert is a reason-giving property; it provides a moral reason to treat persons as they deserve. The weight of this reason, I suspect, is typically minimal, and has substantial weight only when the most monstrous crimes are perpetrated. We need not decide whether or not intrinsic goodness is produced when we act on this reason.[16] Maybe it is; maybe it is not. Or maybe intrinsic goodness is produced sometimes but not always, depending on further details of the case.

I believe desert provides something approximating a *necessary* condition for justified punishment. But if the strength of the reason supplied by desert is minimal—as I believe it to be—the *absence* of this reason might not seem to be so crucial either. Why not punish the innocent? This question is yet another example of an issue that need not detain us. One response is that the reason *not* to punish that applies to those who do not deserve to be punished is much more stringent than the reason *to* punish that applies to those who *do* deserve to be punished. This claim is not ad hoc. The negative public

[15] For a nice discussion, see Jakob Elster, "How Outlandish Can Imaginary Cases Be?" 28 *Journal of Applied Philosophy* 241 (2011).

[16] For further speculation, see Douglas Husak, "Retributivism in Extremis," 32 *Law and Philosophy* 3 (2013).

reaction to the punishment of the innocent is much stronger than the negative public reaction to the failure to punish the guilty,[17] and all non-consequentialists recognize a weighty deontological constraint against punishing those who lack negative desert.[18] Still, it is inevitable that any system of penal justice in the real world will punish innocent persons. The inevitability of this injustice does not show that a rationale for punitive sanctions cannot be based on desert.[19] At the end of the day, theorists should be willing to bite the bullet on the morality of punishing the innocent. If the instrumental value of punishment is sufficiently great, it may well be permissible, all things considered, to punish someone who lacks negative desert. This concession is not as startling as it may appear. As I have indicated, we are unlikely to know that the conditions in the familiar thought experiments designed to give us pause—which typically stipulate supreme confidence that the injustice will never be detected—obtain in the real world.[20] Finally, hard questions about the moral status of punishing the innocent should be posed to all theorists, regardless of the jurisprudential tradition to which they belong. We should not allow difficulties that plague all theories of justified punishment to raise special problems for attempts to defend a desert-based account.

III. Where Research should be Focused

I have identified several questions about punishment which legal philosophers should *not* spend too much time addressing—either because they are not directly relevant to the topic at hand or because we cannot be expected to answer them adequately. My contribution thus far, of course, has been entirely negative. So let us move on now to ask: what issues *should* legal philosophers confront if we want to advance the inquiry about the role of desert in punishment? In what follows, I identify the particular topics I hope will repay further thought and investigation.

I accept Feinberg's insight that punishment should be understood to include two components—which I have called condemnation and hard treatment—and that separate justifications are needed for each. It might be thought that a defense of the first is easy. Indeed, defending the first *is* easier than defending the second, although perplexities lurk even here. I begin with Antony Duff's observation.

> Whatever puzzles there might be about the general idea that crimes 'deserve' punishment, puzzles of which some anti-retributivists make quite a meal, there is surely nothing puzzling about the idea that wrongdoing deserves censure. An honest response to another's culpable wrongdoing—a response that respects and treats her as a responsible moral agent—is to criticize or censure that conduct; and if we think we have the moral standing to pass moral comment on her conduct, we may indeed sometimes

[17] Supporters of the death penalty, for example, are and ought to be far more worried that an innocent person is executed than that a guilty person is spared.

[18] The importance of not punishing those who lack desert provides a plausible normative defense for the presumption of innocence in Anglo-American law. See the symposia in 8 *Criminal Law and Philosophy* 283–525 (2014).

[19] For possible worries about the moral ramifications of punishing the innocent, see George Schedler, "Retributivism and Fallible Systems of Punishment," 30 *Criminal Justice Ethics* 240 (2011).

[20] The debate on this point goes back decades. See, for example, T. L. S. Sprigge, "A Utilitarian Reply to Dr. McCloskey," 8 *Inquiry* 264 (1963).

> think that we *ought* to censure her—that we owe it to those she wronged, to the values she flouted, and also to her, to censure her.[21]

As I will indicate, however, Duff moves a bit too fast. He identifies *censure* as what is not puzzling about what wrongdoers deserve. To which of the foregoing two questions is his answer relevant? Is censure what criminals deserve, or is it relevant to whether we should actually treat criminals as they deserve?

To help answer this question, let me contrast four analytically distinct stages through which responses to wrongdoing might (and often do but need not) pass.[22] Suppose Harry knowingly and inexcusably rapes Sally. I assume without argument that a set of Strawsonian reactive attitudes are apt or appropriate for Sally. As Strawson famously indicates, normal individuals feel indignation and resentment toward those who wrong them.[23] What is fitting and appropriate for Sally is a *feeling* and/or an *attitude*.[24] The fact that persons have these feelings and attitudes, it seems to me, is the clearest and least controversial part of what wrongdoers deserve. That is, Harry deserves that Sally feels resentment and indignation and has negative attitudes about him (and almost certainly much more) in virtue of the rape he has perpetrated.[25] I think we should say—although Strawson himself did not express the matter in quite this way—that it is fitting and appropriate for Sally to judge Harry to be *blameworthy* for what he has done. Still, Sally might decline to share her feelings and attitudes with anyone, regardless of how fitting and appropriate they may be. Thus a second stage through which her response to wrongdoing might pass takes place when she expresses her feelings and attitudes through verbal or non-verbal behavior. She might confide in her friends or therapist, for example. If and when Sally moves to this second stage, we might say that she no longer merely judges Harry to be *blameworthy*; she *blames* him. Next, these feelings and attitudes might be conveyed or somehow made known to the wrongdoer himself. The expression of Sally's feelings and attitudes *to Harry* represents yet a third contingent stage in her response to Harry's act. Blame expressed to the wrongdoer himself might be called *directed blame*.[26] Finally, these feelings and attitudes might be expressed to the wrongdoer in some sort of public, formal setting. As I will indicate, it seems to me that Duff has this fourth stage in mind in characterizing what wrongdoers deserve as *censure*.

It *might* be thought that the desert of wrongdoers is exhausted at the first of these four stages. If what Harry deserves is that Sally has a set of reactive attitudes about him that are fitting and appropriate, how can his desert extend to any of the subsequent

[21] R. A. Duff, "Punishment, Communication, and Community," in Matt Matravers (ed.), *Punishment and Political Theory* (Oxford: Hart Publishing. Co., 1999) 48, 50 (italics in original).

[22] Finer gradations might be drawn between each of these four stages.

[23] Peter F. Strawson, "Freedom and Resentment," 48 *Proceedings of the British Academy* (1962), 1.

[24] These feelings and attitudes are effectively beyond our control. As David Hume observed, "the mind of man is so formed by nature that, upon the appearance of certain characters, dispositions, and actions, it immediately feels the sentiment of approbation or blame . . . [T]hese sentiments are not to be controlled or altered by any philosophical theory or speculation whatsoever." *An Enquiry Concerning Human Understanding* (ed.), Eric Steinberg (Indianapolis: Hackett, 1977) 68.

[25] For a sustained effort to defend a reactive theory of desert, see Brooke S. Roberts, *A Reactive Attitudes Account of Desert* (dissertation manuscript on file with author).

[26] See Michael McKenna, "Directed Blame and Conversation," in D. Justin Coates and Neal A. Tognazzini (eds.), *Blame: Its Nature and Norms* (Oxford: Oxford University Press, 2013), 119.

stages—to the outward expression of these attitudes to others, let alone to Harry himself? The expression of a reactive attitude is not easily defended by the very same rationale that pertains to the attitude itself; the aptness or appropriateness of feelings or attitudes do not obviously transmit to their expression. What, then, is the rationale for making wrongdoers like Harry aware of the attitudes victims such as Sally hold about them? The answer, I think, is fairly clear. Isn't it equally appropriate that persons other than Sally have feelings and attitudes about Harry too? If so, these persons must be made aware of what Harry has done. Harry, in turn, deserves not only that other persons have attitudes and feelings about him in virtue of his deed. He also deserves to know that others have these feelings and attitudes. After all, we are primarily interested in knowing what *wrongdoers* deserve, not in knowing how victims are entitled to feel when they are wronged. It is hard to see that what Harry deserves is merely that other persons have whatever feelings or attitudes are appropriate under the circumstances. The most obvious way to ensure that Harry is made aware of these feelings and attitudes is for Sally (or someone on her behalf) to direct them to him. According to this account, to blame someone is to target him with the appropriate reactive emotions; blame is typically what is *deserved* by the blameworthy.[27]

Thus I think a defense of what I have called stages two and three can also be given in terms of desert. But what about stage four? Even if wrongdoers deserve that others react to their deeds in an appropriate way—which I have characterized as *blame*—how have we shown that institutions of criminal justice are needed to communicate these feelings to wrongdoers? By the time we have made the transition to the final stage, I suspect we have moved from the first to the second of the two questions I have distinguished. That is, we are no longer merely inquiring about what wrongdoers deserve, but rather about the reasons for treating them in a certain way—for constructing formal, public institutions to express these feelings to them and to others. Although Harry deserves to be made aware of the feelings and attitudes others have about him that are apt and appropriate in virtue of his wrongdoing, we should not say that he deserves that penal institutions be created in which these feelings and attitudes are expressed. The rationale for creating these formal institutions is not based on desert per se, but rather on additional concerns. Although a number of such concerns might be identified, two seem especially prominent. Unless such institutions exist, real and potential wrongdoers may be less likely, first, to fully appreciate the wrongfulness of what they have done and, second, to change their behavior accordingly. The particular structures we create should have whatever features increase the probability that these two goals will be achieved. Our formal institutions should be restructured if they do not help real or potential wrongdoers to improve their conduct or to understand the gravity of their wrongs. Philosophers of punishment should be sensitive to empirical inquiries about how to shape and reform our penal institutions to better serve these instrumentalist purposes.

27 For a list of several philosophers who subscribe to this account and a discussion of how it is often taken for granted by others, see D. Justin Coates and Neal A. Tognazzini: "The Contours of Blame," in Coates and Tognazzini, *Blame: Its Nature and Norms*, 3, 13. I am unsure, however, whether to include Moore among these philosophers. Despite the title of his opus—*Placing Blame*—Moore actually says surprisingly little about blame itself in 795 pages of text.

If it were true that *no* particular institutions would further these objectives, we would lack sufficient reason to create them.[28]

I hope that Duff concurs. He defends institutions through which censure is communicated to wrongdoers by appeals to the effects we hope such communications will produce. In particular, he alleges "punishment aims to induce a process of repentance, self-reform, and reconciliation."[29] These objectives, however worthy, provide reasons to treat criminals as they deserve. They are not a part of what criminals deserve per se. After all, defendants do not *deserve* to be repentant or to reform. Thus we should be cautious before agreeing that it is clear that wrongdoers deserve *censure*. Although both the presence as well as the expression of attitudes and feelings about wrongdoers can be defended by reference to desert, the creation of institutional structures through which these feelings and attitudes are conveyed to wrongdoers cannot be defended similarly. The condemnation that censure expresses may be deserved, but censure itself requires something more. Although Sally's feelings and attitudes may be apt even in a state of nature, I doubt we would say she has the capacity to censure Harry, as opposed to merely condemning him, unless formal institutions for this purpose are available. The creation and maintenance of a system of penal justice requires a separate rationale, and appeals to desert take us only so far.

Apart from the response Duff indicates that censure is designed to evoke in wrongdoers, I have not paid attention to the psychological state of the wrongdoer who is made aware of the reactive attitudes of others. The contested issue might be introduced by returning to a crucial part of Moore's defense of retributivism. Although he does not explicitly distinguish the two components of punishment that require justification, Moore undertakes a lengthy discussion not of how victims such as Sally should *react*, but rather of how wrongdoers such as Harry ought to *feel* when they commit monstrous crimes. Generalizing from what he is sure *he* would feel if he committed the gruesome murder of Bonnie Garland perpetrated by Richard Herrin, for example, he infers that wrongdoers would experience tremendous guilt.[30] Of course, we have empirical grounds to be skeptical that anyone can predict accurately how he would feel in very unusual circumstances he has not experienced. But even if his prediction is correct, Moore has been attacked for supposing that the emotional base of a response is relevant to the truth of the corresponding moral judgment.[31] To my mind, however, another problem is more worrisome for present purposes. Even if both of the foregoing problems can be overcome, Moore may have misconstrued the *content* of his feelings. He writes: "[S]uch guilt feelings typically engender the judgment that we deserve

[28] In "Expressive Function," Feinberg insightfully includes authoritative disavowal, symbolic non-acquiescence, vindication of the law, and absolution of others among the functions of punishment that would be difficult or impossible to achieve in the absence of its expressive dimension. These purposes might best be attained through hard treatment, giving us *some* reason to create penal institutions even if they did not help real and potential wrongdoers to understand the gravity of their wrong and to improve their conduct. But these reasons, it seems to me, would not suffice to justify such institutions.

[29] Duff, "Punishment, Communication, and Community," 52.

[30] See Willard Gaylin, *The Killing of Bonnie Garland* (New York: Simon and Schuster, 1982).

[31] See Jeffrie G. Murphy: "Moral Epistemology, the Retributive Emotions and the 'Clumsy Moral Philosophy' of Jesus Christ," in Jeffrie G. Murphy (ed.), *Punishment and the Moral Emotions: Essays in Law, Morality, and Religion* (Oxford: Oxford University Press, 2012) 21; Brian Rosebury, "Moore's Moral Facts and the Gap in the Retributive Theory," 5 *Criminal Law and Philosophy* (2011); and John Gardner, "Wrongdoing By Results," 18 *Legal Theory* 459 (2012).

punishment."[32] Perhaps he is correct. But what is it *about* punishment we think we deserve when we feel guilty? We might concede that such feelings indicate that we deserve the *condemnation* we have received, but is it also clear they "engender the judgment" that we deserve something more? Moore answers affirmatively: "To feel guilty is to judge that we must suffer . . . Our feelings of guilt thus generate a judgment that we deserve the suffering that is punishment."[33]

But what exactly *is* the "suffering that is punishment"? Two possibilities exist. First, it is clear that guilt alone typically causes an acute negative psychological state that might be characterized as suffering. A person who admits he is blameworthy, that is, a legitimate target of condemnation, recognizes the gravity of the wrong he has perpetrated, but does not feel awful about what he has done is a curious creature indeed. Something is defective about the psychology of the culpable wrongdoer who does not feel terrible under these circumstances. Clearly, Harry will not relish his status as a target of Sally's feelings; being blamed is not the sort of thing persons welcome and (if their psychology is normal) is bound to decrease their welfare or utility. Harry *deserves* to feel bad. Even so, Moore is *not* referring merely to feelings of guilt in describing the "suffering that is punishment." He has something altogether different in mind. Even if the censure communicated through institutional structures can be defended, a chasm remains to be bridged before a justification of punishment is complete. No system of criminal justice is content merely to impose censure. Even when wrongdoers feel guilty and remorseful and thus experience a decrease in welfare or utility, the state rarely if ever allows this loss to suffice as punishment.[34] Criminal punishment necessarily involves a second component I have characterized as *hard treatment*—some *extra* deprivation or loss of rights imposed by the state. Fines and imprisonment are the most familiar modes of deprivation, but other kinds of hardship might be imposed as well.[35] How is *this* component of punishment to be justified? Unless this question can be answered, we have failed to produce a complete justification of punishment.

Only two kinds of answer are available. The first is that this extra hardship is justified in terms of desert itself. Criminal defendants deserve not only to be made aware of the condemnation of others and to feel the guilt and remorse such awareness almost inevitably causes, but also deserve the additional deprivation the state inflicts. The second alternative is that this additional hardship is not justified in terms of desert, but depends on some other objective—in all likelihood, on instrumental goals. Deterrence and crime control are the most plausible candidates for these instrumental goals. The state imposes additional deprivations on criminals not because they deserve it, but because they are used for the greater good of public safety and crime reduction. Unfortunately, we will not have made much progress in producing a theory of justified punishment if we adopt this latter alternative. The deprivations imposed by penal sanctions such as imprisonment are problematic because they seem to treat persons in ways that violate

[32] Moore, 1997b, 148–9. [33] Moore, 1997b, 148.

[34] It is an open question, however, whether such losses should ever count *against* the quantum of hard treatment criminals deserve. See Douglas Husak, "Already Punished Enough," in Husak, *Philosophy of Criminal Law*, 433.

[35] Decisions about the particular mode of hardship provide yet another opportunity to ensure that punishments attain instrumental objectives such as crime reduction. Even if hard treatment itself is deserved, the *form* it must take need not be governed by desert.

their rights and/or infringe the Kantian principle against treating persons merely as a means. Desert is a promising rationale for infringing rights or for allowing persons to be treated as a means; as we have seen, it provides the basis for condemnation. This second alternative, however, explicitly denies that the additional hardship imposed by the state is justified in terms of desert. Thus only a little headway has been made in producing a justification of punishment.[36] Hence, the first alternative would make punishment easier to defend than the second.

Return, then, to the first kind of answer. Why *might* criminals deserve the additional deprivation or hardship imposed by the state when they already experience a loss of welfare or utility due to the guilt and remorse they feel (and ought to feel) in response to their wrongdoing and the condemnation directed against them? To my mind, this is the single most difficult question to answer in constructing a defense of punishment based on desert. One possible answer is that remorse and guilt are necessarily inadequate. The loss of welfare or utility such feelings cause is less than the loss of welfare or utility wrongdoers deserve to experience when they are blamed. The state fills the lacuna by inflicting an extra hardship. If I understand him correctly, Moore adopts this position. In reporting what he believes and hopes he would feel were he to have committed a gruesome act like the killing of Bonnie Garland, Moore writes: "I would feel guilty unto death. I could not imagine any suffering that could be imposed upon me that would be unfair because it exceeded what I deserved."[37] He does not even entertain the possibility that the suffering he might inflict upon himself might be adequate. After all, he might say, guilt tends to be fleeting and temporary; Richard Herrin's suffering may have been a distant memory a year after Bonnie Garland died. More is therefore needed, and the state steps in to supply the remainder.

It is arguable, however, that any plausibility in this position is due to an unwarranted generalization from the facts of the extreme case Moore presents. Even if he is correct that no one could possibly feel sufficiently guilty for committing such a horrible murder as that by Richard Herrin, I see no reason to conclude that no one could possibly experience enough of a loss of welfare or utility after feeling guilty and remorseful for committing any crime whatever. After all, nearly all punishable offenses are far less serious. Suppose I steal a bottle of wine from your cellar—a relatively minor crime that presumably merits punishment. I might be wracked with guilt and remorse for my deed. The loss of welfare or utility caused by my guilt might far exceed any loss of welfare or utility I deserve or can be caused by the extra hardship or deprivation imposed by the state that is proportionate to the gravity of my offense. The quantum of guilt people are able to feel is a contingent feature of their particular psychology. As novelists and therapists are well aware, feelings of guilt and remorse *can* cause a substantial amount of suffering in many individuals—sometimes far greater than what is produced by the extra hardship or deprivation imposed by the state (when hardship or deprivation is proportionate to the seriousness of the crime). Therefore, even if more hardship is generally needed when monstrous acts are perpetrated, persons who

[36] Whether or not they are persuasive, communicative defenses of hard treatment seem to abandon the hope of justifying this feature of punishment in terms of desert.

[37] Moore, 1997b, 145.

commit ordinary crimes may not deserve additional deprivations. For relatively minor offenses, *perhaps* the negative feelings of guilt are all that wrongdoers deserve.

Of course, we lack reliable means to *know* whether and to what extent offenders are wracked with negative feelings when they breach given statutes. A criminal has ample incentive to feign guilt and remorse, especially when the severity of her sentence is influenced by this display. The extent of these feelings, I am willing to suppose, is probably less than what is deserved in the majority of cases of criminality. Perhaps hard treatment is needed because of the epistemological difficulties state officials encounter when they try to ascertain whether offenders have experienced the degree of negative feelings they deserve.[38] Admittedly, this attempt to defend the deprivation or hard treatment component of punishment is not unproblematic. If state officials *could* determine that particular defendants had suffered to the extent of their desert, hard treatment would not be justified.

John Kleinig makes a different attempt to show that criminals deserve hard treatment. He alleges that "more than [censure, rebuke, and condemnation] is deserved. For though such expressions of blame constitute some kind of practical response to wrongdoing, they fail to 'embody' it. That is why desert defeasibly requires not merely a response, but a proportionate one. One cannot separate out the 'blame' from something more."[39] If the state does not impose an additional deprivation, it simply does not take wrongdoing sufficiently seriously. In describing why "something more" than condemnation is required, Kleinig invites us to shift our perspective: "To think otherwise is to make the same mistake as would be involved were someone to take the view that appropriate responses of gratitude to benefaction could always consist of sincere expressions of thanks."[40] Kleinig's argument invites the rejoinder that positive and negative desert may be asymmetrical. Persons who perform exceptionally good deeds might deserve more from their benefactors than praise, but persons who perform extraordinarily bad deeds may not deserve more from their victims than condemnation. After all, the challenge is to explain how the loss of welfare and disutility that results from hard treatment *can* be deserved.

Apart from the possible asymmetry of punishments and rewards, Kleinig's observation is trenchant. Although good deeds are sometimes said to be their own reward, something is deficient about a response to a massively generous act that consists solely in an expression of gratitude. If the beneficiary is *really* as grateful as he claims to be, some additional benefit—a gift or a return favor of roughly comparable value—is required to supplement the expression itself. Otherwise, he might add, the benefactor has not been treated as he deserves. As so construed, however, Kleinig's strategy is vulnerable to the same difficulty as Moore's. Although a gift may be needed when great favors are bestowed, mere expressions of gratitude suffice when more ordinary acts of

[38] Those who believe hard treatment is needed because wrongdoers cannot feel guilty enough when they perpetrate serious crimes would be attracted to the position that the severity of deprivations should be measured by their impact on the criminal rather than by some "objective" gauge. For commentary, see Adam J. Kolber, "The Subjective Experience of Punishment," 109 *Columbia Law Review* 182 (2009).

[39] John Kleinig, "What Does Wrongdoing Deserve?" in Michael Tonry (ed.), *Retributivism Has a Past. Has it a Future?* (Oxford: Oxford University Press, 2011) 46, 54.

[40] Kleinig, "Wrongdoing," attributes this argument to Terrance McConnell, *Gratitude* (Philadelphia: Temple University Press, 1993).

beneficence are performed. When someone in the front of a queue goes to the small effort of holding a door open for the person behind him, a small expression of thanks is all that is needed and all that is deserved. We should not reach conclusions about all good or bad acts by generalizing from the most extreme cases.

It may seem I have not succeeded in my endeavor to explain how state impositions of hard treatment or deprivation, layered on top of the loss of welfare or utility caused by the experience of guilt and remorse, can be justified on grounds of desert. If this conclusion were correct, I would have failed to produce a desert-based justification of hard treatment and thus would have failed to produce a complete desert-based justification of punishment. What I called the "most difficult question to answer" in justifying punishment has not been solved. Still, this conclusion may be overly pessimistic. I have long concurred (along with Moore) that theories of justified punishment have profound implications for the content of the substantive criminal law itself.[41] As we have seen, the foregoing attempts to explain how hard treatment might be deserved are most plausible when applied to serious crimes. It is unlikely that the crimes to which this rationale applies need be comparable in severity to the brutal murder of Bonnie Garland. A desert-based rationale for punishment may be persuasive even for lesser crimes that cross a given threshold of severity. It is hard to know how to characterize the level of seriousness that is required; our theories and even our vocabulary to quantify degrees of wrongdoing may not be up to the task. The worry about this strategy, of course, is that it may fail to justify hard treatment for relatively minor offenses that intuitively merit deprivations—such as my example of the theft of a single wine bottle. Still, it is no surprise to learn that the wrongdoing inherent in conduct must be sufficiently serious before the state is justified in proscribing it and imposing hard treatment on grounds of desert on those persons who engage in it.[42] Thus my attempt to defend a desert-based theory of punishment might show why some instances of wrongdoing—those that cross an unspecified threshold of severity—are eligible for state punishment. If this effort is successful, I have made *some* progress in specifying the role of desert in a theory of justified punishment.

I repeat, however, that, whether or not the deprivations imposed by the state could have been shown to be deserved, we still would not have offered a complete desert-based justification of penal institutions as they exist in the real world. Reasonable taxpayers might balk when asked to fund a system of penal justice that deliberately imposes censure and hard treatment on persons who perform wrongful acts—even those acts that cross a given threshold of severity. We should not expect to overcome their reservations by pointing out that wrongdoers, upon reflection, would admit that their suffering did not exceed their desert or that their suffering was inseparable from the condemnation legitimately directed against them. Crime control and public safety must enter the picture at this juncture. Thus it is crucial to remember that my comments are directed as much as possible toward the question of what wrongdoers deserve. We should not invoke desert to try to answer the separate question of why penal institutions should actually be created to treat wrongdoers accordingly.

[41] Douglas Husak, *Overcriminalization* (Oxford: Oxford University Press, 2008).

[42] For further thoughts on trivial offenses, see Douglas Husak, "The *De Minimis* 'Defense' to Criminal Liability," in Husak, *Philosophy of Criminal Law*, 362.

5

Retributive Desert as Fair Play

*Peter Westen**

I. Introduction

Michael Moore is the most distinguished living advocate of "positive retributivism,"[1] the normative claim that persons who culpably violate legal and moral norms deserve to suffer for their wrongdoing, and that their deserving to suffer is always a reason for the state to make them suffer, though not necessarily an indefeasible reason.[2]

Moore defends his claim by relying entirely on the force of retributive emotions and intuitions;[3] and, in doing so, he explicitly foregoes the correlative approach of showing that the claim can be derived from broader moral principles.[4] It is hardly surprising that Moore eschews trying to explain retributive desert in terms of broader principles of justice.[5] The most promising to do so—and the only effort that Moore concedes may have merit[6]—is Herbert Morris's celebrated theory that retributive desert consists of suffering that malefactors owe society to negate the unfair advantage they would otherwise reap from their wrongdoing.[7] Morris's 1968 essay, "Persons and Punishment," is "one of

* I am deeply indebted to Philip Soper and to Mitch Berman, David Brink, Kim Ferzan, Doug Husak, Michael Shapiro, Alan Schwartz, and other participants at the Chicago Round-table of July 18, 2013, for their insights and wisdom regarding an earlier draft.

1 J. L. Mackie, "Retributivism: A Test Case for Ethical Objectivity," in Joel Feinberg and Hyman Gross (eds.), *Philosophy of Law*, 4th edn. (Belmont, CA: Wadsworth, 1991), 677; J. L. Mackie, "Morality and the Retributive Emotions," 1 *Criminal Justice Ethics* 3 (1982), 4 (coining the term "positive retributivism").

2 See Joel Feinberg, *Doing and Deserving: Essays in the Theory of Responsibility* (Princeton, NJ: Princeton University Press, 1970); John Finnis, "The Restoration of Retribution," 32 *Analysis* 131 (1972); Douglas Husak, "Why Punish the Deserving?," 26 *Nous* 447 (1992). Contrary to what is sometimes implied, Michael Moore does not contend that the state should invariably punish the deserving "whatever the cost," R. A. Duff, "Penal Communications: Recent Work in the Philosophy of Punishment," 20 *Crime & Justice* 28 (1996). Rather, Moore argues that the state's categorical obligation to punish the deserving is an instance of "threshold deontology," that is, an instance of an obligation that, though superficially absolute, can nonetheless be defeated by strong countervailing considerations. See Moore, 1997b, 158 & n. 13, 173–4. For the various ways in which Moore defines retribution, see Moore, 1997b, 83, 87, 91, 153–4, 174 (n. 3). For criticism of Moore's threshold deontology, see Larry Alexander, "Deontology at the Threshold," 37 *San Diego Law Review* (2000), 893.

3 See, e.g., Moore, 1997b, 104–88 (n 2). For criticism of this approach, see David Boonin, *The Problem of Punishment* (Cambridge: Cambridge University Press, 2008), 85–93.

4 See Moore, 1997b, 106, 110 (n 2).

5 Cf. Victor Tadros, *The Ends of Harm* (Oxford: Oxford University Press, 2011), 84; Stephen Kershnar, "The Justification of Deserved Punishment," 33 *Southern Journal of Philosophy* 461 (1995); Moore, 1997b, 170 & n. 29 (n 2) ("The battleground of . . . the philosophy of punishment is littered with the corpses of supposed general principles from which the retributive principle is supposed to follow.").

6 See Moore, 1997b, 170 & n. 29 (n 2).

7 See Herbert Morris, "Persons and Punishment," in *On Guilt and Innocence* (Berkeley: University of California, 1976), ch. 2, originally published in 52 *Monist* 475 (1968).

the classics of 20th Century jurisprudence,"[8] and his theory still has followers.[9] Yet Morris's theory has been subjected to such criticism[10] that many of its original exponents—though (contrary to reports) not Morris himself[11]—have since distanced themselves from it.[12]

I believe it is time to revisit Herbert Morris's theory of fair play. Despite its celebrity, Morris's theory has not received the sympathetic analysis it deserves. Part of the problem is that Morris does not clearly specify the precise *benefits* and *burdens* that collective guarantees of security confer and impose on citizens. Another problem is that Morris invokes "burden" where other concepts would better serve his purpose. The most serious problem, however, is that Morris states his theory elliptically, leaving it to readers to fill in the blanks. Critics and supporters alike have responded to the gap by framing Morris's theory in weak forms rather than its strongest form. Viewed sympathetically, Morris's unfair-advantage theory not only provides principled content to what everyone concedes to be a widely held intuition that culpable wrongdoers deserve to suffer for what they have done, but also provides a standard—albeit an approximate one—by which to measure deserved punishment.

I will: (1) begin with Herbert Morris's canonical statement of his theory of unfair advantage, juxtaposing it with ungenerous ways in which commentators have interpreted it and to resulting criticisms raised; (2) restate Morris's theory in a form that I believe is faithful to it and yet strong enough to negate the aforementioned criticisms; and (3) address some additional criticisms of unfair-advantage theory.

[8] Jeffrie Murphy, "Legal Moralism and Retribution Revisited," 1 *Criminal Law and Philosophy* 12 (2007). See also Boonin, *The Problem of Punishment*, 120 (Morris's theory is "the preeminent form of retributivism in the current literature"); Richard Burgh, "Do the Guilty Deserve Punishment?", 79 *Journal of Philosophy* 193 (1982), 202 ("the most powerful and persuasive defense of the view that the offender deserves to be punished"); David Dolinko, "Some Thoughts About Retributivism," 101 *Ethics* 537 (1991), 545 ("probably the most influential contemporary defense of retributivism"); Jeffrie Murphy, "Some Second Thoughts on Retributivism," in Mark White (ed.), *Retributivism: Essays on Theory and Policy* (Oxford: Oxford University Press, 2011), 97 ("[Morris's] essay . . . almost single-handedly rescued robust retributivism from obscurity and rendered it philosophically respectable again").

[9] See, e.g., Richard Dagger, "Social Contracts, Fair Play, and the Justification of Punishment," 8 *Ohio State Journal of Criminal Law* 341 (2011); Michael Davis, "Criminal Desert and Unfair Advantage: What's the Connection?," 12 *Law and Philosophy* 133 (1993); Finnis, "Restoration of Retribution"; Wojciech Sadurski, "Theory of Punishment, Social Justice, and Liberal Neutrality," 7 *Law and Philosophy* 351 (1989).

[10] See R. A. Duff, *Punishment, Communication and Community* (Oxford: Oxford University Press, 2001), 22 (criticism of Morris has been "conclusive").

[11] Morris is said to have "questioned" his unfair-advantage theory and "moved away from it." Andrew Von Hirsch, "Proportionality in the Philosophy of Punishment: From 'Why Punish?' to 'How Much?,'" 1 *Criminal Law Forum* 259 (1990), 264 & n.19. That is not so. Morris makes a number of claims in "Persons and Punishment," including that offenders have a "right" to be punished and that the state has a "duty" to punish. Although Morris has since questioned the latter claims, see Herbert Morris, "A Paternalistic Theory of Punishment," 18 *American Philosophical Quarterly* 263 (1981), he has not questioned his contention that unfair advantage explains widely held notions of retributive desert.

[12] *Compare* Jeffrie Murphy, "Legal Moralism," 13, *with* Jeffrie Murphy, "Three Mistakes About Retributivism," 31 *Analysis* 166 (1971); *compare* Andrew von Hirsch, "Proportionality in the Philosophy of Punishment," 265 n. 21, *with* Andrew von Hirsch, *Doing Justice: The Choice of Punishments* (New York: Hill and Wang, 1976), 47–8; *compare* George Sher, "Deserved Punishment Revisited," in George Sher, *Approximate Justice: Studies in Non-Ideal Theory* (New York: Rowman and Littlefield, 1997), 177, *with* George Sher, "Deserved Punishment," in *Desert* (Princeton: Princeton University Press, 1987), ch. 5.

II. Herbert Morris—His Supporters and Critics

Herbert Morris derives his theory from a broader political theory first advanced by H. L. A. Hart and John Rawls.[13] Hart and Rawls argue that by virtue of benefitting from a jointly beneficial, collective enterprise, citizens are politically obliged to bear burdens necessary to sustain the enterprise.[14] Morris, in turn, argues the protection and personal security that citizens derive from jointly beneficial regimes of criminal law oblige them to respect the reciprocal rights of others on which such regimes are premised; that citizens who reap the benefits of such protection and security without according others the reciprocal respect due them become free riders; and that it is only fair for the state to negate free riding by subjecting such citizens to suffering commensurate with the benefits they would otherwise unfairly retain. As Morris puts it:

> Let us [imagine] . . . a group of rules . . . which closely resemble the core rules of our criminal law, rules that prohibit violence and deception and compliance with which provides benefits for all persons. These benefits consist of noninterference by others with what each person values. . . . Making possible this mutual benefit is the assumption by individual of a burden. The burden consists in the exercise of self-restraint by individuals. . . .
>
> * * *
>
> A person who violates the rules has something others have—the benefits of the system—but by renouncing what other have assumed, the burdens of self-restraint, he has acquired an unfair advantage. . . . Another way of putting it is that he owes something to others, for he has something that does not rightfully belong to him. Justice—that is punishing such individuals—restores the equilibrium of benefits and burdens by taking from the individual what he owns, that is, exacting the debt.[15]

This elliptical statement constitutes nearly the entirety of what Morris says about unfair advantage because he devotes most of the essay to other claims. As a result, Morris has left space to supporters and critics alike to specify more precisely what they believe to be the supposed (A) "benefits," (B) "burdens," and (C) the relationship of hard treatment to "unfairness."

A. The supposed benefits

Commentators, including supporters as well as critics, differ about how to interpret Morris's reference to benefits. The differences are two-fold: (1) commentators who interpret the benefits to refer to boons that malefactors gain *by* wrongdoing, that is, *fruits of crime* that no one should accrue; and (2) commentators who interpret benefits to refer to boons that malefactors gain *prior* to wrongdoing, that is, things that even law-abiding persons enjoy but that a malefactor's wrongdoing now renders it unfair for him to retain.

[13] See C. L. Ten, *Crime, Guilt, and Punishment* (New York: Oxford University Press, 1987), 55.

[14] H. L. A. Hart, "Are There Any Natural Rights?," 64 *Philosophical Review* 175 (1955). See also John Rawls, "Legal Obligation and the Duty of Fair Play," in Sidney Hook (ed.), *Law and Philosophy: A Symposium*, (New York: New York University Press, 1964), 9–10.

[15] Morris, "Persons and Punishment," 33–4.

1. *Benefits gained by wrongdoing*

Most commentators interpret Morris's benefits to consist of what wrongdoers gain by wrongdoing.[16] These interpretations are not only normatively implausible, but also, as we shall see, misreadings of Morris.

a. Proceeds of crime. Richard Wasserstrom (a critic of Morris) takes the benefits at issue to be the ill-gotten gains that wrongdoers reap from their crimes, e.g., the articles of value that thieves and robbers obtain from their victims.[17] Wasserstrom's view is implausible on its face, however, because it would leave whole classes of crimes non-punishable, including: (i) crimes such as attempts, conspiracies, and offenses of reckless endangerment, all which are defined without reference to resulting harm; and (ii) all offenses for which offenders are prepared to pay restitution in lieu of punishment.[18]

b. Freedom from constraining rules. Numerous commentators, including both supporters and critics alike, take the benefit at issue to be the *freedom* that wrongdoers enjoy in committing crimes.[19] However, as Jorge Garcia (a Morris critic) rightly observes, this is normatively untenable, regardless of how "freedom" is defined. If freedom is defined normatively by reference to the liberties people *ought* to possess, wrongdoers enjoy no more of such freedom than law-abiding citizens, because normative standards of freedom apply to law-abiding and wrongful actors alike, regardless of whether wrongdoers comply with them. Alternatively, if freedom is defined empirically by what wrongdoers are *capable* of doing, wrongdoers possess no more of such freedom than law-abiding citizens, because law-abiding citizens are equally capable of violating the law, if they choose to do so. Finally, if freedom is defined by the license that wrongdoers actually *appropriate* for themselves, albeit wrongfully, wrongdoers may, indeed, end up possessing more such freedom than law-abiding citizens, but it is hard to see how society can regard such licentious behavior as a benefit of which law-abiding citizens are deprived.[20]

c. The pleasure of yielding to forbidden desires. Some commentators argue that the benefit at issue is the pleasure or thrill of indulging forbidden desires.[21] As critics point out, however, this view of benefits possesses at least two flaws. First, because transgressors tend to have *more* conflicted and tormented feelings about serious crimes that carry haunting taboos (e.g., parricide) than about trivial offenses (e.g., shoplifting or tax

[16] See, e.g., Shawn Bayern, "The Significance of Private Burdens and Lost Benefits for a Fair-Play Analysis of Punishment," 12 *New Criminal Law Review* 21 (2009); Andrew von Hirsch, *Censure and Sanctions* (Oxford: Clarendon Press, 1993), 8; Jean Hampton, "Correcting Harms Versus Righting Wrongs: The Goal of Retribution," 39 *UCLA Law Review* 1660 (1992).

[17] See Richard Wasserstrom, "Punishment," in Richard Wasserstrom, *Philosophy and Social Issues: Five Studies* (Notre Dame: University of Notre Dame Press, 1980), 145. See also Mackie, "Morality and the Retributive Emotions," 5.

[18] See Mackie, "Retributivism," 680; Leo Zaibert, *Punishment and Retribution* (Aldershot: Ashgate, 2006), 122.

[19] See, e.g., Sher, "Deserved Punishment," 74–90; von Hirsch, "Proportionality in the Philosophy of Punishment," 266.

[20] See Jorge Garcia, "Deserved Punishment," 8 *Law and Philosophy* 272 (1989). See also Boonin, *The Problem of Punishment*, 128; Dolinko, "Some Thoughts About Retributivism," 547–8; von Hirsch, *Censure and Sanctions*, 8–9; Russ Shafer-Landau, "Retributivism and Desert," 81 *Pacific Philosophical Quarterly* 189 (2000).

[21] See, e.g., Ted Honderich, *Punishment: The Supposed Justifications Revisited* (Ann Arbor: Pluto Press, 2006), 55; Ten, *Crime, Guilt, and Punishment*, 55.

evasion), malefactors under this view would reap lesser benefits from serious offenses than from trivial offenses, and hence, would deserve less punishment for serious offenses than for trivial ones.[22] Second, the view implausibly assumes that yielding to forbidden desires, e.g., to rape a person, is a benefit that law-abiding persons must deny themselves rather than evil to be abhorred.[23]

d. Indulgence of one's will. John Finnis (a Morris supporter) argues that the relevant benefit is not the emotional pleasure a malefactor experiences in yielding to forbidden desires but, rather, the mere act of indulging his will in disregard of social obligations, regardless of pleasures derived from it.[24] As with other accounts of benefits derived by offending, however, Finnis's account raises difficulties. First, Finnis does not explain why indulging an evil will in disregard of social obligations constitutes a benefit to be begrudged in malefactors rather than a failing for which they should be despised and pitied. Second, Finnis begs the question regarding the way criminal offenses should be graded. He assumes that serious offenses like criminal homicide should indeed be punished more severely than less heinous offenses like tax evasion. Yet to justify such grading, Finnis would have to show that malefactors consciously act more willfully in committing serious offenses like negligent homicide than in committing trivial offenses like shoplifting. Instead, he begs the question by simply declaring that because people who commit more serious offenses are aware or should be aware of the greater degree of seriousness of their conduct, they *must* be acting more willfully and *must* be deriving greater benefits than those who commit less serious offenses.[25]

2. *Benefits gained previous to wrongdoing*

The aforementioned commentators misunderstand Morris. As Morris makes clear, the relevant benefits for him are ones that malefactors gain not *by* wrongdoing but *prior to* wrongdoing. They consist of the boons that citizens enjoy by living in societies committed to the protection of life, liberty, and property; boons that a malefactor's newly committed crime and lack of reciprocal respect for others render it unfair for him to retain.[26]

To be sure, not all commentators misunderstand Morris. Yet even those who understand him have criticisms that, I believe, fall short. Richard Burgh is a good example. Burgh's criticism consists of three steps, the first two of which are sound. First, Burgh rightly observes that any conception of desert, including Morris's, must account for shared intuitions regarding not only *whom* should be punished but also *how much*. Second, Burgh rightly observes that, if relevant benefits consist of the protective shield of

[22] See Burgh, "Do the Guilty Deserve Punishment?," 209–10; Dolinko, "Some Thoughts About Retributivism," 545.

[23] See Margaret Falls, "Retribution, Reciprocity, and Respect for Persons," 6 *Law and Philosophy* 31 (1987), 31–5.

[24] See John Finnis, "Retribution: Punishment's Formative Aim," 44 *American Journal of Jurisprudence* 91 (1999); Finnis, "The Restoration of Retribution."

[25] See Bernard Gert, "Review of George Sher, Desert," 99 *Ethics* 426 (1989); Michael Zimmerman, "Review of George Sher, Desert," 29 *Nous* 248 (1995).

[26] Morris, "Persons and Punishment," 33–4.

criminal law that malefactors receive in advance of offending, such protection must take one or the other of three specific forms:

Benefit 1: protection derived from the existence of the particular criminal statute that a malefactor violates, e.g., a statute against theft or robbery;

Benefit 2: protection derived from the existence of criminal statutes as a whole; and

Benefit 3: protection derived from the prima facie duty of citizens to obey the law.[27]

Third, Burgh argues that, regardless of which form they take, the three benefits fail to account for shared intuitions regarding the combination of whom should be punished and how much. Thus, benefit (1) fails to account for intuitions regarding *who* should be punished because it would unjustly exonerate a substantive number of clearly culpable malefactors, namely malefactors who do not personally benefit from the existence of the particular statutes they violate (e.g., homeless persons who commit criminal trespass, destitute persons who steal, male rapists in no danger of being raped). Benefit (2) does not account for intuitions regarding *how much* malefactors should be punished because, given that all persons within society benefit enormously from the existence of criminal laws as a whole, benefit (2) would require that malefactors all be punished quite severely, regardless of how minor their offenses might be. Finally, benefit (3) fails to account for intuitions regarding how much malefactors should be punished because, given that all persons benefit—slightly—from the prima facie duty of others to obey the law, benefit (3) would require that all malefactors be punished rather slightly, regardless of how heinous their offenses might be.[28]

This argument of Burgh's, as well as the two arguments of Duff's that follow below, are not unfair, but, rather, are products of the elliptical way in which Morris frames his thesis. Nonetheless, as I shall argue in section III, they are also products of failing to interpret Morris's theory in its strongest form.

B. The supposed burdens

Commentators generally agree that the relevant burden for Morris consists of constraints that criminal law imposes on persons to refrain from criminally preying upon others. Nonetheless, Antony Duff and others find fault in the notion of "burden." Duff denies that it constitutes a *burden* upon citizens—that is, a sacrifice that they must begrudgingly make—to refrain from preying on the lives, personal security, and property of fellow citizens. The truth, he says, is precisely the opposite. Society does not regard the requirements of the criminal law as burdens to be begrudgingly borne but, rather, obligations that people tend to welcome, at least with respect to serious offenses.[29]

27 See Richard Dagger, "Punishment as Fair Play," 14 *Res Publica* 259 (2008), 263–4.

28 See also Boonin, *The Problem of Punishment*, 196–8.

29 See R. A. Duff, "The Incompleteness of 'Punishment as Fair Play': A Response to Dagger," 14 *Res Publica* 277 (2008); R. A. Duff, *Trials and Punishments* (Cambridge: Cambridge University Press, 1986), 213–14. See also George Fletcher, *Rethinking Criminal Law* (Boston: Little, Brown, 1978), 417–18; Hampton, "Correcting Harms," 1660; Ten, *Crime, Guilt, and Punishment*, 64.

C. The supposed relationship of hard treatment to unfairness

Morris, as we have seen, argues that, in benefitting from criminal-law protections that they are unwilling to extend to others, malefactors enjoy benefits that it is unfair for them to retain and, as such, owe "debt[s]" of suffering to "society" that, until paid, leave them in the position of free riders.[30]

Critics fault Morris for distorting what wrongdoers *are* and what they should be punished *for*. Some relatively minor crimes, they say, are indeed crimes of free riding, and their perpetrators are indeed free riders.[31] Thus, people who engage in tax evasion tend to realize that they are engaged in gaming a system that provides them with benefits on the condition that they pay their fare share, which they choose not to do. And with respect to such offenders, critics say, it may indeed be appropriate to punish them for free riding. However, they say, it trivializes grave offenses like murder and rape to equate their gravity with free riding. The wrong that a rapist commits is not a wrong of free riding. It is the wrong of violating another person's sexual autonomy. Antony Duff puts the argument particularly strongly:

> A man is convicted of rape. We might expect the judge to address him in these terms: "You committed a violent and degrading assault on this woman; you showed a callous disregard for her rights and interests; you caused her serious harm; and for this you must be punished." But now it seems the judge should not talk in these terms; if she is to capture the criminal wrongness of the rapist's action she should say: "You refused to restrain your violent and anti-social impulses; you thus took for yourself an unfair advantage over those who do restrain themselves; and for *this* you must be punished."[32]

III. Morris's Theory in a Stronger Form

Morris's theory is widely criticized, and nowhere more effectively than by Burgh and Duff. However, Burgh's and Duff's criticisms are a function of the respective ways in which they interpret "benefits," "burdens," and the relationship of hard treatment to "unfairness." I believe that Morris's theory is capable of being interpreted in a form that negates their criticisms.

A. Stronger interpretation

Suppose that persons live within a society in which they possess the means to invade and destroy the lives, personal well-being, and security of their fellow citizens. Like persons everywhere, they have a moral obligation to refrain from thus preying upon fellow citizens. Suppose, too, that the society is sufficiently organized, politically, to enact laws demanding that every citizen, under penalty of condemnation, respect those moral rights in others. Suppose, finally, that members of the society generally respect those moral and legally declared rights, even if they do not do so universally.

All persons who continue to live in such an organized society, even those who are occasionally victimized, reap enormous benefits in well-being vis-à-vis the fate they

30 Morris, "Persons and Punishment," 34. 31 See Fletcher, *Rethinking Criminal Law*, 417.
32 Duff, *Trials and Punishments*, 211–12; see also Murphy, "Legal Moralism," 14.

would suffer in alternative, predatory societies in which such moral and legally declared rights are lacking. An actor in such a society who fails to show others the respect that morality and law rightly expect of him should be officially condemned for it. In addition, because he has benefitted enormously from the existence and general recognition of moral and legal rights that he has not respected in others, it is just that he forfeit, and that the society compel him to forfeit, a portion of those benefits—namely the portion that his lack of reciprocal respect renders it unfair for him to retain—and that society do so by inflicting suffering commensurate with that portion.

This reinterpretation negates Burgh's and Duff's criticisms. For one thing, it deems a wrongdoer's unfair advantage to consist of so-called "benefit (2)" under Burgh's taxonomy (i.e. protection derived from the existence of criminal statutes as a whole) and, in doing so, undermines Burgh's criticisms of Benefit (2). Burgh argues that, because every wrongdoer benefits equally and benefits greatly from such protection, benefit (2) dictates that all wrongdoers be punished the same—and punished quite severely—regardless of the gravity of their respective offenses. However, that would mean attributing one of two positions to Morris, both of which are implausible: either that every wrongdoer who fails to show others the respect he owes them thereby forfeits *all* prior societal benefits, regardless of the gravity of his particular failure; or that all failures to respect others are *equally grave*. It is more plausible to interpret Morris as taking the position that wrongdoers forfeit only as much of their unfairly retained welfare as is commensurate with the lack of respect that they have manifested toward others.

Furthermore, by framing Morris's view in terms of the *rightful expectations* of respect that actors owe others, this reinterpretation addresses Duff's complaint that unfair-advantage theory falsely asserts that complying with the law is a *burden* on law-abiding citizens. To be sure, Morris himself coins the term "burden of self-restraint," and he uses it repeatedly.[33] However, I believe that Morris's essential meaning is captured as well, if not better, by conceptualizing what he calls "burdens of self-restraint" as the respect that society rightly expects persons to show one another, because the latter explanation not only subsumes the former but also avoids false connotations of begrudging self-sacrifice. Most actors who respect the rights of others are not even tempted to prey upon others and, hence, do not experience compliance with the law as burden. Actors with less respect for others may experience temptation and may feel self-restraint to be a burden. Yet most of them, too, possess sufficient respect to overcome their temptations, and those who do not are to be faulted not for failure to bear burdens but for failure to respect others.

Finally, this reinterpretation undermines Duff's charge that Morris turns the explicit punishment of *wrongs* into the explicit punishment of *free riding*, for three reasons. First, in focusing upon hard treatment (and upon Morris's free-rider justification for it), Duff wrongly overlooks its companion component, namely *condemnation*. Condemnation is easily overlooked because, as between the two components of punishment, condemnation (in contrast to hard treatment) is morally and politically easily justified.[34] But to punish culpable wrongdoers, including in Morris's view, is to condemn

[33] Morris, "Persons and Punishment," 33–4.

[34] See von Hirsch, *Censure and Sanctions*, 9–12. But see Husak, "Why Punish the Deserving?," 456–7.

them. And to condemn them is to reprove them in the name of the specific wrongs that the state so deeply resents their committing, for example rape.

Second, Duff wrongly assumes that, if hard treatment is designed to negate free riding, the expressive content of punishment must consist, at least in part, of *saying so* in so many words. On the contrary, consider a society that adheres to the view that persons should be subjected to hard treatment if, and only if, (i) they deserve such hard treatment, and (ii) the hard treatment produces more consequential good than harm. Now assume that a sentencing judge comes to sentence on a culpable rapist. The judge can justly say a number of things. He can justly say "I condemn you for having committed the heinous act of rape, and I sentence you to ten years in prison"—without mentioning the purpose of hard treatment. Or he can say, "I condemn you for having committed the heinous act of rape, and I sentence you to the term of prison you deserve, namely ten years"—without mentioning the *consequential* purpose of punishment. Or he can say, "I condemn you for having committed the heinous act of rape, and I give a sentence of five years because you *deserve* it and because doing so will produce more consequential good in the way of deterrence than harm"—without expounding upon "desert" in terms of unfair advantage. In each case, the trial judge justly condemns and punishes the rapist without reference to unfair advantage or free riding.

Third, and most importantly, Duff wrongly assumes that, if a sentencing judge were to express the full purpose for which he imposes hard treatment under Morris's theory, the judge would have to state that its purpose is to negate unfair advantage and would have to refrain from mentioning rape. On the contrary, the specific wrongs that Duff wishes to foreground, for example rape, continue to remain salient under the proposed interpretation, because they constitute the *metric* by which the defendant's hard treatment is determined. A malefactor's wrongful act, such as rape, establishes the extent and the limit of the hard treatment to which he is being subjected, and, hence, it is inherent in a judge's full expression of the hard treatment he imposes.

IV. Additional Criticisms of Morris's Theory

I have previously addressed critics who formulate Morris's theory in less than its strongest form. I shall now discuss criticisms of Morris's theory that apply to it even when formulated in its stronger form. (I shall not discuss broader criticisms that have been leveled against retributivism in all its forms,[35] though I think they can and should be separately addressed).

A. Contested premise of political obligation

Morris, as we have seen, derives his unfair-advantage theory of punishment from an anterior political theory regarding fair play. Thus, just as Hart and Rawls argue that the receipt of benefits from a mutually advantageous collective enterprise renders it fair that the recipients sustain the enterprise, Morris argues that the great benefit a person

[35] See, e.g., Deidre Golash, *The Case Against Punishment* (New York: New York University Press, 2005), 74–94; Shafer-Landau, "Retribution and Desert"; Tadros, *The Ends of Harm*, 60–87; Michael Zimmerman, *The Immorality of Punishment* (Ontario: Broadview Press, 2011), 63–120.

receives from the collective willingness of others in society to forbear from preying upon him obliges him to forbear from preying upon them.[36]

Political theorists, starting with Robert Nozick, have challenged Hart and Rawls's fair-play theory, creating uncertainty regarding whether B's receipt of collective benefits from A obligates B to sustain the collective enterprise that provides them.[37] These theorists may or may not be right regarding the particular collective benefits on which they happen to focus; and, even if they are, they may or may not also be right regarding *all* collective benefits, including essential protections of life, personal security, and property. Even if they are, however, their critique does not undermine Morris's theory of criminal desert, because Hart and Rawls look to fair play for something that Morris's theory of punishment does not require. Hart and Rawls look to fairness—specifically, the fairness of obliging a person to sustain collective enterprise from which he benefits—to *generate* political and moral obligations that do not otherwise exist. However, there is no need to look to fairness to generate a person's political and moral obligations in the event he *already possesses* them based upon independent moral grounds.[38] In that event, rather than playing the primary role of creating a moral obligation out of whole cloth, fairness plays a derivative role: it explains why a person who fails to comply with an independent moral obligation to support a collective enterprise can be justly required to disgorge benefits he has received from the enterprise—because he would otherwise constitute a free rider on the enterprise.

The same is true with respect to the collective enterprise of criminal law (though Morris himself may not have realized it). One does not have to look to fairness to explain why persons have a moral obligation to refrain from committing *mala in se* offenses and other crimes against morals.[39] Regardless of one's political theory, citizens surely have a moral right to be free from being killed, assaulted, or deprived by force or stealth of property to which they are entitled,[40] just as their compatriots have a moral

[36] See text accompanying notes 14–16.

[37] See Philip Soper, *The Ethics of Deference: Learning from Law's Morals* (Cambridge: Cambridge University Press, 2002), 140–52.

[38] See Rawls, "Legal Obligation and the Duty of Fair Play," 4 ("It would be incorrect to say that our duty not to commit any of the legal offenses, specifying crimes of violence, is based on the duty of fair play, at least entirely. These crimes involve wrongs as such, and with such offenses, as with the vices of cruelty and greed, our doing them is wrong independently of there being a legal system the benefits of which we have voluntarily accepted.").

[39] Duff and Green argue that prohibitions of moral wrongs extend beyond traditional *mala in se* offenses. See R. A. Duff, "Political Retributivism and Legal Moralism," 1 *Virginia Journal of Criminal Law* 179 (2012); R. A. Duff, "Crime, Prohibition, and Punishment," 19 *Journal of Applied Philosophy* 97 (2002); and Stuart Green, "Why It's a Crime to Tear the Tag Off a Mattress," 46 *Emory Law Journal* 1533 (1997). See also Soper, *The Ethics of Deference*, 159–83 (arguing that a citizen has a prima facie obligation to obey *mala prohibita* regulations, provided the regulations are as reasonable as others that citizen might prefer, because the benefits of having criminal laws entail a duty to defer to the normative judgments of those in charge, even when one believes them to be wrong). For arguments that Duff's and Green's claims do not extend as far as they contend, see Douglas Husak, "Malum Prohibitum and Retributivism," in R. A. Duff and Stuart Green (eds.), *Defining Crimes: Essays on the Special Part in Criminal Law* (Oxford: Oxford University Press, 2005), ch. 3; Larry Alexander and Kimberly Kessler Ferzan, *Crime and Culpability: A Theory of Criminal Law* (Cambridge: Cambridge University Press, 2009), 295–303.

[40] Norms against robbery and theft presuppose norms in support of "property"; and the latter are not natural rights but expectations based upon distributive institutions that, if they are just, must be independently justified, e.g., through contractarian theory like Rawls's. See Emmanuel Melissaris, "Property Offences as Crimes of Injustice," 6 *Criminal Law and Philosophy* 149 (2012). If thieves and robbers "deserve" to suffer,

duty to refrain from such harm. In that event, fairness comes into play not to create moral obligations that do not otherwise exist but to show that malefactors who benefit from the existence of criminal law but fail to comply with their obligation to respect it deserve to suffer.[41]

Now it might be argued the foregoing argument is circular. Fair play cannot operate derivatively to justify hard treatment, so the argument goes, without presupposing the very thing that it would justify—namely a just regime of criminal law that consists of stated offenses and that enforces their violation through hard treatment.[42] However, the argument is not circular. The primary principle of justice of which fair play is derivative is not the combination of just criminal prohibitions and *just hard treatment* for those who violate it (for then the claim would, indeed, be circular) but the just commands themselves, e.g., "Thou shalt not kill," plus the condemnation that justly accompanies their violation. Given that the commands themselves are independently justified, fair play comes in as a derivative principle to justify the imposition of hard treatment upon those who violate the commands.

B. Punishing malefactors who have previously been victimized

Critics contend that Morris's theory is vulnerable to a *reductio ad absurdum*. Morris's justification of hard treatment is premised upon a malefactor's having enjoyed benefits prior to committing his offense; benefits of personal welfare from having lived within a society dedicated to the preservation of life, personal security, and property. Yet, according to critics, some malefactors lack such benefits, namely malefactors who are *victimized by third persons* prior to committing crimes.[43] Thus, critics say, Morris's theory produces the absurd result that previously wronged malefactors cannot be justly punished for offenses they now commit, regardless of how heinous the offenses may be.

This *reductio* would have force if fair-play theory required that the beneficial protections of the criminal law are fully and universally enjoyed—that is, that every subject of punishment has enjoyed the same full benefits of criminal protection as others. However, fair play does not require that. It requires only that a malefactor has benefitted vis-à-vis what his fate would have been within a Hobbesian existence of *bellum omnium contra omnes*.[44] In Western democratic societies, that includes everyone, including those who have been wrongly victimized in the past.[45]

therefore, it is not a preinstitutional notion of desert but desert based on invading owners' legitimate, institutionally based expectations. See Samuel Scheffler, "Justice and Desert in Liberal Theory," 88 *California Law Review* 965 (2000).

41 If Morris's unfair-advantage theory is unable to account for *malum prohibitum* offenses (see Ten, *Crime, Guilt, and Punishment*, 64), it is not alone. The same is true of all theories of criminal desert, including theories of positive and negative retribution alike. See Husak, "Malum Prohibitum," 70.

42 See Duff, *Trials and Punishment*, 215 (making such an argument).

43 See Boonin, *The Problem of Punishment*, 135–7.

44 James Sterba would measure an actor's unfair advantage by whether his crime redistributes wealth and welfare unjustly, thereby immunizing actors who steal from the rich and give to the poor. See James Sterba, "Is There A Rationale For Punishment?," 29 *American Journal of Jurisprudence* 29 (1984). The appropriate baseline, I believe, is not the justice of the redistributions of wealth that crimes effectuate but the absence of moral and criminal-law protections for life, personal security, and property.

45 A class of person remains who, perhaps, cannot justly be subjected to hard treatment, namely persons who, having been falsely and unjustly condemned and subjected to hard treatment for committing a crime,

C. Justifying punishment at the hands of private individuals

Critics claim that Morris's theory is vulnerable to another *reductio*: if malefactors truly owe debts to society of death, imprisonment, or severe corporal suffering, it must follow that private individuals may act as vigilantes to collect society's debts for it.[46]

Vigilante justice is, indeed, unjust.[47] However, there are at least two reasons why fair-play retributivism does not legitimate private punishment. The first reason is contingent upon the kind of communicative act that all punishment consists of, including the punishment that fair play theory seeks to justify. What fair-play theory seeks to justify is not a communication by A of outright *hatred or contempt* toward B as a *person*. Nor is it a communication by A of *personal* condemnation of B's conduct. Nor does it consist of a communication by A of *pleasure* on A's part in B's suffering. Rather, it is a communication by A to B of *society's* moral condemnation of B's *motivation in acting as he did*, and A's imposition of suffering upon B that A communicates is being imposed not for the purpose of giving A personal pleasure but for the sorrowful purpose of negating wellbeing that *society* believes B's culpable wrongdoing renders it unfair for him to retain.[48] (Indeed, those communicative requirements explain why death-row inmates to whom they cannot be communicated may not be executed).[49] Private punishment is contingently unjust because it tends to be imposed by persons who are themselves victims of malefactors' wrongdoing, and, therefore, it tends (1) to express outright hatred and contempt toward malefactors (rather than mere resentment of their actions); (2) to express personal condemnation toward malefactors (rather than society's condemnation); (3) to express that punishers derive pleasure from malefactors' suffering (rather than sorrow at their suffering); (4) to express that malefactors owe a debt of suffering to them personally (rather than to society as a whole); and (5) to overestimate the amount of suffering that malefactors must incur to negate their debt to society.

To be sure, the foregoing objections are contingent upon private punishment, not inherent in it. Each of the objections could be neutralized by fashioning private punishment with proper safeguards. However, at least one element of punishment is inherently inconsistent with private punishment, at least regarding severe hard treatments of death, imprisonment, or severe corporal suffering. Hard treatment exacts from malefactors suffering that they owe *to society*.[50] As a creditor, society is free to decide whether the debts are paid, and, if so, their scale. Society may demand that malefactors

e.g., armed robbery in 1990, are now convicted of committing the same offense at a different time, i.e., armed robbery in 2000. Such persons can be rightly *condemned* for their new offenses. But with respect to *hard treatment*, they have already been deprived of the benefits of the criminal law that their culpability for armed robbery reveals them not to have deserved. For a contrary conclusion, see Bayern, "The Significance of Private Burdens," 19–20.

46 See Bayern, "The Significance of Private Burdens," 13.

47 See Zimmerman, *The Immorality of Punishment*, 98–9. This is not to say that punishments *less* than death, imprisonment, and severe corporal punishment must be imposed exclusively by the state. Private individuals such as parents, teachers, and fellow community members routinely and appropriately impose such lesser punishments. Cf. Zaibert, *Punishment and Retribution*, 16–24.

48 See Finnis, "Retribution," 99.

49 See *Ford v, Wainwright*, 477 US 399 (1986).

50 See Jeffrie Murphy, "Retributivism, Moral Education, and the Liberal State," 4 *Criminal Justice Ethics* 3 (1985), 7 ("'debt' is owed to his fellow citizens"); Jeffrie Murphy, "Three Mistakes," 167 ("the debt [is] owed to the law-abiding members of one's community").

pay their debts of suffering in full. Or it may choose to forgive—that is, to pardon—their debts, in whole or in part.[51] More importantly, society not only *may* make that decision itself, it *must* make that decision, because no other person or body can speak for it. When society imposes the full hard treatment a malefactor deserves, it implicitly decides not to forgive or partially pardon him. In contrast, when a private person decides to impose hard treatment, whether it is all or less than a malefactor deserves, he, too, is implicitly making a decision regarding forgiveness. But it is not a decision for him to make.[52]

D. Fair play in an unjust state

Jeffrie Murphy was originally among Morris's strongest supporters. But Murphy famously came to harbor doubts, in large part because he worried that governments were incapable in practice of providing their citizens with the kind of fair distributions of benefits and burdens that he believed Morris's fair-play theory presupposes. In expressing his doubts, Murphy, and others whom he has influenced,[53] reason as follows:

> ***Fair distribution.*** Citizens are obliged to bear the burden of restraining themselves from harming others if, and only if, the benefits of collective life are distributed among them fairly.
>
> ***Unfair advantage.*** Wrongdoers who fail to restrain themselves gain an unfair advantage vis-à-vis others if, and only if, the benefits and burdens of collective life are fairly distributed among them.
>
> ***Punishment.*** Punishment is just if, and only if, it negates what would otherwise constitute unfair advantages in wrongdoers.
>
> ***Unjust states.*** Although governments may *in theory* be capable of distributing the benefits and burdens of collective life fairly, they invariably fail *in practice.*
>
> ***Conclusion.*** Governments do not act justly in practice in punishing wrongdoers.[54]

Murphy's criticism is based upon an assumption that we have seen is flawed—an assumption regarding the *source* of a citizen's obligation to refrain from violating the lives, personal security, and property of others. Murphy assumes that the obligation derives its existence, if it all, from a fair distribution of benefits and burdens. However, we have seen that the obligation of persons to refrain from invading the lives, personal security, and property[55] of others exists independently of fair-play theory. The benefit

[51] Morris, "Persons and Punishment," 34.

[52] See Alon Harel, "Why Only the State May Inflict Criminal Sanctions: The Case Against Privately Inflicted Sanctions," 14 *Legal Theory* 113 (2008). This does not mean that when the state comes to punish a person who has been privately punished, it should deny him credit for suffering he has already incurred. See Douglas Husak, "Already Punished Enough," in Douglas Husak, *The Philosophy of Criminal Law* (Oxford: Oxford University Press, 2010), ch. 17. Nor does it mean that private individuals may not act as agents of the state, provided that safeguards against contingent objections are in place, e.g., executioners.

[53] See also Ted Honderich, *Punishment*, 56; Jami L. Anderson, "Reciprocity as a Justification for Retributivism," 16 *Criminal Justice Ethics* 13 (1997); Ten, *Crime, Guilt, and Punishment*, 63–4; Duff, *Trials and Punishment*, 209–10; Alan H. Goldman, "Toward a New Theory of Punishment," 1 *Law and Philosophy* 57 (1982).

[54] Murphy, "Legal Moralism," 12–13.

[55] For property entitlements, see note 41.

of living within societies that are committed to such norms is measured not by the fairness of initial distributions of benefits and burdens and not by the comparative advantage others may reap but by the non-comparative benefit of escaping Hobbesian existence in which life is "solitary, poor, nasty, brutish and short". One can perhaps imagine societies in which the benefits of escaping such Hobbesian existence are questionable, such as those torn apart by war, those that use death camps, or those operating race-based slave systems. But the benefits are surely not questionable within modern democratic societies.[56]

E. A "Somali pirate" hypothetical

Consider the following scenario. Somali pirates capture a German ship in the Indian Ocean and threaten its crew with death. The pirates are captured and put on trial in Germany. Surely the pirates deserve punishment. Yet, critics say, it is hard to rationalize their desert on fair-play grounds, because (1) Somalia is practically a failed state, (2) the pirates preyed on no fellow Somalis, and (3) they have received no benefits from Germany.[57]

This hypothetical misconceives the source and content of the benefits that all persons enjoy, including Somali pirates. The benefits have their source in the moral rights against violence that are universal to all persons and that are further reinforced by being embodied in law as *mala in se* offenses. The content of the benefits is what results from this rejection in morals and law of the Hobbesian alternative of *bellum omnium contra omnes*. Persons who commit *mala in se* offenses deserve to suffer to negate the portion of those benefits that their wrongdoing renders it unfair for them to retain. The fact that Somali pirates have survived the helplessness of infancy and childhood, possess life skills learned from others, operate in cooperative groups, and find sanctuary at home is evidence of how much they owe to this shared morality and to its rejection of the alternative.

There remains the issue of Germany's standing to prosecute. Significantly, there is increasing recognition that some *mala in se* offenses, for example war crimes, are crimes of universal jurisdiction that can be prosecuted by any state anywhere. And piracy, too, may be such a wrong. Even if it is not, however, Germany certainly has moral and legal standing to prosecute piracy—and to dictate punishment for it—when it is committed against German nationals.

F. An imprecise metric for fixing and grading criminal penalties

Critics fault Morris for failing to provide one of the two essential elements that retributive desert theory must supply, namely a determinate standard for fixing and grading criminal penalties.[58]

[56] See Michael Davis, "Criminal Desert, Harm, and Fairness," 25 *Israel Law Review* 524 (1991).

[57] I owe this hypothetical to Mitch Berman and Kim Ferzan.

[58] See Duff, "The Incompleteness of "Punishment as Fair Play," 280; Zachary Hoskins, "Fair Play, Political Obligation, and Punishment," 5 *Criminal Law and Philosophy* 37 (2011); Von Hirsch, *Censure and Sanctions*, 8; Zimmerman, *The Immorality of Punishment*, 95, 97.

With due respect, these critics misunderstand the benefits that define criminal desert for Morris and, hence, misunderstand the metric by which criminal desert and penalties are measured. Thus, von Hirsch and Shafer-Landau both assume that the benefit which criminal penalties negate consists of the excessive *freedom* that malefactors arrogate to themselves.[59] And Murphy assumes that the relevant benefit consists of a malefactor's conscious pleasure in giving in to temptation.[60] Neither of these assumptions, however, is consistent with the strongest interpretation of Morris's theory. Interpreted strongly, Morris's metric for measuring penalties is a function of his standard for deserved suffering: the degree of suffering that a culpable malefactor deserves is the degree of well-being at society's hands that he previously enjoyed, that, in the prosecuting society's judgment, his disregard of others reveals it is unfair for him to retain.

Contrary to his critics, therefore, Morris does provide a "fact of the matter about what sanctions a wrongdoer deserves for his offense."[61] This is not to say that Morris's metric provides precise and unchanging guidance in grading offenses. It does not. However, when it comes to grading offenses, immutable exactitude, like that supposedly provided by *lex talionis*, is no virtue. Morris leaves it to each society in its own time to determine the suffering that it regards as morally needed to negate the previously enjoyed welfare that an malefactor's culpable wrongdoing renders it unfair for him to retain—a determination that, though approximate, mutable, and contestable, has the virtue of conforming with a society's assessment of the magnitude of the wrong he committed and with its tolerance for state-imposed suffering.[62]

V. Conclusion

The moral intuition that culpable wrongdoers deserve to suffer is as powerful, pervasive, and persistent as any moral intuition which human beings possess.[63] The intuition is so strong that some advocates of retributivism, including Michael Moore, base their entire positions upon it. Yet, for many students of punishment, the "problem of punishment"[64] is too grave to be resolved on the basis of mere intuition.[65] The problem is that punishment consists of the most fearsome harm that an organized state is capable of inflicting upon its members: it is the practice by which the state, speaking

59 von Hirsch, *Censure and Sanctions*, 8; Shafer-Landau, "Retributivism and Desert," 206.

60 See Murphy, "Legal Moralism," 13–14.

61 Shafer-Landau, "Retributivism and Desert," 191.

62 See D. J. Galligan, "The Return to Retribution in Penal Theory," in C. F. H. Tapper (ed.), *Crime, Proof and Punishment: Essays in Memory of Sir Rupert Cross* (London: Butterworth, 1981), 167 ("[I]t must be accepted that . . . the goal of sentencing an offender strictly according to his deserts is . . . inherently approximate. All that can be claimed is that [the gravity of his offense] and therefore desert can be assessed according to broad and approximate categories").

63 See Burgh, "Do the Guilty Deserve Punishment?," 195; Mirko Bagaric and Kumar Amarasekara, "The Errors of Retributivism," 24 *Melbourne University Law Review* 124 (2000).

64 Boonin, *The Problem of Punishment*, 1; Tadros, *The Ends of Harm*, 1.

65 See Burgh, "Do the Guilty Deserve Punishment?," 195–6 ("People's immediate, intuitive response [to wrongdoing] is that the wrongdoer deserves to suffer . . . However, insofar as we are unable to [show that this response is grounded on principles of justice], we must begin to take seriously the question whether perhaps we should cease responding in this way"); Duff, "Penal Communications," 29 ("A feeling of guilt might indeed, for many people, generate the judgment that one ought to suffer punishment . . . . But, first, we must surely *explain*, rather than just appeal to, that thought: *what*, and *why*, do the guilty deserve to suffer?") (emphasis added); von Hirsch, *Censure and Sanctions*, 6.

publicly on behalf of all its members, purposely subjects some of them to suffering, and even to death, while publicly declaring them to deserve it by virtue of moral failings on their part. If, as John Mackie suggests, "deserving to suffer" lacks principled content,[66] punishment becomes a great moral wrong. If punishment is to be sustained, it is incumbent upon its advocates to articulate the principles, if any, that underlie their and others' intuitions of desert.

Every student of punishment has a stake in this inquiry. Positive retributivists like Michael Moore have a stake in it because their position *wholly* consists of desert. Negative retributivists, that is those who believe that punishment is just if and only if it is both deserved and productive of good consequences, also have a stake in it because their position *partly* consists of desert.[67] And those who reject desert altogether[68] have a stake in it because their position depends upon showing that desert lacks moral force.

The moral principle that I believe most plausibly explains and justifies desert is Herbert Morris's theory of fair play. I have argued that commentators have failed to address Morris's theory in its strongest possible form and have failed to critically examine the arguments against it. Morris's theory not only supplies normative content to assertions and intuitions of desert, it also reveals that "paying back a debt"—the original meaning of the Latin *retributio*—is not a "faded and dead metaphor"[69] but an apt description of what it is to deserve suffering for culpable wrongdoing.

[66] Mackie, "Morality and the Retributive Emotions," 3.

[67] Positive retributivism is the claim that culpable wrongdoing is always a *reason* to punish, though not an indefeasible reason; negative retributivism is the claim that desert is necessary but not sufficient to justify punishment.

[68] For commentators who reject desert altogether, see Kershnar, "Retributivism"; Tadros, *The Ends of Harm*, 60–87; Zimmerman, *The Immorality of Punishment*, 63–120.

[69] Moore, 1999a, 84. See also Dolinko, "Some Thoughts About Retributivism," 539 (referring to "paying one's debt" as a "puzzling" metaphor).

6

The Wrong and the Free

Victor *Tadros**

I. Introduction

If there was no Michael Moore, no one could invent him. His vigor, enthusiasm, clarity, originality, and acuity are almost unparalleled in the philosophy of criminal law. For these reasons alone, I am delighted to contribute to this volume in his honor.

Moore's books are big and brilliant. However, brilliant though I find his work, and even though we share some basic non-consequentialist commitments, I don't agree with too many of Moore's main ideas about criminal justice. This is partly due to a deep disagreement about retributive desert—the idea that wrongdoers deserve to suffer the burdens of punishment in virtue of having acted wrongly. Moore is retributive desert's best friend; I am its most hostile enemy. But as long as they do not persuade too many people, I'm delighted that Moore has defended his ideas so forcefully. My own thinking about all of the central topics in the philosophy of criminal law, as well as fundamental topics in moral philosophy, has been advanced in no small measure by engaging with Moore's work.

The three of Moore's ideas that will concern me in this chapter have to do with criminalization, and are as follows: (1) there is a presumption of liberty, which amounts to a uniform reason against the use of the criminal law (or any coercive law); (2) all moral wrongs should be prohibited, for the reason that those who perform morally wrongful actions deserve punishment; and (3) the only aim that the state should have in criminalizing conduct is to ensure that wrongdoers get what they deserve. These three ideas are the central components of Moore's theory of criminalization.

I think that any interesting interpretation of these ideas will find all three to be false; as I believe that Moore is more likely to be wrong than boring, I think that these ideas, as Moore himself understands them, are false. Moore's commitment to retributive desert structures his thinking about these ideas, but I think they are false, even if (heaven forefend!) Moore is right in thinking that wrongdoers deserve to suffer the burdens of punishment.

II. Is there a Presumption of Liberty?

Moore thinks that there is a general presumption against the use of the criminal law in virtue of the value of liberty. The kind of liberty that he is interested in is liberty to act

* In thinking about the topic of this chapter, I have benefited from discussions with a whole host of people in the Arts and Humanities Council-funded Criminalization project, which I co-organize with Antony Duff, Lindsay Farmer, Sandra Marshall, and Massimo Renzo. Special thanks to Mitch Berman for comments.

without being subject to coercive legal sanctions. He argues that "there is an intelligible set of values served by negative liberty as such, values which apply equally to all actions no matter what their moral quality."[1] He does not believe that there is a general "right to liberty" that must be defeated if the use of the criminal law is to be shown to be legitimate. But he does think that there is always a reason not to legally coerce behavior, even if that reason will often be defeated by legitimate reasons in favor of criminalization.[2] Scrutinizing Moore's arguments is worthwhile not only because the question of whether there is a presumption of liberty is interesting in itself; it is also worthwhile because it helps us to assess the success of different liberty-based arguments that might be offered against criminalization.

Moore offers four arguments in favor of the presumption of liberty. First, he claims that it is good that citizens have a large opportunity set because that provides citizens with "a large and diverse set of projects with some realistic hope of success."[3] Freedom from legal coercion, Moore thinks, is a universal means to secure this good. He explains: "the having of more opportunities is good because it allows you to get what you want, whatever it may be that you want."[4] Let us call this the opportunity argument.

Second, he suggests that the value of a morally good action depends on the reasons why it is performed. If one is legally coerced to do a morally good action, one is less likely to perform that action for good reasons. Hence, legal coercion tends to diminish the value of good actions. Let us call this the argument of the value of actions.

Third, he argues that as almost all people prefer to make their own decisions rather than make decisions under interference from others we have good reasons to favor liberty. We can call this the free-choice argument.

Fourth, he argues that criminal prohibitions use up scarce social resources.

I will leave the fourth argument aside after making the following brief comment. While it is true that expending resources is almost always a reason against criminalization, this reason is not operative when the resources that one spends are more than compensated for by resources gained. There is no reason, not even a defeated reason, against exchanging £5 for £10. As criminalization can sometimes protect as well as expend resources, for example by providing the conditions in which enterprise flourishes, resources are not always a reason against criminalization.[5]

In assessing Moore's other arguments, note that everyone accepts that liberty is sometimes important in an argument against some criminal prohibitions. Furthermore, everyone accepts that some of the reasons that Moore offers against criminalizing conduct are sometimes valid. The interesting question concerns how general their application is. After all, Moore is arguing for the interesting and controversial thesis that there is a general presumption of liberty, and not for the weak, boring, and universally accepted thesis that there are sometimes reasons of liberty not to criminalize conduct. Let us assess Moore's arguments in turn.

[1] Moore, 1997b, 746. [2] Moore, 1997b, 749. [3] Moore, 1997b, 747.

[4] Moore, 1997b, 747.

[5] Of course, we need to show that we can criminalize in part to secure resources to make this argument valid. That relies on an instrumental justification of punishment. I leave defense of such a justification aside here, as I develop one at length in *The Ends of Harm: The Moral Foundations of Criminal Law* (Oxford: Oxford University Press, 2011).

A. The opportunity argument

One problem with Moore's opportunity argument is that it rests on the controversial view, which he attributes to Rawls,[6] that it is good that people get what they want, whatever it may be. Here, there are two doubts.

The first is familiar—whether it is good for a person to get what she wants depends on whether she has good reason to want it. Recall that Moore thinks that his arguments apply whatever the moral quality of actions. Moore thus seems to imply that if D wants to torture babies, it is good that D gets what he wants. To be clear, Moore would not advocate decriminalization of baby-torture, all things considered, on this basis. However, he implies that there is a reason against criminalization that needs to be outweighed.

But the fact that D wants to torture babies is not a reason for D to do so; and if it is not, it is also not a reason to allow D the option of torturing babies. Perhaps Moore might argue that if D wants to torture babies, it would be enjoyable for him to torture babies, and D's enjoyment is good. But enjoying torturing babies is not a reason to do so—the torturer should reject any enjoyment he feels at baby-torture.

Perhaps "feeling like *v*ing" can sometimes provide a reason to *v*.[7] Feeling like doing a cartwheel perhaps provides a reason to do a cartwheel. It does not follow that "feeling like *v*ing" *always* provides a reason to *v*; it does not where the agent has a decisive reason to distance himself from his feelings. A person who feels like torturing babies has every reason to distance himself from this feeling.

Furthermore, D might not want to torture babies because he feels like it. We can want things because we see those things as worthwhile, even if getting those things is not accompanied by positive feelings. D may misguidedly want to torture babies only because he mistakenly thinks God commands it. He may hate following these commands, but believe he is obliged to follow them. D's judgments about both the existence and value of such commands are mistaken. It is difficult to see how these mistaken judgments supply him with reasons. Thus, wanting *v* does not supply a reason to *v*, even if enjoyment at *v*ing always confers reasons to *v*.

The second challenge accepts, for the sake of argument, that it is good that people get what they want. Even if so, the presumption of liberty, as Moore understands it, does not follow. We are concerned with liberty in the following sense: D is at liberty to *v* if D is not legally coerced not to *v*. D is legally coerced not to *v* if D is threatened with punishment if he *v*s. But being threatened with punishment if one *v*s does not necessarily reduce one's opportunities, not even one's opportunities to do what one wants.

If D is credibly threatened with punishment for *v*ing, D lacks an opportunity to *v* without being punished. But he is supplied with an opportunity to *v* and to be punished. If we are neutral about the quality of the opportunities that one has, being threatened with punishment for *v*ing neither increases nor decreases one's opportunities.

[6] The passage that Moore cites is *A Theory of Justice* (Cambridge, Mass.: Harvard University Press, 1971) 396. Rawls's text, though, is (I feel compelled to say, characteristically) unclear. He talks of what a rational individual would prefer in order to carry out their plans of life. He is not clearly committed to claiming that it is good that individuals have opportunities to carry out abhorrent life plans.

[7] For an argument that it can, see R. Chang, "Can Desires Provide Reasons for Action?" in R. J. Wallace, P. Pettit, S. Scheffler, and M. Smith, *Reason and Value: Themes from the Moral Philosophy of Joseph Raz* (Oxford: Oxford University Press, 2004).

Moore might argue that being threatened with punishment for *v*ing necessarily decreases one's opportunities to get what one wants. Not so. That depends on what one wants. If D wants to be punished by the state for torturing babies, D can get what she wants only if torturing babies is criminalized. Prohibiting baby torture supplies D with an opportunity to get what she wants. And if retributivism is true, wrongdoers *should* prefer to be punished for their wrongdoing. They should prefer that they get what they deserve. So, in Moore's own view, the preference that one be punished if one acts wrongly is not even perverse.

Or suppose D wishes to get away with torturing babies. D prefers that torturing babies is prohibited—the value she finds in getting away with torturing babies may depend on baby torture being prohibited. This is less uncommon than it might seem. Some people value taking proscribed drugs in virtue of the fact that doing so is cool. It is cool partly in virtue of the prohibition on drug possession.

If Moore claims that it is good that those who wish to torture babies get what they want, he can hardly deny that it is good that those people just considered get what they want. Of course, it will often be true that people prefer not to be punished for doing what they want. But Moore's argument lacks the universal scope it is supposed to have.

The view that we ought to prohibit baby torture in order that baby torturers who want punishment can get what they want is, of course, silly. But this argument is silly for just the same reason that the view that we ought not to prohibit baby torture so that baby torturers can get what they want is silly. The silliness of both views is exposed by the proper response to the first challenge I posed to Moore: where one has plenty of opportunities to develop and execute life plans, it is not good to have opportunities to do seriously wrongful things, whatever one wants. The value of one's opportunities depends on their quality.

B. **Reasons and the value of action**

Consider Moore's argument from the value of actions. While there is disagreement about whether intentions are relevant to permissibility, everyone agrees that intentions are relevant to the value of actions. We have good reason to celebrate those who sacrifice themselves for the sake of others, for example, but not (or not so much) if this was done only for personal glory.

Moore thinks this implies a uniform reason against criminalizing wrongful action. Moore's argument, I think, is this:

1. Criminalizing any wrongful action, *v*, supplies people with a prudential reason to refrain from *v*ing.
2. Because some people will refrain from *v*ing for prudential reasons, criminalizing *v*ing decreases the number of people who will refrain from *v*ing for moral reasons.
3. The value of refraining from *v*ing for prudential reasons is less than the value of refraining from *v*ing for moral reasons.
4. Therefore, criminalization diminishes the value of permissible actions.
5. Therefore, we have reason not to criminalize wrongful action.

This argument is suspect. One problem is that premise (2) is empirical. Moore does not support it. Why believe that it is uniformly true that criminalization corrupts? If the prudential reasons offered by criminal law are rationally decisive, some people who refrain from *v*ing will do so for prudential reasons. But this does not imply that they will not be guided by moral reasons. They may consider both reasons as sufficient. This seems the normal case: people typically refrain from murdering both because it is wrong and because they will be punished for it.

And here is a general reason to doubt premise (2). In criminalizing *v*, the state indicates public abhorrence at *v*ing. As a result, people may come to recognize that the relevant conduct is wrong, and refrain from acting in that way. Of course, I don't claim that this is always true. But for Moore's argument to work, it must never be true.

Consider domestic abuse. Enforcement and development of the law applying to domestic abuse has contributed to recognition that domestic abuse is wrong, and that in turn may have reduced the instances of domestic abuse. It doesn't seem likely that many who now refrain from domestic abuse out of fear of the law would have refrained from domestic abuse out of duty had domestic abuse been decriminalized. It seems more likely that the use of the criminal law has enhanced people's ability to recognize that domestic abuse is wrong. At any rate, criminalization surely sometimes improves people's ability to act for moral reasons.

A second problem is that Moore's argument proves too much. Consider the following. Many men refrain from attempting rape because they are concerned that the women they would like to rape will fight back, call for help, or go to the authorities. Moore's argument implies these women have a reason to render themselves unable to fight back, call for help, or go to the authorities. For if they do so, men will be more likely to refrain from raping them because rape is wrong, and not because they are likely to fight back, call for help, or go to the authorities. The police also have a reason not to listen to their accusations. For if they refuse to listen, men will be more likely to refrain from raping because rape is wrong rather than because they are afraid of the authorities. As women clearly have no reason to disable themselves, and the authorities clearly lack this reason not to listen to rape accusations, the argument from the value of action fails.

Moore might object that it is surely better that a person refrains from raping another because he recognizes that doing so is wrong than it is that he refrains from raping due to fear of the law. But the truth of this does not provide others with a reason to bring it about in the way specified. A woman has no reason to consider whether to disable herself to bring about this increase in value. It is irrelevant to her. If people refrain from raping her only because she will fight back, they are worse people. It is a shame if her willingness to fight back results in them being worse in this way. But this cannot provide her with a reason to disable herself. The same goes for the law. If the law encourages people not to act wrongly only because they are coerced, and not because they recognize that the acts are wrong, that is a shame. But that is not a reason for the state to refrain from holding people to account for serious wrongdoing. The fact that it is a shame that something occurs does not always supply a reason to avoid that thing.

C. The argument against interference

Moore claims that one uniform reason against criminalization is that people prefer to make their own decisions rather than having decisions made for them. The reference to preferences in Moore's discussion is once again a distraction. If we have a reason to let people decide what to do for themselves rather than interfering with their decisions, this is not due to their preferences. It is because people have reason to value making decisions for themselves.

Here is one familiar doubt. It is not plausible that reasonable citizens see criminalization of serious wrongdoing as a form of interference. Reasonable citizens already rule out serious wrongdoing in deciding what to do.

Here is another. The justification of criminalizing some conduct depends on that conduct being condemnable and punishable. In the case of serious wrongdoing, the state has a duty to condemn and punish wrongful conduct. Of course, it is controversial what explains this duty. That there is such a duty is relatively uncontroversial.[8] In criminalizing seriously wrongful conduct, the state indicates its intention to condemn and punish those who perform such actions. In indicating that it has this intention it simply announces that it will do its duty.

If so, in criminalizing seriously wrongful conduct the state does not threaten to punish wrongdoers. It warns wrongdoers that if they act wrongly the state will fulfill its duty and punish them. Threats plausibly interfere with liberty. Warnings that one will fulfill one's duty if such a duty arises do not. Hence, an indication by the state that it will do its duty in responding to wrongdoing by punishing wrongdoers is not best seen as a form of interference.

Moore may object that it is permissible for the state to condemn and punish offenders only on condition that it has indicated in advance that it will do so.[9] Criminalization thus affects the liberty of citizens—it creates the conditions under which conduct may be publicly condemned and punished.

However, the state plausibly has a duty to condemn and punish seriously wrongful conduct even if it has not criminalized that conduct. If it fails to abide by the rule of law, it ought nevertheless to condemn and punish wrongdoers for what they have done. Moore himself accepts this in the case of the Nazis, who, he thinks, the state rightly punished in contravention of the rule of law.[10] The same is true in domestic contexts. Suppose that even very violent and forcible rape within marriage is not prohibited and, due to a very sexist political arrangement, this conduct is unlikely to be criminalized in the near future. Police, prosecutors, and courts ought nevertheless to try and convict these rapists. Failure to do so would add insult to injury: the failure of the state to criminalize rape is compounded by its inaction in the face of rapes.

[8] There are those who doubt that the state has a general duty to punish, at least on retributivist grounds—they think that the state has at most a reason to punish. See, for example, D. Husak, "Retributivism *In Extremis*" 32 *Law and Philosophy* 3 (2013), 3; L. Zaibert, "Instruments of Abolition, or Why Retributivism is the Only Real Justification of Punishment" 32 *Law and Philosophy* 33 (2013). It is difficult to believe, though, that it lacks a duty to punish serious wrongdoing. A state that fails to punish rapists and murderers surely fails to satisfy a duty that it owes to those who receive inadequate protection from being raped or murdered.

[9] See Moore, 2009c, 27, 31.

[10] Moore, 2009c, 45.

Perhaps if there is some reason to doubt whether some conduct should be classified as rape, the state should refrain from punishing that conduct until it has clarified the law. But this concern does not arise for all instances of rape within marriage. Of course, punishing these rapists would violate the rule of law. But the rule of law is not the only thing that matters in decisions whether to punish.

Furthermore, even if the state is permitted to punish only if it adheres to the rule of law, this does not alter the fact that the criminal law, at least in the case of core crimes, offers warnings rather than making threats. It is sometimes permissible to harm a person only if one has warned other people in advance that one will do so. But even when this is so, giving the person the warning does not interfere with their liberty. The state only expresses something that is true independently of the criminalization of the conduct—that it has a conditional duty to punish offenders for their wrongdoing. In criminalizing the conduct, the state satisfies the condition, triggering the duty.

Perhaps it might be argued that criminalization does not only amount to an indication that those who act in certain ways will be condemned and punished. It also determines police preventive action. And this action interferes with liberty. But it is even less plausible that securing preventive justice depends on criminalization. Anyone is permitted to prevent seriously harmful wrongdoing, whether or not it has been criminalized.

Another response that Moore might offer to the view that the criminal law, in the case of core crimes, warns rather than threatens builds on a point that I noticed earlier: The boundaries of any serious crime are the subject of reasonable disagreement. Criminalization determines what these boundaries are, and thus changes the normative position of citizens. But even if so, the general presumption of liberty that Moore argues for cannot be vindicated on this basis. The permissibility of prevention would not be altered through criminalization with respect to core cases of seriously harmful wrongdoing. A narrow criminal law could be created without altering the circumstances of citizens. Hence, the argument against interference does not support a general presumption of liberty.

III. Ought All Wrongdoing to be Prohibited?

Moore claims that the state has a duty to prohibit all wrongful conduct. He does not endorse the silly view that all wrongdoing ought to be prohibited *all things considered*. He claims that we have a *pro tanto* duty to criminalize all wrongdoing.

As Moore notes, the view that we ought to prohibit all moral wrongdoing need not be illiberal. This is not only because the *pro tanto* duty to prohibit wrongful conduct might be defeated by reasons against criminalization, such as reasons of liberty. It is also because the scope of the alleged duty depends on what is wrong. A person with liberal moral views will have liberal views about the scope of the criminal law. This describes Moore.

For example, one familiar concern with Moore's legal moralism is that it implies a duty on the state to prohibit unconventional sexual behavior. Whether that is true depends on whether unconventional sexual behavior is wrong. Moore briefly outlines a liberal view about when sexual behavior is wrong—who cares who sticks what into which bits of whom (as long as they consent, etc., etc.)?

Some Millian liberals might respond that Moore's view at least threatens illiberality: if legislatures believe legal moralism, they will tend to criminalize those things they find immoral. If legislatures are guided by legal moralism, they will criminalize the (not) wrong stuff. But, as Moore argues, even if legal moralism ought not to guide legislatures, given their fallibility, legal moralism may be true.[11] States may have a duty to criminalize all wrongful conduct, even if they ought not always to try to fulfill that duty.

Millians, though, typically offer a more principled objection to legal moralism. They claim that there is no reason to prohibit wrongful behavior if others are unaffected by it. Whereas Moore sees a powerful reason to punish immoral behavior, a reason that must be defeated by liberty-based arguments, Millian liberals see no reason to punish such behavior at all. For, recall, Mill famously thought that "the sole end for which mankind are warranted, individually or collectively, in interfering with the liberty of action of any of their number, is self-protection."[12]

It is worth noting that, given Mill's commitment to utilitarianism, it is not clear that Mill can endorse a principled argument for his own version of the harm principle. He is best seen as endorsing the harm principle because doing so will best promote the good, rather than because there is no reason to prevent people from doing what is bad.[13] However, Millian liberals who are unsympathetic to Mill's utilitarianism might find principled reasons to endorse the harm principle. For example, they might think that there is no reason to prevent people performing self-regarding wrongs, such as the wrong of corrupting oneself, because doing so is paternalistic.

In response, Moore offers the following argument:[14]

1. If some conduct, *v*, is wrong, those who *v* deserve punishment.
2. The state ought to ensure that those who deserve punishment get what they deserve.
3. The state ought to punish a person for acting in a certain way only if it has criminalized acting in that way.
4. Therefore, the state ought to criminalize all wrongful conduct.

While I am not a Millian liberal,[15] Moore's argument is suspect, even if (as I doubt) premise (1) is true.[16]

[11] See, further, Moore, 2014c.

[12] *On Liberty and Other Essays* (Oxford: Oxford University Press, 1991) 14.

[13] For a good discussion see D. O. Brink, *Mill's Progressive Principles* (Oxford: Oxford University Press, 2013). Moore thinks that Mill must have believed that only actions which harm others are wrongful. But even if he did believe this, his version of the harm principle would be in conflict with his utilitarianism—utilitarianism would support the use of the criminal law to benefit people in conflict with Mill's harm principle.

[14] I'm confident that this is the argument that Moore intends, though he does not spell it out quite like this. See Moore, 1997b, 754.

[15] See, further, V. Tadros, "Harm, Sovereignty, and Prohibition" 17 *Legal Theory* 35 (2011).

[16] For doubts about this premise, see V. Tadros, *The Ends of Harm: The Moral Foundations of the Criminal Law* (Oxford: Oxford University Press, 2011) ch. 4, 'Responses,' 251–82.

There are various middle positions between Moore's and mine. The kinds of thought experiment that retributivists like Moore appeal to in support of their view—the experiment where serious wrongdoers continue to live happy lives without bad consequences—does not support the view that all wrongdoers deserve to suffer. Many people who share the retributivist reaction to serious wrongdoing will not react in the same way to the person who fails to wash the dishes when it is her turn.

Furthermore, even if Moore's wide-scope view of desert is right, Moore's legal moralism does not follow. State punishment is a sledgehammer. Trivial wrongdoing is a nut. We lack a duty, even a defeasible duty, to use this sledgehammer to crack this nut.

Moore's argument depends on the idea that all wrongdoers deserve the kind of suffering or deprivation involved in state punishment. But those who endorse Moore's claims about desert need not believe that all wrongdoers deserve the kind of suffering and deprivation that the state inflicts through punishment. For example, the suffering that trivial wrongdoers deserve might be limited to weak pangs of guilt. State punishment inevitably inflicts suffering and deprivation that is different in kind and degree from weak pangs of guilt. Trivial wrongdoers who are punished by the state inevitably suffer disproportionately. Even tiny fines would be disproportionate. To see this, imagine that the state fines you for failing to wash the dishes when it is your turn. Hence, even friends of Moore's wide-scope desert should acknowledge that the state lacks a duty to criminalize trivial wrongdoing.

Moore might respond that even if some wrongdoer only deserves pangs of guilt, there would always be a duty to punish the wrongdoer—the duty to bring about pangs of guilt. Given that it will inevitably do much more than this, the state ought not to do its duty. That does not demonstrate that it lacks the duty.

Here are two doubts about this response. First, there would be a duty to punish wrongdoers only if the state can cause trivial wrongdoers to feel pangs of guilt that they would not otherwise feel—"ought" implies "can" (at least in this case). It may not be able to do this, either because trivial wrongdoers will already be very likely to feel pangs of guilt, or, more importantly, because using the state's machinery will inevitably cause such resentment that any pangs of guilt will be expunged. Whether these things are true, of course, is an empirical question. But as Moore's view is that the state ought to punish all wrongdoing, his argument will fail if they are ever true.

A second worry takes a little longer to flesh out. Moore's analysis implies that the state has a duty to punish trivial wrongdoing, even though, given that it will inevitably punish the wrongdoers disproportionately, it ought never to punish those wrongdoers. To support this view, Moore might reasonably argue that we sometimes have duties that we ought not to fulfill, because fulfilling them would be disproportionate.

However, with respect to trivial wrongdoing not only does giving trivial wrongdoers what they deserve harm them disproportionately in some cases, it will *inevitably* be disproportionate. To vindicate his view Moore needs to show that the state is required to punish trivial wrongdoers even though it ought *never* to fulfill such duties. We might doubt that we have duties that we ought never to fulfill in any circumstances that are likely to arise. Or, more modestly, we might doubt that the state has such duties in this case.

To investigate further, suppose that the following three things are true of some agent, D:

a. D would have a duty to *x* if D could *x* and not *y*.
b. In all nearby possible worlds where D can *x*, D can either (1) not *x* or (2) both *x* and *y*. D cannot *x* without *y*ing.
c. It is, all things considered, wrong for D to *x* and *y*.

The question is whether, in these circumstances, D has a duty to *x*. Moore might claim that, although, given that he will inevitably *y*, D ought not to *x*, all things considered, nevertheless D has a duty to *x*. When D refrains from *x*ing, he violates a *pro tanto* duty to *x*. He ought to violate this duty in virtue of the fact that if he *x*s he will also certainly *y*.

This view is coherent, in virtue of the fact just noticed: that a person can have a duty that she ought not to fulfill. There are three possible views that one might take for the set of circumstances where (a), (b), and (c) are true:

1. It is always true that D ought to *x*.
2. It is always false that D ought to *x*.
3. There are some cases where it is true D ought to *x* but others where it is false that D ought to *x*.

Which view is correct? Moore moves quickly from the view that wrongdoers deserve to suffer, and that this can ground a duty to give them what they deserve, to the view that there is always a *pro tanto* duty to do this, even where this duty is defeated, for example, by reasons of liberty. As he seems to think that no further argument is needed for this transition, perhaps he believes (1).

Here is a *reductio* of (1). Suppose that if I devoted all of my time and resources to rescuing others, causing me to suffer a great deal over the course of my life, I could rescue one million people from serious disease. If I could rescue this same group of people at no cost to myself I would have a duty to do so, on the relatively uncontroversial assumption that there is a duty of easy rescue. (1) implies that I have a *pro tanto* duty to rescue one million people from serious disease, even though I could only do so by devoting all of my time and resources to rescuing these others. But this is not plausible. In pursuing other projects, I do not infringe a *pro tanto* duty to rescue one million people. I lack that duty altogether. Hence, (1) is false.

To support this view, notice that (1) implies that my range of *pro tanto* duties is absurdly vast—there is a vast number of things that I would have a duty to do if I could do them at no cost. If the fact that doing these things is costly does not vitiate these duties, I retain a vast number of *pro tanto* duties.

If (2) is true, Moore is wrong to think that the state has a *pro tanto* duty to punish trivial wrongdoing. For, if (2) is true, the fact that state punishment for some kinds of wrong is inevitably disproportionate vitiates any *pro tanto* duty to give trivial wrongdoers what they deserve. Moore might claim, though, that the example that I have used to demonstrate the falsity of (1) does not demonstrate that (2) rather than (3) is true. (3) leaves open the possibility that the state has a *pro tanto* duty to punish trivial wrongdoing, even though doing so would be, all things considered, wrong in every case.

However, even if (3) is true, I doubt that the state has a duty to punish trivial wrongdoing. It seems more plausible that the fact that the state cannot punish trivial wrongdoing without doing so excessively vitiates any duty that it would otherwise have to punish trivial wrongdoing. To see why, let's extend the sledgehammer–nut analogy. Consider:

> *Nuts*: I visit a friend and he is hungry, but not starving. I have nuts and a sledgehammer. As we are in an ice storm, I can only crack the nuts indoors. If I use my sledgehammer to crack the nuts, he can eat the nuts, but I will also severely damage his house.

Suppose that I would have a duty to crack the nuts were I able to do so without causing any damage. Nevertheless, I lack a duty to crack the nuts. This is true even if there is no one else around who can crack the nuts with something smaller than a sledgehammer. It is especially true where other people have other tools better than sledgehammers for cracking nuts.

By analogy, even if there were no other social mechanisms to ensure that trivial wrongdoers get what they deserve, the state lacks a duty to punish trivial wrongdoers. Given that there are other mechanisms, such as social mechanisms, to ensure that wrongdoers feel the pangs of guilt that they deserve for wrongdoing (if, indeed, they do deserve these pangs of guilt), this verdict is especially compelling.

Some may argue that my argument against Moore is trivial; for there is no reason for us to determine whether the state ought not to fulfill its duty to punish trivial wrongdoing or whether it lacks that duty. To respond, let us explore further the distinction between (a) having a duty to *v* that it would be wrong, all things considered, to fulfill; and (b) lacking a duty to *v*.

Here are two reasons to distinguish between (a) and (b). First, consider the implications of *pro tanto* duties for practical reasoning. A person who has a *pro tanto* duty to *v* typically must give *v*ing weight in his practical reasoning. He ought not to rule out *v*ing in advance of considering the reasons to violate his duty to *v*. In deciding not to *v*, he ought to acknowledge to himself that he is violating his duty.[17] This is not so where the person lacks a duty.

Second, consider the implications for a person who has a *pro tanto* duty that he justifiably violates. Secondary duties typically arise that would not arise were the person to have lacked the *pro tanto* duty. There are various secondary duties that might arise, the most familiar of which are the duty to apologize and the duty to pay compensation. A person who lacks a *pro tanto* duty to *v* typically need not apologize or pay compensation for failing to *v*.

In deciding what to criminalize, the state need not attend to trivial wrongdoing. It would be right to consider such wrongdoing as "beyond its radar." Furthermore, the state has no reason to apologize to anyone, or to pay compensation, for its failure to punish trivial wrongdoing. This further supports the idea that the state lacks a *pro tanto* duty to punish trivial wrongdoing, even assuming Moore's wide-scope desert view.

17 Perhaps this might help to vindicate Antony Duff's claim, advanced especially in *Answering for Crime* (Oxford: Hart, 2007), that there are some things that are none of the state's business (though not on grounds that Duff would accept). They are none of the state's business, it might be claimed, not because it could not take an interest in them in principle, but rather because any effort that it makes to take an interest in them in practice will be disastrous.

IV. Assurance and Prohibition

Moore claims that: "criminal legislation must exclusively aim at preventing or punishing moral wrongs, and this it can do by prohibiting all and only those behaviors that are in fact morally wrong." [18,19]

Stated like this, Moore's claim is false for reasons that seem to have gone more or less unnoticed in the philosophy of criminal law. Criminalizing is an act, and, like any other act, whether we perform it depends in part on the consequences of performing it. If refraining from doing an act will have very bad consequences, typically we ought to do it, even if doing it is *pro tanto* wrong.

For example, suppose that the US thinks that a Middle Eastern country is not taking seriously enough the War on Terror, and demands that various terrorism offenses are created which prohibit conduct that is not wrong. The Middle Eastern country faces the threat of invasion if it does not comply. Everyone in the country, including those who will be subject to the prohibitions, will be worse off if this happens. That country ought to create these offenses, even if what is criminalized is not wrong either prior to, or in virtue of, it being criminalized. The aim of the legislature is to avert the threat of invasion. This is a legitimate aim.

Decisions on whether to criminalize conduct are often taken in conditions of political pressure, and what we ought to criminalize depends on the pressures we are under. No government can ignore these pressures, and in some instances criminal law will not serve the proper purposes of punishment. However, it does not follow that criminalizing the conduct was not justified, all things considered.

There is room for the philosophy of criminal law to consider not only whether conduct should be criminalized in order that the criminal law serves the ends of punishment, but also whether conduct should be criminalized for other reasons, where this will result in it performing its core functions badly. Real-world expansion of criminal law often arises due to political pressures similar in kind, if not in degree, to those just outlined. It is best not to ignore these pressures in a theory of criminal law.

Moore's view is thus better understood as a view about the proper purposes of punishment. It is better stated thus:

> *Wrongness Constraint*: criminalizing *v* will fulfill the proper purposes of punishment only if *v*ing is wrongful.

The Wrongness Constraint is ambiguous between two claims:[20]

1. *The Strong Wrongness Constraint*: The proper purposes of punishment can justify criminalizing *v* only if *v*ing is wrong independently of its being criminalized.

[18] This section draws on and develops an argument I first made in "Wrongness and Criminalization," in A. Marmor, *The Routledge Companion to the Philosophy of Law* (London: Routledge, 2012).

[19] Moore, 2014c.

[20] Doug Husak sensibly endorses the weaker version of the constraint in *Overcriminalization: The Limits of the Criminal Law* (Oxford: Oxford University Press, 2007).

2. *The Weak Wrongness Constraint*: The proper purposes of punishment can justify criminalizing *v* only if *v*ing is wrong either independently of its being criminalized or as a result of its being criminalized.

Now, recall that Moore thinks that the *only* proper purpose of punishment is to give wrongdoers what they deserve. The fact that he does not endorse the silly view that it should pursue this purpose unconditionally provides room for him to recognize the importance of crime reduction within his theory. Crime reduction can ensure that criminalization is not disproportionate—it can offset the inevitable costs of the pursuit of retributive justice. Hence, recognizing that crime reduction is important is consistent with the view that the only proper purpose of criminal law is to realize just deserts.[21]

However, Moore's view does have implausible implications for *mala prohibita*. These offences, as I will understand them here, are offences that prohibit conduct that becomes wrong only by being prohibited *by the criminal law*. To be clear, there is some conduct that can become wrong in virtue of being prohibited by some other set of laws—for example regulatory laws that solve coordination problems. If these laws are created, those who violate them may act wrongly. As they act wrongly, Moore can consistently argue, they deserve suffering. Hence the criminal law can mimic other parts of the law.[22]

There is some conduct, though, that becomes wrong only if it is criminalized. Moore denies this on the grounds that as we have no obligation to obey the law simply due to its being the law, criminalizing conduct that is permissible cannot render that conduct wrong.[23] But even if Moore's claim about the obligation to obey the law is right (and I am sympathetic to his view), it does not follow that criminalizing conduct cannot render that conduct wrong. Criminalization can render conduct wrong because criminalization affects behavior, and whether some conduct is wrong sometimes depends on what other people are likely to do.

The difficulty for Moore is that if the only purpose of criminal law is to achieve just deserts, the purposes of criminal law cannot justify criminalizing conduct in circumstances where the conduct is wrong only once it is criminalized. For if *v*ing is not wrongful independently of criminal law, those who *v* do not deserve punishment. Hence, the ambition to ensure that wrongdoers get what they deserve cannot motivate the creation of a criminal law prohibiting *v*ing.

To illuminate this problem, consider:

More Spies: X is a member of a group of ten government spies who are undercover in different locations, and who cannot communicate with each other. The nine spies other than X participated in a secret brainwashing programme that prevents them from acting wrongly. X does not know this. All ten have a piece of information. There

[21] See also Moore, 2009c, 44.

[22] Antony Duff uses this kind of argument to show that many offences that are commonly labeled "*mala prohibita*" are consistent with his communicative theory of criminal justice in "Perversions and Subversions of Criminal Law" in R. A. Duff, L. Farmer, S. E. Marshall, M. Renzo and V. Tadros, *Boundaries of the Criminal Law* (Oxford: Oxford University Press, 2010). Duff's argument is also available to pure retributivists like Moore.

[23] See Moore, 2009c, 31–2.

> are 10,000 people whose lives are at risk in a way that is connected to this information. X knows that if all ten keep the information secret for a year, all 10,000 lives will be saved. If X reveals the information now, he can save 9,000 lives, but 1,000 people will be killed. If anyone other than X reveals the information later, all 10,000 will be killed.

Given his epistemic circumstances, what ought X to do? This, of course, depends on what X ought to predict that other nine spies will do. If he should predict that one of the other spies will reveal the information before the year is up, and that will save fewer than 9,000 lives, he ought to reveal the information now.

Suppose that X reasonably but falsely believes that some of the spies are self-interested. If they are not subject to the threat of punishment, X reasonably believes, they will sell the information for profit. If they are subject to the threat of punishment, he reasonably believes, they will not do so. Given his epistemic circumstances, whether he ought to reveal the information now depends on whether revealing the information is criminalized. If it is not, he can confidently predict that he will save the lives of 9,000 people who will otherwise be killed, so that is what he ought to do. If doing so is criminalized, he ought to keep silent, for if he does not he will kill 1,000 people who would otherwise be saved.

Suppose that before this situation arises, the legislature is considering whether to criminalize revealing classified information, knowing that situations like this sometimes arise. If revealing the information is criminalized, 1,000 lives will be saved. This seems a decisive reason to criminalize it. Yet this reason is not available to Moore, for Moore claims that the only purpose of criminalizing conduct is to give people their just deserts.

To clarify why Moore cannot advocate criminalizing the conduct, notice the following. If the conduct is not criminalized, and X reveals the information, no one has acted wrongly. Hence no one deserves punishment. If the conduct is criminalized, and X does not reveal the information, no one has acted wrongly. Hence no one deserves punishment. It follows that criminalization does not improve things with respect to desert.

The conduct clearly ought to be criminalized, but for non-retributivist reasons—to save lives. It is true that those who violate the criminal law in this case will have acted wrongly. Retributivists can conclude that when they are punished they get what they deserve. Giving these people what they deserve, though, cannot supply a reason to criminalize the conduct. Retributivists surely do not advocate criminalizing conduct in order to create wrongs, so that those who perpetrate those wrongs get what they deserve. From the point of view of desert, it is surely better that D is undeserving of punishment and unpunished than that he is deserving of punishment and punished.

Perhaps it might be claimed that the example provided is too esoteric to make an important contribution to debates about criminalization (snore). Not so. The example is simply a clean illustration of a pervasive issue that we find across many areas of criminal law. It is this. What we have reason to do often depends on what we can expect others to do. And what we can expect others to do depends on the implications of doing, or refraining from doing, it. We have reason to alter the expectations that people have about the effects of their actions by changing the incentives to others. We have reason to do this because whether harmful conduct is justified often depends on what others are likely to do.

Changing the circumstances so that people lack good reason to harm others, or to fail to prevent harm to others, is a legitimate function of criminal law. Performing this function often coincides with another function—to ensure that those who act wrongly are called to account for their wrongdoing. For example, people might have good reason to seek personal reprisals against wrongdoers, say for reasons of deterrence, if they were not confident that criminal justice would do so. This creates a reason to assure people that the criminal justice system will function well. One way to do this is to ensure that people do not interfere with the criminal justice process. Hence, we have good reason to endorse there being a range of offences, such as contempt of court, that ensure that criminal justice functions well.

These offences also prohibit wrongdoing, and pure retributivists like Moore can thus endorse them—though that may also lead us not to notice that the rationale that I have offered for these offences is sufficient reason to support them. But, as *More Spies* illustrates, it is not generally true that our ambition to assure people through the existence of criminal law coincides perfectly with any ambition that we might have to secure retributive justice. The former ambition remains, even where the latter ambition cannot be advanced. The assurance function can in and of itself provide a decisive reason in favor of criminalization. When we notice this, we also see that we should reject both the *Strong Wrongness Constraint*, and also Moore's more general claim that the only legitimate aim of criminalization is to ensure that wrongdoers get what they deserve.

I do not claim that we should seek to perform the assurance function unconditionally. It maybe a necessary condition of the legitimate pursuit of the assurance function that those whose conduct is prohibited also act wrongly. This may be so due to of the fact that only wrongdoers should be punished, perhaps because others do not deserve to be, or because criminal law would otherwise condemn those who have acted permissibly. But this condition supports only the *Weak Wrongness Constraint* and not the *Strong Wrongness Constraint* that Moore favors.

Furthermore, just as this argument supports the view that retributivists should be pluralists about criminalization, it also supports the view that retributivists should be pluralists about punishment.[24] For, in cases like *More Spies*, punishment is threatened and carried out to provide assurance about the conduct of others, and through assurance to avert a threat of harm. Retributivists should not be unhappy with this, for punishment is imposed only on condition that those who are punished act wrongfully. Those who do not deserve punishment are not punished. But desert is not the primary rationale for threatening and carrying out punishment. The whole criminalization–punishment machine is directed to harm prevention, and not to achieve retributivist justice, in this case.

[24] Mitch Berman has done a great deal, independently of the arguments presented here, to promote this latter case. See, for example, "Two Kinds of Retributivism," in R. A. Duff and S. P. Green, *Philosophical Foundations of Criminal Law* (Oxford: Oxford University Press, 2010) and "Rehabilitating Retributivism," 13 *Law and Philosophy* 83 (2013).

V. Conclusion

I have attacked some of the central claims that Moore makes in his theory of criminalization, which might seem a bit mean in a volume to celebrate Moore's work. Fortunately, in Anglo-American law and philosophy, attacking a person (or at least their arguments) is a sign of respect. Moore is worthy of attack. Even those, like me, who tend not to agree with his main ideas, can learn a great deal from his work. Even those, unlike me, who are sympathetic to his main retributivist claims, should reject his theory of criminalization, though. Even if criminal law has the function that Moore claims for it, there are limits on the performance of this function. And criminal law has other important functions that can be pursued independently of any function that it has to achieve just deserts. I think that we should want both less from criminal law than what Moore wants, and also more: less vindication of our retributive sentiments, and more prevention of serious harm.

7

Legal Moralism and Public Wrongs

R. A. Duff

I. Introduction: Legal Moralism and Retributivism (and Action Theory)

It is a great pleasure to be able to offer this tribute (one that will be, as philosophical tributes ought to be, critical rather than purely adulatory in tone) to Michael Moore, who has done—and is still doing—so much to advance and enliven philosophical thinking about criminal law. This chapter focuses on Moore's version of legal moralism, which he characterizes as "the theory that all and only moral wrongs should be prohibited by the criminal law."[1] Moore's legal moralism is, however, closely connected to two other dimensions of his work.

It is connected to his version of retributivism, which "demands that criminal punishment be imposed on all and only those who deserve it."[2] For "criminal law is a functional kind whose function is to attain retributive justice," which "demands that those who deserve punishment get it"; criminal law must therefore "punish all and only those who are morally culpable in the doing of some morally wrongful action."[3] But the principle of legality forbids the criminal punishment of conduct that has not been formally criminalized;[4] criminal law should therefore criminalize, in order to punish, "all and only moral wrongs"—all and only actions that deserve punishment.

Second, Moore's legal moralism is also connected to his philosophy of action: what merits criminalization and punishment is not every moral failing, but only moral wrong*doing*. A theory of criminal law requires a theory of action if it is to explain what wrongdoing is; Moore provides this in his sophisticated development of a volitionist theory of action.[5]

There is, of course, much more to be said (and Moore has said much more) about his account of action, and about why criminal law should focus only on action, rather than on other kinds of moral failure; but that is not a topic for this chapter. There is also much more to be said about Moore's version of retributivism: about whether he offers a plausible reading, and defense, of the retributivist intuition that punishment is justified as being deserved for past wrongdoing. Much of that will also remain unsaid here, but I will need to say a little about how Moore understands retributivism, since it bears directly on the form that his legal moralism takes.

In what follows I will first sketch the respects in which Moore and I agree about criminal law and punishment, in order to explore some respects in which we disagree.

[1] Moore, 2014c, 191. See also Moore, 1997b, chs. 1, 16–18; Moore, 2007b; Moore, 2009c; Moore, 2012c.

[2] Moore, 2014c, 191; see also Moore, 1997b, chs. 2–4.

[3] Moore, 1997b, 33, 35.

[4] Moore, 2009c, 31; Moore, 2014c, 191.

[5] See especially Moore, 1993c.

The reason for this is not, I hope, mere self-indulgence:[6] it is rather to further the task of articulating the most plausible version of legal moralism.

II. Agreement—up to a Point

Moore and I agree in espousing legal moralism.[7] Indeed, we agree in espousing not just the negative legal moralist thesis that conduct that is not morally wrong should not be criminalized, but the positive legal moralist thesis that the main (if not the only) good reason for criminalizing a given kind of conduct lies in its moral wrongfulness. The negative thesis is widely shared, even by many who would not count themselves as "legal moralists."[8] The positive thesis is less widely shared, and is sometimes viewed with something approaching horror by liberal critics who see it as a throwback to the Victorian moralism expressed in Stephen's notorious remark that "criminal law is in the nature of a persecution of the grosser forms of vice";[9] we both aspire to persuade such critics that they are wrong.

We also agree that many kinds of morally wrongful action, and many kinds that are thought to be morally wrong, should not be criminalized. Moore argues, indeed, that a Moorean criminal law would not ultimately have a scope very different from that favored by his liberal critics, for two main reasons. First, the scope of the morality of obligation, which is the only morality with which criminal law is properly concerned, is in his eyes narrower than many (often illiberal) people suppose: thus many kinds of conduct which an illiberal legal moralist might see reason to criminalize are not, Moore argues, criminalizable, just because they are not morally wrong; this is especially true of fully consensual sexual conduct.[10] Second, although we have good reason to criminalize every kind of wrongful conduct, we also have stronger reasons, drawn from values outside legal moralism itself, not to criminalize many kinds of wrong. The most important of these reasons are grounded in what Moore calls "the presumption of liberty," and the values that it reflects:[11] that presumption counts strongly, in advance, against criminalization, and although it is sometimes defeated by the demand that we ensure that wrongdoers receive the punishment they deserve, it is often not defeated, even when we are rightly sure that a given kind of conduct is morally wrong. Those who culpably commit moral wrongs always deserve punishment; but other, non-retributive values can outweigh the value of retribution.

[6] Compare Moore, 2009c, 27, on Moore's "not entirely narcissistic" motives for discussing Doug Husak's book *Overcriminalization* "by comparing it to my own theory."

[7] See my *Answering for Crime: Responsibility and Liability in the Criminal Law* (Oxford: Hart Publishing, 2007); and "Towards a Modest Legal Moralism," 8 *Criminal Law and Philosophy* 217 (2014).

[8] For some recent instances, see J. Feinberg, *Harm to Others* (New York: Oxford University Press, 1984); D. Husak, *Overcriminalization: The Limits of the Criminal Law* (Oxford: Oxford University Press, 2007); L. Alexander and K. K. Ferzan (with S. Morse), *Crime and Culpability: A Theory of Criminal Law* (Cambridge: Cambridge University Press, 2009); A. P. Simester and A. von Hirsch, *Crimes, Harms, and Wrongs: On the Principles of Criminalization* (Oxford: Hart Publishing, 2011).

[9] J. F. Stephen, *Liberty, Equality, Fraternity* (1867; ed. R. White; Cambridge: Cambridge University Press, 1973), 152.

[10] See e.g., Moore, 1997b, 662; Moore, 2007b, 1540–1; Moore, 2009c, 32.

[11] See especially Moore, 1997b, ch. 18; Moore, 2009c, 32–3; Moore, 2014c.

We also agree that the primary reason for criminalizing morally wrongful conduct is to make sure (as far as we reasonably can) that it receives an appropriate response. One could espouse a positive legal moralism for preventive reasons: we should criminalize wrongful conduct in order thereby to reduce its incidence.[12] However, although preventive considerations figure in Moore's justifications of legal moralism,[13] they do not provide his main rationale for criminalization: the proper purpose of criminal law is to do retributive justice—to ensure that deserved punishments are inflicted on culpable wrongdoers. If criminal law also has preventive effects, that is a benefit which can help to justify a system of punishment, since it can be weighed in the balance against the system's costs.[14] But there are other ways of preventing wrongful conduct than criminalizing it. If we are to identify the distinctive role that criminal law can play in a political community, we should look not to its instrumental efficiency as one among other techniques for preventing wrongful conduct (which might not be greater than that of other available techniques), but to its intrinsic character as an appropriate way of marking and responding to wrongdoing—to, Moore insists, its function as an agent of retributive justice.

Despite such significant matters of agreement, Moore and I do not find ourselves "holding hands and singing Kumbaya together."[15] There remain significant differences in our accounts of the kind of "appropriate response" that criminal law provides to wrongdoing, and accordingly in our accounts of the kinds of wrongdoing that we have reason to criminalize: so even if we might end up with extensionally similar conceptions of the proper scope of criminal law, we arrive at those conceptions by very different routes.

III. Moore's Retributivism and an Expansive Legal Moralism

Moore's legal moralism, we noted above, flows from his retributivism: what gives us reason to criminalize moral wrongdoing is that by doing so we can bring it about that wrongdoers get the punishments they deserve. It is Moore's particular version of retributivism that generates his distinctively expansive version of legal moralism.

When retributivists say that wrongdoers deserve punishment, it is not always clear just what they are thought to deserve, and how that relates to criminal punishment, understood, roughly, as something intended to be burdensome, imposed by a state authority on an alleged offender for an alleged offence: is it *criminal punishment* that they deserve; or something that punishment is one, but not the only, method of achieving? A crude retributivism, for instance, might demand only that wrongdoers suffer a burden or loss whose severity roughly matches the seriousness of their

[12] We would then need a different reason to espouse negative legal moralism, since there might be ways in which we could efficiently reduce the incidence of wrongful conduct by criminalizing conduct that is not wrongful.

[13] See, e.g., Moore, 2007b, 1550 ("The law does pretty well if it can induce its citizens to keep their moral obligations"); Moore, 2014c, 192 ("Retributivism . . . yields . . . the 'moral wrong principle': criminal legislation must exclusively aim at preventing or punishing moral wrongs"); Moore, 2009c, 44.

[14] See Moore, 2009c, 44.

[15] See Moore, 2009c, 38 on the limited extent of agreement between Moore's theory and Husak's: this will be a relief to those who have heard me try to sing.

wrongdoing, without requiring that it be imposed deliberately, or that it be causally connected to the wrongdoing that calls for it: what retribution requires, according to this view, is a cosmic balance, no matter how it might come about; retribution is achieved even if that balance comes about purely by chance. Others might insist that there must be some connection between the wrongdoing and the suffering that is to constitute retribution: the suffering must be *for* the wrongdoing, which requires that it be somehow a result of it. But that still leaves open the possibility that suffering which is a natural consequence of the wrongdoing could constitute adequate retribution for it; a burglar who is injured attempting to break into a house might thereby receive as much suffering as he deserves.[16] Others might say that what is deserved is suffering that is imposed deliberately, for the wrongdoing: suffering that results from natural causes, even if caused by the wrongdoing itself, cannot constitute or count towards the suffering that is deserved (unless, of course, we see it as being imposed by God). This might still not be to say that what the wrongdoer deserves is *punishment*: the suffering might be imposed by private individuals as revenge, or by vigilantes, rather than formally as punishment by an authorized body; but such privately imposed suffering could satisfy the demands of retributive justice.[17] According to all these views, what wrongdoers deserve is suffering of a kind that can be imposed through formal criminal punishment, but that can also be imposed by other mechanisms: what justifies a system of criminal punishment is that it is an efficient or morally appropriate way of ensuring (as far as we can) that wrongdoers receive as much suffering as (and no more than) they deserve.

Moore's view is of this kind. He might say that what wrongdoers deserve is not "suffering" as such, but suffering that is deliberately imposed for (i.e., as a response to) their wrongdoing:[18] but this leaves it as an open question why the pursuit of retributive justice should be reserved for the state. He answers that question: the state is better placed than are private individuals to determine whether a person culpably committed a wrong, how serious that wrong was, and what degree of penal suffering would be proportionate to it; and a system of state punishment is better placed to reduce the "danger[s] to virtue" that the imposition of punishment involves.[19] Such reasons are, however, extrinsic to retributivism itself: retributive justice is something that can, in principle, be achieved by private individuals who set about imposing deserved suffering on wrongdoers.

I'll suggest later (in section VI) that this is not how we should understand the idea of retribution as the aim of criminal punishment: although we should indeed justify crim inal punishment as a deserved, and deservedly burdensome, response to criminal wrongdoing, we should not conceive it as a matter of inflicting on wrongdoers some quantum of suffering that could instead, in principle, be inflicted by private individuals.

[16] For an insightful discussion of the idea of "natural" punishment, see P. Winch, "Ethical Reward and Punishment" in his *Ethics and Action* (London: Routledge, 1972), 210.

[17] And should then, on this view, be taken into account by a court sentencing the wrongdoer: perhaps he has been "already punished enough"; see D. Husak, "Already Punished Enough," 18 *Philosophical Topics* 79 (1990).

[18] In a private email exchange, he expressed grave doubts about whether suffering that was not both "causally" and "motivationally" connected to the wrongdoing could satisfy the demands of retributive justice.

[19] Moore, 2009c, 42.

The point to notice here, however, is that Moore's version of retributivism generates an expansive version of legal moralism—expansive both as to the kinds of conduct that we have reason to criminalize, and as to the range of agents whose wrongdoing we have reason to criminalize.

Its expansiveness as to the range of criminalizable conduct is often noted: we have reason to criminalize, because we have reason to punish, every kind of moral wrongdoing. What deserves suffering is wrongdoing as such: if a person has culpably committed a moral wrong, he deserves to suffer in proportion to the seriousness of that wrong; his suffering is thus a moral good, which is something that we all have reason to promote.[20] We could promote it by inflicting suffering on the wrongdoer ourselves, but a system of criminal punishment is a morally preferable means of promoting that good; so we have reason to create such a system and bring all wrongdoing within its reach. As citizens, we therefore have reason to argue for the criminalization of every type of wrongdoing; as legislators, we have reason to criminalize every type of wrongdoing, in order to promote retributive justice. This will strike many as implausible: even if only moral wrongdoing, breach of moral obligation, is said to deserve retributive suffering, there are kinds of wrongdoing that it would seem absurd to suggest should be criminalized. Good examples are provided by the obligations that structure the relationships in which so much of human life is lived (and so much of human good is found). I owe obligations to my friends, family, and colleagues; breaches of these obligations are wrongs (often quite serious wrongs), and merit a response from those who are wronged and from others with a legitimate interest in the relationship; but it sounds odd to say that we have reason to criminalize all such breaches—all those betrayals of confidence, all those intimate or collegial wrongs, that we commit against each other. Moore will argue that we have obvious and much stronger reasons not to criminalize many or most such wrongs—reasons to do with the importance of liberty, with the difficulty of establishing the fact and seriousness of the wrong, with the damage that enforcing such criminal laws would do; the oddity of suggesting that such wrongs be criminalized is due, he might say, to the obviously overwhelming strength of the reasons against doing so. But objectors will still argue that things have gone wrong as soon as it is said that there is any reason at all to bring such wrongs within the reach of criminal law.

The expansiveness of Moore's legal moralism as to the agents whose wrongdoing we have reason to criminalize is less often noticed, but it is also important. Moral wrongdoing deserves punitive suffering wherever, by whomever, against whomever it is committed. We all therefore have reason to promote the imposition of such suffering on wrongdoers anywhere in the world, and reason as legislators to bring all wrongdoers within the reach of our criminal law.[21] Those reasons are not geographically restricted. The Illinois legislature has reason to bring within the scope of its criminal law not merely wrongs committed within the state, but wrongs committed anywhere in the world—to count as a crime under Illinois law, triable in the Illinois courts and punishable in its penal system, murder, rape, theft, criminal damage, drunken driving, and so on, committed anywhere in the world; to criminalize and seek to punish

[20] See Moore, 2007b, 1540.

[21] "[T]he world is better if it is morally better, and to the extent legislators can achieve that moral betterment through law, they should do so." Moore, 2007b, 1540.

criminal damage committed by a Turk on the streets of Istanbul. (Correlatively, the Turkish legislature has reason to count as criminal under Turkish law the criminal damage committed by an American in Champaign.) Moore can again point out that there are obvious and conclusive countervailing reasons against giving domestic criminal law such global scope: reasons to do with the practicability and costs of trying to enforce such a globally ambitious criminal law; reasons to do with the importance of respecting other states' sovereignty.[22] However, objectors will still argue that things have gone wrong as soon as it is said that the Illinois legislature has any reason at all to count vandalism in Istanbul as a crime under Illinois law.

Moore might reasonably respond that so far the imagined objectors have not actually *argued* that these implications of his account do anything to undermine it. They have expressed a strong, intuitive feeling that there are kinds of ("private") wrongdoing that are "in brief and crude terms, not the law's business,"[23] and that wrongs committed abroad are likewise not the business of our domestic criminal law:[24] but Moore can explain why such wrongs are indeed, in the end, usually not wrongs that our legislatures should criminalize, even though we have reason to criminalize them; and he can challenge the objectors to offer some rational backing for their intuitions. What rational backing could they offer?

IV. "Public" and "Private" Wrongs

Deferring for the moment the issue of the criminal law's territorial limitations, the objectors might appeal to a distinction between "public" and "private" wrongs, arguing that Moore fails to recognize the category of private wrongs—wrongs that are genuine cases of moral wrongdoing, but that we have no reason at all to criminalize.[25]

A distinction between public and private wrongs is indeed a familiar feature of theories of criminal law. It received its classic formulation by Blackstone: whilst private

[22] Moore might also point, as grist to his mill, to the jurisdiction over "crimes against humanity" that is claimed by international criminal tribunals, and by national legal systems asserting "universal jurisdiction" (see L. Reydams, *Universal Jurisdiction* (Oxford: Oxford University Press, 2003)), even when this infringes the sovereignty of the state within which the crimes were committed: if crimes are so grave that the demands of retributive justice become insistent, but the domestic legal system and its courts are unwilling or unable to meet those demands, international bodies or other states might be justified in intervening to ensure that justice is done.

[23] Sir John Wolfenden, *Report of the Committee on Homosexual Offences and Prostitution* (Cmnd 247; London: HMSO, 1957), para. 61. (Moore would certainly agree that consensual homosexual conduct in private is not, in principle, the criminal law's business; but that, he would argue, is because it is not even wrong.)

[24] I leave aside here the complication (significant though it is) that some states operate with principles of "passive personality" (giving domestic courts jurisdiction over crimes committed abroad against the state's citizens), or of "nationality" (giving domestic courts jurisdiction over crimes committed abroad by the state's citizens): see M. Hirst, *Jurisdiction and the Ambit of the Criminal Law* (Oxford: Oxford University Press, 2003), ch. 5.

[25] More precisely, there are two senses in which wrongs might be "private" (see A. Y. K. Lee, "Public Wrongs and the Criminal Law," 9 *Criminal Law & Philosophy* 155 (2015)): there are wrongs which are not legally cognizable at all; and there are legally cognizable wrongs that should be matters for private law (e.g., for tort law) rather than for public, criminal law. My concern here is with the former notion of privacy. Once a wrong is legally cognizable as such, we can ask what form that legal cognizance should take, and criminalization is then, in principle, on the table as one mode of cognizance.

wrongs infringe "the civil rights which belong to individuals, considered merely as individuals," crimes

> are breach and violation of the public rights and duties, due to the whole community, . . . in its social aggregate capacity. . . . [They] strike at the very being of society, which cannot possibly subsist, where actions of [that] sort are suffered to escape with impunity. In all cases the crime includes an injury: every public offence is also a private wrong, and somewhat more; it affects the individual, and it likewise affects the community.[26]

Doug Husak, Sandra Marshall, and I have appealed to the idea of public wrongs (although not in Blackstone's sense) as a way of marking the proper bounds of the criminal law.[27] Moore objects that we have not offered any substantive, non-question-begging "criterion for the public/private distinction" as "a distinction that is supposed to mark the proper limits of criminal legislation."[28] This objection is in one way well founded. If "the public/private distinction" is meant to provide a criterion for distinguishing criminalizable from non-criminalizable wrongs, or a ground from which we can argue that certain kinds of conduct should not be criminal, we must explain what makes a wrong public rather than private; our explanation cannot simply amount to saying that a wrong is public because it is criminalizable; but what other substantive explanation can we offer?

Blackstone seems to offer two possible criteria: first, a wrong is public if it violates a duty owed "to the whole community," rather than to an individual; second, it is public if it "affects the community" rather than only the individual victim, or "strike[s] at the very being of society." But the first criterion gives us no substantive help: we have then to ask which duties are owed "to the whole community," and the obvious, unhelpful, answer is "those whose violation is criminalizable." The second criterion appears more substantial, if we read it as being concerned with the actual or likely effects of the wrong on the society as a whole: but we should resist the thought that what makes such central *mala in se* as murder, rape, and other attacks on the person criminalizable is not their impact on their individual victims, but their impact on or implications for the wider society; Moore is right that we must criminalize such wrongs precisely because of the wrong that they do to their individual victims. That still leaves us, however, without a substantive criterion for "public wrongs." Nor will it help, Moore argues, simply to talk of the shared values by which the community defines itself: communities "can and do share values . . . about all kinds of human behaviour, incest between adults as much as murder, picking one's nose in public as much as theft"; they can "regard these shared values as constitutive of their being moral communities."[29] Appeals to the idea of "public" wrongs are therefore either empty, if "public" in effect just means "in principle criminalizable"; or vulnerable to the moralizing of different communities: they do not

[26] Sir William Blackstone, *Commentaries on the Laws of England* (Oxford: Clarendon Press, 1765–9; available at <http://avalon.law.yale.edu/subject_menus/blackstone.asp>), Bk IV, ch. 1, p. 5. Blackstone is talking of wrongs that are "private" in the second sense noted in n. 25 above.

[27] See S. E. Marshall and R. A. Duff, "Criminalization and Sharing Wrongs" 11 *Canadian Journal of Law & Jurisprudence* 7 (1998), and "Public and Private Wrongs", in J. Chalmers et al. (eds.), *Essays in Criminal Law in Honour of Sir Gerald Gordon* (Edinburgh: Edinburgh University Press, 2010) 70; Husak, *Overcriminalization* (n. 8 above), esp. 135–9; Duff, "Towards a Modest Legal Moralism" (n. 7 above).

[28] Moore, 2014c, 199; see also Moore, 2009c, 40–1.

[29] Moore, 2014c, 199.

help us set determinate limits to the scope of the criminal law, or provide clear guidelines about what we have good reason to criminalize.

Moore is right on three points. First, the idea of a "public" wrong will not provide a plausible, substantive criterion of criminalizability. Nor, I would add, should it be intended to do so; it is, in this context, a formal rather than a substantive notion, just as "moral wrong" is a formal notion. We might agree, that is, that the criminal law should be concerned with "moral wrongs," or with "public wrongs," though we disagree sharply on the substantive issue of what kinds of conduct constitute moral, or public, wrongs; once we agree on the formal point, we must then move to a more substantive discussion of the content that these formal notions should be given. Someone who believes that sodomy should be criminalized might agree with Moore that the criminal law's proper aim is to achieve retributive justice by punishing all and only culpable moral wrongdoers; but they differ in their views of the content of morality.[30]

Second, it follows that different political communities might accept that criminal law should be concerned only with public wrongs (or only with moral wrongs), but give different contents to their criminal laws, reflecting their different views of what counts as a public (or a moral) wrong. If the members of a polity criminalize adultery as a public wrong, I might agree that adultery is a wrong, and recognize that in counting it as a public wrong they are reflecting their understanding of what constitutes them as a political community; I disagree about whether they should define their community in that (illiberal) way. So too, Moore must recognize that a polity which defines sodomy as a criminalizable wrong might be faithfully reflecting its members' moral beliefs, and criminalizing what they take to be moral wrongdoing; his disagreement with them is not about whether they should criminalize all and only moral wrongs, but about what they should count as a moral wrong.

Third, if we take as our starting point the whole realm of moral wrongs, and then ask how we can distinguish "public" from "private" wrongs within that realm, we will be hard put to offer any plausible, non-vacuous answer—unless we accept Moore's approach, and argue that we should just count as "private" those wrongs which, despite their immorality, we ought not to criminalize because to do so would be to intrude unacceptably on individual liberty or privacy. To take that approach would be to accept Moore's version of legal moralism: we have reason to criminalize every kind of moral wrongdoing, but stronger countervailing reasons not to criminalize many of them; when those reasons are grounded in individual liberty or privacy, we might call the wrongs that are thus exempted from criminalization "private" wrongs.

Is this then to agree with Moore that his is the only viable form of legal moralism; and thus to agree that if we reject a Moorean legal moralism (perhaps because we find its implications, as noted above, quite implausible) we must reject legal moralism as such? Not yet, since there is an alternative: a different form of legal moralism; one which does not have those implications, but which avoids the problems noted above. The key to

[30] This need not reflect the kind of moral relativism or subjectivism that Moore rejects. The point here is simply that to say that criminal law is concerned with moral wrongs, or with public wrongs, is to specify the kind of question we must ask in determining what we have reason to criminalize, but is not yet to answer that question.

recognizing this different form is to see that we must start the discussion in a different place: we must start not with wrongs, but with the idea of the public.

V. Starting with the Public: Professional Ethics

Moore's objections to one version of the "public wrong" conception of criminal wrongs are, we have seen, sound: if we start by taking as our canvas the whole realm of moral wrongdoing, and then ask how within that realm we are to distinguish criminalizable from non-criminalizable wrongs, we will find it hard to develop a non-Moorean answer. But that is an odd starting place, for reasons that should become clearer in this section. I'll argue that if we are to develop a more plausible version of legal moralism, one focused on the idea of "public" wrongs, we must begin not with wrongs (which leads us ask which kinds of wrong should count as "public"), but with the idea of the public realm, as the realm within which wrongs can then be identified as being already public wrongs.

To take what I will suggest is an apt analogy, suppose that we form a committee tasked with creating a new system of governance for a professional body: perhaps for lawyers, or for doctors, or for a new university. The regulations we create for that system of governance will, plausibly, include a code of ethics: that code will define kinds of wrongful conduct that those who are to be bound by it (lawyers, doctors, members of the university) ought to eschew, which will amount to professional *mis*conduct if committed; and it will provide for a process through which charges of misconduct can be adjudicated, and suitable sanctions imposed on those against whom they are proved. Two things should be evident about the logical ordering of the committee's deliberations (whatever their chronological order might be): first, the code of ethics will not be the first matter to be decided; second, when the committee does come to discuss the proper content and scope of the code of ethics, it will not begin with the whole realm of moral wrongdoing as its canvas.

The code of ethics cannot be the first matter for decision because it is a code of *professional* ethics, which defines good and bad, right and wrong, professional conduct: to know what should fall within the scope of such a code, we will need first to work out what falls within the realm of professional conduct. An answer to this question will partly depend on what other regulations we draw up to govern the profession, since professional misconduct often consists in violating such regulations. However, the creation of such a system of governance itself depends on something prior: on a conception of what the practice or profession that is to be regulated *is*. We will need first to consider what it is to be a lawyer, or doctor, or university: what kinds of aim and value define the practice, what sorts of activity fall within its scope?[31] To answer such questions, we might be able to consult a constitution or a charter, or a mission statement, if there is one; or we might need to (re)construct answers from what has so far been implicit in the practices of those involved in the profession, rather than explicit in any document. Our answers will specify what we can call the *res publica* of that profession—the goal-related activities and relationships that constitute the shared

[31] I leave aside here the complicating but not problematic possibility that the account of the aims of the practice might itself be adjusted in the process of working out the governance of the practice.

business (the public affair) of those within the profession. This will also be to define the roles of those within the practice—the role of doctor, or of lawyer, or of professor, and thus also the correlative roles of patient, client, and student.

Given such an understanding of the *res publica* of the practice, we can start to work out what kinds of institution, what kinds of regulation, will serve its proper ends. What will also emerge is a set of ethical norms and expectations: a conception of how members of the profession should behave in their professional lives, what they owe to each other and to those with whom they deal, what should count as professional misconduct—misconduct in the course of one's professional activity. We might then see good reason to formalize such norms and expectations into a code of professional ethics. The point of this will partly be to make clear, to members of the profession and to others, what the profession's ethics are, but it will also be to provide for an appropriate response by the profession to the misconduct of its members: the code will need to include a procedural code under which alleged violations of the ethical code can be adjudicated and, if proved, sanctioned. In drawing up the code, however, we will not start with a blank slate as to either its content or its jurisdiction: we will already have a conception of what the profession, the practice whose ethics are to be formalized, is; and this will already generate a conception both of the kinds of conduct that might be candidates for definition as professional misconduct, and of the agents who are to be bound by the code and answerable to whatever type of disciplinary tribunal it creates. For, as a code of professional ethics, it can claim to govern only those who belong to the profession, and only those aspects of their lives and conduct that constitute their professional activities. The code of medical ethics will govern medical professionals—most obviously doctors and nurses; and it will govern not every aspect of their lives and conduct, but only those aspects that belong to their professional lives—their conduct *as* doctors or nurses.

There will thus be many kinds of moral wrong that we can say, in advance, should not figure in the code of ethics, and many people whose wrongdoings will not fall within the jurisdiction of the profession's disciplinary body: not because we decide that, though we have reason to define such wrongs as species of professional misconduct and to claim jurisdiction over such agents, we have stronger countervailing reasons not to do so; but because we had no reason in the first place to bring them under the code's jurisdiction. We might all believe that marital infidelity is a moral wrong, but that gives us no reason to define it as a type of professional misconduct; we might all believe that lying to someone who depends on your truthfulness is a wrong, but that gives us no reason at all to define as professional misconduct such lies when told by someone who is not a member of the profession. Our concern is with professional misconduct—with wrongful conduct by members of the profession in the course of their professional lives.

There is, of course, room for argument about the profession's *res publica* and about what falls within the scope of a member's professional activities. Such arguments should be worked out by members of the profession through an ongoing process of deliberation by which they define and redefine themselves as a profession. There will be disagreement about the scope of the code of ethics. Universities used, for instance (at least in Britain) to have a "gross moral turpitude" clause in their disciplinary codes, and many have a clause covering conduct that "brings the university into disrepute:" both can be used to treat as disciplinary offences kinds of conduct falling well outside the scope of "professional" activities as narrowly conceived. Any criminal conviction can bring a doctor up before the General Medical Council's Professional Conduct Committee, as can any conduct judged to be "derogatory to the reputation of the profession."[32] However, such broad offences of moral turpitude or of bringing the profession into disrepute could be justified only by arguing that the professional can never put off her professional identity: she is always a doctor, or a professor, and must always behave "appropriately." I do not advocate this view: my point is simply that if such offences are to be justified as part of a profession's code of ethics, what must be argued is not simply that the conduct in question is morally wrong, but that it somehow bears on the person's professional activity, and on the profession's *res publica*.

I suggested that the process of creating a code of professional ethics is usefully analogous to the process of creating a criminal code; it is time now to justify that suggestion.

VI. The Criminal Law as a Code of Civic Conduct?

Suppose now that we are on a committee tasked with drawing up a system of governance not for a profession, but for a polity; we are to be the Founding Parents. It is probable (and desirable) that the system of governance will include a criminal law (although we will need to argue, not just assume, that it should do so), but two things should be evident: first, the criminal law will not be the first matter to be decided; second, when we come to discuss the content and scope of the criminal law, we will probably not begin by taking the whole realm of moral wrongdoing as our canvas.

Our task is to draw up a system of governance for a particular kind of entity—for a polity; in doing so, we will be structuring a state, as the polity's institutional apparatus. We must therefore begin with some notion of the polity's character: what is it for, what are its aims and aspirations, what is its *res publica*? In spelling out this conception of its *res publica*, we will also be spelling out what it is to be a citizen of the polity: for we will be articulating an account of the practice in which the polity's members should take themselves to be engaged—the civic enterprise of living together as citizens. That account will need to include, inter alia, an account of the goals of the enterprise; an account of the values by which it is to be structured; and an account of its scope—of which aspects of its members' lives and activities are to be part of the *res publica*. It will need, that is, to articulate a political theory: for only given such a conception of the polity can we hope to work out what its law, including its criminal law, should be and should do.

Conceptions of the civic enterprise might be found in constitutions, though constitutions are, for obvious reasons, prone to favor rhetoric over determinate substance;[33] but they will need to be worked out in substantive detail through a process of public political deliberation. This is not the place to argue for any particular conception of the civic enterprise: the relevant point is that it is here that the liberal values that Moore and

[32] General Medical Council, *Professional Conduct and Discipline: Fitness to Practise* (London: General Medical Council, 1983), 2–3 and 12–14.

[33] E.g., Article 1 of the Polish Constitution: "The Republic of Poland shall be the common good of all its citizens".

I share will figure—well before we begin to discuss the criminal law. If we are committed to such values as liberty, privacy, and pluralism, a respect for those values, and the promotion of those goods, will be central to our conception of the civic enterprise; one implication of this is that such values will both figure within the civic enterprise and limit its reach. We will be concerned to ensure that large areas of the citizens' lives remain outside the "public" sphere of the civic enterprise—to preserve an extensive "private" sphere in which people can pursue their own conceptions of the good, their own activities, free from the intrusive interest of the polity. The "public" sphere is the sphere that is our collective business, as members of the polity; it includes those aspects of our lives in which other citizens, and the state, are entitled to take an interest. The "private" sphere is that sphere that is not our collective civic business: it includes all those activities and enterprises in which we might engage, and in which what we do (and think or feel) might be the business of other participants, but is not the business of our fellow citizens simply in virtue of their fellow citizenship.[34]

As we work out what falls within the public realm, we will be able to consider what kinds of institution (including legal institutions) and what kinds of regulation will be needed to govern it appropriately. We will probably recognize that the polity's system of governance should include a criminal law, because we realize that members of the polity are likely to misconduct, as well as to conduct, themselves as they act within the public sphere: there will be wrongs committed that should be marked and responded to as wrongs—which is precisely what criminal law does. The primary reason for doing this is not to make sure that those who commit such wrongs receive the suffering they deserve, but to hold them to public account for those wrongs; the punishment they receive is the material form that such holding to account takes. When we say that they deserve to be punished, what we should mean is not that they deserve some quantum of suffering that could in principle be inflicted by anyone, which the criminal court aims to inflict; but that they deserve to be called to such account by those whose business their wrongdoing is—their fellow citizens. Punishment must be understood relationally, as an imposition whose meaning and justification depend not merely on what is imposed, on whom, and for what, but on by whom it is imposed; the claim that A deserves to be punished always needs completion—A deserves to be punished by B, who has the standing to hold A to such punitive account. In deciding on the scope and content of our criminal code, we must thus decide both who is to be bound by it (in relation to whom the polity can claim such standing), and what kinds of wrong should be our collective business.[35]

However, by the time we begin to consider a criminal code, we will already have an idea of the answers to both these questions. For it is to be a criminal code for the polity, and thus a code concerning conduct falling in the public sphere, committed by those over whom the polity can claim authority. Just as a code of medical ethics cannot claim authority over aspects of doctors' conduct that are not part of and do not bear on their

[34] It should be clear that "public" and "private" in this context are not spatial notions: what is done "in public," for instance the colour I paint my door, may be a private matter; what is done "in private," for instance a husband's violent assault on his wife, may be a "public" matter.

[35] For further explanation and justification of the claims in this paragraph, see the items cited in n. 7 above, and Duff, "Relational Reasons and the Criminal Law" 2 *Oxford Studies in Philosophy of Law* 175 (2013).

professional activities, or over those entirely outside the medical profession, the criminal code cannot claim authority over aspects of citizens' conduct that do not fall within or bear on their civic lives in the public sphere, or over those who are not members of the polity.[36] Once we focus our attention in this way, we can identify the two kinds of wrong that are in principle criminalizable. The *mala in se* are wrongs whose wrongness does not depend on their being legally prohibited, or being committed by or against members of the polity; they are the business of this polity's criminal law because they are committed within the polity's public sphere. The *mala prohibita* are those wrongs whose wrongfulness consists in the breach of some public regulation that serves or purports to serve the common good.

Such a formation of a criminal code implies a type of legal moralism: we should criminalize conduct if and because it is morally wrongful, it should be marked as such, and it should receive an appropriate formal, public response. It *could* find room for a Moorean legal moralism, according to which we have reason to criminalize every kind of moral wrong—but only if we began with a distinctly illiberal conception of the public realm and of the polity's aims. One way to arrive at such an expansive legal moralism would be via a totalitarian, rather than a liberal, conception of the polity, according to which the public sphere includes all aspects of its members' lives: there would be no private sphere that was in principle not the polity's business. Moore would reject that approach. He would instead have to argue, as a member of the Founding Parents Committee, that the polity's guiding aims should include the pursuit of retributive justice—retributive justice in relation not merely to wrongs committed within the polity, but to wrongs committed by anyone, anywhere, in any context. But could he argue this?

It is not clear how Moore could offer such an argument, since it seems to be at odds with his liberalism. The core liberal value of liberty requires, inter alia, the maintenance of an extensive private sphere into which the polity has no right to intrude; but the pursuit of retributive justice to which Moore's legal moralism commits him precludes the recognition of any such sphere, since it makes all wrongdoing in principle the polity's business. Breaches of obligations of friendship are moral wrongs, often serious wrongs. Moorean retributivists will therefore see reason to criminalize them, which implies that they belong in the public sphere: for to say that we have reason to criminalize them is to say that they are our business. But a liberal polity should see the relationships within which such obligations arise as falling within the private sphere—the sphere that is precisely *not* the polity's business. This is not to deny that what happens within a friendship can be the business of the polity, and of the criminal law: if I attack and wound my friend in a quarrel, that is the law's business. But that is because such an attack is not just a breach of the obligations of friendship: it is a breach of the obligations that I owe to others simply as fellow citizens, indeed as fellow human beings.

One way to summarize my objection to Moore's legal moralism is that his liberalism comes in too late. His Founding Parents begin with vastly ambitious, far from liberal, ambitions: we all have reason to promote the attainment of whatever is morally good; so insofar as "legislators can achieve [the] moral betterment [of the world] through law,

[36] This last claim needs qualifying to allow the law to claim authority over those temporarily within the polity's territory as guests of various kinds; see "Relational Reasons," 189–90, 207–8.

they should do so."[37] Given this starting point, and a Moorean conception of retribution, they will see reason to criminalize every species of wrongdoing; liberal values then enter the picture as a source of countervailing reasons not to criminalize. That general claim is arguable, even as a claim about the reasons we have as moral agents;[38] as applied to legislators it ignores the limits that legislators (or Founding Parents) should recognize on their roles. Those drawing up a regulatory code for doctors do not begin by asking what would make the world morally better, and then decide which kinds of betterment they can sensibly aim to assist: they begin by asking how a particular practice, medicine, should be governed; and while answering that question they might ask how that practice, medicine, can contribute to some relevant betterment of the world. In doing so, their deliberations will be limited to what can be seen as falling within that practice. The world would be morally better if people did not evade taxes, but that gives the committee no reason at all to include rules about paying taxes, or punishments for tax evasion, in their system of governance, unless it could be argued that this is somehow an aspect of medical practice. Analogously, the Founding Parents should not begin by asking how the world can be morally improved. They must start by asking what should constitute the polity's *res publica*; and any plausible liberal answer to that question will already limit the spheres of life and conduct that fall within the *res publica*. Such limits will also then be limits on what they can have any reason at all to criminalize; if a type of conduct falls within the private sphere, it is not for this committee even to take a view on whether it is morally wrong, let alone to see reason to criminalize it if it is wrong.

VII. Non-concluding Remarks

My argument has been schematic; I have not suggested what content the Founding Parents would give to a criminal code or how they would characterize the *res publica*. Those would be topics for a different debate—for a public deliberation in which the citizens of the polity should engage with each other. Nor have I explored the ways in which the analogy between the task of formulating a criminal code and the task of drawing up a code of professional ethics is imperfect; I do not think that there are enough flaws in the analogy to undermine its usefulness in showing us how the process of law formation must begin with a conception of the *res publica*—a conception that will, in a liberal polity, already limit the kinds of wrong that come to the legislator's formal attention.

There is, of course, no guarantee that such public deliberation will have liberal outcomes. According to the ILGA, seventy-five countries still criminalize consensual same-sex relationships.[39] These polities so define their *res publica* as to include consensual sexual conduct within the public sphere, wherever it takes place, and take homosexual conduct to be a serious wrong within that public sphere. On the account I have

[37] Moore, 2007b, 1540; see text at nn. 20–1 above.

[38] See also J. Gardner, "Relations of Responsibility," in R. Cruft et al. (eds.), *Crime, Punishment, and Responsibility* (Oxford: Oxford University Press, 2011) 87; M. Dempsey, "Public Wrongs and 'the Criminal Law's Business,'" in the same volume, 254; for criticism, see "Relational Reasons" (n. 35 above).

[39] See International Lesbian, Gay, Bisexual, Trans and Intersex Association: A. Carroll and L. Itaborahy, *State Sponsored Homophobia 2015: A World Survey of Laws: Criminalisation, Protection and Recognition of Same-sex Love* (Geneva: ILGA, May 2015).

sketched, we cannot fault the logic of such exercises in criminalization: these polities criminalize what is, in terms of their self-definition, a public wrong. Moore is similarly placed: he must agree that such polities have criminalized what they take to be a serious moral wrong—one serious enough to make it worth incurring the costs of criminalization to ensure that it is punished. That is not to say that either he or I must agree that they are justified in criminalizing homosexual conduct. We can each argue that this is unjustified: Moore on the grounds that such conduct is not morally wrong; I on the grounds that we need not discuss its morality, since it should not fall within the public sphere. Neither of us would probably succeed in persuading these legislatures that such conduct should not be criminalized; but the question that concerns me here is which of us provides the better explanation of why such conduct should not be criminalized.

The difference between Moore and me might seem minor—a small squabble between two legal moralists; and we could end up with similar views about the proper scope of the criminal law—at least, nothing in the structure of our accounts forces us to disagree about that. But the difference still matters: it matters that we get clear about the logic, and the starting points, of the deliberations that should inform criminalization decisions, and about how moral wrongfulness should figure in that deliberative process; it matters that we identify the most plausible version of legal moralism. On these issues, Moore and I disagree; I would like to persuade him that he is wrong.

8

Moore in Jeopardy, Again

Gideon Yaffe

I. Introduction

Michael Moore's intellectual contributions are numerous and important. Even the small ones are important. I personally feel deeply indebted to Moore, and not just for the encouragement he's given me and the great conversations with him that I've been lucky enough to participate in. I also feel indebted to him for the extraordinary work he's done to explain how philosophical reflection on the fundamental natures of things—actions, intentions, beliefs, causation—does and should inform the law. Moore has shown that often the fact that a thing is X if and only if Y—a discovery of analytic philosophy—implies that the law ought to, and sometimes does, *treat it as* X if and only if Y; at least this is true when the law has an interest in Xs. To someone like me, who came to be interested in law out of an interest in philosophy, rather than the other way around, this is both exciting and liberating. Exciting because, if Moore is right, at least sometimes the often technical and abstruse details of philosophical inquiry—details that are the source of endless fascination for those of us who like that kind of thing—make a difference to how we ought to construct the legal institutions that guide how we live together. Liberating because, if Moore is right, to give voice to philosophical discoveries about the fundamental natures of things in a room full of those whose primary interests are legal is nothing to apologize for; quite the reverse. Moore sees the methodology that he adopts—moving from the fundamental aims of a certain area of law, to an account of the natures of the objects that need to be identified and sorted if those aims are to be well-pursued, and back again to law to see how legal institutions are and ought to be constructed in light of what metaphysics teaches—as placing him in a tradition that includes Jeremy Bentham.[1] If I'm working in a tradition that includes Bentham and Moore, then perhaps I'm not wasting my time.

Moore has been close to unflinching in his use of this methodology. But at one important point he flinches, namely in his quite brilliant and under-appreciated discussion of double jeopardy in *Act and Crime*. That discussion has received far less attention than it deserves. I suspect that this is a result of a confluence of historical-sociological forces that have nothing to do with the merits of the discussion. By 1993, when *Act and Crime* was published, the philosophy of action literature had moved away from the question of act individuation, and it has not yet returned to the issue in force; a quick search through *Philosopher's Index* reveals that very little has been written about act individuation in the last twenty years, despite its being a central topic of discussion in the decades prior. So scholars coming to law from philosophy were unlikely to see

[1] See, for instance, Moore, 1997b, 362.

Moore's discussion as engaged with work that they were reading in the recent philosophy journals. Add that the study of principles of individuation—efforts to fill in the blank in schemas of the form "X = Y if and only if ______"—is extremely abstract, notoriously difficult, and seduces even clear-headed people into speaking nonsense, and it is no surprise that those coming to think about double jeopardy from the law side would be frightened away by Moore's discussion. So, there hasn't really been anyone both equipped and motivated to carry the torch. Knowing how important it is to Moore for people to get what they deserve, my goal here is to take some small steps towards giving Moore his due for his discussion of double jeopardy. I am going to try to determine what's right about it and what's not. The issues are too complicated, and Moore's discussion is too rich, however, to make much more than small progress in this endeavor here. I will rest content if I my remarks succeed in prompting Moore to say more in defense of his view.

Moore's discussion begins with a claim about the fundamental point of double-jeopardy restrictions.[2] Starting with the idea that the fundamental goal of criminal law is to apportion punishment to desert, he sees double-jeopardy doctrines as involving extension to our system of what would make sense in a perfect system—the system in which the legislature gets it right in both its definitions of offenses and in its assignment of punishments to offenses, and in which there are no false convictions or false acquittals. In such a system, a second conviction for the same offense is guaranteed to involve over-punishment; a second acquittal for the same offense is guaranteed to involve an unnecessary, harmful, and expensive proceeding for assessing guilt; and, given that the imagined system is perfect, there would never be acquittal in a first trial followed by conviction for the same offense in a second, or vice versa. The result: in a perfect system, the goal of issuing deserved punishments for crimes is served by double-jeopardy restrictions; second jeopardies interfere with the goal. Of course, our system is imperfect, but double jeopardy still makes sense because the best way to fix our system is to improve our definitions of crimes, to improve our apportionments of punishments to crimes, and to improve the accuracy of our verdicts. So double-jeopardy restrictions do what we want them to do when we've gotten it right and leave us to fix things in the way we ought to fix them when we haven't. Section II is devoted to offering a criticism of this picture and to sketching an alternative.

Given his characterization of the fundamental aim of double-jeopardy restrictions, and given his orientation towards the bearing of metaphysical questions on law, you might expect Moore to reason like so: "Token offenses are token acts. So, the fundamental aim of double-jeopardy doctrine can be pursued only if second jeopardies (e.g., second trials following an acquittal in a first trial) are excluded if and only if the token act for which the defendant is in jeopardy the second time is the same token act as that for which he was in jeopardy the first time. So, we need to know the conditions under which token act 1 and token act 2 are the same token act. And from this account we can reconstruct double-jeopardy doctrine in a way that makes sense in light of it." But this is not how Moore reasons. Here he flinches. And, in fact, when criticized for the metaphysical methodology on display in the rest of *Act and Crime*, he responds by citing his

[2] My presentation of Moore's position here differs from his presentation of it. I hope, still, that he will recognize the position that I attribute to him as his own.

approach to double jeopardy as evidence that he is discriminating in his use of metaphysics; after all, if he does not *always* go that route, that's evidence that he goes that way only when it makes sense. He writes,

> [I]f the purposes behind the doctrines in question did not require a metaphysical answer, none was sought [in *Act and Crime*]. For example, on the individuation of 'units of offence' required for double jeopardy, one might think that the metaphysics of event-tokens and of act-tokens should be used to give the legally appropriate answer. In chapter 14 [of *Act and Crime*] I argue to the contrary, setting aside any metaphysics-of-action-answer to the unit of offence question in favour of a 'wrong-relative' mode of individuation. I do this because the dominating purpose animating the double jeopardy requirement—to proportion punishment to desert—requires a count of the separate instances of wrongs done by an accused, not a count of the separate act-tokens he may have done in doing those wrongs.[3]

It seems to me that Moore is committed here to two controversial claims: (1) People are punished under the criminal law for their wrongs, which are individuated differently from their acts, and (2) An account of the principle of individuation of wrongs is not a contribution in metaphysics. I set (2) aside. We can certainly agree that what wrongs a person has done is a function at least in part of what norms she has violated. Whether *that's* a question of metaphysics or not, I don't know. It is a little surprising to find a moral realist like Moore taking the view that it is not. But who cares how we use the term "metaphysical?" Claim (1), however, is interesting and important. The goal of section III is to determine whether it is true. Doing this, as we will see, requires a careful look at Moore's theory of wrong individuation. Ultimately, I will be arguing that Moore's account of the individuation of wrongs is insufficient to the task of guiding double-jeopardy law. What is needed is something closely related, but different: an account that individuates wrongs in part by reference to the agents who do them. As we will see, this in turn has implications for understanding the theory of action relevant to criminal law, and points away from a claim about that theory to which Moore is wedded throughout all of his major works. The claim: An agent's responsibility for a causal consequence of his basic act is solely a function of his degree of causal contribution to that consequence; it is not a function of other facts that modulate our intuitions about the degree to which that consequence is his *doing*. Both this claim, and its relationship to Moore's view of double jeopardy, will become clear, I hope, in section III.

II. The Point of Double Jeopardy

As indicated already, Moore sees double-jeopardy restrictions as primarily playing a role in accomplishing the law's goal of punishing people as much, and no more, than they deserve. He recognizes that double jeopardy also serves, for instance, to limiting the trauma associated with being placed in jeopardy—the trauma of being put on trial, in the paradigm case—but he sees this role as secondary. And that has to be right; after all, that trauma is present in first jeopardies as well as second, but it is worth imposing on people in order to accomplish the fundamental goals of the criminal justice system.

[3] Moore, 1997b, 253–4.

The trauma of second jeopardies, not to mention the state's expenses, would also be worth it if the more fundamental goals involved in placing people in jeopardy in the first place were still served.[4]

The objection I want to press starts by noticing the obvious similarity between double-jeopardy restrictions and rules against do-overs in many games. You can't take moves back in chess, or take mulligans in golf; you can't redo your at bat in baseball after you strike out; you can't return to re-kick the fourth-down field goal in football after you miss it; etc. Of course, this observation should be coupled with another: Often, games do allow do-overs *under certain specific conditions*. You can take moves back in chess, if there's an agreement between the players about it; you can take mulligans in golf in a "friendly" game, but not without limit; you do get another pitch in baseball if you fouled off the last one; you can re-kick the fourth-down field goal if the other team was offside on the play; etc. Still, in many games, the default rule is "no do-overs," even if the rules allow divergence from the default in certain specific circumstances.

These observations alone should give us pause in identifying any goal that is special to the administration of criminal justice as that which is driving double-jeopardy restrictions. There are just too many activities where it makes sense to disallow do-overs by default, activities that do not share any goals at all, to think that such a policy is justified by the specific goals involved in any given activity where the policy is adopted.

In fact, in activities in which the outcome for a given participant is determined in part by chance, and not solely by the merits, the goal of having outcomes determined by the merits is furthered by *allowing* do-overs. The reason for adding up your receipts twice in order to check your work—when calculating a tax deduction, for instance—is precisely that you want the total to be accurate. But if you allow do-overs to a party who seeks an outcome *that is insensitive to the merits*, then you can end up thwarting the goal of achieving outcomes that accord with the merits. If you are going to add up your receipts over and over until you get a total that allows you to pay no taxes, and if there is enough randomness to the calculating procedure to assure that you will eventually reach such a total, then you assure that you will end up using an accurate total only if,

[4] If we focus on the role of double jeopardy in excluding second trials in the case of false acquittal, we can see that Moore is committed to a particular form of reasoning that is common, although controversial, in moral philosophy. Moore's view is that a second trial in the case of false acquittal is excluded, even though it could aid in giving the defendant what he deserves (since the second trial might result in an accurate verdict), because the goal of constructing an institution that gives people what they deserve is best served by improving the accuracy of trials, rather than re-doing them until they yield correct verdicts. The general form of the issue here is this: Rule R is justified because, generally, by following it we further goal G. However, cases exist in which R requires agent S to A, but A-ing in this instance will thwart rather than further G. Rule Utilitarians, and others who believe in rules, will assert that even in such cases, the thing to do is to stick with the rule. The rule, in this view, is detachable from its goal-furthering justification.

It is possible to object to Moore with the standard "rule worship" objection to Rule Utilitarianism: If you like the rule because following it furthers the goal, then you should like defection from the rule when defecting furthers the goal. But I don't want to press this objection against Moore. In part this is because I too am drawn to the idea that a rule can be detachable from its justification—justified rules can be justifiably followed even when following them is unjustifiable on those same grounds. I cannot say that I am sure this is true; but it does not seem impossible to me. Still, it is worth mentioning that if that turns out to be false, then Moore's rationale for the double-jeopardy restriction fails.

by chance, the total is also the actual one. Even if you reach an outcome that accords with the merits, you guarantee that your outcome won't be sensitive to the merits.[5]

Default policies against do-overs, then, make sense when participants have incentive to achieve non-meritorious outcomes but the designers of the policy seek only outcomes for all participants that accord with the merits. And we can also see why, in such cases, divergence from the default policy can be justified under specific circumstances. It can be justified when the specific circumstances make it more likely that outcomes will be assigned in accordance with the merits when do-overs are allowed in such circumstances.

In fact, I suspect that the contours of double jeopardy-law are explicable from this point of view. Consider, for instance, the "same sovereign" rule in double jeopardy: It is double jeopardy to place D in jeopardy a second time for C only if the sovereign who placed him in jeopardy the first time is the same as the sovereign placing him in jeopardy the second time.[6] Under this rule, for instance, double-jeopardy restrictions permit California to try someone for a crime for which he was acquitted in Oregon (in a case in which both states have jurisdiction).[7] Notice that Moore ought to be opposed to this rule, given his view of the fundamental aim of double-jeopardy restrictions. In a perfect system, where there are no false acquittals, this rule will allow an unnecessary, expensive, and potentially traumatic state trial of someone acquitted in anothers state's court. It would allow a defendant to be punished once, in accordance with his desert, for a crime in one state, and then again for the same crime in another. So the rule does not further the goal of apportioning punishment to crime in accord with desert. But the rule makes sense given the general rationale for default no-do-over policies. State actors, like prosecutors, have incentive to get convictions even in the absence of guilt, and so they have incentive to try and retry until a guilty verdict is reached, regardless of the merits. So there's good reason to adopt a default double-jeopardy rule here. But the "same sovereign" rule, allowing retrials by different sovereigns, is compatible with this rationale since the relevant state actors are different. Each individual sovereign cannot avoid deciding on the merits by taking a do-over whenever the outcome is not what the sovereign seeks.

It is important to see that, in a sense, this line of thought involves granting, rather than denying, that the fundamental point of double jeopardy is to help the state to give people what they deserve for their bad behavior. We want a system where the outcomes for those placed in jeopardy of punishment are determined by the merits. If we did not seek a system in which people are punished in accordance with desert, there would be no point in double jeopardy. But the obstacle to achievement of that goal, which double jeopardy remedies, is not that multiple accurate trials necessarily result in either excess punishment or a harmful and unnecessary proceeding. The obstacle is that without a

[5] That the law does, and should, give special attention not just to mechanisms that match As with Bs—e.g., defendants with verdicts—but to mechanisms that do so *non-accidentally* is a theme I have explored in other contexts. See Gideon Yaffe, "'The Government Beguiled Me': The Entrapment Defense and the Problem of Private Entrapment," 1 (1) *The Journal of Ethics and Social Philosophy* 1 (2005); Gideon Yaffe, "Indoctrination, Coercion, and Freedom of Will," 67(2) *Philosophy and Phenomenological Research* 335 (2003).

[6] For discussion of the law in connection with this rule, see Wayne LaFave, *Criminal Law, 5th Edition* (St. Paul: West Publishing, 2010) 243–9.

[7] *Heath v. Alabama* (474 US 82, 106 S Ct 433 (1985)). The Supreme Court in this case upheld the conviction in Alabama of a crime to which the defendant had previously pled guilty in Georgia.

default policy against unlimited jeopardies we assure verdicts that are insensitive to the merits because those with the power to put people in jeopardy have strong incentive to get convictions even when they are not warranted.

There is an apparent problem, although not a real problem, with the line of thought sketched here, consideration of which illuminates the difference between the view I am proposing and Moore's view. The problem is that it appears that, in the account sketched, what is bad, and ruled out by double jeopardy, is unlimited jeopardies. But we could eliminate that problem with a triple jeopardy rule, one that allows a second jeopardy for the same thing (by the same sovereign), but not a third; or, instead, a quadruple or quintuple jeopardy rule, etc. To many, however, even a triple jeopardy rule would be unjust, intuitively speaking. Why? Moore's account can explain this nicely: all it takes is one more good trial leading to conviction to assure that there will be excessive punishment, and all it takes is one more good trial leading to acquittal to assure that you have an unnecessary and harmful adjudicatory proceeding. That Moore's account provides an explanation here is a point in its favor, even if it fails to explain the "same sovereign" rule.

But the view sketched here can also explain why a double-jeopardy rule is better than a triple or quadruple one. The key is to see that, according to the view I am proposing, the double-jeopardy rule undercuts unlimited jeopardies by undercutting the really problematic thing that can lead to them: discretion on the part of the state as to whether or not to take a do-over. Imagine the following game: We flip a fair coin: heads you win; tails I win. But you get to decide whether to do the flip over and I do not have that power. It doesn't take a mathematician to see that you are far more likely than I am to win this game. If you have the right to do-over the do-overs, without limit, then you are guaranteed to win; eventually, a head will come up and then you will choose not to do a do-over. In fact, you are substantially favored in this game even if we adopt a triple jeopardy rule under which you are allowed only one do-over, at your discretion. In that case, you win 75% of the time.[8] If one party, and not the other, has the *discretionary* power to take a do-over or not, then the odds that that party will achieve the outcomes it wants increases.

The point can be extended to systems in which outcomes are sometimes allocated on the merits, but sometimes not. Say that trials reach verdicts on the merits 75% of the time. The other 25% of the time the verdict is randomly assigned as either guilty or not guilty. Of the random verdicts, the guilty verdicts are as likely to be accurate as the defendant is likely to be guilty, the not-guilty as he is not to be not-guilty. So sometimes the trial gets it right for the right reasons, sometimes it gets it wrong, and sometimes it gets it right but not for the right reasons. If the prosecution wants conviction, and can take even a single do-over if it chooses to, then it will subject all of the acquittals *on the merits* to a new trial. Since the new trial will decide the case on the merits only 75% of the time, 75% of those acquittals will not be decided on the merits. But the prosecution will not subject any of the convictions to a new trial.[9] In short, if the triple jeopardy rule does not mandate a second trial, but simply allows the state to bring one if it so chooses,

[8] This is true since, of the four possible two-flip outcomes, you win in three of them.

[9] It will also subject the acquittals not on the merits to a new trial, but that will only improve things for 75% of those—namely 75% of 12.5% of the original verdicts.

then there's a problem. The problem is that the prosecution has the power to magnify the imperfections of the system—the degree to which verdicts are not decided on the merits—in its favor, but the defense has no parallel power to magnify the imperfections in its favor. The result: a double-jeopardy rule is better than a triple jeopardy rule given the aim of deciding cases on the merits, and given that it is always the prosecution, and not the defense, who has the power to place people in jeopardy.[10]

III. Individuating Wrongs

Under both the view of double jeopardy's fundamental purpose advocated by Moore, and under the alternative view I sketched in section II, there would be no good reason for double jeopardy if we really had no interest in deciding cases on the merits. And we agree, for entirely independent reasons, about what the merits are: a case is decided on the merits only if the outcome is that the defendant receives no more nor less than the punishment he deserves.[11] And we both agree that the problem that double jeopardy is intended to remedy is not present when a person is punished once for one thing and then again for something else. We disagree about what the problem is, but that disagreement sits in front of a background of agreement that we need to know under what conditions that thing for which a person is in jeopardy is *the same thing* as that for which she was previously in jeopardy. Moore's answer: it's the same thing just in case it's the same wrong. And the next question is inevitable: Under what conditions is it the same wrong?

Moore sees the individuation of token wrongs as involving the individuation of token acts by reference to certain crucial types to which they belong, namely types like "violations of the norm against drunk driving" and "violations of the norm against reckless manslaughter." Since a single act might violate multiple norms, there might be multiple wrongs where there is only a single act. This view depends upon a very plausible "coarse-grained" view of action individuation, which I also accept, according to which there is not a separate act for each consequence of the relevant basic act, or for each crucial property of it. Rather, the same single act can have multiple consequences, and multiple notable properties, and be described by reference to one rather than another. So if it is true that he drove while drunk and consequently killed someone then he engaged in a single token act that had two properties: the property of being a drunk driving and the property of causing a death. It is false that there are two distinct acts here (driving drunk and killing someone).

Abstractly, then, we can associate token wrongs with ordered pairs of the form (x, N), where x is a token act and N is a norm that x violates. Moore also observes that some norms are violable only by certain agents, and others only when certain people or things are harmed. There is a norm against *Moore* belittling *Yaffe* (remember this when the time comes to write your reply, Moore!). Only Moore can violate that norm, and he does not violate that norm, but a different one, when he belittles someone else. So

[10] If trials were extremely bad at deciding cases on the merits, and if a small percentage of those who are brought to trial are guilty, then a triple or quadruple jeopardy rule might improve things. So, an assumption of the rationale offered here for double jeopardy is that these things are not so.

[11] Moore would say "*if and* only if". But this issue needn't detain us.

wrongs are individuated in part by norms, and norms are individuated in part by the agents and objects they concern. The question then of whether placing some defendant in a second jeopardy is in violation of double jeopardy-restrictions at least sometimes turns on the question of whether the defendant is twice being placed in jeopardy for violation of a single norm; if not, then no problem. And this question will sometimes turn on what, exactly, the norms are to which particular statutory provisions give legal force. If a statute gives legal force to a norm against doing something to *Yaffe*, then someone who also does it to *Moore* has committed two relevant legal wrongs, not one, and so could potentially be placed in jeopardy for both.

So, to talk through one of Moore's examples, consider D., who kills V1 and V2 with a single shot and intends to kill both; the bullet, let's imagine, passes through V1 and kills V2, as intended. Would it be double jeopardy to try D for the murder of V2 following his acquittal for the murder of V1? No, says Moore, for there are different norms being violated by the single act. The wrong of killing V1 can be represented as (shot, "Don't kill V1") and the wrong of killing V2 as (shot, "Don't kill V2"). Add that statutes against murder give legal force not just to the norm "Don't kill people" but to the norms "Don't kill V1" and "Don't kill V2"—the laws give protection, individually to each person—and it follows that here we have the same token act, different norms, and so different wrongs, and so no double-jeopardy problem. So far, so good.[12]

Notice that resolution of this One Shooter–One Shot–Two Intended Victims case requires appeal only to a necessary condition for wrong identity, which it is useful to label:

> *The Norm-Relative View*: Wrong w1 = Wrong w2 *only if* w1 and w2 involve the violation of the same norm.

We do not yet have on the table Moore's view of the relationship between the act tokens involved in w1 and w2 when w1 is or is not the same wrong as w2. And there is a clear need for something to be said about that as we can see by mentioning a different case of Moore's, the One Shooter–Two Shots–One Intended Victim case: D fires twice at V and kills him, acting on an intention to kill him. If D is tried for the first shot, and acquitted, is it double jeopardy to try him again for the second shot? The abstract representations here, if taken naively, would seem to suggest not. After all, (first shot, "Don't kill V") involves the same norm as (second shot, "Don't kill V"), but not the same token act. But we should not naively assume that wrongs are individuated in the way their associated ordered pairs are individuated. Maybe the first shot and the second shot are related to each other in some way that suffices for identity between the relevant wrongs, given that the norms involved are the same. So are the two shots the same wrong, or not? We need more to answer that.

Moore sees this very clearly and supplies an account of the missing piece, which he calls the "wrong-relative" view. Consider the following statement of the view, which Moore makes after describing a case like One Shooter–Two Shots–One Intended Victim:

[12] Moore does a tremendous amount of work in Moore, 1993c to explain the conditions under which norm 1 and norm 2 are the same norms and how we should think about the question of what norm is given legal force by a statute. See Moore, 1993c, ch. 13. The details of that position deserve a careful treatment and will not, sadly, receive it here.

> On the wrong-relative mode of act-token individuation, there is no legally usable answer to the question "How many acts?," until we know what morally salient *type* of act is involved with a given statutory offence. If the question is "How many *murderous* acts were there?" the correct metaphysical and thus legal answer [in a case like One Shooter–Two Shots–One Intended Victim] is "One."[13]

Later, he puts the view with reference to "wrong-making properties."[14] I take it that the wrong-relative view should be understood like so, where x1 and x2 are token acts, and N1 and N2 are norms violated by x1 and x2, respectively:

> *The Wrong-Relative View*: Wrong (x1, N1) = Wrong (x2, N2) *only if* x1 and x2 both have property P, where x1 violates N1 thanks to possessing P, and x2 violates N2 thanks to possessing P.[15]

I think, also, that Moore takes the two necessary conditions for wrong identity articulated to be jointly sufficient, leading us to the following account of his principle of individuation of wrongs:

> *The Norm- and Wrong-Relative Theory (NWR)*: Wrong (x1, N1) = Wrong (x2, N2) *if and only if* (1) N1 = N2, and (2) x1 and x2 both have property P, where x1 violates N1 thanks to possessing P, and x2 violates N2 thanks to possessing P.[16]

To illustrate the work that is done by the Wrong-Relative Theory, consider a hypothetical example. Say that D goes to the public square, stands on a box, and, with a crowd assembled, yells, "The Cardinal is a pedophile! The Cardinal is a pedophile!" The left side of the crowd heard the first sentence but not the second. The right side heard the second sentence but not the first. In fact, the Cardinal is no pedophile and D has said this, not once but twice, to harm the Cardinal's reputation. The Cardinal was severely diminished in the eyes of everyone present; his reputation was badly damaged, just as D intended. D is acquitted at trial of slander despite evidence supplied by a witness who heard the first sentence, but not the second. He is then later tried for slander on evidence supplied by a witness who heard the second sentence but not the first. Is the second trial a violation of double-jeopardy restrictions under NWR?

[13] Moore, 1993c, 385. [14] Moore, 1993c, 386.

[15] The "where" clause here is intended to capture the idea of a wrong-making property. The token act is wrong thanks to violating the associated norm, which it does thanks to the fact that it possesses property P. If a better account of what makes a property "wrong-making" is proposed, I would advise substituting it for what appears in the "where" clause here.

[16] In *Act and Crime*, Moore uses a misleading example to illustrate the theory. He applies the theory to a version of One Shooter–Two Shots–One Intended Victim where *both* shots are causally necessary for the death and they simultaneously strike the victim. (Actually, in his example there are five shots. See Moore, 1993c, 386. But the point is the same.) The relevant wrong-making property is *causing the death*. That property is not borne by either the first shot or the second shot; it is borne by the conjunction of the two. So, neither act individually bears the wrong-making property of interest. The result is that in the example so construed neither act is individually violative of the norm against killing the victim; rather, the more complex act that consists of firing-the-first-and-the-second-shot is violative of that norm. The result is that we are able to resolve the case without appeal to the Wrong-Relative Theory; the Norm-Relative Theory does all the work. The two acts are different wrongs because they are violative of different norms. The first violates the norm against causing the damage the first shot caused; the second violates the norm against causing the damage the second shot caused. So there could be guilt for two counts of grievous battery consistent with double-jeopardy restrictions. But neither of the norms that distinguish the wrongs here is a norm against killing. To generate a double-jeopardy problem that needs appeal to the Wrong-Relative Theory for resolution, we need each act individually to be violative of *the very same norm*.

In answering this question, let's assume that any given lie is slanderous only if it causes at least half the crowd to think ill of the Cardinal. That's the minimum number that need to think ill of him if his reputation is to be damaged. Does Moore's view imply that there is double jeopardy here? Under NWR, are the wrongs represented as (first utterance, "Don't slander the Cardinal") and (second utterance, "Don't slander the Cardinal") the same wrong? The case for "yes": Both are violative of the norm thanks to the fact that they bear the same wrong-making property, namely the property of causing at least half the crowd to think ill of the Cardinal. The case for "no": The first utterance bears the wrong-making property of causing the left side of the crowd to think ill of the Cardinal; the second utterance bears the distinct wrong-making property of causing the right side of the crowd to think ill of the Cardinal. But here the case for "yes" wins, or, rather, it does so given some plausible assumptions about what legislatures are up to in criminalizing slander. Spoken lies damaging to reputation are wrongful not because thanks to them any particular set of people think ill of the victim, but because *the public* does. That is, the norm in question is not sensitive to the difference in effect between the first utterance and the second; the norm, rather, picks out that which they have in common as crucial, namely that each results in *the public* thinking ill of the Cardinal.

Moore has offered a powerful and plausible theory. But does Moore's proposed theory of wrong individuation capture the sense of "the same" that matters for purposes of double jeopardy? Given, for the sake of argument, that the purpose of double-jeopardy restrictions is to avoid undeserved punishments, the question is really whether that which we punish *for* are wrongs in the sense identified by Moore's theory of wrong individuation. I'm not sure, but I'm doubtful.

The source of my doubts comes from the application of Moore's theory to cases involving multiple perpetrators. To see the point, start with a kind of case that Moore explicitly discusses. Cases of this kind are just like One Shooter–Two Shots–One Intended Victim, except that the separate token acts are performed by separate agents. In Two Shooters–Two Shots–One Intended Victim, for instance, D1 and D2 each fires a shot that kills V. We have in hand an explanation for why it is double jeopardy to bring to trial for the second shot following acquittal for the first in One Shooter–Two Shots –One Intended Victim: the two token acts violate the same norm thanks to bearing the same wrong-making property, namely the property of causing V's death. But in Two Shooters–Two Shots–One Intended Victim, it would seem that the same logic would allow us to try only D1 or D2, but not both, consistent with double-jeopardy restrictions. Moore's move here is to distinguish the norms in the two cases. The norm is not "Don't kill V." Rather, there are two norms: "D1 does not kill V" and "D2 does not kill V."[17] When coupled with NWR this has the implication that D1 and D2 committed distinct wrongs even though the two shots in One Shooter–Two Shots–One Intended Victim were the same wrong. So NWR explains why it would be double jeopardy to try the one shooter first for the first shot, then later for the second, but it would not be double jeopardy to try the first shooter for his shot and then later try the second for his.

But notice that we could have reached the same result with an importantly different theory of wrong individuation. We might have thought that a wrong is not just a token

[17] Moore, 1993c, 358.

act that violates a norm, but is, instead, a token act *by an agent* that violates a norm. We might have suggested that the abstract objects to associate wrongs with are not ordered *pairs*, but ordered *triples* of the form (S, x, N) where, as before, x and N are, respectively, a token act and a norm it violates, but where S is the agent who performs x. This then yields a competing theory of wrong individuation:

> *The Agent-, Norm-, and Wrong-Relative Theory (ANWR):* Wrong (S1, x1, N1) = Wrong (S2, x2, N2) *if and only if* (1) N1 = N2; (2) x1 and x2 both have property P, where x1 violates N1 thanks to possessing P, and x2 violates N2 thanks to possessing P; and (3) S1 = S2.

This theory of wrong individuation allows us to admit that D1 and D2, in Two Shooters–Two Shots–One Intended Victim, violate exactly the same norm, namely "Don't kill V," while still reaching the conclusion that D1 and D2 did not commit the same wrong, since wrongs are individuated not just by norms, but also by agents. Of course, whether this is a better way to explain what's going on will depend on whether D1 and D2 really have violated the same norm. It's hard to see how to go about adjudicating that question in that case.

In other kinds of cases there is more to say about the difference between NWR and ANWR. Consider the case of *People v. Russell* (91 N.Y.2d 280, 693 N.E.2d 193 (1998)). The three defendants (let's call them D1, D2, and D3) had a gun battle with each other across a courtyard. A passerby (V) was killed by a single shot and it was impossible to determine who fired the shot that killed him. The theory that the court accepts for convicting all three of depraved-heart murder is that each participated in the gun battle and it was the gun battle that caused the death. Now imagine, counter to fact, that two of the three were tried and acquitted. When the the third is then tried for the same crime he objects on double-jeopardy grounds. As an intuitive matter, this argument, I believe, should be rejected. Consider two different ways of constructing the norm(s) here:

> The One Norm Theory: The legally relevant norm is the one that all three violated: "Don't have gun battles that kill V."
>
> The Three Norm Theory: There are three legally relevant norms, one for each defendant. D1 violated the legally relevant norm, "D1 does not participate in gun battles that kill V," and D2 and D3 violated similar norms that refer to them in particular.

Moore needs the Three Norm Theory to be true if he is to explain why D3's double-jeopardy argument should be rejected. The reason is that the three token acts have the very same wrong-making property: *contributing to a lethal gun battle.* Since NWR, Moore's theory of wrong individuation, sees wrong identity as turning only on norms and wrong-making properties, it follows that to distinguish the wrongs of the three defendants, Moore must distinguish the norms violated by their individual acts. And the tool that he has at his disposal for doing so, at work in his resolution of Two Shooters–Two Shots–One Intended Victim, is to assert that the norms in question make reference to particular agents.

Is this a problem? Perhaps, for while there's sufficient evidence that the gun battle caused V's death, there's insufficient evidence that D3's *participation* in the gun battle was anything more than a tiny causal contributor to the death, if that. Let's assume, to start, that D1 and D2 would have battled it out even if D3 hadn't been there to join them. Still, thanks to D3's participation there were more bullets flying around in the gun battle than there would have been otherwise. And let's grant that even if D3's bullet did not cause V's death, the increased dangerousness of the gun battle deriving from D3's participation was a causal contributor to it. But now consider the general view that a reckless homicide is a better candidate for depraved-heart murder if the probability of the death was very high.[18] The probability that a passerby would die *as a result of the gun battle* was very high, we can assume; that was surely part of what justified the court in finding guilt for depraved heart-murder rather than reckless manslaughter. But the probability that a passerby would die *as a result of D3's participation* in the gun battle was certainly lower and perhaps substantially lower; *ceteris paribus*, it was a third as large. The result is that the case for predicating depraved-heart murder on D3's *participation in the gun battle* is much weaker than the case for predicating that crime on *the gun battle*, of which D3's participation is at most a part. So, Moore's theory, NWR, can support rejection of D3's double-jeopardy argument, but only by seriously weakening the case for thinking of D3 (or D1 and D2) as having committed a depraved-heart murder. And this result is not particular to depraved-heart murder. We will have the same result in any case in which the requisite crime turns on the degree to which the predicate act made a harm more likely; this will include, in addition, all the endangerment crimes and perhaps more.

By contrast, the competing theory of wrong-individuation, ANWR, the theory that takes agent identity to be part of what is involved in wrong-identity, involves rejection of the double-jeopardy argument, but does so in a way that preserves the strength of the case for depraved-heart murder in *Russell*. The reason is that ANWR allows us to accept the One Norm Theory, and its consequent support for the intuitively appealing case for depraved-heart murder, and still reject the double-jeopardy argument offered by our hypothetical D3 following the acquittal of D1 and D2. The point is perhaps most intuitively put in the language of joint perpetration. D1, D2, and D3 are being punished for *the gun battle*, which was something that the three of them engaged in together, and which caused a death. They are not being punished each individually for *his* participation in the gun battle. Further, they all violated the same norm: "Don't have gun battles that kill V." There is just one relevant (joint) act here violative of one norm, but there is no double-jeopardy problem because there are three wrongs. But to reach that result we need to reject Moore's theory of wrong individuation in favor of the alternative view; we need to reject NWR and accept ANWR.

I suspect that at this point Moore will bite the bullet. Or, rather, to put the point in a more charitable tone (this is a festschrift, after all), Moore will accept this as a consequence of his view, articulated in his book *Causation and Responsibility*, that criminal responsibility is a function of causal contribution. The gun battle is a large causal contributor to the death because it pools the causal contributions of all three defendants. But Moore holds that if each defendant's causal contribution to the death is

[18] I am certain that the discussion to follow here would be better if developed with reference to Moore's discussion of cases in which small risks aggregate to produce risks large enough for negligence, or bear other more complicated relations to the risks required for negligence. See, especially, Moore, 2009d, 185–94. One can only do so much.

small, then each bears a small amount of criminal responsibility for it. So, he is likely to see his need for accepting the Three Norm Theory in order to rebut the double-jeopardy argument as merely demonstrating how the truth in one domain hangs together with the truth in another. He is thus likely to accept the conclusion that D1, D2, and D3 might not be guilty, individually, of depraved-heart murder. We have here, instead, just three reckless manslaughters. Or, similarly, if the issue was not the causation of death, but endangerment, it might turn out that three people can be not guilty of endangerment even though they participated jointly in an activity that was endangering. To this, I'm afraid I have little to say except to point to the relative elegance, and normative appeal, of the competing view that draws on ANWR.

Although it is little more than an additional intuition-pull, consider an imaginary case much like *Russell* but with a large number of defendants. A gun is on a timer and set to fire at V's head at midnight. The gun has 1,000 empty cylinders. D1 puts a bullet in cylinder 1, D2 in cylinder 2, and so on all the way up to D1,000. They do this simultaneously. At the end all the cylinders are full. D1–D1,000 all know exactly what is going on here. At midnight the gun fires and miraculously misses. D1–D999 are acquitted in separate trials of endangerment, a crime that requires an act that imposes a risk of death strictly greater than 1 in 1,000. Is it double jeopardy to try D1,000 for the same crime? Moore can say "no" only by also accepting that the verdict in the first 999 trials was correct. There were 1,000 wrongs here, but none of those was in violation of the norm given legal force by the endangerment statute. To me, that's a big bullet to bite. There's a single joint act here—filling the gun with bullets—that is violative of the very norm to which the endangerment statute gives legal force. It is D1's act, it is D2's, and it is D1,000's. But that one act is 1,000 wrongs because there are 1,000 agents here, all of whom imposed a huge risk of death on V. This is not the only way to say what's going on here, but isn't it better than Moore's?

Let me end by noting one subtler way in which the view of wrong individuation that Moore accepts fits in to larger themes in his philosophy concerning his conception of action. Moore thinks of actions as events, like bodily movements, bearing a causal relation to volition, and with further consequences that are sometimes appealed to in describing those acts. Further, he holds that once we have found a consequence of an act, the question of the agent's responsibility for that consequence turns only on facts about the causal relation between the agent's act and that consequence—the greater the causal contribution, the more the responsibility—and on facts bearing on the agent's culpability for it, facts about his mental representation of that consequence. So, in *Russell*, the defendant D1's degree of responsibility for the death is a function of the causal contribution that his act made to the death and a function of his awareness of the possibility that an innocent bystander would die.

This is the positive side of the picture. The negative side is that under Moore's view many things that contribute to our conception of an agent *as active with respect to* a particular consequence of his bodily movement are irrelevant to his responsibility for that consequence. This can be illustrated with cases of so called "non-proxyable" acts; cases in which a description of the act by reference to a consequence applies only if the consequence involves the agent of the act in an intimate way. Causing something to be acquired is not *acquiring* it unless it is *you* who has the thing in the end. This is why sellers don't acquire the objects they sell, even though they do indeed cause them to be had by someone (namely by buyers). Causing something to be crushed is not *crushing* it, unless *your* body is directly involved in the physical pressure placed on the thing. This is why the woman who pays the late-term abortion doctor to crush the fetus' skull has not crushed anything.

One hypothesis about what is going on in these cases is that (1) facts about identity or distinction between the agent and the protagonist of an event make a contribution to the degree to which the agent is active with respect to that event, and (2) that, in turn, makes a contribution to the degree to which the agent is responsible for the event. More activity, more responsibility; and identity is a contributor to activity and so a contributor to responsibility. Since identity is different from causal contribution, if this hypothesis is right then something more than causal contribution can be relevant to one's responsibility for the consequences of one's act.

Moore denies both halves of this hypothesis.[19] I mention this not to adjudicate the issue here—although it may be obvious even from as little as I have just said about it which side I am on—but because it is interesting to see how Moore's view on this issue connects to his view about double jeopardy. Moore cannot (1) assert that people are held criminally responsible for their wrongs, (2) deny that wrongs are essentially individuated by agents, and (3) agree that facts about agents are essential to the determination of that for which a person is held criminally responsible. He does both (1) and (2), so it is no surprise that he does not do (3). Or, to put the point as a challenge, we might say that given that one *should* do (3), one ought not to do both (1) and (2). Moore's views about the individuation of wrongs, that is, fit with his broader philosophy of action so snugly that doubts about the latter, of the sort offered here, should lead us to doubts also about the former.

IV. Conclusion

Has anything that Moore really cares to argue for been placed in jeopardy by the discussion here? I'm not sure. I do not take myself to have offered decisive criticisms against his position. Like I said at the beginning, if all this chapter serves to do is to prompt Moore to clarify his position by defending it further, then I will have succeeded. My goal here has been to give him a do-over; and if what he offers is, instead, an encore, I'll applaud for that, too.

[19] I press the issue in Gideon Yaffe, "Moore on Causing, Acting and Complicity," 18 *Legal Theory* 437 (2012). Moore replies in Moore, 2012a, 513–26.

9

Do We Need a Doctrine of Complicity?

Leo Katz

I. Introduction: Moore's Claim

Causation would surely make it onto anyone's top-five list of concepts philosophers have had to struggle with. As a legal topic, it might rank even more highly. Until recently, the unsurpassed treatment of the legal aspects of causation was Hart and Honoré's *Causation and the Law*. Recently, however, their book *has* been surpassed—by Michael Moore's *Causation and Responsibility*, which has rightly received an enormous amount of attention from philosophers and legal scholars alike.

One of the reasons for the sheer size of Moore's book is that there are in fact few legal doctrines that do not in some way depend on our understanding of causation, and whatever alterations in our understanding Moore proposes are therefore likely to have untold ripple effects throughout the law, only the most important of which he is able to pursue in his book. One of those ripple effects has to do with the doctrine of complicity. A proper understanding of causation, argues Moore, will allow us to dispense with a separate doctrine of complicity, at least in the criminal law, and if he is right, perhaps even in other contexts in which collective action is the subject of legal regulation.

My purpose in this chapter is to explore this particular claim, one of an extraordinary number of provocative claims that Moore makes. I am going to suggest that he is partly right and partly wrong: that some cases of complicity could indeed be unproblematically dealt with without a complicity doctrine, but that many crucial cases cannot. The benefit of working through Moore's claim is thus twofold. To begin with, it shows us to what extent complicity is in fact an unnecessary doctrine, despite the seemingly central place it occupies; but even where one disagrees, as I do, one is forced to isolate in a way one has not had to previously exactly what it is that the doctrine adds—that is, what it adds that an improved understanding of causation, of the kind provided by Moore, would not take care of.

To fully appreciate the boldness of Moore's claim, it is worth contrasting it with a related, more familiar, less bold claim, with which it might easily be confused—the idea that the doctrine of *conspiracy* is an unnecessary doctrine. Conspiracy, like complicity, is a doctrine meant to deal with collective action. It imposes liability, first, on the participants in a collective enterprise for crimes which other members of the collectivity committed (under the *Pinkerton* doctrine), and second, on the would-be participants of such an enterprise, who never did more than agree to carry it out (under the inchoate liability portion of the doctrine). Numerous scholars have pointed out that minor extensions of the doctrines of complicity and attempt would suffice to take care of conspirators, and that many legal regimes have for that reason happily dispensed with a conspiracy doctrine altogether. That's a fairly intuitive claim, whether one agrees with it or not.

Moore, however, wants to claim that all participants in collective wrongdoing whom we want to legitimately punish can be satisfactorily dealt with either by holding them liable as principals or as attempters. In other words, he thinks that not only conspiracy, but complicity as well, is a redundant doctrine. What he suggests is that on a proper understanding of causation—the kind he propagates in his book—accomplices can simply be characterized as either having caused a forbidden state of affairs, just as a principal is usually held liable for doing, or perhaps as *omitting* to prevent such a state of affairs, just as a principal is usually held liable for omitting, or as *attempting* to bring about a forbidden state of affairs, and therefore as guilty of a criminal attempt. Either way, we don't need the doctrine of complicity to impose liability on them—he argues.

Moore's claim is probably most persuasive with regard to the following kind of case: A asks P to kill V. Black letter doctrine does not allow us to hold A liable as principal in the killing of V, because P was an intervening actor. On the other hand, A can be held liable as the accomplice of P. In this way, Moore writes,

> [T]he doctrines of accomplice liability fit like soft clay around the shape of intervening causation. Wherever an intervening agent is himself guilty of a crime and is an intervening cause vis à vis some earlier act by another, that other is eligible for accomplice liability; whereas if the intervening agent is not an intervening cause, then the earlier actor is eligible for liability as a principal. The picture is reminiscent of the hit tune by the former punk rocker, Blondie: we are going to get you, "one way or the other." Intervening-cause doctrine will determine which way that will be.[1]

But there is really no good reason to go about the business in this convoluted way, Moore persuasively argues. It is hard to give a metaphysical or ethical justification for the intervening-cause doctrine, and so we might as well acknowledge that when A tells P to kill V, he is not any less the cause of V's death than if he had fired a bullet at him. And if we dispense with the intervening-cause doctrine, we will no longer need the complicity doctrine to hold A liable.

Where things get controversial is in connection with what are arguably the core cases of complicity, exemplified by the three casebook stalwarts, *Tally*, *Wilcox*, and *Hicks*. In *Tally*, a group of men, the Skelton brothers, set out to kill one Ross, a married man, who had conducted an affair with the Skelton's younger sister, Annie Skelton. For a while Ross had successfully evaded their wrath by escaping into other parts. But when news got around that he had briefly returned, and paid Annie a visit to boot, they tried to track him down at the railway depot of a nearby town where they had been informed he was about to make his latest escape. As they were riding out of town toward the railway depot, Ross's brother saw what they were up to, and immediately handed a telegram to the local telegraph operator, hoping to warn Ross, when he reached the railway depot, about the posse trying to kill him. A relative of the Skelton brothers, one Judge Tally (married to another Skelton sister) saw what Ross's brother had done, and immediately fired off another telegram from the same telegraph office telling the telegraph operator at the other end, whom he apparently knew, not to deliver the warning telegram from

[1] Moore, 2009d, 289.

Ross's brother. The warning telegram in fact never reached Ross, whether because of Tally's intervention is unclear. Whether or not it would have made a difference, if it had been delivered, is also unclear. The only thing that is clear is that the Skelton brothers did catch up with Ross and killed him before he managed to catch the train out of town. Tally was held liable as an accomplice, and the conventional view of the matter is that we need the complicity doctrine to bring about that result, because we cannot really say that he caused Ross's death as a principal. He does not meet what is commonly referred to as the requirement of factual causation, usually identified with the so-called "but for" test, which says that but for the defendant's actions the victim would not be dead. We cannot say with any degree of confidence that but for Tally's actions Ross would not be dead. Complicity does not require the certainty of a "but for" connection that the liability of principals requires.

Next consider the *Wilcox* case. Wilcox was a journalist who attended an illegal concert. He was held liable for assisting in the illegal performance, in other words, as an accomplice to the musician who was the perpetrator of this offense. If we sought to hold him liable for causing the illegal performance, we would not be able to, it would seem, because the performance would have occurred whether or not he participated as a spectator or not.

Finally, consider the *Hicks* case. Hicks watched the perpetrator, Stand Rowe, kill a third man, one Culvert. He shouted words of encouragement at him. Stand Rowe really did not need any encouragement; he was clearly resolved to kill Culvert no matter what. Given the superfluousness of the encouragement Hicks provided, it would have been hard to hold him liable as a principal for causing the victim's death.

Two factors here stand in the way of liability as a principal. In *Wilcox* and *Hicks* it is the redundancy, or near-redundancy, of what the defendants are doing; in other words, the fact that the outcome is, as it were, over-determined. In *Tally*, there is the additional element of uncertainty about whether Tally did or did not make a difference to the outcome. Redundancy and uncertainty are the hallmark of collective action. And so it would seem that if we want to impose liability in the most typical of collective action cases, we need to have a doctrine that waives the usual requirement of *causation proven beyond a reasonable doubt, just as the complicity doctrine does.*

Not so, argues Moore. Where we go wrong is in misidentifying causation with the "but for" relationship. It is tempting to so identify them, which is why the law does it, but it is nonetheless erroneous, as Moore persuasively explains:

> If causation is counterfactual (i.e. "but for") dependence, then it can have no properties not possessed by counterfactual dependence and vice versa. Yet causation is a transitive relation: with qualifications not here important, if c causes e, and e causes f, then c causes f. It is well known that counterfactual dependence is not transitive: f may counterfactually depend on e, and e may counterfactually depend on c, and yet f may not counterfactually depend on c. Moreover, causation (again with qualifications not here relevant) is an asymmetric relation: if c causes e, e does not cause c. Counterfactual dependence is not necessarily asymmetric; e can counterfactually depend on c, even while c counterfactually depends on e. Finally, causation relates temporally ordered states of affairs; if c causes e, then e must not precede c in time—causation does not work backwards through time. Whereas counterfactual dependence knows no

> such limitation; e can counterfactually depend on c without regard to whether c precedes or succeeds or is simultaneous with e in time.[2]

He argues for a different conception of causation, which is in fact not devoid of legal pedigree. What he proposes we do instead is that we

> treat causation as a primitive—a "factor"—save for one characteristic, namely that there can be more or less of it. Causation needs to be a scalar quality, a matter of continuous variation, as opposed to a binary, black and white sort of relationship. Then—[consistent] with section 431 of the Restatement of Torts First and Second—we mark causal responsibility by using some quantitative measure; x causes y if and only if x is (say) a "substantial" cause of y. *De minimis* amounts of causal contribution do not make for cause-based responsibility. This line (between substantial versus *de minimis* amounts of causal contribution) is not governed by counterfactual dependence; x can be a substantial cause of y without x's being necessary for y—witness the fire that joins another fire of equal size, and the two together jointly burn down the victim's house. Moreover, x can be a *de minimis* causal contributor even though x was necessary for y—as where I remind you of how much you hate V, and (with that reminder) you go off and kill V, when otherwise you would not have. (p. 300)[3]

This then allows him to deal with the core case of complicity, that involving overdetermination, in a neat way, by asking whether the various overdetermining influences on the victim's death were substantial causes. What he would say about *Hicks* is this: The principal who shoots Culvert, and would have shot him with or without Hicks's encouragement, can be viewed as doing the equivalent of sending a fire the victim's way; Hicks in turn can be viewed as setting a second fire, which joins with the first. He has increased Stand Rowe's resolution, without however making a difference to the outcome. Notwithstanding that lack of making a difference, both arsonists, in Moore's view, can be regarded as substantial causes of the eventual conflagration, to wit, Culvert's death.

What he has to say about *Wilcox* is this:

> It is important first to see that Wilcox did causally contribute to the legally prohibited result here—the performance for pay of an alien musician. That is because Wilcox was a member of the paid audience, and presumably the presence of a paid audience entered into the motivations of the saxophonist who played. Wilcox is in this respect like others of what we earlier . . . called mixed concurrent cause cases, like pollution and elections. Suppose it requires five units of pollution to cause harm, but each of several hundred polluters contributes one unit; or suppose it requires 51 votes to win an election, but 90 people vote for the winner. In such mixed, concurrent cause cases no individual polluter, voter, or audience member is necessary to the harm occurring, nor are they sufficient; still they are the causes of that harm.
>
> Yet they are, considered individually, very small causal contributors to the result. At some point, surely, they become *de minimis* causes, to be treated for moral and legal purposes not as causers at all. Wherever that point is, it should be the same for causes where the result is the action of someone else (as in Wilcox) or where the result is an event that is not a human action (as in the pollution and election examples). Whatever is sufficient causal contribution for liability as a principal, in other words, should be

[2] Moore, 2009d, 287. [3] Moore, 2009d, 300.

> sufficient for liability as an accomplice, and vice versa. Causal accomplices should again be treated like principals, because both groups equally cause the harm. (p. 302)[4]

Tally is a trickier case for him. The fact that Tally stands in a potential, albeit unproven, relationship of counterfactual dependence to the victim's death might at first seem to make things easier for him in establishing liability without a doctrine of complicity—but not once we remember that the existence of such a relationship does not establish causation in Moore's view. He views the relationship between Tally and his victim as one of what he calls "double prevention," and double prevention, as he sees it, is not a form of causation, just as omitting to rescue someone is not a form of causation. What Tally did was to prevent someone (Ross's brother) from preventing someone's (Ross's) death. On the other hand, a counterfactual relationship of this sort, he says, is as deserving of principal liability as another non-causal counterfactual relationship, such as omissions. Just as we do not hesitate to hold a parent liable for omitting to rescue, we should not hesitate to hold someone liable who prevents someone else from preventing death. (He acknowledges the possibility that the level of culpability might be slightly less than in cases of actual causation.)

What about the uncertainty element of *Tally*? Here he appeals to the

> moral fact that risk imposition is a desert basis independent of causation and of counterfactual dependence. . . . [T]o unreasonably risk is to be blameworthy, the degree of blame here (like for causing) depending on the culpability with which the risking is done. . . . [The *Tally* court found Tally] guilty of aiding murder even though the warning telegram would not have saved Ross even if that telegram had been delivered to Ross; so long as Tally's prevention of the delivery of the warning telegram raised the chances of success of the Skeltons in their killing of Ross. This is chance-raising (or risk-based) liability, pure and simple, [not a special kind of accomplice liability]. (p. 309)[5]

Not too difficult for him now are so-called cases of preemptive causation, such as McLaughlin's, in which the victim is about to trek through the desert, and just before he does, enemy 1 puts poison in his water canteen, and enemy 2 drills a hole, draining out the water along with the poison, whereupon the victim, caught in the desert without water, dies of thirst. He would presumably find enemy 2 to be the only substantial cause of the victim's death.

This then is how Moore would reduce all complicity cases to instances of principal liability.

Has he demonstrated that we do not need a doctrine of complicity?

II. The Issue Sharpened: The Attempt Analogy

It will prove useful to step back a bit and ask what exactly one would need to show to establish a raison d'être for complicity. It will help to do so by looking at a parallel problem that is easier to solve; finding a raison d'être for the doctrine of attempts.

[4] Moore, 2009d, 302. [5] Moore, 2009d, 309.

A crime is defined, roughly, as the creation by a principal, by way of causation or omission, of a forbidden state of affairs. The defendant who never brings that state of affairs off cannot be held liable as a principal. But if he was in the process of trying to bring it off, we still want to hold him liable, which is what the doctrine of attempts allows us to do.

Ideally one would like to able to say a bit more about the doctrine of attempts. Ideally, one would like to be able to deduce the various peculiarities of that doctrine—what sets it apart from ordinary liability as a principal—from its unique function.

There is, to begin with, the distinctively unsettled debate about where to draw the line between preparation and attempt. When has the defendant done enough to merit being found guilty of an attempt? It is pretty clear how this facet of attempt doctrine flows from those features which set it apart from the more standard kind of principal liability. Principal liability involves our focusing on a wrongful action, or to be more precise, the creation of a certain undesirable state of affairs, and then inquiring whether he did so with the requisite mental state, with regard to the various elements of the offense. The thing we don't want to happen defines the actus reus of the offense. With attempts, things are more difficult because, from a purely objective point of view, there is nothing problematic about what the defendant actually did. Otherwise we could hold him for an actual offense. He is being held liable only because of what was going on in in his mind as he carried out objectively innocent actions. The puzzle then arises as to what fraction of his mental design he must have realized before he can be found guilty of an attempt; ten percent? fifty percent? ninety percent? Many of the various criteria for defining an attempt are meant to address this problem.

The next distinctive feature of attempt law is the defense of abandonment, which is not ordinarily available to someone committing an offense as a principal. It would not be theoretically inconceivable to do so. We might for instance have something like the give-back defense for theft, and permit the defendant who returns what he has stolen to go scot-free, but we don't, though that is precisely what we do in attempt law. Why? Can we somehow show that having such a defense follows from the raison d'être for attempt doctrine?

I don't have a complete answer, but the recent book by Alexander, Ferzan, and Morse at least suggests one. It's not that the raison d'être we gave entails an answer, but it suggests why one might be friendlier to an abandonment defense in the context of attempt law than in the context of a more ordinary offense. Alexander et al. emphasize the connection between defendants who perform actions with a conditional intent and someone who attempts a crime. In particular, they note how thin the line is that differentiates, say, someone who carries drugs illegally into a country intending to consume them himself—who is guilty of various completed offenses having to do with illegal drug imports and consumption—and someone who is guilty of the more serious offense of attempting to distribute illegal drugs to the public at large. The person who imports for his own use might well be willing to sell to the public at large if the price is high enough, but he is not with the price as it is. He therefore has the conditional intent to sell illegal drugs to the public at large, and takes certain preparatory actions with that conditional intent. But, so long as the intent is conditional, we are not willing to find him liable for an attempt. (I say this the suggestion to the contrary in the Model Penal

Code notwithstanding, which neither tracks the cases nor our intuitions on this.) Now suppose that the conditions on which his intent is conditioned come to pass. The defendant is offered enough money that his conditional intent now becomes unconditional. At this point of course he has the intent required for an attempt as well as probably having done enough to effectuate it. Now imagine that at some point he abandons his plans because he learns that the price being offered for these drugs is in fact lower than he thought at first. The intent now goes back to being conditional. We could of course say that since it was unconditional for a certain period he is guilty of having committed an attempt at that time. But it is equally natural to say that since his intent was always conditional on being offered a high enough price, it never really became genuinely unconditional, or even if it did, since it reverted to being conditional, the intermittent period of an unconditional intent is not enough to render him guilty of an attempt. It is in this way that the abandonment doctrine is a very natural one to incorporate into the doctrine of attempts.[6]

Finally, how can one understand the *mens rea* requirement for attempts as a natural outgrowth of its raison d'être? It is not hard to see why recklessness is not sufficient for an attempt. The defendant has engaged in conduct creating the risk of many different kinds of offenses, and so it is not clear which of those he could be judged to have attempted. Things are different with the requirement of an actual purpose, as opposed to mere knowledge or a prediction that one is going to produce a certain forbidden state of affairs. Many have thought there is no good justification for this feature of attempt doctrine and suggested it ought to be reformed. However, once we have something like the abandonment defense it would be strange not to insist on the purpose requirement. Let us see why.

Imagine the proverbial case of the defendant who is trying to kill the queen while she is riding in her coach. He plans to plant a bomb inside the coach. He fully expects that this will also kill the coachman, even though he does not have a true purpose with regard to harming the coachman. Suppose that after planting the bomb, he decides to move it slightly, thus incrementally increasing the chance of the coachman's surviving. Arguably we have an abandonment of his plan to kill the coachman, but then planting the bomb with the hope of sparing the coachman surely should be treated the same way. In other words, if we treat the person who exhibits mere knowledge vis-a-vis a certain victim, such as the coachman, the same way we would if he exhibited an actual purpose, we thereby introduce an extremely disturbing asymmetry, or discontinuity between the case in which someone gets the abandonment defense because he moved the bomb incrementally and is therefore not guilty of an attempt, and the case in which he does not move the bomb incrementally, but puts it in that location from the very beginning, in the hope that the coachman will be spared: in the latter case he would be liable for an attempt—unless, that is, we insist on a requirement of true purpose, in which case he is not guilty.

The question that we face regarding complicity is most illuminatingly posed by analogy to the law of attempts. Does complicity contribute a separate form of liability in the

[6] I am blithely passing over a certain complication here: It isn't crystal clear that the abandonment defense would in fact apply in this case, since abandonment only works if it occurs for the "right" kind of reason. Is this the "right" kind of reason? Arguably, but only arguably.

same way that the attempt doctrine does? Does it allow us to hold liable defendants who could not be held liable using other available doctrine, as Moore claims? And if it does in fact allow us to impose liability where other doctrines fail to do so—as I shall contend, contra Moore—does this help to explain the idiosyncracies of complicity law?

III. A Useful Detour: Utilitarianism and Cooperation

It will be helpful for shedding light on these matters to turn our attention to a book that might at first glance appear to have little bearing on the subject, Donald Regan's *Utilitarianism and Cooperation*. The most obvious purpose of that book is to explore various alternative forms of utilitarianism and show that all of them have some highly counterintuitive properties that have not been generally appreciated, as well as to propose a form of utilitarianism that is more intuitive in most (though not all) respects. Once we understand its arguments, however, we will see that it can help us considerably in understanding the need for a doctrine of complicity, which is after all a doctrine meant to deal with the phenomenon of cooperative wrongdoing.

Regan considers four forms of utilitarianism: act utilitarianism, rule utilitarianism, utilitarian generalization, and a special brand he is the first to introduce, which he calls cooperative utilitarianism. He draws attention to three properties that we would want a utilitarian value system to have and shows that of the four types of utilitarianism only one has them all, albeit at the price of a fourth somewhat counterintuitive property.

The first such property he calls "PropAU." A moral theory T has PropAU, says Regan, provided that: "For any agent, in any choice situation, if the agent satisfies T in that situation, he produces by his act the best consequences he can possibly produce in that situation." This of course is the defining property of act utilitarianism. That's what it means to be an act utilitarian—to act so as to produce the best possible consequences in the situation one finds oneself in.

The second property Regan asks us to consider is what he calls "PropCOP." To say that a moral theory T has PropCOP is to say that "If all agents satisfy T in all choice situations, then the class of all agents produce by their acts taken together the best consequences that they can possibly produce by any pattern of behavior." Regan's first interesting point here is that act utilitarianism does not have this property, as illustrated by the following simple schematic example. Let us imagine two actors, Whiff and Poof, who have the choice between two courses of action which he refers to as "pushing" and "not-pushing." If both push, they will generate an outcome of 10 units. If both not-push, they will generate an outcome of 6 units. If one of them pushes and the other does not, they will generate an outcome of zero units. Now consider a situation in which both parties not-push. Then both parties are in fact doing what act utilitarianism requires them to do: they could not produce a better overall outcome by taking a different action. If either chose to push, while the other not-pushed, the outcome would be zero. This demonstrates that act utilitarianism does not have PropCOP.

Next he points out that rule utilitarianism, while it has PropCOP, does not have PropAU. There are many forms of rule utilitarianism, but the point is most readily seen by focusing on the most standard case. Let us suppose that the rules of the particular form of rule utilitarianism we are looking at require each party to push. This form of utilitarianism satisfies PropCOP, because, if each party does what this form of rule utilitarianism calls for, the overall optimum outcome is in fact obtained, a crucial difference as compared with act utilitarianism. But this type of rule utilitarianism does not have PropAU. To see this, imagine that Whiff not-pushes. What should Poof do? According to this form of rule utilitarianism, Poof should do what would be optimal if everybody did the optimal thing, namely push. But in that case the outcome is zero. It is not the outcome that is the best possible one that Poof could produce, which is why PropAU is not satisfied. Other variants of utilitarianism suffer analogous problems.

Neither of the familiar forms of utilitarianism thus manages to satisfy both of these fairly basic requirements one might want to impose on them. There is yet a third property to which Regan draws attention, which one might expect a plausible form of utilitarianism to have but which none of the foregoing in fact do have. It is a property he calls "adaptability." He defines it thus: "In any situation involving choices by any number of agents, the agents who satisfy T in that situation produce by their acts taken together the best consequences that they can possibly produce by any pattern of behavior, given the behavior of agents who do not satisfy T." In other words, "a theory T is adaptable if and only if the agents who satisfy T, whoever and however numerous they may be, are guaranteed to produce the best possible consequences possible as a group, given the behavior of everyone else." We can readily see that neither act utilitarianism nor rule utilitarianism is adaptable. If both Whiff and Poof engage in not-pushing, they are satisfying the requirements of act utilitarianism, despite the fact that they are not producing the optimal outcome which they have it in their power to bring about if they jointly engaged in different behavior, namely pushing. We can also readily see that rule utilitarianism is not adaptable because if Whiff not-pushes and Poof pushes, Poof would be satisfying the rule utilitarian requirement despite the fact that he is not producing the best possible outcome that it is in his power to produce, which is what adaptability would under the circumstances call for.

Regan points out, however, that there is a form of utilitarianism which exhibits all of these desirable properties, PropAU, PropCOP, and adaptability. It is what he calls cooperative utilitarianism.

> The basic idea of cooperative utilitarianism is really very simple. The basic idea is that each agent should proceed in two steps: First he should identify the other agents who are willing and able to co-operate in the production of best possible consequences. Then he should do his part in the best plan of behavior for the group consisting of himself and the others so identified.

Now there is something very special about this type of utilitarianism, Regan points out, that sets it apart from other more familiar types: It is not what he calls "exclusively act-oriented." To determine whether someone has engaged in the right sort of behavior demanded by the situation, it will not suffice to simply focus on the person's actions, which is all that is required by the previously considered types of utilitarianism. Whether he is compliant will depend on what is going on in his mind as he does what he does. To be more precise, he must be engaged in an effort to coordinate his own actions with those of other compliant parties. And that involves a complicated hierarchy of beliefs to the effect that he must want to take actions that mesh with someone else whom he expects to be trying to do the same, and who moreover does so in the expectation that the other actors expect him to do so, and so on, up a hierarchy of complicated interlocking beliefs and expectations. That does not mean that anyone is actually caused to have a certain belief or expectation by what anyone else is believing or expecting; they operate entirely without communication, but they base their actions on these complicated expectations and beliefs about what other willing cooperators are expecting and believing. It is the sort of coordination game famously described by Thomas Schelling: Scenarios in which people are instructed to try to meet someone else at a place and time of their choosing, based on nothing more than the knowledge that other party he is trying to meet has been told the same thing. Cooperative utilitarianism satisfies PropAU, PropCOP, and adaptability. It does, however, have the unusual characteristic, which sets it apart from the previously discussed forms of utilitarianism, that we need to look into the actor's mind to determine whether he satisfies the theory. Simply observing his actions will not do.

IV. A Return to the Main Road: Applying the Lessons from Cooperative Utilitarianism

Let's reconsider McLaughlin's famous case about the man about to go into the desert, one of whose enemies puts poison into his water canteen, and the other of whose enemies drills a hole in it, as a result of which the water drains out, and he dies of thirst.

Here is how Moore's approach would apply to this case. The driller is a substantial factor in the victim's death. He thus meets the actus reus requirement for liability. If he acted with the level of awareness required for culpability, in other words, an intention, or knowledge, or recklessness as to that outcome, he is liable. He would probably not find the poisoner to be such a substantial factor in the victim's death and thus dismiss the possibility of holding him as a principal in the completed offense out of hand.

Now I haven't said much so far about how it came about that these two determined enemies of the victim happened to end up in this curious "preemptive causation" situation. I am surmising that most readers pictured them as each independently conceiving of his deadly design and then proceeding, oblivious to the other actor's nefarious doings. But let us suppose that it was not like that at all. Instead, let us imagine that they are in fact proceeding collaboratively. In other words, let us imagine that P, the poisoner, and D, the driller, wanted it to be the case that one put poison into the canteen and the other drilled a hole. Not that they communicated about that with each other. Rather they cooperated in the same way that Schelling's subjects cooperated. They each tried to adjust their actions and expectations to what they surmised were the actions and expectations of the other, surmising further that that person in turn was trying to do the same with respect to them. Why would they want to cooperate in this redundant fashion? There are many possibilities. Perhaps they hoped to escape liability, inasmuch as neither could now be regarded as standing in a but-for relationship to the outcome. Or perhaps the driller did not quite trust the potency of the poison. Or possibly the poisoner wanted to make sure that if some water was left over, it would not serve to keep the victim alive. Or maybe he just wanted to be part of this enterprise inasmuch as he wholeheartedly endorsed it. Regardless, in any of these alternatives we would presumably want to hold both liable. Yet the approach Moore advocates is impervious to these new fact patterns. Because nothing has changed with regard to the driller's still being a substantial cause of the bad outcome, and the defendant having the requisite level of awareness with regard to it. (To be sure, Moore might be willing to hold the driller liable under the "extension" principles he uses to impose liability on Tally for accomplices who create risks or are engaged in mere attempts. More on that below.)

And yet the difference seems to matter. If by contrast the poisoner did not know about the driller, we would want to let him go. Or if the driller wanted to spare the victim death by poison, then too we would want to let him go. The actions, or even the level of awareness the defendant has with regard to these actions, are not enough to mark the necessary boundaries between guilt and innocence. Even Moore's "extension" principles regarding attempts and risk creation would not really satisfactorily handle this aspect of the matter.

What we are running into here is closely analogous to the phenomenon laid bare by Regan. He noted that the necessary distinctions a utilitarian moral theory must mark cannot be marked by what he calls an "exclusively act-oriented theory." Something similar is happening in the context of criminal liability. When we apply the principal liability approach, we are asking first whether the defendant committed a wrongful act and then checking whether he did so with the requisite level of awareness. That's a close analogue to the "exclusively act-oriented" approach. When we inquire whether they cooperated, with all the complexities that entails, we are of course departing from that act-oriented approach, and using instead a cooperation-informed approach closely analogous to the cooperative utilitarianism advocated by Regan.

Let me try to restate the point in a slightly different way. Let's imagine a different case of overdetermination, this one also involving two actors, D1 and D2, each of whom is going to be firing a bullet at the victim, V. Let's add a third actor, T, to the situation, who is in communication with both D1 and D2. To be precise, he sends a note to D1, telling him that he knows for a fact that D2 is about to shoot V, and will do so regardless of what D1 does. He offers D1 a substantial sum of money if he would be willing to fire at V at the same time. Let us suppose that this is money that D1 desperately wants because it would enable him to help a relative obtain treatment for a painful disease. Let us further suppose that T sends a similar note to D2, telling him that he knows for a fact that D1 is resolved to kill V, and will do so regardless of what D2 does. He offers him too a large sum of money if he will arrange to simultaneously fire at V. And let us suppose that D2 as well has good reasons for wanting that money: he too could help a relative get treatment for a painful disease. They both fire at V, killing him. Are they guilty of murder? Don't be too hasty to say "of course." They had morally important reasons for acting as they did. Those reasons would not of course justify them if they were counterfactually connected with V's death, that is if they each were a sole shooter. But they are not. Each defendant sees himself as doing nothing worse than firing a redundant bullet into V's body, as a result of which the defendant obtains morally valuable benefits for someone else. His situation, as he sees it, is no different, than if he had been asked to fire such a bullet into V as a boulder is about to run over him. Intuitively, I think we would be inclined to grant them each a necessity defense.

Now contrast this with a variation of the same facts. T explains first to D1 and then to D2 that he wants each of them to fire at V, and that he has told the other the same thing, and that they should attempt to simultaneously fire their bullets into V. In return, he promises them each the aforementioned sum of money. Now we have a simple complicitous murder, in return for which each of them obtain benefits that would not of course entitle them to a necessity defense. Note that, as in the original scenario, neither actor: is having a causal impact on the other. Note that as in the original scenario, he does not stand in a relationship of counterfactual dependence to the outcome. Note that as in the original scenario, he is a substantial cause, in the Moorean sense, of V's death. But note that, unlike the original scenario, we are perfectly comfortable denying the necessity defense in this one. The difference is entirely non-causal. It has to do with the particular kind of cooperative mindset in which they stand to each other. What they think about their causal role is not decisive, because, in both scenarios, they are entitled to think about their causal role in the same way. It is the presence of a peculiarly cooperative mindset in the second scenario that makes the difference here. It is a subtle difference, then, but an important one that distinguishes the two scenarios, and it is the one that I believe the complicity doctrine, albeit in somewhat imperfect fashion, tries to mark. If we look at the purpose of the complicity doctrine in this way, it helps account for a variety of its peculiarities. Let's begin with its dispensation of the requirement of counterfactual dependence, which looms so large in the liability of principals, although it is not in fact indispensable, since we are willing to impose liability for cases in which someone was a substantial factor without being a but-for cause (as Moore rightly points out). In McLaughlin's canteen hypothetical, neither counterfactual dependence nor "factor-substantiality" will mark the relevant difference between cases in which we want liability to be imposed and those in which we do not. What is more, cases of this sort are far from exotic. Situations in which many parties interact in such a way that if the contribution of one of them does not do the trick, those of numerous others will, are perfectly commonplace forms of complicity.

Let's consider next the special *mens rea* requirement for complicity, which seems to go beyond a mere awareness or an intention that one is doing what one is doing. The statement of the *mens rea* requirement is often left obscure, but what it appears to be getting at is the idea that something beyond that kind of awareness or intention is required. What is being groped for, I am surmising, is the somewhat complicated cooperative mindset Regan has identified. It is also now clear why that mindset typically precludes mere recklessness as an adequate basis of liability. It is almost inherently bound up with a fair amount of purposefulness.

The odd "derivative" aspect of accomplice liability now also appears to make more sense. For there to be complicity liability, a cooperative mindset on the part of several people would seem to be required, or at least a somewhat derivative mindset, in the sense that one of them needs to be in a cooperative frame of mind vis-a-vis a hypothetical second agent. The requirement of derivative liability seems born out of that realization, even if it does not perfectly capture it.

Abandonment is a doctrine which complicity law shares with attempt law, and which principal liability, as we already noted, lacks. Are we in a position to explain this? To some extent, yes. Like an attempter, an accomplice is required to exhibit purposefulness, and like an attempter he is interacting with his compatriot in a manner that is fundamentally ineffectual, that is, which does not make a difference, which does not help to precipitate a bad outcome in a strict bout for sense. If that purpose subsides, we should be inclined to treat it as we would such intermittent purpose in the context of attempts.

V. Conclusion

Maybe the best way to convey the gist of Moore's analysis is with the help of three leading stalwarts from the casebooks, *Tally, Wilcox*, and *Hicks*. In each of those cases we can imagine versions that lack the cooperative mindset while still exhibiting everything usually required for liability as a principal, and versions in which that cooperative mindset is present. We would, intuitively, want to avoid liability in the former case, and impose liability in the latter. The only way to do that is by using the special doctrine that makes the relevant distinction relevant: the doctrine of complicity, which imposes liability despite the lack of the standard causal nexus, but requires by way of compensation, as it were, the presence of a suitably cooperative disposition.

10

Reluctant Pluralist

Moore on Negligence

*Kenneth W. Simons**

I. Introduction

Is negligence blameworthy? Does it deserve moral sanction? Is it a proper basis of tort liability? Of criminal punishment? If the answer is, "Only sometimes," further questions remain: When? And why only then?

These perennial questions in moral, tort, and criminal law theory continue to provoke debate. In Michael Moore's earlier writings, he addressed these issues thoughtfully but not thoroughly. However, a recent article that he co-authored with Heidi Hurd provides a systematic analysis of different conceptions of negligence and of different accounts of its moral and legal significance.[1]

The results of this new analysis are surprising. Reluctantly, Moore has become a pluralist, acknowledging a range of types of negligence that are sometimes morally blameworthy and sometimes appropriately sanctioned by the law—even by the criminal law. Moreover, he has also become (to use the technical term) squishy. Despite his usual fondness for sharply defined categories and exhaustive subcategories, he has come to acknowledge that the distinctions between negligence and recklessness, and between negligence and faultless conduct, are often a matter of degree. Moore's willingness to question and modify his earlier views is laudable, and not just because his current views are much closer to my own.

This chapter first discusses Moore's earlier forays into the topic, and then reviews his recent co-authored article. It concludes with some ruminations about different dimensions of negligence, and about the distinction between negligence and recklessness, that deserve fuller attention than scholars have provided to date.

II. Earlier Writings

This section sets forth some key arguments that Moore presents in his earlier writings about negligence, arguments that analyze negligence both as a form of wrongdoing and as a category of culpability, and that are especially skeptical of negligence in the latter guise. I also offer some criticisms of and questions about those arguments.

* Much of section III of this chapter is derived from Kenneth W. Simons, "When is Negligent Inadvertence Culpable? Introduction to Symposium, Negligence in Criminal Law and Morality," 5 *Criminal Law & Philosophy* 97 (2011), DOI:10.1007/s11572-011-9116-y.

[1] Moore and Hurd, 2011d. This article is an expanded version of a book chapter, Moore and Hurd, 2011e.

In his 1984 book, *Law and Psychiatry*,[2] Moore makes some rather broad generalizations about negligence that are in need of refinement. Thus, he observes that negligence is much more central to tort than to criminal law, because intention is central in the latter.[3] This is an overstatement, in light of the widespread use of recklessness, negligence, and even strict liability as elements of modern crimes. He also refers approvingly to what he calls the "classical" definition of negligence as behavior that is suboptimal from the perspective of cost–benefit analysis, under the test made famous by Judge Learned Hand in *United States v. Carroll Towing Co.*[4] "Negligence, in short, is the failure to make, or to make badly, a cost/benefit calculation about the desirability of an action."[5] This definition, alas, is also somewhat misleading. In actual jury instructions and tort law opinions, the Hand formula is rarely invoked. To be sure, some appellate court decisions do discuss that formula. However, it is not clear from those discussions what the formula is meant to express—a wholly utilitarian metric, or instead a pluralistic balancing test that is consistent with deontological principles.[6]

Moore further contends that negligence is intended as a culpability requirement, and not merely a criterion of justifiable or permissible conduct. Indeed, Moore explains, the surprisingly anthropomorphic reasonable person test "makes explicit the connection of negligence to culpability only implicit in Hand's kind of formula."[7] The Hand formula tells us what acts are permissible and impermissible; the reasonable person test gives us a standard for judging whether the actor has culpably failed to satisfy the standard.

Or so Moore claims. Yet when he attempts to clarify the relationship between wrongdoing and culpability in the context of negligence, Moore muddies the waters:

> [T]he average reasonable person . . . embodies those qualities of character that we think persons should possess, and those capacities of mind we think all persons do possess. The average reasonable person is benevolently motivated—he counts all persons' interests as equal to his own; he is thus neither unduly selfish nor unrealistically altruistic. . . . He is also capable of calculating what actions are likely to lead to what results and even to assign relative probabilities to each. He is, in other words, a preeminent practical reasoner, finding the morally and legally correct major premises (in terms of costs and benefits) for his practical syllogisms, and forming the accurate means/end beliefs (in terms of probabilities) for his minor premises.

"[The] failure to make the right cost/benefit calculation," he further explains, makes people culpable only if they have the capacity to reason in this way.[8]

Here we confront one of the most challenging difficulties in making sense of negligence. Is it a kind of wrongdoing, consisting in posing unjustifiable risks to others and thereby harming them? Or is it a category of culpability, describing actors who display a modest rather than serious degree of fault in violating a primary prohibition? Or, as Moore here suggests, is it a bit of both? Moore seems to assume that wrongdoing

[2] Moore, 1984d. [3] Moore, 1984d, 81–3. [4] Moore, 1984d, 81. [5] Moore, 1984d, 82.

[6] See Kenneth W. Simons, "Tort Negligence, Cost-Benefit Analysis, and Tradeoffs: A Closer Look at the Controversy," 41 *Loyola of Los Angeles Law Review* 1171 (2008); Kenneth W. Simons, "The Hand Formula in the Draft Restatement (Third) of Torts: Encompassing Fairness As Well as Efficiency Values," 54 *Vanderbilt Law Review* 901 (2001); Richard Wright, "Hand, Posner, and the Myth of the 'Hand Formula,'" 4 *Theoretical Inquiries in Law* 145 (2003).

[7] Moore, 1984d, 83. [8] Moore, 1984d, 83.

depends on one (unspecified) type of cost–benefit analysis, while culpability depends on capacities for benevolence, prediction, and calculation of probabilities. But this bifurcated approach is problematic, for it is difficult to see how wrongdoing of the negligence variety can be identified without calculating probabilities and making predictions (at least on the Hand formula account of negligence as wrongdoing), and without providing a normative framework for judging the significance of various costs and benefits. The relevant framework, Moore says, is "benevolence." But the concept of benevolence is itself equivocal. Does it refer to a utilitarian consideration of all the consequences that one's conduct is expected to produce for the interests of all affected persons? Or does it refer to a character trait disposing an actor to care about others as much as she cares about herself?

In a more recent and more extended discussion of negligence in his book on causation, Moore gives similarly ambiguous guidance on the characterization difficulty. He explains tort negligence, again, in terms of a "calculus of risk," and explores in some detail the Learned Hand formula, suggesting a number of plausible ways in which the formula should be extended:

> Hand's calculus of risk . . . requires one to weigh the total harms risked versus the total benefits risked if a given precaution is not taken, considered for each level of each kind of precautionary action possible, for all levels and kinds of activities in which the defendant might be engaged. An action is negligent, on this holistic view, "if its disadvantages exceed its advantages."[9]

In defending this extended Hand formula, Moore appears to be analyzing negligence as wrongdoing. He notes that the "reasonable person" test is frequently used in tort law, but suggests that this test might not actually vary the content of the Hand formula. Rather, the "reasonable person" standard is a potentially useful heuristic for fact-finders trying to apply the Hand formula, and it also specifies the epistemic vantage point from which the actor's compliance with the Hand formula should be measured.[10]

This discussion, while illuminating, again provokes questions about how negligence is best characterized. The *ex ante* epistemic perspective seems to be a necessary part of defining what risks are wrongful to take; its relevance is not limited to assessing the degree of the actor's culpability. As Moore notes, risks are always 1 or 0 *ex post*. Moreover, one factor that Moore (properly) would include as part of the "expanded" Hand formula is information/calculation costs. These (secondary) costs of continuing to calculate the (primary) costs and benefits that must be considered under the Hand formula sometimes outweigh the benefits of securing greater optimization at the primary level. Moore's point is quite correct, but it reveals a problem: in identifying what an actor should do or permissibly may do, according to the Hand formula criterion of wrongdoing, we also need to examine what efforts an actor should make to determine the facts relevant to whether he or she is negligent.

[9] Moore, 2009d, 185 (citing Restatement (Third) of Torts, § 4, comment k).

[10] At the same time, Moore does concede that the reasonable person formulation might actually support "true divergence" from the Hand formula: it might permit a deontological deviation from the consequentialist calculus, permitting actors to engage in some activities that are not permitted under the calculus and obligating actors to refrain from some activities that are cost-justified under that calculus. Moore, 2009d, 180. This is a welcome concession.

To be sure, the characterization difficulty is less pronounced (or is it simply less transparent?) when negligence pertains only to one of several elements of a moral or legal norm. If the primary norm is "Do not unjustifiably harm V," and if D is accused of negligently harming V, the characterization difficulty is grave. But if the primary norm is "Do not have sexual contact with V unless V consents," then it is natural to characterize as a mere question of culpability the question whether the actor was "negligent" as to the element of V's non-consent. In parallel fashion, it is natural to characterize an actor who is reckless as to non-consent as somewhat more culpable, and a knowing actor as even more culpable.

And yet, even in this context, negligence might be characterized as a criterion of wrongdoing, not as a degree of culpability. Here is how. Suppose A and V consensually kiss on a first date. Then A touches V's genitals. V expresses objection, A withdraws his/her hand, and they resume kissing. Assume that V did not consent to the more intimate touching. Has A acted impermissibly but non-culpably? Or has A acted permissibly?[11]

According to one view, the non-consensual touching of any part of V's body is what is impermissible. According to another, what is impermissible is acting in a way that poses an unjustifiably high risk of a non-consensual touching in light of the other values at stake, where "unjustifiably" takes into account both the significance of those other values (such as spontaneity in romantic encounters and the benefit of mutually desired sexual intimacy), and the risks that those values will not be realized. On the second view, we might conclude that A has not acted impermissibly. After all, one reason for characterizing conduct as permissible (rather than impermissible but non-culpable) is to provide action guidance. And we might conclude that actors seeking physical intimacy should feel free to take very small risks that their conduct of mildly escalating the level of intimacy will be mildly objectionable to the other actor.[12]

This characterization problem has implications for other issues in moral and legal theory, especially for the question of how to analyze reasonable and unreasonable mistakes (about the elements of an offense, or about defenses). Such mistakes are plausibly viewed as just a subset of reasonable and unreasonable conduct (at least when the mistake plays, or should play, a role in the actor's practical reasoning). So the question becomes: if A makes a reasonable mistake in believing that V consents, has he non-culpably committed a wrong, or has he not committed a wrong in the first instance? In one important sense, I believe, he has not committed a wrong at all, for it is often

[11] A third possibility is that A has acted both impermissibly and culpably. However, the example is meant to instantiate a "reasonable" escalation of intimacy in light of the current level of intimacy; the reader can supply an even smaller escalation if this example is not persuasive. (The example is of sexual contact, not sexual intercourse, because greater controversy attends the question whether and when it is culpable for an actor to unilaterally escalate intimacy from sexual touching to sexual intercourse.)

[12] Stephen Schulhofer, in arguing for an "only YES means YES" definition of consent in the context of sexual intercourse, has emphasized the comparative error costs to the initiating party and the other party. If affirmative consent by words or conduct is required, this does impose costs on the initiating party (including the need to ask for more explicit consent, or to wait or forego intercourse), but those costs are outweighed, Schulhofer believes, by the costs to the other person of submitting to sexual intercourse that the person finds objectionable. Stephen J. Schulhofer, *Unwanted Sex: The Culture of Intimidation and the Failure of Law* (Cambridge, MA: Harvard University Press, 1998). I agree that comparative error costs are relevant to the analysis of permissible risks in sexual encounters, but I also believe that in some cases, such as the example in the text, the *ex ante* quantitative and qualitative "costs" or burdens of not proceeding outweigh the burdens of proceeding.

socially desirable for actors to proceed upon reasonable appearances—for police to arrest upon probable cause, for actors to use defensive force when this reasonably appears necessary, and so forth.[13]

Moore's other forays into the negligence jungle are mainly explorations of negligence as culpability, not as wrongdoing. In the 1990 essay, "Choice, Character, and Excuse,"[14] slightly revised for publication as Chapter 13 in the book *Placing Blame*,[15] Moore considers whether a choice or character conception of culpability is able to explain moral responsibility for negligence, and thus to justify criminal liability for negligence. His answer is no. The choice conception does not suffice, because although a negligent actor makes choices, they are not of the right kind: the actor "does not choose to do the kind of complex action forbidden by morality and law (such as killing the man standing behind the target) because his mind was not adverting to that aspect of his action."[16] Moore is basically correct here, though we must be careful not to overstate the extent to which even an advertent actor "chooses" to impose the risk to which he adverts (as I note in this chapter's Conclusion).

Moore believes that the character theorist is also unable to accommodate the culpability of negligence. First, an act of negligence can be isolated, and need not spring from a general tendency to be inadvertent. Second, even a general tendency towards inadvertence and mistakes need not flow from a bad character, such as an indifference to the interests protected by the criminal law. "Such carelessness can be due to awkwardness and stupidity as easily as indifference. And, again, we blame for carelessness irrespective of *why* one is careless."[17] This analysis is largely persuasive, though I also believe that some forms of indifference are a suitable basis for moral blame and criminal liability, as I explore in the Conclusion.

In his original article, Moore concluded from this analysis that negligence might not merit moral blame, and that legal liability for negligence can only be justified on utilitarian grounds. However, by the time of the publication of his 1997 book, *Placing Blame*, he had changed his view, now believing that "morally . . . it seems wrong to say that we are not at least somewhat blameworthy for negligent conduct."[18] The third form of culpability that negligence reflects is, according to Moore, H. L. A. Hart's notion of the culpability of unexercised capacity. Still, Moore believes there is a basic difference between that very modest form of culpability and the more robust form that occurs when an actor knows he is doing a wrongful sort of action and nevertheless chooses to do it.

One important response to Moore's argument here is that only a *subset* of negligence cases are sufficiently morally blameworthy to be fit subjects of criminal punishment—namely, those that reflect, not mere carelessness, but culpable indifference.[19] Suppose

[13] For further discussion of this argument, see Kenneth W. Simons, "Self-Defense: Reasonable Beliefs or Reasonable Self-Control?," 11 *New Criminal Law Review* 51 (2008); R. A. Duff, "Rethinking Justifications," 39 *Tulsa Law Review* 829 (2004); but see Heidi Hurd, "Justification and Excuse, Wrongdoing and Culpability," 74 *Notre Dame Law Review* 1551 (1999), for a contrary view.

[14] 7 *Social Philosophy & Policy* 29 (1990).

[15] Moore, 1997b.

[16] Moore, 1997b, 589.

[17] Moore, 1997b, 590–1.

[18] Moore, 1997b, 591.

[19] For further discussion of this concept, and the promise and perils of employing it as a legal standard, see Kenneth W. Simons, "Does Punishment for 'Culpable Indifference' Simply Punish for 'Bad Character'? Examining the Requisite Connection between Mens Rea and Actus Reus," 6 *Buffalo Criminal Law Review* 219 (2002).

Sam pays no attention whatsoever to whether Victoria consents to his sexual advances, because he is entirely focused on his own pleasure. This reason for unawareness is, under the circumstances, highly culpable, even if it does not flow from a general character flaw, and even though Sam does not choose to proceed with intercourse by consciously disregarding a risk that Victoria does not consent. Now consider the following passage from Moore, in which he is responding to Hart's effort to characterize the choice theory itself as an instance of a capacity theory:

> What makes the intentional or reckless wrongdoer so culpable is not unexercised capacity—although that is necessary—but the way such capacity to avoid evil goes unexercised; *such wrongdoers are not even trying to get it right.* Their capacity goes unexercised because that is what they choose.[20]

This argument proves too little, however. It is indeed persuasive as applied to Sam, an actor who is "not even trying to get it right." By contrast, one plausible *negative* criterion of culpable indifference is good faith: an actor is not culpably indifferent if she *is* "trying to get it right"—if she tries to conform to moral and legal norms and her failure to conform is due only to lack of skill or judgment.[21] Moore is right to emphasize that culpability depends on the *way* in which an actor fails to exercise his capacity to avoid harm, and not merely on the fact that he has failed to exercise his capacity. But a culpably indifferent actor can be distinguished from a simply negligent actor in this respect, because the fault of the former requires more than his mere failure to exercise a capacity.[22]

III. Moore's Current Views on the Culpability of Negligence

Moore's most recent and most detailed analysis of the culpability of negligence is contained in an article he co-authored with Heidi Hurd, "Blaming the Awkward, the Stupid, the Weak, and the Selfish: The Culpability of Negligence." The article is a tour de force, addressing and clarifying an enormous range of conceptual, moral, and legal issues that are relevant to the judgment of whether negligence is an apt basis for moral blame or for legal sanction.

20 Moore, 1997b, 590 (emphasis added).

21 See Simons, "Punishment for 'Culpable Indifference.'"

22 In Chapter 9 of *Placing Blame*, "Prima Facie Moral Culpability," originally published in Moore, 1995b, Moore returns to the topic of negligence, and reiterates his view that its culpability cannot be compared to the culpability of intentional or reckless conduct:

> Culpably inadvertent risk-taking . . . involves a kind of epistemic failure. One who *acts* unreasonably is one who *believes* unreasonably in the sense that an inference about unjustified risk-taking is not drawn when it should be. . . . Culpability as negligence blames us despite our acting rightly in the world as we see it. Although we can be somewhat culpable in not seeing the world more clearly, such culpability pales before that of wrongdoers who choose to do their wrongs in a world they see clearly.
>
> Moore, 1997b, 412.

And he suggests that choice is the appropriate minimal culpability for a criminal law that seeks to achieve retributive justice, while unexercised capacity is an appropriate culpability for a tort law that seeks to achieve corrective justice; this explains why negligence is central in tort law but not criminal law.

As a crude generalization, this is a plausible analysis, though (as Moore recognizes) tort law contains significant elements of strict liability, too. For example, tort law's "reasonable person" test pays very little attention to individual cognitive capacities.

Moore and Hurd begin their wide-ranging article by clarifying that they understand the concept of negligence as some form of unreasonable risk-taking. They prescind from questions about what makes the risk-taking unreasonable. But, they add, they do not presuppose that the balance of risks and benefits that the negligence inquiry often requires is necessarily a utilitarian calculus, and they are open to a non-consequentialist account. This is a very welcome evolution in Moore's views.

The authors plausibly view *criminal* negligence as requiring a "gross" degree of negligence, unlike tort negligence, which simply requires a departure from the standard of reasonable care. They then distinguish recklessness from criminal negligence in two respects. First, a reckless actor must be advertent, while a negligent actor need not be. The authors also emphasize, correctly, that while advertence is necessary for recklessness, it is not sufficient: some instances of advertent negligence do not and should not count as reckless. In my view (but apparently not theirs),[23] recklessness requires not just awareness of a risk of harm, no matter how miniscule, but awareness of a substantial or at least non-trivial risk of harm.[24] This threshold is, I believe, what the Model Penal Code means to require, and also is a normatively appropriate criterion of recklessness, insofar as recklessness warrants more punishment than negligence (or warrants punishment when negligence would be insufficient). If you decide to drive very safely to the store rather than walk two blocks, you are imposing a miniscule additional risk of harm, but even if you offer no justification for your choice, you should not be considered reckless.[25]

Second, the authors assert that a reckless actor must be "grossly, grossly" negligent, and not, as in the case of the criminally negligent actor, merely grossly negligent. I disagree with this assertion as a descriptive matter; the law does not actually draw the distinction in this manner.[26] Moreover, it is highly doubtful that such a "gross, gross" deviation requirement for reckless liability would be a sensible legal standard. As applied, such a requirement would often make proof of recklessness unduly difficult. If an actor subjectively believes there is only a small risk that the victim of his sexual advances is not consenting, but fails to communicate with the victim to be sure that she consents, a jury might plausibly find gross but not "gross, gross" negligence, yet the conduct seems egregious enough to justify punishing for recklessness rather than negligence.

Furthermore, such a requirement would place extraordinary demands on the judge and, especially, the jury. It is challenging enough to explain the difference between

[23] The authors at one point assert that an actor who believes the risk is small is not reckless because he does not grossly, grossly depart from reasonable care. At another point, however, they say that awareness of the substantiality of risk is not a requirement of recklessness.

[24] See Kenneth W. Simons, "Should the Model Penal Code's Mens Rea Provisions Be Amended?," 1 *Ohio State Journal of Criminal Law* 179 (2003).

[25] How that threshold ("substantial" or "non-trivial") should be defined is, to be sure, a difficult question.

[26] See Simons, "When is Negligent Inadvertence Culpable," 111. To be sure, the Model Penal Code treats reckless actors as categorically more culpable than negligent actors. But that is because they, unlike negligent actors, knowingly endanger others, not because their acts of endangerment are necessarily a greater deviation from reasonable care. Compare Delbert, who speeds through an intersection, knowingly creating a 1 in 1,000 risk of injuring a pedestrian; with Elbert, a beginning driver who unknowingly creates a 1 in 3 risk of injuring another driver on the highway because he does not check his mirrors before changing lanes. Given the level and type of risk that Delbert creates, he departs less from a standard of reasonable care than Elbert. But the Code will treat Delbert as reckless and Elbert as negligent.

ordinary civil negligence and "gross" criminal negligence. Explaining the difference between "gross" and "gross, gross" negligence would be even more daunting. The authors, unfortunately, offer little guidance on this score. They refer several times to Judge Magruder's distinction between being a "fool" (ordinary negligence) and a "damned fool" (gross negligence), and they suggest that recklessness requires that one be a "damned damned fool" or (in Magruder's phrase) a "God-damned fool." Lord help us if this language finds its way into a jury instruction.[27]

Even if some negligence is advertent, the question remains: can criminal punishment for inadvertent negligence be justified? The authors pay special attention to the details of H. L. A. Hart's affirmative answer. Hart claimed that we are culpable, not just for our choices, but for our unexercised individual capacities. The authors pose several challenging and central questions about this account. What does it mean to have the capacity to advert to a risk? Do people actually have that capacity? And, finally, if they do have such a capacity but fail to exercise it, are they morally culpable in such a way and degree as to deserve criminal punishment?

In their thorough responses to these questions, the authors clarify a range of critical conceptual and normative issues. Thus, they helpfully identify the many features of "advertence" that require clarification, including the requisite object of the belief, the requisite accuracy and specificity of the actor's typing of the risk, the requisite vividness of the phenomenological experience (if any is indeed required), and the relevance of cognitive dissonance, wishful thinking, and self-deception. They observe, plausibly, that many of these issues are questions of degree. They conclude, less persuasively, that we can therefore throw many of these scalar questions into the hopper with other aspects of the recklessness criterion: thus, they claim, an especially unjustifiable risk might counterbalance an especially dim awareness so that we can still legitimately consider the actor to be reckless. This is not a recipe for a determinate rule to guide actors or legal decision-makers. And such a sliding-scale approach demands a deeper justification. If recklessness is more culpable because it demonstrates a deliberate and impermissible trade-off—a definite choice to act in the face of a risk—then it seems that some minimal threshold of awareness should be established, a threshold that "dim" would fall short of. Moreover, the view that recklessness is just one point on a sliding scale that balances numerous culpability factors is problematic. Such a conception of culpability is quite foreign to criminal law grading distinctions and seems inconsistent with widespread intuitions.[28]

Turning to the question of the meaning of "capacity," the authors point out that in the present context, the contra-causal sense of capacity—whether the actor "could" have done otherwise than he did in light of sufficient antecedent causes of his behavior—is

[27] Moreover, the enormous trouble that courts have encountered making sense of "depraved heart" or "extreme indifference" murder is a worrisome precedent. Indeed, if recklessness requires a "gross, gross" departure from reasonable care, then presumably the more culpable state of mind of "extreme indifference" would require an even more extreme departure. Should judges instruct the jury, in extreme indifference murder cases, that they must find that the actor's conduct was a "gross, gross, gross" departure from proper behavior?

[28] But see Larry Alexander and Kim Ferzan, *Crime and Culpability: A Theory of Criminal Law* (Cambridge: Cambridge University Press, 2009). For criticism, see Kenneth W. Simons, "Book Review: Retributivism Refined—Or Run Amok?," 77 *University of Chicago Law Review* 551 (2010).

not the relevant notion. And they correctly note that capacity statements are at least implicitly conditional, translatable into "would (or could) have A'ed if C." The capacity question for negligent inadvertence, they claim, is whether the actor could have adverted to a risk "if condition X," where X is a plausible desert basis, just as the capacity question for intentional and reckless wrongs is whether the actor could have acted differently if he had chosen differently.[29]

So far, so good. But then the authors flatly assert: "[T]here can be no culpability of unexercised capacity." If negligent inadvertence is culpable, they argue, it is because of the underlying source, X, of the incapacity, which directly grounds the culpability of negligence. "[T]he 'capacity to advert if X' judgment" is "a mere implication of the independent moral significance of X.... Until X is specified, judgments of unexercised capacity lack sense; once it is specified, judgments of unexercised capacity have no justificatory work left to do."[30]

The authors seem to be claiming that the capacity judgment is irrelevant to culpability. That claim is unconvincing. They are, of course, correct that the mere failure to exercise a capacity to advert is not always culpable. Culpability requires something more, such as (in my words, not theirs) an "unreasonable" failure, or a failure to act with the concern fairly to be expected of a member of the community.[31] But the "something more" does not by itself justify blame or punishment for inadvertent negligence. Rather, only the combination of that extra something and the *capacity* to have adverted (and to have acted differently) can justify negligence liability.[32] A failure to advert can only matter, morally or legally, if the actor ought to have adverted. And "ought" (the last time I checked) implies "can"—here, a capacity to have adverted and then to have acted differently. To be sure, we must examine the deeper explanations for that failure to advert if we wish to offer a full account of negligence liability. But capacity to advert is a crucial component of the analysis.

Addressing the possible culpable sources of inadvertence, the authors helpfully identify four categories, each of which is a distinct type of practical reasoning defect. These are flaws in motor control (e.g., clumsiness), in cognition (e.g., stupidity or short attention span), in conation (e.g., weakness of will), and in motivation (e.g., character flaws such as selfishness or indifference). Of these, the most clearly blameworthy are the motivational flaws, so the authors concentrate on these.

The authors raise a number of objections to premising criminal punishment for inadvertent negligence on underlying vices such as jealousy, selfishness, or arrogance. One is our inability to rank these vices in any reliable way. Sometimes, they claim,

[29] The authors aptly criticize Alexander and Ferzan for conflating these inquiries. Alexander and Ferzan seem to claim that we can advert to a risk only if we can choose to advert to the risk, yet actors only rarely choose to advert to a risk. Moore and Hurd are right to respond that this begs the question of when advertence is culpable, because the capacity to advert to risk might be subject to specifiable and defensible conditions other than choice.

[30] Moore and Hurd, 2011d, 164.

[31] The authors appear to criticize Hart for asserting that culpability depends merely on unexercised capacity, but this criticism is unfounded; Hart does recognize that the ultimate criterion of negligence considers whether the failure to exercise that capacity is unreasonable.

[32] Recall Hart's point that certain gross incapacities—of children or the insane—negate responsibility, even for negligence. H. L. A. Hart, *Punishment and Responsibility*, 2nd edn. (Oxford: Oxford University Press, 2008).

inadvertence caused by jealousy is worse than inadvertence caused by selfishness, but sometimes the contrary is true.

This objection is overstated.[33] First, they give no concrete examples in which the relative "viciousness" of two vices such as jealousy and selfishness differs. Perhaps, in any real-world example in which our relative evaluation of two vices seems to change, other factors actually change and explain the apparently inconsistent evaluation.[34] Second, given the limited occasions on which criminal law does, or at least should, impose liability for negligent inadvertence, fine gradations between different vices need not be made. Rather, we only need to be confident that the legal decision-maker is imposing criminal liability on actors who have exceeded some appropriate threshold level of culpability (whether due to jealousy or selfishness or indifference or some other culpable trait) in light of other relevant features of his conduct (such as the degree of risk that he is imposing and the extent of his awareness of the surrounding circumstances). Third, the authors' objection, if valid, would similarly doom our ability to employ recklessness as a culpability criterion. Recklessness requires, in addition to advertence, a gross deviation from a standard of reasonable or law-abiding conduct, in light of the "unjustifiability" and "substantiality" of the risk. Yet the authors raise no similar objection to recklessness liability.

Consider, by comparison, how negligence operates within the Model Penal Code's homicide structure. Negligent homicide is the least culpable category of homicide, reckless manslaughter is the intermediate category, and murder (which requires purpose, knowledge, or extreme indifference) is the most culpable category. Placing all negligent homicide cases in the same grading category does not produce serious problems of inconsistency. The overall standard might be as specified in the Model Penal Code (requiring gross deviation from a reasonable standard of care in light of the unjustifiable and substantial risks), or it might also include more explicit language identifying the relevance of culpable reasons for inadvertence, such as "inadvertent because of a seriously culpable desire or emotion."[35] Though imprecise, these standards are no more vague than "unjustifiable" in definitions of negligence and recklessness.

The authors express another worry: an analysis of negligence based on character or motivational flaws cannot explain why wrongful *action* is required. "The theorist who takes inadvertence to be blameworthy when and because it manifests poor character

[33] The authors also worry about character theories insofar as one person's vice might be another's virtue. Although this is a valid concern in some contexts in which the state is enforcing a particular view of virtue and vice, here it has little purchase, because reasonable and significant disagreements only rarely occur with respect to whether specific vices are relevant to conduct that creates serious risks of harm to others. "I was so hungry that I took my eyes off the road for a few seconds to grab more fries"; most will agree that this is blameworthy, even if, as a general matter, we might be uncertain whether or to what extent gluttony is a vice or is blameworthy.

[34] For example, suppose A loses control of his car and injures passenger B because B had just informed A that B is sleeping with someone A desperately wishes to date, while C loses control of his car and injures D because C is selfishly preoccupied with combing his hair over his bald spot. A seems less culpable for losing control than C, but not because jealousy is always a less culpable reason for posing a risk than selfishness; rather, it is because reacting jealously and emotionally when suddenly confronted with evidence that triggers that reaction is less culpable than choosing to groom oneself while driving.

I do agree with the authors that, in principle, it is possible that a moral factor that has a particular valence in one situation has a different or even opposite valence in another. See Jonathan Dancy, *Ethics Without Principles* (Oxford: Clarendon Press, 2004).

[35] Simons, "Punishment for 'Culpable Indifference.'"

has to have an argument for why poor character is not itself sufficient for punishment if it is confidently known." This worry is misplaced. Yes, a supporter of negligence liability does need an argument for an act requirement, but so does a supporter of liability for reckless and intentional wrongs. Why not impose liability simply for harboring a reckless or intentional state of mind, even if it does not result in wrongful action? Respect for autonomy, concern about excessive state power, and other values explain why it is not justifiable to punish someone who has decided to kill but has taken no steps yet to effectuate that desire. Suppose Michael gets out of bed, planning to go for a drive, and he forgets that his car's brakes are not in working order. If he has not left his bedroom when apprehended by the ever-vigilant police, he, too, should be shielded from criminal liability.[36]

The authors then raise a more fundamental concern: why, in a character theory, is inadvertence required? "If inadvertence is blameworthy when and because it is the product of unfortunate character, it would seem that inadvertence is morally irrelevant."[37] Again, however, this ignores the relevant context. Self-absorption, for example, is sometimes but not always a vice or a culpable trait. We should be grateful that Matisse, Prokofiev, Coltrane, and Sontag were self-absorbed. But an actor is indeed culpable if, while driving in traffic, he is selfishly preoccupied with finding the best song on his car radio for five seconds while he pays no attention to the risks he is creating. When a particular character trait foreseeably increases the risk that the actor will be unaware of serious risks of harm, one might be culpable for acting in accordance with that trait under those circumstances. The authors, by eliminating the actor's inadvertence and risk-creation from their analysis of negligence culpability, ignore much of what is morally salient in the situation.

After persuasively rejecting the "tracing" strategy,[38] the authors turn to what they call "free-standing" instances of negligence that is, those that do not derive from the four categories of defects in practical reasoning. An example is a loving parent who forgets a young child in a car, causing the child's death by suffocation. They plausibly argue that the parent's mistake need not flow from a character flaw or a flaw in practical reasoning. Yet many would blame her for negligence.

What could account for such blame? One possibility they mention, here and in other "free-standing" negligence cases, is that the parent knowingly failed to obey a sensible and well-known action-guiding rule. Perhaps it is that rule-violation that explains our judgment of blame. The authors argue that we can indeed blame a parent for knowingly violating the rule against leaving a young child unattended in a car or in the bath, and that the culpability involved in such a rule-violation is, at least sometimes, a good enough

[36] To be sure, we should take this worry more seriously when the actor has (albeit unknowingly) taken substantial steps towards causing the relevant harm or wrong. If Michael is actually driving the car with bad brakes, should he be guilty of attempted negligent homicide? This raises distinct concerns, however. And we might address these concerns by limiting attempt liability to purposeful and knowing (and perhaps reckless) risk-creation, notwithstanding strong arguments in favor of attempt liability for actors who proceed to the very last act of risk-creation, whether the actor was purposeful, knowing, reckless, or negligent.

[37] Moore and Hurd, 2011d, 175.

[38] In an illuminating analysis, the authors address the "tracing" strategy in some detail, explicating the different senses in which inadvertence can arguably be traced to a prior culpable act, and advancing some telling objections to each.

substitute for the culpability of inadvertent negligence. Their argument for this conclusion is complex and cogent, but in two respects problematic.

First, the authors claim that the rules in question cannot be understood as deontological prohibitions, because the rules are not categorical and are sometimes subject to consequentialist overrides; thus, the rules must be interpreted as epistemic rules of thumb that give useful guidance for conforming with cost–benefit consequentialist principles. This claim is dubious in two ways. Deontological principles need not be categorical. And, even in the particular context of rules for permissible risks, the principles justifying the proper trade-off of benefits and disadvantages of precautions against risk need not be entirely consequentialist in structure and content (just as the defenses of self-defense and necessity need not be consequentialist).[39]

Second, consider their qualified endorsement of what they aptly call the substitution principle:

> One can . . . use [an actor's] deliberate rule violation as a 'substitute' for a finding that she subjectively appreciated the risks that then materialized, for the one has a 'closeness' to the other that makes such a substitution morally inoffensive. Thus the actor who knowingly violates the rule against pointing a gun at another almost knows that he is risking that other; the parent who knowingly violates the rule against leaving the child in the bathtub cannot claim inadvertence to the possibility of his death . . .[40]

The authors do not confront the far-reaching implications of employing a substitution principle to "approximate" fault in this manner. An armed robber accidentally drops a loaded gun that discharges and kills a confederate. Why doesn't the robber's knowing violation of the rule against armed robbery "substitute" for the intent to kill otherwise required for murder? Although I am sympathetic to a very narrow version of the principle,[41] it is surprising that the authors endorse it without much qualification.

In the end, however, the authors conclude that the intuition behind punishing the parent of the child who suffocates cannot be explained by this rule-violation argument, since there is no known safety rule that the parent violated. I am not so sure. Perhaps she violated a rule requiring parents of young children always to check the back seat of their automobile before locking the car. On the other hand, such a rule is not widely known and followed. And in other cases they mention, such as inadvertently leaving a pot on the stove to boil over (resulting, say, in burns to a child), this is even more clearly true, yet the actor clearly seems negligent. So the authors are indeed justified in concluding that some negligent inadvertence cases in which the actor intuitively seems culpable cannot easily be explained. (One partial solution that the authors do not fully explore is the demand for a *gross* deviation from reasonable care for criminal negligence liability. Some conduct that intuitively qualifies as negligent does not so clearly qualify as grossly negligent; leaving the pot on the stove that boils over is an example.)

Despite the relentlessly skeptical tone of most of the paper, the authors conclude by listing eight categories in which criminal liability for negligence is sometimes

39 See Kenneth W. Simons, "Deontology, Negligence, Tort, and Crime," 76 *Boston University Law Review* 273 (1996).

40 Moore and Hurd, 2011d, 191.

41 See Kenneth W. Simons, "Is Strict Criminal Liability in the Grading of Offences Consistent with Retributive Desert?," 32 *Oxford Journal of Legal Studies* 445 (2012).

justifiable.[42] They honestly admit that the eight types are a hodge-podge: "[N]egligence is not a single continent with a unified nature. It is more like an archipelago of islands, each with its own distinct nature."[43] This is quite a concession from two decidedly orderly and systematic thinkers. I feel their pain. But I think they are quite right about the pluralistic nature of negligence liability. Indeed, one could take the point much further; other types of culpability, especially recklessness, but also knowledge and purpose, are also plausibly viewed as pluralistic.[44]

IV. Conclusion

Negligence is indeed a surprisingly complex and pluralist concept. As suggested earlier, it would be very fruitful for scholars to more fully explore two issues that it raises. First, to what extent is negligence a matter of wrongdoing, and to what extent a matter of culpability? How do these two understandings of negligence relate to one another?[45]

Second, the subcategory of negligence cases involving "culpable indifference" deserves special attention. Culpable indifference is an unusually protean concept. Some treat it essentially as a term of art for whatever forms of culpability our moral theory or legal doctrine recognizes.[46] So understood, it does not help in the task of determining when negligence is sufficient for legal liability. But others treat it as a distinctive form or type of culpability, distinguishable both from intentional wrongdoing and from acting

[42] The eight categories are as follows:

(1) The actor possessed full awareness of the risk created by his conduct, but the imbalance of detriment to benefit is not so great as to make his risk-taking reckless.
(2) The actor was less than fully aware of the risk created by his conduct: he possessed a dim awareness, an inkling, or a mere suspicion that his conduct might create peril.
(3) The actor possessed a dispositional awareness of the risk created by his conduct, but had no phenomenological awareness of that risk.
(4) The actor possessed either phenomenological or dispositional awareness of general types of risk associated with his conduct, of which the risk taken by him on the particular occasion was an instance (although he failed to see it as such).
(5) The actor's inadvertence was caused by flaws in his character against which he took no precautions.
(6) The actor's inadvertence was caused by physical or psychological defects that are not flaws of character, but against which precautions could have been, but were not, taken.
(7) The actor adverted at some earlier time to risks that were created by later behavior.
(8) The actor may have deliberately violated a known mini-maxim, the spirit of which is to protect against the risks his ensuing conduct created.

Moore and Hurd, 2011d, 192–4.

[43] Moore and Hurd, 2011d, 192.

[44] See Kenneth W. Simons, "Rethinking Mental States," 72 *Boston University Law Review* 463 (1992); Simons, "Punishment for 'Culpable Indifference.'"

[45] See Kenneth W. Simons, "Dimensions of Negligence in Criminal and Tort Law," 3 *Theoretical Inquiries in Law* 283 (2002) (distinguishing between the unreasonably risky conduct conception of negligence, which might be understood as a wrongfulness conception, and cognitive negligence, which is a culpability conception; and noting the function of negligence as a secondary legal norm parasitic on a primary legal norm).

Moore incorrectly attributes to me the view that negligence is a conduct requirement, not a mental state requirement. Moore, 1997b, 411. My actual view is that some conceptions of negligence emphasize unreasonable conduct more than unreasonable beliefs or attitudes; but that even the unreasonable conduct conception ordinarily employs the idea of epistemic risk. See Simons, "Rethinking Mental States"; Simons, "Dimensions."

[46] This seems to be the view espoused in Alexander and Ferzan, *Crime and Culpability*.

recklessly, that is, acting with knowledge of the risks or the other relevant features of one's conduct.[47] A more careful analysis of the concept would facilitate analysis of moral and criminal culpability generally, and negligence culpability in particular.

Let me conclude with some observations about the distinction between negligence and recklessness. As Moore and Hurd recognize in their recent article, the contrast between culpability for inadvertent negligence and culpability for recklessness is much blurrier than usually supposed. There are many reasons for this. I will mention two.

First, characterizing the reckless actor as "choosing" to impose a risk is a form of rhetorical embellishment, because the characterization is usually inaccurate. Typically, such an actor, although aware of a risk of harm, proceeds despite that risk, not because of it. A reckless driver prefers speeding to slowing down and reducing the risks of injury to others. A reckless rapist prefers his own immediate pleasure to pausing and ensuring that he has the victim's consent. On rare occasions, to be sure, such an actor affirmatively desires to endanger another, as when two actors dare each other to a drag race in a busy parking lot rather than an empty one because they value the excitement of posing a risk to others, or when two actors play Russian roulette with a loaded gun. But ordinarily, the risk to others is not the actor's objective. Granted, every reckless actor "chooses" (in a weak sense of the term) to endanger the other when he makes a choice to act despite *knowing* that there is a risk to the other. However, this is also true of the negligent actor: he "chooses" to endanger another in precisely this same (weak) sense when he makes a choice to proceed with his conduct despite not paying sufficient attention to whether he is posing a risk to the other. The point is nicely illustrated by cases in which the negligent actor chooses specifically *not* to pay attention to a risk. If, on a dare, the actor decides to drive blindfolded for 100 yards at night on an apparently deserted stretch of road, or if a sexually aggressive actor decides to close his or her eyes and pay no attention to whether the victim consents, each actor has made a choice that may be just as culpable as if he or she had been aware of a significant risk of causing harm.[48] In short, although the reckless actor is sometimes indeed more culpable than the negligent actor, this is not because the first has "chosen" to endanger the other while the second has not, in either the robust or the weak sense of choice.

Second, the conduct of a reckless actor is properly viewed as culpable (and often more culpable than the conduct of a negligent actor) even though the reckless actor almost never is aware of, much less consciously chooses, *all* of the morally and legally relevant features of his act. Thus, most commentators agree that the actor need not be aware of the illegality, or perhaps even the immorality, of his act, in order to deserve blame and punishment; nor must he believe that the risk he is running is unjustifiable. And conversely, the culpability of so-called "inadvertent" risk-creation depends in significant part on both the conscious choices that the actor made and the actual beliefs

[47] See, e.g., R. A. Duff, *Intention, Agency and Criminal Liability* (Oxford: Blackwell, 1990); Simons, "Punishment for 'Culpable Indifference.'"

[48] Suppose the blindfolded actor believes there is only a one in a million risk she will cause injury, but also realizes that the blindfold reduces her ability to perceive such a risk from 95% to zero. Compare a speeding but not blindfolded actor who believes there is a one in 100,000 risk that her speeding will cause injury. It would be plausible to treat the two actors as roughly equal in culpability. And clearly both actors "choose" in a similar (weak) sense to endanger others. (Of course, in many actual scenarios with greater traffic or population density, the blindfolded actor will actually be aware of a significant risk of injury.)

that he embraced. A driver is culpable for taking his eyes of the road for several seconds only if he is knowingly driving in traffic; a babysitter is culpable for not attending to the baby only if she knows at the relevant time that she is the sole or primary caregiver; and so forth. If the actor is so detached from reality that he possesses no beliefs whatsoever about the circumstances that would put a reasonable person on notice of a risk, then he cannot be culpably negligent.

These observations do not imply that the distinction between culpable inadvertence and culpable advertence is meaningless or pointless. But they do suggest that the distinction is one of degree, not kind, and that it depends crucially on context. Accordingly, future analysis of the culpability of negligence might profitably focus more on the trees, and less on the forest.

11

Putting (and Keeping) Proximate Cause in its Place

*John Oberdiek**

I. Introduction

Before one can recover for an injury sounding in negligence, one must establish that the defendant more likely than not proximately caused the injury. That the positive law of negligence imposes this requirement is beyond controversy. What is more controversial is whether the requirement is conceptually and morally defensible. Michael Moore, singly as well as in tandem with Heidi Hurd, powerfully argues that it is neither. Specifically, Moore contends that the harm-within-the-risk test of proximate causation, despite its venerable history in tort law and reaffirmation in the latest *Restatement*,[1] is "incoherent" and "morally undesirable."[2] It is bad enough, in Moore's view, that negligence law bifurcates its causal inquiry, distinguishing as it does the question of actual causation from that of proximate causation, rather than pursuing a unified naturalistic inquiry into the substantiality of causal contribution. What is worse is that tort law can't even get its own misguided causal inquiry half-right.

I do not share Moore's jaundiced view of the harm-within-the-risk test of proximate cause—what I will call the "risk rule" for short. I begin by questioning his understanding of the risk rule as it figures in tort law, and go on to argue that neither his conceptual nor his moral criticism of the risk rule is decisive. In the course of rebutting Moore's criticisms, I outline what I take to be the most compelling account of the risk rule in the law of torts. What emerges is a conception of proximate cause that is thoroughly moralized. Of course moral premises must be invoked to defend the risk rule's moral merit, but, I argue, they must also be invoked to defend its conceptual coherence. In my view, the risk rule is both morally and conceptually sound.

* I have been a lucky beneficiary of Michael Moore's generosity for twenty years now. Between entertaining the questions that I mailed him (!) about legal interpretation as a college junior studying abroad, welcoming me into the JD/PhD program that he helped create, convincing a law school to hire me before I even went on the market, hosting me at roundtables from Drum Moir to Timberline Lodge and countless places in between, and entrusting a journal to me—to say nothing of all the encouragement he provided and confidence he instilled—I am very deep in Michael's debt. Luckier for me still, his generosity lies also in the fact that he keeps no ledger. This chapter is a small token of appreciation for all that Michael has done for me—though as the chapter shows, he never could set me straight—and I am grateful to Kim Ferzan and Stephen Morse for inviting me to write it.

[1] Restatement (Third) of Torts: Liability for Physical and Emotional Harm.

[2] Moore, 2009d, ix.

II. The Risk Rule in the Tort of Negligence

Before turning to Moore's attack on the risk rule, it is important to clarify the risk rule itself, as well as Moore's understanding of it. As a threshold matter, it is worth observing that Moore assumes that the risk rule is the same in both tort law and criminal law and indeed plays the same role in each domain, *mutatis mutandis*. His is an all-purpose, all-encompassing analysis. His criticisms are similarly generalized. But in what follows, I focus only on tort law, and on the tort of negligence in particular, which is where tort law employs the risk rule most explicitly. A key reason why my ambitious are lower than Moore's, or at any rate narrower, is that I doubt that his initial assumption is safe. Tort law and criminal law are different enough that it would seem highly unlikely that an all-purpose assessment of the risk rule could be sound. And I think that Moore's analysis of the risk rule justifies my caution, as I will explain below. In any case, in what follows I focus exclusively on the risk rule's incarnation in the tort of negligence.

To make out the prima facie case of negligence, it is necessary for the plaintiff to establish by a preponderance of the evidence each of the tort's constituent elements: injury, duty, breach, and actual and proximate cause. But dividing the tort of negligence into these constituent elements, which are individually necessary and jointly sufficient for establishing prima facie liability, has the potential to mislead. For it suggests that each individual element demands an independent and free-standing analysis. That is most clearly false with respect to proximate cause.

It is impossible to conceptualize proximate cause generally, and the risk rule specifically, without understanding the relationship between the breach and injury elements in the prima facie case. This is because proximate cause is an "alignment concept."[3] To assess proximate cause is to assess the alignment between the defendant's breach and the plaintiff's injury. In querying proximate cause, one asks: Did the defendant's breach (actually) cause the plaintiff's injury in the right way? The risk rule offers the following answer: If the injury was one of the harms whose likelihood made the careless conduct careless, then the injury was a harm within the risk, and the careless conduct constitutes a proximate cause of the injury. Moore would seem to share this understanding of the risk rule, aptly posing the relevant question, "Was the harm that happened to this plaintiff within the risk that made it negligent for the defendant to have acted as he did?"[4]

So far, so good. Moore recognizes that proximate cause is not a free-standing concept in that the risk rule conception of proximate cause cannot be analyzed in isolation from the duty and breach elements of the tort of negligence. What is troubling, though, is that he also thinks this inquiry revolves around culpability. He maintains that "[p]roximate-cause tests . . . should serve the function of grading offenders between the more blameworthy causers of harm, and the less blameworthy riskers . . . of such harm," and that the risk rule in particular "connects a defendant's culpability to particular

[3] John Goldberg, Anthony Sebok, and Benjamin Zipursky, *Tort Law: Responsibilities and Redress*, 3rd edn. (New York: WoltersKluwer, 2012), 289.

[4] Moore, 2009d, 157.

harms."[5] A distinctive feature of the risk rule, according to Moore, is that it tracks the "desert-determiner" of *mens rea*.[6] This is fundamentally misguided. It is also clear evidence that Moore's ambition in providing an all-purpose analysis of the risk rule is misconceived. For although there is no question that culpability is central to criminal law, it plays no role in the tort of negligence.

Moore may well be right that assessing *mens rea* introduces what he calls a "fit problem," in which the defendant's mental state must closely "fit" whatever consequence has occurred.[7] It is also true that the fit problem resembles the risk rule's test of alignment between the breach and injury elements in the prima facie case of negligence. But Moore is nevertheless mistaken when he holds both that "the essential claim behind the harm-within-the-risk test is that 'legal cause' is the label lawyers should put on a problem of culpability, the problem I call the fit problem," and that advocates of the risk rule are committed to treating the risk rule as a *mens rea* doctrine.[8] These are puzzling claims. In tort law, the risk rule does not revolve around mental states, culpability, or desert at all. The risk rule is not in the business of, as Moore puts it, "grading by culpable mental states."[9] How *could* it be? Moore admits that it is mental states that must face the fit problem and concedes that negligence is not a mental state, such that negligence does not—indeed cannot—have a fit problem.[10] Yet Moore seems to think that this undermines the risk rule, rather than his analysis of it. Damning by faint praise, he says, "[t]he harm-within-the-risk test asks a good question, but it asks it in the wrong place."[11] Moore's criticism misses the mark. The tort of negligence employs the risk rule to identify not *culpability* but *responsibility*.

It is a platitude of tort law, and of the tort of negligence in particular, that one's liability can far outstrip one's culpability. Tort law casebooks are full of cases where a mere lapse in a defendant's attention has disastrous results for the plaintiff, such that the defendant is now duty-bound to compensate the plaintiff for the full extent of his or her injuries. The same casebooks are also replete with cases where a defendant does not accidentally injure another but does so intentionally, and yet the defendant's remedial duty to the plaintiff is identical.[12] The intentional tortfeasor's liability thus matches the negligent tortfeasor's, other things being equal, even though intentional harming is far more culpable than careless harming. This is possible because negligence liability, and tort liability generally, tracks a defendant's responsibility, not culpability.

It is perfectly understandable why criminal law's regime of punishment should be (perhaps even exclusively) sensitive to a defendant's culpability. But this just underscores how profoundly different criminal law is from tort law. Tort law and criminal law prohibit much of the same conduct, to be sure, imposing similar primary obligations. But each imposes entirely different secondary obligations, should the primary obligations be violated: a compensatory damages award, which is the form of

[5] Moore, 2009d, 97–8. [6] Moore, 2009d, 98. [7] Moore, 2009d, 100.

[8] Moore, 2009d, 100 ("Proponents of this test urge that legal cause, properly understood, is really a *mens rea* doctrine, not a doctrine of causation at all.")

[9] Moore, 2009d, 100.

[10] Moore, 2009d, 102 n. 69 ("With respect to negligence, which is not a mental state, I shall urge . . . that we should not ask the fit question at all, anywhere.").

[11] Moore, 2009d, 102.

[12] It is at least typically identical. "Typically," because if intentional wrongdoing is also willful and wanton, it can ground punitive damages in addition to compensatory damages.

redress that tort law typically offers, is fundamentally unlike the punishment that criminal law doles out. Driving this difference is the fact that tort liability is keyed to facts about plaintiffs—namely their injuries—whereas criminal punishment is keyed to facts about defendants—namely their culpability.[13] Tort law's focus on the injuries suffered by plaintiffs explains why tort law revolves around responsibility, not culpability: tort law enables plaintiffs to shift losses imposed on them by tortious conduct to those defendants responsible for them. Thus, when Moore claims that the risk rule is in the business of testing for "both moral blameworthiness and duties to compensate," it is he who is only half-right.[14]

Moore seems to go wrong in his analysis of the risk rule because he identifies conduct constituting breach of duty with conduct that is culpable. This identification is clearest when Moore states that the risk rule "connects a defendant's culpability to particular harms."[15] The risk rule, however, connects a defendant's *breach* to particular harms, aligning the breach and injury elements in the prima facie case of negligence. Breaches of duty are not necessarily culpable, which is why the alignment between the breach and injury elements is not identical to Moore's so-called fit problem. One breaches one's duty of care simply by failing to conduct oneself as a reasonable person would under the circumstances—it need not involve any particular *mens rea*. When one negligently injures another, one's carelessness does not consist in a state of mind, it consists only in one's faulty conduct. Fault does not require a guilty mind. Perhaps there is something to be said for demanding that negligence liability answer to blameworthiness more than it does,[16] but there is nothing to be said for collapsing the responsibility that negligence liability tracks into culpability.

That Moore apparently disagrees is likely a consequence of his view that the standard conception of the breach element in the prima facie case of negligence is defective. On the standard conception, again, one breaches one's duty of care if and only if one's conduct is not reasonable, that is, if one fails to act as a reasonable person would act in the circumstances. Moore's conceptual and moral criticisms of the risk rule extend to the reasonable person standard at the heart of the tort of negligence. So, the importance to the risk rule that Moore assigns to culpability perhaps owes to a belief that some substitute for the reasonable person standard is needed. To get to the bottom of Moore's understanding of the risk rule, then, it is necessary to explore his conceptual and moral arguments against it.

[13] Of course, facts about the defendant's action also matter to tort liability, just as facts about the victim's injury also matter to criminal punishment: negligence defendants are only liable if they have acted unreasonably, while a punishment's severity is greater if the defendant actually injured someone.

[14] Moore, 2009d, 98. [15] Moore, 2009d, 98.

[16] Tony Honoré, for example, argues that corrective justice should be tempered by retributive justice: "even when fault is genuinely a condition of tort liability . . . the compensation payable may be disproportionate to what is often a minor fault. To avoid this disproportion, the retributive principle insists that defendants should not be exposed to disproportionately heavy losses. If the claims of corrective justice are to be morally viable, ways must therefore be found of spreading such losses." Tony Honoré, "The Morality of Tort Law: Questions and Answers," in Aileen Kavanagh and John Oberdiek (eds.), *Arguing About Law* (New York: Routledge, 2009), 539.

III. On the Conceptual Coherence and Moral Justification of the Risk Rule

Moore first charges that the risk rule suffers from fatal conceptual problems. He identifies two of these, which he respectively calls the "all-inclusiveness problem" and the "description problem."[17] Moore introduces these problems by exploring what he calls the "expanded Hand formula for negligence."[18] The Hand formula, famously articulated by Judge Hand in *United States v. Carroll Towing*,[19] treats carelessness as a function of three variables: the burden of taking precautions adequate to prevent some harm or loss (B); the probability that some loss will eventuate should no precautions be taken (P); and the magnitude of that loss (L). According to Hand, as everyone knows, if the precautionary burden (B) is less than the product of the probability (P) and magnitude (L) of the loss, then failing to take the requisite precautions is careless (B<PL). If B exceeds PL (B>PL), on the other hand, it is not careless to forgo the precautions that would have prevented the loss. The problem with the Hand formula, by Moore's lights, is that it vastly oversimplifies the necessary calculus, even on its own terms. Moore maintains that a suitably amended Hand formula "requires one to weight the total harms risked versus the total benefits risked if a given precaution is not taken, considered for each level of each kind of precautionary action possible, for all levels and kinds of activities in which the defendant might be engaged."[20] These emendations may well help the Hand formula stay truer to its aspirations, but they also stimulate the two conceptual problems that Moore thinks plague the risk rule.

The open-ended expansiveness of Moore's more detailed Hand formula brings the all-inclusiveness problem to the fore because "once one appreciates that *all* risks created by a defendant count in an assessment of his negligence, it would appear that *any* and *all* harms that materialize from the defendant's conduct are within the category of risks that make such conduct negligent."[21] And it raises the description problem, "for how one describes the risk(s) that make(s) the defendant's conduct negligent does all the work to place the harm(s) in question either within or outside the stated risk(s)."[22] Each of these problems is a significant challenge to the conceptual coherence of the risk rule.

The all-inclusiveness problem holds that the risk rule fails to rule out any harms because *all* harms are within the risk that makes a defendant's conduct careless.[23] In Moore's words, "[i]f a harm materializes from a defendant's conduct, then necessarily there was some risk of it so doing, and that risk was on the list of risks created by the defendant's conduct, the cumulative total of which make the defendant's conduct unjustified."[24] If all harms are within the risk, however, then any harm due to a defendant's carelessness is within the risk that makes the defendant's careless conduct careless, which in turn entails that the risk rule is "impotent," for it is no independent

17 Moore, 2009d, 185.

18 Moore, 2009d, 181.

19 159 F. 2d 169 (2d Cir. 1947).

20 Moore, 2009d, 185.

21 Moore, 2009d, 185.

22 Moore, 2009d, 185.

23 The next two paragraphs draw from John Oberdiek, "Philosophical Issues in Tort Law," 3 *Philosophy Compass* 734 (2008), 744–5. But, as will become clear, my argument here extends and indeed departs from that discussion.

24 Moore, 2009d, 185–6.

check on liability owing to actual causation.[25] Even were one to assume away the all-inclusiveness problem, though, the description problem would remain; namely how one describes the risk-taking that makes the defendant's conduct careless determines whether the harm at issue is within the risk so described. Basically, as one re-describes a risk in ever more general terms—for example, as risking property damage instead of as risking flooded property caused when one improperly secured ship becomes unmoored and creates a dam with a second ship that it dislodged while careening down river—the harm falls evermore within the risk.[26] Moore contends that "[i]nasmuch as any given harm instantiates any number of types of harm, all levels of description of the harm risked can be equally accurate; it would thus appear that any choice of a description is inherently arbitrary," which makes the risk rule itself inherently arbitrary.[27] Moore's twin conceptual criticisms are indeed fatal if it is the case that there is no principled way to isolate *the* risk that is imposed when negligence is alleged. But if it is possible to privilege some particular description or characterization of a risk, and do so in a way that narrows what harms can be fairly attributed to that risk, then it should be possible to fend of Moore's attack on the risk rule.

On this front, Stephen Perry's elaboration of H. L. A. Hart and Tony Honoré's broad approach to these problems is notable.[28] In *Causation in the Law*, Hart and Honoré propose tackling the seeming indeterminacy of proximate causation by asking not about the foreseeability of harm as such but "[u]nder what specific description which fits this harm experience taught us to anticipate harm?"[29] In their view, one cannot be liable for unusual harms that experience has not taught us to expect or that are "very unlikely in the light of the knowledge available to ordinary men."[30] Perry observes that Hart and Honoré seem to suggest that that "the capacity of the *ordinary* person to foresee harm" is the appropriate benchmark for proximate cause in tort law.[31]

Perry identifies two considerations that proximate cause is sensitive to in this approach: "(1) the level of generalization that ordinary persons typically bring to bear in describing or categorizing relevant event-types, and (2) the common knowledge that can be expected to be available to ordinary persons regarding the probability of those event-types."[32] Perry further observes that this is an entirely natural (and naturalistic) way to think about the matter, for "typical human beings . . . share a roughly similar way of conceptualizing the world in which they live."[33] The general similarity of our conceptual schemes, moreover, extends to "the categories we use to anticipate events in the future."[34] In this way, according to Perry, risk is only hypothetically indeterminate

25 Moore, 2009d, 186.

26 *Petition of Kinsman Transport Co.*, 338 F.2d 708 (2d Cir. 1964).

27 Moore, 2009d, 194.

28 See Stephen Perry, "Responsibility for Outcomes, Risk, and the Law of Torts," in Gerald Postema (ed.), *Philosophy and the Law of Torts* (New York: Cambridge University Press, 2001), 99–101. Perry is in fact responding to Moore's early rendition of the arguments later memorialized in *Causation and Responsibility*. See Moore, 1993a.

29 H. L. A. Hart and Tony Honoré, *Causation in the Law*, 2nd edn. (Oxford: Oxford University Press, 1985), 258. Hart and Honoré are discussing the foreseeability account of proximate cause, not the risk rule formulation, but the problem besetting each is the same.

30 Hart and Honoré, *Causation in the Law*, 80.

31 Perry, "Responsibility for Outcomes, Risk, and the Law of Torts," 100 (emphasis in the original).

32 Perry, "Responsibility for Outcomes, Risk, and the Law of Torts," 100.

33 Perry, "Responsibility for Outcomes, Risk, and the Law of Torts," 100.

34 Perry, "Responsibility for Outcomes, Risk, and the Law of Torts," 100.

and the skepticism about proximate cause purely academic because it is a brute fact that people characterize risks similarly. A non-normative evolutionary process might well explain why ordinary persons share a roughly similar conceptual scheme, yet Perry believes that "[a] shared conceptual scheme, however it might have come about, is morally significant just by virtue of its existence."[35] Perry does not elaborate, but the best case for the moral significance of a shared conceptual scheme, it seems to me, is that such a scheme holds out the hope of making something like interpersonal moral accountability in the characterization of risk possible.[36] In Perry's view, then, one need not embrace any ontologically robust and therefore metaphysically suspect conception of risk to respond to the conceptual challenges that Moore issues, for appealing to the construct of an ordinary person exercising reasonable care allows one to characterize *the* risk that is relevant in the analysis of proximate cause—namely the risk whose imposition constitutes a breach of the duty of care.

Yet while Perry's elaboration of Hart and Honoré's approach certainly helps to deflate the practical indeterminacy of risk, its overtly naturalistic basis limits its normative power. These limitations can be brought into relief by considering Thomas Schelling's notion of a focal point, which Schelling famously introduced to solve game-theoretic coordination problems.[37] In one of Schelling's examples, a person is given the task of meeting a stranger in New York City without the ability to communicate with the stranger in advance. When and where should the person go to meet the stranger? There are, of course, any number of times and places where the two people *could* meet. Any such combination would be suitable to the two parties, given their aims, and would thus be a so-called equilibrium solution. Still, some times and places are more salient than others. In fact, as reported by Schelling, most would seek to meet the stranger at noon in Grand Central Station. The salience of that time and place (at least when Schelling was writing) make it a good choice—the correct choice even—as a meeting place precisely because others are likely to recognize its salience and so to select it as well. It is a focal point. The precise cause of its salience is irrelevant. It is a focal point simply because each believes that the other will regard it as a good meeting place and both know this. The prudential goal of meeting drives each party to the interpersonally salient choice.

In much the same way that there are any number of places and times that two strangers could meet in New York City, there any number of different characterizations of any particular risk that different parties could converge on. And just as any of those meeting places and times would serve as a game-theoretic equilibrium solution, any characterization of a particular risk would be a sufficiently determinate predicate for interpersonally robust moral valuation so long as it is shared. Finally, just as some meeting places and times are more salient than others, so too, some characterizations of risk are more salient than others, serving as focal points. Echoing Perry, people just do typically agree on the characterization of risk in virtue of their shared conceptual scheme.

[35] Perry, "Responsibility for Outcomes, Risk, and the Law of Torts," 101.

[36] Perry, "Responsibility for Outcomes, Risk, and the Law of Torts," 100–1. I discuss this at greater length in John Oberdiek, *Imposing Risk: A Normative Framework* (Oxford: Oxford University Press, forthcoming), chs. 1 and 2.

[37] Thomas Schelling, *The Strategy of Conflict* (Cambridge, MA: Harvard University Press, 1960), 57.

Indeed, this convergence helps to explain the phenomenology of (determinate) risk imposition.

There is, however, a significant weakness in Perry's appeal to a shared conceptual scheme as a way of cutting through the indeterminacy of risk. It can be highlighted by posing this question: If Schelling's strangers are not drawn to the same focal point and so fail to meet, does either party have grounds for complaint? Clearly not. They might be disappointed, but they cannot justifiably complain. This is no embarrassment to Schelling's own use of the notion of focal points because his is not a normative aim, but an empirical/predictive one. His contention is simply that the parties likely *will* meet due to the existence of the focal point. In a normative context, however, the standards are different: It is important for present purposes that the party who is left waiting in Grand Central Station be able to hold accountable the individual who failed to show up.

The concept of proximate cause, and the risk rule conception of it, has a normative function; namely to identify whether someone who imposed risk upon another is liable to them for the resulting harm. Given this aspiration, it is crucial that we be able to hold each other accountable for our respective characterizations of risk. Interpersonal moral justification demands this. Perry observes that, as a matter of fact, people just will typically agree on how to characterize various risks. But he offers no normative basis for holding people accountable for those characterizations, or for the relevant parties themselves to hold each other accountable. Perry is surely right that most people most of the time characterize risks similarly, but they do not always do so, and the exceptions matter. And yet though these exceptions matter, they actually matter less, philosophically speaking, than the nature of both divergent and even convergent characterizations of risk. The deeper problem with Perry's account of (admittedly widespread) convergent characterizations of risk is that even the convergent characterizations are not normative. It is not enough that any such convergence exists and has an explanation. It must have a justification.

This point is underscored by the fact that even certain convergent characterizations of risk can be morally unacceptable. If Schelling's strangers meet at a seemingly random location, it is all to the good, for there is no point to their meeting but meeting. In contrast, convergence has instrumental importance in the context of negligence law, and risk imposition generally. The further purpose of coming to a shared characterization of risk is to reason about and act in the face of uncertainty in a way that is mutually morally justifiable; the justifiability of negligence liability depends on this. This further aim exerts normative pressure not simply to converge on some characterization of risk, but to converge on one that can stand up to moral scrutiny. That any number of people might come to share a conceptual scheme of event-types concerning risk might be welcome and remarkable, but unless that scheme is somehow anchored in a cogent characterization of risk, it is bound to yield morally indefensible conduct and morally indefensible attributions of responsibility and liability. Morality demands that people take reasonable care in assessing the facts upon which their conduct depends. This is no less true with respect to risk, for when imposing risk, the fact at issue is the risk whose justified imposition is in question.

Still, Perry is right to hold that though risk may be perspective-dependent, it need not be perspective-indifferent. For if among the indefinitely many perspectives from which risk might be characterized there is one perspective that is best, the fact that risk is nevertheless perspective-dependent will not entail that risk impositions are indeterminate. Furthermore, I do not criticize Perry's candidate perspective as such but his overly descriptive and naturalistic understanding of it. To do the work that it must, the risk rule must employ a moralized conception of risk imposition. The perspective on risk that matters is not that of an ordinary person understood in purely descriptive terms, then, but of a person understood in normative and indeed in moral terms. Tort law gets this right. The reasonable person standard of course has descriptive features, but it is at bottom an irreducibly normative standard.[38] I contend that it is a reasonable person standard that allows risk to be perspective-dependent but not perspective-indifferent, and which illuminates the way to a defensible understanding of the risk rule. Meeting Moore's conceptual challenge to the risk rule in this way, moreover, shows why the reasonable person standard's "idealized epistemic situation" has "normative relevance" even though Moore seems to dismiss it because the reasonable person's perspective is "not that of either victim or injurer."[39]

Now, there are any number of candidate perspectives that might be thought to be the best one from which to characterize the risk that certain conduct poses and that informs the analysis of the breach element. The reasonable person perspective that tort law endorses is a version of what we can follow Derek Parfit in calling an evidence-relative perspective.[40] It is evidence-relative because the reasonable person perspective incorporates a subjective conception of risk that is nevertheless objectively based and broadly evidentialist.[41] But how can relying on an evidence-relative reasonable person perspective help characterize risk in the face of risk's seemingly intractable indeterminacy, thus providing the risk rule with the determinacy that it needs to fend off Moore's conceptual criticism?

Much as beliefs about causal facts that it would be reasonable to hold are imputed to an agent to provide content to an evidence-relative perspective, a particular reasonable characterization of risk can also be imputed. Ultimately, while there are any number of factually accurate characterizations of a given risk, one must be settled on, and the evidence-relative reasonable person perspective will select as most apt that

[38] See *The T.J. Hooper*, 60 F.2d 737 (2d Cir.), cert. denied, 287 US 662 (1932).

[39] Moore, 2009d, 172. I say "seems" here because Moore also maintains, at 201, that "risks as used in the culpability assessments of negligence constitute probabilistic calculations about future events that a reasonable person would make if he were in the defendant's situation."

[40] Derek Parfit, *On What Matters: Volume 1* (New York: Oxford University Press, 2011), 151. Parfit holds that an act is "*wrong* in the *evidence-relative* sense just when this act would be wrong in the ordinary sense if we believed what the available evidence gives us decisive reasons to believe, and these beliefs were true." A more straightforward formulation of the view holds that an act is wrong just when the available evidence that we have decisive reason to believe would make the act wrong. In Parfit's schema, evidence-relativity sits between the two poles of belief- and fact-relativity. This tripartite distinction is more precise than the more common objective/subjective distinction. According to Shelly Kagan's typical rendering, "[w]e can maintain an *objective* account of rightness, holding that whether an act is right is a matter of the facts as they actually are; or we could adopt instead a *subjective* account of rightness, holding that whether an act is right is a matter of what the agent believes, or perhaps what a reasonable person would believe." Shelly Kagan, *Normative Ethics* (Boulder, CO: Westview Press, 1998), 65. The advantage of Parfit's tripartite distinction is that it distinguishes the two possible interpretations of the subjective account that Kagan notes, which alternately track what an agent believes (belief-relative) and what a reasonable person would believe (evidence-relative).

[41] I explore this conception of risk in detail in John Oberdiek, *Imposing Risk*, chs. 1 and 2.

characterization of risk that can be morally justified to both defendant and plaintiff, as a matter of mutual moral accountability. In this way, the very characterization of risk is morally laden.

Moore often refers to "trivial risks," a familiar enough concept, and his fanciful example of one that attends driving a car is as good as any: "a seagull might bounce off the car's roof and hit an old lady."[42] Why does Moore call this risk trivial? The most obvious reason is that the relevant causal facts—those that would have to be true in order for such a risk to ripen into the risked harm—are so *unusual*. Without more, nothing about driving a car would give a driver reason to consider, much less expect, such a bizarre mishap. It is for that reason that, from the evidence-relative perspective, the risk in Moore's example is trivial. Compare Hart and Honoré's claim, as quoted earlier, that one cannot be liable in tort law for causing injuries that are "very unlikely in the light of the knowledge available to ordinary men."[43] They are getting at the same point, but from tort law's retrospective angle. When causal facts are highly unusual, they will usually remain reasonably beyond one's ken.

Now, one must always be on the lookout for the causal facts surrounding one's conduct.[44] This is a fundamental epistemically inflected moral duty.[45] That one must be on the lookout in this way is important both prospectively, to determine whether such causal facts bear on the permissibility of acting, and also retrospectively, as ascribing liability depends upon ascertaining what a reasonable lookout would have revealed about those causal facts. While we can all agree that it is usually wrong to engage in conduct that results in harm to another person, we do not always know or even have an inkling whether our conduct will have that result—the relevant causal facts can be elusive. In such cases, moral responsibility entails epistemic responsibility: One needs to make a reasonable effort to discover any morally relevant causal facts.

Sometimes, a reasonable inspection fails to uncover all of the relevant causal facts. And sometimes, this failure can have terrible, harmful consequences, grounding regret in the agent who caused them.[46] Still, according to the evidence-relative perspective, if a reasonable effort to discern the causal facts would uncover no evidence that one's conduct will result in harm to another, then on the simplifying assumption that that's the only morally relevant consideration, one's conduct is straightforwardly permissible and one should not be held liable for any resulting harm. As Thomas Scanlon explains, after taking reasonable steps to uncover any relevant causal facts surrounding some prospective action and finding nothing that should give one pause, what makes it permissible to go ahead and act "is the fact about the world that taking these steps puts us in a position to see: that the available evidence does not indicate that our action poses such a danger."[47] The same is true retrospectively. If a reasonable review of the available evidence did not reveal any danger, we ought not to be held liable for any resulting harm.

[42] Moore, 2009d, 200.

[43] Hart and Honoré, *Causation in the Law*, 80 (cited at fn. 29).

[44] See T. M. Scanlon, *Moral Dimensions: Permissibility, Meaning, Blame* (Cambridge, MA: Harvard University Press, 2008), 50–1.

[45] See John Oberdiek, *Imposing Risk*, chs. 1 and 2.

[46] See Bernard Williams, *Moral Luck* (Cambridge: Cambridge University Press, 1981), 27–30.

[47] Scanlon, *Moral Dimensions*, 50–1.

This is not to say that uncovering such causal facts would be impossible. But the bare possibility of discovery is irrelevant, for there is a limit to the search that morality requires us to make for such causal facts. This, in turn, is because there is a limit to what anyone who might be affected by our conduct can expect of us epistemically. In the context of negligence law, our "lookout duties" must be mutually justifiable between plaintiff and defendant. That anyone's duties are limited in this way is why tort law valorizes the reasonable person and not the omniscient person or the epistemically supererogatory person.

Moore himself defends something very close to this, although he erroneously couches the claim in terms of culpability. He maintains that "risks as used in the culpability assessments of negligence constitute probabilistic calculations about future events that a reasonable person would make if he were in the defendant's situation."[48] Risks, in Moore's view, are the product of a reasonable person's judgment of relevant causal facts. Thus, risks are emphatically *not* mere possibilities of harm—something that only an omniscient person would know. Herein lies the rub. For Moore is therefore flatly mistaken when he makes the claim, central to his all-inclusiveness conceptual challenge and quoted earlier, that "[i]f a harm materializes from a defendant's conduct, then necessarily there was some risk of it so doing, and that risk was on the list of risks created by the defendant's conduct, the cumulative total of which make the defendant's conduct unjustified."[49] This is wrong because a harm that eventuates from someone's conduct may not have been a risk in the only sense of that concept that Moore himself believes matters in this context: the resulting harm could be owed to a mere possibility of which the defendant was reasonably unaware. But a mere possibility of which the defendant was reasonably unaware is not a risk in the relevant sense. As Moore himself says, there can be no "Monday-morning-quarterbacking": "the risks ascribed to the defendant's Saturday conduct must be those that could have been assessed on Saturday, not those only knowable on Monday."[50] And again: "risks only made apparent as a result of, or after, the defendant's conduct do not belong in the [negligence] calculus."[51] Of course anything that happens has to have been possible. If someone's conduct harms another, then certainly, it was possible for the conduct to cause the harm. It is this that gives some plausibility to Moore's all-inclusiveness challenge. But possibility is not the issue in negligence, and Moore himself agrees, despite himself. The all-inclusiveness problem can therefore be safely set aside.

Extending this line of reasoning also solves the description problem, bringing determinacy to the characterization of risk, which in turn supports the risk rule. To recount, I have argued that the limits to anyone's duty to be on the lookout for relevant causal facts underwrite the evidence-relative reasonable person standard. The limits to our lookout duties are themselves a function of the kind of inspection that would be mutually morally justifiable, that is, justifiable to both agents and those whom they subject to risk. Nothing more robust than the reasonable person standard can be right, then, because anything more robust would be too epistemically burdensome to be plausible. Just as certain moral theories are unduly demanding for all that they would require agents to do and sacrifice, the fact-relative perspective asks too much of agents

[48] Moore, 2009d, 201. [49] Moore, 2009d, 185–6. [50] Moore, 2009d, 200.
[51] Moore, 2009d, 201.

epistemically. Anything weaker, though, would commit the opposite mistake: too little would be asked of agents, selling short the interests of potential plaintiffs. It is more plausible to suppose that some inspection must be made of the causal facts surrounding one's conduct but that there are limits to that inspection. The evidence-relative reasonable person perspective takes seriously everyone's competing interests—that perspective is mutually morally justifiable.

The limits placed on how much anyone must be on the lookout for relevant causal facts suggest how determinacy can be brought to the characterization of risk. As Moore illustrates, there are countless ways of characterizing a risk imposition. As I have just argued, one reason why the evidence-relative reasonable person perspective will rule out relying on certain facts in characterizing a given risk is that their discovery would be unreasonably demanding on the agent. So, when one drives, the risk of a seagull hitting one's roof and ricocheting into an old lady really is negligible, absent some very special facts that a reasonable person would notice, because the evidence to which one has reasonable access gives one reason to believe that one is imposing a negligible risk, no matter what the actual causal facts happen to be. The set of facts that might be thought to shape the characterization of a particular risk, then, will be diminished at the outset by the demandingness constraints generated by the reasonable person perspective. This will help cut through risk's indeterminacy because fewer facts generate fewer possible characterizations of risk. It will not typically be enough to solve the problem, however, because it will still be possible to characterize a given risk in many ways by recourse only to what it would be reasonable to believe about the morally relevant causal facts. Still, the path forward is illuminated.

If we can rule out appeal to certain causal facts in characterizing risk because it would demand too much of agents, we can also rule out appeal to certain characterizations of risk for paying insufficient heed to the interests of potential patients. In fact, through considering the myriad interests of would-be defendants and plaintiffs, a single characterization of a risk imposition—*the* risk—can be isolated. For example, while one could characterize the risk that a particular person poses to others in driving a car by reference to general statistics about the dangers of driving, it would nevertheless be unjustifiable to do so if the particular driver in question were driving drunk. Drunk drivers pose a greater risk to others (and themselves) than sober drivers, after all, and thus it would not take due account of the interests of those in the drunk driver's orbit—the potential victims—to characterize the risk that the driver poses as if they were just any sober driver. It is true that each of the characterizations of the risk in this example would be fitting and accurate, but moral considerations can be brought to bear to rule out the one characterization for failing to weigh the interests of potential plaintiffs appropriately.

This is just one example of the exercise that will isolate a particular factually accurate but also morally justifiable characterization of risk. There are any number of other examples that illustrate the idea. To take a few: it would not show due regard for the interests of coal miners in West Virginia to characterize the risk they face in the mines as the average faced by all West Virginians; nor for the interests of Japanese farmers whose (radioactive) land is near the devastated Fukushima Daiichi nuclear power plant to characterize the risk they face in farming as the average faced by farmers generally;

nor for the interests of public utility workers who install and repair high-voltage power lines to characterize the risk they face on the job as the average faced by the utility's employees generally. In all of these cases, while either of the reference classes mentioned would yield a factually accurate characterization of the risk, only the more specific member of the pair would yield a morally justifiable characterization.

What makes the more specific characterization in these examples the sole characterization that could be justified to potential plaintiffs? A common thread in all of the examples is that the more specific characterization of the prospective risk imposition reveals a more dangerous risk imposition than the more general characterization. The more specific characterization, in other words, reveals more causal facts that the potential plaintiff has reason to care about than does the more general characterization—the patient is revealed to be at greater risk when the risk imposition is characterized more specifically.

Note, though, that it is not the specificity as such of the characterization that necessarily makes the difference in these examples. A. J. Ayer made this mistake in proposing that the best characterization of risk was that yielded by the narrowest applicable reference class.[52] Specificity sometimes captures the proper characterization of risk, but not always. The chief reason that Ayer's proposal fails is that there is usually more than one narrowest reference class and there is no guarantee that the different narrowest reference classes will generate the same risk. This fact gets masked in the examples above because I simply stipulate reference classes: "West Virginia coal miners," "Japanese farmers near a radioactive site," and "public utility employees working with high-voltage lines," respectively. The reason, of course, is that when we evaluate conduct, we evaluate it under a particular description—a point Hart and Honoré were right to think important. We want to know what the risk is of doing things like mining for coal, farming near a radioactive site, and working with high voltages. If we approach the risk more abstractly, though, we see that Ayer's proposal cannot succeed for the reasons noted above.

But why should it be that the greatest risk yielded by taking up the evidence-relative reasonable person perspective is the correct, morally justifiable characterization of the risk? Ayer's attempt to circumvent the reference class problem fails because there may be no narrowest reference class—just many different ones. Winnowing down reference classes, in other words, does not necessarily yield a single characterization of risk. Now consider an example of risk imposition that implicates moral norms: When one drives, one ought to be reasonably aware that one is imposing a risk on pedestrians and other drivers—a risk that can be variously characterized. The potential victims of one's driving have a stake in how the risk is characterized. For the characterization of the risk will be uploaded to a normative ethical theory governing, inter alia, the imposition of risk, determining how much care one must exercise in driving. In any plausible moral theory, the greater the risk imposed, the harder the risk will be to justify. The potential victims of one's driving, then, have reason to want the risk imposed on them to be characterized so that, ultimately, under whatever moral theory governs risk impositions,

[52] A. J. Ayer, "Two Notes on Probability," in Ayer, *The Concept of a Person and Other Essays* (London: Macmillan, 1963), 202. I discuss and reject Ayer's strategy of overcoming the reference class problem in John Oberdiek, *Imposing Risk*, ch. 1.

their interests are maximally protected. The proper characterization of the risk that the agent would be imposing must account for this in order to do justice to their interests. This is why, in the examples above, the characterization revealing the greater risk was appropriate. It remains the case that the characterization must be *mutually* justifiable—justifiable to the would-be plaintiffs as well as to the would-be defendant whose conduct is at issue. This simply means, though, that the risk imposition must be given the gravest characterization compatible with the agent's evidence-relative reasonable person perspective.

In a moral and legal context, the proper characterization of a risk imposition is that which reveals the greatest risk to the patient, as judged from the agent's evidence-relative reasonable person perspective. The agent is responsible for acting in light of whatever morally relevant causal facts a reasonable search would discover, which is a middle way between excessive and insufficient epistemic demandingness, thus giving due regard to both agent and patient. But of course the patient remains the most vulnerable party, for it is the patient who is put at risk. To make up for this fact, the characterization of the risk imposed upon the patient must be construed as favorably to them as is compatible with the agent's evidence-relative reasonable person perspective: The greater the risk, the stronger the potential plaintiff's claim will be under any plausible moral framework of risk imposition. So in this way and for this reason, risk must be characterized to be least objectionable to the individual to whom it is most objectionable. The broader conclusion is that moral considerations play a central and ineliminable role in the fundamental task of characterizing risk. Before risk impositions can be morally assessed, moral premises must be invoked at the threshold to characterize risk itself. No purely empirical account of risk will be adequate.

The risk rule, then, is on a secure conceptual foundation after all. The all-inclusiveness and description challenges can both be met. In meeting these, moreover, the normative problems that supposedly beset the risk rule are much easier to diffuse, for they depend upon Moore's conceptual claims. For reasons of space, I focus on what I take to be Moore's most fundamental normative criticism of the risk rule.

Moore targets what he accurately takes to be the risk rule's core moral claim, namely "[w]hen a risk materializes from a defendant's conduct in a manner that would surprise a reasonable person, it is flatly unfair to exact compensation for it from the defendant."[53] The flaw in the risk rule's moral logic, according to Moore, comes to this: the defendant is *ex hypothesi* careless—if the goal is to align the breach and injury elements appropriately, breach has been established—so the defendant has no grounds to complain about being held liable for any harm to the plaintiff that that carelessness has caused. Thus, if faced with the choice of allowing an innocent victim to go uncompensated, or forcing a careless defendant to pay damages, Moore would make the careless defendant pay.[54] Moore thus meets the risk rule's core moral claim head-on and attempts to turn it back: In his view, there is "no unfairness in holding defendants liable for 'harms *outside* the risk.'"[55]

The source of the problem with Moore's position on this score is conceptual and familiar. When we hold that a defendant has imposed a risk, Moore says, we mean that

[53] Moore, 2009d, 198. [54] Moore, 2009d, 203. [55] Moore, 2009d, 202.

"from the epistemic situation of the defendant, it was possible to predict, with a certain degree of confidence, that the conduct would cause a harm."[56] But that is not true. The *possibility* of predicting harm is irrelevant—lookout duties in morality and tort law are not that onerous. Indeed, they are not so onerous precisely because it would be unfair to defendants and agents generally if they were. Moore mistakenly denies this because he mistakenly believes that, "*because they are knowable to him*," it is appropriate to hold a defendant liable for the materialization of any such "knowable" risk that he imposes on a plaintiff.[57] What is "knowable" is inapposite because the standard is not that of the omniscient person or even the epistemically supererogatory person, but of the reasonable person. What is *reasonably knowable* is therefore what matters. And in negligence cases, that difference makes all the difference.[58]

It is of course true that the upshot of all of this is that an admittedly careless defendant who did in fact cause harm to an innocent plaintiff can be found not liable, but then the fairness of that possibility is precisely what is at issue. And Moore would be among the last whom I would expect to treat being soft-hearted as an argument unto itself.

[56] Moore, 2009d, 200 (emphasis in original).

[57] Moore, 2009d, 201. Italics in the original.

[58] In this way, Moore is insufficiently careful in stating: "That people often do not consciously calculate the myriad risks created by their conduct is no argument that they should not or could not calculate such risks." Moore, 2009d, 202. It is true that if one should calculate the myriad risks created by one's conduct, then it follows that one could do so; the reverse, however, is not true.

12

Causation: Metaphysics or Intuition?

*Richard W. Wright**

I. Introduction: Causation, Culpability, and Responsibility

In his magnum opus, *Causation and Responsibility: An Essay in Law, Morals, and Metaphysics*,[1] Michael Moore seeks to elucidate the nature of causation and its role in determining moral and especially legal responsibility and blame. Following the lead of Herbert Hart and Tony Honoré,[2] he claims that causation plays a pervasive and dominant role. Although he purports to disavow Hart and Honoré's reliance on ordinary language usage as an indicator of actual causal relations,[3] his frequent and often heavy reliance on supposed common intuitions to support his arguments[4] belies that disavowal.

I agree with Moore that causation plays a major role in assessments of legal responsibility. However, I disagree with his account of the nature of and relationships among causation, responsibility, culpability, and blameworthiness, which, among other errors, reflects the frequent tendency among criminal law theorists to misunderstand tort law as being concerned, like criminal law, with culpability and blameworthiness. My initial idea in writing this chapter was to address those issues. However, trying to sort out and address all of the complex and often inconsistent strands in Moore's arguments proved too difficult to accomplish in the available time and allotted space. So I have instead picked up the strands of my ongoing debates with Moore regarding the nature of causation per se, in particular his criticism of my NESS (*n*ecessary *e*lement of a *s*ufficient *s*et) account and his espousal of an "I know it when I see it" primitivist singularist theory.

II. The NESS Account

According to the NESS account as initially elaborated, a condition *c* was a cause of a consequence *e* if and only if it was necessary for the sufficiency of a set of existing

[1] Moore, 2009d.

[2] H. L. A. Hart and A. M. Honoré, *Causation in the Law* (Oxford: Oxford University Press, 1959).

[3] Moore, 2009d, 255–60; see Richard Wright, "Causation in Tort Law," 73 *California Law Review* 1735 (1985), 1788–803; Richard Wright, "The Nightmare and the Noble Dream: Causation and Responsibility," in Matthew Kramer et al. (eds.), *The Legacy of H. L. A. Hart: Legal, Political and Moral Philosophy* (Oxford: Oxford University Press, 2008), 165.

[4] E.g., Moore, 2009d, x–xii, 29–33, 38–9, 55–8, 66, 347, 445–7, 507.

antecedent conditions that was sufficient for the occurrence of *e*.[5] Subsequently, after recognizing that the necessity aspect of the NESS criterion need only be incorporated in the definition of a causal law, I recast the test for singular instances of causation as follows: an actual condition *c* was a cause of an actual condition *e* if and only if *c* was a part of (rather than being necessary for) the instantiation of one of the abstract conditions in the completely instantiated antecedent of a causal law, the consequent of which was instantiated by *e* immediately after the complete instantiation of its antecedent, or (as is more often the case) if *c* is connected to *e* through a sequence of such instantiations of causal laws.[6]

This test for singular causes obviously puts great weight on the definition of a causal law. Recently, I have tightened up my past descriptions of what constitutes a causal law, although the core idea remains the same:

> A causal law is an empirically derived statement that describes a successional relation between a set of abstract conditions (properties or features of possible events and states of affairs in our real world) that constitute the antecedent and one or more specified conditions of a distinct abstract event or state of affairs that constitute the consequent such that, regardless of the state of any other conditions, the instantiation of all the conditions in the antecedent entails the immediate instantiation of the consequent, which would not be entailed if less than all of the conditions in the antecedent were instantiated.[7]

I use the phrase "causal sufficiency" to refer to the requirement in the above definition of a causal law that all of the conditions in the antecedent of the causal law must be instantiated on the particular occasion. This complete instantiation requirement is critical and distinguishes the required sense of sufficiency in a causal law from mere lawful sufficiency, in the sense of a guarantee of the occurrence of the relevant consequence, which Moore refers to as "nomic sufficiency."[8] Contrary to Moore's assumption[9]—which unfortunately is shared by many—*guaranteeing* the occurrence of some result is not the same as *causing* that result.[10]

Our knowledge of causal laws generally is incomplete. Even if it were complete, we rarely refer to completely specified causal laws, since such complete specification would

[5] This definition was a clarification of my initial description of a NESS condition as a *n*ecessary *e*lement of a *s*ufficient *s*et, which was ambiguous and thus failed to clearly incorporate the requirement, which has always been stated in my elaborations of the NESS account, that a NESS condition must be necessary for the sufficiency of the sufficient set. See e.g., Wright, "Causation in Tort Law," 1790; Richard Wright, "Causation, Responsibility, Risk, Probability, Naked Statistics, and Proof: Pruning the Bramble Bush by Clarifying the Concepts" ["Pruning the Bramble Bush"], 73 *Iowa Law Review* 1001 (1988), 1019, 1021, 1041. For the history and defense of a similar account, developed independently a few years earlier by Ingeborg Puppe, which makes almost all of the points that I make in this chapter, often better than me, see Ingeborg Puppe, "The Concept of Causation in the Law," in Benedikt Kahmen and Markus Stepanians (eds.), *Critical Essays on "Causation and Responsibility"* (Berlin: De Gruyter, 2013), 67 [Kahmen and Stepanians, *Critical Essays*].

[6] Richard Wright, "Acts and Omissions as Positive and Negative Causes" ["Acts and Omissions"], in Jason W. Neyers et al. (eds.), *Emerging Issues in Tort Law* (Oxford: Hart, 2007), 297–8; Wright, "Pruning the Bramble Bush," 1045.

[7] Richard Wright, "The NESS Account of Natural Causation: A Response to Criticisms" ["NESS Account"], in Richard Goldberg (ed.), *Perspectives on Causation* (Oxford: Hart, 2011), 289; cf e.g., Wright, "Acts and Omissions," 293–4 and n. 18 therein.

[8] Moore, 2009d, 475. [9] Moore, 2009d, 474.

[10] Wright, "Acts and Omissions," 298–300; see section III.D of this chapter.

be extremely burdensome and unnecessarily detailed and lengthy. We rather employ causal generalizations, which refer to only some of the antecedent conditions in the relevant causal laws and have only as much specificity as is possible and needed in the particular situation. However, when we make an assertion regarding a singular instance of causation, we are implicitly asserting that all the unstated as well as the stated conditions in the relevant causal generalizations and all the unknown as well as known conditions in the causal laws underlying the causal generalizations were instantiated on the particular occasion. Even when the inference of an applicable causal generalization (and the underlying causal laws) is based on a single observation of a singular instance of causation, the inference of causation in the singular instance comes after and depends upon the inference of the applicable causal generalization. In such instances the order is: (1) observation of the occurrence, (2) inference of the causal generalization based on the observation, and (3) assertion of causation through enunciation of the singular causal statement, which implicitly invokes the causal generalization.

III. Alleged Deficiencies of the NESS Account

A. Definitional issues

Moore claims that the NESS account is "viciously circular," since causal terminology is often used in its elaboration and it relies upon the concept of causal laws.[11] However, one need merely look at the definition of a causal law in section II of this chapter, as well as the definitions in my prior work,[12] to see that, whatever other flaws they may have, they do not contain any causal language or suppositions. Similarly, the concept of causal sufficiency is defined non-circularly as the complete instantiation of all the conditions in the antecedent of a causal law (the definition of which contains no causal language or suppositions and thus could be substituted for "causal law" to produce a definition of causal sufficiency that contains no causal language), or, alternatively, as the label for that aspect of the non-circularly defined causal law. There is no conceptual circularity here, vicious or otherwise.

Moore complains that my definition of a causal law, which requires that it be "an *empirically derived* statement that describes a successional relation between ... *distinct* abstract event[s] or state[s] of affairs," excludes merely analytic, logical, identity, or mereological (part to its whole) relations. Although he and everyone else agrees that these are not causal relations and should be excluded,[13] he declares that my defining a causal law so as to exclude them, while not circular, is "ad hoc in that it is unmotivated by the nature being attributed to causation."[14] Really?!

B. Causal directionality

Under a mere nomic (lawful) sufficiency conception of causation, which fails to encompass causal directionality, consequents can be treated as causes of one of their antecedent conditions by simply inverting the relevant law. For example, we could treat

[11] Moore, 2009d, 477, 484, 494–5. [12] E.g., Wright, "Acts and Omissions," 293–4 and n. 18.
[13] See Wright, "NESS Account," 286, n. 9. [14] Moore, 2013b, 331, 336; see Moore, 2009d, 477.

the shadow cast by a flagpole as a cause of the flagpole's height, since, given the shadow, the laws of geometry, and all the conditions in the antecedent of the law for casting shadows other than the flagpole's height, including the location of the sun, we can infer the height.[15] However, if the relevant law has directionality, that is, is a causal law as I have defined it, this maneuver is blocked. Through experience and/or education, we know that the relevant causal law has the height of the flagpole as one of the conditions in the antecedent of the causal law and the shadow as the consequent.

In his most recent criticism of the NESS account, after initially accusing me of "particularly blatant" circularity for "attempt[ing] to smuggle the asymmetricality and time-directionality of causation into his notion of [causal] sufficiency,"[16] Moore retreats to an assertion of ad hoc, unmotivated stipulation similar to the one that he made regarding my defining causal laws so as to exclude analytical and mereological relations. Noting my inclusion of the terms "successive relation" and "immediate" in my definition of a causal law, he states:

> [A]symmetricality and temporal order ("successive relation," "immediate") are merely stipulative add-ons to nomic sufficiency that in no way follow from the supposed nature of causation (viz, nomic sufficiency). Sure, causation is an asymmetrical and time-ordered relation, and nomic sufficiency as such is not. But *causal* sufficiency has these features—once one by fiat adds these features of causation to nomic sufficiency. . . . One can fairly demand . . . that [Wright] show us how an asymmetric and time-ordered relation (causation) can be identified as a seemingly different relation (nomic sufficiency . . .) that is neither.[17]

Either Moore doesn't get it, or he refuses to accept it. From the beginning my effort has been to provide an account of causation, and from the beginning it was clear to me, as it is to Moore, that simple nomic (lawful) sufficiency does not fully capture the concept of causation, for all the reasons that Moore explains, which I also have elaborated in my work. I have emphasized the necessity of developing and employing a conception of causal laws and of the sufficiency employed in them that is distinct from mere lawful sufficiency, which, in order to flag the distinction, I call causal sufficiency.

Moore commends John Mackie for treating the directionality of causation, which Mackie calls "causal priority" and which both he and Mackie agree is a fundamental aspect of causation, as an addition to, rather than as an essential constitutive element of, the sense of "sufficiency" when employed in causal analysis.[18] Mackie acknowledged the use of the more discriminating sense of causal sufficiency in common discourse, but he thought it better for the sake of clarity in language use to reserve "sufficiency" for use in its simplest sense: mere lawful sufficiency.[19] I have hoped to preserve clarity while not letting language use govern metaphysics by distinguishing between causal sufficiency and mere lawful sufficiency.

[15] Moore, 2009d, 477. [16] Moore, 2013b, 334; see Moore, 2009d, 483–5.

[17] Moore, 2013b, 335. [18] Moore, 2009d, 482–5.

[19] J. L. Mackie, *The Cement of the Universe: A Study of Causation* (Oxford: Clarendon, 1974), 51–3, 190–2.

C. Epiphenomena

When a condition is a common cause of two different causal sequences, employing mere lawful sufficiency rather than causal sufficiency can result in erroneously treating conditions in one sequence as causes of the conditions in the other sequence.[20] Moore claims that my definition of a causal law does not prevent treating the earlier occurring event on one fork of such an epiphenomenal relation from being treated as a cause of the later occurring event on the other fork:

> Let c be a common cause of e1 and e2; let c occur at t1, e1 at t2, and e2 at t3; let t3 succeed t2 by as small an interval of time as Wright means by "immediate." The occurrence of e1 can be sufficient of the occurrence of e2 (the cases are legion – use your imagination); unless "successive" means something causal (Wright's "causal process"?), Wright has no way not to conclude that e1 causes e2, contrary to what we all know to be true.[21]

Moore is wrong. He is paying attention only to the words "successional" and "immediate" in my definition of a causal law, while ignoring the rest of the definition. Given the epiphenomenal situation assumed by Moore, there is no empirically derivable abstract set of antecedent conditions containing a condition of type e1 that, if fully instantiated, would be sufficient for the occurrence of e2 unless a condition of type c also were part of the set, but if that were true then conditions of type e1 would be unnecessary for the sufficiency of the set. Conversely, if the set did not contain a condition of type c, it would be insufficient regardless of the inclusion of a condition of type e1.

Of course, this conclusion, like every other causal conclusion, depends upon our having sufficient knowledge of the relevant causal laws or, more likely, their incomplete generalizations. Without such knowledge and pending sufficient experimentation or experience, one might infer a causal relation between e1 and e2, as with any other set of successive or concurrent events (e.g., the shadow and height of the flagpole). However, for there actually to be a causal relation, causal sufficiency (complete instantiation of the relevant causal laws) must have occurred.

D. Pre-emptive causation

Moore and others have criticized the NESS account for allegedly being unable to handle properly some types of pre-emptive causation situations. Once again, the criticisms erroneously assume that the NESS account merely requires lawful sufficiency, rather than causal sufficiency. Consider the following often discussed hypothetical:

> C is a traveler in the desert, whose only source of water is a keg full of water. A adds a fatal dose of undetectable poison to the water in the keg, for which there is no antidote. C remains unaware of the poison in the water. Subsequently, before C drinks any of the poisoned water, B dumps the poisoned water out of the keg. When C attempts to drink water from the keg, she discovers that it is empty. C dies because of dehydration.

[20] See Wright, "NESS Account," 297.

[21] Moore, 2013b, 335–6 (citation omitted).

If we merely require lawful sufficiency and do not qualify the consequence by the time of its occurrence—or perhaps even if we do—we would incorrectly treat the poison as well as the emptying of the keg as duplicative causes of C's death. The poison in the water, along with the other existing conditions, guarantees C's death and thus is lawfully sufficient for its occurrence. On the other hand, if we require necessity—that the condition "made a difference" as a "but for" cause—we would be forced to conclude that neither condition was a cause.

In the NESS account, we require causal sufficiency rather than necessity or mere lawful sufficiency—an approach that Moore again incorrectly claims is viciously circular.[22] The causal generalization for death by poisoning includes the victim's drinking the poison, a condition that was not instantiated since the keg was emptied before C was able to drink from it. On the other hand, the causal generalization and the underlying causal laws for death by dehydration, which include as a necessary condition lack of water (and the physical bodily processes that occur as a result of the lack of water), were fully instantiated. Thus, B's emptying of the keg, but not A's poisoning of its contents, caused C's death, even though C may have lived longer as a result of the emptying of the keg.

Since Moore refuses to treat negative conditions such as lack of water as causes or effects (but what about the positive condition of the poison in the water?), he denies that either A or B caused C's death, thereby treating the death as an uncaused miracle.[23] He stands alone in this conclusion, and I have a hard time believing that it fits even his intuitions.

Moore until recently argued that attempts to use the NESS account to resolve the causal issue in "late pre-emption" situations are circular and question-begging, because they allegedly simply amount to requiring that the effect was not already caused by something else.[24] However, his argument failed to distinguish the necessary conditions in the antecedent of a causal generalization and the distinct condition that constitutes the consequent of the causal generalization.[25] For example, although to say that an entity exists or is alive at a certain time obviously entails (in our world) that nothing has caused the entity's destruction or death prior to that time, it should also be obvious that the entity's existence or being alive at a certain time is a state of affairs that is distinct from and not simply the converse of the destruction, death, or non-existence of the entity at a later (remote or immediate) time;[26] rather, it is one of the necessary but by itself insufficient conditions for the occurrence of the later event or state of affairs.

In his most recent critique of the NESS account, Moore has apparently given up on his claim that the NESS analysis of pre-emption is circular. Instead, he puts forth a new argument:

> Wright's definition [of a causal law] does not rule out (as being causal) pre-empted factors in pre-emptive overdetermination cases. In the case of the poison victim about to die from his poisoning who is then shot dead immediately by a second wrongdoer, the

[22] Moore, 2009d, 495. [23] Moore, 2009d, 144, 466–7. [24] Moore, 2009d, 494–5.

[25] See Wright, "NESS Account," 300–2.

[26] It is unfortunate that on this issue Moore fails to recognize or employ the rigorous distinction between distinct states of affairs that he elsewhere employs (Moore, 2009d, 14–19, 281–2) to distinguish between acts and consequences to rebut arguments that there is no causation requirement in inchoate crimes.

> "poison leads to death" causal law was about to be instantiated in however small an interval of time as Wright means by "immediate." (It's my hypo so I can assure of this with the certainty of an omniscient novelist.) The "instantiation of the consequent" (i.e., here, death) immediately followed the set of conditions (of which poison was here a necessary member) sufficient for death, and that set . . . was "fully instantiated." Yet we know that the even more immediately acting bullet killed him, pre-empting the poison.[27]

If we know (with Moore's omniscience) that the bullet killed the victim, not the poison (or both), then clearly the causal set containing the poison was not fully instantiated; some micro-process had yet to be completed, the completion of which required more time than remained before the bullet killed the victim. Or would Moore put the universe on hold? Alternatively, "immediate" means simultaneous with the instantiation of the last condition to be instantiated in the fully instantiated antecedent of the relevant causal law. Either way, the poison was not a cause.

E. Duplicative causation

Moore acknowledges that the NESS account properly handles situations involving duplicative causation by two or more independently sufficient conditions, such as two independently sufficient fires or floods that merge and destroy a building, which the *sine qua non* account mishandles since none of the conditions "made a difference" by being a "but for" cause.[28] He also acknowledges the validity and usefulness of the NESS account's ability to identify as causes conditions that were neither strongly necessary nor independently strongly sufficient—for example, each of ten drops of poison or discharges of pollution when only three such drops or discharges were necessary for the occurrence of the relevant harm[29]—while criticizing the proliferation of causes.[30]

IV. Omissions and negative causation

A "positive" condition is the presence of some act, event, or entity in a particular situation; a "negative" condition is the absence of some act, event, or entity in a particular situation. A "positive" or "producing" causal process is one in which all the steps in the process consist of the complete instantiation of one or more causal laws. A "negative" causal process is one in which at least one step in the process involves the failure of a causal law to be completely instantiated.[31]

Many philosophers believe that a negative condition cannot be a positive cause, but rather, at best, only a negative cause.[32] Some argue that negative conditions cannot be

[27] Moore, 2013b, 336. [28] Moore, 2009d, 474. [29] See Wright, "NESS Account," 303–5.

[30] Moore, 2009d, 487–91.

[31] These definitions of positive and negative causal processes differ slightly from my prior definitions, but the underlying idea is the same. See Wright, "NESS Account," 312.

[32] E.g., Ned Hall, "Two Concepts of Causation," in John Collins, Ned Hall, and L. A. Paul (eds.), *Causation and Counterfactuals* (Cambridge MA: MIT Press, 1994), 225, 253, 260; Jonathan Schaffer, "Causes need not be Physically Connected to their Effects: The Case for Negative Causation" ["Negative Causation"], in Christopher Hitchcock (ed.), *Contemporary Debates in Philosophy of Science* (Oxford: Blackwell, 2004) 197, 197–8.

part of any plausible account of reality and thus cannot be any sort of cause or effect. Moore is most insistent on this point. He notes, correctly, that there are no negative conditions in the sense of the negative opposite of a positive condition, for example non-tramplings by non-elephants. Rather, a negative condition must be understood to be the absence of some positive condition, rather than the "ghostly" reality of its negative opposite.[33]

Yet, as Jonathan Schaffer has pointed out, all voluntary human actions and many other actual conditions take place through causal processes in which absences play a critical role:

> The pattern of negative causation features in even the most *paradigmatically causal* cases. Suppose that the sniper feels murderous, pulls the trigger, fires a bullet through the victim's heart, and the victim dies. Here is a paradigmatic causal sequence, *every step of which* is negative causation.
>
> Working backwards, *surely* the firing of the bullet through the victim's heart causes the victim to die. But heart damage only causes death by negative causation: [firing the bullet] (*c*) causes [a hole (~*d*) in the wall of the heart, which allows the blood in the heart to flow out of the heart (*e*). The flow of the blood out of the heart (*c*) causes][34] an absence of oxygenated blood flow to the brain (~*d*), which [causes an absence of oxygen in the brain cells (~*d*), which] causes the cells to starve [(~*e*)] [and die] . . .
>
> At the next step backwards, *surely* the pulling of the trigger causes the bullet to fire. But trigger pullings only cause bullet firings by negative causation: pulling the trigger (*c*) causes the removal of the sear from the spring (~*d*), which causes the spring to uncoil, thereby compressing the gunpowder and causing an explosion, which causes the bullet to fire (*e*) . . .
>
> At the third and final step backwards, *surely* the sniper's feeling murderous causes him to pull the trigger. But nerve signals only cause muscle contractions (such as that of the sniper's trigger finger) by negative causation: the firing of the nerve (*c*) causes a calcium cascade through the muscle fiber, which causes calcium–troponin binding, which causes the removal of [the inhibitor] tropomyosin from the binding sites on the actin (~*d*), which causes myocin–actin binding, and thereby causes the actin to be pulled in and the muscle to contract (*e*) . . .
>
> Since all voluntary human actions are due to muscle contractions, it therefore follows that *all voluntary human actions* (perhaps the most paradigmatic of all causes) involve negative causation.[35]

Although there is no *physical* connection between causal process *c* and causal process *e* or ~*e* in each step of this causal process, there is a *causal* connection via the failure (~*d*) of causal process *d*. This failure either enables causal process *e*, which was previously blocked by causal process *d*, to go forward or by its failure also causes the failure of causal process *e*, which previously was ongoing.[36] This is how absences generally (but

[33] Moore, 2009d, 53–5, 399–400, 436–7, 444–5, 460–1.

[34] And/or the hole in the heart causes the failure of the heart to keep pumping, which causes an absence of oxygenated blood flow to the brain.

[35] Schaffer, "Negative Causation," 199–200 (emphasis by Schaffer). I have added steps overlooked by Schaffer.

[36] Jonathan Schaffer, "Disconnection and Responsibility," 18 *Legal Theory* 399 (2012), 426–7.

not always)[37] do their causal work, not by *initiating or maintaining* a positive causal process, but rather by necessitating the *failure* of a positive causal process. No implausible ontology is required; no ghostly entities are involved. No positive "production" is occurring; instead, negative "allowance" is occurring. Both types of operation are part of the causal processes at work in our world.

As Schaffer's example indicates, acts (e.g., the pulling of the trigger) as well as omissions can be negative causes; indeed, given Schaffer's argument, they are always negative causes! In particular, acts of shooting, stabbing, strangling, and removal of water or food all similarly cause the negative condition of the absence of life by causing the absence of one or more of the necessary conditions for the positive causal processes involved in maintaining life. Although Moore argues otherwise,[38] death as an event is a transition from a positive state, being alive (with a functioning heart or brain, depending on one's preferred definition), to a negative state, the absence of life—which, unfortunately, for each of us is an ultimately certain real state of affairs. The relevant positive causal processes for the maintenance of human life, at least as we know it, include as necessary positive conditions the presence of sufficient amounts of water, oxygen, and certain nutrients, as well as functioning organs (e.g., lungs, hearts, arteries, veins, stomachs, livers) for keeping these items in place and processing them in the body. The negative condition of an absence of any of these things is a negative cause of the negative condition of death (the absence of life).

Acts as well as omissions also cause positive conditions through negative causation, by preventing a positive causal process that would have prevented the occurrence of the positive condition. For example, the act of removing a safety device or damaging it so that it no longer works results in the same negative state of affairs—the lack of a working safety device, which if present and working would have prevented some injury—that exists if there is no working safety device in the first place.

Moore notes that nomic sufficiency theorists have a way to account for negative conditions as causes (and effects):

> If "instantiation" means that there must exist some token of the type instantiated, then ... NESS and other generalists are not committed to omissions being singular causes. Yet this cannot be what generalists mean by "instantiated." When they are asking after the truth makers for the negative conditions in laws, they are not looking for negative tokens of negative types. Rather, the truth-maker for negative conditions is the absence of any positive instances of some type. The law is "instantiated" in this sense whenever its negative conditions are made true by the world. In that sense, negative conditions can be "instantiated," and so omissions will be causes.[39]

Moore considers the ability of counterfactual and nomic sufficiency theories to treat omissions and other absences as causes as a mark against those theories, and the inability of some singularist theories to do so a virtue.[40] Treating them as non-causal enables him to explain and support the "intuition of difference" in responsibility for misfeasance and nonfeasance, or doings and allowings, as being based on the presence or absence of

[37] See Wright, "Acts and Omissions," 291.

[38] Moore, 2009d, 53–5, 303, 442.

[39] Moore, 2009d, 479.

[40] Moore, 2013b, 333, 340–1; Moore, 2009d, 461, 478–80, 508–9.

causation, respectively. Legal responsibility for omissions, allowings, and other absences, he argues, is a lesser form of responsibility based on non-causal counterfactual dependence.[41]

Although treating liability for omissions and other absences as being based on non-causal counterfactual dependence substantially undercuts Moore's initial assertion of the pervasive "causation-drenched" nature of legal responsibility,[42] it is a price he apparently is willing to pay to be able to explain differences in responsibility and liability as being based almost entirely on differences in causation—a motivation that also underlies his attempt to replace all of the doctrines of attributable responsibility (so-called "proximate causation") with the alleged "scalarity" of causation.[43] However, as Schaffer has pointed out, Moore seems not to have realized that opening the door to counterfactual dependence as a desert determiner permits—indeed requires—holding anyone who contributes to one fork of an epiphenomenal relation liable for every condition in the other fork and anyone who contributed to an effect liable for all the conditions that were necessary for that effect.[44] Moore has reacted to Schaffer's pointing this out by stipulating restrictions on the employment of counterfactual dependency to avoid these results.[45] Apparently, such stipulations, when employed by Moore rather than others, are not considered by him to be ad hoc, contrived, or viciously circular.

Moore's byzantine conceptual structure collapses entirely when Schaffer's basic point is understood: All human actions take place through the occurrence of an absence. If, as Moore asserts, absences cannot be causes or effects, then, rather than causation being a pervasive, dominant determinant of moral and legal responsibility, it plays no role at all. Worse yet, despite our beliefs to the contrary, human actions cannot cause anything.

Moore attempts to avoid these disastrous consequences for his theory by employing an expanded version of the ad hoc tactic that he uses to avoid applying the doctrine of double effect, which he now supports, when it leads to unacceptable results. That doctrine asserts that merely knowing or believing that some consequence will occur as a result of your actions incurs less moral responsibility for the consequence than when you act with the purpose of causing it. Moore employs the doctrine not only to justify lesser moral responsibility for knowingly causing something rather than purposely causing it, but also to authorize utilitarian consequentialist departures from his alleged deontological, justice-based theory of moral and legal responsibility when knowledge rather than purpose is involved. The tactic is to "get sloppy" in our descriptions of distinct states of affairs and thereby treat them as the same state of affairs, but only when necessary to avoid an unacceptable result.[46]

To deal with Schaffer's demonstration that all human actions (and many other events) take place through the occurrence of an absence, Moore similarly "gets sloppy" when dealing with the steps in a causal chain that contain such absences by treating the distinct states of affairs that existed prior to and after the absence as being the same state of affairs if their descriptions are sufficiently "close." He asserts: "the moral difference (like the metaphysical difference) tends to evaporate."[47] If need be, considerable

[41] Moore, 2009d, 426, 435–67. [42] Moore, 2009d, vii. [43] See section V of this chapter.
[44] Schaffer, "Disconnection and Responsibility," 413–15. [45] Moore, 2012a, 503–5.
[46] Moore, 2009d, 45–7, 462–3. [47] Moore, 2009d, 457; see Moore, 2009d, 461–3, 465–6.

sloppiness is allowed: "A ruptured heart is not literally the same state of affairs as cellular death [of brain cells] in the person whose heart it is; but it is pretty close."[48]

Note that the relevant conditions in the states of affairs identified by Moore—the hole in the heart and the lack of life in the brain cells—are absences, so he has not avoided the problem of absences even by skipping over several intermediate steps in the relevant causal process: the hole in the heart (caused positively by the bullet's hitting the heart) caused negatively (a) the failure of the causal processes that were keeping the blood contained in the heart, arteries, and veins, which allowed the positive causal process of the blood's escaping containment to occur, and/or (b) the failure of the positive causal process of the heart's pumping blood; and one or both of these failures caused negatively an absence of oxygenated blood going to the cells in the brain, which caused negatively the failure of the causal processes keeping the brain functioning, which caused negatively the death (lack of life) of the victim.

Moore's willingness to "get sloppy" varies depending on the argument. For example, when rebutting arguments by others that there is no causation requirement for inchoate crimes, such as attempts, he insists on an extremely rigorous and minute distinction between states of affairs in order to distinguish between acts and consequences.[49]

Putting aside Moore's inconsistency and the very ad hoc and contrived nature of his attempted fixes to his theory, in the end these fixes do not rescue his theory as a matter of metaphysics, but rather (following in Hart and Honoré's footsteps) only as a matter of linguistics and common sense morality, as he himself admits:[50]

> Decapitations and deaths are close enough that we should say that to intend the first is to intend the second. Analogously, we should say that to do an act causing the first is to do an act causing the second. In each case this is true irrespective of the actual metaphysics of event-individuation or the true identity of states of affairs and of mental representations. Even if Herod didn't literally either cause or intend John's death [when Herod had John's head cut off and delivered on a platter to please his wife], what he did cause and intend is close enough that his moral responsibility is that of an intender and a causer of death.[51]

Moore's adherence to the position that omissions and other absences cannot be causes or effects leads to the conclusion, as a matter of metaphysics, that human actions do not cause anything and that causation can play no role in determining moral and legal responsibility, which is not only highly implausible but in direct contradiction of his major thesis in *Causation and Responsibility*.

Moore's response to my, Ingeborg Puppe's,[52] and Schaffer's each noting the devastating consequences for his theory of Schaffer's demonstration that absences are pervasive in causal processes is to dodge: "Schaffer's considered view is not that [absences can be the relata of singular causal relations, but rather that] items that look like absences are really positive presences."[53] Schaffer does try to make that argument work.[54] However, Moore fails to note that he,[55] Dieter Birnbacher, and David Hommen[56] have all demolished that

[48] Moore, 2009d, 461–2. [49] Moore, 2009d, 14–19, 281–2. [50] Moore, 2012a, 501–2.
[51] Moore, 2009d, 463. [52] Puppe, "The Concept of Causation in the Law," 80–5.
[53] Moore, 2013b, 340. [54] Schaffer, "Disconnection and Responsibility," 416–26.
[55] Moore, 2009d, 437–9.

argument, and that Schaffer states that, if that argument fails and omission claims reference absences, he would bite the bullet and acknowledge that absences can be the relata of singular causal relations, rather than having to accept, as Moore must, that chopping off heads doesn't kill people and, worse, that humans cannot cause anything.[57]

I am with Schaffer, although not needing to be driven to that position as a last resort. As Moore has acknowledged, there is no obstacle to treating absences as causes under the NESS account.[58] Indeed, absences as specific time-and-place-located features of actual states of affairs—for example, the absence of a stop sign at an intersection—are real enough to be perceived by others, and that perception often leads to some action being taken by those others.

The critical distinction for purposes of causal analysis is not the distinction between positive and negative conditions (e.g., acts versus omissions), but rather between positive and negative causal processes, each of which may be initiated by either positive or negative conditions and have positive or negative conditions as the ultimate effect. This distinction is critical because the analysis of each type of causation, although based on the same underlying (NESS) account of causation, differs owing to their differing focus.

A negative condition—for example, being dead—is the absence of a positive condition—for example, being alive. Such absences exist owing to the lack of occurrence of the positive causal process(es) that would have produced or maintained the relevant positive conditions. Thus, while the analysis of positive causation focuses on the successful completion of the relevant positive causal process(es), the analysis of negative causation focuses on the failure of a positive causal process. To know that a positive causal process succeeded, we need to know that all of the necessary conditions in the antecedents of the relevant causal generalizations and their underlying causal laws were instantiated on the particular occasion. To know how one or more of them was instantiated, we need to go one or more levels deeper in the causal web. To know that a positive causal process failed, we need to know that at least one of the necessary conditions in the antecedents of the relevant causal generalizations and their underlying causal laws was not instantiated. To know what caused its failure we need to know at what point it failed and go one or more levels deeper in the causal web to find out why it failed at that point.[59]

V. Moore's Primitivist Singularism

Moore is a self-described "reluctant primitivist" (or perhaps "physical reductionist") type of "back door singularist."[60] According to Moore, the distinction between generalist accounts and singularist accounts "is the distinction between accounts that do, and accounts that do not, reduce statements of singular causal relations to statements of instantiated laws."[61] A primitivist singularist denies not merely the reduction of

[56] Dieter Birnbacher and David Hommen, "Omissions as Causes—Genuine, Quasi, or Not At All?" in Kahmen and Stepanians, *Critical Essays*, 133, 140–1; David Hommen, "Moore and Schaffer on the Ontology of Omissions," 45 *Journal for General Philosophy of Science* 71 (2014), 82–5.

[57] Schaffer, "Disconnection and Responsibility," 417, 427.

[58] Moore, 2009d, 479.

[59] See Wright, "NESS Account," 311–21.

[60] Moore, 2009d, xii, 506–7.

[61] Moore, 2009d, 497.

[62] Moore, 2009d, 499.

[63] Moore, 2009d, 499–502.

singular relations to causal laws, but also their reduction to anything else.[62] A physical reduction singularist reduces singular causal relations to physical processes, qualities, or quantities, which persist along the chains of causation.[63] Given Schaffer's demonstration, which Moore accepts, of the lack of physical connection in the causal processes involved in all human action and many other causal processes due to the presence of absences in those processes, physical reduction singularism is a non-starter. In any event, Moore consistently favors the primitivist approach.

The "back door" and "reluctant" qualifiers are due to Moore's supposedly having arrived at these positions by finding all extant alternative theories lacking,[64] but he also greatly appreciates not having to say anything about what causation really is:

> [P]rimitivism frees us from having to deal with all the counterexamples adduced against [reductionist theories, which] juxtapose our pre-theoretical causal intuitions against the seeming dictates of the preferred reduction bases for causation. . . . [P]rimitivism offers up no non-causal facts with which to compare our causal intuitions. Causation can be just what those intuitions say that it is, on the primitivist view. [¶] "[A] cause is a cause" is the most that can be said . . ..[65]

In a few conclusory, *ipse dixit* statements, Moore claims that the various alleged defects of generalist theories disappear under singularist theories, especially primitivist singularism. For example, although conditions and stipulations in generalist theories that are designed to avoid overbreadth are "ad hoc," "unmotivated," and "viciously circular," primitivists "have license to shape causation to their pre-theoretical intuitions, so their theory cannot suffer from overbreadth."[66] More particularly,

> Primitivists, of course, can simply endow their primitive relation with temporal direction and asymmetry and be done with it. Physical reductionist singularists have to do a bit more work, here as elsewhere. The reduction-bases need to have these two features, but that seems unproblematic.[67]

Moore claims that singularists "of all stripes" have no problem distinguishing causal relations from non-causal epiphenomenal relations: "There is no causal chain between co-effects of a common cause on any of these theories, making them invulnerable to objections along these lines."[68] He similarly brusquely claims that "we all know (with a certainty that borders on the a priori)"[69] that in pre-emptive causation cases the pre-emptive condition was a cause and the preempted condition was not:

> Singularist theories slice through [over-determined causation] cases like the proverbial hot knife through butter. There are continuous causal chains for each factor in all of these cases, save for the pre-empted factor in pre-emptive-cause cases (which strong causal intuition does not regard as causal).[70]

Moore provides no explanation of the nature of causal chains or, more importantly, how we are supposed to be able to perceive their existence or non-existence, when, as Moore himself insists, the notion that "we can directly observe singular causal

[64] Moore, 2009d, 506–7. [65] Moore, 2009d, 505. [66] Moore, 2009d, 508.
[67] Moore, 2009d, 509. [68] Moore, 2009d, 509. [69] Moore, 2009d, 507.
[70] Moore, 2009d, 510.

relations . . . [is a] hogchoker of a premise."[71] He ignores the many debates about what was a cause of what in these situations in the academic literature, including discussions of differing intuitions by academics and others.

For Moore, "[o]ne of the great strengths of most singularisms—namely all forms of singularism that deny action at a distance—is that they get it right in how they classify omissions, preventions, and double-preventions as non-causal."[72] He admits that this is strongly contrary to common intuition in the sorts of "double-prevention" cases that Schaffer has discussed, such as cutting off someone's head. Yet, he asserts,

> a properly regimented intuition—one recognizing that omissions and preventions cannot be non-causal unless double-preventions are also non-causal, and which recognizes that there is no causal distinction between double-preventions which are allowings and double-preventions which are not—must at the end of the day treat double-preventions as non-causal.[73]

Moore ignores the fact, discussed in section V of this chapter, that this position commits him to concluding that humans cannot really (metaphysically) cause anything, which destroys the fundamental premise of his book, which is intended to demonstrate the pervasive role that causation plays in assessments of moral and legal responsibility.

Moore claims that, as a primitivist, he can stipulate that causation is "scalar" and thus "peters out" over extended chains or after repeated interventions and does not exist for trivial contributing conditions.[74] The notion that causation, a purely natural relation, peters out is naive scientifically and metaphysically, as one can see by positioning oneself at any point in a lengthening chain or expanding web of causation: it just keeps going on. It is responsibility, rather than causation, that peters out or is terminated, and assessments of responsibility are not merely or even primarily based on a simplistic measuring of causal chains, counting of interventions, or comparing of the sizes of different causal contributions (if the latter is even possible in most situations).[75]

Moore needs to stipulate causal scalarity to make good on his assertion that causation plays a pervasive role in attributing responsibility. He needs a (supposed) metaphysical basis for his jettisoning all of the standard legal limitations on attributable responsibility (so-called "proximate" causation) and replacing them with the allegedly primitivist "substantial factor" criterion, despite widespread criticism of that criterion in the legal literature, including the Restatement Third of Torts.[76] In furtherance of his argument, he misstates the history and content of the substantial-factor criterion. As created by Jeremiah Smith and incorporated in the first and second Restatements, it was not, contrary to Moore's descriptions,[77] an unelaborated primitivist concept. Rather, to

71 Moore, 2009d, 363; see also Moore, 2009d, 511–12.

72 Moore, 2009d, 508.

73 Moore, 2009d, 508–9.

74 Moore, 2009d, 508; see also Moore, 2009d, ix, 61, 70–1, 102, 105, 121–2, 223–5, 275, 357–8.

75 To avoid treating events that occur as a result of numerous small contributions, each trivial when compared to the aggregate contributions, as unexplained miracles, Moore turns to a favorite (yet seriously defective) tactic of criminal lawyers—treating the aggregate contributions as the cause—hoping, I assume, that no one will notice his trenchant criticism of that tactic a few pages later, relying on arguments in his book. Moore, 2013b, 340, 348–50 (citing Moore, 2009d, 354–5, 410 n. 44); see Wright, "Causation in Tort Law," 1780–1.

76 Moore, 2009d, xii, 88–9, 104–5, 276–8, 505–6.

77 Moore, 2009d, 88–9, 104–5, 299–300, 505–6.

be a "substantial factor" in the production of some harm, it was necessary but not sufficient that the condition at issue be either necessary or independently strongly sufficient for the occurrence of the harm.[78]

After reading Moore's criticisms of generalist theories and praise of primitivist "theories," it is a bit of a shock to learn that Moore rejects "extreme," "wild-eyed" singularism, as argued for by Mackie[79] and Elizabeth Anscombe,[80] according to which "singular causal relations either do or at least can exist in the absence of any pertinent causal laws."[81] Moore is forced to admit the necessity of causal laws, composed of abstract conditions that describe specific properties or features of events and states of affairs, by his acceptance, after long opposition, of the feature-driven nature of singular causal relations: It is the properties or features of events or states of affairs, rather than the events or states of affairs in their entirety, that, when concretely instantiated in particular situations, are the relata of singular causal relations.[82] Properties, Moore correctly notes, "play too important a role in both events and states of affairs as causal relata to countenance extreme singularism."[83]

Yet Moore resists what would seem to follow: The necessity of some generalist "covering law" theory of causation, such as the NESS account. His resistance likely is based on his recognizing that such accounts open the door to treating absences as causes and on his erroneous belief that treating the properties of events or states of affairs as the relata of singular causal relations would require acceptance of the "harm within the risk" (HWR) limitation on attributions of legal responsibility—which, however, focuses on risks rather than on causation.[84] He therefore employs the same linguistic dodge that he employs in dealing with absences. He erroneously claims that it is unclear whether the law requires event-causation or feature-causation and states that, in order to avoid the problems raised by the HWR limitation, the law should employ (metaphysically incorrect) event-causation.[85] Although a few legal theorists in the past have argued for event-causation, they were (as Moore fails to note) HWR proponents, who relied on the HWR limitation to avoid extremely overbroad findings of causation

[78] See Wright, "Causation in Tort Law," 1781–4; Wright, "Once More Into the Bramble Bush: Duty, Causal Contribution, and the Extent of Legal Responsibility" ["Once More"], 54 *Vanderbilt Law Review* 1071 (2001), 1075–80.

[79] Mackie, "Cement of the Universe," 40–58, 76–8, 120–2; see also Wright, "Pruning the Bramble Bush," 1023–4.

[80] Moore, 2009d, 362, 472, 496.

[81] Moore, 2009d, 506.

[82] Moore, 2009d, 361–5, 368 n. 61.

[83] Moore, 2009d, 506; see also Moore, 2009d, 472.

[84] Although at one point Moore seems to recognize this distinction (Moore, 2009d, 104), he continues to assert that I, as the primary legal expositor and supporter of feature-causation rather than event-causation, support the HWR limitation and opposed the Restatement Third's rejection of that limitation as a duty limitation. Moore, 2009d, 166–7 and nn. 49 and 50. To the contrary, I have from the beginning been a vigorous critic of the HWR limitation as either a duty limitation or a scope-of-liability limitation, arguing instead for a "harm results from the risk" scope-of-liability limitation, which does not suffer from the defects that Moore correctly attributes to the HWR limitation. Wright, "Causation in Tort Law," 1759, 1773–4; Wright, "Once More," 1091–6 (miscited by Moore); Richard Wright, "The Grounds and Extent of Legal Responsibility" ["Legal Responsibility"], 40 *San Diego Law Review* 1425 (2003), 1479–1531. I led the way in getting the American Law Institute to shift from HWR to "harm results from the risk" language in the Restatement Third, a development Moore fails to note. Moore, 2009d, 168, 221 n. 17. See American Law Institute, *80th Annual Meeting, Proceedings 2003* (St. Paul: ALI, 2004), 57–8, 62–4, 67–8, 70–1; American Law Institute, *Restatement of the Law Third, Torts: Liability for Physical Harm* (Proposed Final Draft No. 1*) (St Paul: ALI, 2005), § 29.

[85] Moore, 2009d, 329–32, 366–8.

and liability based on event-causation. As virtually every current legal theorist other than Moore acknowledges, the law should and does require feature-causation rather than event-causation.[86]

To avoid acceptance of a generalist "covering law" theory of causation, Moore argues for a "moderate" form of singularism, according to which no singular causal relation can exist unless it instantiates a causal law that "accompanies" or "stands behind" the singular causal relation. The "accompanies" and "stands behind" terms indicate what distinguishes moderate singularists from generalists: Generalists view the causal laws as basic and singular relations as "simply" instantiations of those laws, while singularists insist that singular relations are basic and that causal laws are "mere constructions" derived inductively from the singular relations.[87]

Our knowledge of causal laws is empirically derived.[88] However, the notion that causal laws are "mere constructions," the existence of which depends on their being derived inductively from observation of singular causal relations—which supposedly are prior to and independent of the causal laws, yet which, for some unexplained reason, cannot exist unless they happen to be instantiations of the causal laws—is bizarre. This theory makes the existence of causal laws—the laws of nature—contingent and dependent on our "constructing" them. If we weren't around, there apparently would be no laws of nature.

Moore's attempt to treat singular causal relations as primitivist in nature, with the relevant causal laws idly "standing behind" them, makes no sense unless his moderate singularism is a "dualist" rather than, as he claims, a "generalizing" theory.[89] Even as a dualist theory, his requirement that the singular relations from which the causal laws are constructed must be instantiations of those laws makes moderate singularism subject to each objection that Moore raises against nomic sufficiency theories.

At one point Moore claims that causal generalists follow Hume in believing that the existence of singular causal relations is an illusion.[90] I don't believe that, and I am not aware of any other causal generalist who believes that. Singular causal relations are real; indeed, causation only actually occurs within singular causal relations. However, what makes them causal relations is their being complete instantiations of the relevant causal laws. As Moore himself states, when accepting David Armstrong's reductionist identification of singular causal relations as instantiations of causal laws as a singularist theory,

> the 'glue' of causation, its necessitating [sufficiency] power, resides as much in the singular causal relation as in the relation between types (the subject of a law). Indeed, it is the same 'glue'. It is as completely present in singular causal relations as in causal laws. One is not more basic than the other, not because these are different but equally basic relations; rather, the mysterious ('primitive') element is the same thing in each relation.[91]

[86] Wright, "Causation in Tort Law," 1759–74; Wright, "Legal Responsibility," 1494–9; David Robertson, "The Common Sense of Cause in Fact," 75 *Texas Law Review* 1765 (1997), 1770 n. 19.

[87] Moore, 2009d, 361, 472–3, 496–9, 506.

[88] See Wright, "NESS Account," 289–90.

[89] Moore, 2009d, 499, 506.

[90] Moore, 2009d, 263–4.

[91] Moore, 2009d, 498.

13

The Moral Asymmetry Between Acts And Omissions*

Horacio Spector

I. Introduction

Michael Moore claims that sometimes we can justify an omission by its good consequences, whereas we cannot justify a paired action by its equally good consequences.[1] I think that this claim can only be plausible as a corollary of a more abstract view that we can call the *moral asymmetry view* (or *asymmetry view*). This view says that acts resulting in θ are morally worse than omissions that fail to prevent θ, where θ is any bad or harmful state of affairs. We can formulate the view even more briefly by introducing a term of art. Let's say that acts resulting in θ and omissions that fail to prevent θ are *equiconsequential.*[2] Therefore, it is necessarily true that the harm generated by a harmful act is equivalent, both qualitatively and quantitatively, to the harm allowed by the equiconsequential omission. Then the asymmetry view says that harmful acts are morally worse than equiconsequential omissions. The defense of the asymmetry view is not otiose, because many contemporary moral philosophers reject it.[3]

The moral difference between acts and equiconsequential omissions is also captured by related contrasts like doing/allowing, making/letting, and so on. These labels are not interchangeable, for omissions have peculiar nuances that are absent in mere refrainings. Thus it is reasonable to say that non-preventive omissions presuppose the agent's practical possibility to prevent or counteract the relevant causal process. Sometimes other features are also included within the concept of omission, such as the agent's awareness of her possibility to intervene, her intention not to intervene, and a moral duty or a customary requirement to avert or thwart the production of the harm. Because I need to distinguish acts from omissions in causal terms, that is, in a non-subjectivist and non-normative fashion, I ignore these further features in this chapter.[4]

Other authors have defended the moral asymmetry view as well, and there are substantial similarities but also dissimilarities between the various versions.[5] In this chapter I will try to delineate what I consider to be the most plausible formulation of the

* I am grateful for helpful comments made by Marcelo Ferrante and Eduardo Rivera López.

1 Moore, 2009d, 55.

2 I do not mean that equiconsequential acts and omissions have the same *causal* consequences.

3 For instance, Shelly Kagan, *The Limits of Morality* (Oxford: Oxford University Press, 1989); Ingmar Persson, *From Morality to the End of Reason* (Oxford: Oxford University Press, 2013).

4 I have discussed some of them in *Autonomy and Rights* (Oxford: Oxford University Press, 1992), 117–22.

5 *Autonomy and Rights*, Ch. IV.

asymmetry view, even though it is a formulation that Moore himself does not fully embrace.

A complete defense of the asymmetry view requires three interconnected arguments. First, we need the *causal argument*. Because the asymmetry view is a moral claim, and assuming that moral evaluations supervene on factual properties, we should be able to discover a *factual difference* that grounds the moral difference between acts and equiconsequential omissions.[6] A moral difference between *a* and *b* supervenes on a factual difference between *a* and *b* only if there is a factual feature that is typically true of *a* and typically false of *b* such that the moral difference is grounded on that factual feature. Moore also thinks that we need a basis for the asymmetry view, but he thinks that the grounding distinction is *metaphysical* rather than factual. He says: "[Y]ou cannot cause 'a nothing' any more than you can be caused by 'a nothing.'"[7] He adds, later on in the same book: "If negative events and negative states of affairs neither are referred to nor exist to be referred to by talk of omissions, it is baffling how there could be relata for singular causal relations involving omissions."[8] I made similar claims many years ago.[9] Whether described as factual or metaphysical, Moore and I think that the difference grounding the moral inequivalence is a causal distinction. The causal argument says that acts cause harms in a sense in which equiconsequential omissions do not.

Second, according to any reasonable conception of reflective equilibrium, the moral asymmetry view should cohere with our stable intuitions in concrete actual or hypothetical cases. This is the *intuitional argument*. The asymmetry view has considerable intuitional support within a large range of cases. So, for instance, most people would agree that if a stranger *A* kills *C*, he does something morally worse than a stranger *B* does in failing to give *C* money to get life-sustaining medical treatment, even though *B* could afford to do so. Yet our intuitions might be mistaken or distorted by emotional mechanisms and so it is important to establish what their strength and scope really are.

Finally, we need an argument that explains why the intuitions that the intuitional argument relies on supervene on the factual or metaphysical differences that the causal argument stresses. The *transcendental argument* views our moral intuitions on acting and failing to prevent as manifestations of a deeper understanding of our sense of moral responsibility and individual agency. The idea is that the moral asymmetry view is a condition of possibility or transcendental presupposition of our basic idea of individual agency and responsibility. A condition of possibility of a pattern of thought is a condition in the absence of which the pattern is meaningless, unstable, or inescapably imprecise. We see ourselves as separate persons when we visualize ourselves as morally responsible agents. This self-perception becomes unstable or inescapably imprecise if we reject the moral asymmetry view.

[6] In *Autonomy and Rights* I made the same point: "...if our ethical consciousness draws a moral distinction between doing and allowing, there should also be a factual difference between doing and allowing, not any factual difference whatever, but rather one which might be intuitively pointed to as the reason for the moral distinction in question. This follows from the general point that moral properties are *supervenient* upon factual ones." (146) (italics in the original).

[7] Moore, 2009d, 54. [8] Moore, 2009d, 445.

[9] *Autonomy and Rights*, 150–1. I have further discussed this problem in my recent article on causation in law and morality: "The MMTS Analysis of Causation," in Richard Goldberg (ed.), *Perspectives on Causation* (Oxford: Hart, 2011).

This chapter is organized into three further sections, each respectively devoted to the three arguments enumerated above. In section II, I discuss the causal argument.[10] I use the label *agent-conditioning* to dub all the ways in which agents can control changes in the world.[11] I distinguish causation proper from counterfactual dependence. Causation proper holds between events: a cause is an *event* that is the truth-maker of a particular proposition that instantiates an antecedent in a relevant set of generalizations; the effect is an *event* that makes true a particular proposition that belongs to a set of consequent propositions that can be deduced from the union of two sets, the set of antecedent propositions and the set of generalizations, but not from each set on its own.[12] In counterfactual dependence, a counterfactual determiner is an event in the absence of which the effect would not have occurred (or would not have occurred to a certain degree of probability). Whereas harming is a form of *sensu stricto* causation, failing to prevent harm is generally a form of counterfactual dependence. In section III, I show that the asymmetry view must be defended in its *moderate version*. The view does not say that harming is always worse than failing to prevent the same harm. It claims that causing harm is, in the absence of disturbing factors, morally worse than omitting to prevent the same harm. As a result, a harmful act is worse than its equiconsequential omission in all those cases in which the omission is unaccompanied by factors that can compound it or affect its intuitional assessment. In section IV I discuss the moral asymmetry view as a presupposition of our deep-seated conception of ourselves as individually responsible agents. I conclude in section V.

II. The Causal Argument

The factual difference between acts and equiconsequential omissions is causal. Whereas doing harm is a form of causation, failing to prevent harm generally is a form of counterfactual determination. When the harm occurs, the non-preventive omission is not a cause of the allowed harm. In contrast, it holds a relation of counterfactual dependence to some causal conditions of the harm. However, it is true that both acts and non-preventive omissions are ways in which an agent can control changes in the world. Agent-conditioning is a complex phenomenon that requires a dual explanation, that is, an explanation that appeals both to causation and counterfactual dependence. Agents do harms, fail to prevent harms, or remove obstacles that would otherwise prevent harms. Making things happen (acts), failing to prevent things from happening (omissions), and enabling things to happen (double-preventions) are three fundamental forms of agent-conditioning. (This list is not exhaustive as agents also contribute to things and collaborate with things in various ways.) Acts are events (i.e., bodily movements) that make true certain *positive causal conditions* established as antecedents in a set of generalizations. Omissions are *negative* counterfactual determiners of *causal*

[10] This section draws on section VI of "The MMTS Analysis of Causation" but I have modified some aspects of the previous account.

[11] Agent-conditioning is different from *agent causation*, which denotes the relation of volitions to external outcomes.

[12] I have submitted a three-set analysis of causation in "The MMTS Analysis of Causation."

conditions established as antecedents in a set of generalizations.[13] Though many examples of omissions involve negative causal conditions, omissions are negative counterfactual determiners of *negative or positive* conditions. For instance, a kindergarten teacher may fail to prevent the children's sunburn by not falsifying the negative condition "non-application of sunscreen" or the positive condition "sun exposure" (or both). Enabling harms (i.e., preventing their prevention) are *positive* counterfactual determiners of negative causal conditions. Enabling harms are acts that resemble omissions in that they operate as counterfactual determiners of some causal condition of the harm.

Consider the following case:

> *Hurried Pedestrian.* A hurried pedestrian sees an old lady being robbed by a mugger on a crowded street of the city, but fails to aid her, though he could easily do so.

The pedestrian's behavior is wrong as a failure to aid. It could be claimed that the mugger's intervention preempts the pedestrian's moral responsibility. But our business now is to establish not whether the behavior is wrong but whether the pedestrian has *caused* via his omission the lady being robbed. Some authors defend what we can call the *plain view*. In this view, non-preventive omissions are truth-makers of negative conditions in a causal generalization, just as acts are truth-makers of positive causal conditions. For instance, Richard Wright and Ingmar Persson claim that omissions to act are negative causes or conditions.[14] Plain view theorists would say that the pedestrian's failure to stop the mugger is a negative condition that is necessary for the relevant event to be a cause of the undesirable outcome (robbery). This is an erroneous claim, however. To be sure, the set of causal conditions of the robbery must include the negative condition that the thief is not stopped, but the pedestrian's omission is not logically equivalent to this negative condition. Hence, the omission cannot be a truth-maker of that negative condition.

The plain view conflates non-preventive omissions with causal conditions. But omissions are not logically equivalent to negative (or positive) causal conditions. We can clarify this point by focusing on the logical behavior of omissions. The occurrence of the condition *non-C* entails that no one prevented *non-C* by causing *C* (by the same token, the occurrence of the condition *C* entails that no one prevented *C* by causing *non-C*).[15] In turn, the proposition that says that no one prevented *non-C* by causing *C* entails, for any agent *A*, that *A* did not prevent *non-C*. Non-preventions could then be thought to be logical consequences of negative causal conditions. However, we have said that omissions, unlike mere refrainings or non-preventions, presuppose the agent's practical possibility to prevent a causal condition of the harm. The condition *non-C* says nothing about any agent's practical possibilities. Therefore, *omissions* to prevent are not logical consequences of causal conditions. Conversely, *A*'s omitting to prevent *non-C* is not a logically sufficient condition of *non-C*. Though the set of causal conditions of the

[13] As I will show later on, some omissions play a different role.

[14] Richard W Wright, "Acts and Omissions as Positive and Negative Causes," in J. W. Neyers et al. (eds.), *Emerging Issues in Tort Law* (Oxford: Hart, 2007), 291; Ingmar Persson, *From Morality to the End of Reason*, (n. 4) 81.

[15] Eric Mack makes a similar point. He points out that the non-obtention of falsifying preventions "is implied by the satisfaction of the initial statement of jointly sufficient conditions." Eric Mack, "Bad Samaritanism and the Causation of Harm," 9 *Philosophy and Public Affairs* 258 (1980).

lady's being robbed must include the negative condition that the lady was not aided, the hurried pedestrian's omission does not guarantee that negative causal condition. In effect, we can hypothesize that another pedestrian or the police aided the lady, or could have aided the lady. In this case we would still want to say that our pedestrian omitted to stop the robbery. Suppose another pedestrian negated the negative condition "non-aid" by protecting the lady just in time to prevent the robbery. Still we would want to say that the first pedestrian omitted to save the lady, rather than merely to say that he *attempted to omit* to protect the lady.[16] Therefore, non-preventive omissions are not logically equivalent to the negative (or positive) causal conditions they fail to prevent.

The correct view about non-preventive omissions is as follows. Prevention occurs, or could occur, by negating one of the negative or positive conditions stated in the antecedent of the causal generalization. So the hurried pedestrian could have made the negative condition "non-aid" false by stopping the mugger. Therefore, the negative condition indicated would have been falsified in the absence of the pedestrian's omission (i.e., in case the pedestrian had performed the relevant preventing act). It is easy to realize, then, that omissions are *negative counterfactual determiners* of a negative or positive condition that figures in the antecedent of a causal generalization. By failing to prevent a causal condition, an agent "collaborates" with a causal process. An omission is not necessarily a causal condition, but the conditions that counterfactually depend on omissions are conditions of the relevant outcome in accordance with a causal generalization. That is, "non-aid" is a causal condition of the lady's robbery.

Saying that non-preventive omissions are counterfactual determiners of causal conditions is quite different from asserting that omissions are counterfactual determiners of the harm. The latter is the position that Moore explicitly adopts. He says: "If omissions give rise to a moral responsibility for some harm that is not based on there being a causal relationship between the omission and the harm, it is pretty clear that counterfactual dependence is the relation between the omission and the harm that is doing the moral work here."[17] While it is not uncommon to regard a failure to prevent as a counterfactual determiner of the relevant effect (i.e., the harm), I have been unable to find an account of omissions to prevent as counterfactual determiners of causal conditions.[18]

It is easy to explain why a non-preventive omission is not necessarily a counterfactual determiner of the harm. Consider the following example, in which a non-preventive omission preempts a later non-preventive omission:

[16] In contrast, other phrases that denote refrainings, like "allowing" and "letting," seem to have a different implication. Thus, if *A* let *B* die, *B*'s death seems to be entailed by *A*'s abstention, though we might try to say that *A*'s letting *B* die only entails that *B* would have died save for some fortunate thwarting factor.

[17] Moore, 2009d, 451–2. Moore says that an omission has a relation of counterfactual dependence to the harm: Moore, 2009d, 452. However, he also appeals to an idea borrowed from Phil Dowe, who analyzes omissions and double preventions in terms of counterfactual claims about "genuine" causal processes: Phil Dowe, *Physical Causation* (Cambridge: Cambridge University Press, 2000), 136–40. Moore says in this connection: "...when I am blamed for omitting to save you, the relevant counterfactual asserts that had I done a certain act (such as throw a rope) it would have *caused* a certain state of affairs (such as you being pulled ashore) that is incompatible with your drowning." Moore, 2009d, 455. The view defended here is different because it analyzes omissions (and double preventions) as counterfactual determiners of negative causal conditions.

[18] See, for instance: Jane Stapleton, "Choosing What We Mean by 'Causation' in the Law" 73 *Missouri Law Review* 433 (2008), 436–7.

Unreliable Guards. Two guards must take care of a prisoner in a cell. Sally must give him water, Bert must supply bread. Neither guard fulfilled their duty, but the prisoner dies from dehydration rather than starvation.[19]

Neither Sally's nor Bert's omissions are counterfactual determiners of the prisoner's death, because this event would have occurred anyway in the absence of each omission on its own. Whereas Sally's omission is a counterfactual determiner of the causal negative condition "no water," Bert's omission is a counterfactual determiner of the negative condition "no bread." However, generalizations relative to starvation do not fit the whole domain of empirical facts in this example. In contrast, generalizations relative to dehydration do match those empirical facts. For this reason, it is Sally's omission that is relevant in relation to the applicable set of generalizations.

Non-preventive omissions are *negative* counterfactual determiners of negative (or positive) conditions, but they are not necessarily truth-makers of those conditions. However, a subclass of omissions, which I propose to call *endogenous omissions*, has a different structure. These omissions are truth-makers of negative causal conditions of the outcome. To explain its nature, I need to use the concept of a "causal system." A causal system *S* is a fragment of the history of the world transpiring in a certain spatiotemporal region and defined by a series of states and a set of causal generalizations whose state variables are instantiated by the successive states of *S*.[20] An endogenous omission can be true of an agent *A* in a system *S* only if the complete description of *S* for some initial period essentially includes physical, mental, and/or social properties of *A*. Because *A* is involved in *S*, it is possible for a single omission of *S*'s to be truth-making (rather than counterfactually determining) of a negative condition at a certain state in *S*. If these conditions are not met, an omission is *exogenous*. Consider the following case:

Lethal Treadmill. A war prisoner is cheated into a perverse ergometric treadmill test. The equipment has been modified in such a way that if he stops running he will turn on an electric chair that will electrocute his fellow prisoner in the next room. He stops running.

In this example we have a causal system that ends up with the fellow prisoner's electrocution and that begins with the prisoner's running on the treadmill. The complete description of this system must cite the prisoner's running on the treadmill as an initial state. The prisoner's omitting to continue running on the treadmill is an endogenous omission because it is a truth-maker of a negative causal condition in the system. It is true that if the prisoner had continued running on the treadmill, the electric chair would have remained off and the system would not have ended in electrocution. But this is so only in the trivial sense in which a truth-maker is a determiner of the proposition that it makes true. Relative to the relevant set of generalizations, one state in the system includes the condition that the prisoner stops running and other omissions are

[19] Judith Jarvis Thomson, "Causation: Omissions," 66 *Philosophy and Phenomenological Research* 81 (2003).

[20] Broadly speaking, I have borrowed this concept from Georg Henrik von Wright, *Explanation and Understanding* (Cornell: Cornell University Press, 1971), 49.

irrelevant. Endogenous omissions resemble acts in that they are also truth-makers of causal conditions.

I have argued that whereas acts involve causation, omissions generally are negative counterfactual determiners of negative (or positive) causal factors, except in cases like *Lethal Treadmill*, where an omission can be causal in a form similar to an act. Just as omissions can sometimes resemble acts, acts can resemble (exogenous) omissions if they enable harms to occur. Acts enable harms to occur when they are *positive* counterfactual determiners of *negative* causal factors. This takes place in cases where an agent positively removes an obstacle or impediment (e.g., a safety device). *Double preventions*, as they are often called, are acts that prevent a preventive causal process thus allowing a certain effect to occur. A more careful analysis of double preventions exceeds the scope of this chapter.

III. The Intuitional Argument

Although the moral asymmetry view has strong intuitional support, there are cases in which acts causing harm are morally on a par with their equiconsequential omissions. For instance, Michael Tooley has argued that the moral asymmetry view is false by adducing the following pair of examples:

> *Babysitting Device 1*. One is confronted with a machine that contains a child and a military secret. The machine is so constructed that unless one pushes a button, the child will be tortured and the secret will be destroyed. If one pushes the button, the child will emerge unharmed, but the secret will be transmitted to the enemy. One fails to push the button.
>
> *Babysitting Device 2*. One is confronted with a machine that contains a child and a military secret. The machine is so constructed that unless one pushes a button, a secret will be transmitted to the enemy, while a child will emerge unharmed. If one pushes the button, the secret will be destroyed, but the child will be tortured. One pushes the button.[21]

It is hardly imaginable that our moral intuitions could find any moral difference between the omission in *Babysitting Device 1* and the equiconsequential act in *Babysitting Device 2*.

Other cases seem to refute a corollary of the asymmetry view, namely the proposition that, whereas it is permissible to allow some harm θ in order to prevent greater harm, it is impermissible to cause harm θ in order to prevent the same greater harm. For instance, it might be thought that the famous trolley case, in Thomson's bystander version, is a counterexample to Moore's defense of the asymmetry view.[22] In this case a bystander can flip a switch diverting the trolley onto a side track in such a way that he will save five people trapped on the main track but will kill one person trapped on the

[21] Michael Tooley, "An Irrelevant Consideration: Killing versus Letting Die," in Bonnie Steinbock (ed.), *Killing and Letting Die* (Englewood Cliffs, NJ: Prentice-Hall, 1980), 58–9. The names of the examples have been added.

[22] Carolina Sartorio, "Moore on Doing versus Allowing Harm," 42 *Rutgers Law Journal* 442 (2011).

side track.[23] Most people believe that the bystander may turn the trolley, which seems to run counter to the asymmety view.

One way of discarding such puzzling cases is by distinguishing between two different versions of the asymmetry view: the *absolutist version* and the *moderate version*. The absolutist version holds that an act is worse than its equiconsequential omission no matter what other factors attend the act and the omission. The moderate version includes the clause "in the absence of *disturbing factors*," which covers relevant properties that could be contingently true of an omission and that modify its moral assessment. Among disturbing factors are differences that violate the *ceteris paribus* proviso ("all else being equal"). The moderate version affirms that a wrong act is worse than the equiconsequential omission provided disturbing factors are not present. This version does not rule out the possibility that some factors could interact with the doing/allowing contrast in such a way that one particular omission is as bad as or even worse than the equiconsequential act. Of course, we need further indications about the class of disturbing factors to avoid a merely tautological formulation of the moderate view.

It is the moderate version of the asymmetry view that has powerful intuitional support; the absolutist version is counterintuitive. Indeed, many omissions are morally so serious that they can hardly be less serious than any other act. The asymmetry view claims that, in the absence of disturbing factors, doing harm is morally worse than the equiconsequential omission. But disturbing factors are often present. Well understood, the asymmetry view claims that doing harm is *more generally* bad than allowing the same harm. This can only be the case if a property necessarily true of doings makes a moral difference that the same or other properties can only contingently match or surpass in the case of equiconsequential omissions. The moderate view is compatible with claiming that failing to prevent harm is morally as bad as doing the same harm *within a certain range of cases in which disturbing factors are present*. Conversely, doing harm would be morally worse than allowing the same harm in all those cases in which the behaviors are unaccompanied by disturbing factors. The intuitional support of the moderate asymmetry view then remains unaffected if all the problematic cases belong in the range of cases in which disturbing factors are present.

Disturbing factors are properties that are contingently true of some omissions and that can aggravate the verdict on their moral seriousness up to the point at which it parallels the seriousness of the equiconsequential act. In the following I will focus on two groups of disturbing factors: (a) social dysfunction factors (e.g., agent's cost, effort, or risk), and (b) division-of-labor factors (e.g., agent's role, responsibility, or special position).

The agent's costs, effort, or risk are the most obvious social dysfunction factors. Doing harm is robustly wrong across various degrees of cost, effort, or risk involved in not doing the act. For example, one should not kill another person even if that is indispensable for saving one's life; there are obvious exceptions, like self-defense. In contrast, letting a person die is permissible if the only way to prevent it is by seriously risking one's own life. When the costs, effort, or risk are minimal, a moral constraint on allowing harm cannot be exploited by other people to externalize substantial costs to

[23] Judith Jarvis Thomson, "Killing, Letting Die, and the Trolley Problem," 59 *The Monist* 204 (1976).

the agent. It has been argued that one social function of the moral asymmetry is to avoid prisoner's dilemma situations that could be generated by a constraint on allowing harm (i.e., an obligation to prevent harm), especially if the constraint is strong and broad.[24] More specifically, a limitless duty to prevent harm can lead to (1) a dramatic waste of social resources caused by the moral hazard effect involved in cheap and comprehensive insurance, and/or (2) a tragedy of the commons by which the supply of communalized harm avoidance gets depleted in a prisoner's dilemma fashion.[25] It seems obvious that our moral intuitions are shaped by beliefs about serious potential dysfunctions in the operation of the social world. Given that the agent's prevention in the *Babysitting Device* cases involves minimal effort, and that the cases are so constructed that they can seldom occur in practice, the possibility of creating a prisoner's dilemma situation is unrealistic and the moral difference between pressing the button and failing to press the button then gets masked.

Among division-of-labor factors there is, first and foremost, the agent's special position. Thus, it is often claimed that the moral wrongness of not helping someone increases and may even equate the wrongness of positively harming the same person if one is causally or morally responsible for the creation of that person's position of need or vulnerability.[26]

Other cases of special position are more intricate. Non-preventive omissions are counterfactual determiners of negative (or positive) conditions in causal generalizations, but they are not logically sufficient conditions of such conditions. Indeed, an agent's non-preventive omission is compatible with the falsification of the relevant negative condition if someone else succeeds in negating it. Agents do not always have the unique possibility to prevent a certain result that is under the control of their non-preventive omissions (though this is often the case in endogenous omissions). In contrast, agents do typically have the unique possibility to prevent a certain result controlled by their acts. However, when an agent is placed in such special position that she alone has the possibility to negate a negative condition of a causal process, her omission incorporates one property that is true of acts, and it is then no surprise that the immorality of the omission approximates or equals the immorality of the equiconsequential act, especially if other disturbing factors are also present (for instance, the agent's cost, effort, or risk is minimal). The *Babysitting Device* cases are so designed that they suggest, even if only through a conversational implicature, that you (the reader) have the unique possibility to operate the machine. This means that you are the only person who can possibly push the button to alter the programmed result. The initial wording of the examples ("one is confronted") also suggests that you have no alternative but to take a decision. The examples also suggest that the process cannot be altered by natural causes. From the description of the cases it follows that your involvement in not pushing the button is similar to your causal involvement in pushing it. As there is no other agent or force in the setting that can possibly negate the negative condition

[24] David McCarthy, "Harming and Allowing Harm," 110 *Ethics* 749 (2000), 756–7; 766–9.

[25] Point (2) is also explored in: David Schmidtz, "Islands in a Sea of Obligation: An Essay on the Duty to Rescue," 19 *Law & Philosophy* 683 (2000), 686; 696; 700.

[26] Richard Louis Trammell, "Saving Life and Taking Life," in Bonnie Steinbock (ed.), *Killing and Letting Die* (Englewood Cliffs, NJ: Prentice-Hall, 1980), 170; Bruce Russell, "On the Relative Strictness of Negative and Positive Duties," in Steinbock (ed.), *Killing and Letting Die*, 223.

"button not being pushed" by pushing the button, your omission to push the button is a logically sufficient condition of that negative condition. Therefore, some exogenous omissions resemble endogenous omissions in that they have a relation to negative conditions that is stronger than mere counterfactual dependence. Still, making allowance for these complexities is different from returning to the plain view.

The agent's role and responsibility in relation to the harm is a widely accepted disturbing factor. Thus, a mother's allowing her baby to die by failing to feed him is aggravated by her role and responsibility and is possibly as serious as her suffocating the baby. In legal and political settings, the government's systematic omission to protect fundamental rights can be as bad as the government's positive violation of the same rights. This particular factor is so important that when it is present, the asymmetry between doing harm and failing to prevent harm tends to vanish.

When disturbing factors are absent, the asymmetry view has strong intuitional support. Thomson's trolley case requires a more detailed discussion. The moderate version of the asymmetry view does not entail the counterintuitive proposition that it is impermissible for the bystander to throw the switch, for there are disturbing factors that are present in the trolley case. First, the cost, effort, or risk of the bystander's flipping the switch is minimal; virtually the same as the cost, effort, or risk of the bystander's abstaining from flipping the switch. Since the cost, effort, or risk is minimal, its externalization can hardly generate a dynamic leading to a tragedy of the commons or other related social dysfunctionalities. In addition, the standard intuition in the trolley case is that the bystander's act (i.e., flipping the switch) is morally optional, as something different from being required by a moral constraint on the bystander's omission. Moral options cannot be exploited or manipulated to externalize costs in the same way as moral constraints can. In any case, discounting the influence of this effect magnifies our perception of the moral reasons in favor of flipping the switch, so that the moral status of this act can shift from being wrong to being morally optional.

Second, the example is so designed that the bystander is suggested to be the only agent in the setting that can throw the switch, so that his omission is a logically sufficient condition of the switch not being flipped. The example could have been worded by saying: "One (a bystander) is confronted with a runaway trolley that will. . . . The "one is confronted" clause is crucial because it individualizes a certain agent as the only person who can prevent the harm by falsifying a causal condition. The wording of the hypothetical already includes a factor that exerts a subtle influence on the intuitions of colleagues and students. In fact, the clause makes the omission causally similar to the positive action, because the omission is not merely a counterfactual determiner of the switch not being flipped (this is a necessary property of non-preventive omissions) but also a logically sufficient condition.

Third, the bystander does have a role, responsibility, or special position with respect to the harm in the extraordinary circumstances of the trolley case. In Foot's original case the agent was the trolley driver, which used to prompt the usual reply that the driver has a role or responsibility in assuring that the trolley he drives does not kill people. But the substitution of the bystander for the driver does not eliminate the influence of this factor altogether. The bystander's role is not attributed by legal or railroad norms, but is ipso facto imposed by social norms of emergency management. In fact, a sort of commonsensical norm is probably assumed to assign an ad hoc role to a non-appointee in an emergency situation in which the specialized professional or officer is not available and the delay of the relevant performance is dangerous. (A similar kind of norm indicates that health-care workers can be called on to attend an emergency patient when a physician is not available.) The usual understanding of the trolley case suggests that (1) the railroad switch operator is not available to perform the relevant maneuver, and (2) the bystander has sufficient basic knowledge or experience about switch operation to become an ad hoc emergency operator. These two conditions are not included in the wording of the example, and must often be added by professors in classroom discussion. In the absence of the two conditions, the bystander's intervention would probably be considered unjustifiable. In normal circumstances a regular railroad switchman would have to confront the situation, but emergency management requires extraordinary ad hoc solutions. Our moral intuitions when confronted with the trolley case are probably shaped by this kind of social norm.

What is the role of the bystander as a kind of emergency switch operator? I believe that colleagues and students who are inclined to think that it is morally optional for the bystander to flip the switch tend to visualize the situation as one in which the six trapped people form a *shared-risk group*. Those few who think that it is forbidden for the bystander to flip the switch are reluctant to accept the existence of shared-risk groups that are not created by explicit agreements. In fact, the trolley problem has a sociopolitical component that is related to the extent to which we are prepared to collectivize risks and resources on a non-voluntary basis.[27] Collectivization of risk or resources seems like an essential ingredient in the standard intuition that it is permissible to minimize the group members' overall risk of death. For instance, if the six people are railroad workers, this perception is a plausible one because we assume, albeit unconsciously, that the railroad company has created a shared-risk group that encompasses all workers situated in the same risk scenario. A similar example is a group of six firemen who get trapped in a fire. The fire deparment has placed them in a shared-risk group. Creation of shared-risk groups is done by explicit bylaws or customary norms. But even if the six people are private parties, we can view the situation as one in which six people are exposed in the setting to the same kind of risk. In social practice common risk exposure is often associated with the existence of a shared-risk group. For instance, people trapped in a fire form a shared-risk group from the perspective of the firemen. Now, when we assume that there is a shared-risk group, it is natural to think that there is one distributor that has a role, responsibility, or special position in minimizing the overall risk by allocating the available scarce resources. In the trolley example, safety from the trolley's threat is a scarce resource that can be enjoyed either by the one person or by the five-person group, but not jointly by all six people. We usually assign government officers or other specialized agents (captains, CEOs, etc.) the role or responsibility to minimize overall risk in shared-risk groups. When such specialized agents are not available, we might think it natural to assign the distributive role or responsibility to the one person who can de facto perform that role or responsibility, and in this case that

[27] Guido Pincione has argued that the trolley case supports a redistributive permission that is incompatible with the priority of negative duties over positive duties: "The Trolley Problem as a Problem for Libertarians," 19 *Utilitas* (2007).

person is simply the bystander, who becomes accordingly a sort of ad hoc distributor. Therefore, the bystander's failure to save the five people is more serious than an ordinary non-preventive omission, thus contributing to the aggravation already produced by the other factors. Of course, our resistance to accept the existence of shared-risk groups, that is, our tendency to reject collectivization of risk or resources, can influence our intuitions in the trolley example. It is only natural for uncompromising individualists to maintain that it is morally impermissible for the bystander to deflect the trolley.[28]

IV. The Trascendental Argument

The causal argument specifies the factual difference on which the moral asymmetry supervenes, but this is not the whole story. We also need an argument that explains why the causal difference is morally relevant. Here the transcendental argument comes into play. It says that the asymmetry view is a condition of possibility of any moral system that establishes a regime of individual responsibility. We can understand the concept of individual responsibility through the idea of *agent-separateness*. I have argued elsewhere that personal separateness has two sides: patient-separateness and agent-separateness.[29] Patient-separateness requires us to treat individuals that are potential beneficiaries or victims of our actions on a separate basis, in principle ruling out maximization of their overall utility. According to agent-separateness, my responsibility as a moral agent is limited to *my own behavior*. If someone else violates a moral duty, in principle it is not me who must answer for the violation; it is the other person. Individual responsibility is a form of *agent-relativity*, because in a moral system that establishes individual responsibility understood as agent-separateness each agent has a different moral aim. In contrast, *agent-neutrality* prescribes that all agents should share the same moral aim.[30]

The concept of individual moral responsibility presupposes a distinction between one's own conduct and someone else's conduct. Does the moral asymmetry view entail a principle of individual responsibility? Bernard Williams argues that utilitarianism fades out the contours of individual agency in postulating a strong *doctrine of negative responsibility* that makes our agency encompass all consequences of our behavior broadly defined.[31] The doctrine says that "if I am ever responsible for anything, then I must be just as much responsible for things that I allow or fail to prevent, as I am for things that I myself, in the more everyday restricted sense, bring about."[32] Williams seems to equate in this passage *doing* (as opposed to allowing or failing to prevent) and *my bringing about* (as opposed to someone else's bringing about). The problem is that

[28] Thomson eventually abandoned her life-long solution to the problem: Judith Jarvis Thomson "Turning the Trolley," 36 *Philosophy and Public Affairs* 359 (2008).

[29] Horacio Spector, *Autonomy and Rights*, (n. 4) 177–8; Horacio Spector, "The Reflective Nature of Moral Rights," 2 *Metodo. International Studies in Phenomenology and Philosophy* (2014) (freely available on the Web).

[30] Derek Parfit, *Reasons and Persons* (Oxford: Oxford University Press, 1984), 104.

[31] Bernard Williams, "A Critique of Utilitarianism," in J. J. C. Smart and Bernard Williams (eds.), *Utilitarianism For & Against* (Cambridge: Cambridge University Press, 1973), 93–5.

[32] Williams, "A Critique of Utilitarianism," 95.

the distinction between doing and failing to prevent cuts across the distinction between one's own conduct and someone else's conduct. The moral asymmetry view attaches special importance to causing harm, but its capacity to generate a regime of individual responsibility depends on whether we adopt an agent-neutral or agent-relative interpretation of the view. In fact, the moral asymmetry view does not entail a regime of individual moral responsibility. This is easy to establish. The moral asymmetry view fails to entail individual moral responsibility when it is formulated in an agent-neutral fashion. The reason is that, if doing harm (whoever does it) is worse than allowing harm (whoever allows it), then one should be morally required to prevent someone else's *doing harm* whenever the prevention is possible, and, therefore, norms of individual responsibility would lose their practical significance. In other words, the moral asymmetry view is not a logically sufficient condition of a regime of individual responsibility. What about the other direction (from individual responsibility to the moral asymmetry view)? Does a regime of individual moral responsibility entail or presuppose the moral asymmetry view?

Though the moral asymmetry view is not equivalent to a regime of individual responsibility, it is not conceptually independent from it. Indeed, in the other direction (from the regime of individual responsibility to the moral asymmetry view) there is not a relation of logical entailment, but the transcendental argument claims that a regime of individual responsibility *presupposes* the moral asymmetry view. The argument states that the moral asymmetry view is a condition of possibility of a stable and precise regime of individual responsibility. Scheffler pursues this line of thought. He claims that we ordinarily distinguish between the "primary" and the "secondary" manifestations of our agency and that, "in general, the norms of individual responsibility attach much greater weight to the primary than to the secondary manifestations".[33] However, Scheffler says that he does not aim to provide a precise formulation of the distinction between primary and secondary manifestations of agency, which renders his position accordingly imprecise.[34] Yet Scheffler takes a shot at stating the connection between individual responsibility and the moral asymmetry view:

> To see oneself as subject to norms of responsibility is to see oneself as having reason to bring one's conduct into conformity with those norms. But bringing one's conduct into conformity with norms of individual responsibility is itself something that one does, and not something that one merely allows to happen.[35]

In this passage, Scheffler's notion of doing is so formal and abstract that it embraces both doing and allowing. So one could reject the moral asymmetry view and still maintain the distinction between one's doing and someone else's doing (in the formal or abstract sense of doing). In fact, the moral asymmetry view could be rejected by holding that (1) one's doing is morally equivalent to one's omitting, and still claiming that (2) one's doing/omitting is morally different from someone else's doing/omitting. Scheffler recognizes this point when he says that "it does not follow from this [the formal idea of doing implicated in subjecting oneself to norms of moral responsibility] that the norms

[33] Samuel Scheffler, "Doing and Allowing," 114 *Ethics* 216 (2004).

[34] Scheffler, "Doing and Allowing," 218.

[35] Scheffler, "Doing and Allowing," 222.

to which one views oneself as subject must, as part of their content, attach significance to the distinction between what one does and what one allows."[36]

Scheffler argues that, though the norms of individual responsibility do not entail the moral asymmetry view, the rejection of the latter view makes the difference between one's own agency and someone else's agency untenable. He invites us to imagine an agent who views himself as subject to norms of individual responsibility but who at the same time rejects the moral distinction between doing and allowing:

> Insofar as he is determined to comply with the norms of responsibility, he treats the distinction as significant, for securing compliance with the norms is itself a primary manifestation of his agency. But insofar as he treats the outcomes he directly brings about and those that he fails to prevent as having equal weight in determining the rightness or wrongness of his actions, he denies that the distinction is significant.[37]

Unfortunately, Scheffler's argument is unsound because there is no incoherence or tension between recognizing the significance of the formal sense of doing implicated in subjecting oneself to norms of individual responsibility, and rejecting the significance of the substantive sense of doing that is contrasted with allowing in the moral asymmetry view. Since the two senses of doing (formal and substantive) are clearly different, it is perfectly possible to dismiss the moral asymmetry view with respect to the substantive sense while maintaining the moral relevance of the formal sense of doing.

The fundamental question is whether a regime of individual moral responsibility presupposes a *substantive* asymmetry between acts and omissions. Indeed, the rejection of the moral distinction between doing and omitting seems to be at odds with a stable and well-demarcated notion of individual agency and responsibility. However, I have for a long time been unable to find an argument that could prove that a regime of individual responsibility *requires* the moral difference between acts and omissions. Though this is a complex puzzle, I think I can now offer a solution. The strategy is to demonstrate that a set of plausible substantive claims, including the rejection of the moral asymmetry view, is incoherent. If my *reductio* is successful, the obvious way out is to endorse the moral asymmetry view. The argument runs as follows.

Assume our universe of discourse includes possible behaviors θ, such that θ is morally wrong and, when it is possible for someone else to commit θ, we can make him commit θ or prevent him from committing θ. In other words, it is necessarily true that we can control someone else's doing θ. Therefore, it is necessary (within our universe of discourse) that

(1) If someone else makes/omits θ, I omit to prevent that someone from making/omitting θ.

Suppose one rejects the moral asymmetry view. Then one accepts the moral equivalence principle (*E*):

(2) One's making θ is morally equivalent to one's omitting to prevent θ.

[36] Scheffler, "Doing and Allowing," 227. [37] Scheffler, "Doing and Allowing," 228.

A well-demarcated notion of individual moral responsibility requires that my conduct engage my own responsibility more stringently than someone else's conduct does. That is, we must endorse the principle of individual responsibility (*R*):

(3) My own making/omitting θ engages my responsibility more seriously than someone else's making/omitting θ does.

However, if (2) is accepted, one cannot endorse (3) within our universe of discourse. Let's see why. In accordance with (2) we must hold

(4) My making someone else make/omit θ is morally equivalent to my omitting to prevent someone else from making/omitting θ.

Now, making someone else do something wrong makes that someone's doing it engage my responsibility as seriously as my own doing it does. Therefore, it also seems reasonable to accept the *control principle* (*C*):

(5) If I make someone else make/omit θ, that someone's making/omitting θ engages my responsibility as seriously as my own making/omitting θ does.

This moral principle seems true, but we must be careful to exclude cases of full control of another person from its scope. In such cases (e.g., physical compulsion, brainwashing, etc.), the concept of making someone else commit an *action* is meaningless, because this person is not then an agent but a kind of automaton. The principle justifies a great variety of doctrines, both in municipal and international criminal law. Thus it is generally recognized that a person can commit a crime by using another person as instrument or executer. We find examples of an agent making someone else perpetrate a crime in cases of duress, manipulation of information, and solicitation, and in various ways in which a person incites, encourages, offers money, persuades, or, generally speaking, gives another a powerful motive to commit a crime.[38] The direct perpetrator can be held responsible or be absolved from any legal liability depending on her culpability and other circumstances; in any case, by committing solicitation or incitement an agent engages his responsibility as seriously as he would do if he himself had perpetrated the crime (though the penalties could be different). German criminal law even regards the "man behind" as an indirect or mediate perpetrator on the basis of his ability to control the crime. In the early sixties Claus Roxin extended the "mastery of the fact" theory to crimes perpetrated through organizational power structures. According to this view, the person who controls an illegal organizational power structure bears responsibility as indirect perpetrator of the crimes that he has made the structure's personnel commit.[39] In general, the indirect perpetrator makes someone else commit a crime by "pressing the button" of a power apparatus that controls the commission of the crime by one or another of its agents.

[38] According to the Model Penal Law, a person is liable for the conduct of another in various cases; for instance, if he causes an innocent person to commit a crime, or if he solicits another person to commit it: American Law Institute, MPC (1985), s. 2.06 (2)(a) and (3)(a)(i).

[39] Claus Roxin, *Autoría y dominio del hecho en Derecho Penal*, Joaquín Cuello Contreras and José Luis Serrano González de Murillo (trans.), (Madrid: Marcial Pons, 2000), ch. 6. Roxin gives the example of Adolf Eichmann's crimes: 273–5.

Now, by the rule of substitution of equivalents, we can infer from (4) and (5) that

(6) If I omit to prevent someone else from making/omitting θ, that someone's making/omitting θ engages my responsibility as seriously as my own making/omitting θ does.

By hypothetical syllogism we can infer from (1) and (6) that

(7) If someone else makes/omits θ, that someone's making/omitting θ engages my responsibility as seriously as my own making/omitting θ does.

Clearly, (7) is in contradiction with (3). If someone else's behavior engages my moral responsibility *as seriously as* my own behavior does, my own behavior does not engage my responsibility *more seriously than* someone else's behavior, and, therefore, a well-demarcated notion of individual moral responsibility vanishes.

The trascendental argument can also be viewed as an *impossibility theorem*. It shows that any moral system that includes principles *E*, *R*, and *C* is logically incoherent. In a nutshell, the moral significance of the argument is as follows. If we want to accept (3), that is, the regime of individual moral responsibility, we must reject either (2) or (5). But (5) is much less contestable than (2). So the obvious option is to reject (2), that is, the moral equivalence principle, and rejecting (2) is tantamount to accepting the moral asymmetry view.

If the transcendental argument is correct, rejecting the moral asymmetry view carries with it giving up deep conceptions of individual agency and moral responsibility that are at the bottom of our moral intuitions and thought. This perhaps does not show that the moral asymmetry view is true in an external, objectivist sense. But it shows that its dismissal is not a practical option, as it would involve reshaping human personhood to an extent that escapes the limits of our ethical consciousness. Therefore, moral reasons against the moral asymmetry view are condemned to be counterintuitive or paradoxical.

V. Conclusion

Though the three arguments for the moral asymmetry view can work jointly or separately, the trascendental argument (i.e., the impossibility theorem) is the fundamental one. The causal argument shows that the moral distinction between acts resulting in θ and omissions that fail to prevent θ is *possible* because it is grounded on a factual or metaphysical difference. The intuitional argument indicates that, as a matter of fact, we recognize the moral distinction in passing particular judgments on the morality of various alternatives of action. The trascendental argument establishes in the abstract that the moral asymmetry view is a *condition of possibility* of a regime of individual moral agency. The rejection of the moral asymmetry view would involve, under the plausible assumption of the control principle, giving up the idea of individual moral responsibility. That would mean a drastic reshaping of our moral life.

14

Moore and the Metaphysics of Causation

*Richard Fumerton**

I. Introduction

Moore's book, *Causation and the Law*, is accurately described by many as monumental both in terms of its scope and sophistication. An understanding of causation and subjunctive (sometimes called counterfactual) conditionals seems to be critical to a full understanding of a legal system that deploys both in attempting to articulate law and legal responsibility. But the importance of finding a philosophically satisfactory understanding of the truth conditions for causal claims and counterfactual assertions goes far beyond the philosophy of law. In many plausible views, explicit or implicit appeals to causation and the relations expressed by subjunctive conditionals (hereafter subjunctive connections) permeate our thought about both the mind and the external world. Behaviorists used to turn to subjunctives about how people would behave under certain conditions in an (always quixotic) attempt to analyze ordinary assertions about the mental states of others. These days some version of functionalism seems to have replaced behaviorism as the best hope for physicalist reductions of the mental, and again the functionalists explicitly appeal to our understanding of causal inputs and outputs in order to locate their functionally understood mental states.

Ironically, perhaps, while physicalists were turning to subjunctives and causation to understand *mental* states, earlier philosophers (and a few contemporary retros) did precisely the same thing to capture the truth conditions for commonplace assertions about the *physical* world. The classic analysis of a secondary property explicitly appealed either to facts about what sensations a subject would have under certain conditions, or to facts about the causal "powers" of objects to produce subjective appearances in sentient beings. And when under philosophical pressure the distinction between primary and secondary qualities collapsed, phenomenalists attempted to understand *everything* we say about the external world in terms of subjunctive or causal connection. According to this view, to say anything about properties of physical objects is to say something about the exemplification of properties (unknown or even unknowable) which are understood only in terms of their causal role in affecting sentient beings. Whether or not one is prepared to follow philosophers down that exotic metaphysical trail, the same reliance on our understanding of causation is critical to contemporary "reference fixers." To fix the reference of terms for properties and natural

* I would like to thank all of the participants in the University of San Diego Conference on "What Do Compensatory Damages Compensate?" and, particularly, Michael Moore, for discussion that helped me see more clearly some of the issues discussed in this chapter.

kinds, such philosophers typically employ definite descriptions that they hope will denote micro-structures causally responsible for more accessible macro-properties.[1]

It is an understatement, then, to suggest that it would be really nice to get a plausible philosophical account of both causation and the truth conditions for subjunctives. The first step in getting such an account is to ask the right questions. As is so typical of all of his work, Moore does just that. A chapter of his book that I will discuss extensively later on focuses on the relata of causal connection. It is a critical for as Moore would admit, I think, the plausibility of some of the main contenders for a successful analysis of causation depends critically on what the relata of causal connection are. As he might also admit, key claims he makes about what *cannot* stand in causal relations may also hinge on the answers to these preliminary questions. Taking his inspiriation from "Something Good" in *The Sound of Music*, Moore has famously emphasized his conviction that "Nothing comes from nothing; nothing ever could." By contrast, I'm willing to embrace negative facts and even claim that one can be directly aware of some such facts. (I'm what P. L. Heath described in his hilarious piece on "Nothing" in the *Encylopedia of Philosophy*[2] as a "know nothing.") And since I have got negative facts I'll take my own inspiration from the old cliché that absence really does (sometimes) make the heart grow fonder.

II. Issues of Conceptual Priority

Before we search for the relata of causal connection (and the relations and relata relevant to the truth of subjunctive conditionals) it's probably a good idea to follow Moore in briefly reminding ourselves of key controversies concerning conceptual priority. Three questions have long plagued philosophers of science—What is a scientific law? What is causation? What are the truth conditions for contingent subjunctive conditionals? It has always been tempting to think that if one could just get an answer to one of these questions, one could use that answer to find answers to the other two. Generalists are convinced that the key to unlocking philosophical mysteries about causation and subjunctives is the concept of law. Put crudely (far too crudely), the generalist suggests that X causes Y when there is a law L (a covering law) that together with X entails Y. The beginning of a generalist approach to our understanding contingent subjunctive conditionals might suggest that the subjunctive, If X were to occur then Y would occur, is true just in case there is some law L which together with X entails that Y occurs. But neither approach is even close to capturing our ordinary talk about causation or our ordinary use of the subjunctive conditionals.

Let us say that X is lawfully *sufficient* for Y when there is a law L such that (X and L) entails Y where neither X nor L *alone* entails Y. The causes we talk about in ordinary language are rarely lawfully sufficient for their effects. We think it might be true that his cigarette smoking caused his cancer, that her exposure to the flu caused her to catch the

[1] So, Kripke argues that we use the description "the cause of sensation S" (where "S" refers to the phenomenal property of feeling hot) to assign reference to "heat." The meaning of heat is (I think, miraculously) supposed to be distinct from the definite description that breathed life into it—"heat" is supposed to "directly" refer to something like molecular motion. See Saul Kripke, *Naming and Necessity*. (Cambridge, MA: Harvard University Press, 1980).

[2] P. L. Heath, "Nothing," *Encyclopedia of Philosophy* (New York: Macmillan, 1967).

disease, and that his flipping the switch caused the light to go on. But it isn't even remotely plausible to suppose that there is some law asserting a *universal* correlation between cigarette smoking and cancer, exposure to the flu and catching the disease, or flipping a switch and a light's going on. We all know that what we identify as "the" cause is only a *part* of a very complex state that is responsible for that kind of thing we call the effect. Moreover, we all know that there are causal *chains* and that we typically focus on only one link (or series of links) in verbally identifying "the" cause of a given phenomenon.

The same is true of subjunctives. I say truly that if I were to drop that ball it would fall to the ground, that if I were to flip the switch the light would go on, and that if I were to be obnoxious to my wife one more time today I'd pay a fairly high price. But there are no laws connecting the kind of phenomena referred to in the antecedents of these conditionals with the kind of state referred to in their consequents. For both causation and *certain* sorts of contingent subjunctive conditionals, the obvious fix for the generalist might be appeal to something like Mackie's old idea of the INUS condition.[3] "INUS" is an acronym for "*I*nsufficient but *N*ecessary part of an *U*nnecessary but *S*ufficient condition." So to use Mackie's illustration of the concept, we might say of the electrical short circuit that it caused the fire because the short circuit, though not sufficient for the fire, is a critical part of a very complex state of affairs that obtained (one that includes the presence of oxygen, the absence of sprinkler systems, the absence of people to put out the fire in its early stages, the composition of the house, and so on); conditions which aren't lawfully necessary for the fire, but are when conjoined with the short circuit lawfully sufficient for the fire.[4]

One might try the same general approach with certain sorts of contingent subjunctive conditionals. The use of the subjunctive mood usually either implies (or at the very least, leaves open) that the conditions described in the antecedent do not obtain. Not all subjunctives, however, even appear to have as their truth-maker the existence of *lawful* regularity. As I sit alone in my office right now, it is true that if another person were to enter the office there would be at least two people in the office. In this example, the subjunctive is true simply because the occurrence of the state of affairs specified in the antecedent together with the conditions that currently obtain (my being alone in the office) entail the truth of the conditional's consequent. Even more straightforwardly, it seems true to say that if I were to draw a square on a sheet of paper, I would have drawn a rectangle. Here the relevant connection between antecedent and consequent is analytic entailment. But the truth-makers for *other* subjunctives do seem to involve lawful connections. Put another way, some subjunctives seem to be made true by something more like a causal connection between the state of affairs referred to in the antecedent and

[3] J. L. Mackie, "Causes and Conditions," 2 *American Philosophical Quarterly* 245(1965).

[4] Leaving aside the many problems facing the INUS analysis of causation, there are technical problems with this characterization of the condition. Take some state of affairs completely unrelated to Y; call it U. And let a lawfully sufficient condition for Y be S. Then U will be an INUS condition for Y because U conjoined with the disjunctive state of affairs (not-U or S) is a necessary part of an unnecessary but sufficient condition for Y (the complex state of affairs that is: U and (not-U or S)). The problem can be fixed, but one needs to specify that an INUS condition is not a part of a truthfunctionally complex state of affairs that includes that condition as a part. (Alternatively, one can place restrictions on what counts as a genuine state of affairs.

that referred to in the consequent (the kind of connection one could not discover, for example, a priori).

When I assert that if I were to heat that wax it would melt, I say something that is true partly because of nomological connections between the heating of wax and its melting. But again, as we normally use subjunctives it is rarely the case that conditions described in the antecedent would be lawfully *sufficient* for the obtaining of the conditions described in the consequent. It is true that if I were to flip the light switch in this room the light would go off, that if I were to turn my head I would seem to see a bookshelf, and that if I were to stab my hand with the letter opener on my desk I would feel pain, but the states of affairs described in the antecedents of these conditionals are not lawfully sufficient for the states of affairs described in their consequents. Borrowing again the idea of an INUS condition, perhaps we might plausibly suggest that when we assert that if X were the case, Y would be the case, we are at least *sometimes* asserting that while X itself isn't sufficient for Y, there is some set of conditions C that obtains which with X is lawfully sufficient for Y (where C itself is insufficient for Y).

As Moore argues in his book, there are all kinds of serious prima facie difficulties for covering law models of both causation and (nomological) contingent subjunctive conditionals. The first and most obvious is that if one is intent on analyzing causation and subjunctives by appeal to lawful regularity one needs an account of what makes a regularity lawful. To avoid circularity, that account cannot employ either the concept of causation or the relation expressed by contingent subjunctives. And that's a problem. The most obvious difference between lawful generalizations (e.g., that all metal expands when heated), and accidental generalizations (e.g., that all of the coins in my pocket now are quarters), is that the former's being lawful entails that if this wood *were* metal it *would* expand when heated, while the latter's being accidental does not entail that if this penny were in my pocket it would be a quarter. But if we are to offer a non-circular covering law account, we can't say this.

There have been many heroic attempts to analyze the distinction between lawful and accidental generalizations within the framework of a Humean regularity theory of law, but it is an understatement to suggest that such accounts have not met with unqualified success.[5] One need not, of course, embrace a regularity theory of law to offer a covering law account of counterfactuals. We might embrace Armstrong's suggestion that there are genuine metaphysically necessary connections holding between universals.[6] However wrong-headed Hume's positive account of law might be, however, he did have some pretty good reasons for rejecting this sort of Armstrongian necessary connection. The necessary connection between universals holds, presumably, in virtue of the intrinsic character of the universals. Since it doesn't make sense to suppose that a universal could be intrinsically different than it is, the necessary connection would need to be an *internal* relation (one that necessarily holds given the existence of the relata). But

[5] The most promising are so-called contextualist accounts. I have in the past suggested that the lawful generalizations occupy a place in a hierarchy of generalizations such that if that hierarchy conflicts with any other hierarchy, the hierarchy with which it conflicts has fewer instances. Two hierarchies conflict when each includes a generalization that conflicts with a generalization in the other. Two generalizations conflict when their conjunction with the proposition that they have instances is a contradiction. I can do a decent job defending this approach but I can't really bring myself to believe it.

[6] See D. M. Armstrong, *What is a Law of Nature?* (Cambridge: Cambridge University Press, 1983).

internal relations seem to be such that we can know a priori that they obtain (provided that we can know a priori the intrinsic character of the relata). Unfortunately for the necessitarians, and I suppose for the progress of science, one simply can't discover scientific laws just by reflecting hard on the nature of the properties whose exemplification they describe.

Even if we were to successfully capture a distinction between lawful and accidental regularity, we are by no means home free when it comes to analyzing *causation*. The concept of lawful sufficiency is indifferent to time. X can be lawfully sufficient for Y whether X occurs before or after Y. But there is a strong intuition (perhaps defeasible)[7] that effects cannot precede their causes. Furthermore there are well-known examples of what appear to be lawful, but not *causal* regularities involving phenomena even where there is the right sort of temporal relation. The barometer's falling is non-accidentally connected to the storm, but it isn't the cause of the storm. Increases in the sale of ice cream are non-accidentally connected to warmer weather, but they don't cause the warmer weather. So the covering law account of causation is going to need an account of the distinction between *causal* laws and non-causal laws, an account that doesn't invoke the concept of causal connection!

In the face of these intimidating problems confronting generality theorists, it is tempting to abandon that approach and adopt as one's conceptual building blocks either subjunctives or causation, but, as we shall see, this is easier said than done. To see clearly the difficulties faced by those who reject generality theorists it will be helpful to return now to the question of what constitute the relata of causal connection, and the relata of whatever relations are asserted by subjunctive conditionals.

III. The Relata of Causal and Subjunctive Connection

Let's start by talking about causation. The topic is in one respect easier because the indicative claim that X caused Y (where X and Y describe particular occurrences) presupposes the existence of both X and Y. Subjunctives, by contrast, often "describe" what is not, and, sometimes, has not been, and never will be the case. We make both general causal claims and particular or singular causal claims. We say, for example, that smoking causes cancer, and that Bogart's smoking four packs a day caused his cancer. It is surely *tempting* to think that our understanding of *some* general causal claims is parasitic upon our understanding of particular claims. As we ordinarily talk, the general claim about smoking and its causal connection to cancer is probably pretty loose. It will be regarded by us as true if instances of smoking usually cause cancer, or even if there is a much higher incidence of cancer among smokers than among non-smokers.[8]

[7] Chisholm and Taylor have a really interesting discussion of backward causation and generality theories of causation in "Making Things to Have Happened," 20.4 *Analysis* 73 (1960).

[8] One might take this to be in itself a crucial problem for generalist theories. In "Studies in the Logic of Explanation," 15 *Philosophy of Science* 135 (1948), Hempel and Oppenheim argued that many of our causal claims (general and singular) are simply incomplete. Others suggest that in explaining events we are often content with the statistical information (though again one will need to distinguish between accidental and lawful statistical regularity). It is an open question as to just what the connection is between explaining an event and identifying the cause of an event.

As Hume pointed out in his revolutionary discussion of the topic, causation seems to be a *relation*.[9] And where we have a relation we need to figure out what the relata of that relation are. Hume himself often spoke of one *object's* causing another (see, for example, his famous definitions of cause),[10], but when he was careful, he made very clear that it is objects' exemplifying properties that are properly viewed as causes and effects.[11]

In Chapter 15 of *Causation and Responsibility* Moore importantly distinguishes facts from events, but he and I use the term "fact" in different ways. For Moore, a fact is a *truth*. For me, a fact is a potential truth-maker and just *is* the exemplification of a property or properties at a time. As I understand Moore, my facts are what he calls facta, or states of affairs. So in my view an object's being red at time t is one fact (facta or state of affairs) involving that object and the property of being red as constitutents.[12] That same object's being round is a different fact involving the same particular but a different property. In this way of thinking, there are at least as many facts as there are property exemplfications. So if there are both determinate and determinable properties, if, for example, the property of being cherry red is distinct from the property of being red, then there are two properties exemplified when cherry red is exemplified—being cherry red, and being red. And there are, similarly, two facts—the fact that the object is cherry red and the fact that the object is red. But again, in my view, facts are not truths, though they are (potentially) truth-makers. I say *potentially*, for I would argue that the primary bearers of truth value are thoughts; the kinds of things that wouldn't exist in a world without conscious beings. Strictly speaking, then, we can't really make sense of a world in which there are truths but no thoughts (representations) of reality, though we can make sense of a world in which there are facts that could have made thoughts true, had those thoughts existed. [13]

The distinction between truths and facts is clouded by the way we often talk. The locution "It is a fact that..." is often used primarily as a way of emphasizing the assertion that follows. And so-called redundancy theorists are convinced, as Moore's terminology suggests, that fact talk just *is* truth talk. That's why they reject as almost a bad

[9] David Hume, *A Treatise of Human Nature* (ed. L. A. Selby-Bigge), (London: Oxford University Press, 1888). Prior to Hume, there was very little discussion of just what causation is. Philosophers were content to talk about mysterious powers that were "in" causes. Sometimes this idea of the effect being in the cause seems to have been taken almost literally.

[10] Hume, *A Treatise of Human Nature*, 172.

[11] See Rule 5 of his "Rules by which to judge of causes and effects," in Hume, *A Treatise of Human Nature*, 174.

[12] In addition to the object and the property there is, of course, exemplification to deal with. We surely can't treat exemplification as a relation (that is itself exemplified) without facing Bradley's vicious regress. See F. H. Bradley, *Appearance and Reality* (London: Swan Sonnenschein, 1893), chs. II and III. Armstrong's discussion of this issue is still one of the best, in *A World of States of Affairs* (New York: Cambridge University Press, 1997).

[13] There are some potentially problematic consequences of taking thoughts to be the bearers of truth value, at least if thoughts are treated as the exemplification of certain mental properties. If we define a necessary truth as one that is true in all possible worlds, then there are no necessary truths, for there will always be worlds in which there are no thoughts. If we say that a necessary truth is one that is true in all worlds in which the relevant thought exists then we are forced to the conclusion that it is necessarily the case that there are thoughts. One escape is to construe the thoughts that are the bearers of truth value as universals and argue that universals exist in all possible worlds, whether exemplified or not. That's a steep price to pay to guarantee the existence of truth bearers in all possible worlds. I discuss all this in some detail in Richard Fumerton, *Realism and the Correspondence Theory of Truth* (Totawa, N.J.: Rowman and Littlefield, 2002), chs. 1 and 2.

joke the kind of correspondence theory of truth stated in terms of facts. In one version of the correspondence theory (the one I defend in *Realism and the Correspondence Theory of Truth*), the *thought* that P is true just when it corresponds to the *fact* that P. It is false when there is no fact to which it corresponds. If talk about the fact that P is just another way of talking about P's being true, we obviously aren't making any progress when we try to understand the property of being true in terms of the property of corresponding to a fact.

If facts were just truths, then I would agree completely with Moore in rejecting them as candidates for the relata of causal connections. Just as it seems obvious that the world could have contained all sorts of objects with their properties even if conscious life had never evolved anywhere, so also it seems obvious that there would have been causation even if conscious life had never evolved. Boulders crashing into trees would have caused those trees to be leveled, droughts would have caused plants to die, and the moon would still have had its effects on the tides. Causation doesn't require conscious beings, and since without conscious beings there would be no truths (in my view), causation doesn't require truths. But facts aren't truths. It doesn't even make sense to describe most facts as true or false (though in my view *thoughts*, e.g., my thinking that I am hungry, are facts and a thought is the *one* sort of fact that can correspond or fail to correspond to other facts, and thus be true or false).

Another candidate for a relatum of the causal connection is a state of affairs. There is even less consensus on how to use the expression "state of affairs" than there is on how to understand the expression "fact." I use "fact" and "state of affairs" interchangeably, but I do so primarily because I don't include in my ontology so-called non-obtaining states of affairs. To my way of thinking, a non-obtaining state of affairs is every bit as bad as a Meinongian object that has being but doesn't exist. One doesn't need much of a taste for desert landscapes to worry about including among the things that *are*: a non-existent Pegasus, a non-existent Golden Mountain, or a non-existent (non-obtaining) Romney's having been elected President of the US. It's not as if Meinongians didn't feel *driven* towards their ontological commitment.[14] The more convinced you are that intentional states are relations, the more hard-pressed you will be to find plausible relata for those relations. Grammatically, the sentence "Jones fears ghosts" looks as if it reports a relation of fearing that holds between Jones and ghosts. The sentence, after all, has a subject followed by a transitive verb that is itself followed by an object. If you take the surface grammar of the sentence at face value, you might find yourself desperately searching for *some* kind of ghost (even if it is only a "subsistent" ghost) to be what Jones fears. But this is surely to take the wrong road. Surface grammar can and often is misleading, and I am entirely sympathetic with the so-called adverbialists who take "ghosts" in the sentence above to be a modification of the kind of fearing in which Jones is engaged. In any event, if one doesn't allow for the possibility of a non-obtaining state of affairs, I don't think there is any good reason to distinguish a state of affairs from a fact.[15]

[14] It is hard to remember the philosophical landscape before Bertrand Russell's "On Denoting," 14 *Mind* 479 (1905). The idea that a name's meaning was its referent, together with the seemingly undeniable fact that names like "Pegasus" have meaning, presented an enormous problem.

[15] Dialectically, non-obtaining states of affairs might do wonders for a nice clean analysis of truth. If one understands the distinction between obtaining and non-obtaining states of affairs one can simply identify

That really leaves us with events as the main competitors to facts (again Moore's facta or states of affairs) as the relata of causal connection. Moore anticipates most objections to most views, and he correctly supposes that many of us will worry about precisely how to understand what an event is (*Causation and Responibility*, 348). When I played the "The Star Spangled Banner" loudly on the piano last night, waking up my neighbor whose mood quickly turned ugly, how many events occurred? Was my playing the piano the same as my playing the piano loudly? Was it the same as my playing "The Star Spangled Banner"? Was it the same as my waking my neighbor? Was it the same as my annoying my neighbor? I think Moore believes he knows how to count events, or at least that the problem of individuating events isn't any *more* difficult than the problem of individuating truths, facta, or states of affairs. But I don't agree, precisely because I think I have a much better grasp of properties than I have of the kinds of things that might exemplify properties. If I know how to individuate properties, I also know how to individuate facts. The fact that I played the piano is a different fact from the fact that I played "The Star Spangled Banner," a fact that is in turn different from the fact of my annoying my neighbor. To use an old philosophical example, the fact that Oedipus killed the King of Thebes is different from the fact that Oedipus killed his father. Again, I know how to individuate facts, because facts are individuated in terms of their constituent properties, and I know how to individuate properties.[16] The property of being a father isn't identical with the property of being a king; the former is not a constitutent of the fact of Oedipus's killing the king, though it is a constituent of the fact of Oedipus's killing his father.

To be sure, there is a vague sense that even if Oedipus's killing his father is in some sense a different fact from Oedipus's killing the king of Thebes, *only one thing happened*. I suppose one can give intuitive sense to the idea by thinking about how, for example, one might have filmed the deed. It's not as if one would have needed two cameras or two camera angles to film what happened. The killing (one might argue) was a relation between two entities, Oedipus and his father. And while we can pick out the relata of the killing relations in all sorts of different ways, the relata are what they are independently of their descriptions. But I don't know how far one can get with this vague idea. Return to my playing the piano. I suppose one would need only one camera to film both my playing the piano last night and my playing "The Star Spangled Banner." But there is another sense in which the audio would be critical to depicting precisely what tune I was playing and to capturing how loudly I was playing it. And if you were trying to capture my waking up the neighbor, wouldn't one need to get my neighbor into the picture?

Even if one could capture some notion of events that tells us which properties of an event are relevant to its identification, it is not clear that this would be a good reason for taking events to be the relata of causal connection. Donald Davidson adopts perhaps the most extreme, but also the most pure, version of an event-based theory of

the bearer of truth value with a state of affairs, and its being true as its obtaining. Its being false would be its failure to obtain. But simplicity and plausibility aren't the same thing.

[16] I say that I know how to individuate properties. But Moore is right to suggest that there are deep philosophical controversies about how that story goes. For a development of my own view, see Richard Fumerton, *Knowledge, Thought, and the Case for Dualism* (Cambridge: Cambridge University Press, 2013), ch. 5.

causation.[17] As I understand his view, events are temporally extended analogues of "bare" particulars. A bare particular, in a view like Armstrong's[18] or Bergmann's,[19] is a temporally non-extended constituent of a fact that is the bearer of properties—it's *bare* in the sense that *qua* particular it isn't individuated by its properties (even though it couldn't exist without having properties). For Davidson an event is similarly a bearer of properties. Causation, for Davidson, is an unanalyzed relation between these "bare" events. Causal laws are generalizations about *kinds* of events standing in causal relations. So it might be a law that every event that has the property of being a heating of wax to 60 degrees centigrade is causally connected to an event that has the property of being a melting of wax. But the causal connection is not to be *analyzed* in terms of the causal law. Davidson does claim that whenever there is a causal connection between events there is a causal law, but it is not clear what grounds he has for making such a claim (more about this in section IV(A)).

It is important to note that (as I understand him) Moore himself shies away from the kind of extreme view that I am attributing to Davidson. In *Causation and Responsibility*, he first nicely summarizes what amounts to an argument for thinking that it is really property exemplifications (my facts) that serve as the relata of causal connection. He imagines someone arguing as follows:

> [I]f causal relata are whole events, then such events are causes in virtue of their possessing just those properties that figure in the necessarily accompanying causal laws. This is the idea that many philosophers call the 'feature-driven' nature of causal relata. The idea is that it is not incidental that the things that are causal relata either are, or at least possess, features allowing causal laws to exist. Rather, what makes something be a cause is that it either is, or possesses, features described by a causal law.[20]

He then suggests that there is nothing in this basic idea with which a Davidsonian need disagree. But Moore *does* argue that the Davidsonian must resist the following step in the reasoning:

> [I]f causal relata must be feature-driven, then such relata are simply to be identified as those features.[21]

And he goes on to say:

> I find this quite intuitive: why is it not simplest to identify the relata as those features, and not as the whole events which have such features? Why is the driver [of a feature-driven relation like causation] not the better candidate for the cause, rather than the passenger or vehicle driven. Less metaphorically: if what makes an event a cause of some other event is some feature that the first event possesses, then why is the feature not really the cause? On the feature-driven view of causality, it is the feature

[17] Donald Davidson, "Causal relations," 64 *Journal of Philosophy* 691 (1967). I should mention in passing that Davidson claims that the "slingshot" argument establishes that facts cannot stand in causal relations. The argument is a bit complicated but it rests on the supposition that causal claims are referentially transparent, a claim that no "fact" theorist would accept.

[18] Armstrong, *A World of States of Affairs*.

[19] Gustav Bergmann, *Logic and Reality* (Madison: University of Wisconsin Press, 1967).

[20] Moore, 2009d, 364.

[21] Moore, 2009d, 365.

> that imparts to the event its causal character, so it is the feature that, at the most basic level, must be the cause.[22]

Moore further suggests that the only reason to resist this conclusion is that features might be thought of as universals, and universals can't stand in causal connections. But, as he correctly notes, the view is not really that the *properties* stand in singular causal relations, but that property *exemplifications* (again my facts) are the relevant relata.

This seems right to me. Even *if* we include events in our ontology, it is only an event's exemplifying a property or properties that is properly viewed as a cause or an effect. And if that's correct, then we are right back to facts as the relata of causal connections. Remember that, in my characterization of a fact, a fact just is the exemplification of a property or properties. *If* one can distinguish particulars from events as the bearers of properties then there will be two sorts of facts—one sort whose constituents involve particulars; another whose constituents include events. Either way, facts end up being the relata of causal connections.

IV. The Implication of Taking Facts to be the Relata of Causal Connection

A. Facts and generality

We noted earlier that Davidson argued that there couldn't be a case of a singular causation without a related causal law. According to Davidson a causal law is a generalization about kinds of events standing in causal relations. As I understand him, Moore is sympathetic to this claim, but insists that it is perfectly compatible with the rejection of a generality theory of causation. A generality theory of causation purports to give an *analysis* of what causation is. It doesn't deny that where there is singular causation there is also a causal law. But it is not clear how a pure event theorist can argue for the strong modal claim that *necessarily* where there is singular causation there is a causal law. Davidson, for example, takes causation to be an unanalyzed relation between events. I presume the relation is contingent. But if all that is so, then why should we assume that every time there is a singular causal fact of the form e causes d (where "e" and "d" refer to events) there is some general truth of the form: for all x and for all y if x is an event that is F and y is an event that is G, then x causes y). It might be true as a matter of contingent fact that we can generalize over kinds of events standing in causal connection, but how could it be anything other than contingent?

Once one has a feature-driven account of event causation, then one is back in business arguing that it is a *necessary* truth that when e's being F causes f to be G there is a causal law. The whole point of a feature-driven account is to emphasize that it is the exemplification of F that causes the exemplification of G where F and G are properties. To be sure, singular causation holds only between the exemplification of properties, not the properties themselves. And I suppose one might argue that it is at least coherent to claim that F's being exemplified at t was the full cause of G's being exemplified at t + 1, even though F's being exemplified at t + 10 wasn't followed by an exemplification of G.

[22] Moore, 2009d, 365.

Of course, we would surely take the causal claim involving the first exemplification of F to be *disconfirmed* by the fact that we later had F without G. But one cannot in general reach a metaphysical conclusion from an epistemological observation. The real question, though, is whether one can even make *sense* of a *feature-driven* account of causation while one admits that the exemplification of the relevant features sometimes does and sometimes doesn't have a given effect. If the features can be present without the causal connection, then in what sense is causation a function of the *features* exemplified by the event? The generality theorist has a simple account of the necessary connection between the singular causal truth and the existence of causal laws. The singular causation is ontologically parasitic upon the lawful connection between property exemplifications.

B. Facts and logical relations

By taking facts to be truth-makers whose existence is independent of their being represented, we can let them be the relata of causal connection while making causal connection mind-dependent. That's a good thing. But if we are at all inclined towards a generality theory of causation, we are in danger of losing one of the most important benefits of construing causation as a relation between facts. Consider a crude generality theory that takes a fact X to be the *complete* and immediate cause of a fact Y if and only if there is some causal law L such that (X and L) entails Y (where neither X nor L alone entails Y).[23] If we construe facts as Moore does—as truths—all is well and good. We can make perfectly good sense of one proposition entailing another. But on the face of it, facts aren't even the *kinds* of things that can stand in logical relations. P entails Q when it is impossible for P to be true while Q is false, *but only when P and Q are truth-bearers.* I suppose that it is impossible for the lamp to be true while the piano is false just because it is impossible for lamps or pianos to have truth value. But there is no interesting sense in which for that reason we should say that the lamp *entails* the piano.

So the covering law theorist who takes facts about lawful regularity between property exemplifications to be part of the analysis of causal claims and who takes facts to be the relata of causal connection is going to need at least a derivative concept of entailment that can capture a relationship between facts (and thus capture the "covering" in the "covering law" model). Fortunately, it may not be that difficult to develop such a concept. Facts are, after all, truth-*makers*. In one classic version of the correspondence theory of truth, truth-bearers and truth-makers have a common structure.[24] In trying to understand necessary connections between concepts or thoughts, philosophers as different as Hume and Kant have talked about relations between ideas. So Kant, for example, would ground the analyticity of the proposition that bachelors are unmarried in the fact that the concept of a bachelor contains the concept of being unmarried. Hume would ground the necessity of the proposition that what is blue all over is not red

[23] Also remember the earlier footnote in which I suggested that there would need to be some technical adjustments to this suggestion.

[24] In Russell's somewhat idiosyncratic version of a correspondence theory, both a thought and its truth maker have the same constituents. The constituents are "connected" by the belief state in the case of thought, and by exemplification in the case of the fact that makes the thought true. See Bertrand Russell, *The Problems of Philosophy* (Oxford: Oxford University Press, 1967), ch. 12.

all over in a relation of exclusion between the idea of being blue and the idea of being red. But interestingly, almost every philosopher who grounded the necessity of propositions in terms of relations between concepts, thoughts, or ideas, *also* thought you could "read off" features of the world by reflecting on these relations between *representations* of that world. I know that all bachelors are unmarried. That's a truth about the world. It is a truth about bachelors, even though I don't need to *empirically* investigate any bachelors to discover it. I can know truths about the world based on what I know about the character of my thoughts, because I know that a truth-maker for that thought must have the same structural properties of the thought. Just as the thought that there are bachelors contains the thought that there are men, so also, the *fact* that there are bachelors contains as a constitutent the fact that there are men, and in that sense we can talk about a necessary connection between the relevant facts (and the relevant properties involved in the respective facts). We can't *define* entailment relations between propositions in terms of necessary connections between *facts* because propositions can entail other propositions even if they are false, even if there are no facts to which they correspond. But when there are truth-makers for propositions, a necessary connection between propositions is *usually* paralleled by a necessary connection between the truth-makers (I'll explain the qualification in the following section).

V. What Kinds of Facts are There?

Because we have distinguished facts from truths, we have not settled one of the controversies on which Moore takes a firm stand. If facts *were* truths, then, since there are uncontroversially true negative propositions (e.g., that there are no unicorns, that there are no people over twelve feet tall, that there are no horses in my room right now), we would have no principled reason to reject the view that omissions or failures to act can be causes. But we have distinguished true propositions from facts. Furthermore, it is not clear that we need a distinct fact as the truth-maker for every distinct true proposition. Consider, for example, true disjunctions. It is true that either the Moon is made of green cheese or Chicago is in Illinois. It is also true, of course, that Chicago is in Illinois. The disjunctive *proposition* is uncontroversially distinct from each of its disjuncts, but it is not clear that it is anything other than the fact that Chicago is in Illinois that *makes* true *both* propositions. I suggested earlier that the truth-maker for a proposition (thought, representation) often has the same structure as the proposition. But if what I said about disjunctions is plausible then that will not always be the case. Nor will every necessary connection between facts be paralleled by a necessary connection between propositions made true by those facts. The fact that Chicago is in Illinois is necessarily connected to there being an Illinois, but the proposition that either the Moon is made of green cheese or Chicago is in Illinois does not entail that there is an Illinois.

The controversy over what sorts of facts we should include in our ontology was one of the key issues debated by the logical atomists. It is a controversy that is not easy to resolve. For our present purposes the most crucial question is whether or not there are *negative* facts. Consider the truth that that there are no horses in this room. What fact about the world makes that proposition true? One might, of course, start listing facts about the properties exemplified in this room, but none of these facts about objects and their properties seem to make it true that there are no horses in the room until one *adds* to the list the fact that there is nothing else in the room. But there being nothing else in the room is a negative fact. It is not clear to me that one can rely too much on the example of disjunctions discussed above to avoid commitment to such other controversial facts as existential facts, universal facts, or negative facts. Arguably one doesn't need a disjunctive fact as a truth-maker precisely because there are disjunctive thoughts—thoughts that are complex in such a way that they can contain two quite distinct representations of how the world is. But the thought that there are no horses in the room doesn't seem to be indeterminate in that way.

In addition to the sheer difficulty of finding something other than a negative fact to serve as the truth-maker for a negative proposition, is there any other reason for including in one's ontology negative facts? Well, I referred in the introduction to the "know-nothings"—the philosophers who actually claim to find themselves aware of absences. In my (highly controversial) view, phenomenological awareness is the ultimate ground of *all* ontological commitment. Direct awareness is a relation that can hold between a person and a property or a fact. Eliminative materialism isn't just a false view, it is a *crazy* view. And it is crazy because I am directly aware of such facts as that I am in pain. Through that awareness I have the best justification possible for believing both that I am in pain and that there is such a property as being in pain. But ask yourself how you know that you are *not* in pain right now (assuming that you are not). You can talk about all the mental states you are aware of—boredom, apparent memories, visual experience—but those facts won't be identical with the fact that you are not in pain, and your awareness of them won't give you any justification for believing that you are not in pain. I am directly aware of the absence of pain, and that is what justifies me in believing that I'm not in pain. One can't reduce any of this to propositional knowledge. All sides agree that there are negative propositions, and that we can know such propositions to be true. But I'm talking here about the epistemic ground of such knowledge. As a classical foundationalist I look for the ground of direct knowledge in non-propositional awareness of facts. And to ground knowledge of negative propositions, I need direct awareness of negative facts.

VI. If You Got Them, Use Them

So since I've got negative facts in my ontology, I might as well use them. Moore presents a pretty strong case for taking facta (my facts) to be the relata of causal connection, though he also thinks it is harmless to allow that one can also identify events as standing in causal connection. He also admits that we often speak as if omissions (and absences) can be causes. We say that the cause of the derailment was the conductor failing to apply the brakes. My failing to water the plant caused the plant to die. And absence really does sometimes make the heart grow fonder. We also hold people morally and legally responsible not just for what they do, but for what they fail to do. Of course, Moore wants to capture the content of "causal" claims about omissions by turning to subjunctives. He certainly wants to admit that had the conductor applied the brakes, the derailment wouldn't have occurred; that if I had watered the plant, it wouldn't have died; and if my love had been present, perhaps I wouldn't have been as fond of her. But we still need to find truth-makers for the relevant subjunctive conditionals.

In the final analysis, I'm inclined to agree with Chisholm's view that subjunctives simply have no determinate truth value.[25] They always seem to have *something* to do with the derivability of the consequent of the conditional from the antecedent and *some* set of conditions. But while the context sometimes makes clear which conditions we hold constant in asserting the conditionals, it often doesn't. So as Chisholm suggests we can assert all of the following (with appropriate emphasis):

1. If that piece of metal had been heated, then it wouldn't have been true that all metal expands when heated (where here we hold constant that it didn't expand).
2. If that piece of metal had been heated, then it would have expanded (where here we hold constant the law that metal expands when heated).
3. If that had been heated it wouldn't have been metal (where here we hold constant both the law and that it didn't expand).

Don't even *try* to get involved in a discussion about what would be happening in the Middle East if Jane Fonda were the U S Secretary of State without first just asking what the person who makes the assertion wants you to hold constant.

At least sometimes, in a view like Chisholm's, the relevant conditions that we hold constant, and that are critical to an assessment of the truth of the conditional, are *causal* facts (the truth-makers for causal laws). As we saw earlier, sometimes the truth-makers *don't* involve causal laws. The subjunctive that if that were a triangle then it would be a plane figure enclosed by three straight lines isn't made true by causal laws that hold. But "If I were to heat that wax to 60 degrees centigrade it would expand" is made true, in part, by the existence of lawful connections between heating wax and wax melting.

Can we avoid a commitment to negative facts or causation by omission by turning to subjunctives? The question will inevitably take us right back to the issue of what can stand in causal connections and what can stand in lawful connection. If there can be lawful connections (not just true statements about lawful connections) that obtain between certain properties *not* being exemplified and others *not* being exemplified, then those lawful connections will play a critical role in making true subjunctives. And there is as much plausibility in claiming that there are such connections as there is in claiming that there can be singular causal connections between someone's failing to do something and something happening.

Moore correctly rejects truths as the relata of causal connection by appealing to the obvious fact that causation doesn't require conscious beings to represent the world in certain ways. But common sense also suggests that wax would melt were it heated to 60 degrees centigrade whether or not anyone ever asserted the relevant subjunctive. And it is no less plausible to suggest that the truth-makers for some subjunctives involve negative facts or negative properties than it is to suggest that the truth-makers for some singular causal claims involve negative facts.[26]

[25] R. M. Chisholm, "Law Statements and Counterfactual Inference," 25 *Analysis* 73(1955).

[26] It is an understatement to suggest that this discussion of subjunctives is highly cryptic. One could literally write a series of books on how to understand subjunctive conditionals. There is, however, one truth we should all remember. Everything that is true is made true by some feature of the one and only actual

VII. Conclusion

Moore wants causation to do a lot of work in fixing moral and legal responsibility. Anyone with that goal would do well to resist the idea that there are such facts as omissions that stand in causal connections. Indeed, anyone with such a goal would probably do well to avoid, if possible, a generality theory of causation. If there are failures to act, then such failures can obviously be INUS conditions. And lawful connections extend indefinitely into the past and the future. My stabbing you with my knife is an INUS condition of your dying, but so is your failing to stop me, and Obama's failing to stop me, and your failure to carry a loaded gun that you would have used to stop me, and my mother's giving birth to me, and so on. INUS conditions are all over the place and we will need to rely heavily on pragmatic and evaluative considerations to select from among the lawfully relevant conditions those for which we hold a person responsible. Once we accept a generality theory, it is also difficult (though perhaps not impossible) to argue, as Moore does, that causation (as opposed to responsibility) comes in degrees. A generality theory will inevitably adopt something like an INUS account of causation, and the concepts of necessity and sufficiency that the analysis of an INUS condition relies upon do not admit of degrees. One proposition cannot entail a proposition "more" than another.[27]

I want to close this discussion, however, by recognizing the obvious. In a chapter of this length it is simply impossible to do anything more than scratch the surface of some of the critical metaphysical controversies that are intimately connected to what we should say about the nature of causation. These involve the nature of truth, truth-making, and truth-makers, and the existence of such problematic categories of being as properties, events, states of affairs, and facts. The issues are among the most complex and difficult in all of philosophy. It is again a credit to Moore's work on causation and responsibility that he is willing to take these controversies head on and to do so in a way that is extraordinarily detailed, subtle, and sophisticated. Whether or not one accepts his ultimate conclusions, one comes away from reading *Causation and Responsibility* with a much finer appreciation of how to frame the relevant debates.

world. The *metaphor* of possible worlds might be harmless as long as we do the philosophical work necessary to discover what precisely the metaphor is a metaphor for.

[27] The idea of recognizing degrees of causation is still intriguing in some contexts. When we are dealing with the exercise of force that brings about some effect, and there is more than one person employing force, we might still be able to develop a sense in which the force you applied was a relatively small fraction of the total force required for the effect. I'm not sure, however, that this will always, or even usually, parallel our intuitive idea of how we are going to divvy up legal and moral responsibility.

15

Self-Defense: Tell Me Moore

Kimberly Kessler Ferzan[*]

I. Introduction

Michael Moore is a master architect in criminal law theory. Each piece of his theorizing neatly and completely coheres with others. Moore's views are often so clear and well argued that if one spends enough time with his work, one can generally predict his answers to any question. Every brick has its place. And there's more. Moore also has a thoroughly worked out shtick for explaining his theories. His writings are replete with citations to movies, songs, and even Sunday comics, including *The Princess Bride*,[1] Blondie,[2] and *The Sound of Music*.[3] Indeed, sometimes it seems that reading Moore's work is an exercise in bad popular culture references.

One of the most predictable of Moore's references is when he needs to talk about self-defense. In the movie, *History of the World Part I*, Moses drops one of the tablets, leaving ten instead of fifteen commandments. That third tablet, argues Moore, included exceptions to deontological norms such as the exception for self-defense.[4] It's Moore's clever way of asserting that even deontology does not really mean "thou shalt not kill" full stop.

Like Moses' third tablet, Moore's work seems to have dropped self-defense. It is almost an afterthought in his theorizing about the relationship between deontology and consequentialism. *Placing Blame* contains a handful of pages.[5] Self-defense gets two pages in *Causation and Responsibility*.[6] Even when he discusses targeted killings in *Targeted Killings and the Morality of Hard Choices*, Moore quickly moves beyond a self-defense justification.[7]

Self-defense fascinates me, and I have questions for Moore. I just wish that he would say more about the positions that he holds. More troubling, I worry that the sparse commitments he has may be difficult to square with some of his other criminal law positions. Putting the pieces together of that broken tablet may ultimately yield that Moore's architecture is left askew.

In what follows, I will first give a brief overview of the current theorizing about self-defense. Next, I will set forth Moore's arguments about when self-defense is

* For comments on this manuscript, I thank Stephen Morse.

[1] For dismissing the distinction between being "almost dead" and "all dead." Moore, 2009d, 66.

[2] For the point that between causation and accomplice liability, the criminal law is gonna get you "one way or another." Moore, 2009d, 289.

[3] To do the work essential to Moore's view on omissions that "nothing comes from nothing." Moore, 2009d, 54–5.

[4] Despite having heard Moore make this reference at several conferences, I could not find an instance in which he used it in his writing. He alludes to it in Moore, 2012b, 449.

[5] Moore, 1997b, 711–17. [6] Moore, 2009d, 38–40. [7] Moore, 2012b.

justified and why. I will then raise a series of questions, both about the content of Moore's view and its implications for other positions he holds.

II. Self-Defense Theorizing: The State of the Art in a Nutshell

When one endeavors to give an account of "self-defense," the initial question is what one means by "self-defense." As a matter of ordinary language, our use of the term is quite extensive. If a culpable aggressor tries to kill me and I kill him, I will justify my action by claiming "self-defense." The term can also be applied to the killing of an innocent aggressor, that is, a person who lacks culpability but whose act will kill me, such as a child who mistakenly believes a real gun to be a toy. And, we can certainly say that one acts in self-defense when one kills an innocent threat, that is, an individual who does not even voluntarily act but whose body nevertheless threatens me, such as the large man who will fall on me and kill me if I do not disintegrate him immediately.[8] Indeed, "self-defense" would likewise be an explanation for why I shot a rabid dog that was about to attack me or maybe even why I disintegrated your television set that was about to smash into me during a tornado.

Given that all instances of self-defense are "defensive" in nature, it is tempting to think that there must be a unifying explanation. I think we ought to resist that temptation. Because we can meaningfully employ the term "self-defense" to justify our killing of a culpable aggressor or destroying a neighbor's television, the explanation would likely have to be so broad as to run roughshod over relevant moral nuances. It is thus more fruitful to think of self-defense as a type of defense, where some tokens may be permissible (or justified) and others will not.[9]

One of the most important normative and conceptual moves in the self-defense literature in the last decade or so has been to carve out liability as a distinct route to permissibility.[10] Previously, it seemed that one must opt to either take an "aggressor-centered" approach or a "defender-centered" perspective. The assumption was that we needed to pick which approach should govern self-defense. However, this assumption is false. One may believe that both perspectives are morally relevant. A liability approach focuses on what an aggressor must do to be liable to defensive force, that is, to have forfeited his right against being defensively harmed. A permission-based view focuses on when a defender may harm a person who is, or is perceived to be, an attacker. It is coherent to say that an individual is liable to be killed but it is impermissible for the defender to do so, and it is also coherent to claim that an agent may permissibly kill someone who is not liable to be killed.

As one brief example of this severance, consider the well-known trolley problem. It is generally assumed that one may turn the runaway trolley away from five trapped workers to one trapped worker. Many theorists maintain that the one worker's rights

[8] These cases were originally imagined by Robert Nozick. Robert Nozick, *Anarchy, State, and Utopia* (New York: Basic Books, 1974), 34–5.

[9] As suggested by Victor Tadros, *Criminal Responsibility* (Oxford: Oxford University Press, 2005), 117; Jeff McMahan, "Self-Defense and the Problem of the Innocent Attacker," 104 *Ethics* 252 (1994), 256.

[10] This suggestion seems to originate in McMahan, "Innocent Attacker." McMahan has continually distinguished these concepts in his work. It was made quite explicit by Helen Frowe, "A Practical Account of Self-Defence," 29 *Law & Philosophy* 245 (2010).

will be infringed, but not violated, because the action is justified. Notably, the worker has certainly done nothing to lose his right to life. The worker is not liable to be killed. Contrast this with a culpable aggressor, where we would say that the attacker's rights are neither infringed nor violated. His own actions have forfeited his moral complaint against being killed defensively.

Allowing liability to serve as a route to permissibility opens up various possibilities. For instance, one may maintain that (1) the moral basis for liability to defensive killing is intending a culpable attack or so appearing; (2) a moral permission to kill another may be based on the agent-relative permission to give one's life greater weight; and that (3) as a matter of the usage of the term, "self-defense," it may be appropriate to call actions under either (1) or (2) (or both), instances of "self-defense." This means that not only do you get to kill bad guys who are trying to kill you for the reason that they have forfeited their rights but you also get to kill an innocent aggressor (at least sometimes) because you are entitled to give your life more weight.

To this point we have seen that the term "self-defense" is quite promiscuous and that different justifications may ground different routes to permissible self-defense. Let us now turn directly to liability accounts. Liability accounts hold that what the aggressor does grounds why he forfeits his rights against defensive force being employed to stop him. Elsewhere, I have defended the following disjunctive conditions for liability to defensive killing:[11]

(1a) The aggressor forms an intention to purposefully, knowingly, or recklessly kill the defender, the aggressor lacks a justification or excuse, and the aggressor will kill the defender unless defensive force is used; or

(1b) the aggressor purposefully, knowingly, or recklessly engages in conduct that he is aware may lead the defender to believe that that (1a) is true, and the aggressor lacks a justification or excuse for so doing; AND

(2) based on his belief that he is subject to attack, the defender acts to repel the perceived attack.

That is, I argue that culpable attackers who will kill their victims are liable to defensive force by the defender. I have defended the position that this (1a) forfeiture is a fitting and appropriate response to a culpable attack by the aggressor. If the aggressor were permitted to attack, thus ignoring the rights of others while maintaining his own rights, it would be fundamentally unfair.[12] The grounding of the forfeiture for (1b) is distinct. For this sort of forfeiture, I maintain that when we insincerely evince the exercise of a normative power or a change in normative relations, that power is exercised or those relations are truly altered, or so I have argued.[13] This forfeiture by insincere act is fitting and appropriate because the faker would otherwise make the interpreter normatively vulnerable. The interpreter no longer knows what rights and duties he has. The idea is that if someone points an unloaded gun at you but makes you believe the gun is loaded,

[11] Kimberly Kessler Ferzan, "Culpable Aggression: The Basis for Moral Liability to Defensive Killing," 9 *Ohio State Journal of Criminal Law* 669 (2012).

[12] Kimberly Kessler Ferzan, "Forfeiture and Self-Defense," in Michael Weber and Christian Coons (eds.), *The Ethics of Self-Defense* (Oxford: Oxford University Press, forthcoming).

[13] Kimberly Kessler Ferzan, "The Bluff: The Power of Insincere Acts," (manuscript on file with author).

you mistakenly believe that he has forfeited his rights. Because he is the one who has culpably created this belief, he forfeits his rights such that he is not wronged by your using the force you believe is necessary to defend yourself.

Other self-defense theorists offer disparate views. To take two other views in the literature, Jeff McMahan grounds forfeiture in moral responsibility, which is best understood as unjustified, foreseeable risk imposition.[14] Jonathan Quong grounds forfeiture in the failure to attribute to someone his full moral status.[15] We can contrast the claims by considering the following three cases.

> *Falling Large Man.*[16] Victor falls to the bottom of a well. His arch-enemy, Abe, sees this. When Tony, a very large man, walks by, Abe pushes Tony down the well. If Tony lands on Victor, Victor will die but Tony will live. Victor has in his possession a ray gun with which he can disintegrate Tony.
>
> *Conscientious Driver.*[17] Darla is driving her well-maintained car down the road. Suddenly, her car malfunctions such that it veers toward Peter, a pedestrian. If Darla hits Peter, he will die. Peter can throw a grenade at Darla's car such that it will blow up and kill only her.
>
> *The Resident.*[18] An identical twin of a vicious killer is driving down the road when his car malfunctions. He is non-culpably unaware of the fact that his brother has escaped from prison and local news channels have warned residents to be on the lookout. Moreover, his evil twin has a modus operandi of knocking on the door to a home and then immediately killing the occupant. The innocent twin knocks on the Resident's door. She believes he is his evil twin brother; she raises her pistol (that she just happens to be holding) to shoot him. The innocent twin sees what the Resident is about to do. (To be clear, in *The Resident*, the question is whether the Resident is liable to be killed because she mistakenly believes the innocent twin to be the evil one and acts on that mistaken belief.)

Falling Large Man is commonly viewed as an instance of an innocent threat because the fact that he is threatening Victor with harm is not attributable to a voluntary act.[19] Conscientious Driver and the Resident are innocent aggressors because they have acted voluntarily but have not culpably chosen to attack.

I have defended the claim that none of these actors is liable to be killed as none of them are culpable.[20] (I do maintain that with respect to non-culpable attackers, it is plausible that one has an agent-relative permission to give one's own life greater weight vis-à-vis innocent aggressors.)[21] In contrast, Jeff McMahan claims that anyone who (1) will in fact cause an unjustified harm (as is true in each of these cases because in each case, from an omniscient point of view, none of these actors is behaving justifiably) and

[14] Jeff McMahan, "The Basis of Moral Liability to Defensive Killing," 15 *Philosophical Issues* 386 (2005).

[15] Jonathan Quong, "Liability to Defensive Harm," 40 *Philosophy & Public Affairs* 45 (2012).

[16] Nozick, *Anarchy, State, and Utopia*, 34–5.

[17] McMahan, "Basis of Moral Liability," 393–4.

[18] McMahan, "Basis of Moral Liability," 387.

[19] For some doubts about deeming the innocent threat as distinguishable from the innocent aggressor, see Kimberly Kessler Ferzan, "Jeffrie Murphy's 'Involuntary Acts and Criminal Liability' Revisited," 125 *Ethics* 1119 (2015); Ferzan, "Culpable Aggression," 682; Michael Otsuka, "Killing the Innocent in Self-Defense," 23 *Philosophy & Public Affairs* 81 (1994).

[20] Ferzan, "Culpable Aggression."

[21] Larry Alexander and Kimberly Kessler Ferzan, with Stephen J. Morse, *Crime and Culpability: A Theory of Criminal Law* (New York: Cambridge University Press, 2009), 136–41.

(2) has engaged in foreseeable non-reciprocal risk imposition (as is true in the latter two cases because in those two cases the innocent aggressors know they are engaging in behavior that creates a risk of harming an innocent—the driver chooses to drive and the resident chooses to shoot) is liable because the aggressor is morally responsible.[22] Jonathan Quong argues that only the Resident is liable because she makes a mistake as to the twin's liability (she believes he is attacking her and has forfeited a right when in fact he has not) and it is the failure to accord someone his full moral status that makes the aggressor liable.[23] In contrast, according to Quong, because the Conscientious Driver's risk calculation already takes into account the value of both his life and that of the pedestrian (the determination that it is safe to drive conscientiously already includes in the calculation, and gives due value to, the possibility of harming a pedestrian), the driver is not liable. Neither Quong nor McMahan maintains that the Falling Large Man is liable as he has not chosen to impose any risk at all.

Beyond liability itself, theorists must address proportionality and necessity. Consider proportionality first. Most theorists agree that the harm employed defensively must be in proportion to the harm threatened.[24] One way to understand this is that the aggressor only forfeits rights against a certain amount of force. Anything beyond that amount is a harm that would violate his rights. Proportionality then is typically seen as internal to liability.[25]

There is more significant debate over the question of necessity. McMahan, for example, crafts liability in such a way that it entails necessity. An aggressor is only liable to harm if it is necessary to harm him to protect oneself.[26] The reason that one acts, then, is built into the liability/forfeiture condition. In contrast, one might claim that the loss of a right is independent of the reason to harm the aggressor. The attack forfeits rights, and the attack provides a reason to harm the aggressor, but these two can come apart: if, for example, the culpable attacker is only bluffing—his attack forfeits his right without providing a reason to harm him.[27] Both views still require that the defender *believe* force is necessary, either because the intention is relevant to permissibility or because the rights forfeiture is nuanced so that rights are only forfeited vis-à-vis actors who believe the harm they are inflicting will prevent the attack.[28]

A final consideration for liability accounts is the possibility of more than one aggressor or threat. What if, instead of a large man, Abe goes to the nearby hospital, takes fifty newborn babies, ties them together with twine, and hurls the ball of babies at Victor?

[22] McMahan, "Basis of Moral Liability."

[23] Quong, "Liability to Defensive Harm." For doubts about Quong's view, see Larry Alexander, "Recipe for a Theory of Self-Defense: The Ingredients, and Some Cooking Suggestions," in Weber and Coons (eds.), *The Ethics of Self-Defense*.

[24] But see Peter Vallentyne, "Defense of Self and Others against Culpable Rights-Violators," in Weber and Coons (eds.), *The Ethics of Self-Defense*.

[25] This sort of proportionality is called "narrow proportionality," a requirement that the harm to the aggressor be in proportion to what he has threatened. In contrast, if the defender will also injure bystanders, this brings in questions of "wide proportionality." This sort of proportionality is not internal to liability. It is the restriction that even if the aggressor has no rights against you harming him, the two innocent actors beside him, who will be killed as well, do have such rights and thereby restrict what you may do.

[26] Jeff McMahan, "The Limits of Self-Defense," in Weber and Coons (eds.), *The Ethics of Self-Defense*.

[27] Ferzan, "The Bluff."

[28] I endorse the latter position in "Forfeiture and Self-Defense."

What if, instead of Conscientious Driver, Peter, the pedestrian, must kill fifteen individuals who have chosen to drive their cars?

I suspect that most people would think that it is wrong to kill the fifty babies or fifteen non-culpable drivers. This gives us reason to reject the view that these threats/aggressors are liable to be killed. This intuition is likely even stronger when we appeal to the question of what third parties should do. Why would a third party have to pick Victor over fifty babies? What is the argument for that?

Some theorists, who are sympathetic to the claim that innocent aggressors can be liable to defensive force, have offered alternative accounts for what to do when these "minimally responsible threats" are aggregated. McMahan and Saba Bazargan advocate hybrid justifications that contain elements of liability and elements of a lesser-evils justification.[29] The idea is that a conscientious driver may be partially liable. The reason it is permissible to kill him, then, is because he counts as less of a person when weighed against the pedestrian. Because this is a lesser-evils balancing, continuing to increase the number of conscientious drivers ultimately leads to a point at which the pedestrian may no longer kill the conscientious drivers because their deaths are no longer the lesser evil. To be sure, increasing the number of aggressors raises puzzles for those who take innocent aggressors to be liable.

Although these are clearly divergent views and this is a superficial overview, even now, we can see that these views share certain core assumptions. The first is that individuals can forfeit rights by what they do, and that one can provide a principled account of why the individual is responsible in such a way that it is fitting and appropriate for his rights to be forfeited. The second is that this forfeiture can be nuanced. It is not an assumption that we get to boil aggressors in oil for kicks. It is an assumption that for so long as you are a threat, you cannot complain if someone stops you. Thus, though self-defense theorists might quibble over the grounds for rights-forfeiture, we share certain assumptions about what such a theory needs and what such a theory does.

I cannot possibly do justice to the complexity of the arguments in the self-defense scholarship. If anyone could master the mechanics, it would be Michael Moore. Any subject matter is the better for Moore's engagement with it. Where, then, should we situate Moore's views on defensive force?

III. Moore on Self-Defense

Moore typically substantially and thoroughly analyzes topics within criminal law. Unfortunately, he has spent less of his career grappling with self-defense. If I had to diagnose the cause of this lack of attention, it would not be that Moore is reluctant to confront a challenge. Quite the contrary. I suspect he thinks self-defense is easy. Hopefully, I can convince him that this is not so.

Moore's most recent articulation of his position is in *Targeted Killings and the Morality of Hard Choices*.[30] He begins with the claim that we have a "strong permission" to

[29] Saba Bazargan, "The Liability of Minimally Responsible Threats," 125 *Ethics* 114 (2014); Jeff McMahan, "Liability, Proportionality, and the Number of Aggressors," in Saba Bazargan and Samuel Rickless (eds.), *The Ethics of War* (New York: Oxford University Press, forthcoming).

[30] Moore, 2012b.

engage in self-defense such that we are permitted to defend ourselves even if the consequentialist balance tips otherwise.[31] Following Phillip Montague, he takes self-defense to be an instance of a "general moral principle": "he who culpably causes the necessity of some harm being visited on somebody, is himself the right person to be made to suffer such harm."[32] This principle is supported by "robust intuitions of fairness and appropriateness."[33] There is a "divine justice" when the bad guy gets the harm he had intended for the innocent victim.[34]

Moore then turns to innocent aggressors and threats. In 2009, in *Causation and Responsibility*, Moore was tentative about his conclusion that one is justified in killing two innocent threats.[35] In *Targeted Killings*, Moore no longer finds the question hard. He admits the question is "a close one" but concludes that one is justified in killing innocent aggressors and threats, seemingly no matter how numerous.[36] Ball o' babies beware!

Moore rejects victim-based accounts that culpable actors may forfeit their rights, thus creating a weak permission that is then open to consequentialist balancing.[37] He thus reaffirms a position he set forth in *Placing Blame*. In his earlier discussion, Moore maintains that forfeiture accounts cannot supply a reason why innocent aggressors forfeit their rights nor can they provide an explanation for why, when an attack is over, the aggressor regains his rights.[38]

In sum, Moore offers a distributive justice account of self-defense, wherein harm ought to fall upon its culpable cause. He maintains this account is a strong permission, immune to consequentialist balancing. He believes this permission also applies to *Falling Large Man, Conscientious Driver*, and *The Resident*, and he maintains that this position holds even when the innocent aggressors outnumber the defenders. Finally, he rejects forfeiture accounts as implausible.

In what follows, I wish to question these claims. First, it is unclear what grounds Moore's extension from the redistribution of harm to its culpable cause to the redistribution of harm to its innocent cause. Moreover, I am unsure why a causal account would necessarily yield that defenders get to kill innocent threats; I would think that for Moore this would be empirically contingent on the degree of causal contribution. Second, I worry that self-defense is not best understood as a mechanism of distributive justice as it ignores the aggressor's ability to stop attacking thereby preventing the need for anyone to be harmed. Third, I query whether Moore's dismissal of forfeiture is warranted, both because forfeiture views rely on changes of normative relations, which in other contexts Moore takes to be quite possible, and because the sort of underlying moral justification at work in Moore's theory seems in harmony with the claims made by forfeiture theorists. Finally, I question whether Moore's theory of self-defense might justify a deterrence-based criminal law. Indeed, I wonder whether he might be committed to punishing the innocent.

[31] Moore, 2012b, 457.
[32] Moore, 2012b, 457.
[33] Moore, 2012b, 457.
[34] Moore, 2012b, 457.
[35] Moore, 2009d, 40.
[36] Moore, 2012b, 458.
[37] Moore, 2012b, 464.
[38] Moore, 1997b, 713.

A. What grounds killing innocent aggressors?

The first puzzle is how Moore grounds the extension of "divine justice" from culpable aggressors to innocent threats. He asserts that the reason why it is justifiable to kill culpable aggressors is that (1) culpable actors who (2) cause (3) the need for someone to be harmed are the ones who should therefore be harmed. This is grounded in robust intuitions of fairness that bad guys get their due. He then goes on to say that defenders can kill innocent threats as well.

I don't get it. Nothing about the fittingness and appropriateness of culpable actors being harmed defensively seems to commit us to any particular view of innocent actors. With respect to innocent aggressors, Moore abandons requirement (1). He never fully articulates an argument for why it is permissible to kill Falling Large Man, Conscientious Driver, or The Resident.

Without culpability, Moore is left with only causation and necessity. Perhaps Moore thinks that is enough.[39] However, as Coase has shown, causation is reciprocal.[40] The only reason the large man falling down the well is a threat to the defender at the bottom is because the defender found himself at the bottom of a well. Aren't they both causes?

Indeed, Moore believes that causation is scalar. Is it not possible then that there will be cases in which the defender is more of the cause than the innocent threat? After all, we imagine in these cases that Victor, the person at the bottom of the well, is somehow motivating Abe, the pusher, to try to kill him. When Abe grabs the large man (who may just be on his way to the post office), why should we assume that the large man is more of a cause of the predicament than the defender? Causation does not seem to be able to discriminate between innocent aggressor and defender as Moore would have it.

If not culpability (or causation), then what makes this fitting? It is hard to see this account as an account of distributive justice. Should it not matter what the probability of being victim and defender are? If we are interested in "fairness and appropriateness," it seems the calculation should be sensitive to whether one is more likely to be victim or defender. As Larry Alexander has argued, if it is much less likely that you will kill someone as an innocent aggressor than that you will become an innocent aggressor and be killed, perhaps we should not so easily decide that killing innocent aggressors is permissible.[41]

There does not seem to be a moral principle that can be added to do the normative work. Besides the fact that, as Jimbo on *South Park* would say,[42] "they're coming right for us!" there does not seem to be any normative grounding that would undergird killing for such a reason. At one point, Moore seems to indicate that "he's coming right for us" is a moral ownership. More specifically, it is about "risk ownership." However, Moore has the ownership of the risk argument exactly backwards. Consider what Moore says about innocent shields. He imagines the following case:

[39] He suggests as much in Moore, 1997b, 714.

[40] R. H. Coase, "The Problem of Social Cost," 3 *Journal of Law & Economics* 1 (1960).

[41] Larry Alexander, "Self-Defense, Justification and Excuse," 22 *Philosophy & Public Affairs* 53 (1993).

[42] I've got my bad popular culture references too. There is a great episode of *South Park* where Jimbo, a hunter, is told he may only kill animals who are attacking him. The episode proceeds with innocent animals frolicking in the woods and Jimbo continuously asserting that "they're coming right for us" so that he may shoot them.

> Consider the situation in which a terrorist ("T") takes an innocent bystander ("V") as a shield to use as T seeks to kill another ("D"). If D's only way to defend himself against T is to shoot through V, it is common to suppose, morally and legally, that he may do so. The reason for this, I would think, lies in the "ownership" of the risk (of T's violence) that V, through no fault of his own, has acquired. T's taking V as a shield was V's misfortune; V did nothing to deserve it but it's his nonetheless, like disease or natural catastrophe. D is entitled to resist the shifting of that risk from V to himself, not because V caused the risk, but because it's his risk nonetheless.[43]

Why can it not be equally maintained that the person stuck owning the risk is D? As it stands, V's being strapped to T creates no risk to V whatsoever. The unlucky person is D. So why is it that D gets to shift the risk to V? And why isn't T entitled to resist the shifting of the risk? If "shit happens"[44] to the innocent who are then stuck with their misfortunes, it isn't remotely clear why the person who is stuck is V and not D.

Compare Jeff McMahan's dismissal of this kind of reasoning in the falling man cases:

> It is, however, not the falling man who has bad luck. If no one does anything, he will not be harmed, for there is a cushion below him. It is that cushion, an immobilized person, who has bad luck. May he transfer that bad luck to an innocent person, the falling man, by killing him? To override the presumption against killing, there must be a basis of liability. That basis is lacking in this case, just as it is when a person can save himself only by killing an innocent bystander.[45]

It seems that Moore has yet to come up with an argument that would decisively yield that defenders may kill innocent threats.[46]

I wonder what Moore believes he would lose by abandoning the strong-permission approach in favor of an agent-relative permission to kill innocent aggressors. Moore's view on innocent aggressors is not in accord with that of Phillip Montague, upon whom Moore claims to be relying. In "Self-Defence and Innocence: Aggressors and Active Threats,"[47] Montague distinguishes between culpable and innocent aggressors. Montague does not maintain that we have a claim right to kill innocent aggressors, holding instead that one has a liberty with which third parties may interfere. Montague's argument stands in stark contrast with Moore's robust position that self-defense against innocent aggressors is a strong permission.

Moore has been sympathetic to agent-relative obligations in other work. He notes, for example, that if an evil threatener threatens to kill a parent's child unless the parent produces some *greater* evil, the parent is *justified* because the parent has an agent-relative obligation to safeguard her child.[48] As mentioned earlier, some theorists do maintain that one has an agent-relative *permission* to give one's own life greater weight. Moore goes farther in other work, arguing that one has an agent-relative *obligation* to

[43] Moore, 1997b, 714. [44] "[A]s a popular '90s bumper sticker had it." Moore, 2009d, 290.

[45] Jeff McMahan, "Reply," in Paul H. Robinson, Stephen P. Garvey, and Kimberly Kessler Ferzan (eds.), *Criminal Law Conversations* (New York: Oxford University Press, 2009), 404–5.

[46] The most famous defender of the permissibility of killing the Falling Large Man is Judith Thomson. Judith Jarvis Thomson, "Self-Defense," 20 *Philosophy& Public Affairs* 283 (1991). For critiques, see Alexander, "Self-Defense, Justification and Excuse"; McMahan, "Basis of Moral Liability"; Ferzan, "Culpable Aggression."

[47] 12 *Utilitas* 62 (2000).

[48] Moore, 2014d. He also mentions the possibility of "skewing" in Moore, 2012b, 463.

safeguard one's child. I wonder why Moore resists the agent-relative route. There must be something more at work for Moore that allows defenders to kill many innocent people. I wish he would, as the Pink Ladies and the T-Birds request, "tell me more."

B. Is self-defense best understood as a mechanism for the distribution of harm?

More generally, I doubt that seeing self-defense as a mechanism for the distribution of inevitable harm is the most perspicuous way to see it.[49] As David Wasserman points out, unlike true distributive questions (in which someone's gotta die), in self-defense cases, no one has to die.[50] The culpable aggressor could just change his mind, and he certainly has it within his power to eliminate the existence of any distributive problem.

Indeed, Montague's solution to this problem is one Moore would most certainly reject. Montague makes the necessity dependent on the agent's perspective. After assuming that Alice is attacking Al, and Arliss is a third party who can intervene, Montague says of Al and Arliss: "They are respectively permitted and required to [harm Alice] as a matter of justice in the distribution of harms that are unavoidable *from their standpoints*."[51] To Moore, justice isn't a matter of perspective. Moore would thus need to take the position that because it is necessary in fact (because the culpable aggressor will pull the trigger), the defender may act now to distribute a harm. But taking this approach seemingly ignores that self-defense is preemptive and there is something important about the fact that the culpable aggressor can still prevent the creation of any harm.

Moreover, as Wasserman also notes, once the harm is already out there and we are truly distributing it (for instance, the culpable aggressor has already sunk the ship and everyone is scrambling for planks), then lots of factors may count.[52] Provocateurs nicely raise this. Assume that Iago provokes Othello into trying to kill Desdemona, but this is a modern version where Othello sets up a machine gun to fire where Desdemona is sleeping. Iago and Othello are both waiting in the wings. All that you, a third party, can do is to push either Iago or Othello into the line of fire. Who gets the bullet? And, now, add another character in the wings—Claudius, who, from another play, is already responsible for at least one death. He is a bad guy who has not gotten the punishment he deserves. How do we factor him into the mix if we are distributing this harm? There are degrees of culpability, degrees of causal responsibility, and degrees of moral desert

[49] Admittedly, I was tempted by this view in earlier work. See Kimberly Kessler Ferzan, "Justifying Self-Defense," 24 *Law & Philosophy* 711 (2005). But I have come to see that the grounding of the forfeiture is what does the heavy lifting.

[50] David Wasserman, "Justifying Self-Defense," 16 *Philosophy & Public Affairs* 356 (1987).

[51] Phillip Montague, "Self-Defense, Culpability, and Distributive Justice," 29 *Law and Philosophy* 75 (2009), 84 (emphasis added).

[52] Phillip Montague, "Self-Defense and Choosing Between Lives," 40 *Philosophical Studies* 207 (1981), 211 (arguing that in forced-choice situations, "special moral significance" does attach to the situation's being caused by someone's culpable behavior); David Wasserman, "Justifying Self-Defense," (rejecting Montague's theory and arguing "that greater fault is not a sufficient condition for choosing one life over another").

and who takes the bullet might just be complicated.[53] I certainly do not disagree that in this sort of case, one must distribute the certain harm. I merely think that such distributions are complex beyond Moore's simple justice. At most it seems that a distributive justice account may explain some instances of self-defense some of the time.[54] That's fine in the sense that we need not have only one account. However, Moore must then concede that more work must be done to cover other cases.

C. Why isn't Moore a fan of forfeiture?

Moore dismisses forfeiture theories as implausible. I demur. Moore needs forfeiture.

It may be that Moore dismisses the "full surrender" robust forfeiture that we think of with respect to some legal rights. Here, he is surely right. If you give something up for ever and ever, well, then you don't get it back just by lowering your gun. I take the real objection here to be not that these things are restored, but rather whether this "now you have it, now you don't, now you have it again" process is best viewed as one of forfeiture. As Richard Lippke argues in the punishment context, "Offenders might be understood to suffer other losses with regard to their rights besides forfeiture. Specifically, their rights might be curtailed or suspended, instead of forfeited. Forfeiture theorists need to show forfeiture, rather than curtailment or suspension, is the best characterization of the losses that are justifiably imposed on offenders."[55]

Elsewhere I have speculated that because forfeiture seems so final, the literature has gravitated toward "liability." However, because "liability" in the self-defense literature is neither legal liability nor Hohfeldian liability, I am skeptical that this terminological shift was actually for the better. Nevertheless, even if the objection goes beyond nomenclature to a claim that there is something deeper at stake with respect to getting the shift in normative relations right, that still does not mean that offhanded dismissal of forfeiture is warranted. Rather, what liability theorists claim is that there is a shift in the aggressor's rights.

Certainly, there is nothing odd about thinking that we can shift our rights and others' duties. I can change my moral relationship with you by giving you permission to drive my car. I can obligate myself through making a promise. I can give you a new reason for acting by making a request. Why isn't it plausible that self-defense likewise involves such a shifting of moral relations?

[53] For the argument that it is Iago, see Kimberly Kessler Ferzan, "Provocateurs," 7 *Criminal Law and Philosophy* 597 (2013). For the argument that it is Othello, see Daniel M. Farrell, "What Should We Say about Contrived 'Self-Defense' Defenses?" 7 *Criminal Law and Philosophy* 571 (2013). David Rodin might also opt for Othello. See David Rodin, "Justifying Harm," 122 *Ethics* 74 (2011), 91 ("where two or more persons share responsibility for unjust threatened harm, defensive force should be presumptively directed at the agent whose intervening action is most proximate to the threat."). For the argument that Claudius ought to be considered, see Alexander, "Recipe." As for Montague's distributive claim, Montague notes, "the distribution thesis makes no mention of comparative fault, and is therefore inapplicable to cases in which the victims of aggression are to some extent blameworthy for their predicaments." Phillip Montague, "The Morality of Self-Defense: A Reply to Wasserman," 18 *Philosophy & Public Affairs* 81 (1989), 86.

[54] This is Montague's position. He claims that his distributive justice account "does yield an explanation of permissible self-defense against culpable attackers, but it implies nothing about self-defense against innocent attackers." Phillip Montague, "Self-Defense, Culpability, and Distributive Justice," 88.

[55] Richard L. Lippke, "Criminal Offenders and Right Forfeiture," 32 *Journal of Social Philosophy* 79 (2001), 84.

Indeed, as a retributivist, Moore certainly needs an account of how it becomes the case that it is permissible to harm someone because she deserves it. Either our rights are specified such that they are not infringed when we are given deserved punishment,[56] or we forfeit our rights in such cases.[57] Indeed, Moore allows of such a possibility, noting that we can punish offenders because no non-forfeited right stands in the state's way, "since [offenders] forfeit such rights precisely by the culpable wrongdoing that constitutes desert."[58] If Moore does not deny that defendants may be permissibly punished—that is harmed without their rights standing in the punisher's way—then why does he deny that rights may shift in self-defense cases?[59]

Finally, one wonders whether Moore implicitly brings to bear the very same moral facts, just in a different package. If self-defense is about distributing harm, there is a reason why the bad guy gets that harm and the good guy does not.[60] That reason, that alteration in moral standing vis-à-vis others, looks quite like what liability theorists are after. Perhaps Moore has good arguments for why these accounts are importantly different. I wish he would tell us what those are.

D. A deterrence theorist after all?

To this point I have offered concerns about Moore's commitments within self-defense theory, but if Moore is right, I wonder whether his theory of self-defense leads to a very different justification for punishment. Notably, I share with Moore a commitment to retributivism. I just wonder whether he is actually a back door deterrence theorist. Here is how the argument runs.

The concern with deterrence theories of punishment is that they countenance punishing the innocent, and in particular, using the innocent as a means. A pure utilitarian theory would allow good consequences to justify scapegoating someone wholly unconnected with the crime.[61] Because utilitarian theories condone the punishment of the undeserving, and because mixed theories seem to exempt the punishment of the deserving where no further good is accomplished, Moore declares that the last theory standing is retributivism. This is what he calls "an argument from the back door for retributivism."[62]

The question, though, is whether Moore's commitments to a distributive justice view of self-defense can go some distance toward establishing a distinct justification for punishment. Maybe there is more than one back door to the house.

Notice that the first chink in the armor, as Victor Tadros has shown, is that the prohibition on punishing, or using, the innocent, requires a deontological account of why

[56] Mitchell N. Berman, "Punishment and Justification," 118 *Ethics* 258 (2008).

[57] Christopher Heath Wellman, "The Rights Forfeiture Theory of Punishment," 122 *Ethics* 371 (2012).

[58] Moore, 1993b, 36.

[59] Moore can't, at this level of analysis, avail himself of the fact that punishment is state imposed. Moore believes that desert can justify targeted killings and does not rely on the fact that punishment is public state action in his justification. Moral desert does all the work. See Moore, 2012b, 458–9. Thanks to Stephen Morse for suggesting this potential rejoinder by Moore.

[60] I owe this observation to a paper I anonymously refereed. The journal was unwilling to allow me to waive anonymity in exchange for learning the author's identity to properly cite the author.

[61] Moore, 1997b, 94–7. [62] Moore, 1997b, 103.

harming this particular person is not using him as a means.[63] Retributivism furnishes such a reason, but Tadros has argued that if the wrongdoer has a duty to suffer then he is not being used. If I push you into the lake, I have a duty to rescue you. If Alex points a gun at me to enforce that duty, he is not using me as I am already required to rescue you from drowning. The duty provides all the justification we need for why I am not being used as a means when Alex forces me to save you. Now, one need not agree with Tadros about his duty view for the criminal law (I doubt Moore does, and I don't) to see the force of the argument, which is that a deontological account need not be a retributive account. One just needs an account of why the person does not have a right that stands in the way.

Now consider Moore's commitments to self-defense as a form of distributive justice. If one is culpable in forcing a choice, then one ought to be the one to suffer the harm. The culpable cause of the peril is the person who should suffer the harm. Here, too, we have a deontological account of when it is permissible to harm others.

In reaching this theory, Moore endorses Philip Montague's work. Let us consider another Montague fan. Daniel Farrell also endorses Montague's views, but for an entirely different end. He employs Montague's theory to justify specific and general deterrence.[64]

Farrell's brief for specific deterrence is a rather clear case. If someone hurts you, and by virtue of that attack, she makes it more likely that you will not be able to resist subsequent attacks from her, then she is the culpable cause of your peril. If harming her abates these potential injuries, then, according to Montague's theory, claims Farrell, one is justified in harming the attacker.[65]

Consider also his claim for general deterrence. "[S]omeone might attack me, in the state of nature, and someone else, observing this attack, and observing as well that it goes unpunished, might be inspired by what she sees to attack me subsequently herself, even though she would not have dared to do this if my original attacker had been punished for his attack."[66] Now, admittedly, there are some steps required to get from this point to a system of general deterrence. Farrell endorses the view that one is harmed when one is presented with an "increased probability of being harmed sometime in the future."[67] Moore would never accept that. He does not take risks to be harms. Still, Moore cannot avoid the point that, given his endorsement of Montague's theory, on self-defense and defense-of-others grounds we may be justified in harming someone if he makes an attack by others inevitable.

It may be that such a theory is too convoluted for application in the real world. It may simply be impossible to determine how much harm may be visited on a defendant for the peril he creates in the future.[68] Perhaps, via this reasoning, deterrence may be theoretically justified but not practically implemented.

63 Victor Tadros, *The Ends of Harm: The Moral Foundations of the Criminal Law* (Oxford: Oxford University Press, 2011).

64 Daniel M. Farrell, "Punishment without the State," 22 *Noûs* 437 (1988); Daniel M. Farrell, "The Justification of General Deterrence," 94 *Philosphical Review* 367 (1985).

65 Farrell, "Justification of General Deterrence," 370.

66 Farrell, "Punishment without the State," 444.

67 Farrell, "Punishment without the State," 444.

68 For questions of this sort about Tadros' theory, see Vera Bergelson, "The Duty to Protect the Victim—or the Duty to Suffer Punishment?" 32 *Law & Philosophy* 199 (2013).

Still, I am somewhat curious what would happen in the (nearby?) possible world where Moore pursues these questions with the same sort of ruthless resolve with which he has subjected action theory or causal metaphysics. Would Moore endorse the position that his distributive justice commitments yield an entirely different justification for punishment?

Indeed, consider what the content of our criminal law would look like if Moore took his theory of self-defense *and maintained his view that it applies to innocent threats.* Consider cases of non-deserving actors in the retributive sense. Sometimes utilitarian arguments are made that an excuse should not be recognized because recognition will open up the floodgates to abuse by others. Mistake of law, duress, and insanity are classic instances where such a claim arises. This sort of argument is antithetical to retributivism, but it isn't to Moore's distributive justice account of self-defense. If your innocent mistake makes me vulnerable to ploys by non-mistaken actors, you have made me worse off, and thus, you ought to be the one to suffer the harm. Punishment of the (morally) innocent is justified after all. I suppose that in Moore's book, they just own that risk they've done nothing to deserve.

IV. Conclusion

Michael Moore does not just engage topics. He conquers them. I have learned more from him than any other theorist. I am grateful to have had him as a teacher. I am grateful to call him my friend. But most importantly, I am grateful that such a brilliant mind has done such tremendous work in a field I love, and that I get to engage with his ideas. Now, Michael, please come and conquer self-defense.

16

Moore on the Mind

Stephen J. Morse

I. Introduction

Michael Moore has been much and consistently on my mind since I first became acquainted with him by reading his early paper, "Some Myths About 'Mental Illness.'"[1] Michael had applied for a faculty position at USC School of Law, and I was on the appointments committee. I was bowled over by the paper's conceptual clarity, the depth of the analysis, and the sheer analytic penetration. It was an easy case for appointment, and those same formidable intellectual powers have never waned and indeed have waxed over Michael's long and distinguished career. It has been my clichéd but genuine pleasure and privilege to have been his friend and colleague for four decades. With respect to the exceptional other colleagues from whom I have learned so much, including the authors in this volume, Michael has been the most powerful and enduring influence on my thought and scholarship.

Michael and I agree about almost everything methodologically and substantively. As a result, one wag referred to us as the "USC Twins." I took this as a compliment to me and backhanded dig at Michael. There are differences, to be sure, but they have little practical importance and they are swamped by the similarities. I attribute this mostly to Michael's outsized influence as a result of his power and erudition. Thus, this chapter is an homage to Michael, who is henceforth conventionally called, Moore.

The next section of this chapter addresses metaphysical and other philosophical foundational problems. Section III addresses the criteria for action in the context of cases in which consciousness is divided. Section IV considers whether mental disorder sometimes excuses because it is a status excuse. The following section covers the continuing controversy about the validity of a control ("volitional") excuse. Section VI surveys the burgeoning but vexed relation of neuroscience to law. A brief conclusion follows.

II. Philosophical Foundations and Spockian Methodology

As Moore—famously a metaphysical realist about law, morality, and the relations between them (and much else)—would observe, one is always wittingly or unwittingly "doing" metaphysics. I agree. About some issues, it scarcely matters, but about the types of issues that mutually concern us, such as the causation of action (the mind–body problem) and the criteria for responsibility (compatibilism v. incompatibilism),

[1] Moore, 1975b.

metaphysical assumptions matter. The question is whether one must resolve or even defend one's metaphysical and other philosophical foundations in these fraught areas. Moore thinks that one must, but I disagree for legal purposes. I make no claim for metaphysical or philosophical quietism because I believe that metaphysical questions are conceptually and practically important in many cases.[2] I shall suggest, however, that when one's philosophical position is foundational and practically important, it must be acknowledged, but need not be defended or, *a fortiori*, resolved.

Please do the following thought experiment. Imagine that you do a content analysis of high-level introductory texts in metaphysics or in any other area in philosophy, such as the philosophy of mind and action. The intrepid investigator will find, without exception, that each text will describe many different, often contradictory, approaches to the central questions. What is the relation of the potential truth of determinism to the possibility of "free will" and responsibility? Every text will discuss libertarianism, hard determinism, and compatibilism. Are there moral truths independent of our constructs and practices? Every text will discuss varieties of realism, antirealism, and everything in between. What is the relation of the brain to consciousness, mind, and action? Every text will present various forms of physicalism and the like. There will almost always be good arguments for and against the various positions, but among the survivors of ongoing philosophical dialogue none, will have clearly dominated. Consequently, all the contenders will be left standing. To paraphrase the noted metaphysician, Lewis Carroll, everyone has won (at least in their own eyes) and all must have prizes.

What is a poor country lawyer-scholar supposed to do in such circumstances when trying to make normative arguments about doctrine, practice, and policy? One possibility is to master all the metaphysical arguments relevant to the question being addressed, take a position, and try to defend it against the counter-arguments. This seems like a bootless enterprise because arguing the metaphysics or other basic philosophical issues is not the country lawyer-scholar's comparative advantage and it will not lead to an uncontroversial position. Further, the history of the law suggests that country lawyers can "run the railroad" without even recognizing the foundational issues that are implicated. If philosophical understanding is not the primary goal, it is in large measure a distraction. So, the original question remains: What to do?

My current preferred approach is what I call Spockian solutions or, what to do until the doctors of metaphysics and science arrive to cure our metaphysical and empirical ills. By Spockian, I do not mean the cold-bloodedly rational Vulcan, Mr. Spock, of *Star Trek* fame. I refer to the famous pediatrician and author, Dr. Benjamin M. Spock, whose many editions of the influential childcare manual, *Baby and Child Care*,[3] guided young parents over many generations. The book is replete with home remedy formulas for ameliorating the common ills that beset children until the doctor came or until the parents and child could make it to the doctor.

[2] See generally, Charles Barzun, "Metaphysical Quietism and Functional Explanation in the Law," 34 *Law & Philosophy* 89 (2014) (arguing for metaphysical engagement).

[3] Benjamin Spock and Robert Needlman, *Baby and Child Care*, 9th edn. (New York: Pocket Books, 2011).

In the spirit of Dr. Spock, my legal home remedy is to start with a normative position that is attractive at the non-metaphysical level of applied ethical, moral, political, and legal theory. If this position is consistent with a reasonable metaphysics that does not conflict with relatively uncontroversial or at least plausible empirical assumptions and with other reasonable philosophical theories, then one can proceed without defending the philosophical position. Importantly, common sense should enter the analysis, too. Any position that violates common sense should meet the most demanding burden of persuasion. The scholar does have the duty, however, to avoid adopting normative positions that require inconsistent metaphysical positions unless there is good reason for the inconsistency.

The home remedy requires intellectual effort. A plausible basic position must be taken, which requires reasonable understanding. If a critic points out the reasons that the chosen philosophical position is problematic, we know that a sophisticated metaphysician who adheres to the chosen metaphysics would have answers and there would be no decisive arguments to refute the sophisticate. Trying to defend a metaphysical position at the level of professional philosophy involves too much "inside baseball" analysis when one is trying to "do" law.

Let us turn to examples of the home remedy that are relevant to the topics this chapter addresses. The basic questions that run through most are the relation of the brain to mind and action and the implications of the truth of determinism. I am a physicalist about the former. The brain enables the mind and action, but we have no idea how, despite all the astonishing advances in neuroscience and other disciplines.[4] The problem of consciousness may be insoluble,[5] but perhaps progress can be made on mental states and actions.[6] How do we know that the brain enables the mind and action? Well, if your brain is dead, you are dead and, to the best of our knowledge, you have no mental states.

Assuming that the brain enables the mind and action, is the relation reductive or not? Is property dualism true? Can mental states cause changes in physical states or does the exclusion principle require that causation can only run from the physical to the mental? At present, non-reductive physicalism is probably the dominant view, but neither I nor anyone else can decisively answer the foregoing and similar questions.

Like Moore,[7] I subscribe to the causal theory of action (CTA), of which there are many forms and many criticisms.[8] CTA roughly holds that an event (behavioral or mental) is an action if it is caused in the right way by mental states. In his recent chapter,[9] Moore ably updates his earlier account and defends it against various critics. The critics will not be persuaded, but I am happy to adopt the same or a similar view, not least because it accords with common sense and the folk-psychological theory that we always use to explain ourselves to ourselves and to others. I have elsewhere addressed

[4] Ralph Adolphs, "The Unsolved Problems in Neuroscience," 3 *Trends in Cognitive Sciences (TiCS)* 173 (2015), 175; Paul McHugh and Philip Slavney, *The Perspectives of Psychiatry*, 2nd edn. (1998), 11–12.

[5] See, e.g., Colin McGinn, *The Mysterious Flame: Conscious Minds in a Material World* (New York: Basic Books, 1999).

[6] Adolphs, "The Unsolved Problems in Neuroscience."

[7] Moore, 1993c; Moore, 2010.

[8] Jesus H. Aguilar and Andrei A. Buckareff, "The Causal Theory of Action: Origins and Issues," in Aguilar and Buckareff (eds.), *Causing Human Actions* (Cambridge, MA: MIT Press, 2010), 1 (providing a useful overview).

[9] Moore, 2010.

whether recent work in neuroscience and psychology proves, as some claim,[10] that we are not agents and concluded that such claims are unconvincing at present.[11] As Jerry Fodor wrote, if we are wrong about the common-sense causation of action, that is the wrongest we've been about anything except belief in the supernatural.[12] It would be a disaster to believe the contrary, even if we were capable of doing so, which Fodor doubts. Moreover, there is a plausible philosophical argument that causation can run from the mental to the physical, despite the exclusion principle.[13] I am not suggesting anything mysterious or any form of *sui generis* agent causation. How action happens will be explicable according to whatever scientific laws that govern the rest of the universe might be discovered. The task of neuroscience should be to explain agency, not to explain it away reductively.

Moore is a reductive identity theorist about brain and mental states. He believes that brain states simply are mental states and vice versa. I assume, however, that in his account the reduction only runs downward from the mental to the physical. Nonetheless, because Moore adheres to CTA, he must accept the standard view that mental causation that is itself non-actional can cause actions (or omissions). This is the role volitions play in his theory. In contrast, I am most attracted to non-reductive physicalism. We have a mind/brain, which is only one substance, but it has both physical and mental properties. The latter are emergent and cannot be reduced fully to the former. This appears the most commonsensical view and there is no scientific reason to doubt it at present. The greatest experts cannot resolve this issue, much less a poor country lawyer-scholar. Luckily I do not have to. It is sufficient that there are plausible philosophical accounts that are consistent with CTA and folk-psychological explanations. I am perfectly content opportunistically to adopt any of them.

I take no position on the vexed question concerning responsibility of whether anyone can do otherwise even if the CTA is true. There is dispute about how the principle of alternative possibilities (PAP) should be interpreted, and, like Jay Wallace, I doubt that foundational questions of responsibility will be decided by exquisite deployment of modal logic.[14] There are sufficient, albeit controversial, arguments to suggest that PAP is not a problem.[15] This question will not be solved to everyone's satisfaction and we have a railroad to run. I am a compatibilist, a perfectly plausible metaphysics, and will continue to believe that robust responsibility is possible until an incontrovertible argument that all would accept requires me to jettison this view.

In short, CTA and compatibilism are my bedrock metaphysics. If Moore or anyone else claims that I need a particular type of CTA theory or compatibilism, I am happy to

[10] Joshua Greene and Jonathan Cohen, "For the Law, Neuroscience Changes Nothing and Everything," in S. Zeki and O. Goodenough (eds.), *Law & the Brain* (Oxford: Oxford University Press, 2006), 207, 217–18; Daniel M. Wegner, *The Illusion of Conscious Will* (Cambridge, MA: MIT Press, 2002).

[11] E.g., Stephen J. Morse, "Lost in Translation: An Essay on Neuroscience and Law," in Michael Freeman (ed.), *Law and Neuroscience* 529 (Oxford: Oxford University Press, 2011).

[12] Jerry A. Fodor, *Psychosemantics: The Problem of Meaning in the Philosophy of Mind* (Cambridge, MA: M.I.T. Press, 1987), xii.

[13] Christian List and Peter Menzies, "Non-Reductive Physicalism and the Limits of the Exclusion Principle," 106 *Journal of Philosophy* 425 (2009).

[14] R. Jay Wallace, *Responsibility and the Moral Sentiments* (Cambridge, MA: Harvard Univeristy Press, 1994).

[15] E.g., Kadri Vihvelin, *Causes, Laws and Free Will* (New York: Oxford University Press, 2013).

take that as a friendly amendment. Giving up CTA or compatibilism would undermine my work, but, happily, nothing in philosophy or science suggests that I must do so.

III. At Action's Border

The title of this section is taken from my contribution[16] to a symposium celebrating the publication of Moore's brilliant book, *Act and Crime*, which is still the most important contribution to action theory in criminal law jurisprudence. I took issue with Moore's view that bodily movements performed while the agent is in a dissociative state are not actions and therefore do not meet the criminal law's prima facie culpability requirement of a "voluntary act." I believed with reservations that such movements are actions, a view that Bernard Williams also adopted (1994).[17] I suggested that if the dissociation was sufficiently severe, the agent should be excused. I argued this position using Moore's own theory of action in *Act and Crime* and in his magisterial, *Law and Psychiatry: Rethinking the Relationship*.[18] Moore's reply[19] was a paragon of gracious courtesy and friendly dispute that stuck to his guns but concluded that there was little space between us.

I'm still not certain if dissociated movements should legally be treated as "voluntary actions," but I am increasingly sure that that the philosophy of mind and action and the relevant sciences cannot answer this question because it is unlikely that action is a natural kind with clear boundaries. There are clear cases, to be sure, but there is a huge range of intermediate cases that resist easy classification.

Let us begin with the relatively uncontroversial phenomenology. At one end of the continuum are consciously intentional movements, such as booting up my computer to work on this chapter. At the other are movements, such as spasms and reflexes, which are not intentional. How should we think about movements that appear automatic, habitual, or thoughtless, such as the body language we use when we lecture? These movements are not consciously intentional, but we rightly believe that they can be brought under conscious intentional control if we have reason to do so. These types of habitual or automatic movements are treated by both common sense and by the criminal law as actions. There is nothing wrong with the agent's consciousness and he can bring it to bear if necessary. How should we treat movements performed thoughtlessly on the impulsive spur of the moment or in cases involving intense emotions such as anger? It may be difficult for such agents to be self-conscious and to bring reason to bear, but once again we think the agent is capable of doing so in virtually all cases.

But then there are dissociated movements, what I call the "actish" cases, such as sleepwalking or severe intoxication. The agent's movements indicate awareness of the environment, accurate feedback from it, and goal-directedness. Consider Ms. Cogdon, who very effectively axe-murdered her adult daughter while sleepwalking. Moore believes that access to the full reasons for action is "sealed off" and cannot be retrieved. Ms. Cogdon had good reasons not to kill her innocent daughter, but at that moment

16 Stephen J. Morse, "Culpability and Control," 142 *University of Pennsylvania Law Review* 1587 (1994).

17 Bernard Williams, "The Actus Reus of Dr. Caligari," 142 *University of Pennsylvania aw. Review* 1661 (1994).

18 Moore, 1984d.

19 Moore, 1994c.

could not access them. Her consciousness was transiently partial, divided, dissociated, or the like. We know many of the causes of such states, but we do not well understand the neural mechanisms.

Are dissociated movements more like clear cases of action or non-action? This question ignores, however, the continuous nature of dissociation. An agent may be more or less dissociated. Imagine someone who is continuously drinking alcohol and becoming progressively more intoxicated. At first the intoxication will be slight and the agent can force herself to snap back to self-consciousness and to regain access to countervailing reasons. As the level of intoxication increases, this will be increasingly difficult. Finally, it will be supremely difficult and perhaps impossible. Where on the continuum should we draw the line between action and non-action? Even if we had a complete neural description of each discrete level of dissociation—a science fiction fantasy—it would not answer the question. Where on the continuum we should draw the line is a moral and legal question not answered by saying that action is a natural kind and the line should be drawn at its border.

Why does the criminal care about whether something is an action or not? Criminal responsibility is based on a folk-psychological concept of agency and instantiates the moral consequences of that conception. Our underlying moral and legal theory will guide our concept of action and not the reverse. I continue to think that whether dissociated movements are not actions or are excused actions is a very difficult question. I believe that the argument for excused action is stronger, but still inconclusive. Alas, the philosophy of mind and action and the new neuroscience cannot neatly resolve the issue.

In either case, the defendant is found not responsible, but there are doctrinal issues that suggest that treating dissociated movements as excused actions makes more legal sense. Retrospective mental state evaluations are difficult to make, but deciding how dissociated an agent was in the past can be fearsomely difficult. It is an easy claim to make and hard to disprove if the prosecution must prove the act element beyond a reasonable doubt because the usual inferences about mental states from behavior do not apply in cases of dissociation. If dissociation is an excusing condition, however, the burden of persuasion can be placed on the defendant, reducing the risk of wrongful acquittals.

If the defendant is acquitted because the prima facie case is negated, the defendant is freed entirely. Much like an acquittal by reason of legal insanity, an acquittal by reason of dissociation would provide the state with a justification for some form of commitment in appropriate cases.[20] Unlike present English law and in some US jurisdictions, dissociation or automatism should not be considered under the rubric of legal insanity, however. Most cases of automatism do not arise from mental disorder. Furthermore, many dissociated defendants do not need involuntary mental hospitalization or compelled treatment because the cause of the dissociation is transient or can be medically managed. Shoehorning these cases into legal insanity makes no sense, but some form of commitment or quarantine might be needed in some cases of untreatable, permanent conditions.

[20] *Jones v. United States*, 463 US 354 (1983) (upholding the constitutionality of indefinite civil commitment for insanity acquittees).

The most attractive reason to treat dissociation as an excusing condition is moral because it permits more finely calibrated responsibility ascription. Whether dissociated movements are actions is a binary decision. Dissociation is a degree phenomenon, however, and it lends itself to a continuum of moral ascription ranging from full responsibility through mitigation to full excuse, depending on the resulting level of rationality impairment. No legislature has adopted a generic mitigating verdict, but this would be a perfect vehicle for having the finder of fact reach more morally responsive decisions in cases of dissociation and other rationality impairments. At present, then, if dissociation were considered an excusing condition, sentencing would be the only option for considering it in cases not warranting a full excuse.

IV. Legal Insanity

Michael Moore has intermittently and illuminatingly written about law and mental disorder for over four decades. His most recent foray[21] brilliantly distills his thinking in this field, demonstrating the influence of his general thought about philosophy of mind, action, and personhood. Moore and I concur that a test for legal insanity is morally required and inevitably legal and moral, and that we cannot use medical, psychiatric, or psychological proxies for the moral and legal judgment that must be made. We also agree that testifying mental health professionals often fail to distinguish moral/legal from medical/psychological judgments. Finally, for decades we have tried to correct what I have termed the "fundamental psycholegal error," the benighted, misguided claim that causation, including abnormal causation, is per se an excusing condition.[22] Even if abnormal mental states play a causal role in explaining criminal behavior, it does not follow that the person must be excused. The abnormal mental states must satisfy the law's genuine excusing criteria.

We disagree about why mental disorder sometimes warrants an excuse. I am more skeptical than Moore about the validity of the diagnostic categories in the American Psychiatric Association's diagnostic manual,[23] but there is no doubt that severely abnormal mental phenomena, such as delusions and hallucinations, exist, and we agree that what is relevantly wrong with such people is usually a severe cognitive defect that impairs reality testing. We disagree, however, about whether mental disorder justifies legal insanity because it is the basis of a status excuse.

Before continuing, it is useful to ask whether Moore's account is meant to be a "goodness of fit" positive account of current Anglo-American and perhaps continental tests or whether it is his normative vision of what the test should be. Even if a different view better explains our actual practices, Moore's view may still be normatively desirable. I conclude that his account is not the best positive explanation and his proposal would lead to undesirable outcomes for the law and for people with mental disabilities.

Moore claims that at least some people with severe mental disorder lack fundamental conditions for personhood and are not moral agents. Severe disorder is a status excuse and thus deprives people of responsibility *tout court*. In short, such people are not

[21] Moore, 2014f. [22] Morse, "Culpability and Control," 592–4.

[23] American Psychiatric Association, *Diagnostic and Statistical Manual of Mental Disorders* (5th edn.), (DSM-5) (Washington, DC: American Psychiatric Association, 2013).

excused for specific actions, but instead are simply exempt from responsibility ascription. Moore lists nine criteria for moral personhood: (1) mental states; (2) consciousness (i): phenomenal experience; (3) consciousness (ii): privileged access; (4) intentionality; (5) three parts to the soul (the platonic functional appetitive, rational, and executory); (6) practical rationality; (7) emotionality and the rationality of emotion; (8) character structure at a time and over time; and (9) autonomy. These criteria are an attractive account of agency, but I fear they will not do the work for *moral* agency that Moore wishes.

Many people who are clearly legally insane and most 10 to 13 year olds meet these nine criteria, but Moore nonetheless (correctly) denies their status as potential moral agents. Needed is a particular deficit that unites those we potentially excuse. In other parts of the paper, Moore notes that practical rationality, his sixth criterion, must involve some degree of substantive and not simply instrumental rationality. I think that this is the key to understanding the excusing condition rather than severe "madness" itself. We excuse when substantive irrationality impairs the agent's practical reasoning in the context in question.

People with severe mental disorder are not their disorders. They are persons with a disability, which is why the preferred locution at present is not to characterize people as their disorder, for example, a "schizophrenic," but as a "person with" schizophrenia. This is cumbersome, but it is all too easy, in contrast to cases of physical disease, to think mistakenly that mental disorder is the entirety of a person. As DSM-5 recognizes, all mental disorders, including the most severe, are heterogeneous in presentation. Severe disorder heterogeneously affects the sufferer's life depending on a large number of factors, many of which are external. It need not affect every aspect of their lives. The category of "Delusional Disorder" is an example. Sufferers are psychotic but their delusional beliefs operate only in those contexts in which the belief is motivating. People with psychotic disorders may be perfectly capable of substantive and instrumental rationality in some, indeed most, areas of their lives. Contra Bleuler, who Moore quotes approvingly, they are not "stranger to us than the birds in our gardens," nor are they "beyond good and evil" in the non-Nietzchean sense, as Moore claims. Each is recognizably one of us.

Moore draws an analogy to children; but even with children, the law does not uniformly treat infancy as an excuse and takes different views of their capacities depending on their age and what is at stake. Consider the common-law excuse of infancy, which is often considered a status excuse: children aged six and younger are categorically exempt; children of seven to thirteen are presumed non-responsible; and children fourteen and older are presumed responsible. This is quite consistent with what we know about cognitive development. Although some outlier youngsters who are six or younger might have the cognitive ability to be responsible, these would be such rare cases that individuation would be inefficient. For the intermediate group, cognitive development is generally incomplete, but the presumption of non-responsibility is rebuttable. Infancy is simply a proxy for lacking certain cognitive capacities and isn't really a status excuse.

The United States Supreme Court has held that minors categorically are insufficiently rational to deserve the death penalty or to be sentenced to mandatory life without parole for non-homicide crimes,[24] but there was a strong argument that the decisions should have permitted individuation, at least for older adolescents. I believe the Court drew a bright line for the sake of administrative convenience and to avoid the horrendous error of potentially wrongfully imposing these dreadful sentences. In *Miller v. Alabama*, the Court rejected mandatory life without parole for minors committed of homicide crimes, but permitted individuation in imposing this sentence.[25] In many jurisdictions, minors are considered sufficiently rational to make an independent decision about whether to use birth control or to have an abortion. Even infancy is not clearly a "status" for all purposes.

"Intellectual Disability" (ID; formerly retardation or developmental disability) is a similar example. The Supreme Court categorically excluded people with ID from capital punishment because of rationality defects that mark this condition,[26] but conceded that such people could be criminally responsible and insisted on careful decision-making about whether the convicted capital defendant did have ID. The Court could have once again insisted on individuation even for those defendants concededly suffering from ID, which also presents heterogeneously, but for the same reasons as in *Roper* and *Graham*, opted for a categorical rule. Finally, in the civil context, whether people with ID should be treated as competent is a functional test that differs from context to context.

The same considerations are true of people with severe mental disorders. They may be competent or morally responsible for some conduct. Involuntary civil commitment, for example, no longer has the consequence of declaring the person committed civilly incompetent for all purposes, such as making contracts or voting. Moreover, those people who are omni-disabled are usually too disorganized to engage in criminal conduct other than simple assaultive or disorderly conduct, for which no sensible defendant raises an insanity defense. Those with severe disorders who commit crimes are usually quite instrumentally rational and mostly substantively rational as well. A specific cognitive deficit that irrationally and materially motivated the defendant is doing the work in most legal insanity cases. Consider McNaughton, who delusionally believed the Tories were persecuting him and were a threat to his life,[27] or Andrea Yates, who delusionally believed that she was morally corrupting her children and thus they would be tortured for all eternity in Hell unless she killed them when they were still "innocent."[28] Both carefully planned their conduct and executed it successfully (although McNaughton's victim was Peele's private secretary, Drummond, who McNaughton non-delusionally but mistakenly believed was Peele).

Moreover, the moral compass of those with severe disorders is often unimpaired. Suppose one believed what Andrea Yates believed. If these facts were true, as Ms. Yates sincerely believed, then it would be morally permissible and perhaps obligatory to kill one's children. To suggest that Ms. Yates or other legally insane people lack all moral agency is contrary to the facts and I fear demeans them. It is preferable to say that she is

24 *Roper v. Simmons*, 543 US 551 (2005); *Graham v. Florida*, 130 S Ct 2011, (2010).

25 *Miller v. Alabama*, 132 S Ct 2455 (2012).

26 *Atkins v. Virginia*, 536 US 304 (2002).

27 Richard Moran, *Knowing Right From Wrong: The Insanity Defense of Daniel M'Naghten* (New York: The Free Press, 1981).

28 Deborah W. Denno, "Who Is Andrea Yates? A Short Story About Legal Insanity," 10 *Duke Journal of Gender Law and Policy* 1 (2003).

not responsible for killing the children because she was psychotically motivated to do this particular crime, but she was responsible for much else in her life that had moral import.

It is useful to compare psychopathy to assess this issue. At the extreme, people with psychopathy, a personality disorder of unknown origin, completely or almost completely lack conscience, a sense of morality, and the capacity for empathy.[29] They are incapable of recognizing the normatively best reasons for respecting the rights of others. I believe that they are morally irrational, although they can be instrumentally rational and do understand criminal prohibitions and the potential costs of offending. I have argued elsewhere that severe psychopathy should be a predicate for excuse.[30] If the law permitted using psychopathy as a basis for legal insanity, it would best be explained by the lack of moral rational capacity, and not because psychopathy is a status.

Although plausible insanity defense cases are akin to mistakes of fact and law, the materially irrational motivation is the foundation of the excuse. Moore's views and mine are very similar, but I do not agree that a delusional person who engages in criminal behavior unrelated to his delusion is not responsible because he is not a moral agent. If his conduct is rationally motivated—even though he is wildly out of touch with reality in other domains of his life, which is commonly the case—what good moral theory would exempt him from responsibility for rationally motivated actions?

Moore is correct that knowledge of right and wrong or knowledge of what one is doing is not precisely the issue because everything turns on how narrowly knowledge is interpreted. This is a normative question unanswered by adopting equally vague terms such as "understand" or "appreciate." As an aside, most legally insane defendants did think their conduct was permissible or necessary, even according to conventional reality, if the facts were as the defendant believed. Consider Andrea Yates again.

If "knowledge" is properly interpreted morally, most people who are legally insane do not know what they are doing in the sense that they are motivated by a non-culpable error about reality. The deific decree exception to a narrowly interpreted *M'Naghten* test does not prove that madness itself excuses. It confirms that material, irrational motivation about what one is doing is necessary for excuse. Contra Moore, we do need mental disorder plus Factor X, and mental disorder must "cause" the criminal conduct by severely impairing the person's practical rationality in the particular circumstances. We have a mental disorder criterion and do not treat Factor X independently not because madness is a status excuse. As many have pointed out, mental disorder is used as an objective indicator that proves that the defendant's mistake about the motivating reality is not an "ordinary" mistake.

The hardest case for my view is the person who is materially delusionally motivated, but knows that what he is doing is wrong. An example is the person who delusionally believes that his spouse is unfaithful, is wildly jealous, cannot be convinced by evidence or logic to the contrary, and indeed weaves counter-evidence and logic into the delusional belief system and thereby reinforces it. If he kills his spouse, should he be excused? He is clearly and severely mad. The DSM-5 diagnosis would be "Delusional

[29] See Robert M. Hare, *Without Conscience: The Disturbing World of the Psychopaths Among Us* (New York: Pocket Books, 1999).

[30] Stephen J. Morse, "Psychopathy and Criminal Responsibility," 3 *Neuroethics* 205 (2008).

Disorder, jealous type"—a psychotic disorder—but note that the law virtually everywhere would not find him legally insane because he knew that what he was doing is wrong. Would Moore's status view excuse him? Perhaps so, because a psychotic belief motivated him. But is he a non-responsible agent generally? Seemingly not. If he committed theft, he should surely be responsible. For years I waffled on this issue, but now believe that the delusional spouse must be convicted, unless his moral compass is independently compromised by mental disorder. Even if all the facts and circumstances as he believes them to be were true, he would still be guilty of a crime. Faithlessness does not justify intentional homicide even if it reduces the degree of guilt in some circumstances. I would convict him of murder, but this might well be an appropriate case for my proposed "guilty but partially responsible" verdict because he had a severe rationality defect in the context.[31]

In conclusion, I don't think that the status account of legal insanity best explains current law. More important, I worry that if adopted, it would contribute, albeit marginally, to common misunderstandings and fear of mental disorder that continue to stigmatize and exclude people with such disorders.

V. The "Volitional" Excuse

The first major, modern proponents of a control test were Sir James Fitzjames Stephen[32] and the Alabama Supreme Court, which adopted the "irresistible impulse" test.[33] Both specified the folk-psychological mechanism that caused the failure of control. Fitzjames believed that the problem was the failure to keep future consequences firmly in mind.[34] The *Parsons* decision spoke of the destruction of the power to choose between right and wrong, and, quoting an authority on medical jurisprudence, attributed this to reason losing its "empire" over the passions.[35] In short, both proposed a rationality defect as the source of loss of control capacity. By the time of the *Hinckley* verdict in 1982, the Model Penal Code test, which famously includes a "control" prong, was dominant, but that dominance came to an end. In the wake of the unpopular acquittal, the American Psychiatric Association and the American Bar Association criticized control tests for failure of conceptualization and operationalization, and political pressure led to abolition of the control test in all but a small minority of jurisdictions.

I think that the APA and the ABA were right. All cases that plausibly seem to require a control test are in fact better explained, as Fitzjames and *Parsons* understood, as involving rationality defects. I am not an opponent in principle of a control test *independent* of a rationality defect if such a test has a conceptual and operational foundation. By an independent test, I mean cases in which there is no rationality problem,

31 Stephen J. Morse, "Diminished Rationality, Diminished Responsbility," 1 *Ohio St. J. Crim. L* 289 (2003).

32 James Fitzjames Stephen, *II History Of The Criminal Law of England* 120 (London: Macmillan and Co.:1883).

33 *Parsons v. State*, 81 Ala. 854,859 (1887).

34 Stephen, *History*, 120.

35 *Parsons v. State*, 859.

but, in folk-psychological parlance, the agent "can't help himself." This is precisely what Leroy Hendricks, a serial child molester, said about himself.[36]

As Moore notes, I have challenged control test proponents to provide the non-cognitive folk-psychological mechanism that causes loss of control and a method for its accurate identification. In his excellent paper on the volitional excuse,[37] Moore accepts the challenge and defends a volitional test. I will focus on his analysis of the "incapacity" justification for a control excuse and not on the interesting things he writes about the "fair opportunity" justification. Although I am willing in principle and mostly in fact to accept Moore's premises, I do not think that the conclusion he draws follows. His analysis of doctrine is better explained by a different rationale.

A preliminary word on terminology and the subjects of agreement is in order. Moore holds that volitions are independent executory intentions.[38] In virtually all cases that involve the control excuse Moore defends, he recognizes that volitions successfully execute the defendant's motivating intentions. Thus, it is somewhat strange for him to talk about a volitional excuse rather than a control or compulsion excuse. Consequently, I shall use the term "control" because it more accurately describes what ordinary morality and the law care about—the capacity to control oneself. Moore and I agree about virtually everything, including the following: There are cases calling for excuse that go beyond the strictures of current cognitive tests; the defendant must not be culpable for causing the condition of his own excuse; the defendant's capacity is the crucial question; the can't/won't distinction is actually scalar, although the law treats it as binary; and counterfactual analysis will be necessary to draw the can't/won't line.

Moore's characterization of cases requiring a control excuse are those in which the defendant did not do "what he most wants to do," either because the agent is unable to form the "right intention" or because the agent is able to form the "right" intention but is unable to execute it. Moore begins his analysis of the folk psychology of loss of control with a number of stipulations about "desire, strongest desire, and intention" that he concedes are contested in the philosophy of mind and action. I accept his stipulations, but, once again, what is a poor country lawyer-scholar to do if others contest them? Moore then proposes and evaluates six models of the folk psychology of the lack of control, ranging from desire bypassing the will entirely to unstable preference shifts (described in terms of hyperbolic discounting by many addiction specialists). He is properly skeptical that most of the models he canvasses are the underlying, unitary foundation for a control excuse, but he does settle on one of them: motivation by "ego-alien desires that refuse to be integrated into one's sense of the self," that "seem alien to [rather than part of] the reason-responsive, responsible self." I would analyze the folk psychology differently and paradoxically think that Moore underweights some of the models he rejects, but I will accept his psychology for the purpose of analysis.

I concede the psychology because all the models exemplify rationality defects if those defects are properly understood. Moore's preferred model of ego-alien desires is a prime example. Generically, the "ego-alienated" agent's desires are sealed off from the

[36] *Kansas v. Hendricks*, 521 US 346 (1997) (upholding the constitutionality of involuntary civil commitment for "mentally abnormal sexually violent predators"). See also, *Kansas v. Crane*, 534 US 407 (2002) (requiring a "serious difficulty" controlling oneself criterion for committing sexual predators).

[37] Moore, 2014d. [38] Moore, 1993c, 113-65; Moore, 2014d.

reason-responsive self. Moore quotes from many other thinkers who have reached similar conclusions about cases "when a strong, emotion-laden, not-identified-with-self desire conflicts with a less strong, probably less emotion-laden but more identified-with-self desire, and wins." The essence of all, I believe, is that the disjunct occurs because the agent is not fully rational, as M. Smith, who Moore cites approvingly, suggests.

All core criminal offenses infringe on the rights of victims and communicate disrespect for the victim and for society. Everyone thus has supremely good reason not to commit core criminal law offenses. I could quibble with how often genuinely ego-alien desires arise in criminal law cases and with Moore's account of them, but even if Moore's psychology is accepted, the problem that might excuse is a rationality defect best explained by the agent's inability to "think straight"—to access the good reasons not to offend—under circumstances that seem to disable those abilities, such as craving, intense emotion, and the other variables Moore properly notes. I think this better explains the excusing and mitigating conditions in law that Moore addresses, such as provocation/passion, "diminished capacity," involuntary intoxication, and legal insanity. The other doctrines Moore adduces, such as necessity, duress, and innocent aggressor, are better explained by a common-sense hard choice situation the agent does not create and in which the agent on balance whole-heartedly harms another. No control excuse is necessary.

Even if a control test may be justified, Moore argues that it should only apply if the agent cannot, as opposed to will not, control himself. This is a scalar concept and probably every agent has this capacity to some degree, as demonstrated by the assumption that all those agents with a control problem would manage to resist offending if they were threatened with instant death. The ability of an agent to exercise control under such circumstances does not entail that he must be responsible. No just legal regime would be so unforgiving. It is sufficient to excuse if the agent lacks "substantial" capacity, with that lack given varying normative content depending on the general stance of the legal system to the expansiveness of excuses.

Moore and I agree that counterfactual analysis is the primary way to evaluate an agent's control capacity. It is no surprise to learn that Moore metaphysically analyzes capacity using David Lewis's possible worlds modal logic. The concept of capacity is contested within professional philosophy and Moore freely concedes some of the problems with his approach. More fundamentally for the law, how could the legal system ever practically use Lewis's methodology, even if it is metaphysically the most potent? Even Lewissians differ about how close the possible worlds must be. What is a country lawyer-scholar supposed to do?

I start, of course, by conceptualizing control capacity in terms of cognitive deficits and then suggest a purely common-sense folk-psychological counterfactual methodology. Consider that refraining from most core criminal behavior, such as not killing, not raping, not burning, not stealing, and so on, is low-skill behavior. If one has the general capacity to refrain as demonstrated by the agent's behavior in other, similar circumstances—Does the agent always attempt to kill people who provoke him to anger? Does the pedophile always touch kids when there is no witness?—then it is fair to infer that the agent probably had similar capacity at the time when the prohibited action occurred.[39] This conclusion is defeasible by showing that the specific circumstances of the instant case make it distinguishable from apparently similar circumstances, but the metaphysics of counterfactuals will not help with the practical determination that must be made. There will be no easy answers in many cases, but all one can do is attend to the relevant history and compare it to the present facts and circumstances.

Neuroscience and psychology simply cannot help solve these problems. What good research now exists isn't remotely ecologically valid and there is serious question whether such research could be successfully performed, even if an institutional review board would allow the types of experimental interventions that would be necessary. We shall have to accept the necessity of behavioral evaluation.

In short, I welcome Moore to the ranks of those who understand control problems as rationality problems (anyone wants Moore as an ally) and hope that he will join me in challenging the proponents of control tests to provide a test independent of rationality defects.

VI. The New Neuroscience and Law, especially Criminal Law

In a 2002 editorial published in *The Economist*, the following warning was given: "Genetics may yet threaten privacy, kill autonomy, make society homogeneous and gut the concept of human nature. But neuroscience could do all of these things first."[40] This type of claim was fueled by the early 1990s discovery of non-invasive functional magnetic resonance imaging (fMRI) that permits neuroscientists to study not only brain structure, but also brain physiology. Scanners for non-clinical purposes became common in academic departments of psychology and neuroscience in the early part of this century and there has been a logarithmic increase in studies of cognitive, affective, and social neuroscience, which are the subfields of neuroscience most relevant to law.

Those bedazzled by the impressiveness of the technique and the cascade of data have succumbed to what I call "brain overclaim syndrome."[41] Sufferers from this dire malady claim that the new neuroscience will revolutionize law and especially criminal law. Moore, as is so often the case, pinpoints the critical issues. He distinguishes nine challenges to responsibility that allegedly flow from the new neuroscience that include, inter alia, eliminativism, epiphenomonalism, and hard determinist incompatibilsm.[42] All, I believe, are forms of the claims that neuroscience "proves" that determinism is true, that no one is responsible and the even more extravagant assertion that we are not really agents. According to neuroscientists Joshua Greene and Jonathan Cohen, for example, neuroscience allegedly proves that we are only "victims of neuronal circumstances" and the law should adapt accordingly.[43] Traditional notions of responsibility,

[39] I am assuming that the notion of a general capacity is coherent. It is controversial among some philosophers, but many think it is coherent and it accords with common sense.

[40] "The Ethics of Brain Sciences: Open Your Mind," *The Economist*, May 23, 2002, 77, <http://www.economist.com/node/1143317/print> (accessed October 5, 2011).

[41] Stephen J. Morse, "Brain Overclaim Syndrome and Criminal Responsibility: A Diagnostic Note," 3 *Ohio State Journal of Criminal Law* 397 (2006).

[42] Moore, 2011a; Moore, 2012g; Moore, 2014b.

[43] Greene and Cohen, "For the law, neuroscience changes nothing and everything," 217–18.

desert, and morally justified punishment that are at the core of current criminal justice should be replaced with a consequentially justified prediction and prevention scheme of social control.

The new neuroscience is indeed impressive, but virtually all these claims are based on too little data[44] and often on conceptual confusion.[45] Moore has entered the overclaiming thicket to clarify the conceptual space as only he can do. He has shown the following. Compatibilism is not defeated and should be embraced by neuroscientists. Wegner's claims in *The Illusion of Conscious Will* that virtually all actions are automatisms and mental states are post hoc rationalizations the brain creates are conceptually confused and empirically incorrect. Also confused and false is the claim that neuroscientist Benjamin Libet's demonstration that brain activity in the supplemental motor area precedes conscious awareness of an urge to move proves that one's brain is the only cause of the behavior and that mental states play no causal role. The neuroscience of the can't/won't distinction will be fearsomely hard to perform and probably will not answer the question of when an agent can and cannot control himself. And, finally, eliminativists and epiphenomenalists will have immense and perhaps insurmountable difficulties proving their case with neuroscience, even if they understand the precise nature of their claims, which the neuroscientists often do not. Many others and I[46] have also addressed these issues, but no one has done so with the overwhelming sophistication and depth that Moore deploys. And I am happy to report that the "Libet industry" that overclaimed about its alleged moral and legal implications appears bankrupt on empirical and conceptual grounds[47] and I doubt that it will emerge.

I agree with Moore completely about all the foregoing. We may disagree about brain/mind identity and reductionism, but since we agree on the CTA and its implications for responsibility, the disagreement scarcely matters for legal purposes. Our bedrock core agreement is that folk psychology is the foundation of law and criminal law in particular. We so thoroughly agree about the relation of current neuroscience to criminal law, that I will focus briefly on issues that are not central to Moore's writing, but which are complementary to it.

In virtually all cases, good psychology precedes good behavioral neuroscience. Neuroscientists do not go on fishing expeditions.[48] They begin with a behaviorally well-characterized condition or task and then correlate brain activity with it. For example, to

[44] Morse, "Lost in Translation."

[45] Michael Pardo and Dennis Patterson, *Minds, Brains and Law: The Conceptual Foundations of Law and Neuroscience* (New York: Oxford University Press, 2013).

[46] E.g., Stephen J. Morse, "Lost in Translation."

[47] E.g., Alfred Mele, *Effective Intentions: The Power of Conscious Will* (New York: Oxford Univerity Press, 2009); Moore, 2011a; Parashkev Nachev and Peter Hacker, "The Neural Antecdents of Voluntary Action: A Conceptual Analysis," 5 *Cognitive Neruocience* 193 (2014); Aaron Schurger, Jacobo D. Sitt, and Stanislas Dehaene, "An Accumulator Model for Spontaneous Neural Activity prior to Self-Initiated Movement," 109 *Proceedings of the National Academy of Sciences* E2904 (2012); Aaron Schurger and Sebo Uithol, "Nowhere and Everywhere: The Causal Origin of Voluntary Action," *The Review of Philosophy and Psychology* (2015), available at DOI 10.1007/s13164-014-0223-2.

[48] There is one amusing exception. Craig M. Bennett et al., "Neural correlates of interspecies perspective taking in the post-mortem Atlantic Salmon: An argument for multiple comparisons correction," 1 *Journal of Serendipitous and Unexpected Results* (2009), 1. Available at <http://citeseerx.ist.psu.edu/viewdoc/download?doi=10.1.1.161.8384&rep=rep1&type=pdf>. The study scanned a dead Atlantic salmon to demonstrate that significant results can be obtained from the most unpromising investigation unless the research design properly controls for chance findings (false positives).

determine the structural or functional brain correlates of schizophrenia, one must first clearly identify based on behavioral criteria an "experimental" group of subjects who have the disorder and a comparison group that does not. Legally relevant and valid neuroscience will always depend on clear behavioral criteria. If the behavioral differences are clear, we do not need the neuroscience because the law's criteria are behavioral, although it is comforting if the neuroscience is consistent with behavioral observation. Further, actions speak louder than images. If there is a disjunct between the two, malingering aside (which neuroscience cannot diagnose for behavioral disorders), we must believe the behavior. For example, if structural images showed no difference on average between adolescent and adult brains, we would not conclude that adolescents behaved no differently than adults or that their rational capacities were identical to those of adults.

Most of what we know about cognitive, affective, and social neuroscience is correlational and coarse-grained, rather than causal and fine-grained.[49] fMRI is a relatively recent technique and we are constantly discovering new methodological artifacts as this young science progresses.[50] The publication bias that exists in the social sciences generally exists in neuroscience.[51] Virtually no current neuroscience addresses legal issues, virtually none is directly legally relevant, and only a small amount is inferentially relevant, though often requiring extravagant chains of inference. Replications are seldom attempted. None of this is a critique generally of behavioral neuroscience. It is a young field using new technologies that is addressed to one of the thorniest problems in science and philosophy: the relation of the brain to the mind and action. It is not surprising that progress, impressive as it is, is slow.

Neuroscience also shares with other sciences the G2i problem, which is how to make inferences about a particular individual based on group data.[52] Scientists are interested in how the world works and produce general information. Law is often concerned with individual cases and it is difficult to know how properly to apply relevant group data. For example, a neuroscience study that reports increased activation in some brain region of interest bases its conclusion on averaging the activation across all the subjects, but no subject's brain may have activated precisely in the area identified. If such group data are permitted, as they now are for functions such as predictions, the question is how to use probabilistic data to answer what is often a binary question.

Finally, suppose, counterfactually, that the radical critics are right. We are not agents and our mental states do no work (if they exist at all). We are simply victims of neuronal circumstances. What follows? Greene and Cohen think consequentialism follows. In contrast, I think nothing does because the radical position is normatively inert, a thought first prompted by Mitch Berman in the context of determinism.[53] Reasons

[49] Gregory A. Miller, "Mistreating Psychology in the Decades of the Brain," 5 *Perspectives on Psychological Science* 716 (2010).

[50] E.g., Craig M. Bennett et al., "The Principled Control of False Positives in Neuroimaging," 4 *Social, Cognitive and Affective Neuroscience* 417 (2009).

[51] E.g., John P. A. Ioannidis, "Excess Significance Bias in the Literature on Brain Volume Abnormalities," 68 *Archives of General Psychiatry* 773 (2011).

[52] David L. Faigman, John Monahan, and Christopher Slobogin, "Group to Individual Inference (G2i) in Scientific Expert Testimony," 81 *University of Chicago Law Review* 417 (2014).

[53] Mitchell Berman, "Punishment and Justification," 118 *Ethics* 258 (2008), 271.

are mental states. If the reasons we believe motivate action are not real or lack causal efficacy, then we have no reason to do anything, except perhaps to wait for determinism to happen. I certainly do not deserve criticism or blame for failing to accede to the truth that Greene and Cohen propose. My brain made me do it.

VII. Conclusion

In this contribution, I have tried to cover the immense influence Moore has had on my work on issues of mutual interest and to explore our disgreements and our vastly greater areas of agreement. No legal scholar and few philosophers have written as illuminatingly about the mind as Michael Moore. That is why he is continuously on my mind and will be as long as I continue to think about and work on these issues.

17

The Means Principle

*Larry Alexander**

I. Introduction

Michael Moore believes there are deontological constraints on actors' pursuit of good consequences. He believes these constraints are best conceived of as agent-relative and intention-focused prohibitions such as "you must not intentionally kill, batter, rape, steal, etc."[1] I, joined in recent years by Kimberly Ferzan, believe that the best interpretation of deontological constraints—the interpretation that best accounts for our intuitions about certain stock cases—is that they are constraints on the causal means by which good consequences may be achieved.[2] We believe those constraints can be unified under a single deontological principle, what we call the "means principle." It forbids actors from achieving otherwise good consequences by using, without their consent, others' bodies, labor, talents, or other resources that are rightfully theirs. The means principle can be viewed as a jurisdictional limitation on the reach of strong (legitimately enforceable) moral obligations.[3] Its focus is on the causal structure of how good consequences are to be achieved, not on the mental states of those attempting to achieve them. Actors' mental states can affect their culpability but not whether their acts are morally permissible. Even with respect to culpability, actors' beliefs rather than their intentions are the primary determinants. Their intentions can affect only the level of their culpability if they are culpable, but cannot render an otherwise non-culpable act culpable. Thus, the means principle is a stark contrast to Moore's agent-relative, intention-focused account of deontological constraints.[4]

* This chapter is a seriously abbreviated version, stripped of numerous citations of supporting literature as well as some supporting arguments, of the paper that can be found at <http://ssrn.com/abstract=2378608>. I presented the longer version of this chapter at a conference celebrating Michael Moore's seventieth birthday and then again at a conference on Deontological Principles and the Criminal Law hosted by the Rutgers Institute for Law and Philosophy. I owe thanks to the many people at those events who commented on the paper. In particular, I should like to thank David Brink, Kim Ferzan, Adil Haque, Heidi Hurd, Doug Husak, Michael Moore, Govind Persad, Re'em Segev, Victor Tadros, Peter Vallentyne, and Alec Walen.

[1] See, e.g., Moore, 2009d, 34–77; For Moore's conception of the morally and legally relevant notion of intention, see Moore, 2008a, 47–59.

[2] Larry Alexander and Kimberly Kessler Ferzan, *Crime and Culpability: A Theory of Criminal Law* (New York: Cambridge University Press, 2009), 96–100.

[3] See Larry Alexander, "The Jurisdiction of Justice: Two Conceptions of Political Morality," 41 *San Diego Law Review* 949 (2004). When I speak of strong moral obligations, I am referring to those the violation of which can be legitimately punished and thus result in a deprivation of certain rights. Weaker moral obligations are those the violation of which can be criticized and rightfully blamed. The means principle is a constraint on the former but not the latter.

[4] Moore views deontological constraints as agent-relative, moral-agent focused. See Moore, 2009d, ch. 3; Moore, 2012d, 459–61.

II. The Consequentialist Background

Deontological constraints do not and cannot exhaust all of our enforceable moral duties. Many of our acts are assessable only through a consequentialist lens. In the famous *Trolley* hypothetical, turning the trolley to save the five trapped workers but killing the one worker trapped on the siding is generally believed to be a morally permissible act. (Nor should it matter whether one is *deflecting* the trolley or instead *initiating* a new force, such as lowering a drawbridge that will stop the trolley but crush a bystander; deflection is, after all, a form of initiating.) If such acts are permissible, however, it is because they produce good consequences, the saving of a net four lives.[5] By the same token, turning the trolley from the track on which the one is trapped to the track on which five are trapped is a morally impermissible act because of its consequences.

I am going to assume that a consequentialist moral theory provides the backdrop to my discussion of deontological constraints and governs acts that do not fall afoul of those constraints or fall within the prerogatives that are the flipsides of those constraints. I shall not elaborate on what that consequentialist moral theory—call it C—looks like. For example, it is a matter of indifference for my discussion here whether "The Good" in C is monolithic or pluralistic. The nature of C, important as it is, is not my topic here.

III. The Means Principle

The means principle (MP) is the principal deontological constraint on the pursuit of C. In other words, an act that is required by C but forbidden by the MP is morally forbidden. The MP trumps C.

What is the MP? As I said in the introductory paragraph, the best interpretation of the MP is a causal one. An act required or permitted by C is nonetheless forbidden if the good consequences that are the bases of its endorsement by C are produced by the unconsented-to use of persons' bodies, labor, or talents.[6] In other words, the MP enjoins the appropriation of another's body, labor, or talents without that person's consent where appropriation is the causal path by which otherwise good consequences are produced. Put somewhat differently, the MP is a jurisdictional notion: A person's body,

[5] Note that I am assuming that the numbers (of persons saved) do count. On the question of whether and why the numbers count, given that each person suffers only his own harm, see John M. Taurek, "Should the Numbers Count?," 6 *Philosophy & Public Affairs* 293 (1977). Taurek's answer to his question was "no," an answer for which I have some sympathy. After all, if five people die, it is not as if there is someone who will suffer the aggregate of five deaths. (One who *kills* five is, however, a worse killer than one who kills only one.) Most who have written in response to Taurek accept the non-aggregation of harms to different people but still seek an argument in support of the proposition that one should save the greater number in situations where not everyone can be saved.

[6] The MP also forbids unconsented-to use of resources that could not have been obtained except by the possessor's use of his body, labor, or talents; or of resources conveyed to him by others who obtained them similarly. See text accompanying n. 10. However, for the most part I will drop the reference to such resources in elaborating the MP. One's resources come within the MP only derivatively by virtue of the MP's prohibition of unconsented-to uses of one's body, labor, and talents.

labor, and talents are beyond the jurisdiction of strong (enforceable) morality unless the person consents to subjecting his body, labor, and talents to its jurisdiction.[7]

The MP explains the intuitions behind *Trolley* and other stock hypotheticals. In *Trolley*, turning the trolley to the siding is not a "using" of the one trapped worker's body, labor, or talents. One would turn the trolley to the siding even if the one worker were not there or could escape, because turning the trolley itself saves the five whether or not the siding is occupied. The presence of the one trapped worker only reduces the amount of C-benefit turning the trolley produces. And the same applies to *Drawbridge*, in which lowering the drawbridge saves the five by stopping the trolley but kills a bystander who otherwise would not have been harmed by the trolley.

On the other hand, in *Fat Man*, where pushing the fat man onto the track is the only way to prevent the trolley from killing the five workers, the fat man's body is the means by which the five are saved. Thus, pushing the fat man *is* a violation of the MP. So, too, in *Transplant*, is carving up the one patient to harvest his organs and save five dying patients. In both *Fat Man* and *Transplant*, the causal path by which the saving of lives is brought about runs through the unconsented-to use of a person's body. In *Trolley*, it does not.[8]

[7] See Alexander, "The Jurisdiction of Justice: Two Conceptions of Political Morality." I should also point out that the MP is not violated by an unconsented-to use of another's body if one is not touching his body and is merely somehow taking advantage of it while rightfully occupying certain space. Examples would be standing in the shade of another's body or admiring another's body.

On the other hand, things are less clear in the case where the *Strategic Bomber* targets the civilians but only because their location is his best evidence for the location of the munitions, his real quarry. Is targeting them a violation of the MP? I am inclined to say it is, but without strong conviction. See Victor Tadros, "Wrongful Intentions Without Closeness," 43 *Philosophy & Public Affairs* 52 (2015), 63–5; Neil F. Delaney, "Two Cheers for 'Closeness': Terror, Targeting and Double Effect," 137 *Philosophical Studies* 335 (2008).

[8] In certain of the trolley loop hypotheticals, where turning the trolley will not by itself save the five trapped workers (because the siding rejoins the main track short of the five), but there is a worker trapped on the siding whose body will stop the trolley, turning the trolley violates the MP unless there is a C-benefit to turning it other than the use of the trapped worker's body. For example, if distance over the siding loop to the main track were longer than the distance down the main track to that junction, and turning the trolley would thus give the five workers more time to escape (or at least more time to live), turning the trolley would produce C-benefits other than use of the one worker's body. That would also be true if there were a heavy object further down the siding that would stop the trolley were it not stopped by the one worker. See also Ingmar Persson, *From Morality to the End of Reason* (New York: Oxford, 2013), 146–7 (his example of *Double Saving*, which is analogous to the trolley loop hypothetical with a greater distance for the trolley to go if it is switched).

In other trolley loop hypotheticals, where the track past the switch is nothing but a loop, switching the trolley to the section of the loop on which one worker is trapped will save the five on the other section only by using the body of the one to stop the trolley, a violation of the MP. However, not switching the trolley will save the one only by using the bodies of the five to stop the trolley, which would also violate the MP, or so it might seem. See Alec Walen, "Transcending the Means Principle," 33 *Law & Philosophy* 427 (2014). Yet, in the latter case, it is chance (the position of the switch) that will "use" the bodies of the five to save the one. It is as if lightning has killed five members of a shipwrecked crew, whose corpses can now be eaten to sustain the one remaining. Switching the trolley, however, would be like throwing a meatier crew member into the path of the lightning to kill him and save the leaner members, who otherwise would have been struck, killed, and eaten by the meatier one. Switching the trolley from the five to the one seems permissible only if there is some reason to do so other than using the one's body (perhaps the loop towards the one would require the trolley to travel more distance before reaching the five, giving them more time to live or to escape). The same analysis applies to other trolley hypotheticals similar to the loop hypotheticals in structure. For example, in the *Lazy Susan* scenario, where the five trapped workers are on a segment of track that can be switched 180 degrees, and Fat Man is also on that segment but farther away from the oncoming trolley, there is a C-benefit, (more time to escape or live) other than the use of Fat Man for rotating the Lazy Susan segment and positioning Fat Man rather than the five trapped workers closer to the oncoming trolley. Thus, in my

In every case, the relevant question is: How does the act in question satisfy C? If the answer is that it satisfies C only by using someone's body, labor, or talents as a resource without the person's consent, then the act violates the constraint by virtue of the causal path between it and satisfying C.[9]

I have thus far spoken of the MP as encompassing unconsented-to appropriation of another's body, labor, or talents. The talents part is perhaps redundant, as in the absence of the ability to read minds one can only appropriate another's talents through his labor. I include the reference to talents merely to make clear that appropriation without consent of another's intellectual or artistic creations violates the MP even if the creation is a song, a poem, or an idea for an invention or a story that has not yet been reduced to a tangible form.

In addition, the MP extends not only to the products of intellectual labor that do not employ any resources other than mental ones but also to the products of labor that employ one's rightful share of external resources, resources the rightful shares of which are determined by C. If one takes one's rightful share of external resources, then no one else has a claim on one's improvements of them. For were that not so, others would be appropriating not only one's rightful share under C, but the improvements produced by one's labor and talents.

Moreover, not only does the deontological constraint extend to the products of one's labor and talents that have used only one's rightful (under C) share of external resources, but it extends as well to products and resources that belonged to another but have been consensually transferred to one through gift, bequest, or exchange. (I leave open, however, whether one's C share of resources should be sensitive to one's other sources of well-being, namely the willingness of others to exchange with one or donate to one.)

One important point here, neglected by so-called "left libertarians," who endorse something like the MP but who advocate the equal distribution of natural resources, is that the MP potentially blocks such a distribution. The reason can be illustrated by a simple example I have used in an earlier article.[10] Suppose there are two people, Short and Tall, and one natural resource, apples on an apple tree. Some of those apples are on the low branches, within easy reach of Short. Tall, however, cannot bend low enough to pick them. Other apples are on the high branches, out of Short's reach but within Tall's. And some of the apples are on the intermediate branches, within the reach of both Short and Tall. The MP dictates that only the intermediate apples are subject to whatever C's distributive principle is, whether that is equality, priority, utility maximization, or

account, rotating the Lazy Susan does not use Fat Man as a means and is permissible. But see Persson, *From Morality to the End of Reason*, 146–7. On the other hand, in the standard trolley hypothetical, with five trapped on the main track and one trapped on the siding, it is not permissible to switch the trolley to the siding if there are six trapped workers behind the one on the siding and who will be saved only because the one is in front of them and his body will stop the trolley. For there is no C-benefit in such a case for switching the trolley other than to use the one as a means of saving the six. And Michael Moore's example of wearing a vest that gives one's dance partner an allergic rash, the treatment of which saves her doctor's practice—the C-benefit that outweighs the harm of her rash—*is* a using. See Michael S. Moore, "Responses and Appreciations," in this volume. The causal path by which C is promoted goes through an unconsented-to production of a bodily condition.

9 Alec Walen's notion of an unrestricted claim is almost identical to my jurisdictional version of the MP. See Walen, "Transcending the Means Principle."

10 See Alexander, "The Jurisdiction of Justice: Two Conceptions of Political Morality."

something else. For if the low apples were to be distributed to Tall, or the high apples to Short, that could only happen if Short were compelled to pick the low apples and Tall were compelled to pick the high ones. That is, without Short's labor, Tall would be unable to obtain the low apples; and without Tall's labor, Short would be unable to obtain the high ones. The MP thus requires that a C distribution of natural resources does not distribute any to persons who could not obtain them except through others' labor.

There is a further extension of the MP worth mentioning. Suppose Al engages in conduct solely to make Barb suffer psychologically because Al derives enjoyment from Barb's psychological suffering. Were Barb not to exist, or exist but not suffer, Al would be less happy. Now Al might be violating C. But suppose his conduct is actually furthering C. Perhaps he gains more happiness from Barb's suffering than Barb loses. Perhaps Al is even among the worst off and Barb among the better off. Still, Al's furthering C through Barb's psychological suffering violates the MP. Al's using Barb's psychological suffering to further C is no different from his furthering C by using the fat man's body to save the five trapped workers.

Reflection on the preceding examples might lead one to the conclusion that the MP is really just equivalent to the following norm N: "Do not make yourself better off than had another person not existed by making the latter worse off than had you not existed."[11] And indeed, most cases of violation of the MP will be violations of N, and vice versa. Moreover, N would even appear to solve the so-called paradox of blackmail; for blackmail is conduct that violates N.[12]

There are two reasons for not equating the MP with N, however. First, N takes no account of whether the baselines for determining "worse off" and "better off" are justifiable. Suppose Barb, a candidate for high office, has cheated on Carl, her husband, and Al learns of this. Al can sell his information to a news outlet and make a lot of money. So suppose he does so. He is now better off than he would have been had Barb not existed, and Barb is now worse off than had Al not existed. Al has violated N, but he has done nothing wrong; for Barb does not deserve to be as well off as she would have been in Al's absence. She has been "used" but has not been wronged.[13]

Perhaps we could save N by adding a proviso that "better off" and "worse off" are to be gauged relative to a baseline of deserved well-being. There is another reason, however, not to reduce the MP to N. For the MP is violated, or so I would contend, even when the used person is, without his consent, made *better off* through the appropriation of his body, labor, talents, or psychological states. In other words, the MP is a constraint on paternalism (which might otherwise be required by C), whereas N is not. Even forcing another to labor or use his body, not only in furtherance of C, but for the benefit of the person himself, is a violation of the MP. So too is getting him to labor or use his talents by manipulating him psychologically through deception or through

[11] Walen appears to endorse N. See Alec Walen, "Wrongdoing Without Motives: Why Victor Tadros is Wrong About Wrongdoing and Motivation," 32 *Law & Philosophy* 217 (2013), 235–40.

[12] Other violations of N, similar to blackmail, are the so-called "spite fence" and other uses of property that the owner values only because his neighbors will pay him to stop.

[13] As I shall point out in the text at n.18, the MP can permissibly be cancelled and one thus permissibly "used" if one has acted culpably and is deserving of punishment.

inducing unpleasant emotions, even if the deception and the unpleasant emotions will ultimately cause him to benefit and are consistent with C.[14]

One final point about the MP. It, like its close relative N, does not govern activities that we would and could carry on in the absence of those who might be harmed by those activities. For those activities, even if they harm others, do not use their bodies, labor, or talents without their consent. C, not the MP, governs those risky activities. Reckless behaviors are culpable and, if they harm others, impermissible.[15] But they are so generally by virtue of C, not the MP.

That is all I want to say about the MP itself. The core idea is that we are not resources for others' benefit without our consent. Nor are we resources for our own benefit except insofar as we ourselves determine. Enforceable morality has no jurisdiction over us as resources for its ends.

IV. The Flipside of the MP: The Prerogative

The logical corollary of the MP is a prerogative not to be compelled to further C.[16] In other words, the MP entails a realm of moral freedom. (C itself may, and if C is indirect will, contain its own domain of prerogatives in addition to the realm carved out by the MP.)

To see this, consider *Trolley* again. As discussed, it is permissible to turn the trolley from the track with five trapped workers to the track with one. Such an act, which saves a net four lives, would further C, or so I shall assume. But even if turning the trolley furthers C, the person at the switch cannot be enforceably morally obligated to throw the switch. For to compel him thusly would be to use him as a resource without his consent and violate the MP, just as would compelling him to lie down in front of the trolley if there were no siding. Throwing the switch or not throwing it, lying down in front of the trolley or not doing so—these are all within the actor's prerogative. They are in a realm of moral freedom, not in the sense that they are beyond moral criticism, but in the sense that they are beyond rightful coercion.

On the other hand, if the trolley is heading toward the one rather than the five, switching it to the track with the five is not within the switcher's prerogative defined by the MP. The act violates C; and in prohibiting the act, the actor is not being used as a resource without his consent. Thus, his act violates C, and its prohibition does not violate the MP. His act can legitimately be forbidden on pain of punishment.

I said that the prerogative that is the flipside of the MP is an area of moral freedom but also that acts within the prerogative are morally assessable. What I mean is that the prerogative is the realm of the super- and suberogatory; the realm of virtue and vice. If one acts within one's moral prerogative, one cannot be deemed culpable—and thus justifiably punishable—for not furthering C, even if one could do so at little cost of time,

[14] Is so-called "soft paternalism" a wrongful violation of the MP? If so, does that undermine the tenability of the MP? Or is it an exception to the MP? Paternalism is in general a difficult issue, and it is particularly difficult if one wishes to maintain that "hard paternalism" is wrong but "soft paternalism" is not. See Larry Alexander, "Scalar Properties, Binary Judgments," 25 *Journal of Applied Philosophy* 85 (2008), 96–7.

[15] More on the distinction between impermissible acts and culpable acts in Section V, and on risking and the MP in Section VI.

[16] Just as the logical corollary of a prerogative is a deontological constraint (such as the MP) on others.

effort, or expense. Not furthering C under such circumstances may well be suberogatory and thus morally discreditable. But it is not culpable and thus not deserving of sanction.[17]

V. Limitations on the MP

Is the MP absolute, or is it subject to limits, and if so, which? Consenting and promising are non-controversial limits on the MP. Indeed, I would argue that they are really internal to the MP, which refers to *unconsented-to* uses of one's body, labor, and talents—not limits on it. There are other possible limits on the MP that are worth discussing. One stems from acts that have imperiled others and that will result in a violation of C unless the one whose acts are the source of the peril uses his body, labor, or talents to avert the peril. For example, if a man has accidentally thrown the trolley switch and redirected the trolley from the track with one worker to the track with five, and still has time to throw the switch again and redirect the trolley back to the one worker, he has an affirmative duty to do so. His original act, however non-culpable it was, will violate C unless he throws the switch. And he can be legitimately coerced to do so without violating the MP.

Are there other affirmative duties to act, ones not based on one's promises to do so (as might be the case with lifeguards, nannies, spouses, police officers, etc.), or based on one's acts that have imperiled others? The duty of parents to care for their children comes to mind. Does that duty apply only to parents who have voluntarily assumed it, or does it apply to all parents, regardless of how voluntarily they became parents? That is a deep and difficult issue that I will sidestep here.

Another possible external limit on the MP is also controversial, but it is one on which I have previously taken a stand. I have argued that a culpable actor who has yet to be punished to the full extent he deserves may be used as a means to further C or to protect others' rights. The use of the culpable is itself limited by the amount of suffering he deserves for his culpable acts(s) in excess of the amount he has already been punished.[18]

The final possible (and again controversial) external limit on the MP comes under the heading of "threshold deontology." If the actor need only lift his finger to save a drowning infant, or if the sacrifice of his life would save a million lives, does the MP nonetheless protect him from being coerced to do so? Most deontologists believe that the MP does not. They believe the consequences of honoring the MP should matter and limit the MP's scope. The MP restricts the scope of C, but C restricts the scope of the MP, or so it is argued.

[17] Note that the MP and its corollary prerogative *can* generate intransitive options. One can permissibly breach a promise in order to risk one's life to save a stranger, permissibly go to the movies rather than risk one's life to save a stranger (per the prerogative), but cannot permissibly breach a promise in order to go to the movies.

[18] See Larry Alexander, "Recipe for a Theory of Self-Defense: The Ingredients, and Some Cooking Suggestions," in Christian L. Coons and Michael Eric Weber (eds.), *The Ethics of Self-Defense* (forthcoming, 2015). There I also suggest that if an innocent bystander could justifiably be harmed as a side-effect of use of defensive force, perhaps he could also then be used as a shield—a means—for defense, if the amount of harm he would suffer as a shield were less than the amount he would suffer as a side-effect.

Again, I need not settle the issue here. My interest is in the nature of the MP, not its limits. I have written on threshold deontology, not to take a final stand on it, but to point out its theoretical difficulties.[19] But, whether or not it is a plausible limitation on the MP, it does not bear on the nature of the MP within the limits it imposes.[20]

VI. Permissibility versus Culpability

Moral permissibility turns on how things really are, not on what an actor believes. It is an ontic matter rather than an epistemic one. If there are five workers who will be saved by turning the trolley at the cost of the one worker on the siding, then unless there are qualitative factors that relevantly distinguish the one worker from the five, switching the trolley to the siding is morally permissible in fact, irrespective of the switcher's beliefs or motivations.

Culpability, on the other hand, *is* a matter of the actor's beliefs. If the actor who switches the trolley is unaware that he is saving the five trapped workers and aware that he is probably killing the one, his act of switching, though morally permissible, is highly culpable. Conversely, if the actor believes that by switching the trolley he will save the five trapped workers at the cost of the life of the one on the siding, then he acts non-culpably in switching the trolley, even if it turns out that the five workers were not trapped, or were not on the track, or were an optical illusion. For though his act was morally impermissible, his belief that he was saving the five and thus was acting permissibly renders him non-culpable.[21]

So far, nothing that I have said should be controversial. We recognize that one can be culpable for attempting to harm or for unjustifiably risking harm, even if the attempt turns out to be harmless or beneficial, or the "risk" of harm turns out to be zero. Indeed, we recognize as well that the culpable attempter or risker who is unknowingly performing a permissible act can be encouraged by third parties. By the same token, those whose mistaken beliefs lead them to perform morally impermissible acts—who in the self-defense literature are referred to as "innocent aggressors"—may be permissibly restrained but not punished for their non-culpable acts.

My next points *are* controversial, however. First, although the actor's beliefs affect his culpability, his intentions cannot render an otherwise permissible act impermissible. At most, the actor's intentions may aggravate his culpability if he *is* culpable. But his intentions cannot render him culpable.

[19] Larry Alexander, "Deontology at the Threshold," 37 *San Diego Law Review* 893 (2000).

[20] Suppose we can prevent the violation of the MP in *Fat Man* by merely snapping our fingers (an easy rescue) but doing so will result in the deaths of the five trapped workers. If ordinarily our prerogative against being used as a means is overridden in cases of such really easy rescues (the deontological threshold is surpassed), must we prevent the MP violation at the cost of the five? Is it different if Fat Man is just trapped on the tracks, and we can easily save him but cannot then save the five? Similarly, if we must choose between saving two people from a deadly natural threat or one person from a deadly MP violation, should we choose the latter?

For discussion of this issue, see Re'em Segev, "Should We Prevent Deontological Wrongdoing?" (forthcoming).

[21] Put differently, culpability is a function of the actor's beliefs regarding the magnitude of the risks of various harms that his act presents and the presence of any facts that could potentially justify imposing those risks, discounted by the probabilities of those facts. Culpability is thus solely belief-based, unlike permissibility, which is solely fact-based.

To see this, consider the actor who switches the trolley. If switching the trolley to save the five is morally permissible, and if the switcher believes switching will save the five, then his switching the trolley is non-culpable *even if his only reason for doing so is to kill the one on the siding.*[22] We want him to switch the trolley (it furthers C). And he has the prerogative not to switch it (by virtue of the MP). If the only motivation he has for switching the trolley is his desire to kill the one, then that motivation is C-useful. And if he will not switch if we will regard him as culpable for switching in order to kill the one, then it would be C-useful not to regard him as culpable.

Now I realize that this is not an argument that will convince the skeptics. For not every belief that it would be useful to hold is true. In Kavka's Toxin Puzzle, the fact that it would be useful to believe that one will drink the toxin tomorrow does not mean that one can so believe. Beliefs aim at truth, not usefulness.[23]

So consider these analogs of the ill-motivated trolley switcher. We may need people to carry out various tawdry but morally permissible and even morally compelling tasks. We may need CIA assassins. We may need executioners for murderers. And so on. The MP prevents us from compelling people to perform these tasks. So suppose that the only volunteers we get for the jobs of assassin or executioner are people who will enjoy the jobs. Should we regard the executioner who enjoys executing convicted murderers, or the CIA operative who enjoys assassinating terrorists, as having acted *culpably* in executing or assassinating if their acts were morally permissible and they were aware of the facts that made the acts permissible?

I would contend that the answer should be "no." I believe that the temptation to say otherwise stems from confusing an assessment of character with an assessment of culpability. The executioner and assassin who enjoy their jobs may have character flaws that make them quite unsavory people. But that does not show their morally permissible acts of execution and assassination to be culpable. So long as they act on the intentions in question only when the acts are morally permissible—or would be morally permissible if what they believed to be true were true[24]—they should not be blamed or punished. And if they should not be blamed or punished, that must be because they have not acted culpably.[25] (Likewise, if a dosage of morphine is proper for a terminal patient even though it will hasten his death, then if the doctor who knows this nevertheless administers it only because he believes in euthanasia, he should not be deemed culpable for doing so even if euthanasia is otherwise impermissible. And if a bombing run has been pre-programmed by the Strategic Bomber and will permissibly bomb a

[22] See Judith J. Thomson, "Physician-Assisted Suicide: Two Moral Arguments," 109 *Ethics* 497 (1999), and many others in accord.

[23] Gregory Kavka, "The Toxin Puzzle," 43 *Analysis* 33 (1983).

[24] Applying this to what I have said regarding intentions, the one who switches the trolley with the intention of killing the one worker but believing that he is also saving the five workers on the main track is acting non-culpably *even if the five workers were not in fact trapped on the main track and were in no danger.*

[25] I thus disagree with Matthew Liao, who argues that because one can permissibly refrain from switching the trolley, one should do so if one's only reason for switching is to kill the one worker. S. Matthew Liao, "Intentions and Moral Permissibility: The Case of Acting Permissibly with Bad Intentions," 31 *Law & Philosophy* 703 (2012), 715–17. But the reason one is permitted not to turn the trolley is because, by virtue of the MP, one cannot be used as a means to save the five. If, however, one is willing to turn the trolley (in order to kill the one trapped worker), then it is good that one does so (as it will save the five), regardless of one's intent. Moreover, if *we* believe his act will save the five, we can urge him to switch, even if to get him to do so requires us to point out that the one worker on the siding is someone he hates.

munitions factory and in so doing also kill and terrorize some civilians, the Terrorist Bomber, who knows this, may non-culpably fly the plane as programmed when the Strategic Bomber falls ill, even though his only reason to make the run is to kill and terrorize the civilians.)

If unsavory intentions cannot render a morally permissible act either impermissible or culpable,[26] good intentions cannot render a morally impermissible act permissible or non-culpable. The one who pushes the fat man onto the trolley track with the intention of saving the five, and who regrets having to kill the fat man, has still violated the MP and thereby acted impermissibly and culpably. A bad intention—say, the desire to kill the fat man and indifference to the fact that the death will save the five workers—will aggravate the culpability of the pusher. But the good intention will not eradicate his culpability any more than it will render his act permissible.

And now for a perhaps even more controversial point. Just as a bad intention will not render a morally permissible act impermissible or culpable (so long as the actor believes the circumstances render his act morally permissible), neither will it render a permissible act impermissible or culpable when it leads the actor to choose an act that is non-optimal according to C. So let us return again to *Trolley*. This time, however, in addition to the main track with five trapped workers and the siding with one trapped worker, there is a second siding with no one on it. Clearly, it would be C-optimal for the trolley to be switched to the unoccupied siding. But suppose our switcher, while aware of the five workers on the main track and of the fact that the second siding is unoccupied, is not motivated to switch the trolley to the unoccupied siding. He is motivated, however, by the prospect of killing the one worker on the first siding. So suppose he does switch the trolley to the first siding, killing the one worker. I would contend that he has acted permissibly and non-culpably, though surely non-optimally. He has revealed his character to be morally flawed, but in switching the trolley he has not acted in a way that merits punishment. Given that the MP permitted him to refrain from any switching, we should be grateful that his unsavory character led him at least to save the trapped five. Had he been unaware of them, then although his act would still have been morally permissible (because it would have saved a net four lives and furthered C), he would have been culpable for the switching. But because he was aware of the trapped five, his act was neither impermissible nor culpable. (Nor would the verdict change had he been motivated to kill the one in order to transplant the one's organs to save some dying friends—in other words, had he been trying to violate the MP. For, given that he was aware of the five, and the switching the trolley was not itself a violation of the MP vis-à-vis the one, it is immaterial why the switcher wanted to kill him.)[27]

[26] I think we should be happy to conclude that unsavory intentions cannot render an otherwise morally permissible act impermissible. For that allows us to skirt the issue that bedevils those of the opposite persuasion, such as Moore and those who hold an intention-focused version of the Doctrine of Double Effect, namely how to distinguish what one intends from what one believes will result from what one intends. See, e.g., Moore, 2008a, 47–59. For an excellent critical analysis of the intention versus foresight literature and a proposed solution to its central problem, see Kimberly Kessler Ferzan, "Beyond Intention," 29 *Cardozo Law Review* 1147 (2008).

[27] My claim in this paragraph is bound to meet resistance. Here is how one line of resistance might run: Suppose that in order switch the trolley to the siding with the one worker, the actor must first switch it to the unoccupied siding and then switch it again. In other words, switching the trolley from the main track with the five workers to the siding with the one worker requires two discrete acts, the first of which is switching

Some contend that using someone as a means itself relies on intention—the intention to cause another's body, labor, or talents to produce a good result. This is not true, however. Consider this example. We have the runaway trolley, the five trapped workers, and Fat Man on the drawbridge over the trolley tracks. The drawbridge in its current position is crushing some lovely flowers, and Al decides to alter its position to save the flowers from being crushed. Al foresees—but does not intend—that altering the position of the drawbridge will cause Fat Man to tumble onto the tracks and get killed by the trolley. That would surely not be a justifiable cost for saving the flowers. However, Fat Man's death will save the five workers, which would make saving the flowers overall justified were Fat Man not being used as a means. Nevertheless, he *would* be being so used, *despite the fact that Al does not intend his use but only foresees it.* (Al indeed regrets that the Fat Man would be used as a means because were the Fat Man absent, Al could justifiably save the flowers.) Using as a means does not require an intent to use. It only requires that the use is necessary to justify the act, and it is culpable if the actor foresees that the use is necessary to justify the act.

Here's another issue. May Al refuse to rescue Fat Man, who is on the trolley tracks, because if he is not rescued, the five workers will be saved? If one has no duty to rescue Fat Man, then refusing to rescue him for the stated reason is not wrong. Nor would one have a duty to prevent another from pushing Fat Man onto the tracks. On the other hand, rescuing him would not be wrong even though it sets back C (because four lives net are lost). For C is only set back by virtue of Fat Man's not being a means to C's promotion; and acts that set back C are not impermissible if they set back C only by saving someone from being an involuntary means of promoting C. And, *a fortiori,* if one has a *duty* to rescue Fat Man—for example, he's one's child, or one caused him to fall onto the tracks—then that duty is not canceled by the setback to C.

Finally, just as one's intentions cannot render one's act a violation of the MP if its causal structure is that it furthers C without an unconsented-to using of another's body, labor, or talents, so too is the act–omission distinction immaterial to the MP. Both acts and omissions are encompassed by the prerogative that is the MP's flipside. One who sees a rock thrown in his direction may duck it—an act—even if he is aware that it will

to the unoccupied siding. Given that at the completion of the first act, no one is in danger, would not the second act be an impermissible killing of the one worker because it is not a saving of any workers?

This line of resistance, which is limited to two-act scenarios, is quite powerful, and I am tempted to accept it as an exception to the claim in the text. Countering that temptation is this thought, however: If the actor will only switch the trolley away from the five if he can non-culpably switch two times and direct the trolley to the occupied siding, then should we not welcome his ability to do so? The point applies to all "package-deal" rescues that, because of the MP, one has no duty to undertake. If the package deal is that the actor will rescue the victim if and only if the actor may thereafter slug the victim, have sex with the victim, take the victim's money, etc., may the actor permissibly and non-culpably rescue and then slug, etc.?

Here is another line of resistance: Suppose there is a deontological threshold such that the MP is overridden if the mere movement of the actor's finger will save a life. And suppose this time that the first act of switching, which requires great strength, will direct the trolley toward the one worker. The second act of switching, which will direct the trolley toward the unoccupied siding, requires only the movement of the actor's finger. Because of the MP, the actor is not required to switch the trolley to the occupied siding. Once he does, however, because the MP is now overridden, must not he now switch the trolley to the unoccupied siding?

Again, I find this line of resistance quite tempting when applied to scenarios that are structurally similar. Countering the temptation is the worry that an actor who will be culpable and thus punishable were he to stop after the first switching will just not switch at all, and the five workers will die.

probably then strike and harm someone behind him, *and even if he himself would not be harmed by it were he not to duck*. Nor does one have to remain standing against Balanced Rock when one realizes that it has become unbalanced and will crush some picnickers below if one ceases to be its doorstop. "Ducking" by walking away is both an act and an omission (to remain in place) but is within the prerogative. For one has no duty to use his body to shield others even at little or no cost (unless his not doing so crosses the threshold of threshold deontology). Again his ducking may be criticizable as suberogatory, but it is not impermissible or culpable.[28]

VII. When is Risking Violating the MP Culpable?

What risk of violating the MP are we permitted to take without being culpable? Assume, for example, that the agent is attempting to promote C (or attempting to act within his prerogative without reducing C). He estimates that his act is 80% likely to do so without violating the MP. But is that probability sufficient to avoid culpability? Consider, by analogy, whether an 80% probability of not punishing a criminal more than he deserves (including the risk of not punishing him if he is innocent) is sufficient to render us nonculpable in punishing him? Holly Smith argues that in assessing whether to acquire additional information in order to avoid breaking a promise, we should count the promise itself, as opposed to the harm to the promisee if the promise is broken, as having zero weight.[29] Assuming Smith is correct, should we treat the MP, as opposed to the harm to the one used, similarly? I cannot see how we could do that and still regard the MP as a deontological constraint on C. For if we assess only the underlying harm to the one used in deciding how to act in light of our estimate of the probabilities, we are engaged in precisely the decisionmaking that C, stripped of the MP constraint, requires. So we must give the deontological constraint of the MP a value apart from the harm of the using. Because we always run the risk of violating the MP—which includes punishing people more than they deserve when doing so furthers C—and of breaking promises, we need a theory for assigning such a value.

Here is the approach that I believe makes sense. First, the objective, God's-eye view of deontological constraints looks like this: If the benefits of an act exceed its costs, it furthers C and is permissible. However, one counts as C-benefits only those that are not caused by usings (MP violations, including undeserved punishments) or caused by breaches of promises. On the other hand, one *does* count the harms to those used and harms to the promisees from breaches. Put differently, an act is objectively permissible if its benefits, excluding those causally derived from usings or breaches of promises, exceed all of its costs, including those caused by usings and breaches of promises. In *Trolley*, for example, one counts as a benefit the saving of the five workers, but one excludes as benefits the saving of lives produced by harvesting organs from the dead worker. The benefits of using him cannot be part of the calculus; only the harm of his death counts.

[28] But if the picnickers had used their property as a brace to keep Balanced Rock in place, and someone removes it, thereby resulting in their deaths, his act is not within the prerogative but is a wrongful killing.

[29] Holly M. Smith, "The Subjective Moral Duty to Inform Oneself Before Acting," 125 *Ethics* 11 (2014).

Moving from the objective view to the subjective, culpability-determining estimates of the actor is now straightforward. The actor estimates the probability that his act will be permissible by estimating the probabilities and magnitudes of benefits not produced by usings or breaches of promises and the probabilities and magnitudes of all harms. If the net of permissible benefits over all harms, discounted by the actor's estimates of their probabilities, is positive, his act is not culpable (even if, from the God's-eye objective perspective, it will turn out to be impermissible). The key, I believe, to solving the problem raised by Smith is excluding all benefits derived from deontological violations but not excluding the harms.

VIII. Other Deontological Constraints?

Is the MP the only deontological constraint on the furthering of C? That is hard to say, because C itself has not been specified. I believe that most acts that we believe are impermissible and legitimately punished, at least if committed culpably, are either violations of C or violations of the MP. But I cannot rule out the possibility that there are some acts that are impermissible in this strong sense but that violate neither C nor the MP.

First, let me explain why most acts that we believe are wrongful, if not violations of the MP, are violations of C. If I knowingly drive dangerously and injure or kill someone, or damage her property, I will not have violated the MP. I would have happily driven the same way had she not existed. The impermissibility of my act must come from its setting back C. For if it furthered C despite the harm to the victim and did not use the victim, it is hard to see wherein its impermissibility lies. Of course, if I did not believe my act was furthering C but believed instead it was setting back C, then my act was culpable. But if it furthered C, then even if culpable, it was permissible. So again, most acts we believe are wrongful will be so either because they violate the MP or C.

Perhaps some acts of deception, for example, could change the deceived's behavior in ways that promote C but not by "using" the deceived in the ways the MP prohibits. I confess that I have a difficult time thinking of such a case. The MP protects people from the unconsented-to use of their bodies, labor, and talents to promote C, but it does not protect them from being prevented from performing acts that set back C, where the baseline for gauging such a setback does not rely on the use of the person's body, labor, or talent. If deceiving someone does not violate the MP and is a means of preventing him from setting back C, then the deception is C-permitted and not MP-proscribed. If, on the other hand, the deception furthers C by getting the deceived to use his body, labor, and talent to further C, then it is MP-prohibited if the deception vitiates the deceived's consent. So the question is, are there acts of deception that promote C but do not violate the MP? If not, then C and the MP together handle all cases of deception.[30]

What, then, about killings or other uses of force that promote C but do not violate the MP because they do not promote C by using the victim's body, labor, or talents? This might be thought possible. Suppose C is maximizing utilitarianism. And suppose that if

[30] Deception is, of course, a quite variegated phenomenon, and the moral assessments of acts of deception will often be quite controversial. For an excellent analysis of the various forms of deception and their moral statuses, see Collin O'Neil, "Lying, Trust, and Gratitude," 40 *Philosophy & Public Affairs* 301 (2012).

Al kills Barb, everyone else will gain more utility than will be lost by Barb's death. Killing Barb does not use her as a means. Rather, it eliminates her as a source of utility and disutility.

Utilitarianism of either the total or average variety would thus have space for a deontological constraint on killing to promote C in addition to the constraint provided by the MP. However, in a moral realm that recognizes deontological constraints such as the MP, utilitarianism seems a very unlikely candidate for C. Rather, deontological constraints fit more easily with a more egalitarian or prioritarian form of C. And an "eliminative" killing would probably be a violation of C because it is inconsistent with the impartial concern that is at the core of such forms of C.[31] Therefore, C and the MP may together exhaust strong (enforceable) morality.

IX. Conclusion

Michael Moore has taken many heterodox positions in his writings, but his position that deontological constraints are agent-relative and intention-focused is quite an orthodox one. Most of the explication of the Doctrine of Double Effect makes the intention of the actor central to the doctrine, and Moore is right in step with this.

I believe, however, that Moore and the orthodoxy are mistaken. The MP that I hold to be the quintessential deontological constraint on the pursuit of C demotes the role of the actor's intention. Facts, not the actor's intentions, determine his act's permissibility. And the actor's beliefs, not his intentions, are the determinants of whether he is culpable in acting. Intentions may reflect our character but not the moral status or culpability of our acts.[32]

[31] Michael Moore thinks that all unjustified killings must be deontological wrongs and not merely consequentialist wrongs. Moore, "Responses and Appreciations." I see no good reason, however, to deny that some killings and other intended or knowing harms can be C wrongs but not deontological violations.

[32] The longer paper to which I referred in this chapter's first n. contains a section on three problems for the MP: the paradox of deontology; how MP reasons compare to other reasons for acting; and the culpability of MP violators.

18

Moral Dilemmas and Moral Theory

Toward a Viable Deontology

Phillip Montague

I. Introduction

Michael Moore has emphasized two important ways in which examining moral dilemmas can fruitfully go hand-in-hand with moral theorizing. He describes one way in this passage:

> The sad fact is that the world is full of . . . moral dilemmas, the general form of which is the same. To resolve any of them adequately demands recourse to something equally general, viz., something no less general than our overall deontic framework for all obligatory/permissible actions.[1]

In other words, problems presented by moral dilemmas should be approached by way of general moral theory. But Moore also points to the possibility of proceeding in the reverse direction:

> [T]o see what general shape moral norms possess, the best heuristic is to look to the issues of justification. For it is here, where there is much to be said for doing something that is normally quite wrongful, that we can work our intuition pumps most vigorously in seeing the general shape of morality. Hard cases may make bad law, as Holmes warned us, but in ethics they are indispensable for sorting out what we think.[2]

That is, "the general shape of morality" can be revealed through an investigation of hard cases. Interpreted as referring to fundamentals, the second passage implies that examining the structure of moral dilemmas (or "hard cases") is an especially good way in which to pursue the goal of formulating an acceptable moral theory. It is this view that motivates and guides my discussion in this chapter.

My inquiry begins with an examination of the relation between moral dilemmas and moral reasons for action. It then moves to a consideration of these reasons understood as premises of inferences from moral principles to conclusions about the moral status of particular actions. This discussion introduces the companion questions of how to interpret the logical form of moral principles, and how to understand the logic of principle-based moral inferences. Although these questions are of fundamental importance to moral theory, they are almost entirely ignored in contemporary moral

[1] Moore, 2012b, 438. [2] Moore, 1997b, 670.

philosophy.[3] Of particular relevance here is the more specific question of whether the logical form of moral principles and the logic of moral reasoning are open to interpretations under which they accommodate moral dilemmas while avoiding serious logical problems. I will argue that the most satisfactory affirmative answer to this question is provided by a pluralistic deontological theory that interprets principle-based moral inferences non-deductively. As will become clear during the course of the discussion, the sort of theory to which I am referring differs significantly from a type that is largely deontological (and of which Moore's own view is arguably an instance), and which I will argue is seriously problematic.

II. Moral Dilemmas and Moral Reasons for Action

We can usefully begin our examination of moral dilemmas by imagining the following scenario:

> Al is with his elderly mother when she is informed by her physician that she is terminally ill. Al's mother prevails on him to promise not to tell anyone what the doctor has said. She places particular emphasis on Al's not telling his sister Alice, because she knows that such news would distress Alice greatly. Although reluctant to do so, Al does promise. Shortly thereafter, Al learns that he is being transferred to another state—which will leave his mother's care in Alice's hands. He asks his mother to release him from his promise, but she remains firm in her insistence that her condition should remain a secret.

Such situations exemplify moral dilemmas, the most common characterizations of which appeal to the notions of conflicting reasons for action, or reasons for performing incompatible actions or for performing and refraining from performing the same action. To avoid needless complexities in the following discussion, I will assume that a moral dilemma involves reasons for performing—and also reasons for refraining from performing—one and the same action. Although references to reasons for action in the literature suggest that there are various ways in which they can be categorized, perhaps the most fundamental of these categorizations of reasons concerns their ontological status.

In one interpretation of reasons for action, they are concrete entities—more specifically, psychological states such as beliefs, desires, motives, or preferences. This interpretation is particularly appropriate when reasons for action are referred to in explaining why someone has acted. So, for example, suppose that Al breaks his promise; and that he does so because, in the circumstances, he wants more than anything to protect his mother's welfare, and believes that he can do so by (and only by) informing Alice about their mother's illness. The combination of Al's desire and belief (that is, his *desiring* and his *believing*) is his reason for informing Alice, and appealing to it explains why he acted as he did.[4] Note, however, that although these reasons explain Al's action,

[3] To some extent, inattention to these issues reflects a preference among contemporary moral philosophers for versions of consequentialism. However, while the latter might not directly raise logical questions, they are commonly linked with pluralistic value theories that do raise such questions.

[4] Here I follow Donald Davidson, whose account of explanatory reasons for action is the best one I know of. See Donald Davidson, "Actions, Reasons, and Causes," 60 *The Journal of Philosophy* 685 (1963).

they aren't *moral* reasons. Here is an explanation that does refer to moral reasons: Al wants to do what morality requires of him, and he believes that he is morally required to inform Alice.

In contrast to this interpretation of reasons for action as concrete psychological states (references to which can explain actions) is the idea that reasons for action are certain types of abstract entities. Under this interpretation, reasons for action are propositions (or statements, or the *contents* of psychological states like beliefs or desires) that logically support conclusions about the moral status of particular actions.[5] Although the notion of logical support as used in this context needs clarification (and will be examined shortly), propositions that function in this way are fairly easy to identify. For example, the proposition that Al promised his mother to keep her illness secret, when conjoined with the proposition that promise-keeping is morally required, certainly seems to provide logical support for the conclusion that Al is morally required to refrain from informing Alice.[6] Note that appealing to such propositions can't by itself *explain* any actions performed by people to whom the propositions refer. Thus, suppose that Al doesn't inform Alice. His action can't be explained by simply invoking the propositions that promise-keeping is morally required and that Al's not informing Alice is an instance of promise-keeping. And although appealing to Al's *believing* that these propositions are true (and his desiring a certain outcome) would explain why he didn't inform Alice, such an appeal would change the focus from reasons as propositions to reasons as psychological states.[7]

Given what has just been said about the psychological and propositional interpretations of reasons for action, it isn't at all surprising that they are often referred to respectively as "explanatory" and "justificatory" reasons. However, references to "subjective" and "objective" reasons will be more convenient in the present context.[8] We can then distinguish between subjective and objective moral dilemmas, as determined

[5] On its face, the distinction between these two types of reasons for action seems quite straightforward. However, writers on the topic of reasons for action often equate them with one type rather than the other—or they at least emphasize one type over the other. For examples of these various interpretations, see Joseph Raz, *Practical Reason and Norms* (Princeton, NJ: Princeton University Press, 1990), 17, 18; Thomas Nagel, *The Possibility of Altruism* (Princeton: Princeton University Press, 1970), 13–15, 47; Shelly Kagan, *The Limits of Morality* (Oxford: Clarendon Press, 1989), 65, 275; and Donald Davidson "How is Weakness of the Will Possible?" in Joel Feinberg (ed.), *Moral Concepts* (New York: Oxford University Press, 1969), 93–113, 105. Despite the apparent reference to reasons as propositions in this passage, in "Actions, Reasons, and Causes" Davidson seems to assume that all reasons for action are psychological states.

[6] As this example suggests, "logical support" is being used here as an abbreviation for "principle-based logical support." Moreover, while logical support in the example might seem to consist in entailment, whether it does depends on how the logical form of the principle is interpreted. This issue will be addressed in Section II.

[7] It might be important for some purposes to distinguish reasons for action from reasons for belief. (On this topic, see Alan Millar, "How Reasons for Action Differ from Reasons for Belief," in Simon Robertson (ed.), *Spheres of Reason* (Oxford: Oxford University Press, 2009), 140–63.) For example, rather than saying of a proposition P that it is a moral reason for Al to inform Alice, P might be characterized as a reason for believing that Al is morally required to inform Alice. There is no need to worry about this here, however. The important point for my purposes is that situations can evidently arise in which there are true propositions that logically support conclusions that particular actions are morally required and also true propositions that logically support conclusions that refraining from performing those very same actions is morally required.

[8] Although Nagel also distinguishes subjective from objective reasons for action, his distinction is very different from mine (*The Possibility of Altruism*, 90). Nagel's is a version of the familiar distinction between "agent-relative" and "agent-neutral" reasons. Although writers on the topic explain this latter distinction in

by the presence—respectively—of subjective and objective moral reasons for action.[9] However, while we can make sense of moral dilemmas that are associated with subjective reasons for action, and while such subjective dilemmas might be philosophically interesting in certain contexts, they are only tangentially relevant to the issues that will be focused on here. With this in mind, let us look more closely at the idea that when person x faces an objective moral dilemma there are objective moral reasons for x to perform an action y and also objective moral reasons for x to refrain from performing y. That is, if x faces an objective moral dilemma regarding whether to perform y, then there are propositions that logically support the conclusion that x is morally required to do y and also propositions that logically support the conclusion that x is morally required to refrain from doing y.[10]

Although this condition is necessary, however, it isn't sufficient. The condition isn't sufficient because x faces a genuine objective moral dilemma only if the propositions that logically support the two moral conclusions are both true. Thus, suppose that Al is mistaken in thinking that keeping his promise would jeopardize his mother's welfare. Then, in the absence of other morally significant factors, Al doesn't face an objective moral dilemma. In this circumstance, if Al faces a moral dilemma regarding whether to inform Alice, it is entirely subjective in character.

Generalizing, we can say that x faces an objective moral dilemma regarding whether to perform y if and only if there is a true proposition that logically supports the conclusion that x is morally required to perform y, and also a true proposition that logically supports the conclusion that x is morally required to refrain from performing y. As we shall see, however, satisfying this condition is problematic for any moral theory, and indeed is impossible for some theories. According to these latter theories, there are no objective moral dilemmas.

III. The Problem of Logical Contradictions

If Al faces an objective moral dilemma regarding whether to inform Alice, then, arguably at least, this is because propositions like the following are true:

(P1) People are morally required to refrain from breaking their promises, and Al's telling Alice about their mother's illness would break a promise.

various ways, all (including Nagel) seem clearly to assume that both agent-relative and agent-neutral reasons fall within the category of reasons for action that I am calling "objective." Within this category, moreover, there is nothing about the difference between agent-relative and agent-neutral reasons that is relevant to the present discussion.

[9] According to "reason internalists," all reasons for action are necessarily motivational. On one interpretation of this view, however, it casts no doubt at all on the distinction I am drawing between objective and subjective reasons. I have in mind the idea that, if x *has* a reason to do y, then x is motivated to do y, where the notion of having a reason is cashed out in terms of references to certain psychological states. More interesting in the present context, is whether there can be a reason for x to do y even if x isn't motivated to do y, and regardless of whether x has that reason. I don't see why not, although I won't argue the point here. As was pointed out in a previous note, all that matters here is whether situations can arise in which true propositions logically support moral conclusions that conflict with each other in a certain way.

[10] Moore seems to have in mind something like what I am referring to as objective moral dilemmas in stating that "moral dilemmas are found whenever two or more quite plausible moral principles recommend diverging courses of action on particular occasions." Moore, 2012b, 437.

(P2) People are morally required to protect the welfare of their elderly parents, and Al's telling Alice about their mother's illness would protect their mother's welfare.

The first proposition seems logically to support the conclusion that

(C1) Al is morally required to refrain from informing Alice about their mother's illness,

while the second proposition seems logically to support the conclusion that

(C2) Al is morally required to inform Alice about their mother's illness.

P1 and P2 seem to provide logical support for C1 and C2 respectively because the principles contained in the former propositions are most naturally interpreted as universalized conditionals.

That is, "People are morally required to refrain from breaking their promises" is most naturally interpreted as "For all x and y, if x would break a promise by doing y, then x is morally required to refrain from doing y." And "People are morally required to protect the welfare of their elderly parents" is naturally interpreted in a parallel fashion. Under these interpretations of their incorporated principles, P1 and P2 logically support C1 and C2 respectively because they *entail* C1 and C2. We will refer to this way of thinking about moral principles and inferences from those principles to conclusions about the moral status of particular actions as "the deductive model of moral reasoning"—"the deductive model" for short.

The conjunction of C1 and C2 is problematic from both practical and theoretical standpoints, although we will restrict our attention to problems of the latter sort. The most serious of these problems is that, although the conjunction of C1 and C2 isn't explicitly contradictory, it implies a contradiction when taken together with certain other propositions, all of which are eminently plausible. If these latter propositions are true, then, of course, the conjunction of C1 and C2 is false. It would follow that, if this conjunction is entailed by P1 and P2, then at least one of these two propositions is false, and hence (relative to those propositions) Al doesn't face an objective moral dilemma regarding whether to inform Alice.

The "eminently plausible" propositions just referred to include axioms or theorems of standard systems of deontic logic, as well as the principle that "ought" implies "can." Although the contradictions generated by the conjunction of these propositions with C1 and C2 might seem avoidable by rejecting at least some of the former, this maneuver would represent a sort of "nuclear option" that won't be pursued here.[11] Instead, we

[11] The propositions in question are divisible into two sets:

Set 1

If x is morally required to refrain from doing y, then x isn't permitted to do y.

If x is morally required to do y, then x is permitted to do y.

Set 2

If x is morally required to do y, then x is able to do y.

No one is able both to perform and to refrain from performing any action.

If x is morally required to do y and morally required to do z, then x is morally required to do y and z; and hence if x is morally required to do y and morally required to refrain from doing y, then x is morally required to do y and to refrain from doing y.

will consider approaches from within moral theory that are alternatives to the idea that P1 and P2 are true propositions from which C1 and C2 are respectively deducible.

First of all, consider monistic moral theories, each of which has one basic principle that attributes inherent moral significance to a single property of actions—a property whose possession by actions is necessary and sufficient for the actions to be morally required.[12] Monistic theories therefore presuppose the deductive model; and a monistic theory can avoid contradictions only by interpreting the property to which it attributes inherent moral significance so that it can't be simultaneously possessed both by an action and by refraining from that action. (For example, a consequentialist could avoid contradictions by designating the property in question as corresponding to "maximizes overall intrinsic value.") Clearly, then, monistic theories that avoid contradictions in this way exclude the possibility that there are true propositions that logically support conclusions of the form "x is morally required and refraining from x is morally required." The theories are therefore incapable of accommodating objective moral dilemmas. And because a monistic theory treats the possession of some particular property by an action as necessary and sufficient for the action to be morally required, monistic theories should exclude principles like those contained in P1 and P2 if the principles are interpreted as universalized conditionals. Accepting any principle of the latter sort could create problems because situations could arise in which the principle conflicts with the monistic theory itself.

It is therefore unclear to me how a moral monist would characterize Al's situation—except, perhaps, to allow that he would face a subjective moral dilemma if he accepted P1 and P2 under their problematic interpretations.[13] From a monistic perspective, of course, Al *shouldn't* accept P1 and P2 under these interpretations. Regardless of how proponents of monistic theories might explain Al's situation, however, I will have no more to say about such theories here. My concern is with theories that can accommodate objective moral dilemmas while avoiding contradictions, and I don't see how any monistic theory could do both. So we will now focus on pluralistic moral theories—theories that have multiple basic principles that attribute inherent moral significance to a variety of logically unrelated properties of actions. We will attempt to determine whether any such theory can accommodate objective moral dilemmas without producing contradictions. As the preceding discussion suggests, whether any particular pluralistic theory can do so depends on how its incorporated principles are formalized. We will begin by examining a type of pluralistic theory that is regarded by its proponents as combining the intuitive appeal of both consequentialism and deontology. The underlying idea is that consequentialism is constrained by deontological

The conjunction of C1 and C2 with the propositions from either of these sets results in explicit contradictions.

[12] Consequentialism—that is, "act" consequentialism—is monistic in this sense. But so are standard versions of "rule" consequentialism. Each of the latter has one basic principle. And although this principle, when conjoined with appropriate non-moral propositions, can imply that various properties are morally significant, their significance would be derivative—not inherent.

[13] A consequentialist might attempt to connect Al's promise-keeping, or perhaps promise-keeping in general, with intrinsic value. However, working this out would require at least the beginnings of a theory of intrinsic value, together with some indication of how the problems referred to in n. 3 would be solved. The fact would remain in any case that Al wouldn't be dealing with a conflict of *moral* considerations, and hence wouldn't be facing an objective moral dilemma.

considerations, and so this type of theory will be referred to here as "consequentialism with constraints," or CWC.

IV. Can Consequentialism be Constrained?

CWC is most closely associated with Robert Nozick's suggestion that rights function as side constraints on the goal of value-maximization. In Nozick's words,

> In contrast to incorporating rights into the end state to be achieved, one might place them as side constraints upon the action to be done: don't violate constraints C. The rights of others determine the constraints upon your actions. (A goal-directed view with constraints added would be: among those acts available to you that don't violate constrains C, act so as to maximize goal G. Here, the rights of others would constrain your goal-directed behavior.) This view differs from one that tries to build the side constraints C into the goal G. The side-constraint view forbids you to violate these moral constraints in the pursuit of your goals, whereas the view whose objective is to minimize the violation of these rights allows you to violate the rights (the constraints) in order to lessen their total violation in the society.[14]

Versions of CWC that appear in the literature differ from Nozick's view in two respects: they typically contain more explicit endorsements of consequentialism, and the constraints to which they refer aren't limited to rights. Moore's own "three level" theory appears to exemplify this kind of approach, although whether it actually does depends on how one of its components should be understood.

To explain what I'm getting at here, a distinction must be drawn between, on one hand, consequentialism (the theory), and, on the other, pluralistic moral theories that attribute inherent moral significance to what I shall call "consequentialist properties." The latter are properties of actions that refer (implicitly or explicitly) to the consequences of their possessors. So, for example, "is harmful," "is beneficial," and "prevents harm" all correspond to consequentialist properties. Clearly, a theory can attribute inherent moral significance to such properties and still be incompatible with all versions of consequentialism. W. D. Ross's pluralism belongs in this category, since it includes prima facie duties of non-maleficence and of beneficence, yet it implicitly denies that an action's maximizing value is always sufficient for the action to be morally required.[15]

In explaining his own theory, Moore refers repeatedly to *consequentialist reasons* and to *consequentialist obligations*. Now, consequentialist reasons and consequentialist obligations can easily be interpreted in terms of the concept of a consequentialist property. Thus, consider Moore's own "drowning baby" example. He claims that someone in a position to save the baby has a consequentialist obligation to do so. True enough. But the obligation is consequentialist because "saves the baby's life" corresponds to a consequentialist property—a property to which moral significance could be attributed by a theory that incorporates the principle that people are obligated to prevent others from being harmed, and yet is incompatible with consequentialism.

[14] Robert Nozick, *Anarchy, State, and Utopia* (New York: Basic Books, 1974), 29.

[15] W. D. Ross, *The Right and the Good* (Oxford: The Clarendon Press, 1930).

So nothing Moore says about consequentialist reasons and obligations requires that his theory contains consequentialism as a component. Yet he endorses consequentialism. In his words, "consequentialism . . . [is] a true general principle of practical rationality"[16] and also "a principle of morality."[17] Granted, he doesn't believe that consequentialism can stand alone, claiming that it needs "two sorts of supplements."[18] The reasonable conclusion to draw here, I think, is that Moore regards his theory as combining *consequentialism* with certain moral considerations that are independent of consequentialism—a version of CWC, in other words. However, for reasons touched on earlier (and which will now be explained further), no such combination is possible.

Moore characterizes consequentialism in this way: "right action . . . consists of those actions . . . that maximally produce intrinsically good states of affairs."[19] Since Moore also connects consequentialism with obligations, I will assume that he would agree that, according to consequentialism, obligatory action consists in those actions that maximally produce intrinsically good states of affairs. Or, put in terms of the vocabulary and format that I am employing: x is morally required if and only if x maximizes intrinsic value. The requisite "supplements" include considerations that are commonly associated with deontology, in that they require or permit people to act in ways that don't maximize intrinsic value in certain circumstances.[20] We will ignore deontological permissions, and focus exclusively on deontological requirements. These are referred to in principles that require the performance of types of actions that have no necessary connections with consequences. In Moore's view, consequentialism determines what is morally required of people in situations to which deontological principles are inapplicable, but deontological principles determine moral requirements in situations to which they do apply. In these latter situations, people can be morally required to refrain from performing actions that would maximize intrinsic value.[21]

But suppose now that, if x does y, x will maximize intrinsic value and also break a promise. Then Moore's view implies that x is morally required to refrain from doing y on deontological grounds. If consequentialism is true as Moore claims, however, then it—in conjunction with the proposition that x's doing y maximizes value—implies that x is required to do y. There is nothing in Moore's position that blocks inferences to such conclusions.[22] Moreover, given what Moore says about deontological requirements, it

16 Moore, 2008a, 38. 17 Moore, 2008a, 39. 18 Moore, 2008a, 40.

19 Moore, 2008a, 39. Moore also states that, according to consequentialism, "we *generally* have reason to maximize good states of affairs and minimize bad ones," and "Maximizing the good . . . *sometimes* gives us . . . a moral obligation." Moore, 2008a, 38, 39 (respectively, my italics in both cases). But interpreting consequentialism as incorporating such qualifiers is incompatible with claiming that, according to consequentialism, right action *consists in* maximizing value.

20 Moore's theory must also be supplemented by principles that express requirements of justice in the distribution of benefits and burdens—if for no other reason than to provide support for his position on the morality of other-defense. See Moore, 2012b, 457. These principles neither follow from consequentialism nor can be characterized in terms of the concept of agent-relativity (which is how Moore characterizes his other supplements to consequentialism).

21 I take Larry Alexander to be endorsing much the same view in "The Means Principle," this volume.

22 Certain remarks of Moore's *would* block such conclusions if they could be made to cohere with other things he says. First of all there are the qualifications that he sometimes inserts into his statements of consequentialism (referred to in n. 17). Then too there are the qualifications he places on deontological considerations. For example, he claims that they don't apply to situations involving "moral horror." Moore, 2008a, 44. This qualification fits with Moore's characterization of his project as concerned with "the scope of permissible consequentialist justification of *prima facie* prohibited actions." Moore, 2008a, 42 (my italics).

is difficult to avoid concluding that his position can yield conclusions of the form "x is required to do y and x is required to refrain from doing y," and that it is therefore implicitly contradictory.[23] In any case, if people can indeed be required by deontological considerations to refrain from performing actions that maximize intrinsic value, then consequentialism isn't constrained; rather, it is refuted.

Any version of CWC that purports to contain consequentialism as a component is bound to be similarly self-refuting. Of course a theory can include consequentialist considerations without incorporating consequentialism per se. For example, consider the following alternative interpretation of CWC:

> (CWC1) If x's doing y maximizes intrinsic value, then x is morally required to do y if and only if no deontological principles apply to x's doing y.

Now, while CWC1 might capture the spirit of Nozick's remarks, it represents an implicit rejection of consequentialism. It also invites the question "What about situations like Al's to which deontological principles *do* apply?" The clear answer to this question is that CWC1 provides no basis for drawing conclusions about the moral status of Al's informing Alice or of any others that fall within the scope of deontological principles.

We are therefore returned to the problem of identifying the principles that apply to Al's situation, and explaining how they provide logical support for a conclusion regarding whether Al is morally required to inform Alice. P1 and P2 seem to include applicable principles but, as we have seen, these principles can't be interpreted as highly general universalized conditionals since this interpretation generates implicitly contradictory conclusions. However, moral principles could have the form of universalized conditionals, but lack the generality of those contained in P1 and P2. In this vein, we might take our cue from CWC1 and interpret moral principles along these lines: If x's doing y is an instance of promise-keeping, then x is required to do y if (and only if) no other principles apply to x's doing y. This method of formulating moral principles is one version of an approach commonly called "specification."[24] Unfortunately, the principles that result from employing this particular version of specification can't provide bases for drawing conclusions about the moral status of actions to which more than one principle applies—as is the case in Al's situation, for example.

In an effort to avoid this problem, a specifier might interpret moral principles as having exceptions referred to explicitly. As it pertains to our Al/Alice example, this approach suggests these principles: "People are morally required to keep their promises if and only if their doing so doesn't prevent them from protecting the welfare of their elderly parents," and "People are morally required to protect the welfare of their elderly parents if and only if their doing so wouldn't break a promise."[25] When applied to Al's

However, I don't see how these references to qualifications on consequentialist and deontological considerations *can* be made to cohere with the main thrust of Moore's remarks.

[23] That is, barring reliance on the "nuclear option" referred to earlier in the text.

[24] I believe that Judith Thomson originated this use of "specification" in her discussion of how rights-principles might be interpreted. See Judith Thomson, "Self-defense and Rights," *Findley Lecture*, 1976 (Lawrence, Kansas: University of Kansas Press, 1977).

[25] Moore seems to have something like this in mind in claiming that moral norms must have exceptions implicit in them to have any moral plausibility. To be morally plausible, "thou shalt not kill" must be taken to be an elliptical reference to a much more complicated norm: "Don't' kill unless in self-defense, to protect

situation, however, these principles imply that he is neither required to inform Alice nor required to refrain. Perhaps this result makes sense on the assumption that the situation contains no other morally significant factors. However, the principles are useless in the presence of other such factors and, indeed, they are false as they stand.

Regardless of how exactly specification is interpreted, all versions have the same basic aim: to provide a method by which moral pluralists can formulate their principles so that conclusions regarding the moral status of particular actions are deducible without generating contradictions. While I doubt that this method can deliver principles satisfying these conditions that are useful to people who find themselves in morally complex situations, I will set this point aside. I will focus instead on the idea, central to specification, that principle-based moral inferences are deductive. I will argue that specification presupposes that there are non-deductive moral inferences, and that, once the existence of these inferences is recognized, employing the method of specification is revealed to be at best dispensable, and perhaps completely pointless.

V. The Unavoidable Generality of Moral Principles

If Al is to be helped by specification in deciding whether he is required to inform Alice, then he must be able to formulate a principle that refers to all and only the morally significant features of the courses of action open to him. This principle must have the form of a universalized conditional so that it, in conjunction with corresponding subsidiary premises, entails that Al is required to inform Alice or that he is required to refrain. We have been assuming that these subsidiary premises would refer to Al's having promised not to inform Alice, and also to his endangering their mother by not informing Alice. But Al's informing Alice has other morally significant features, references to which would need to be included in Al's principle. For example, Al's informing Alice might fail to respect their mother's autonomy in making decisions regarding her own welfare.

Clearly, the morally significant features of actions open to Al would be morally significant features of any actions possessing them. Hence, the method of specification presupposes that there are *principles* that identify morally significant features of actions. Moreover, these principles don't simply affirm that certain features of actions are morally significant. They also reveal the kinds of contributions that these features make to the moral status of actions possessing them; and they do so without implying that the features' presence is sufficient for the actions to possess moral properties. These conditions are satisfied if the principles in question are interpreted as affirming that the possession of morally significant features by actions creates presumptions that the actions are morally required, or presumptions that they are prohibited. So, for example, being an instance of promise-keeping is a morally significant feature of actions, and its being possessed by an action creates a presumption that performing the action is morally required. Or, the principle can be stated more succinctly as "promise-keeping is presumptively required."[26]

your family, to aid in a just war lawfully declared, to execute those deserving of the death penalty such as Adolph Eichmann, ...," etc. Moore, 1997b, 706.

[26] My use of "presumptively" and my interpretation of moral principles are obviously reminiscent of W. D. Ross's "prima facie" and his interpretation of principles.

If specification is to work, then these "presumptive principles" must be the raw materials from which "specifying principles" are constructed—where the latter are the principles that are supposed to be used to deduce conclusions regarding the moral status of particular actions. And if it is indeed possible to construct specifying principles from presumptive principles, then this process is presumably a kind of reasoning, albeit non-deductive reasoning.[27] Hence, principle-based reasoning is, for specifiers, a two-step process—a process in which presumptive principles are implicitly recognized as the basic components of principle-based moral inferences. This process begins with non-deductive inferences from presumptive principles to specifying principles, and then moves to deductive inferences from specifying principles to conclusions regarding the moral status of particular actions. However, there are reasons for believing that this process can be short-circuited by eliminating the inferences from presumptive principles to specifying principles.

Note first of all that presumptive principles provide direct logical support for propositions regarding the moral status of particular actions in situations with only one morally significant feature. For example, suppose that Brenda faces a decision whether to keep her promise to perform action A, and that no other morally significant features are present. Then the principle that promise-keeping is morally required, in conjunction with the proposition that Brenda promised to do A, logically supports (but, of course, doesn't entail) the proposition that Brenda is required to do A. So inferences from presumptive principles to conclusions about the moral status of particular actions needn't proceed by way of inferences from presumptive principles to specifying principles.[28]

Moreover, even assuming that specifying principles could be inferred from conflicting presumptive principles, this process would consist in weighing the competing presumptions against each other, for the purpose of determining which are defeated and which are the defeaters. However, while this weighing process might be capable of providing logical support for specifying principles, the very same process could just as easily be used to make a direct determination of the moral status of the action to which the relevant presumptive principles apply. In other words, it is possible even in morally complex cases to reason from presumptive principles to moral conclusions about particular actions without the aid of specifying principles.

These points can be illustrated by returning to our example in which we have been assuming that these three presumptive principles apply: refraining from promise-breaking is presumptively required; protecting the welfare of one's elderly parents is presumptively required; and respecting others' autonomy is presumptively required. Let us also assume that the competition among these presumptions can reasonably be

[27] It is important to recognize, however, that specifying principles couldn't be inferred from presumptive principles by anything resembling inductive generalization. The reasoning would be nothing like inferences from "This particular thing is A and also B, and this other thing is A and B, and . . ." to "All As are Bs."

Moore also suggests that non-deductive reasoning can be used to derive moral principles, but the premises that he envisions would be used in this reasoning are very different from the presumptive principles to which I am referring. Moore, 1997b, 224.

[28] Davidson's account of the logical form of "prima facie" moral principles and of principle-based inferences can easily be restated in terms of references to presumptive principles ("How is Weakness of the Will Possible?" 108). I develop a somewhat different and much more detailed account of (non-deductive) principle-based inferences in *Evaluative Reasoning and Its Relation to Inductive Reasoning*, doctoral dissertation, Stanford University, 1966.

regarded as logically supporting the specifying principle "People are morally required to keep their promises even if their doing so jeopardizes the welfare of their elderly parents, provided that they would be respecting their parents' autonomy." It is surely just as reasonable to regard the competition as directly supporting the conclusion that Al's informing Alice (in which he would keep a promise, endanger their mother's welfare, but respect her autonomy) is morally required.[29]

Regardless of how the relation between presumptive and specifying principles is interpreted, pluralistic moral theories that incorporate presumptive principles can accommodate objective moral dilemmas without generating contradictions. Although such theories block certain sorts of contradictory conclusions, however, they don't seem to provide a way in which to arrive at *any* conclusions about the moral status (all things considered) of particular actions. In particular, they don't seem to explain how to conclude either that Al is morally required to inform Alice, or that he is morally required to refrain from doing so. True enough. But we shouldn't infer from this that the suggested account precludes the possibility of *knowing* what Al is required to do in the circumstances. Some analogies will help explain why I say this.

The inferences by which we acquire day-to-day knowledge of factual propositions are seldom (if ever) deductive. For example, I can know that my daughter will arrive soon, or that the trash is being picked up, or that my computer is malfunctioning, even though I haven't deduced those propositions from any other propositions. More dramatically, the jurors in a criminal trial can know that the defendant is guilty by having weighed the evidence provided by the defense and the prosecution, even though no part of that evidence entails that a guilty verdict is appropriate. Similarly, a paleontologist can know that certain species of prehistoric creatures lived in a particular location without having deduced that conclusion from the evidence presently available to her. Granted, these examples are of empirical knowledge, and the claims made in the previous paragraph are about moral knowledge, but there is no reason to think that the *logic* involved in acquiring one type of knowledge should differ significantly from that involved in acquiring the other type just because of substantive differences between what is known in each case. Hence, interpreting principle-based moral inferences as fundamentally non-deductive casts no doubt at all on the possibility of acquiring knowledge of the moral status of particular actions.

VI. Conclusion

I'll close with a brief summary of the preceding discussion, along with some concluding remarks.

Situations can arise in which there certainly appear to be objective moral reasons for people to perform particular actions and also objective moral reasons for them to refrain from performing those very same actions. These objective moral dilemmas

[29] To be sure, this result can be generalized. That is, if Al's refraining from informing Alice is morally required, then so is any *relevantly similar* action—leading to the principle "People are morally required to keep their promises even if their doing so jeopardizes the welfare of their elderly parents, provided that they would be respecting their parents' autonomy." However, since we have already used presumptive principles to infer that Al is required to refrain from informing Alice, the specifying principle plays no useful role in Al's reasoning about what he is required to do.

deserve careful attention because examining their structure focuses needed attention on the basic principles of moral theories in their role as premises of moral inferences, thereby underscoring the importance of clarifying the logical form of these principles. Monistic moral theories can't accommodate objective moral dilemmas. Pluralistic theories *can* accommodate them (while avoiding contradictions) but only if their basic principles are formulated so that inferences from them to conclusions regarding the overall moral status of particular actions are fundamentally non-deductive. Principle-based moral inferences are *fundamentally* non-deductive in that they are required even if specification has some role to play in moral reasoning.

Moore's pluralistic theory combines consequentialism with deontological principles. It must be distinguished from versions of deontology that don't incorporate consequentialism, but that attribute inherent moral significance to consequentialist properties (such as being maleficent) as well as to standard deontological properties (such as being an instance of promise-keeping). I have suggested that the principles of these latter theories should be interpreted as presumptive, inferences from which would necessarily be non-deductive. It is unclear, however, how moral reasoning is meant to work within Moore's theory. Inferences from consequentialism would be deductive; and, while it might seem that Moore's deontological principles could be interpreted as presumptive, and inferences from them as non-deductive, it is hard to see how the two types of inferences could function together in particular situations.

Of course, Moore does attempt to segregate the two types of inferences from each other by claiming that the actions to which consequentialism applies are distinct from those to which deontological principles apply. But consequentialism purports to provide conditions that are necessary and sufficient for *any* action to be morally required. Hence, if consequentialism is true, then whether an action is morally required is determined by whether it satisfies consequentialism's necessary and sufficient conditions—and this regardless of what might be non-deductively inferable from applicable presumptive principles. In other words, consequentialism would always trump preemptive deontological principles, rendering the latter entirely useless when reasoning about the moral status of particular actions.

Perhaps it is possible to produce a consistent version of moral pluralism that combines consequentialism with deontological principles, but I don't think so. Rather, a choice would need to be made between some standard (monistic) version of consequentialism and a pluralistic deontology within which principle-based inferences are non-deductive. It seems to me that a theory of the latter sort that incorporated principles attributing moral significance to consequentialist properties would square quite well with Moore's views on specific moral issues; and I don't see anything in these views that depends on support from consequentialism.

19

"Just No Damned Good"

*Jeremy Waldron**

I. Introduction

One of the best classes I ever taught was a class on "Legal and Moral Theory," co-taught with Michael Moore at Boalt Hall, at the University of California, Berkeley, in the Jurisprudence and Social Policy Program. In 1987 I had just arrived from Scotland and Moore and I wrestled to make our respective meta-ethical positions commensurable so that we could have a productive dispute about them. Moore was a moral realist, motivated by impatience at many of the fallacies and misconceptions that emerged in the work of his relativist colleagues in legal academia. I was brought up as a non-cognitivist in the tradition of Hume and Hare and it only later occurred to me that my meta-ethics was a burning provocation to realists like Moore. I believed that by and large a sophisticated non-cognitivist could say more or less everything about his moral convictions that a realist wanted to say: that they were true, that he firmly believed them, that their truth wasn't conditional on his attachment to them, and so on. I guess I was a "quasi-realist," to use a term introduced by my friend Simon Blackburn, and I tried to persuade Moore to take this set of options seriously.[1] He was interested, but resisted; and he strove valiantly, for his part, to introduce me to the arguments that had convinced him of the realist position.

I shall examine one of those arguments here. I think I can show it is a bad argument. But as indicated at the end, such a showing does not discredit moral realism. A position can be good and valid even though one of the arguments for it has been undermined. Equally, the fact that this chapter is an argument against a position held by Moore should not be read as anything other than an adversarial tribute to his philosophical work and to my happy memories of many good arguments in California, in the classroom and in the mountains, in the late 1980s.

My aim in this chapter is to discuss and criticize one of the more powerful arguments put forward in favor of the objective reality of moral values: the argument based on the indispensability of such values in the explanation of historical and psychological events.

* An earlier version of this chapter was presented at the American Philosophical Association Meetings in Washington DC, in December 1992. I am grateful to Simon Blackburn, Leslie Green, Kenneth Kress, Michael Moore, and Dennis Patterson for their comments on that occasion. The years since have not diminished the convictions that the chapter conveys.

[1] See Simon Blackburn, *Essays in Quasi-Realism* (Oxford: Oxford University Press, 1993).

II. The Argument from Best Explanation

"[I]t seems plausible," writes Nicholas Sturgeon, "to cite moral facts as part of an explanation of non-moral facts."[2] And it is appropriate, writes Moore, to infer ontological conclusions from the plausibility of such explanations:

> [T]o discover whether some particular entity or quality exists is to determine whether that thing has a necessary place in the best explanation of some features of the natural world that we take (for these purposes) to exist. We are justified in believing, for example, that intentions, electrons, or propositions exist just in case our best explanations of human behavior, chemical structure, or linguistic behavior commit us to their existence. The question about moral entities such as rights, or moral qualities such as justice or culpability, is whether there are any natural phenomena (that we are confident exist) that the existence of these moral entities or qualities best explains.[3]

In presenting this argument, Sturgeon talks of "moral facts" while Moore talks about "moral entities." The two terms are connected in a pretty straightforward way. We can explain their relation via the idea of a moral statement. A moral statement is a statement that makes direct use of some moral expression like "good," "evil," "wrong," "virtue," "a right to," "just," "culpable," etc. The use of these expressions can be understood in all sorts of ways. The philosophical hypothesis under consideration—moral realism—makes the claim that moral expressions like the ones just mentioned are used to pick out real entities—real qualities or relations in the world that persons, institutions, or actions might possess. If this hypothesis is true, then a statement like "Hitler was evil" describes a moral fact in just the same way as "Hitler died in 1945" describes an historical fact. Just as the expression "in 1945" picks out a time so that it can be associated with an event, so the term "evil" picks out an attribute that can be associated with a person's character. The Sturgeon/Moore claim is that we may infer the truth of this realist hypothesis (e.g. about the semantic relation between "evil" and some real quality, evil) from the indispensability of moral statements in the explanation of non-moral facts, that is facts which can be described or picked out without using moral expressions.

I think Moore is convinced, by the way, that this is the best means of establishing the ontological *bona fides* as it were, of moral entities. He has argued that the "explanationist" argument is the best riposte to those, like J. L. Mackie, who have complained that moral entities would be ontologically "queer." That such entities situate themselves naturally in explanatory discourse means that they take their place, and are taken seriously, in the whole web of explanation that comprises physical science and ordinary persons, actions, and objects in the world.[4] Of course all sorts of things look queer in our explanatory scheme—like neutrinos, quarks, and so on. But we seem to have no

[2] Nicholas L. Sturgeon, "Moral Explanations," in Geoffrey Sayre-McCord (ed.), *Essays in Moral Realism* (Ithaca: Cornell University Press, 1988), 243.

[3] Moore, 1992b, 2492–3. Moore also cites a similar strategy in an argument for realism about the entities picked out by certain legal expressions in Moore, 2002b, 619.

[4] See Moore, 2002b, 664–5.

choice but to countenance such objects if we are to explain what is going on in the world, and the same may be true of rightness, evil, desert, and justice.[5]

III. Conditions of Validity

Later (in section V), I shall explain why this inference is inappropriate. To begin with, let me note three necessary conditions for its validity.

(1) The premise of the inference must be not merely that we tend to use moral statements when we explain certain facts, but that the use of moral statements in the explanation of those facts is indispensable. Moore expresses this requirement by saying that the moral statement must play a part in "the *best* explanation" available (my emphasis)—and that will do. The idea must be that an explanation of the facts in question which does not involve the use of moral statements would be unsatisfactory from the point of view of our desire to develop good explanatory schemes. If it is controversial whether a moral statement is superior as an explanation to a non-moral statement, then the Sturgeon/Moore inference to the reality of moral qualities is to that extent thrown into doubt. And of course if the controversy about the quality of moral versus non-moral explanations itself involves the philosophical issues at stake between moral realists and their opponents, then both sides will have to concede that the argument is inconclusive. Nothing interesting about the truth of moral realism can be inferred from claims about the superiority of certain explanations if those claims themselves presuppose the truth of the realist view or the denial of some hypothesis that contradicts moral realism. What Moore calls the "explanationist" strategy is supposed to be a way of making progress in this debate, not merely a way of parading progress that one side or the other tendentiously claims has been made in the debate already.

(2) Before we can infer the reality of evil as a moral quality from the indispensability in explanation of a statement like "Hitler was evil," we must show that the term "evil" functions in a variety of ways in a variety of contexts where statements using it are explanatorily indispensable. The aim is to avoid being duped by syncategorematic terms. It would be unwise, for example, to infer the existence of *sakes* from the fact that "He did it for her sake" provides the best explanation of some event. Only if there were a variety of sentences using "sake" in a variety of ways—"The sakes were against her," "He had one sake too many"; each of which furnished the best explanation of some phenomenon—would we want to conclude that there are such things as sakes and objective truths about their presence, their properties, the relations they enter into, and their behavior. This may mean that we have to adduce several explanations involving statements like "X was evil," or "The evil that men do lives after them," or "Y was the lesser of two evils," and show that they are, in each case, the best explanation of some non-moral fact associated with them.

(3) We must also be sure that the moral statements that figure in the allegedly best explanations have all the features that characterize moral statements as they figure in the most robust meta-ethical controversy. In this regard, the most striking feature of

[5] For an example of Moore's putting this line of argument to work in jurisprudence, see his account of statements about desert as indicating the best explanation of our retributivist intuitions in Moore, 1997b, 177–80.

moral statements is their normativity: the entities and facts that they seem to refer to are such that their apprehension directs us as a practical matter towards certain actions and decisions. To say, for example, that Hitler is evil is not just to make an observation; it is to prescribe the avoidance (to say the least) of Hitler and all his works and perhaps to prescribe militant action against him. Assuming (as the realist must) that non-cognitivism is false, this is not all there is to the statement that Hitler is evil; but it is an indispensable part of it. Now we know that moral statements also have ironic uses where one can appear to endorse them in a non-committal way; but these uses are not primary; they are parasitic. If it appeared that the moral statements that are supposed to figure in best explanations were operating like these, then their explanatory power would prove very little. For the moral realist's claim is that moral statements *in their full and ordinary use* pick out moral entities (*with the full and ordinary commitments* that they seem inherently to elicit). Some philosophers have argued that the best-explanation strategy may fail on this ground.[6]

I am sure there are also other conditions for the validity of a best-explanation inference to realist conclusions.[7] Condition (1) will be quite important in the discussion that follows. But I have spelled out all three conditions here in order to emphasize that the explanationist strategy is not to be taken lightly, either by anti-realists or by realists. The strategy is being used to defend a position that is—independently and importantly—controversial in philosophy. Realists are right to point out that our existential claims are not independent of our overall explanatory scheme. But anti-realists are right to insist that we should be very cautious in the meta-ethical claims we make along these lines. For (1) we do not want the argument to be question-begging; (2) we do not want the conclusion tritely to assimilate the mere fact that a word or phrase has *a use* in some explanatory statement to the claim that it must therefore denote some real entity; and (3) we want the conclusion to convince us that moral statements are explanatory in their fullest normative sense.

IV. Other Explananda

The most striking vindication of the explanationist strategy in this debate would be if its proponents could point to large areas of understanding where clearly and indisputably moral concepts were deployed and deployed commonly in order to explain ordinary events. It would be great if they could show that we are in some sense *driven* by the undeniable frequency and prominence of such explanations to accord reality to the values and moral qualities to which the statements made in the course of such explanations appear to refer.

[6] See David Copp, "Explanation and Justification in Ethics," 100 *Ethics* 237 (1990), 246–8. See, however, the discussion in Edward Sherline, "Confirmation Theory and Moral Justification," 73 *Philosophical Studies* 225 (1994).

[7] See Arthur Fine, "The Natural Ontological Attitude," in Jarrett Leplin (ed.), *Scientific Realism* (Berkeley, CA: University of California Press, 1985), 86, for the claim that arguments for ontological conclusions—where those conclusions are philosophically controversial—must have a better grounding than ordinary empirical claims.

For what it's worth, I want to note that this is not what is going on. Instead, the sense one gets—particularly from Moore's discussion—is that moral realists are casting around, *trying to find* evidence of explanations that will best make their case.

Moore is quite unashamed about this; the title of one section in his article "Moral Reality Revisited" is "In Search of an Explanandum." Far from being *driven* to postulate the reality of values as the best explanation of some phenomena, we have to *search* for facts concerning which we may perhaps, at a stretch, construct a sort of plausible case for saying they may best be explained using moral ideas.[8]

The two possible explananda that Moore considers seriously are (A) the existence (and character) of our moral beliefs *qua* beliefs—for example, the fact that we believe that torturing terrorist suspects is wrong and are unwilling to budge from that belief even in the face of social pressure—and (B) various other pieces of human behavior or historical fact that can be described without using moral language—for example, the fact that in the eighteenth century, slavery evoked more opposition in Britain than it did in Spain. If the best explanation of (A) our believing that torturing terrorist suspects is wrong is that torturing terrorist suspects really is wrong, or if the best explanation of (B) the existence of greater opposition to slavery in Britain is that slavery in the British colonies was more unjust than slavery in Latin America, then we will have moral statements on our list of indispensable explanations and we will be well on the way—provided we can also satisfy conditions (2) and (3) mentioned above—to establishing rightness and wrongness, justice and injustice, as real properties that may be attributed to actions and institutions respectively.

Moore focuses his discussion on explananda of type (A) rather than type (B), although he concedes that the latter are "more promising" from an explanationist point of view.[9] His reason for choosing the existence and character of our moral beliefs as his favored explanandum seems to be the following. If we succeed in showing (e.g.) that the wrongness of torturing terrorist suspects explains why we believe it is wrong to torture them, then we will have killed two philosophical birds with one stone. Not only will we have initiated a best-explanation argument for the reality of wrongness as a moral property, but we will also have answered various epistemological questions that would otherwise embarrass moral realism. It is, after all, not enough to simply announce that entities of a certain category exist; one must also give an account of how we acquire information about those entities:

> Such an account gives us reason to credit certain of our experiences—what we often call observational experiences—as constituting evidence of a deeper reality causing them. The causal theory of perceptual belief offers such an account for our observations of many ordinary (and some not so ordinary) objects in the world. If moral qualities also exist, we need some account of the origins of our moral beliefs analogous to the causal theory of perceptual belief. Otherwise the realist cannot show our moral observations to be reliable evidence of a deeper reality.[10]

[8] However, the argument in Moore, 1997b, 177–80, about the way in which facts about desert might explain retributivist beliefs seems much less strained than this.

[9] Moore, 1992b, 2508. [10] Moore, 1992b, 2508.

This is true and it is important. But I think it is a mistake to suggest that this challenge and the challenge of finding cases of explanation from which realist conclusions can be inferred can be met at a stroke. For one thing, the best-explanation strategy will work only if the alleged moral fact really *explains* the existence of the moral belief, and so it will work only if the challenge articulated in the passage I have just quoted has *already* been met. Unless we are in a position to say *how* moral reality affects our experiences (including our beliefs), we cannot say that the former provides an explanation, let alone the best explanation, of the latter. The assertion of an explanatory relation is not enough. But it is unlikely that we would be in this position to say how, if we were (as Moore concedes) still at the stage of having to establish that there are such things as moral facts and having no better basis to establish that than that the alleged facts are plausibly cited as explanations of our experiences and beliefs.

In other words, if the ontological issue is still open or still controversial, it seems better to move one step at a time. First, we should show that referring to moral facts is the best strategy for explaining events other than beliefs about or experiences of the alleged facts in question. Then second, once that is settled, we can move from the ontological to the epistemological issue: do these moral facts, whose reality has now been established, cause humans to have certain experiences which might plausibly be described as *beliefs* about those facts? Do humans acquire beliefs about them in some other way (e.g., by God's imprinting them innately in our minds)? For this reason (that is, to avoid begging the question), I am going to focus my comments on the second class of explananda.

There are also three other reasons for this. First, in category (A) the nature of the alleged explananda is seriously in dispute between moral realists and at least some of their opponents. Though both sides may casually describe a person's moral views as her *beliefs*, anti-realists who are also non-cognitivists will be reluctant to place much weight on that description. They may prefer to talk about her attitudes or her disposition to issue certain prescriptions. Realists, on the other hand, will insist that they are philosophically quite serious in using the same label ("beliefs") to describe a person's moral views as they would use to describe her views about whether or not it is raining. Clearly, this dispute—about how to characterize the explanandum—goes to the heart of the philosophical disagreement between realists and non-cognitivists. It seems to me quite unlikely that it can be isolated from the issue of what counts as a good explanation of people's having the moral views that they do. Thus it is unlikely that the explanationist strategy will settle anything; non-cognitivists will probably regard it as question-begging. Since we all have an interest in settling this philosophical dispute on terms that have some prospect of convincing people on both sides, we would be well advised to avoid cases where the dispute itself is implicated in our characterization of the very premises of the argument that is supposed to be helping to settle it.

Second, if we focus exclusively on explananda of class (A) there is a danger that we will be confused and distracted by certain linguistic relationships between the explanandum and the alleged explanans. Clearly, as a matter of semantics, there is a relation between X's belief that torturing terrorist suspects is wrong and the wrongness of torturing terrorist suspects. Because beliefs are propositional attitudes, there is a connection between a belief that P and P, and no doubt some suitably looser version of this can also be applied to views, feelings, attitudes, etc. Anti-realists will regard this purely as a matter of disquotation: according to them, saying "I believe that torturing terrorist suspects is wrong" is just another way of saying "Torturing terrorist suspects is wrong." Realists, on the other hand, will take the connection to be one between a mental state and a state of affairs in the world. Once again, it is likely that this semantic issue will become entangled in the explanationist strategy. It seems wiser to try out the strategy on cases where no such question-begging entanglement is likely to arise.

Third, I emphasized—as condition (2), above—that the explanationist strategy will not yield reliable ontological conclusions unless it works in a variety of contexts for the term or the alleged entity in question. So even if we were to focus on explananda of type (A), we should *still* want to look at explananda of type (B). And if we found that the best-explanation strategy failed with regard to explananda of type (B), we should take that as grounds for questioning the reliability of the inferences we had drawn from cases of type (A).

V. Passed Midshipman Woodworth

Let us focus then on the historical cases. Various examples have been cited. Joshua Cohen and Alan Gilbert maintain that the restiveness of slaves in the ancient world is best explained by the fact that slavery violates the inherent rights of human personality.[11] Michael Moore suggests that it is plausible to cite Adolf Hitler's moral depravity in any reasonable explanation of his conduct.[12] And Nicholas Sturgeon has furnished a striking example in Bernard DeVoto's account of the failure of an attempt to rescue the Donner party, trapped by snow in the High Sierras, in his book *The Year of Decision: 1846.*[13]

I am going to focus on this third of these examples. In the summary given in Sturgeon's paper,[14]

> [T]he relief efforts were put under the direction of a recent arrival, Passed Midshipman Selim Woodworth, described by a previous acquaintance as "a great busybody and ambitious of taking a command among the emigrants."[[15]] But Woodworth not only failed to lead rescue parties into the mountains himself, where other rescuers were counting on him . . ., but had to be "shamed, threatened, and bullied" even into organizing the efforts of others willing to take the risk; he spent time arranging comforts for himself in camp, preening himself on the importance of his position; and as a predictable result of his cowardice and his exercises in vainglory, many died who might have been saved, including four known still to be alive when he turned back for the last time in mid-March. DeVoto concludes: "Passed Midshipman Woodworth was just no damned good."[[16]] [17]

[11] Joshua Cohen, "Do Values Explain Facts?—The Case of Slavery," in *American Political Science Proceedings* (Ann Arbor, MI: University of Michigan Press, 1986), 30–1; Alan Gilbert, *Democratic Individuality* (Cambridge: Cambridge University Press, 1990), 153–4.

[12] Moore, 1992b, 2508.

[13] Bernard Devoto, *The Year of Decision: 1846* (New York: Little, Brown & Company, 1943).

[14] Sturgeon, "Moral Explanations," 244; see also Moore, 1992b, 2508.

[15] DeVoto, *The Year of Decision*, 426.

[16] DeVoto, *The Year of Decision*, 442. Intriguingly, the same phrase once arose in a free speech case, in the military, concerning someone who was charged with disloyalty for saying that his captain was "no damned good." (See *US v. Gustafson* 1952 WL 2161 CGCMR, 1952.)

[17] Sturgeon, "Moral Explanations."

Says Sturgeon, "I cite this case partly because it has so clearly the structure of an inference to a reasonable explanation."[18] It looks like the Passed Midshipman's lack of goodness is being invoked as the only possible basis for accounting for the failure of the rescue expeditions that were supposedly under his command. It looks like the anti-realist can deny the existence of goodness only by insisting that DeVoto's explanation is not an explanation or the best explanation of the failure. But as Sturgeon complains, in defense of this and the other examples he cites, "What is supposed to be wrong with all these explanations?"[19]

The answer is, of course, "Nothing." DeVoto's account of the failure of the efforts to rescue the Donner party is illuminating and convincing. The fault lies in Sturgeon's and Moore's over-eager application of the explanationist strategy to examples like this. It lies in their suggestion that we can infer immediately from the reasonableness of DeVoto's account that being no damned good is a real property that individuals (like Woodworth) may possess. DeVoto for his part is much less impatient. For he continues the passage quoted by Sturgeon as follows: "Passed Midshipman Woodworth was just no damned good. His stomach would not take danger, and besides the audience was in the settlements.... Woodworth was timid and with slack leadership the men were slack."[20] Clearly the last two of these three sentences have at least as much claim to provide an explanation of the expedition's failure as the first. Woodworth was timid and had no stomach for danger (and the rescue party would have had to face danger); that is one reason why the effort failed. The audience was in the settlements not in the mountains, and Woodworth enjoyed playing to the audience; that is another reason. Woodworth's lack of discipline (his "slackness") affected the discipline of his men; there's a third. None of *these* explanations involves any appeal to moral facts. Sturgeon points out that DeVoto wrote "with more moral intensity (and with more of a flourish) than academic historians usually permit themselves."[21] But he fails to draw the obvious conclusion. A

[18] Sturgeon, "Moral Explanations," 244.

[19] Sturgeon, "Moral Explanations," 245.

[20] DeVoto, *The Year of Decision*, 442.

[21] Sturgeon, "Moral Explanations," 244. Compare, for example, the opening paragraphs of a review by Christopher Hitchens of Walter Isaacson's biography of Henry Kissinger (*London Review of Books*, October 22, 1992, 12):

> In a rather more judgmental time, history was sometimes written like this: "The evils produced by his wickedness were felt in lands where the name of Prussia was unknown; and in order that he might rob a neighbour whom he had promised to defend, black men fought on the coast of Coromandel, and red men scalped each other by the Great Lakes of North America." "Evil"? "Wickedness"? The ability to employ these terms without awkwardness or embarrassment has declined, while the capacity of modern statesmen to live up to them has undergone an exponential rise since Lord Macauley so crisply profiled Frederick "the Great". Walter Isaacson's new study of Kissinger shows beyond doubt that he rose to power by intriguing for and against an ally, the South Vietnam's military junta, whom he had sworn to defend, and that in the process of covering his tracks, consolidating and extending his power and justifying his original duplicity, he was knowingly responsible for the deaths of hundreds of thousands of non-combatants in lands where his name was hitherto unknown.
>
> Walter Isaacson is one of the best magazine journalists in America, but he moves in a world where the worst that is often said of some near-genocidal policy is that it sends the wrong "signal". He accordingly approaches the problem of evil with some circumspection.... [T]here is a limit, imposed by the tradition of New York–Washington "objectivity", on his willingness to call things by their right names. It became very plain to me, as I finished the book, that if I were to employ the *argot* of popular psychology I could say that I had been reading the profile of a serial murderer.

modern historian might omit the sentence "Passed Midshipman Woodworth was just no damned good" from the last passage I quoted and still have a good explanation (*three* good explanations) of why the rescue failed.

Suppose, however, he had omitted the last two sentences and just left us the first, as his explanation. Would it be a satisfying account, considered on its own—that is apart from whatever else we could gather from the rest of Sturgeon's summary? Surely not, for we would ask, "No damned good—*how*?" There are all sorts of ways in which a person can be no damned good: he may be a heavy drinker, a fornicator, a devil-worshipper, a tone-deaf singer, a bad philosopher. But only some of these vices would tend to contribute to the failure of efforts to rescue the Donner party.[22] "No damned good," then, is too general to be the best explanation.[23] The best explanation is found in the specific claims that follow it.

Sturgeon fails to see this difficulty, though he labors another point. He says:

> One can think of competing explanations, but the evidence points against them. It isn't, for example, that Woodworth was a basically decent person who simply proved too weak when thrust into a situation that placed heroic demands on him. He volunteered, he put no serious effort even into tasks that required no heroism, and it seems clear that concern for his own position and reputation played a much larger role in his motivation than did any concern for the people he was expected to save.[24]

But the problem is not that there are alternative explanations to DeVoto's characterization of Woodworth as no damned good. The problem is that that characterization intimates an explanation only to the extent that we go on to say exactly the sort of thing that Sturgeon said in the second half of this passage: "he put no serious effort into tasks that required no heroism," etc.

What, then, is the place of statements like "Woodworth was just no damned good" in historical explanation? We are dealing, I think, with relations between statements of three kinds:

1. The rescue effort failed. [*explanandum*]
2. Woodworth was no damned good.
3. Woodworth had no stomach for danger.

Evidently (3), together with the claim that successful rescuers would have had to risk danger, provides a good explanation of (1); and because it is more specific it provides a

Nothing in my criticism of the metaphysical inferences that Sturgeon and Moore want to draw from DeVoto's book is intended to disparage the way of writing history that Hitchens urges and that Sturgeon and Moore celebrate.

[22] Something similar is true of Moore's claim that Hitler's depravity explains his genocidal conduct. One might assent to "Hitler was depraved" and not think that it contributed one iota to the explanation of the Holocaust, if the depravity one had in mind was reading pornography. It is only because *one already has in mind* the sort of depravity that would explain the Holocaust that the bare statement "Hitler was depraved" can seem like any sort of explanation at all.

[23] A similar criticism is developed by Warren Quinn, "Truth and Explanation in Ethics," 96 *Ethics* 524 (1986), 534: "even if someone were badly behaved in every way . . . it would seem odd to think that this could be better explained by saying that he was no good than by saying that he happened to have all the particular vices. For a reference to his general badness would in no way help us understand the odd coincidence of his bad qualities."

[24] Sturgeon, "Moral Explanations," 244.

better explanation than (2) does, at least if (2) is considered on its own. Sturgeon, in the passage just quoted, does an excellent job of showing why the truth of (3) explains our readiness to say (2), but that of course is unhelpful to him since (3) is not a moral claim.

However, one important use that (2) might have, in this context, is to indicate that (3) provides an explanation for (1). After all, Woodworth might have had no stomach for danger, he might have had all his other character traits, and yet the rescue party might have succeeded, by some fortuitous conjunction of his character traits and what turned out to be called for in the circumstances.[25] As a gloss on (3), (2) indicates its significance as an explanation. We can see this if we rephrase it slightly as:

2A. Woodworth was no damned good at running a rescue effort.

(2A) does not itself provide an explanation of (1), any more than (2) does. But it indicates that there is an explanation, and it locates it in Woodworth's character. It provides, in other words, a bridge between (3)—or something like it—and (1), and it proclaims that connection as an explanatory connection. This is clearest when "good" and "no damned good" are being used in the functional sense indicated by (2A). To see the point, consider a straightforward functional claim that some implement fulfills its function—that it is, for example, a good knife. Now we may cite this in explaining why the implement was able to cut through a rope. But the real explanation would be that the implement was (a) strong, (b) rigid, (c) straight-edged, and (d) sharp. Saying that it was a good knife would be a way of saying that its possession of properties (a)–(d) explained its ability to cut things like the rope mentioned in the specific explanandum. A good knife just is a knife whose specific properties explain its ability to cut.

The same point can be put another way. Suppose somebody utters (2) with the intention of *condemning* or *blaming* Woodworth. (Whatever else its meaning may be, (2) may surely be used to perform that sort of speech act. This is the point we made in section III, under presupposition (3).) Another person may ask, "Why are you condemning Woodworth?" The first person's reply is likely to be something along these lines: "Because (3) is true." If he is asked why that is a reason for condemning a man, he will add, "And what's more (3) explains (1)." Now this last statement is important and revealing. In a paradisal world where humans were never in peril, the fact that a person had no stomach for danger might not be a reason for condemning him.[26] But we happen to live in a world where the truth of statements like (3) explains the truth of statements like (1): individuals' having no stomach for danger often leads to catastrophe for others. That is why we say things like (2).

If this is the case then the explanationist strategy is in tatters. Far from (2) being the best explanation of (1), (2) gets its distinctive condemnatory force from the fact that (3) is the best explanation of (1). To repeat: we say (2), intending to *blame* people like Woodworth, only because we believe that many catastrophes like that described in (1) are best explained by character traits like that described in (3).

[25] Imagine, for example, that the expedition had been successful and that it had been *because* they turned back (through Woodworth's timidity) that they came across the survivors and were able to rescue them.

[26] Cf. Michael Sandel, *Liberalism and the Limits of Justice* (Cambridge: Cambridge University Press, 1982), 32 and 35: "[P]hysical courage is a virtue only in the face of injurious conditions. . . . Gratuitous displays of physical courage in the midst of tranquil conditions can prove disruptive of the very tranquility they fail to appreciate. . . .

I said I was going to concentrate only on cases where moral facts allegedly provide good historical explanations: cases of type (B) as I called them in section III. But it is worth adding a comment or two on another view that Sturgeon holds about Passed Midshipman Woodworth—namely that his being no damned good provides the best explanation of DeVoto's *belief* that he was no damned good.[27] I never met Mr. DeVoto but I suspect that had he been asked for an explanation of his belief, he would not have couched it in those terms. He would have said perhaps, "What explains my belief that Woodworth was no damned good is that he was vain, timid, slack, incompetent, etc." In other words, he would have used statements of type (3) to justify his believing (2). Once again, then, the specifically moral statement, (2), is not itself being used to explain anything. It indicates perhaps that there is some explaining going on, and it stands itself in need of explanation. But it has no status as explanans in its own right that could possibly be appealed to in order to justify a best-explanation inference to the reality of no-damned-goodness.

VI. Supervenience

The issue of course is partly to do with supervenience. Moral predicates like "no damned good" behave as though they denote properties that supervene upon properties like "no stomach for danger." (I say "behave as though" because most technical definitions of supervenience stipulate that it is a relation between sets of properties,[28] and of course non-cognitivists deny that there *are* moral properties.)

I used to think that supervenience posed an insurmountable difficulty for proponents of the explanationist strategy. The difficulty went as follows. If a moral property M supervenes upon a set of non-moral properties $N^1 \ldots N^n$, then anything that is explained by a moral fact is also necessarily explained by the corresponding non-moral fact. That is, if the explanation of some event E is that person P was M (to a given degree)—for example, that P was no damned good—then E would also be explained by the fact that P had property N^i, where N^i is the supervened-upon property corresponding to the possession of M (to the degree stated). We could not say therefore that "P was M" was the *best* explanation of E, nor even that it was explanatorily indispensable, because its place could always be taken in explanation by "P was N^i." Thus an anti-realist opponent could always resist a best-explanation inference to the reality of M by denying the indispensability of moral explanations of this sort.

In fact, this is not a cast-iron rebuttal of the explanationist strategy. For explanation is not just a relation between particular events (like E and P's being N^i). We have an explanation only if two events are related via some general law. Now it may be the case that, although M is supervenient upon $N^1 \ldots N^n$, we are unable to formulate law-like

27 Sturgeon, "Moral Explanations," 244: "If DeVoto is right about this evidence, moreover, it seems reasonable that part of the explanation of his believing that Woodworth was no damned good is just that Woodworth was no damned good."

28 See, for example, Blackburn's definition in his article "Moral Realism," in John Casey (ed.), *Morality and Moral Reasoning: Five Essays in Ethics* (London: Routledge, 2013), 106: "A property M is supervenient upon properties $N^1 \ldots N^n$ if M is not identical with any of $N^1 \ldots$ Nn nor with any truth function of them, and it is logically impossible that a thing should become M, or cease to be M, or become more or less M than before, without changing in respect of some member of $N^1 \ldots N^n$."

statements relating events of type E and events exhibiting properties $N^1 \ldots N^n$. Thus, as Sturgeon points out, social facts like unemployment supervene upon complex histories of many individuals,[29] yet it is unlikely that we could formulate the law-like relations between inflation and unemployment that some economists claim to have discovered if we had to replace all references to unemployment with a mass of complex individual histories. Similarly, as Alan Gilbert points out, the element oxygen supervenes upon a complex microphysical structure, but reference to oxygen seems ineliminable in our explanations of phenomena like combustion.[30] Thus, even if a particular explanans such as "P was M" is replaceable by "P was N^i" because of supervenience, still the former may be better as an explanation than the latter inasmuch as the latter offers us no clue to the shape of the general laws that are being appealed to when we cite it in order to explain event E.[31] This is sufficient to preclude any broad argument against the best-explanation strategy based on the fact that the explanans supervenes upon another property. Supervenience *as such* does not undermine the strategy.

But that point is not much use to Moore and Sturgeon. For in the example they cited, it was apparent that in fact the explanation disclosed itself at the N-level rather than at the M-level. Whatever the case with unemployment and oxygen, in the case of Passed Midshipman Woodworth we had to descend from "no damned good" to "no stomach for danger" before anything really got explained. "No damned good" was too general a category to explain specific things like the failure of rescue expeditions. The law-like statements that one would be looking for in explanation appeared, in this case, not at the level of the supervening property but at the level of the properties that were supervened upon.

I suspect—though I cannot prove—that this is true of moral properties generally. We talk loosely of the supervenience of moral properties as though it were exactly on a par, logically speaking, with the supervenience of claims about oxygen on statements about microphysical structures. But there are important differences. Supervenience in the case of moral language is best understood in terms of the purposes for which moral language is used. Simon Blackburn states the point like this:

> It seems to be a conceptual matter that moral claims supervene upon natural ones. Anyone failing to realize this . . . would indeed lack something constitutive of competence in the moral practice. And there is good reason for this: it would betray the whole purpose for which we moralize, which is to choose, commend, rank, approve, forbid things on the basis of their natural properties.[32]

[29] Sturgeon, "Moral Explanations," 247 n.

[30] Gilbert, *Democratic Individuality*, 103. Cf. Jeremy Waldron, "On the Objectivity of Morals: Thoughts on Gilbert's *Democratic Individuality*," 80 *California Law Review* 1361 (1992), 1389–91.

[31] I wonder if it is significant that all the philosophically respectable cases in which this strategy is used are cases where we infer ontological conclusions about microstructures (e.g., protons) from the best explanation of macro-events (vapor trails), whereas all the cases in which it is controversial are cases in which the questionable entities (e.g., values or mental states) are supervenient upon some ontologically uncontroversial microstructure (natural properties, neural states).

[32] Simon Blackburn, "Supervenience Revisited," in Sayre-McCord, *Essays in Moral Realism*, (cited by Moore, 1992b, 2520).

Another way of putting this point is that what looks like supervenience in the case of moral statements is best accounted for in terms of the speech acts that are characteristically being performed when moral statements are made.[33] We are commending and condemning persons, actions, and institutions to one another on the basis of the properties $N^1 \ldots N^n$ that they have or lack. We do not do this gratuitously or as a game; we do it because properties $N^1 \ldots N^n$ matter to us. And as I said in section IV, the claim that a particular such property N^i matters to us is often best characterized in terms of its presence explaining things like the failure of rescue expeditions.

Thus once we stop simply repeating the term "supervenience" to ourselves as though it were simply a well-understood logical relation, once we ask ourselves why moral language has this feature, we begin to see why what realists call "moral facts" cannot themselves be explanatory. We make moral statements because we want to draw one another's attention, for purposes of future choice and decision, to the fact that certain natural properties are associated with certain natural outcomes. When we make a moral judgment to the effect that an individual is good or bad, we are likely to be asked *why* we are commending or condemning him. Both the obviousness of the question and our propensity to answer it by citing some natural property are what we mean by supervenience. When we answer it by citing a natural property, we do so because of what that property is or what it does. If it is the latter, it will often be because that property enters into the best explanation of some other event that matters to us. It is because *this* property is the best explanation of *this* event (and others like it) that we cite it when our moral judgment is challenged. An appeal to explanation, then, is often involved in the supervenience of moral judgments. But precisely because of that, we cannot say that those moral judgments themselves figure as the best explanation of the events that are cited to back them up.

VII. Conclusion

My argument in this chapter has been entirely negative. It does nothing to establish the truth of anti-realism—the point that was at issue in the seminar that was taught by Moore and me. It aims simply to undermine a particular strategy of argument. There may be other reasons for asserting the existence of moral properties and maybe for identifying them, naturalistically (as I understand Moore wants to do), with the clusters of properties on which they are supervenient. All I have wanted to show is that the best-explanation strategy adds nothing to whatever other arguments Moore and Sturgeon can concoct in favor of moral realism. The strategy sounded promising because of its success in regard to some of the less discernable entities that physicists postulate. And it

[33] There is still no better account than that set out in R. M. Hare, *The Language of Morals* (Oxford: Clarendon Press, 1952), especially 80 ff., 131, 145 ff., 153, and 159. Hare's account goes as follows. We have in a variety of areas (ranging from driving cars to choosing expedition-leaders) developed practices of discerning, communicating, and teaching ways of responding to the world on the basis of various repeatable natural features that situations may present. The use of evaluative language is characteristic of such practices and it is from such practices that such language takes its primary meaning. It is obvious then why something like supervenience is associated with evaluative meaning. To use moral language non-superveniently would be to fail to use it to discern, communicate, or teach a way of responding to repeatable features of the world.

has been useful philosophically because it has encouraged all of us to think in more complex terms about how ontological claims are made out. But its deployment in the moral realm begs important questions and ignores or overrides many of the distinctive peculiarities of moral language.

And so I guess my conclusion is obvious. Like Passed Midshipman Woodworth, the best-explanation argument for moral realism is full of noise and promise, but it leads nowhere. It is misleading, it is question-begging, it is no damned . . . —well, let's just say it doesn't work.

20

Conceptual Breakage and Reconstruction

Michael S. Moore's Natural Law Theory of Interpretation

Michael H. Shapiro

I. Introduction: Natural Law Interpretation; Moral Reality; Originalism

The first thing I'm not going to do is a number on what "a natural law theory of interpretation" is. Professor Moore is simply referring to moral objectivity or moral realism. The phrase itself is otherwise amusingly ambiguous and a nice target for historians and theologians as well as lawyers and philosophers.[1] His view is that, in reality, some actions are right or wrong, some situations good or bad. There are right answers to moral questions (maybe not as many as the moral realists think). The theory has no necessary connection with religion, but it has some historical association with it because of the general notion of natural law and its theological overtones.

There are, however, differing accounts of natural law theories of text interpretation, some indeed linked (in complex ways) to religion or human nature.[2] I think most of them intersect by affirming that moral claims are meaningful and objectively grounded. I note in advance that the only conceptual link to "nature" presented by Moore arises with the use of the idea of "natural kinds" in ascertaining meaning.[3] It is not an independent ground for moral evaluation, as in "don't do X because it's unnatural."

The question now is: How does searching for and finding moral truth link to legal interpretation and (in this case) specifically to constitutional interpretation? I will suggest some key problems for analysis and ask how Professor Moore's approach would go and what outcomes it would yield, and compare it with other interpretive approaches, especially the originalism of Justice Scalia.

Under Scalian originalism, in Justice Scalia's own words, the task is to "display how the text of the Constitution was originally understood" by the Framers and by "other

[1] See Moore, 1985b, 286. On his interpretive theory: "[T]he interpretive premises necessary to decide any case can and should be derived in part by recourse to the dictates of that moral reality. In short, real morals, not just conventional morality or 'shared values,' have a necessary place in the interpretation of any legal text."

[2] See, e.g., John Finnis, 'Natural Law Theories', *Stanford Encyclopedia of Philosophy*, last modified July 25, 2011, <http://plato.stanford.edu/entries/natural-law-theories/>.

[3] Moore, 1985b, 300 (n. 1):

> The meaning of a word like "death" is only to be found in the best scientific theory we can muster about the true nature of that kind of event. By assuming that there are such true natures of natural kinds of things, the theory of meaning presupposed by our usage is aptly termed a realist theory of meaning.

intelligent and informed people of the time."[4] Choosing among interpretive theories, however, requires both an empirical semantic approach and a moral approach. The former requires that our theory adheres to non-moral constraints of meaning: "meaning" doesn't just mean anything. The latter refers to the exploration of moral reality, and not just to empirical accounts of what moral views people hold—a conventionalist stance. These are, however, entangled approaches, as discussed in what follows. The meaning of "meaning," as argued by Moore, *includes* reference to moral considerations.

As I argue below, Scalian originalism inevitably devolves to a more comprehensive interpretive theory, Moorean or otherwise. In this sense, it is (speaking loosely) a kind of category mistake to compare pristine originalism with natural law as theories of interpretation. This is because the association assimilates a single criterion (authorial understandings) to a complete "algorithm." Originalism is a partial and simply runs out in certain situations, rather more often than Justice Scalia concedes, as we will see. But American courts cannot punt; they cannot declare matters so unclear that there is no law and leave the parties to themselves—a *non liquet* situation. In this sense, originalism is one region within a more complete map of text interpretation. It cannot stand alone; originalists who do not confront this would seem to be in error. Moorean objective reality also may not yield definitive answers, but it doesn't block them and doesn't cover up the interpretive process—and it is, indeed, in principle a text-interpretation process, not a text-displacement one. To be sure, Scalian moral analysis—whether the Justice admits it to be that or not—may be quite different from Moore's, and that is not a pure interpretive point. Their notions of moral reality differ.

II. Constitutional Basics: A Hierarchy of Interests and Their Associated Standards of Review

I can't start from scratch, so some basics must simply be outlined and presupposed. Any coherent constitutional interpretation will yield an *ordered* set of individual rights and government powers—a vector of sorts. Of course, not all interpreters will specify the same set or the same ordering, and some argue that, in an earlier time, the US Supreme Court did not recognize any such ordering. The methods of interpretive derivation that yield the kind of ordering relevant here—some interests are fundamental rights or liberty interests, or involve protection against some forms of classification—should be evident as we move on.

This ordering *entails* as a doctrinal matter that a court take certain *stances* concerning competing claims. It may have to presume that certain claims are sound and demand countervailing justifications from the government on behalf of society. Or it may have to presume that certain claims are unsound. For example, because of the derived "location" of freedom of speech in the constitutional pantheon, a threshold showing of interference with freedom of speech by government action directed at the content of communication is often presumptively unconstitutional and can stand only if it promotes a compelling interest without unduly burdening speech.

[4] Antonin Scalia, "Interpreting the Constitution and Laws," in Antonin Scalia (ed.), *A Matter of Interpretation: Federal Courts and the Law* (Princeton: Princeton University Press, 1997), 38. There are of course different versions of originalism—e.g., mainly semantic and purpose originalisms.

This brief account suggests the origins of constitutional standards of review, which come in various forms and go by different names.[5] They are required by the constitutional ordering of interests (with some accompanying premises), which is itself text-derived. They are thus not the extrajudicial frolics of hyped-up judges. They are constituents of the doctrines that implement basic constitutional values.

The last point requires underscoring: the Constitution is not morally neutral. This does not alone require moral reality to inform its interpretation, but moral conventionalism as a mechanism for implementing moral/constitutional values is not a sound alternative. This is why rigorous scrutiny of government action challenges it to provide credible justifications for some maneuvers (say, telling me I can't write about Jane Austen) and minimal ones for others (say, telling me I have to send my ablutions to the sewer system instead of my septic tank). My preference to keep my precious bodily fluids from entering the sewer system does not rest on a basic constitutional interest.

III. Interpretive Linkages when Originalism Peters Out

A. The *Smith* case

In *Emp't Div., Dept. of Human Res. of Or. v. Smith*,[6] the Supreme Court, per Justice Scalia, changed the triggering mechanism for strict scrutiny of burdens on the free exercise of religion. Before, the Court would examine the gravity of the burden placed on religious exercise, and, if the impact was sufficient, would demand that the government show both a compelling interest for the burden, and also establish that it was the most efficient way of substantially advancing it at the least cost to the protected interest. From now on, however, religious exercise had to be *targeted* by the government action. A law of general application[7] that "incidentally" impacted religion wasn't enough, however serious the burden.

So, the luckless claimants lost: they had been denied unemployment compensation because they had been dismissed for cause from their jobs—as drug rehabilitation counselors! Because the law criminalizing peyote consumption was general—it certainly didn't prohibit *only* religious use—only the rational basis standard of review was applied. In this area of constitutional law, that standard is almost vacuous.

The interpretive steps here are these: the First Amendment's Free Exercise clause says, "Congress shall make no law . . . prohibiting the free exercise [of religion]." This explicit mention, along with historical/traditional understandings of the "free exercise of religion," not only designated certain conduct but reflected the elevated moral status of such freedom. This yields high placement in the constitutional hierarchy. This works for both Moorean natural law and Scalian originalism.

5 The standards, rigorous or otherwise, can be either discontinuous (step) functions or "sliding scales." See Michael H. Shapiro, "Argument Selection in Constitutional Law: Choosing and Reconstructing Conceptual Systems," *18 Southern California Review of Law and Social Justice* 209 (2009), 269–70 (n. 136).

6 *Emp't Div., Dept. of Human Res. of Or. v. Smith*, 494 US 872, 876–9, 110 S Ct 1595 (1990).

7 The anti-peyote law of course specifically deals with *something*, but it is facially general with respect to religion and, absent a hidden malign purpose, thus draws only a minimal burden of justification (however described).

But what does "prohibit" mean? For Justice Scalia, it meant a burden directed at religion. For Justice O'Connor and others, it referred to government action that made a religious practice impossible or at least quite difficult, whether or not this was intended.[8] It is not obvious whether the *de re* or *de dicto* approach is the correct one, either in everyday language or in constitutionalese. Justice Scalia said either reading was permissible, but the *de re* option was correct under prior constitutional decisions.[9]

In fact, the Court's decisions reveal the opposite. But the point here is that the decision was not pitched on understanding the text as the Framers did. Both the *de re* and the *de dicto* understandings of the Clause are "permissible." Justice Scalia thought the *de re* reading was confirmed by precedent, not by what the Framers or contemporary informed observers had in mind.

So, an obvious question: How is this interpretive outcome—"prohibits X" implies "aimed at X"—properly derived from the text via originalism or any other interpretive theory? I see no clear account of Justice Scalia's methodology. He urges that using the compelling government interest requirement in *Smith* would generate "a private right to ignore generally applicable laws," which would be "a constitutional anomaly," enabling a practitioner to "to become a law unto himself."[10] Justice Scalia might have quoted Chief Justice Burger in *Bowen v. Roy* to capture the heart of the non-originalist interpretive argument that applying strict scrutiny to generally applicable rules impinging on religious exercise would (in the Chief's words in *Bowen*) please "libertarians" and "anarchists"; "it is hard to imagine that this is what the Framers intended."[11] True, the Framers clearly endorsed *some* version of the rule of law, but this is hardly decisive, and the approach is too diaphanous to be originalism.

Did Justice Scalia, by his law-unto-himself-anomaly remark, back into an originalist mode by referring to what the Framers probably intended concerning the rule of law? (Again, he might have used a loose *reductio ad absurdum* approach—"You want anarchy?") If so, why did he say that the alternative readings were "permissible"? If either reading is permissible, then the Framers didn't demand one of them. And if they didn't intend one reading over the other, where, in principle, can Justice Scalia go? He went to another standard—a loosely specified notion of (in my words) "what makes the most sense here, with respect to American values of rule of law."[12]

But this sounds suspiciously like his bête noire, "The Living Constitution,"[13] which is roughly equivalent to "the moral reading of the Constitution."[14] Justice Scalia, however, might interpret such reading as purely conventionalist—the result of investigation of public norms, not the demands of moral reality.

[8] Both Justice Scalia and Moore take a dim view of exploring legislative motivation. See Moore, 1985b, 348–58 (n. 1).

[9] *See Emp't Div., Dep't of Human Res. of Or.*, 494 US at 878.

[10] *Emp't Div., Dep't of Human Res. of Or.*, 494 US at 885–6 (quoting *Reynolds v. United States*, 98 US 145, 167 (1878)).

[11] *Bowen v. Roy*, 476 US 693, 707 (n. 17), 106 S Ct 2147, 2156 (1986).

[12] Recall Chief Justice Burger's remark in *Bowen* that "libertarians and anarchists" would "applaud" rejection of his view. This obliquely invokes a coherence-with-American-rule-of-law criterion. Whether this is a purely empirical conventionalist claim or a moral evaluation is unclear.

[13] Scalia, "Interpreting the Constitution and Laws," 38 (n. 4).

[14] Ronald Dworkin, *Freedom's Law: The Moral Reading of the American Constitution* (New York: Oxford University Press, 1996), 4.

Here, then, originalism has devolved into some other theory—perhaps natural law/moral reality, or tradition/conventional morality—derived independently of Framers' intent. Originalism, from a purist standpoint, was bagged. This does not mean that attending to authorial purpose variables was wrong, but this approach is incomplete, and especially opaque here. Although the point is often fuddled in judicial opinions, courts need a methodology for switching from one's default mode of constitutional interpretation to a more comprehensive one, as *Smith* neatly illustrates.

B. The *Cruzan* case

Cruzan v. Director, Missouri Department of Health[15] displays several striking interpretive maneuvers. Chief Justice Rehnquist grudgingly recognized a liberty interest in refusing medical measures, including life-saving treatment. His only assumption *arguendo* was that artificial nutrition and hydration constituted medical treatment. However, the US Supreme Court validated Missouri's rule requiring patient preferences concerning life-saving treatment to be established by clear and convincing evidence, and upheld the Missouri Supreme Court's refusal to authorize withdrawal of treatment.

What commands our attention here is the derivation of the liberty interest,[16] and Justice Scalia's concurrence. Chief Justice Rehnquist's majority opinion was a classic example of recognizing the existence of an important but unexpressed constitutional interest protected by the liberty clause of the Fourteenth Amendment, not backed up by specific language in the Bill of Rights. The interpretive mechanism he used to derive this liberty interest seems to rest on intersubjective meaning informed by historical analysis of American practices. The Supreme Court's confirmation of meaning was fairly simple, as these things go: it described a century-long string of common-law cases upholding a right of competent persons to refuse even life-saving medical treatment. To accept this is, of course, not to assert the irrelevance of either originalism or natural law. Relatively simple derivations based on lexical understanding of "liberty" in American practice are consistent with a natural law approach.[17]

On what interpretive ground did Justice Scalia reject the majority's framework? He expressly recharacterized the issue: it was not (simply) a matter of refusing medical treatment, including life-saving treatment. It was for him a matter of suicide: knowingly and competently refusing life-saving treatment is either an act forthrightly intended to result in death or with foresight of such certainty as to merit being treated as intentional. Because there is no American tradition supporting or tolerating suicide,

[15] See *Cruzan v. Dir., Mo. Dep't of Health*, 497 US 261, 110 S Ct 2841 (1990).

[16] The different terms "liberty interest" and "fundamental right" illustrate the pressure to fractionate the hierarchy of constitutional interests. Fundamental rights, express or implied, are highly ranked and generally draw strict scrutiny. Liberty interests are ranked lower and draw a form of intermediate scrutiny. *Cruzan* used the term "liberty interest" and seemed to invoke heightened but non-strict scrutiny. Compare *Roe v. Wade*, 410 US 113, 152–7, 93 S Ct 705 (1973) (holding that abortion is a fundamental right drawing strict scrutiny) *with Planned Parenthood of Se. Pa. v. Casey*, 505 US 833, 837–8, 112 S Ct 2791 (1992) (holding that abortion is a liberty interest in abortion, to be judged on the "undue burden" test).

[17] But cf. Moore, 1985b, 320 (n. 1) (arguing that it is presumptively desirable to look to ordinary meanings).

there is no liberty interest.[18] (Tradition may support a given view of the Framers' intentions or may represent a conventionalist escape from originalism.)

The Court and Scalia are either not appraising the same thing, or are applying different doctrines to it. Neither Scalian originalism concerning the Fourteenth (or Fifth) Amendment's Due Process Clause nor customary American practice support the view that knowingly and competently refusing life-saving medical assistance is suicide.[19] Most states expressly permit, by statute or common law, the refusal of life-saving medical treatment, doing so *without calling it "suicide"*—although they may explicitly exempt it from the laws prohibiting suicide assistance.[20] Justice Scalia makes no effort to show that his characterization of treatment refusal as suicide is the dominant strain of American tradition. Instead, he attacks the very logic of making such a distinction, *notwithstanding contrary historic lexical understanding*. In fact, our traditions do not view all cases of deliberate self-destruction as suicide. It is not suicide to use your body to block the bullet headed toward your child. Moreover, if *tradition* accepts the refusal vs. suicide distinction in certain situations, *it makes no (necessary) difference if it is philosophically vulnerable.* (To be sure, tradition ought to be rejected in various situations.)[21]

Justice Scalia's concurrence seems to embrace some theories of interpretation he reviles. As we saw, it is not clear what to call them, but they involve testing government action and historic practices for coherence with reigning norms, possibly by looking for deep consensus at higher levels of abstraction,[22] or indeed by exploring moral reality—the natural law way described by Moore. In both *Cruzan* and *Smith*, then, Scalia goes beyond his originalism.

IV. The Interpretive Pentad

Here I reconstruct some basic aspects of the meaning of "meaning," before introducing some demanding interpretive situations. There is nothing new here, but I abbreviate our understanding of meaning in a particular way so as to identify a cluster of entangled elements (axes, dimensions) that compose the idea of meaning. Here is a desiccated functional expression that describes what I mean:

> Meaning = f(authorial variables, intersubjective (lexical) understandings, audience variables, moral/all-things-considered variables, temporal emergence variables)

[18] *Cruzan v. Dir., Mo. Dep't of Health*, 497 US at 293–8 (Scalia, J., concurring). Physician-assisted suicide was indeed left largely unprotected in *Washington v. Glucksberg*, 521 US 702, 117 S Ct 2258 (1997).

[19] There may be conflicts between the Framers' understandings and either concurrent or later-developing customary understandings—an important theoretical problem. Of course, customary understandings at Framing time feed into our knowledge of Framers' understandings.

[20] Alan Meisel and Kathy L. Cerminara, *The Right to Die: The Law of End-of-Life Decisionmaking* (New York: Aspen, 2004), §1.07(D). See *Bartling v. Glendale Adventist Med. Ctr.*, 163 Cal App 3d 186, 195–6, 209 Cal Rptr 220, 225–6 (1984).

[21] See Jacob Gershman, "When Does Tradition Trump the Constitution?" *Wall Street Journal* (January 13, 2014) (discussing the constitutionality of the president's recess appointments). One thinks of *Brown v. Bd. of Educ.*, 347 US 483, 74 S Ct 686 (1954).

[22] *See* Moore, 1985b, 298–9 (n. 1)(discussing "deep conventionalism").

These categories are not all on the same categorical plane, and they overlap and feed into each other. (They are mutual functions, as in $y = f(x)$ and $x = g(y)$.)[23] Thus: if what the authors meant is unclear, we check the dictionary; if the dictionary is unclear, we might return to the author, or ask what various listeners would understand. Some paths may be decisive in some contexts, not others. And they do not form an ordered set across the board. Perhaps some paths are more important in some contexts—authorial intentions if God is the author? Audience understanding in a complex trade regulation area?

Here, then, are some multiple aspects of meaning.

1. The first interpretive axis addresses the *message sources and their intentions and purposes*, including their understandings of the meanings of the language or symbols they use, and—more controversially—their motives for selecting text bearing those meanings. Looking to what authors had in mind is an instinctive course for ascertaining meaning. True, its being instinctive is not decisive, but it's not nothing.[24]

2. A second path runs to the *linguistic/symbolic components of the message and their intersubjective meanings*. Within languages, these meanings generally exist independently of the intentions, motives, and purposes of message sources or receivers.

3. A third dimension is the *understandings of the message receivers*: what meanings are taken by them. Of course, this interpretive element is as problematic as the others. If the listener doesn't understand, she is likely to inquire after what the author meant and to check this by looking for lexical meaning—or the other way around.

4. The fourth dimension reflects a different plane of abstraction: if other paths don't work, what then? Moore answers in part by saying that a court's analysis must include "a judgment checking ordinary meaning, precedent, and purpose against an 'all things considered' value judgment about the best result in this case."[25] To this Moore adds a "balancing" plank for his elements of interpretation.[26] All this, he argues, is how values enter into the interpretive scheme.[27] This is where, on our conceptual map, moral analysis becomes most prominent in interpreting a text.

[23] Mathematical linguists are needed here. See, e.g., Eric W. Weisstein, "*Recursion*," WolframMathWorld, last visited February 28, 2014, <http://mathworld.wolfram.com/Recursion.html>. More generally, some concepts seem to be definitionally linked in an endless referential ping pong—autonomy and personhood may be an example. See Stephen Darwall, *The Second-Person Standpoint: Morality, Respect, and Accountability* (Cambridge, Mass.: Harvard University Press, 2006), 12 (discussing "interdefinability").

[24] The entanglement of some of these axes is displayed in Andrei Marmor, "Truth in Law," in Michael Freeman and Fiona Smith (eds.), *Law & Language: Current Legal Issues* (Oxford: Oxford, 2013), 45, 53:

> [I]n an ordinary conversational context, it is precisely the communication intentions of the speaker that we try to grasp by figuring out what is said (and perhaps implicated, etc.). . . . The assertive content of an utterance is determined by what a reasonable hearer, knowing the relevant conversational background and context, would infer about the speaker's communication intentions from the words or sentences uttered in that context.

[25] Moore, 1985b, 376 (n. 1). Moore is here answering the particular question of how values enter into interpretation.

[26] My interpretive template is meant to include such balancing within the functional relationship among the elements of interpretation.

[27] As Moore argues, the role of moral values is

> . . . first, sometimes (but not always) to aid in the determination of the ordinary meanings of words; second, to enter into the determination of what is the holding of a prior case or line of cases; third, to enter into the formulation of the purpose behind a text; fourth, to determine the

5. Finally (this might be packed into "all-things-considered"), some of the elements of meaning may shift over time. (True, original understanding is theoretically invariant—but not our understanding of that understanding.) We may be able to gauge the *direction and strength of the vectors of change*—but how should this affect interpretation? Although the opinion is hard to parse, *Lawrence v. Texas* seemed to acknowledge the relevance of a "trajectory of conceptual understanding" as part of the interpretation of "liberty." *Lawrence*, as I read it, recognized a liberty interest (entailing elevated scrutiny) in choosing sex partners; it looked to an "emerging awareness" about the expanse of "liberty."[28] Compare this with Justice Scalia's remark that

> [s]ometimes (though not very often) there will be disagreement regarding the original meaning; and sometimes there will be disagreement as to how that original meaning applies to new and unforeseen phenomena [such as sound trucks and television].... In such new fields *the Court must follow the trajectory of the First Amendment*, so to speak, to determine what it requires—and assuredly that enterprise is not entirely cut-and-dried but requires the exercise of judgment.[¶] But the difficulties ... are negligible compared with ... [those] of the philosophy which says that the Constitution *changes*....[29]

What this "trajectory" talk in item no. 5 means is unclear. I simply note that his reference to the "trajectory of the First Amendment" is applied to a trivial conceptual problem. The move from speaking softly to shouting, to using a megaphone, and to operating a sound truck, is a simple linear progression which in no way challenges *our conceptual and moral understanding of the concept of speech or the structure of doctrine.* Sound truck disputes require that we apply our traditional understanding of the value of speech, including access to audiences, and the need for repose and auditory health. But the use of sound trucks doesn't cast doubt on free speech values and their applications. It is *toto caelo* different from, say, asking whether forced biological modification of mental processes—which of course are logical precursors of speech—implicates the First Amendment, or whether the algorithms that computers follow in facilitating traditional speech are themselves speech. This brings us directly to some of the conceptual demands of technology.

V. Technological "Pressure" on Interpretive Processes when the World Deconstructs

Technologies fragment and reassemble nature. This generates new mechanisms, entities, and even interpersonal relationships that are in many respects unfamiliar, confusing, and possibly alarming, as well as interesting. This is especially true when we deconstruct and reconstruct *basic* life processes for specific ends. The results often baffle both description and evaluation: the revised processes and structures may not fit

> all things considered judgment about which interpretation will yield the best results in the particular case; and fifth, to determine the correct balance of each of the preceding four factors.

Moore, 1985b, 376–7 (n. 1).

28 *Lawrence v. Texas*, 539 US 558, 559, 123 S Ct 2472, 2474 (2003).

29 Scalia, "Interpreting the Constitution and Laws," 45 (n. 4) (first emphasis added). My use of "trajectory" is more expansive than Justice Scalia's.

our (seemingly) inert thought frameworks, which rest on a world whose basic features are assumed to endure.

These transfiguring processes seem, at least at first, to deform our conceptual templates. The very power to usefully recombine aspects of life imports an unaccustomed range of choice over matters we historically had to accept as (more or less) given and only marginally adjustable: controlling the traits of future generations, molding our personal attributes while preserving the identities given to us, using sexual recombination as the mode of human reproduction, developing our personal attributes, and controlling the dying process and extending our lives. Is someone who is permanently unconscious a dead person with a living body?[30] If a woman's fertilized ovum is gestated by a second woman, who is "the mother"? Human asexual reproduction (cloning) assails the common understanding of parentage itself: the nuclear source of the offspring's genome is not, biologically, a parent. She is the delayed twin sibling of the nuclear source, whose own parents are—genetically—the offspring's parents.

So, natural kinds may be reassembled—perhaps into largely artificial kinds.[31] Sometimes nature itself does the "reassembly" by defying our expectations, as with intersex persons. (Against whom may intersex athletes compete?) Sometimes it is through accident, as when someone's personality is transformed by brain injury.

This challenge to familiar conceptual realities of moral, legal, and constitutional analysis is what I mean by "technological pressure on constitutional interpretation" (including natural law interpretation). In particular, new powers of control over life processes may result in incentives to construct ever finer calibrations of constitutional values and interests, and thus of their doctrinal implementers—our standards of review. It is one thing to assert that we have a fundamental *right to procreate* that is presumptively abridged by sterilization. It is quite another to assert that we have a *right of person-production* by cloning.

VI. Controlling Human Traits: Natural Law and Originalism Applied to Cloning and Punitive Identity Reconstruction

A. Outlining asexual procreation

Asexual person-production[32] (cloning) is the only extended example I deal with; I refer only briefly to non-voluntary identity reconstruction as a form of punishment.

Cloning refers to producing living entities by replicating an existing genome, rather than sexually recombining portions of two (or more?) genomes. Cloning is now accomplished by inserting the diploid nucleus of a body cell in an enucleated egg, implanting it in a womb, and bringing it to term. Mitochondria (and errors) aside, one gets an exact genomic duplicate of the nuclear source. Eventually, we may develop artificial

[30] See Moore, 1985b, 299, 322–3 (n. 1) (mentioning this in his discussion of death).

[31] For reference to artificial kinds, see Alexander Bird and Emma Tobin, "Natural Kinds", *Stanford Encyclopedia of Philosophy*, first published September 17, 2008, <http://plato.stanford.edu/entries/natural-kinds/>.

[32] By using the term "production," I do not suggest that new procreative techniques objectify persons. Whether this risk would justify interfering with an important constitutional right I cannot address. (I am using "procreation" and "reproduction" interchangeably.)

wombs and the ability to bring diploid nuclei to term without use of ova or pregnancy. The offspring will not be "duplicates" of existing persons; they will not bear their memories and personalities.

Is there a presumptive right (at least in some circumstances) to do this? (Note the "presumptive": this right may exist now even if the risks to the persons produced and to society are so great that governments are justified in preventing cloning. I do not discuss this.)

B. Filling out the hierarchy of constitutional interests and locating procreation within it, via originalism or natural law

We start with procreational autonomy. The bellwether case is *Skinner v. Oklahoma*,[33] where the Court invalidated a law that required sterilization of persons convicted three times of crimes of moral turpitude. Such crimes included larceny but exempted embezzlement. This probably was done because embezzlement requires the victim to have entrusted property to the embezzler, and such trustees are often thought to reside in a different social class from larcenists. The Court, for the first time, said that procreation was the sort of right that triggered strict scrutiny. This was also the first time the Court had expressly announced this argument structure.

The Court's invalidation was based on the Equal Protection Clause. This is interesting and makes for nice academic speculation, but the only way this could have worked is via Justice Douglas's strict scrutiny, which required an independent derivation of the fundamentalness of procreative rights. This—as Chief Justice Stone's concurrence indicated—could not be done solely via the Equal Protection Clause.

"Liberty" is defined nowhere in the Constitution. Not every claim of liberty is presumed to be strongly protected; government could not effectively operate under this burden, and although some might view this as desirable, it is not our world. On the other hand, government can't just operate with minimal scrutiny across the board without trashing our basic values. There must be a hierarchy.

What sort of interpretive account underlies the argument in the preceding paragraph? The Framers of the Due Process Clauses of the Fifth and Fourteenth Amendments didn't present arguments precisely like this, but one might reasonably think they would agree.

But doesn't the account of the two poles of "liberty" (everything/nothing is maximally reviewed) depend on oft-criticized counterfactual analysis?—as in: "What would the Framers have thought about legislative burdens in justifying impingements on different kinds of liberty?"[34] Still, such counterfactual posits seem part of finding what was *meant* by the no-deprivation-of-liberty-without-due-process text in the Constitution.

In any case, if Justice Scalia or other originalists advance this argument-by-counterfactual, are they conflating a principled republican moral/political philosophy, on the one hand, with searching for the Framers' understanding of the Due Process

[33] *Skinner v. Oklahoma*, 316 US 535, 62 S Ct 1110 (1942).

[34] I do not see how any coherent form of originalism can do without counterfactual analysis, but this point is peripheral here. See generally Symposium, "'What If' Counterfactuals in Constitutional History," *45 Indiana Law Review* (2011), 1.

Clauses, on the other? "Conflation" is much too strong. They are using probable Framers' beliefs about political philosophy to infer Framers' lexical understandings, not to aid an independent "moral reading" of the text.

Assume we agree that there is an interests hierarchy and that the interests in the Bill of Rights include many of our top rights. But this leaves open an infinitude of claims of important rights not mentioned, not all of which can be rejected coherently within our normative system, either understood conventionally, or formulated within a moral-realistic framework.

Next: how did procreational autonomy attain high rank on this list? There was a smattering of cases in lower courts saying that certain sterilization statutes were unconstitutional.[35] But there was no extended list of cases—compare *Cruzan*—denying government the power to terminate procreational ability. Then again, American governments did not often seek to burden procreative rights, so the matter rarely arose.

Justice Douglas's somewhat lame argument was that the human race would expire without procreation. Of course, it would expire without food too. (There may be basic rights associated with fair opportunities to avoid inanition.) Perhaps a more persuasive argument would simply have been that there was only the merest sliver of a practice of limiting procreation in America.

We could fancy up the derivation by comparing procreation in America, where it is a personal family-formation project, with its non-parallel in Plato's Republic. The idea there was for the Top People to select persons for mating, the offspring then being removed for raising by another select group.[36] Whether one inspects tradition empirically or pursues true moral analysis, one is likely to find family formation a critical aspect of how we understand "liberty" in any legal text, and in everyday talk. For us, the right to reproduce is not just about creating a child, as the New Jersey Supreme Court foolishly intimated in *In the Matter of Baby M*.[37] There, the court invalidated a traditional surrogacy agreement (the genetic mother also gestated the child), saying:

> The right asserted by the Sterns is the right of procreation; that asserted by Mary Beth Whitehead is the right to the companionship of her child. We find that the right of procreation does not extend as far as claimed by the Sterns.... The right to procreate very simply is the right to have natural children .... It is no more than that. Mr. Stern has not been deprived of that right.[38]

Flapdoodle. Procreation *is* more than that *in context*—and it *generally includes the expectation of companionship with one's offspring*. The distinct line of Supreme Court cases dealing with companionship, rather than procreation, arose when parental (usually paternal) association with the child was compromised, whether through the parent's fault or otherwise. But this does not sever companionship from procreation; they are integral to protected family formation rights in America.[39] We don't just produce

35 E.g., *Smith v. Bd. of Exam'rs of Feeble-Minded*, 85 NJL 46, 88 A 963 (1913).

36 Plato, *The Republic*, Book V. 457–60 (Desmond Lee trans.), (Harmondsworth: Penguin Books, 1955), 211–18.

37 *In re Baby M*, 109 NJ 396, 448–9, 537 A 2d 1227, 1253–4 (1988).

38 *In re Baby M*, 109 NJ at 447–8.

39 See, e.g., *Santosky v. Kramer*, 455 US 745, 747–8, 102 S Ct 1388 (1982) (ruling that due process requires that a state must prove its case by clear and convincing evidence before it can terminate parental rights in their natural child). Genetic connection is not always decisive, however. See *Michael H. v. Gerald D.*, 491 US

persons; we keep and raise them in families, although the family structures may vary widely. Procreation is thus instinct with but distinct from companionship.

Should Justice Douglas have taken such extended routes? Perhaps such derivations seem too complex—a strain on the text—thus casting doubt on their soundness.

In any case, let us take procreation as a fundamental right, without considering what could qualify it, and move on. Human reproduction is a natural kind, but what *kind* of kind? A paradigm that we rely on under any plausible interpretive theory? As we practice it today, it isn't all of a piece, and as a paradigmatic guide, it is fractured and seems to need an overarching meta-paradigm. Thus, we have artificial insemination by donor as well as by husband; *in vitro* fertilization; various forms of implantation of gametes and fertilized ova; surrogacy, traditional and gestational; termination of procreation by abortion; and—to come—artificial gestation entirely outside the woman's body. (What do the abortion cases have to say about extracorporeal gestation? To prevent unplugging the artificial womb is not to prevent *abortion*.) Do these all receive fundamental rights status? We could use some guides for paradigm reconstruction—and the guidance comes from moral analysis, not some handy fixed chief paradigm. Moore did not set out specifically to pursue the task, but Scalia doesn't seem to recognize the problem.

Many writers think that procreational autonomy applies in some strong form to artificial insemination by husband and by donor and to the use of certain fertility techniques (e.g., *in vitro* fertilization). They are less clear about surrogacy and posthumous reproduction.[40] But *some* constitutional protection seems in order for many of these practices, for reasons that parallel those for protecting historical forms of procreation. Indeed, in many of these situations, it is hard to see why anything less than maximal protection should be provided. If gestational surrogacy is the only way a couple can assure that their child is genetically connected to both of them, serious protection seems in order.

But wait. Why should we indulge such a preference? Let them adopt. Recognizing a fundamental right or liberty interest to implement the irrational preference for genetic connection is . . . well, irrational.

It doesn't work that way with fundamental rights, however. For constitutional protection, we don't generally need rational reasons for exercising them—in this case, by generating genetically linked offspring rather than adopting.

Finally, back to the pressure to recalibrate rights: a person's desire to have descendants only after his death is far from the paradigm of nuclear family formation—which usually suggests live parents raising live children. Perhaps it should nevertheless be accorded some intermediate protection.

C. Cloning, originalism, and natural law

Human sexual recombination entails conceptually identifiable mothers and fathers, although gestational surrogacy generates a choice-of-mothers problem (see below).

110, 123–4, 109 S Ct 2333 (1989) (ruling that a genetic father, not married to child's mother, had no liberty interest in a parental relationship with the child).

40 But cf. *Hecht v. Superior Court*, 59 Cal Rptr 2d 222 (Ct. App. 1996) (unpublished) (upholding a woman's right to gain access to sperm of her deceased friend).

With asexual reproduction, matters are more difficult. Many plants reproduce asexually, and some plants and animals do so parthogenetically, but the only confirmed mode of human procreation is sexual union, resulting in offspring with half of each parent's genome. As we saw, the spawn of your body cell nucleus—as opposed to your gametes—is not, biologically, your son or daughter, but your twin.

One would expect some observers to deny this was procreation *at all*, and to hold that it deserves no special protection. Much of the execrable public (and some of the academic) debate on cloning conflates its supposed horrors—some of which *might* justify prohibiting it—with the threshold question whether it is a seriously protected interest. Some even deny it is worth arguing: it is simply too disgusting to tolerate, like bestiality.[41]

On the other hand, cloning is person production and these persons might be intended for inclusion within a family, whether the parents/guardians are genetic strangers, or the nuclear sources, or anyone else. It could also be entirely divorced from family formation of the usual kind (Google as custodian?). We might voluntarily give up our fingernail clippings to the Federal Guardians who would produce persons and raise them, either in foster homes or institutions, for the purpose of raising extraordinary persons who would promote the public welfare. Or something.

It is not easy to specify the paradigm or kind that we are to rely on in the interpretive enterprise. If one checks the traditional meaning of "reproduction," it covers all forms of generating new individuals. But this doesn't tell us whether all such variations can be associated with *human* reproduction.[42] It seems quite a stretch to expect any form of originalism, Scalian or otherwise, to answer whether *the creation of a new person* is all that counts for procreation or the creation of a new person *by sexual recombination* is essential. As Justice Scalia might say, echoing his remarks in *Smith*, either interpretation is permissible. Once again, originalism in any form is *incomplete* as a theory of interpretation. Recall now Justice Scalia's earlier concession that there may be (rare) disagreement about original understanding, but that the Constitution nevertheless cannot change. Change from what to what? Of course, a text is not meaningless even if it seems "empty" in some cases from a particular interpretive framework: there may be no fact of the matter about what the Framers—with or without present-day knowledge— would have thought about cloning, whatever we think they thought about procreation. But if a given interpretive theory yields a blank, it makes little sense to inveigh against "change." How would we be "changing" the Constitution by protecting cloning? There was no exclusion of it. Did Justice Scalia "change the Constitution" in *Smith* by resolving the question of the meaning of "prohibit" left open by the Framers?

Still, "pristine" originalism often includes a "termination" provision: if the search for original text understanding does not tell us whether something is a specially protected right, then it isn't one, and if we don't like it, we should amend the Constitution. Is this instruction a matter of *interpretation* or, instead, of text *displacement* resulting from a moral/political conclusion reached when interpretation—the search for meaning—"runs out"? What seem to be displacements or replacements, however, are not

[41] See Leon R. Kass, "The Wisdom of Repugnance," 216 *New Republic* 17 (June 2, 1997), 17–26.

[42] Noah Porter (ed.), *Webster's Revised Unabridged Dictionary of the English Language* (Springfield, Mass: G. & C. Merriam Co., 1913), 1222.

necessarily wholesale abandonments of the text. The maxim "Resolve doubts against recognizing new fundamental rights, in order to avoid excessively burdening government" *might* be discernible from interpreting larger swaths of constitutional text, or the entire Constitution. One could, of course, defend the squarely opposing maxim, and link the new claim with previous recognitions of right. Cloning, after all, more closely resembles standard procreation than my right to remain unlinked to the sewer system resembles any other precisely defined right.

What does natural law—moral reality—say here? Again, does it serve *as an aspect of text interpretation* or abandonment of the text? On one hand, we are still anchored in the text: *it defines our enterprise's dimensions and thus limits our enterprise*; what we decide *is to be fitted into* our clarified and (possibly) enlarged meaning of the text. On the other hand, our fundamental terms—procreation, mother, parent—have all been assailed, though not fully imploded.

What, then, of cloning? If Scalian originalism didn't work in *Smith*, it's not going to work here. Nor is lexical investigation, whether through dictionaries or polling. One would expect that a reasonable observer would be uncertain whether it would be a form of human reproduction, whether or not they wish it banned. After all, God's creation of Eve from Adam's rib was not a procreative enterprise, whatever it was.

There is a push to view cloning as not within the meaning of procreational autonomy under the Due Process clauses because of its claimed risks and offensiveness. The often hysterical opposition to generally rests on the daft views that persons are being duplicated or made immortal or are "less than human."[43] Sometimes, the state's massive interests suggest that there is no right at the threshold. (There is no fundamental right to practice medicine without a license.) But a different conceptual scheme (with different value overtones) would recognize a threshold right and test it by raising colorable objections—for example, the risk of conditioning, tracking, and enslaving of persons selected for genomic characteristics; and the ensuing reduction of persons to manipulable organisms.

The interpretive enterprise so far has brought us to the two final nodes of the interpretive pentad: the moral analysis and its "all things considered" component, and—possibly included within the latter—the "trajectory" of interpretive developments. Here, the empirical search (full of counterfactuals) for a deep conventional agreement in this uncertain arena might track what we would consider within full-scale moral analysis. (The two are of course conceptually quite distinct.) But, within either track, the moral analysis cannot always rely solely on measuring departures from an agreed-upon paradigm, because the paradigm is contested: if the end stage of person-production is the key, there should be some presumptive constitutional protections for cloning. But if sexual recombination defines human procreation, cloning is out in the constitutional cold.

To be sure, a starting presumption of protection can be overcome, but if constitutional scrutiny is elevated, it cannot rest on misconceptions (cloning is xeroxing) or wild speculation (we will grow hordes of fierce soldiers), or simply on finding it odious. Odiousness may be our stopping point after other analyses have failed—what does one

[43] Jean Bethke Elshtain, "Ewegenics," 216 *New Republic* 25 (March 31, 1997), 25. See also Kass, "The Wisdom of Repugnance," 17–26 (n. 41).

say when others claim that it is fine to torture people just for fun, after one's moral arguments have all been rejected? Revulsion may also be a clue that something may be seriously amiss and requires further analysis. Contrary to Kass's suggestion, however, it is not a morally proper starting-and-ending point for cloning. When rational argument reaches its limits—there are no overarching concepts and arguments left to guide us—then "here I stand" is all we have.[44]

It is time to note Moore's discussion of the definition of "death" and the role of scientific advances in natural law interpretation. There are two striking fractures of life processes involved here. One is the technological separation of the rough concurrence between cardiopulmonary and neurological failure. We can keep persons suffering complete brain failure (including the brain stem) on ventilators that keep their hearts beating.[45] Another is permanent unconsciousness (a vegetative state): the separation of the very possibility of conscious life from the life of the body. Specifying a brain death criterion does not pose huge conceptual challenges, although there are continuing critiques of the concept and disputes over protocols.[46] Learning new scientific facts about something doesn't necessarily change meanings: the centrality of brain failure filled out but didn't trash our understanding of death.

The situation is quite different with permanent unconsciousness. Scientific advances may give us more information about the nature and permanence of unconsciousness in various forms (for example, vegetative states are not comas, from which many patients recover). Nevertheless, *they cannot tell us whether we should truly revise the concept of death* to cover permanent unconsciousness caused by incomplete brain death (the brain stem still functions in vegetative patients), where the living body endures and requires no artificial ventilation to sustain cardiopulmonary functions. This fragmentation poses far more serious conceptual/interpretive problems than those involved in the separation of cardiopulmonary and neurological failure. Thus, one of Moore's points concerning *In re Quinlan*[47] needs elaboration, which he himself supplied in a later observation:

> "Death" is not vague, on a realist theory of meaning, because the word names that natural kind of event whose nature it is the business of science to progressively reveal to us.... That we may not *know* whether the meaning of "death" is such that the word includes in its extension events like those that happened to Karen Quinlan does not entail that meaning itself has run out; only that our present knowledge of it has.[48]

But, as we saw, whether a permanently unconscious person is "really dead" is a far more difficult question than that involved in establishing the brain death criterion, and this is

[44] See generally Michael H. Shapiro, "I Want a Girl (Boy) Just Like the Girl (Boy) that Married Dear Old Dad (Mom): Cloning Lives," 9 *Southern California Interdisciplinary Law Journal* 1 (1999).

[45] One could argue that such *non-spontaneous* heartbeat may signal cardiopulmonary failure.

[46] Supposed "recoveries" from brain death are likely to be diagnostic errors. See Tia Powell, James Zisfein, and Helen Irving, "Letter: We Must Encourage Organ Donors," *Wall St. J.* (March 17, 2012) ("[T]here has never been a documented case of patient recovery after a properly performed determination of death by neurological criteria. Ever.").

[47] Ms. Quinlan was found to be permanently unconscious. Her father sought appointment as guardian of her person so that he could terminate ventilation, and succeeded in the New Jersey Supreme Court. *In re Quinlan*, 70 NJ 10, 54–5, 355 A 2d 647 (1976).

[48] Moore, 1985b, 308–9 (n. 1).

not simply a matter of needing knowledge. It is a matter of moral value, as Moore later indicates:[49]

> Consider (yet again) the word "death." It is plausible to suppose that the best theory of what death is will include some judgments about what attributes are valuable in a person. Consciousness, for example, would be a good candidate for such an attribute. If this is so, a realist court seeking the meaning of "death" would have as part of its job the articulation of those attributes so valuable that loss of their possession entails death.

So it is with cloning. More scientific knowledge may tell us about the risks of the cloning process—such as the incidence of disabilities and defects, including attenuated lifespans from using "old" adult nuclear cells. But this will not inform moral analysis to the point where we can say that "liberty" should include cloning as (at least) a liberty interest drawing non-minimal scrutiny.

D. Applications to punitive identity reconstruction

Suppose the arch-criminal Vladimir is sentenced solely to identity replacement through biological technology. The question for both Scalian originalism and Moorean moral realism is: does the constitutional text (whether we focus on the Eighth Amendment or the more expansive no-deprivation-of-liberty-without-due-process clauses) presuppose that identity endures through punishment in order to constitutionally validate the procedure?

To say that originalism's tank is empty is not to deny all interpretive value to understandings at Framing time. Original understandings are not all-or-nothing matters, despite press reports to the contrary. In *Smith*, for example, we saw that although Scalia invoked the idea of a "constitutional anomaly" related to rule of law, he made little effort to link this to Framers' understandings.

Even at its diaphanous best, it is much harder to apply the counterfactual template "what they must have thought about X" to punitive identity reconstruction using drugs, surgery, and electronic manipulation of the brain.[50] It cannot now be done precisely and satisfactorily, but this may well change. Even with the developing prison system and hints of a rehabilitative ideal at framing time, there is no easy way to fit punitive reconstruction into the exemplars originalists thought the Framers viewed as operationally defining invalid punishments. It may not even be seen as "punishment" in any sense at all. Is it treatment? (For what condition?) Moral enhancement? A reward? Justice Scalia's plurality opinion in *Harmelin v. Michigan* referred to early commentators and courts who spoke of the rack, stake, and "horrid modes of torture."[51] He thus took the Eighth Amendment to ban "only certain modes of punishment."[52] He did not even

[49] Moore, 1985b, 382 (n. 1).

[50] Although not focused on identity reconstruction, this is a useful work: President's Council on Bioethics, *Beyond Therapy: Biotechnology and the Pursuit of Happiness* (Washington, DC: President's Council on Bioethics, 2003). On identity, see Michael H. Shapiro, "The Identity of Identity: Moral and Legal Aspects of Technological Self-Transformation," *22 Social Philosophy and Policy* 308 (2005).

[51] *Harmelin v. Michigan*, 501 US 957, 981, 111 S Ct 2680, 2694 (1991).

[52] *Harmelin v. Michigan*, 501 US at 983.

cite *Trop v. Dulles*, which emphasized the still-operative view that the Eighth Amendment "must draw its meaning from the evolving standards of decency that mark the progress of a maturing society."[53]

The mode of analysis for Justice Scalia's version of originalism thus seems to be comparison of the situation at hand with a relatively small list of standard torments. All are awful in similar ways: the infliction of pain and mutilation. They also impair autonomy and impose humiliating indignities, but *Harmelin* did not indulge such generalizations.

Consider now the interpretive instruction to "compare the case at hand to these illustrations." Doing so doesn't block viewing, as cruel and unusual, situations radically different from what is on the originalists' list of exemplars. Such applications, however, would be beyond anything one would call "originalism." If we do not know whether factor X is central to a paradigm—here, the element of endurance of identity through customary forms of alteration—we do not know the terms of comparison to the standard cases. Advanced technological identity reconstruction might or might not involve gross physical invasion and pain, but this cannot be decisive. "List originalism" can barely address identity reconstruction as either constitutive, or an intended outcome of, punishment. This is particularly so when the changes in one's traits are substantial and discontinuous. The problem is less the absence of disorder model constraints (as with forced medical treatment), but the evanescence of identity.[54] Perhaps some originalists would posit an original understanding that punitive measures applied to persons *already* revamped post-crime would be pointless and thus "cruel and unusual," but this would be difficult for a list originalist. Much the same holds for the question whether it would violate the Eighth Amendment to continue holding or controlling those transformed. After all, they no longer require disablement or specific deterrence, and are probably no longer proper candidates for retribution (A heroic posit, of course.).

Moore's natural law theory, being better grounded than any form of pure originalism because of its proper attention to the interpretive role of objective morality, is more illuminating than its competitors. To be sure, because its mission is to probe value concepts that are imprecise, it will necessarily often yield uncertain results, but at least with him we are on a much better path.

[53] *Trop v. Dulles*, 356 US 86, 101, 78 S Ct 590, 598 (1958).

[54] "Identity change" is a trope for serious trait alteration, even if identity continues.

21

Metaphysical Realism and Legal Reasoning

Brian H. Bix

I. Introduction

Early in my graduate work at Oxford University, I spoke to my supervisor, Joseph Raz, about my interest in studying the intersection of philosophy of language and philosophy of law. One of Professor Raz's recommendations was to read the works of Michael Moore, a theorist with whom at the time I was not familiar. However, I soon learned that Moore was, and is, a highly productive scholar of long, detailed, and important works applying metaphysically realist ideas to legal interpretation, precedent, and theories of the nature of law.[1] By the time I finished my doctoral work, I had probably read more pages written by Moore than I had by any other author on any other topic (with the possible exception of Fyodor Dostoevsky, but I was never able to find a way to incorporate the great Russian novelists into my neo-Wittgensteinian ramblings), and I have added still more hundreds of Moorean pages since then. I have also had the honor and pleasure over the years to learn in person from Moore's incisive verbal responses (to me and others) at numerous legal theory conferences.

My first response to Moore's work on philosophy of language and law was published in the *University of Pennsylvania Law Review*,[2] a text that was subsequently revised as a chapter of my doctoral thesis,[3] and eventually appeared (with further revisions) as a chapter in my book, *Law, Language, and Legal Determinacy*.[4] I have returned to Moore's work sporadically over the twenty or so years since then,[5] as I found his work a rich source of knowledge and challenge as I have worked through my own ideas about legal truth, the role of meaning and authority in law, and the possibility and function of theories of doctrinal areas of law. Overall, I do not think that reading all of those hundreds of pages of his work has (yet) made me into a Moorean acolyte or even a convert to the Moorean project, but I have always left the Moorean texts I have read wiser, and with great respect for the author, even if with less than total agreement. I suspect that

[1] And beyond those, of course, he has produced equally important and voluminous writings on criminal law, causation, constitutional law, and other topics that were outside my graduate-school research agenda and are outside my current expertise.

[2] Brian Bix, "Michael Moore's Realist Approach to Law," 140 *University of Pennsylvania Law Review* 1293 (1992). The principal pieces by Michael Moore discussed in that article were: Moore, 1981; Moore, 1982a; Moore, 1985b; Moore, 1987a; Moore, 1987d; Moore, 1989f; Moore, 1992a; Moore, 1992b. Most of those pieces were subsequently republished in Moore, 2000a.

[3] Brian Bix, "Wittgenstein and Legal Determinacy" (Oxford D. Phil. Thesis, 1991) (on file with author).

[4] Brian Bix, *Law, Language, and Legal Determinacy* (Oxford: Oxford University Press, 1993), 133–77.

[5] Brian H. Bix, "Can Theories of Meaning and Reference Solve the Problem of Legal Determinacy?," 16 *Ratio Juris* 281 (2003); Brian H. Bix, "Global Error and Legal Truth," 29 *Oxford Journal of Legal Studies* 535 (2009).

we now disagree less than we once did, and I would speculate that this is probably more a case of my changing my views (and perhaps also correctly my understanding of Moore's views), in response to his works, than it is a case of Moore's changing his views in response to my comments and criticisms.

Moore's work has advocated a metaphysically realist approach[6] to reference, truth, and meaning, including the meaning and reference of moral terms. He has applied these ideas to law, resulting in what he has characterized as either better practices or a better understanding of our existing practices, in relation to legal reasoning, legal interpretation, and precedent. As regards the nature of law (and theories about the nature of law), Moore has argued that law should be understood as a functional kind (a sort of poor relation to the better known philosophical notion of "natural kinds").[7] He has gone on to show how these approaches collectively constitute necessary, and perhaps sufficient, grounds for believing that propositions within law and about law are objective.

In section II, I consider and raise some questions about Moore's insights regarding the role of metaphysical realism in legal reasoning. Section III looks at a particular subpoint of that general topic, relating to the interaction of authority and metaphysical realism in law. Section IV mentions a distinctive question relating to metaphysical realism—the problem of global error. Section V offers some reflections in response to Moore's idea that law is a functional kind. And section VI concludes.

II. Metaphysical Realism and Legal Interpretation

In earlier writings, my main complaint about Moore's position focused on three different objections: Wittgensteinian doubts about metaphysical realism, questions about whether belief in metaphysical realism would in fact make a difference in legal reasoning, and concerns that Moore's position did not sufficiently take account of the role of authority in law and legislation. There is far too little space to consider here any significant portion of the realist/anti-realist debate (a debate that Moore has portrayed in a number of his publications, and with admirable fairness as well as great sophistication), but I will offer a few comments on the other two themes, and add a few comments on related concerns.

I still hold to the general Wittgensteinian suspicion that our (linguistic and legal) practices are, almost by definition, presumptively fine the way they are[8] (I have offered

[6] I will generally write of "*metaphysical* realism" to distinguish (especially for legal scholars) Michael's preferred approach from American and Scandinavian "legal realism," a quite different set of views. Metaphysical realism "in the widest sense [is] the view that (a) there are real objects ..., (b) they exist independently of our experience or our knowledge of them, and (c) they have properties and enter into relations independently of the concepts with which we understand them or of the language with which we describe them." Robert Audi (ed.), *The Cambridge Dictionary of Philosophy*, 2nd edn. (Cambridge: Cambridge University Press, 1999), 562. On American and Scandinavian legal realism, see, e.g., Brian Bix, *Jurisprudence: Theory and Context*, 6th edn. (London: Sweet & Maxwell, 2012), 193–204, 278–9.

[7] On "natural kinds," see Hilary Putnam, "The Meaning of 'Meaning,'" in *Mind, Language and Reality, Philosophical Papers*, vol. 2 (Cambridge: Cambridge University Press, 1975), 215–71.

[8] See Bix, "Michael Moore's Realist Approach to Law," 1310–13; see also Ludwig Wittgenstein, *Philosophical Investigations* (G. E. M. Anscombe, P. M. S. Hacker, and Joachim Schulte, trans.), rev. 4th edn. (Oxford: Wiley Blackwell, 2009). § 124: "Philosophy must not interfere in any way with the actual use of language, so it can in the end only describe it. For it cannot justify it either. It leaves everything as it is."

this response not only to Moore's metaphysical realist theory, but also to theories that purport to ground their prescriptions for legal practice on Wittgensteinian sources).[9] This may in fact occasion no disagreement. Many of Moore's arguments are probably best understood as (and are, in fact, often expressed as) re-characterizations of what we are already doing: for example, the argument that we are generally metaphysical realists, whether we know it or not; the assertion that lawmakers generally intend the terms of their laws to be understood in a metaphysically realist way, etc. I am far from persuaded, however, that our current legal and linguistic practices require a robust metaphysically realist grounding by way of either explanation or justification.

One of Moore's favorite examples of the presence and value of metaphysically realist approaches to meaning and reference, an example that appears from his early writings to some of his most recent, is the use of the term "death"—for example, in a statute allowing removal of organs for transplant only after a person has died.[10] The concern is that if the statute was written at a time when our more limited ability (e.g.) to revive patients whose heart had stopped led to a conventional equation of death with cessation of heart function, then following conventional understandings of meaning could lead to the absurd and tragic situation of organ removal being authorized for patients who were still capable of being revived.

Advances in medical treatment and technology have granted us not so much greater wisdom about the nature of "death," but rather a greater variety of circumstances when we are both somewhat uncertain about the when to apply the label and at odds among ourselves regarding what is permitted and required in different circumstances. How should we respond to various levels and types of cessation of brain function? If some form of physiological functioning is possible, can treatment be *continued* despite objections of the family (or the patient's prior expressed wishes)?; can treatment be *stopped* despite objections of the family (or the patient's prior expressed wishes)? And so on. I was, and remain, far less convinced than Moore was (and is) that there is something ("death") whose metaphysical nature we now understand better than we once did, or that the seeming exploration of the nature of "death" gives us the right answers to the difficult moral and policy questions we face in the sort of treatment decisions mentioned.[11] If anything, the growing ability to maintain and revive physiological functioning while vast regions of the brain remain non-functional seems only to suggest that the concept "death" may be too simple, and that there might be different types or levels of death.[12]

[9] See, e.g., Brian H. Bix, "Cautions and Caveats for the Application of Wittgenstein to Legal Theory," in Joseph Keim Campbell, Michael O'Rourke, and David Shier (eds.), *Topics in Contemporary Philosophy* (Cambridge, MA: MIT Press, 2005), 217–29.

[10] See, e.g., Moore, 1985b, 293–4, 297–300, 308–9, 322–8, 382; Moore, 2014a.

[11] At the time of writing, there was a legal dispute about whether a woman who is "legally and medically dead" should be kept on life support for the fetus she was (is) carrying, under the apparent requirement of a state statute. Michael Muskal, "What's at Issue in Texas Battle Over Brain-Dead Pregnant Woman," *Los Angeles Times*, January 24, 2014. Eventually a court granted the wish of the woman's family and ordered the woman to be taking off of life support. Manny Fernandez, "Texas Woman is Taken Off Life Support After Order," *N.Y. Times*, January 26, 2014.

[12] Cf. *R. v. Malcherek* [1981] WLR 690, 694 (CA) ("Modern techniques have undoubtedly resulted in the blurring of many of the conventional and traditional concepts of death").

"Death" is an unusual example, to be sure—not quite like the "kinds" or categories that fit most comfortably in the "natural kinds" metaphysically realist approach Moore favors; though neither is it the sort of social practice or human artifact that is most resistant to that sort of analysis. It is more a kind of event, which is independent of our thoughts and perceptions, but not of humanly created complications (through what our medical technology enables).

One can find comparable problems among the sort of terms with which law and legal scholars are commonly concerned. Consider the legal conclusion that two parties had a "valid contract," or that one party's action was the "proximate cause" of the other party's injuries (for the purpose of a tort law claim). Like the conclusion that a patient was "legally dead" for the purpose of an organ donor statute, these are conclusions that contain a mixture of description, morality, and policy. This observation recalls some of H. L. A. Hart's first writings, when he experimented with the idea that legal concepts are "performative utterances"; conclusions that change the (normative) world, rather than being descriptions of that world.[13] This early view by Hart overstated its insight, and Hart correctly retreated from that position in his later works.[14] It is true that court rulings can and do change the normative circumstances, leading to the American legal realist quip that the law is simply (a prediction of) what the judge says it is.[15] At the same time, however, law is not simply a game of (what Hart called) "scorer's discretion."[16] Judicial conclusions are not *merely* performatives, in that they also purport to *describe* the way the (normative and factual) world is, or, perhaps, more precisely, to apply existing (legal) norms to facts—the contract is *declared* to be valid because the judge concludes that under the applicable legal rules *it is (already) valid*. That judges are fallible, and that their decisions, even when erroneous, may yet be final and have legal effects, does not alter the proper characterization of what they do.

At the same time, the fact remains that judges make law, even when they only purport to be describing the existing legal circumstances or to be applying the clear semantic meaning of a legal text. This is partly a function of factors already noted: that judges are both fallible and (sometimes, in some legal systems) authoritative. It is also a function of how judges' decisions (in common-law countries) can change the law, even when judges are only filling in gaps or clarifying ambiguities. The fallible and authoritative aspect of (sometimes unintentional) judicial law-making may be most pronounced and most salient in the interpretation of the broad provisions of constitutions, not least the United States Constitution.[17] However, one might object that all of this has little to do with the value of having the correct theory of meaning and reference. I would respond that the topics area in fact connected, though some of the connections are indirect.

[13] See, e.g., H. L. A. Hart, "The Ascription of Responsibility and Rights," 49 *Proceedings of the Aristotelian Society*, 171–94 (1948–9). The idea of "performative utterances" is taken from J. L. Austin. See J. L. Austin, *How to Do Things with Words* (J. O. Urmson and Marina Sbisá, eds.), (Cambridge, MA: Harvard University Press, 1962).

[14] See, e.g., H. L. A. Hart, *Essays in Jurisprudence and Philosophy* (Oxford: Oxford University Press, 1983), 4–6.

[15] See, e.g., Oliver Wendell Holmes, Jr., "The Path of the Law," 10 *Harvard Law Review*, 457 (1897), 460–1.

[16] H. L. A. Hart, *The Concept of Law*, 3rd edn. (Oxford: Oxford University Press, 2012), 143–6.

[17] See, e.g., Sanford Levinson, "Law as Literature," 60 *Texas Law Review* 373 (1982).

In general, I think that even the theorists who have done the most to bring sophisticated philosophy of language into legal interpretation—like Moore, and, in constitutional interpretation, Lawrence Solum[18]—do not sufficiently note and evaluate how the normative context of language (that terms appear in a rule which requires, prohibits, or authorizes) can affect the words' meaning in application. Moore reports how broad legislative declarations (of "everyone," "no one," or "never," and the like) are frequently understood (or at least judicially interpreted) as included modifications like "unless there is a good reason" or "in a reasonable way,"[19] but draws no further conclusions from this observation. A. M. Honoré once similarly noted[20] that norms (especially legal norms) that contain absolutes—like "all" or "never"—are understood in that context to contain implied exceptions, while such exceptions would rarely be implied or assumed if those same terms appeared in a descriptive sentence.

This point relates to an idea first introduced by H. L. A. Hart, and developed later by other theorists, that defeasibility is common in legal and judicial reasoning.[21] The general notion is that a conclusion—for example that an agreement is a "valid contract," that an action was "reasonable" (in response to a claim of negligence), and so on—is reached tentatively or presumptively, subject to additional facts and considerations. While claims about the defeasibility of or in legal reasoning usually refer to rules as a whole, or the application of rules to particular facts, the basic analysis applies also, directly or by analogy, to single terms within legal norms. That is, whether a particular term within a legal text applies to a set of facts may only be determined tentatively or presumptively by the semantic meaning or realist reference of that term. Additional facts and circumstances brought to the court's attention may persuade (and justify) it in reaching a different conclusion. Because of this sort of dynamic in the understanding and application of legal norms, one should be cautious in applying conventional ideas about semantics, pragmatics, and reference when speaking about the language of legal norms; conventional analysis is best seen as being only *a part* of the overall process of legal reasoning—perhaps a *major* part, and the *starting point* of analysis, but with an important supplement still to be added.

Moore concedes that some legal concepts (his examples include "contract," "malice," and "insanity") should not be treated as natural (or functional) kinds, describing something out in the world whose nature we might come to know better. Rather, he argues, the proper way forward with such legal concepts is to interpret them in light of their purpose.[22] I would go further than Moore, and argue that within legal norms (e.g., statutes, administrative regulations, and constitutional provisions) sometimes even terms that are *not* technical legal terms need to be read in terms of moral, policy, and

[18] See, e.g., Lawrence B. Solum, "The Interpretation–Construction Distinction," 27 *Constitutional Commentary* 95 (2010).

[19] Moore, 2014a.

[20] In a private conversation.

[21] See Hart, "The Ascription of Responsibility and Rights"; Jordi Ferrer Beltrán and Giovanni Battista Ratti (eds.), *The Logic of Legal Requirements: Essays on Defeasibility* (Oxford: Oxford University Press, 2012). Hart's article could be seen as making the argument that defeasibility is essential or intrinsic to law; however, as argued in many of the articles in *The Logic of Legal Requirements*, such an ambitious claim is probably not tenable.

[22] Moore, 2014a.

institutional interests.[23] Admittedly, it is a fine line between saying that the legal norm as a whole should be interpreted a certain way, and stating that the meaning of a term within the norm should be interpreted a certain way—but the ultimate point is that semantic meaning in the context of legal interpretation and legal decision-making is often modified or overridden by moral or policy considerations.

III. Authority, Intention, Interpretation, and Realism

There is a general problem with issues of legal interpretation, a problem which may get the most attention in the United States in interpretation of its Constitution, but comparable issues arise in in all countries, in relation to statutory interpretation and other instances of the interpretation and application of official legal texts.[24] The problem relates to how much attention should be paid to the intention of the lawmakers, and, to the extent that one looks to intention, what resources should be used to discern it.

Within this debate, on one hand is the argument from the central role of authority in law: the claim is that there are officials—executive officers, legislators, administrators, etc.—who are authorized to make choices on behalf of the community, and the role of those (judges and others) who apply legal norms should be focused on recovering the choices made by those decision-makers.[25] This view encourages a focus on lawmakers' intentions, and though one needs to recognize that intentions come at many levels,[26] intentions can be expressed and discerned in different ways,[27] and at least sometimes some of the relevant intentions are specific intentions regarding application. On the other hand are arguments based on "rule-of-law" virtues: citizens should only be bound by the words duly passed by lawmakers following proper procedures, and there should

[23] I discuss this in the context of constitutional interpretation in Brian H. Bix, "Constitutions, Originalism and Meaning," in Grant Huscroft and Bradley W. Miller (eds.), *The Challenge of Originalism: Theories of Constitutional Interpretation* (Cambridge: Cambridge University Press, 2011), 285–99.

[24] See generally Kent Greenawalt, *Legal Interpretation: Perspectives from Other Disciplines and Private Texts* (Oxford: Oxford University Press, 2010); Kent Greenawalt, *Statutory and Common Law Interpretation* (Oxford: Oxford University Press, 2013); Antonin Scalia, *A Matter of Interpretation: Federal Courts and the Law* (Princeton, NJ: Princeton University Press, 1997); Lawrence M. Solan, *The Language of Statutes: Laws and Their Interpretation* (Chicago, IL: University of Chicago Press, 2010); Lawrence B. Solum and Robert W. Bennett, *Constitutional Originalism: A Debate* (Ithaca, NY: Cornell University Press, 2011).

[25] This is the idea of judges as "faithful agents." See, e.g., Greenawalt, *Statutory and Common Law Interpretation*, 20–1; Richard A. Posner, *Law & Literature*, 3rd edn. (Cambridge, MA: Harvard University Press, 2009), 307–8.

[26] At one extreme, lawmakers have at the least the ("minimal") intention to create a (new) legal norm. Lawmakers can intend: that the norm be understood and applied in particular ways in particular circumstances; or that the terms be held to pick out the true nature of some category (whether that category be "fish" or "gold" or "marriage" or "due process") or the conventional understanding of that term (either at the time of law-making or at the time of application); or that decisions about interpretation and application be delegated to judges or other officials. Lawmakers can also intend that particular rules and conventions be used in applying the law. For some overviews of issues relating to intentions, see Richard Ekins, *The Nature of Legislative Intent* (Oxford: Oxford University Press, 2012); see also Greenawalt, *Statutory and Common Law Interpretation*, 33–75; Solan, *The Language of Statutes*, 82–119; Joseph Raz, *Between Authority and Interpretation* (Oxford: Oxford University Press, 2009), 241–98; Ronald Dworkin, *Law's Empire* (Cambridge, MA: Harvard University Press, 1986), 313–54.

[27] When textualists denounce intentionalism, it is usually *not* because textualists deny the importance of determining the intentions of those who made the law, but only because for various reasons (often relating to rule of law concerns) they believe that those intentions can only be discovered through the lawmakers' choice of statutory language.

be due notice to citizens of whatever is required of them. Thus, citizens should not be bound by the privately held intentions of lawmakers or even by "legislative history" if and when (as is usually the case) that record of debates has not been approved through normal voting procedures; additionally, there is the problem that legislative history is not easily accessible to most people.[28] However, being bound "only" by the words still leaves open the question of what the proper focus should be in determining the meaning and application of the legal norms, and we are then brought back to issues about whether to focus on the likely intentions and understandings of the lawmakers at the time of enactment, the reasonable understanding of the citizens at the time of enactment, the reasonable understanding of citizens today, or some other standard.

Moore seems to try to elide the problem of authority and perspective in law by merging and submerging those issues; he does this by declaring that lawmakers (like everyone else, he says) have (or, at least, "should be held to have")[29] the intention that their words be understood according to the words' real (realist) meaning. And while this is likely to be true most of the time, it is not universally or necessarily true, and it seems to be in doubt in some of the most notorious cases. There are instances of legislation where lawmakers intended whales to be included in the definition of fish, and same-sex marriages excluded from the definition of marriage.[30] While it is true that these lawmakers may have thought that these boundary lines reflected the true natures of "fish" and "marriage," it is also true that they almost certainly did not want or intend those boundaries to be re-drawn should experts in the field later come to different conclusions regarding what should be included or excluded. Judges should usually defer to the choices made by lawmakers, and this may sometimes mean selecting against the meaning one would discern from a dictionary or a panel of experts.

Some of Moore's recent work *might* be construed to leave some leeway for the tension between "reason" and "fiat" in lawmaking to play out, though he tends not to emphasize that leeway.[31] Moore writes:

> Over the past quarter century I have used many examples of legal texts where the best interpretation took the words in them to refer to natural or moral kinds. [Giving examples.] In each case the argument was not just that certain natural or moral kinds existed so that they could be referred to by the words in legal texts, nor even that the authors of such texts intended to so refer in the choice of their words. Rather, the complete argument included a moral premise, *viz.*, that the value behind the rule was best

[28] The best-known advocate in recent years of this "rule-of-law" position has been US Supreme Court Justice Antonin Scalia. Scalia, *A Matter of Interpretation*. There may be "rule-of-law" reasons for favoring the conventional understanding of terms over either the best scientific understanding or the lawmakers' intentions. See, e.g., *Nix v. Hedden*, 149 US 304 (1893) ("tomato" should be classified as a vegetable for the purpose of a statute, not as a fruit, even if scientists would classify it as a fruit; the common understanding should prevail over the scientific in applying statutes).

[29] Moore, 1985b, 323.

[30] The reference of the marriage law is of course to the Defense of Marriage Act codified at 1 USC § 7; 28 USC § 1738C. Part of that law was invalidated in *US v. Windsor*, 133 S Ct 2675 (2013).

[31] On reason vs fiat (or "will") in the law, see, e.g., Brian H. Bix, "Will versus Reason: Truth in Natural Law, Positive Law, and Legal Theory," in Kurt Pritzl (ed.), *Truth: Studies of a Robust Presence* (Washington, DC: Catholic University of America Press, 2010), 208–31.

served by construing such words as referring to a kind whose nature was to guide legal meaning.[32]

The argument thus is that in many—perhaps most—occasions, there is a convergence between the metaphysically realist meaning (reference) of terms, the intentions of the lawmakers regarding the meaning and application of terms, and the effectuation of the (moral) purpose behind the rules. However, it also shows, indirectly, how there can be, and likely will be, occasions where the different factors point in different directions: for example, where the lawmakers have meaning and application intentions different from (our current best understanding of) the metaphysically realist meaning of terms, or where the values behind a rule are best served by deviating from the lawmakers' intentions *or* from the metaphysically realist meaning of terms.

While accepting the possibility (or even the probability) of such potential conflicts may complicate Moore's analysis, it need not require any radical alterations in his views. There will simply be occasions where we need to determine the correct or best answer that takes into account different factors (Moore allows for the need of comparable balancing elsewhere in legal reasoning, e.g., in how the proper interpretation of a contract may involve "a functional kind whose nature is partly given by the true metaphysics of events and partly given by conventions and intentions").[33]

IV. Realism and Global Error

One advantage of metaphysical realism, as Moore has pointed out, is that it directs judges and advocates to focus on finding the correct answer rather than holding that language (or law) runs out and we must legislate anew.[34] Meaning is in principle independent of current understandings and beliefs regarding an object, and therefore one can believe that a right answer exists for some dispute (e.g., about the meaning or reference of some term), despite pervasive disagreement, and despite significant changes in related practices and conventions. Similarly, metaphysically realist approaches make it easier to make sense of the understanding and application of terms uttered or written long ago—whether it is the texts of ancient Greek philosophers or the terms of a constitutional text written over 200 years ago.[35]

The danger, however, may be at the opposite side of the analysis. If the right answer in some area of discourse is (largely) independent of our current beliefs and practices, this allows the possibility of radical and global error—that is, situations where everyone is wrong about some matter. In the case of a realist or right-answer approach to propositions of law,[36] then it could be the case that all officials, and all citizens as well, might be wrong on what the law is and what the law requires. The problem of global error for

[32] Moore, 2014a.

[33] See Moore, 2014a (referring to the insurance policy interpretation issue of whether the 9-11 attacks on the World Trade Center constituted "two events" or "one event" for the purpose of the policy coverage).

[34] In this, Moore's view parallels Ronald Dworkin's, though Moore's view of Dworkin's work was that Dworkin's ontological views could not ground the views of justification that he (Dworkin) put forward. See Moore, 1987a (reviewing Ronald Dworkin, *A Matter of Principle* (Cambridge, MA: Harvard University Press, 1985)).

[35] See Moore, 2014a.

[36] Cf. Moore, 2003a.

law is that it seems contrary to basic understandings for such a practice-based discourse.[37] As Andrei Marmor writes: "Surely, no conventional understanding of law could allow for the possibility of an extensive misidentification of the law.... [S]uch an extensive misidentification of the law would seem profoundly mysterious."[38]

Moore might respond that global error is not likely to occur frequently under his approach, and on the rare occasion when it does occur, it would not be problematic. On one hand, the truth of legal propositions for him is partly a function of the actual actions of legal officials (e.g., through the enactment of laws and the promulgation of decisions that have precedential force), so it would be unusual for legal truth to deviate sharply and universally from the beliefs of officials and citizens. On the other hand, those occasions where someone might claim global error under Moore's approach would be situations where such claims would be sensible (i.e., not nonsensical) and relatively unproblematic. For example, there might be a claim of global error where the legal truth of a proposition turned on the proper understanding of some moral or natural kind, and (the claim would continue) current conventional understandings of that kind are all badly mistaken.[39] One possible example would be something like the American prohibition on "cruel and unusual punishment" in the Eighth Amendment to the US Constitution. Altering the facts relating to the Eighth Amendment only slightly: perhaps a vast majority of those who drafted, passed, and ratified that amendment believed that capital punishment would not be prohibited by it, but (an argument could be made that) the proper understanding of the moral standard "no cruel and unusual punishment" would in fact require invalidating any law authorizing capital punishment. The result would be a situation where everyone, or nearly everyone, in some period of time would be mistaken as to the validity of statutes imposing capital punishment for certain offences. In cases like this, where assertions of global error derive from natural kinds, moral kinds, or the like, it seems likely that Moore would endorse (rather than feel the need to deny or flee from) a claim of global error.

V. Law as a Functional Kind

Moore has argued that "law"—in the sense of the category whose nature is sought in jurisprudential theories of law—is best understood *not* as a natural kind (for there is no structural grounding for the kind as there is, e.g., for "gold" or "water")—but rather as

[37] On the problem of global error in law, see, e.g., Brian H. Bix, "Global Error and Legal Truth"; Matthew H. Kramer, "Is Law's Conventionality Consistent with Law's Objectivity?," 14 *Res Publica*, 241 (2008); Andrei Marmor, *Interpretation and Legal Theory* (Oxford: Oxford University Press, 1992), 85–102.

A separate, related objection sometimes raised about metaphysical realism is that it encourages radicals and eccentrics, as claims need no longer be tied to what most people, or at least a significant number of people, believe (of course, others might say this is the *benefit* of metaphysical realism, that it rightly opens up the possibility for prophets and grand reformers).

[38] Marmor, *Interpretation and Legal Theory*, 96–7.

[39] As I discuss in my article, another "acceptable" claim of global error might arise where the legal system gives authoritative status to the historical intentions of the framers of a constitution or some other old legal text, and there is (allegedly) currently widespread error about those intentions. See Bix, "Global Error and Legal Truth," 542–3. However, as Michael believes that lawmakers' intentions are usually to have their texts interpreted in a metaphysically realist way, he would probably doubt that claims of global error would or should arise based on mistakes about intentions.

a "*functional* kind."[40] Functional kinds exist where the category is defined by a common function (e.g., a "knife" might be defined as anything that cuts). Overall, Moore's analysis of law as a functional kind can be seen as an elaboration and improvement on Lon Fuller's "procedural natural law" approach to law (as Moore himself notes).[41] However, Moore remained somewhat agnostic about which distinctive end(s) law might serve, and was not entirely satisfied with the answers to that question given by Fuller, Ronald Dworkin, or John Finnis.[42] John Gardner has recently offered a different understanding of Fuller's approach, an understanding which was also offered as a response to Moore: Gardner sees law *not* as a functional kind (or even a "formal" kind), but rather as a "modal kind" (a view Gardner believes can be attributed also to H. L. A. Hart and Hans Kelsen).[43] This reflects a difficulty Moore had earlier seen in the functional kind approach to law: there are problems in determining the functions *distinctive* to law.[44] Gardner expands the critique, stating: "law is not *distinguished* by its functions .... It is distinguished rather by the distinctive means that it provides for serving whatever ends it serves."[45]

Rather than arbitrate this dispute, one might place it in a larger context. One general problem for those who put forward theories about the nature of law—or views of other scholars' theories about the nature of law—is that the discussion soon seems a practice somewhere between "different views of the cathedral"[46] and six blind men and an elephant. I have written elsewhere on how one can see the disagreement between legal positivists and natural law theorists as in part a difference in focus or emphasis—whether one sees law primarily as a kind of social institution or as a kind of practical reasoning.[47] If one suspects that law is both a type of social institution *and* a central part of practical reasoning, one might reasonably wonder if one could ever find the one "right" theory of law (that could do justice to both aspects of law). One can find many similar broad-scale concerns about the proper approach to theorizing about the nature of law, coming from a variety of directions: for example, arguments that conventional analytical theories are insufficiently concerned about the connection between law and state or insufficiently attentive to forms of law other than municipal legal systems;[48] and arguments that conflicting analytical theories simply reflect either different political cultures[49] or different moral choices.[50] This variety of theoretical (and

[40] Moore, 1992a. As Michael puts it: "Law . . . seem[s] to be good for something more than it seems to have a structural essence ...." Moore, 1992a, 221.

[41] E.g., Lon L. Fuller, *The Morality of Law*, rev. edn. (New Haven, CT: Yale University Press, 1969).

[42] Moore, 1992a, 219–27.

[43] See John Gardner, *Law as a Leap of Faith* (Oxford: Oxford University Press, 2012), 195–220.

[44] The further complication for those who would offer a functional theory as a *natural law* theory of law, as Michael shows, is that the function law serves must be intrinsically good (leading perhaps to an untenable conclusion that law's function might be serving *all* things that are intrinsically good). Moore, 1992a, 217–27.

[45] Gardner, *Law as a Leap of Faith*, 207.

[46] See Guido Calabresi and A. D. Melamed, "Property Rules, Liability Rules, and Inalienability: One View of the Cathedral," 85 *Harvard Law Review* 1089 (1972).

[47] Brian Bix, *Jurisprudence: Theory and Context*, 7th edn. (London: Sweet & Maxwell, 2015), 80–1.

[48] See Keith Culver and Michael Giudice, "Making Old Questions New: Legality, Legal System, and State," in Wil Waluchow and Stefan Sciaraffa (eds.), *Philosophical Foundations of the Nature of Law* (Oxford: Oxford University Press, 2013), 279–300.

[49] See Dan Priel, "Is There One Right Answer to the Question of the Nature of Law?," in Waluchow and Sciaraffa (eds.), *Philosophical Foundations of the Nature of Law*, 322–50.

meta-theoretical) perspectives is substantial, even if one brackets off those (like Brian Leiter) who raise questions about the possibility and value of any general theory about the nature of law.[51] Those of us who continue to work on that most clichéd of jurisprudential questions, "what is law?," need to do more work than we already have to justify both that quest and the assumption that there are correct, valuable, and (perhaps) unique answers to be found.

Returning to Moore's view of law as a "functional kind," one might be skeptical, given the variety of functions that legal systems (in the US and other countries) can and do serve, that a single function can be found for law that is both distinctive to law and that is specific enough to be able to ground theoretical insights about law's nature.

VI. Conclusion

It is a lifetime's work to do justice to the arguments Michael Moore has raised in his works on language, meaning, morality, and the law, and the impressive fact is that these collectively constitute only a fraction of the areas to which Moore has made substantial contributions. If the significance of theorists can be judged by the way that their work continues both to teach and to challenge, Moore's work remains among the most important in legal theory. The relationship between philosophy of language and philosophy of law remains an under-explored area, and legal theorists are tasked with the work of adding to what Moore has already taught us.

In particular, I think that there is still work to be done to determine the limits of realist approaches to interpretation, and to discover a principled guide to when and how realist meanings should be overridden. There are also issues relating to legal truth and when the conventional grounds of law foreclose a claim of global error. And there are further explorations to be made regarding whether law is best thought of as a functional kind or a modal kind, and whether either approach can withstand a naturalism-based challenge to theorizing about law in general.

[50] See, e.g., Stephen R. Perry, "Interpretation and Methodology in Legal Theory," in Andrei Marmor (ed.), *Law and Interpretation* (Oxford: Oxford University Press, 1995), 97–135.

[51] See, e.g., Brian Leiter, *Naturalizing Jurisprudence: Essays on American Legal Realism and Naturalism in Legal Philosophy* (Oxford: Oxford University Press, 2007). Leiter's attack on conceptual analysis in jurisprudence would likely affect a functional kinds analysis as well: at a minimum, it would likely require that the claim be altered from "this is the nature of law" to something like "this accurately tracks our current usage of the term 'law.'"

22

Law and the Role of a Judge

*Leslie Green**

I. Introduction: The Problem

Every society that has law also has people who perform the role of a judge. They need not be called "judges"; they may be "priests," "elders," "kings," or something else. Nor need they be thought of specifically as judges. The society may not distinguish between, say, a judicial role and a priestly role; in religious legal systems it is fairly common for these to be fused. But it is a feature of legal systems of any kind that they have at least some officials who settle disputes by applying pre-existing standards. That marks an important difference between law and other forms of social regulation, such as coercion, mediation, or arbitration. When there is a legal system, there are not only people who can make people do things, guide their conduct, and settle their disputes, but people with a duty to do that by applying law.

That law stands in an important relation to the judicial role is widely agreed among legal theorists. What the relationship amounts to has been disputed. It has been suggested that laws are generalizations that predict the decisions of judges, norms addressed to judges, norms that judges are entitled to enforce, or norms that those subject to judicial decisions are required to obey. The thesis I explore here is different. According to it, laws are *norms that judges have a moral obligation to apply*. Some writers propose a purely negative version of this thesis: a norm that is morally defective—for example, one that is intolerably unjust—is not a legal norm at all, or at least not a standard case of a one: *lex injusta non est lex*. Here, I test a positive version of the thesis. In this version, not only do certain kinds of immorality disqualify standards as law, but moral credentials stand as sufficient affirmative qualifications for something being law. Michael Moore defends a bold version of the positive thesis, so I will take his account as the springboard for my inquiry. He writes, "jurisprudence should tie law strictly to judicial obligation, so that if a standard does not give a judge an obligation it is not part of the law."[1] So far, this is a version of the familiar negative thesis. But Moore also maintains, "Not only is law conceived as whatever obligates judges, but the role of judging is conceived in terms of decision-making constrained by those standards we think of as law."[2] So we have this: law is whatever obligates judges, and judging is a role constituted by the application of all and only those standards that are obligation-imposing.

* I thank the editors, Thomas Adams and James Grant for criticism of an earlier draft of this chapter; I thank Michael Moore for his response, and for many years of generosity and discussion.

[1] Moore, 2000a, 96. [2] Moore, 2000a, 95.

To forestall some possible misunderstandings, let me stress a few initial points about the thesis. First, Moore does not merely mean that laws are such that judges have a *legal* obligation to use them; he means that they have a *moral* obligation to do so. Second, his claim is not that all legally binding standards are themselves obligations—the law also contains norms that confer powers or permissions, as well as things that are not norms of any kind, for instance, definitions and assertions of value. The claim is that these are law if and only if there is a moral obligation to *use* or *apply* them (in the way that a law of that kind is to be used or applied). Third, there is no suggestion that law necessarily imposes moral obligations on its (non-official) subjects. That judges have a moral obligation to apply the law does not presuppose or entail that subjects have a moral obligation to obey the law. It is consistent with Moore's thesis that law's ordinary subjects owe it nothing at all and may blamelessly treat it as a mere price system. (Moore does not endorse that view, but he expressly leaves open what is usually called the "problem of political obligation.") Finally, although the obligation binds people in their role as judges, the obligatory standards have a mutually constitutive relationship to that role. To repeat the passage I quoted above, "the role of judging is conceived in terms of decision-making constrained by those standards we think of as law."[3]

Moore thinks of this as amounting to some kind of "natural law" position, no doubt because it ties the existence of law to the satisfaction of tests of moral propriety. I shall not address this aspect of his view. It is more important to know whether the view is correct than whether it is loyal to the tradition of natural law.[4] Anyway, Moore makes clear, in an ecumenical spirit, that he does not think his is the only possible sort of jurisprudence. The view just described is what he calls "internal" jurisprudence; a theory that approaches the nature of law from within what is assumed to be a legal system and identifies its law in terms of standards that certain actors in that system have reason to think morally binding.[5] But he acknowledges that there is an independent and intelligible project of trying to figure out what sorts of institutions amount to legal systems in the first place. That would be what Moore calls "external" jurisprudence; the sort of project undertaken by Aristotle or Aquinas, Bentham or Kelsen, who ask from a general point of view what is the nature of law as such. External jurisprudence has no ambition to instruct judges in a particular system how to decide their cases; its ambitions are to explain and evaluate familiar social institutions.[6]

My main interest here is in the claim that, within anything that is undeniably a legal system, the law is the set of all and only those standards that are morally binding on its judges, as judges. I have doubts about that. I am not the first to be skeptical: natural

[3] Moore, 2000a, 95.

[4] For contrasting views, which also have some claim to the title "natural law," see the works of Lon Fuller or John Finnis, who think law is something that its subjects have a moral duty to obey, or Ronald Dworkin, who thinks that law is something that justifies the authorities' power to coerce.

[5] Compare Ronald Dworkin's later suggestion that there is both a "sociological" and a "doctrinal" concept of law, in his *Justice in Robes* (Cambridge, Mass: Harvard University Press, 2006), 226–7.

[6] I say "explain and evaluate" because general jurisprudence addresses both descriptive and normative questions, including whether certain evaluative standards apply to law in virtue of the nature of law as a social institution. H. L. A. Hart thought that. He held that we can know whether something is a legal system without engaging in moral evaluation of it, but also that there are moral standards up to which law, as law, should live: H. L. A. Hart, *The Concept of Law*, 3rd edn. (Intro Leslie Green, eds., P. A. Bulloch and J. Raz), (Oxford: Oxford University Press, 2012), 160–7; 193–200.

lawyers and legal positivists have both rejected that thesis, and I rely on some of their arguments here.[7] But I also try to advance the discussion by examining in closer detail what the judicial role amounts to and how law-application figures in it. To anticipate, I argue: (1) Some standards that a judge is morally obligated, *qua* judge, to apply are not law. (2) The role of a judge is not exhaustively constituted by the duty to apply the law, or indeed by any single duty. (3) The other obligations of a judge are related to the obligation to apply the law, but they do not arise from principles of law. The judicial role also includes important creative powers anchored in principles of the rule of law. These principles do bind judges as judges, but they are not principles of law.

II. A Simple View

Let us begin with a simple view according to which any standard whatever that a judge has a moral obligation to use in deciding a case is part of the law. This is not Moore's official view; I will introduce that in section III. But it is helpful to begin by seeing what is wrong with the simple view. It is vastly over-inclusive. Here are three obvious counterexamples.

Consider the law of damages. In a personal injury case, English judges must determine what a successful claimant is owed by combining damages suffered under various "heads": medical expenses, travel costs, loss of future earnings, pain and suffering, loss of amenity, and so forth. How to determine the total owed under any head? That is easy—just add up the relevant costs; take the sum. The same goes for the damages overall. The sums are determined by ordinary principles of arithmetic. Someone who could not do arithmetic (or who could not get it done) would be a very poor judge. Of course, what a judge needs in this department is arithmetic "know-how," not any kind of "knowing-that." He needs to know how to add; he does not need to know the unique-factorization theorem. But if in reckoning damages a judge did anything *other* than add—for instance if he awarded only the amount under the category that registered the highest loss, or if he multiplied the individual components together—it would not merely be an arithmetical error. It is immoral to short-change the claimant or to fleece the defendant; a judge has a duty to get the sums right. Nonetheless, principles of arithmetic are not laws of England. When Korean children learn arithmetic, they have not learned a little English law. Arithmetic is universal in application; its content is unconnected with the activity of any English political institution; it is known and understood in a way different to the law. Contrast the principle that damages must be reckoned as a single, lump sum payment, or the principle that pension contributions are to be deducted before calculating an employee's actual loss of earnings. These principles are law. They are not binding everywhere; they have not always been in force in England, and their existence and content is dependent on decisions of courts and others.[8]

[7] Especially E. Philip Soper, "Legal Theory and the Obligation of a Judge: The Hart/Dworkin Dispute," 73 *Michigan Law Review* 473 (1977); Joseph Raz, "Incorporation by Law," 10 *Legal Theory* 1 (2004) (Reprinted in his *Between Authority and Interpretation: On the Theory of Law and Practical Reason* (Oxford: Oxford University Press, 2009).

[8] *Wells v. Wells* [1998] 3 All ER 481 (lump-sum principle); *Dews v. National Coal Board* [1987] 2 All ER 545 (pension deductions).

What holds for arithmetic also holds for the syntactic, semantic, and pragmatic principles of a natural language. In every jurisdiction, the law has at least one mother tongue—its official language. In England (and elsewhere) the law speaks in English. Judges and lawyers in that jurisdiction therefore have to worry a lot about what English words, sentences, and whole documents mean. It would be wrong of them not to: we depend on the law being intelligible to us, and our lawmakers speak so as to be understood, if not by laypeople then at least by the lawyers who must advise them. But the English lexicon and rules of grammar are not English laws. Does the literal or "plain" meaning rule of interpretation suggest otherwise? Isn't that what makes the stop sign at an intersection mean "Stop"? (Instead of, say, "Call your mother"?) Of course not. English makes it mean that. The plain meaning rule functions in the context of other legal rules. It holds that when the ordinary meaning of a provision is clear, unambiguous, produces no absurdity, and serves some intelligible purpose, then it is to be construed in accordance with that meaning, notwithstanding other available principles of interpretation. But it is not the plain meaning rule that *provides* the ordinary meaning of English words. Like the lump-sum and pension-deduction principles, the plain meaning rule rests on legal sources; its popularity has waxed and waned over time; its merits are arguable.[9] Legislatures and courts control and shape it; they have no similar control over the plain meaning of ordinary English words.

Finally, consider ordinary moral principles. Judges should protect rights, do justice, promote the common good, and more still. Other things being equal, they ought to conform to all these standards whenever and wherever they apply the law. But not because these standards are law, and not because of anything that someone thought, said, or did that made them relevant to legal decisions. As Joseph Raz puts it, "Why are judges, and humans generally, subject to morality? This is due to the nature of morality. It has no doctrine of jurisdiction setting out its conditions of application. It applies universally to all agents capable of understanding it."[10] That is so: if morality applies anywhere, it applies also in court. It is true that special features of adjudication tend to make certain moral principles—such as the requirement for impartiality in decision, or for consistency among decisions—more stringent than they are in other departments of life. It is also true that the law may direct or permit people to do something other than what morality would require in the absence of legal institutions and that, where the authority of law is legitimate, this may be morally justified. But it is wrong to think of any of this as law incorporating morality by reference, or somehow making morality relevant to decisions on which, but for the say-so of some court or legislature, it would not bear.

Like principles of arithmetic or grammar, moral principles apply of their own force to the activities to which they are relevant. Owing to the importance of the interests that law regulates, and the allocative and expressive upshots of judicial decisions, moral principles are inevitably relevant in court. No plug-in or adapter is needed to connect moral standards to judicial decision-making. They are already connected, unless they get (legitimately) disconnected. And, like arithmetic and grammar, sound moral principles do not vary among legal systems except where there is variation in the facts on which they supervene.

9 *Sussex Peerage Case* (1844) 11 Cl & Fin 85: *Fisher v. Bell* [1961] 1 QB 394.
10 Raz, "Incorporation by Law," 2.

In pointing to this analogy between the legal relevance of arithmetic, grammar, and morality I am not, of course, suggesting that these operate in the same ways in the law. For one thing, judges give much more explicit attention to moral standards, and legislators frequently make explicit mention of them when they make law. Arithmetic and grammar, on the other hand, tend to operate more quietly in the background, being used without being mentioned, save in cases of doubt about what they require. Legislators felt no need explain multiplication, division, addition, and subtraction when they said:

> There may be deducted from the amount deemed by subsection 146.3(6) to be received by an annuitant out of or under a registered retirement income fund an amount not exceeding the amount determined by the formula $A \times [1 - ((B + C - D) / (B + C))]$[11]

They did not need to say anything about arithmetic because, well, everyone already knows how to add, subtract, multiply, and divide (and, if they do not, instructions in the "Interpretation" section of the Income Tax Act are unlikely to help).

With respect to morality things are often different. Here, legislators and judges become articulate and sometimes garrulous. Statutes and constitutions explicitly prescribe ideals such as "equality before and under the law"; they expressly prohibit "inhuman and degrading" punishments; they assert all sorts of "human rights." Judicial decisions then comment at length on what these standards require. Even without any invitation from statutory language, judges often explain what they think would be "reasonable," "fair," or required by "common sense" in the case before them. If morality is like arithmetic or grammar, then why does that law mention it so much more often? Is it merely that knowing how to use the concept of "equality" or "degradation" is trickier than knowing how to subtract or divide?

Sometimes—but not always. Even when the force of moral requirements is clear, there are several reasons we hear so much about them in court. First, moral standards may remain crucially relevant to a case even after considering the bearing of positive law, and ordinary moral argument is articulate. If we want to contend that a certain procedure is oppressive, or that a penalty would in the circumstances be unjust, we normally do so explicitly using those terms and explaining why they apply. Second, not all use of moral language in court is what it seems. Some moral terms have legal homonyms. "Equality" is a very broad moral principle; but in court it often picks out a technical, legal principle subject to source-based tests for what it demands: equality before or under the law, "formal" but not "substantive" equality, or the reverse, but in any case equality as the law sees it. Or again: "harm" is a moral notion; but judges who rule that films are criminally obscene only if "harmful" often look to community standards, not to moral arguments, to decide what is harmful.[12] Third, some overt references to morality in the law are there to counteract the effects of legal standards. For example, the Canadian Charter of Rights and Freedoms empowers those whose rights are violated to apply "to obtain such remedy as the court considers appropriate and just in the

[11] Income Tax Act RSC 1985, c. 1 (5th Supp) section 146 (Canada).

[12] For example, *R v. Butler*, [1992] 1 SCR 452 (Supreme Court of Canada). For discussion see Leslie Green, "Men in the Place of Women, from Butler to Little Sisters" 43 *Osgoode Hall Law Journal* 473 (2005), 479–82.

circumstances."[13] Does this make justice a principle of Canadian law? Would it have been fine for judges to grant inappropriate and unjust remedies if that clause had not made it into the final draft of the Charter? Of course not. The quoted provision reclaims space for justice by limiting the impact of legal principles including, here, an express constitutional provision for judicial review together with a long-standing judicial prejudice in favour of striking-down as the sole proper remedy for unconstitutionality. The remedial provision reins that in, and allows moral principles to claim their natural place in crafting remedies. Unless modified by law, these principles bind all judges everywhere, and we know they are binding before we learn anything else about a given legal system.[14] We need to study the law of that system in order to know what is binding there as well as, or instead of, what morality permits and requires.

III. Roles and Obligations

These examples show that the simple view is incorrect. They appeal to our ordinary understanding of law. They can be supported by theoretical considerations that I have not mentioned.[15] But perhaps they miss the point? The counterexamples rely on the fact that it would be wrong for judges not to apply ordinary standards of arithmetic, grammar, or morality in contexts where those are, of their nature, applicable and where legal authority has not intervened to change matters. Judges are obligated to use these standards, in the phrase I quoted from Raz, "because judges are humans": humans who need to calculate, humans who need to use a language, humans who need to conform to moral principles. However—and this is what suggests the counterexamples may miss their target—Moore does not say that whatever is morally binding on a judge (*qua* human) is part of the law. He says that, "Law obligates judges in their role as judges . . ." by which he means law is "that which binds the occupant of [an] office": law is "binding on legal actors *qua* legal actors."[16] Does this qualification make a difference? If it does, perhaps the counterexamples involve standards that judges are morally obligated to apply, but not standards they are morally obligated to apply *as judges*. To know whether this makes a difference, and if so what difference it makes, we need to investigate more closely the relationship between social roles and moral obligations.

Some obligations are binding only on people performing given roles. Only the dog-catcher has a duty to catch stray dogs. Other obligations bind everyone, but they bind people within roles in a different way than they bind people outside them. Anyone is owed an explanation if reprimanded for poor job performance, but the Dean must reprimand an instructor in writing and give an opportunity to respond.

A social role, like the closely related notions of a "station" or "office" or even "job," picks out a set of norms, values, and expectations that apply to people in virtue of the fact that they hold that role. Obligations that come with a role are in some ways like

[13] Canadian Charter of Rights and Freedoms, s. 24(1), Part I of the Constitution Act, 1982, being Schedule B to the Canada Act 1982 (UK), 1982, c. 11.

[14] Can law modify morality? See Leslie Green, "Should Law Improve Morality?," 7 *Criminal Law and Philosophy* 473 (2013).

[15] Hart, *The Concept of Law*, 3rd edn., 200–12; Joseph Raz, "Authority, Law and Morality," 68 *The Monist* 295 (1985). Moore criticizes the second line of argument: 2000a, ch. 5.

[16] Moore, 2000a, 5.

what philosophers call "special obligations" that bind people standing in a particular relationship or performing a particular activity. Yet not all special obligations are role obligations. Consider an ordinary promise. It creates a paradigmatic special obligation: it binds the promisor in particular and does so in virtue of the fact that he made a promise. Nonetheless, "promisor" is not the name of a role; it is merely the logical subject of a promissory obligation. We do not assume the role of promisor and then get a duty to keep our promises; we just promise. In this respect, "promisor" is like "tortfeasor"; it is no more than the name for someone who did a certain morally relevant thing. It is a mark of roles, in contrast, that they consist of norms that cohere in a way that warrants us thinking of the role as a unity different from its occupant, and one that might in principle have another or a different occupant. Legal systems are replete with roles like that: judge, juror, policeperson, bailiff, legislator, sovereign, and so on. Unlike "promisor" or "tortfeasor", these are not merely names for the subjects of special obligations; they have a deeper legal and moral existence.[17]

Four features seem to characterize such roles:

1. A role is cluster of norms (e.g., obligations, powers, permissions) that apply to its occupant, together with virtues and expectations that support those norms.
2. Role-norms apply to the occupant of the role at least partly in virtue of the fact that he occupies that role.
3. A role can have more than one possible occupant, either at the same time or sequentially.
4. Role-norms typically function together as a package: some are binding only because others are; some support conformity to the others; some influence the interpretation of the others.

This characterization attempts to explain, while sharpening, our familiar notion of a role. It does not offer any account of why role-norms are valid, that is, why they are binding on their occupants. It is important to be clear about that. Point (2) is often misunderstood. A role necessarily identifies the obligations of its occupants, but this is not enough to justify those obligations. For that we need to appeal to moral considerations external to the role.[18] What can be misleading is the fact that to someone who asks "Why do I owe my client a duty of confidentiality?" we can informatively answer, "Because you are his lawyer." That will be informative whenever someone knows she is a lawyer but has not yet grasped all that it entails. In such cases, the explanatory "because" does not give the ground of a duty, it merely identifies it *as one of* a lawyer's duties. The identificatory function is also present in roles that are morally repugnant and should not be performed at all, not even by those who voluntarily assume them (Mafia *capo*, Guantanamo torturer, etc.). In such cases we can informatively say that it

[17] How far special obligations are embedded in roles is variable. Is "father" the name of a social role, or only of a special relationship? It is unclear, and it probably varies culturally and historically.

[18] See Michael Stocker, "Moral Duties, Institutions, and Natural Facts," 54 *The Monist* 605 (1970); A. J. Simmons, *Moral Principles and Political Obligations* (Princeton, NJ: Princeton University Press, 1979), 16–23; Leslie Green, *The Authority of the State* (Oxford: Oxford University Press, 1990), 193–215; Michael Hardimon, "Role Obligations," 91 *The Journal of Philosophy* 333 (1994); A. J. Simmons, "External Justifications and Institutional Roles," 93 *The Journal of Philosophy* 28 (1996).

falls to the *capo* to give orders to the *sgarrista*, or that it falls to the torturer to keep the water-tanks full. What we cannot say is that, just because these things are on their job descriptions, the *capo* or torturer have a moral duty to perform them. On the contrary, they have a moral duty *not* to perform them.

The problem of justifying role obligations is, however, more complex than merely identifying reasons for holding people to be subject to the obligations that their roles include. Point (2) entails that we need reasons to think those obligations are binding in virtue of the fact that they help constitute a role.[19] What does that mean? The English philosopher F. H. Bradley believed in the centrality of roles. Against moral individualists, Bradley defended the importance of understanding people's duties in light of their "stations" in life. He wrote, "[A]lthough within limits I may choose my station according to my liking, yet I and everyone else must have some station with duties pertaining to it, and those duties do not depend on our opinion or liking."[20] I am unsure whether everyone has, let alone must have, a station, unless that is understood in an unusually wide sense. Bradley's second point, however—that the duties of a station do not depend on our option or liking—is clearly correct. But he mistakes its significance. It is a general characteristic of all obligations that one must perform them whether one likes to or not. That is true even of voluntary obligations: the obligation of a promise also does not depend on our "opinion or liking." Role obligations have a feature beyond this: they bind *as parts of* a role—in a package deal, so to speak. So it is not merely that the duties do not depend on our liking: which duties constitute a given role does not depend on our liking either. When we assume or fall into a role, we take it as we find it.[21] To justify role obligations one therefore needs to offer reasons why obligations should ever bind in that holistic, package-deal, kind of way.

I do not think there is any general explanation for that feature of roles; but three types of reason are often found (and found in combination). First, because roles can have multiple occupants, it is often important that a new entrant be bound at once by all of its obligations, at the point of entry. The unity of a role facilitates learning what it requires and stabilizes the expectations of those who depend on it being performed. We want the new professor to have all the obligations and powers of a professor, and we want students to know she has them as soon as she takes on the job. Second, there are often reasons for several obligations to be in one set of hands: we want the lawyer who owes us a duty of loyalty also to avoid putting herself in a conflict of interest, and we want her to hold in confidence things that we tell her. These obligations are mutually supporting. It is hard even to make sense of a duty of loyalty where conflicts of interest are permissible, and hard to fulfil such a duty without keeping certain information confidential. Third, many roles have a wider significance in the community; they have a

[19] It need not be the only reason. A witness ought to tell the truth (a) because of a natural duty: everyone should tell the truth; (b) because of a special obligation: he took an oath to do just that; and (c) because of a role obligation: it falls to him as a witness.

[20] F. H. Bradley, *Ethical Studies*, 2nd edn. (Oxford: Oxford University Press, 1962), 176.

[21] Throughout I am considering only social roles like that of a judge. One could always take a piece of paper and write at the top, "My Role," and below that list a set of duties for oneself, putting down only those duties that one would like to perform. If this is a role, it is not the sort of role we are considering here. But some genuine social roles do come with powers to reform that very role. When one assumes such roles one assumes those powers, too—whether one likes it or not.

valuable social aspect precisely because they are roles. There are few if any obligations of a spouse that could not be negotiated separately through ante-nuptial agreements. If there were no common role of "spouse" in our society, very different intimate relationships would likely emerge, depending on the wants and needs of couples (and also on the individual bargaining power of the people entering those relationships). There would be advantages to that arrangement, but also losses. Only when most spouses owe each other similar duties is the status of "spouse" available and generally understood, and only then can people interact on the basis of shared expectations without need for inquiry, possibly an intrusive inquiry, into others' domestic and intimate arrangements. This is not to deny the value of the many creative variations we have on the themes of "husband," "wife," or "spouse." But you cannot have a variation on a theme until you have a theme. It is one of the things that helps sustain a common culture, and a common culture helps us live together in comfort and mutual tolerance.

Such considerations interact with the wider question of why any package of duties ever binds. There are multiple answers here, too, and they vary with the nature of the role. As it is not my aim in this chapter to explain why the judicial role is binding on those who perform it, let me leave this issue with some very brief observations. Sometimes it is important that a role, such as that of spouse or lawyer, be voluntarily assumed. Allowing people control over the incidence of such obligations, even as a package, has a protective function: it gives them the power to shape their lives to suit their own ambitions and characters, and it helps secure their commitment to the role and their motivation to perform its duties. Such considerations explain the omnipresence of judicial oaths. On the other hand, some important roles are non-voluntarily binding, especially when others are dependent on the role being performed, such as the duties of parenthood on which young children depend. In our legal systems, the role of juror is a familiar example. In smaller and more stable societies, the same was probably true of being a neighbor, and possibly of being an elder called on to settle disputes. In such cases, considerations of "natural duty" argue in favor of the obligations being binding without actual or even implied consent. No doubt there are other possibilities as well; but this is a large issue and we do not need to settle it here.[22]

IV. The Role of a Judge

Consider now, in a general and abstract way, the judicial role as we have it.[23] Judges have an obligation to apply the law. That is not in doubt. It is also widely agreed that this obligation is not absolute and can sometimes be cancelled or overridden. Moore appears to share that view. He says, "Law obligates judges *in their role as judges*; that does not mean that sometimes judges will not be justified in stepping out of the judicial role because other values are more important than those (rule-of-law) values that

[22] On the possibility of non-voluntary political duties see Leslie Green, "The Duty to Govern" 13 *Legal Theory* 165 (2007).

[23] Throughout this chapter, I am discussing the judicial role as it actually is in familiar legal systems. I assume that Moore's remarks are intended in the same spirit. The judicial role can change, and has changed, over time. Perhaps it should change in various further ways. I make no claims about these matters here.

normally justify conformity to the judicial role."[24] Thus, if something is law, judges have a role-obligation to apply it, unless they are justified in stepping out of their role. We do not need to think of "stepping out" as a matter of "stepping down." It is doubtful that resignation is a morally necessary precondition for any justified refusal to apply odious laws. Stepping out of role is more like a change of perspective that brings a responsiveness to various considerations that need not, or even may not, be attended to whilst in the role; for instance, in the way a professor might need to step out of the role of teacher in order to help a student in personal distress. In any event, the idea that judges can step outside their role, and may be justified in doing so, presupposes that there is something out of which to step: some kind of boundary—not necessarily sharp—between what falls to judges as judges and what falls to them as moral agents who have immense power over other people's lives.

Many features of a given judge's role are fixed by law and political convention and vary by jurisdiction. In one legal system, a judge may have a duty to strike down unconstitutional legislation; in another he may have no power to do so. In one, a judge must stand ready to rule on the meaning of any constitutional provision if so asked by the Attorney General; in another he may have to await an actual case or controversy. Such local variations do not help us understand how, or which, principles are binding on judges as judges, for they are simply consequences of the judicial duty to conform to the laws of their jurisdiction, including the laws that regulate their own powers. Some law-dependent features of the judicial role are so familiar that we forget their sources. In Number 78 of *The Federalist*, for example, Alexander Hamilton argues that the judicial power to strike down Congressional legislation is on a par with the judicial power to decide which of two conflicting laws should prevail. With respect to the latter, Hamilton writes:

> The rule, which has obtained in the courts for determining their relative validity is, that the last in order of time shall be preferred to the first. But this is a mere rule of construction, not derived from any positive law, but from the nature and reason of the thing. It is a rule not enjoined upon the courts by legislative provision, but adopted by themselves, as consonant to truth and propriety, for the direction of their conduct as interpreters of the law.[25]

In fact, Hamilton is wrong to say that the rule that priority is to be given to the newer law—*lex posterior derogat priori*—is "not derived from any positive law," unless by that he means it was not imposed by legislation.[26] *Lex posterior* was a positive rule of the civil law and of the common law, and so, far from being obviously mandated by "the nature and reason of the thing" or being "consonant to truth and propriety," the merits of *lex posterior* are unclear and are frequently debated by the courts.[27] (And the same is true of the power Hamilton hoped to establish by his strained analogy: judicial review of legislative action.)

[24] Moore, 2000a, 96.

[25] *The Federalist No. 78*, "The Judiciary Department" (1788).

[26] Sometimes, *lex posterior* is imposed by legislation, e.g., in the Vienna Convention on the Law of Treaties, Art 32 (1155 UNTS 331).

[27] In the UK, see *Nwogbe v. Nwogbe* [2000] 2 FLR 744 (Court of Appeal); and *BH and Another v. The Lord Advocate and Another (Scotland)* [2012] UKSC 24 (June 20, 2012).

To make progress here, we need a broader characterization of the socio-political role of a judge, one that is not merely derivative of the requirements of positive law. Although Moore disclaims any interest in "general" jurisprudence, he does need a general jurisprudence, at least of the judicial role, in order to know what would count as judges stepping outside it, and thus what principles are binding on them in virtue of that role. As far as I can see, however, the only direction Moore gives us is the following: "judges are always obligated (in their role as judges) to follow the law and nothing but the law."[28] I argue below that this is incorrect. Be that as it may, the direction is of little help. First, it presupposes rather than explains the idea of a judicial role. Second, it is a single decisional norm alleged to bind all occupants of that role. As we have seen, however, a role is a cluster of norms and related phenomena. "Law-applier," like "promisor," is not a role in the relevant sense. There is more to being a judge than that.

Let us grant that it falls to a judge, as judge, to apply the law, and also to do other things that are instrumentally necessary to the application of law. What else is in the job description? Here is a suggestion derived from some remarks by H. L. A. Hart. Hart holds that where a case cannot be settled by law (owing to indeterminacies caused by vagueness or by conflicts in the law) judges usually have discretion to settle it; but they do not have a free hand. Their discretionary powers are limited: by considerations of judicial craft, by deference to the proper authority of other institutions, but also by something Hart calls the "characteristic judicial virtues." Judges do and should exercise their discretion, he says, while displaying "impartiality and neutrality in surveying the alternatives; consideration for the interest of all who will be affected; and a concern to deploy some acceptable general principle as a reasoned basis for decision."[29] I do not think we should make heavy weather of Hart's use of the word "virtues," as if he were concerned to maintain that these are desirable dispositions for a judge but not matters of obligation. A judge who acts with partiality or bias, or who gives no consideration to the interests those with a stake in a decision, or who utterly fails to decide on the basis of general reasons, does not merely exhibit a weakness of character, he is in breach of moral obligations (and, in most jurisdictions, also of legal obligations).

The question arises, however, how far these virtues involve obligations that are not only "characteristically" judicial, as Hart puts it, but also *constitutively* judicial: part and parcel of the role itself. The first two—impartiality and due consideration—are important, but they do not themselves identify the judicial role. They are general features of moral decision-making that become more exigent whenever one has effective authority to rule on matters affecting people's interests. Arbitrators and mediators, for example, also ought to work impartially and with due consideration for the interests of those they serve. Unlike judges, however, they are not bound as part of their role to apply pre-existing standards in coming to a decision or in issuing advice—it is perfectly acceptable, and even typical, of them to try to bring the parties to a fresh agreement, or to split the difference between them, or to do justice as they see it without regard to what they had done before or what they might do next. Admittedly, obligations of a role do not need to be unique to a role in order to help constitute it. A distinctive role can be a distinctive combination of several non-distinctive obligations. Both professors and

[28] Moore, 2007b, 1537–8. [29] Hart, *The Concept of Law*, 3rd edn., 205.

physicians have a role-based obligation to keep current on research in their field; it is their other obligations and the particular ways those combine that distinguish these roles. My worry is rather that Hart's first two virtues fall to judges as moral agents, something not true of the professor or physician's duty to keep up. There is no general moral obligation to know the latest in numerical analysis or in molecular medicine, not even if these are among your hobbies. The specifically professorial and medical duties to keep up flow from the dependence of others on the skillful performance of the role.

The third virtue, the judicial "concern to deploy some acceptable general principle as a reasoned basis for decision," is different. Understanding the requirement of generality to be not just logical but temporal—a decision is to be applicable not only without reference to proper names, but also to future similar cases—and understanding the reference to "acceptability" to bridge moral correctness as well as some sort of fit with existing law, this does capture a characteristic duty in the role of a judge.[30] Anyone should decide on the basis of reasons, but judges must decide on the basis of reasons of a particular kind. The requirement to use and articulate acceptable general principles applies to judicial decision-making in virtue of that fact the rulings will be used to guide others. The rulings themselves guide the parties and, if necessary, other officials; but rulings can also immediately constitute, or eventually contribute to, general rules of conduct. Providing guidance through such rules is one of the main functions of law. As Lon Fuller stressed, law cannot serve that function unless it contains general rules; rules that are also reasonably clear, consistent, stable, prospective, and actually effective in legal proceedings.[31] Judges are in control of many of the conditions that determine how far those requirements are satisfied, and they stand in a special position to be able to protect the law from the conduct of people who might undermine them.

This points the way to a more complete understanding of the judicial role, one that includes but goes beyond application of valid law, and that draws on the connection between Hart's third virtue and the ideal of the rule of law. So conceived, the judicial role consists of three families of obligations:

1. Law-applying obligations: Judges have an obligation to apply valid law in making rulings, and to do other things necessary to the proper discharge of that duty. For example, they have a duty to make correct findings of fact, to know what the law is, to keep their knowledge of the law up to date, to rule intelligibly so that those to whom the ruling applies know what to do, and so on.
2. Law-improving obligations: Judges have an obligation to keep the law "legally in good shape."[32] Not every improvement in law falls to judges as judges, but many of those required by the rule of law do. If judges find the law unclear, they have a duty to clarify it; if there are conflicts in the law, they should try to resolve them. More generally, they should improve the law's capacity to guide the conduct of its subjects.

[30] Stripping out distracting polemics and purely parochial concerns, I take this to be the sound idea in Herbert Wechsler's, "Toward Neutral Principles of Constitutional Law" 73 *Harvard Law Review* 1 (1959). (And it applies not only to constitutional law, but to all judicial decisions.)

[31] Lon L. Fuller, *The Morality of Law*, rev. edn. (New Haven: Yale University Press, 1969), 46–91.

[32] I borrow this phrase from John Finnis, *Natural Law and Natural Rights* (Oxford: Oxford University Press, 1980), 270.

3. Law-protecting obligations: Judges have obligations to regulate their own processes and the conduct in their courts, and to protect the rule of law and the integrity of their jurisdiction from those who would attack it by undermining judicial independence, by using the legal process oppressively or abusively to subvert the law, or by undermining the effectiveness of the courts in applying the law.

None of these obligations is absolute, and the law-applying obligations are defeated where the laws are egregiously immoral or the law-creating institutions lack the legitimacy to create law at all. The obligations may also conflict. A judge may need to choose between applying existing law or improving it, between clarifying it or keeping it stable over time. But, painting in broad strokes, these obligations characterize the judicial role and help distinguish it from other political roles in our societies.

This account has the following notable features. First, it is not tied to any particular jurisdiction or type of legal system: these are duties of judges in common-law courts, in civil courts, in courts martial, in religious courts, and so on. Second, it describes a social role constituted by several norms, a role that can be occupied by various people. Third, key aspects of the role are unified by the fact that judges have an obligation and power to apply the law. The obligations falling to ordinary subjects in respect of the rule of law are mostly limited to not undermining it: we must not bribe judges, take frivolous lawsuits, break the law without compelling reason, and so forth. But judges, owing to their control over their own procedures and decisions, also have further law-improving and law-protecting duties in the service of that ideal. Fourth, there are reasons for a judge's role-obligations to be binding as a group. It is important that those who apply the law do so in ways and under conditions that help the law guide the conduct of its subjects, and it is important for those in judicial office to be bound by these obligations immediately on assuming the office. They are binding primarily because of the way they serve the rule of law, and secondarily because of the moral force of judicial oaths or their willingness to undertake the job. Fifth, judicial obligations to clarify the law or protect the judicial process are not dependent on the existence of laws imposing those obligations and, like principles of morality, they are unlimited in their jurisdiction. They bind all judges everywhere. As Philip Soper puts it, "Some standards bind judges, not because they are law, but simply because they are part of what it means to be a judge."[33] If this is correct, as I think it is, then the fact some moral principles bind not because judges are humans but because they serve in a particular role does not, after all, change the conclusion of point (2). Many judicial obligations are binding only because the law imposes them; to know what they are we need to know what the law requires. Others are binding in virtue of what "raw" morality requires, or in virtue of what morality requires of people performing a judicial role. But these too are invariant among legal systems; that is why they bind judges as such, as judges. They are not principles of general morality, but like principles of general morality they apply of their own force and without regard to jurisdiction or any connection to particular social or political institutions.

[33] E. Philip Soper, "Legal Theory and the Obligation of a Judge," 477.

V. Understanding Judicial Creativity

It will not have escaped notice that, on my account, the obligations of judges are not only applicative but creative. Complying with a judge's law-improving and law-protecting obligations may require bold rulings that go beyond what pre-existing law requires. Moreover, a judge's obligations under points (2) and (3) above will often be imperfect, leaving them considerable latitude to decide how and when to fulfil them. They may, or may not, decide to distinguish a case; they may choose to overrule earlier decisions; they may re-interpret settled law in new and surprising ways. How then should we think about these, and other, creative aspects of the judicial role?

Moore is clear on how we should *not* think about them:

> Common law distinguishing or overruling, together with purposive interpretation of statutes, are well-accepted aspects of the judge's role as we know it. If we freed law from its close tie to judicial obligation, we might think of these judicial activities as proper but as going *against the law*.[34]

To think of these tame and familiar activities as proper yet "going against" the law would indeed be absurd. It is true that overruling "goes against" the very law (*in sensu diviso*) that it overrules, as would legislative repeal of that law; but it does not go against the law (*in sensu composito*). Each of these activities uses powers that properly fall to any judge, or at least to any judge working in a common-law system. Moore's proposal is that to avoid the absurd conclusion we need to "conceptualize the law as always having been that which the overruling/distinguishing/purposefully interpreting court has discovered for the first time."[35] But that is overkill. Why do we need to think that these creative activities discover what the law was all along in order to show that they do not go against the law? If a legal system had a general norm to the effect that judges may never create law by distinguishing, overruling, or interpreting, then those activities would go against the law in that system. I am not familiar with any legal system, common-law or otherwise, that contains such a norm, and it is not clear that it would be possible for any legal system to wholly lack judicial powers that have law-creating effects, not even one that pledges allegiance to the myth that judges never make law. There will always be some cases not determined by existing law, and I assume that judges will have duties to settle at least some of them. These settlements will be both binding and new. Moreover, whether or not there is a formal doctrine of precedent, repeated interpretations of law, including incorrect ones, can over time build up customs and conventions that will also change the law. All legal systems are dynamic in character, and all judges have (some) creative powers.

To the extent that judicial activities create new law with retrospective effect, they do of course compromise one aspect of the rule of law, namely the principle that laws should be prospective in force. But that ideal is not itself a law, and violation of it does not lead to the invalidity of a law, unless there is some special legal requirement for prospectivity.[36] And anyway no one thinks the requirement of prospectivity dominates all other aspects of the rule of law, any more than they think that the requirement that

[34] Moore, 2000a, 97. [35] Moore, 2000a, 97.

[36] Something that Fuller never denies: *The Morality of Law*, 51–62.

the law should be stable over time means that inconsistency or vagueness in law should never be cured by courts or legislatures.

So these familiar techniques indeed do not "go against the law"; they use legal powers provided by the legal ground rules, whether constitutional norms or, more fundamentally, the rules of recognition and adjudication of that system. In using these powers to shape law, a judge no more goes against the law than does the UK Parliament when it makes valid use of its powers to enact new statutes. Parliament does not deduce or infer statutes from the UK Constitution, as if they were already somehow latent in it, just waiting to be discovered or derived. Parliament takes decisions; it acts. If it acts in one way the law will be one thing; if it acts in another it will be something different. That is why it matters who is elected to Parliament. The same is true of judges and, although their legal powers are much more limited and subject to many more constraints, that is why it matters so much who is appointed, or elected, to the bench.

It is tempting to say that judges may be justified in acting creatively if they are also acting non-judicially, that is, outside their role. But is there really such a place, in Moore's theory? I have argued that the role is bounded by obligations to apply law and certain obligations to improve and protect it. Although Moore mentions the possible justifiability of stepping outside the role, I do not think he has left space for it. He says that in every case, even the easiest one in the most benign legal system, where a judge could apply obvious law to the clearest of facts, the judge always has a duty as a judge to consider whether that should on balance be done:

> The omnipresence of the question whether the obvious law should be followed means that one cannot confine the values justifying a limited judicial role to outside-of-role, "Sunday" musings. Rather, such values enter into each application of the obvious law by a judge, for each application requires a balance of those values against the potential injustice of applying such obvious law to the case before a judge.[37]

In this passage, the province of justice seems to be what the ancients called "general" justice: the realization of all sound moral values in their right relations. (That is, it is not limited to distributive, corrective, or procedural justice in particular.) Indeed, perhaps we should just say "all sound values," for elsewhere Moore signs up to the view that, "morality includes everything that is otherwise a valid and relevant reason within the overall balance of reasons that determines the rightness of our actions."[38] Now, it is true that in the preceding extract Moore explicitly says the values that cannot be consigned to outside-of-role "musings" are those that justify a *limited* judicial role. But if a judge must, as he also says, always consider whether such values outweigh the possible injustice in applying "obvious" law, then *within* their role the judge must always assess the justice of every law. So every valid reason that could be relevant to that issue applies in virtue of the fact that the assessor is a judge. It follows, then, that a judge is never actually justified in "stepping outside the role." If the considerations in favour of doing so were justificatory, they would not lie outside the role, for they bear on the pervasive moral question of whether the law should be applied. Since these values bear on every application of law (and bear as law—though not as "obvious" law) there can be no

[37] Moore, 2007b, 1536. [38] Moore, 2000a, 155.

difference between what a judge is morally obligated to do as a judge and what a judge is morally obligated to do, full stop. The introduction of the judicial role thus turns out to be a fuel-wasting detour on a road back to the unacceptable simple view: scenic, but circular.

Let me emphasise that I am not denying that judges should attend to morality, or that they should remain alert to the question whether they should be applying law at all. Of course they should: the law is morally fallible, and judges exercise great power. The mistake is in thinking that this duty is distinctively judicial, and in thinking that it can help us understand what is, and what is not, law. If the law is whatever standards judges are obliged to apply as judges, and "as judges" they are required to attend to all moral values, then we are back with the simple view and its obvious defects.

VI. Conclusion: Jurisprudence and Conceptual Choices

I want to conclude with a thought about Moore's philosophy of legal philosophy, something that may be the source, or perhaps a consequence, of his ecumenism about jurisprudence, and may also be related to his urge to miniaturize the judicial role so that it consists of a single duty: apply the law and only the law.

Moore says there are four ways that judges ought to use moral principles in deciding cases: judges ought to apply moral principles when those principles are "incorporated" by "obvious" law; judges ought to test the authority of law against those principles; judges ought to use moral principles to settle undetermined cases; and judges ought to use moral principles to decide whether and how to overrule immoral laws. For reasons explained in section V, it is a feature of his account that conforming to those norms is inevitably discovering what the law (already) requires. Moore is well aware that his is a controversial view, and that it faces competition. Other legal philosophers, including me, hold that the law can and does use all sorts of standards without incorporating them into the law, that judges have powers to change and create law even if they do not own up to them, and that there are things that judges must do, as judges, apart from applying the law. Surprisingly, Moore seems to think that, as between his own view and a view like that, it is a close call. He writes,

> We thus face a conceptual choice that is not obvious. The positivist keeps our notion of law simple—law consists of all and only the obvious stuff; but the ethics of obligation then becomes complicated because judges (even in their role as judges) are not always obligated to follow the law, nor are judges limited in their judicial decisions to the law alone. The natural lawyer keeps our ethics simple: judges are always obligated (in their role as judges) to follow the law and nothing but the law; but their notion of law now becomes complicated, because law is not only, and not always, what we take to be obviously law.[39]

Moore favours simple ethics and complicated law, though he does not think the case for that is obvious. He says we face a "conceptual choice."

What is a conceptual choice and what grounds could be relevant to making one? I think that our concepts are what they are. Some, like "fee simple," are complex but at the

[39] Moore, 2007b, 1537–8.

same time fairly sharp. Others, like "reasonableness" are simple but also pretty vague. We work all the time with vague concepts, making them more precise only when we need to. That does pose choices, for there is no single way to make a vague concept more precise; how best to sharpen it depends on our purposes. Perhaps precisification is a kind of conceptual choice.

Like all of our concepts, the concept of law is vague to some degree and in some respects. But it is vague in the respects Moore has in mind? He does not show that it is. What he shows is that there are contending positions in legal philosophy and he claims it is not obvious which of them is correct. Perhaps not. But it is no measure of the vagueness of a concept is that it can attract philosophical disputes, or that it can be difficult to see a clear path through those disputes. Philosophy is difficult, and disputatious. There has been a philosopher willing to deny almost any proposition about law you can think of, no matter how patently true. The nature of the subject, to say nothing of the profession, encourages that, for the rewards in advancing a thesis that is new, even if crazy, can be greater than the rewards in advancing a thesis that is (merely) true. Moreover, at least since Kant we have known that one of the liabilities of free inquiry is that, from time to time, reason gets above itself. How to respond to that, and to rein in the philosophical tendency to generate nonsense, is itself a matter of philosophical dispute. Jurisprudence probably contains no greater proportion of nonsense than do other areas of philosophy, but the fact that there are divergent philosophical opinions on some matter does not set up any problem of "conceptual choice." It merely sets up a problem for philosophy.

Choices about concepts can arise in a second way, however: not in sharpening vague concepts but in reforming existing concepts, including sharp ones. We have a deeply entrenched concept of "race." It is not difficult to grasp—children learn racial classifications easily and early—and though it admits of indeterminacy it is not so vague that there is, for example, no point in trying to ban discrimination "on grounds of race." We understand "race" well enough for that. There is nonetheless no scientific or moral value in what we might call the first-order use of the concept: to sort and rank people into ethno-genetic kinds. There is nothing in the world that answers to our actual concept of a "race." Using the concept in the first-order way has led to grave moral and theoretical errors; so we should live without "race" if we can, and reform it if we cannot. Some philosophers seem to think there are similar stakes in "law." Of course, they do not normally think we should abolish the concept of law, but some do think we should re-shape it with attention to the alleged practical consequences of operating with one concept rather than another. They ask "Would we do better if we think, with Gustav Radbruch, that directives that do not aim at justice are not laws, or if we think that they are laws but evil ones?"[40] To that question, Hart replies that there are good reasons to keep a "broad" concept of law that extends to evil laws instead of adopting a "narrow" one that does not. *To that question*. What Hart does not say is that we have a "choice" about what the concept of law really is, a choice that might be decided by the three pages

[40] Hart, *The Concept of Law*, 3rd edn., 209–12. For discussion see Leslie Green, "The Morality in Law," in L. Duarte d'Almeida, J. Edwards, and A. Dolcetti, eds., *Reading HLA Hart's "The Concept of Law"* (Oxford: Hart Publishing, 2013), 203–7.

of considerations he advances against Radbruch-type proposals. (Had Hart thought that, *The Concept of Law* could have been a very short book.)

It may be that by "conceptual choice" Moore has in mind something along those lines: a pragmatic case for reform of our concepts of law, judicial role, etc. He does claim that, "The main virtue of internal jurisprudence is its practicality."[41] So perhaps that is the light in which we should assess his suggestion that "judges are always obligated (in their role as judges) to follow the law and nothing but the law," the view that "keeps our ethics simple." But what is the gain in this kind of simplicity? Why would that be a good way to reform our concept of law—why not reform it so that only democratic laws, or just laws, or efficient laws henceforth count as laws? We are hearing a lot these days from so-called "legal pluralists" and others who maintain that there is no distinction worth drawing between legal norms and any other social norms. We also hear from some inter- and trans-national legalists that jurisprudence is hung up on an outmoded "Westphalian" statist view; that law is changing around us, already evolving into something bigger and better. If everything now really is law, and familiar juristic distinctions are as phoney as the supposed "races" of our single species, then maybe it is time to retire "law" too.

I do not think that Moore accepts anything of that sort. (At any rate, I hope he does not.) But neither does he present any other case for reforming the concept of law, and I am not sure how one would go. Maybe we could take a lead from something J. S. Mill said about justice. Mill observed that to save a life we may be not only permitted but also obliged to steal food or medicine; we may even be required to conscript an unwilling doctor to help us. Mill then suggested:

> In such cases, as we do not call anything justice which is not a virtue, we usually say, not that justice must give way to some other moral principle, but that what is just in ordinary cases is, by reason of that other principle, not just in the particular case. By this useful accommodation of language, the character of indefeasibility attributed to justice is kept up, and we are saved from the necessity of maintaining that there can be laudable injustice.[42]

Now, this passage is frustrating because it is hard to tell how far Mill is maintaining ironic distance from a habit of speech he actually thinks misleading—a *mere* keeping up of appearances—and how far he holds that the "accommodation of language" actually is useful. Reading it straight up, however, we could plausibly construct the view that practice is one thing and theory another, and the norms by which we should guide our lives may differ from the underlying structure of morality. You can see why Mill might think it playing with fire to acknowledge that some injustices can be justified: it would be like entertaining the idea that torture could be justified in the philosophers' ticking-bomb hypothetical, a hypothetical whose conditions are never satisfied in our world. Mill might reasonably hold that we should try to put some things beyond decision, to the extent that we can, by putting them beyond thought and speech, to the extent that we can. So perhaps that gives us a moral reason make justice indefeasible: we cannot

[41] Moore, 2000a, 97.

[42] J. S. Mill, *Utilitarianism*, ch. V. (*Collected Works*, vol. X, 238) (Toronto: University of Toronto Press, 1969).

trust ourselves to operate with the more complex, if more accurate, judgment; at least not in the normal circumstances of moral decision-making. I am not sure how far Moore's own enthusiasm for "moral realism" permits him to go down a line like this. If it does, might he invoke analogous considerations here?

I cannot see how. In ordinary life there may well be value in working with simple rules such as "Never lie," "Keep all promises," or "Always be just." But what value would there be in charging our judges to work with the rule, "Apply the law and only the law"? Bear in mind that in Moore's view that they need to understand "the law" as including not only positive law, but principles of the rule of law, the values underlying them, and any moral reason that might count against applying a law. If judges fail to do the right thing, then they will have failed to conform to this norm. But there is no reason to think that in attempting to conform to it they would be more likely to do the right thing. For that to be plausible, judges would need an independent test for whether they *are* conforming to the norm, and Moore's capacious idea of "law" deprives them of that. It is a bit like being told that you would do best to follow the simple norm "Keep all promises" but then being informed, "And what you promised is determined by all moral considerations relevant to the decision about whether to keep it." That may not set us back in our moral reasoning, but there is no way it can improve it.

In truth, we have far fewer "conceptual choices" in jurisprudence than some imagine. The concept of law is vague, but not *that* vague: not more vague than, say, the concept of a market or the concept of a political party. We could certainly make the concept of law more precise, and we could reform it if there were any reason to do so. (Though to succeed in the campaign we will need a lot more than a philosophical argument; we will also need to change the way we normally talk and think, and, probably, the way we live. That is why "race" has been so hard to budge.) But we need a better reason to try than that doing so will, by a useful accommodation of language, allow us to keep up the idea that all sound judicial decisions apply the law and only the law, and that this is the beginning and the end of a judge's job. That really is just keeping up appearances. The law is much smaller than that, and the judicial role much larger.

23
Responses and Appreciations

Michael S. Moore

I. Introduction

It shouldn't go without saying how pleased and flattered I am to be the occasion for this collection of essays. It is a privilege to have attracted friendly and critical commentary from as distinguished a group of scholars as have contributed to this volume. In this response I cannot hope to explore adequately the many suggestions and criticisms offered up by this commentary. But I am grateful for the opportunity to expand the horizons of my thinking on some of the diverse issues raised in these essays.

It had been my hope that I might organize this chapter by subject-matter areas, folding in the points of various authors as appropriate. To a limited extent I was able to do that, particularly on the retributivist theory of punishment, the moral wrong theory of criminal legislation, the troublesome issues surrounding omissions and other negative facts, and some issues about judicial obligations to interpret legal texts. But, by and large, the topics raised in the foregoing chapters are too diverse to permit any more of such subject-matter organization. Most of this response thus is organized by author.

II. Retributivism

The three chapters on retributivism by Mitch Berman,[1] Doug Husak,[2] and Peter Westen[3] variously raise a series of questions about retributivism that it is fruitful to explore together. The first of these questions is about the definition of retributivism itself: given the varieties of views labelled "retributivist," how should retributivism as a theory of punishment be defined?

Husak urges that "we should not spin our wheels attempting to define retributivism itself."[4] He notes the variety of views so labeled, and eschews a choice of any of them as constituting the core of retributivism. Yet other theorists' usages of "retributive" should only be of secondary interest to us so long as the definition we seek is stipulative and not lexical. Stipulative definitions do not seek to conform themselves to an existing body of usage and so are undisturbed by fractures in that usage. Rather, stipulative definitions are to be judged by the purpose(s) for which the definition is offered, the question being, does the definition serve those purposes well? My own purpose in defining retributivism was to display as crisply as possible an intellectual debate I early in my career found interesting. This was the debate between those who found it morally unintelligible to think it intrinsically good to make culpable wrongdoers suffer the hard treatment that is punishment because of their culpable wrongdoing, and those who thought the opposite. The uniformity of educated opinion that I, Herbert Morris, Jeff Murphy, and other early retributivists faced was that expressed by H. L. A. Hart: retributivism, Hart said, required some sort of "mysterious alchemy" that could transform "two wrongs into a right."[5] The retributivist I defined was indeed someone who did believe that sometimes (i.e., when deserved) it is intrinsically right, good, and just, to make others suffer. The debate with the retributivist so defined was thus not without interest.

Berman essentially adopts this definition of retributivism in his criterion R; giving culpable wrongdoers the suffering they deserve is an intrinsic good constituting a reason to visit such suffering on them. Berman rightly sees this as the core of retributivism, as does Peter Westen in his chapter. Despite his expressed misgivings about defining retributivism, Husak too implicitly adopts this notion of retributivism when he confesses that he is "inclined to think that some small intrinsic good probably is achieved when persons are treated in accordance with their desert . . ."[6] Yet even so, Husak's philosophical abstemiousness leads him to engage in some excessive hand-wringing over the "morass" (his word) of intrinsic value: how we know what is valuable, how we know what is intrinsically (versus instrumentally) valuable, how we can demonstrate to others the truth of what we claim to know.[7] In point of fact, we all have theories of what is intrinsically valuable, for we could not make evaluations if we did not. So we all need

1 Mitch Berman, "Modest Retributivism," this volume.
2 Douglas Husak, "What Do Criminals Deserve?," this volume.
3 Peter Westen, "Retributive Desert as Fair Play," this volume.
4 Husak, "What Do Criminals Deserve?," 52.
5 H. L. A. Hart, *Punishment and Responsibility* (Oxford: Oxford University Press, 1968), 234.
6 Husak, "What Do Criminals Deserve?," 53.
7 Husak, "What Do Criminals Deserve?," 54.

to hobble along as best we can, and use notions like intrinsic value to allow us to identify things that are worth arguing about—like retributivism as I have defined it.

If we can settle on something like Berman's "R" as the core of retributivism, we can then pursue the two general questions about retributivism that interest me from these three chapters by Berman, Husak, and Westen. First, how much work does R do in justifying the punitive doctrines and institutions of criminal law? And second, how is R itself to be justified?

Berman and Husak say many fruitful things on this first question, so let me pursue the question by working through some of their distinctions as well as some of my own. I shall begin with one of my own distinctions. When we ask how much work R can do in justifying punishment, we should subdivide our concerns in two: (1) How strong a reason (to punish) is R?; and: (2) how strong does R need to be to justify punishment?

With respect to (1), there is some disagreement between myself and Berman/Husak on the strength of the reason (to punish) given by the desert of culpable wrongdoers. I think this is a strong reason; they find it to be a weak reason. How tractable this disagreement is depends on what sort of justificatory support can be mustered one way or the other. I shall thus defer discussion of this until I come to it, as my second topic of discussion with Berman, Husak, and Westen.

My focus here is on (2). Perhaps the work needing to be done by R is so slight that even a weak reason can do it. That depends on a number of distinctions Berman and Husak introduce.

Consider first Berman's distinction between "tailored" versus "all-out" justifications.[8] A tailored justification, as Berman conceives it, is quite a context-sensitive matter: in the context of there being a prima facie reason against a certain act or practice, a justification is *tailored* in the sense that it is aimed at removing the sting of such prima facie reasons against a practice. About punishment specifically, Berman notes the common objection, which is that punishment involves the intentional inflection of suffering, a prima facie bad thing to do. A tailored justification here would be one showing that this generally cogent objection has no force in this context. And Berman concedes, I believe, that R can provide such a tailored justification. That the culpable wrongdoer deserves to suffer plausibly removes this general objection to the intentional infliction of suffering. R makes *permissible*, in other words, what otherwise would be forbidden.

So insofar as the task is to provide a tailored justification, weak as R is taken to be by Husak and Berman, R can do what is needed by way of providing such a justification. Yet this does not establish R's credentials as a justification of punishment. To remove a barrier to doing something—to give a permission—is not to give one a reason to do what one is permitted to do. For that, some kind of what Berman calls an "all-things-considered" justification is needed.

And now we need to employ a second distinction, one dividing up Berman's "all-things-considered" justification into two kinds. One of these I shall call *internal* justifications. An internal justification of a practice, as I would understand it, seeks to provide the good(s) that give one a reason to engage in the practice (that tailored justifications make permissible to engage in). That punishment gives culpable

[8] Berman, "Modest Retributivism," 42.

wrongdoers what they deserve is one such good; so could be prevention of the welfare loss and/or the rights violation that violent crime represents.

Such justifications are internal in the sense that they suspend external considerations such as "how much do punishment institutions cost to all other things we value?" Internal justifications are thus by their nature partial. They only seek to identify the good(s) an institution can achieve that are the reason(s) we have for creating it. They are thus "all-things-considered" only in a limited sense: they deal only with plausible motives for having some institution and make some claim about why one or more of these is "sufficient" to justify the institution in question. (Notice how limited the "sufficient" is in such internal justificatory schemes. It is limited to the universe of possible reasons for having the institution and claims that one is *sufficient* only in the sense that no other of those reasons is *necessary*.)

Notice that for R to play the role of an internal justification of punishment, it needs very little by way of strength. For the claim made on behalf of R as an internal justification is limited to a claim of exclusivity: within the universe of possible reasons served by punishment institutions, R is the good such institutions uniquely serve. The degree of importance of the good that R gives is relevant only indirectly, insofar as strength bears on exclusivity. It is only when R faces the test as an external, all-things–considered justification that strength becomes directly relevant, because it is only here that R has something to outweigh (as opposed to exclude).

Let us turn, then, to external, all-things-considered justifications. (This is roughly equivalent to Husak's second question, which is, "should we give culpable wrongdoers the suffering and censure that they deserve?")[9] Here I have often been mischaracterized in terms of holding some absurdly strong retributivist view. I am gratified that, on the whole, my three commentators here resist these mischaracterizations. Even so, it may be helpful to (re-)state what I do *not* believe here.

I am often quoted for saying that giving culpable wrongdoers the punishment (Husak's censure plus hard treatment) that they deserve is a *sufficient* justification for penal institutions. My meaning was that given above: *internally* (i.e., vis-à-vis other goods proposed as justificatory of punishments), giving just deserts alone is enough, without recourse to other goods such as crime-prevention. Often, however, I am misconstrued as meaning that externally, vis-à-vis all costs and benefits of punishment, the giving of just deserts is sufficient. More specifically, I am supposed to believe that:

(1) Even if doing so causes "the Heavens to fall" in the sense that humanity will perish from the Earth, still the last culpable wrongdoer should be punished; or

(2) Amongst all the duties of the lawmaker, the duty to punish those who deserve it is categorical and not to be balanced off against mere consequences of punishment, however bad; or

(3) Amongst all the goods there are (such as *not* punishing the innocent, preventing the rights-violations that violent crime represents, not punishing those whose moral wrongs have not been legally prohibited in accordance with the dictates of

[9] Husak, "What Do Criminals Deserve?," 50, 51.

legality and the rule of law, achieving non-retributive kinds of justice such as corrective and distributive justice, etc.), giving culpable wrongdoers the punishment they deserve is always the most important.

In truth, I subscribe to none of these beliefs. As to (1), Berman correctly notes[10] that I am generally only a *threshold* deontologist when I am a deontologist at all. If punishing Kant's last murderer left on the island causes humanity to perish from the Earth, don't do it! As to (2), at the level of institutional design and budget appropriation, it is in fact my view that there is no place for supposed categorical obligations to achieve retributive justice. Achieving retributive justice is an intrinsically good state of affairs, but in the budget room its attainment is no more of a categorical obligation than is the attainment of distributive justice, corrective justice, rights-preservation, etc. Trade-offs in terms of how much of these goods we can afford are not only inevitable but desirable. And, relevantly to (3), when these trade-offs are made, sometimes the achieving of retributive justice will lose out to the achievement of other goods as we design the legal institutions that we can actually afford.

None of this is to deny that I am the "bold" and "robust" fellow that Berman, Husak, and others describe me as. I do think that the reason given to punish the deserving is a strong reason, not minimal; that the reason is strong enough to be characterized as an *obligation*; that the obligation is one of justice; and that the duty (to punish) extends from individuals in individual cases to state actors setting up legal institutions that deal with a run of cases. Berman complains that none of these stronger claims follows from (is "entailed by") the simple core of retributivism, R.[11] And of course they do not. But I am a pants-on-one-leg-at-a-time guy. My chief opponents as I saw it in my early defenses of retributivism were those liberal thinkers who found it morally unintelligible to think (as does the retributivist at his/her core) that requiting wrongdoing with suffering was good at all. Enough for the day to send those liberal opponents packing.

Still, Berman might say, the day is now late and my liberal interlocutors have been sent packing. So where is Moore's argument, moving from R (giving culpable wrongdoers what they deserve is *a* reason), to robust retributivism, viz. giving culpable wrongdoers what they deserve is so strong a reason as to constitute an obligation of justice? Let us suppose that I have no such argument (an *arguendo* concession, to be sure, but such concessions help to isolate distinct arguments). Do I need one? Suppose Berman, Husak, and I—three core retributivists all—constitute the budget committee for some society. We are deciding how to set up legal institutions that we can afford so as to maximize all the intrinsically good things there are. Husak and Berman now want to object that although achieving retribution is intrinsically good, it is too slight a good to be worth the high cost of its attainment. Husak: "Although . . . it is plausible to believe that [a judgment of desert] entails ceteris paribus, it would be good if [punishment] were given. . .," unfortunately . . . "other things are not equal because punishment is administered by the state rather than by god; therefore it is inevitable that the practice of punishment . . . will be tremendously expensive, subject to grave error, and susceptible to enormous abuse. . . . These three deficiencies . . . I will call . . . the drawbacks of

[10] Berman, "Modest Retributivism," 41.

[11] Berman, "Modest Retributivism," 40–6.

punishment."[12] Husak's thought (in common with Berman): the good of achieving retributive justice is too modest to justify setting up an institution with such serious drawbacks.

One can hardly dispute that punishment practices in actual human societies involve the costs that Husak identifies as the three drawbacks of punishment. Nor can one dispute that these three costs are significant. Therefore, it might seem that a defense of retributivism (all things considered and externally) must crucially depend on a defense of the strength of the reason described in R. That is, giving the guilty the punishment they deserve must be a really good thing, else how could one justify doing so in the face of such high costs?

Ignored by this line of argument is the idea of *net* costs. For practices like that of punishment not only have drawbacks; there are as often incidental benefits produced by such practices. (Such benefits are incidental in the sense that achieving them is no part of the reason for having practices that generate them; still, they are welcome in any event, as a kind of pleasant bonus.)[13] A big benefit of punishment practices is that it reduces crime in just the ways the utilitarians have charted for centuries: one gains both deterrence and incapacitation of would-be offenders by such familiar forms of punishment practices as incarceration. Factoring this benefit alone in, it is plausible to think that the *net* cost of achieving retributive justice is quite small, perhaps even nonexistent.

Husak thinks (I think) that this turns me into a "mixed theorist" of punishment rather than the "pure retributivist" that I bill myself as. Yet my "purity" is at the level of internal justification solely. In the budget room where trade-offs must be made, I let the kitchen sink in like everyone else. Surely Bob Nozick, John Rawls, and Aristotle all do the same when it comes to funding institutions realizing the natural rights of property, distributive justice, or corrective justice. Real human institutions have real costs, but seeing that obvious truth hardly makes theories of natural right or of distributive or corrective justice "impure" or "mixed."[14]

I turn now to the second general question about retributivism I earlier distinguished, which was: how is the core retributive claim—Berman's "R"—to be justified? My own justification in past papers has been particularist, intuitive, and emotion-based. The alternative mode of justification with which I contrast my own is generalist, deductive, and not based on emotion. The example I give of the latter is Herb Morris's well-known "unjust enrichment" or "fair play" justification of retributivism. Husak concerns himself with the former, Westen with the latter. Let me discuss each in turn.

There are many questions to ask about my particularist justificatory strategy,[15] but in the context of these chapters let me distinguish four such questions. The first is whether

[12] Douglas Husak, "Why Punish the Deserving?," in Thom Brooks (ed.), *Retribution* (Farnham, UK: Ashgate Publishing, 2014), 190–1.

[13] Contrast with Husak, Victor Tadros in his "The Wrong and the Free," this volume, 91. Tadros recognizes that "crime reduction can . . . offset the inevitable costs of the pursuit of retributive justice," and that affirming this "is consistent with the view that the only proper purpose of the criminal law is to realize just deserts."

[14] Nozick, for example, regards the Lockean's use of incentive-effects-benefits from the awarding of property rights to be in no way altering of the natural rights character of Locke's theory of property rights.

[15] I explore five families of these in Moore, 1993b, 15–49, reprinted in Moore, 1997b, 165–87.

the fact that culpable wrongdoing has been done by one person justifies another person in some sort of response. A retributivist answers affirmatively, finding some response rightful and justified, not by "any contingent future benefits that it might bring,"[16] but solely by the culpable wrongdoing to which it is a response. My use of guilt feelings and judgments lines up well with this "core feature" of retributivism, for unless one holds Nietzsche's view that it is irrational to cry over spilled milk (or blood), guilt regards the past as entirely sufficient for one's present deserts.

Second, Husak asks in some detail, *what* response is justified by culpable wrongdoing? Husak rightly distinguishes the censure such a wrongdoer could deserve from the hard treatment also deserved. But in fact the list should be more extensive. Culpable wrongdoing may plausibly enough be thought to justify compelling the wrongdoer to: make restitution or other form of compensation to the victim; answer for his crime; apologize or make some other expression of regret to the victim or to the general public; etc. Despite this richness of justified responses to culpable wrongdoing, Husak like myself focuses on hard treatment. For it is this response that aligns itself with the most troublesome aspect of punishment, which is the state's intentional infliction of suffering on one of its citizens. My particularist mode of justifying this most troublesome aspect of punishment has been in terms of the connection between feelings of guilt on one hand, and judgments of merited suffering on the other. To feel the compelling power of guilt is to judge that one deserves to suffer for what one did.

Third, it is reasonable to ask why there should be a transfer of first-person to third-person judgments: why should it be that because my guilt feelings tell me that I deserve to suffer for my past transgressions, therefore others deserve to suffer for theirs? Here Husak goes a bit awry, for he worries that the capacity to feel guilt varies enormously between people, and that some wrongdoers may have suffered enough just by their having of intense guilt feelings. Yet none of these worries touch my mode of justifying retribution. As I say in my earlier essays, my use of guilt is not as a kind of redemption theory. I use guilt only epistemically, as an indicator that one *is* guilty because one feels guilty. And for that epistemic role there is only one set of guilt feelings that count for any of us and those are our own. It is what my own guilt feelings tell me about what I deserve that matters, and it is what your guilt feelings tell you that should matter to you. I transfer my judgments of what I deserve into a judgment of what you deserve, not by your guilt feelings (if any) but by mine—coupled with a judgment of equality, viz. that you are no less a person than me, no less a subject of responsibility. As Herb Morris would say, you have a *right* to the same judgment of deserved suffering that I make for myself.

The fourth question has to do with a different sense of transferability. This stems from the worry that even if seriously culpable wrongdoers (like one of my examples, Richard Herrin) deserve to suffer for their wrongdoing, the same could not be said of those who with much less culpability do much less serious wrongs. The worry is that desert can only justify the punishment of a small fraction of those whom every criminal law system in fact punishes. Husak worries that I have made an "unwarranted generalization from the facts of the extreme cases ... such ... as that of Richard Herrin," to the

[16] Husak, "What Do Criminals Deserve?," 59.

facts of more modest wrongs such as theft of a bottle of wine from another's wine cellar.[17]

A like criticism has long been expressed by other of my critics, notably David Dolinko.[18] In truth I have never felt there was much sting to the objection. Once one puts aside Husak's empirical concerns about what different wrongdoers will differently *feel* about their wrongdoing—empirical facts to which my defense of retributivism is utterly indifferent—then one is left only with the commonplace observation that lesser emotions produce less clear and less compelling intuitions of justice. Minor breaches of corrective or distributive justice do not give rise to strong emotions and clear and compelling judgments either. Why should they?[19]

I have hitherto been discussing four criticisms of my particularist mode of justifying retributivism. Peter Westen concerns himself with the deductive, generalist mode of justifying a moral view like retributivism, an approach with which I am sympathetic, but one I do not myself take, as Westen observes. Westen's lovely reconstruction of Herb Morris's justly celebrated "fair play" argument for retributivism allows me to comment generally on the relationship between Morris's justificatory approach and my own.

It seems to me that a generalist justificatory scheme such as Morris's should measure the extent of its success by three variables. The first is the differential plausibility of the premise of the argument versus that of the conclusion. *Ceteris paribus*, a deductive justification is stronger the more plausible is its premise vis-à-vis the conclusion the premise is to justify. Great success here is to be found in deriving a counterintuitive conclusion from a rock-solid premise. The second is the plausibility of the connection alleged to exist between the premise and the conclusion. The stronger the connection, the stronger the justificiation. The third is the (at least seeming) inferential distance between premise and conclusion. A justification of the conclusion that wrongdoers should suffer based on the premise that wrongdoers should suffer would be impeccable in terms of the second criterion yet deficient in terms of this third criterion. Successful deductive justifications surprise us by showing us how premises we accept ineluctably lead to conclusions we thought we rejected.

The power of Herb Morris's justification of retributivism is its seeming satisfaction of all three criteria for a strong deductive justification. Many share: Morris's initial premise that we each owe others in our society a reciprocal duty of fair play; Morris's connecting of that primary duty to a secondary duty of wrongdoers to suffer detriments because they have obtained unfair advantages; and Morris's sense that the duty of fair play is quite distinct from the duty to suffer retributive punishment. Morris, in short, seems to strongly derive a surprising, and to many a counterintuitive, conclusion (retributivism) from a strongly intuitive premise (fair sharing of the benefits and burdens of living together).

[17] Husak, "What Do Criminals Deserve?," 60.

[18] I discuss Dolinko's version of this objection in Moore (1993b), reprinted in Moore (1997b), 184–6.

[19] Victor Tadros raises a distinct worry about small-potatoes wrongdoing, a worry unconnected to the diminished epistemic import of such cases. His is the substantive (i.e., non-epistemic) worry that state-inflicted punishments will always exceed what trivial offenders deserve. Tadros, "The Wrong and the Free," 87,89.

As I see it, the trick for Westen is to retain these prima facie high marks on these three criteria for Morris's theory, while deflecting the decades of criticism that have accumulated on that theory. The danger is that Westen's attempt to strengthen the connection between fairness and retributivism might well come at the cost of reducing seeming inferential distance and differential plausibility between premise and conclusion. The limiting case would be where Morris's deductive justification turns into Moore's intuitive, particularist mode of argument: it is right that culpable wrongdoers suffer punishment because it is right that they do so—a strong connection but weak in inferential distance and in differential plausibility!

This danger more specifically arises for Westen because of his (independently quite plausible) objectification of what it is a wrongdoer gains by his crime that he has to disgorge. Westen transforms this from an historically contingent thing—from comparative benefits retained or burdens renounced by the wrongdoer—to non-contingent items. It is thus not a tit-for-tat fairness concern that measures the wrongdoer's gain (such as, he has gained X amount by his not forbearing when others have restrained themselves). Rather the "unfairness" now lies in an objective feature of the moral order—what society "has a right to expect" from each of us.

Notice that in this objective interpretation of Morris the wrongdoer makes no *gain* by his wrongdoing. His not forbearing is not a gain; it is what morality obligates him to do, and his not doing it is no gain to his moral ledger (nor is it a gain by the fruits of crime, as Westen shows). By the same token there is thus no *benefit* retained that needs to be disgorged. Rather, the wrongdoer has done what he was obligated not to do, and thus has suffered a moral detriment. This is true irrespective of whether others have done wrong too and thus whether this wrongdoer is free-riding on their forbearance.

Westen concedes that fair play does not (and cannot) justify why the wrongdoer is obligated not to do wrong. The burden of the theory of fair play, he urges, is only to justify the visitation of punishment on those who have done wrong. Yet what *benefit* (in its usual sense) has been retained by the wrongdoer that he must disgorge? Seemingly only this: that he hasn't yet had to suffer for his wrong. For doing wrong gives him no benefit; and others not doing wrong to him was no benefit either—it is only what he deserved. And if the judgment is that he forfeits that desert of forbearance by others by his own wrongdoing, why is that not just a long-winded way of saying that wrongdoing deserves punishment?

Westen notes that "the moral intuition that culpable wrongdoers deserve to suffer, is as powerful, pervasive, and persistent as any moral intuition which human beings possess."[20] If Westen is right about that, that makes the challenge issued up to deductive justifications like Morris's a steep one. For how are they going to find a premise even more compelling with which to justify the retributive intuition? The danger is that such seemingly separate justifications become no more than a restatement of the intuition to be justified. For my own part I hope that this is not so. Although my own justificatory scheme for retributivism does not require it, I would like Morris's kind of justifications to succeed. However, despite Westen's admirable rescue effort, this is still mostly a hope on my part.

[20] Westen, "Retributive Desert as Fair Play," 77.

III. Legal Moralism

It is usual for criminal law theorists to separate the "why punish?" question from the "what should be punished?" question. The answer to the first is styled a theory of punishment; the answer to the second is usually called a theory of legislation. Although these are distinct theories dealing with distinct subjects, there are nonetheless intimate connections between such theories.

Both Antony Duff[21] and Victor Tadros[22] explore the links between my retributivist theory of punishment and my legal moralist theory of criminal legislation. Duff makes his exploration as a fellow retributivist of a sort; Tadros, not so much, given that he announces himself as retributive desert's "most hostile enemy."[23]

Both Duff and Tadros correctly note that my seemingly conservative legal moralist theory of legislation is nonetheless made liberal in the limits it proposes for criminal legislation by two factors: one, my notion that the moral wrongdoing that is in my view the touchstone for proper criminal prohibition does not include much that social conservatives think it includes, such as sexual practices of various kinds. And two, even when wrongdoing is the target of criminal legislation, the state's hand is rightly stayed from prohibition in cases where the liberty taken by prohibition is too great to outbalance the good (of retributive punishment) obtained by prohibition. Focusing on this second aspect of my theory, both Duff and Tadros worry that my theory makes too much behavior prima facie (or "pro tanto") prohibitable even if liberty comes in later to save the day. Granted, Duff and Tadros concede, liberty and other non-retributive values will stay the hand of a Moorean state in America from criminalizing, for example, lying and promise-breaking in Istanbul; but "things have gone wrong as soon as it is said that there is any reason at all to bring such wrongs within the reach of the criminal law" of a US state.[24]

Notice that Duff focuses on kinds of wrongs and places of their occurrence as his examples of the alleged overreach of my legislative theory. Tadros focuses on a third feature; the quantity of wrongdoing involved. Tadros urges that with regard to trivial wrongs, "we lack a duty, even a defeasible duty," to prohibit them.[25]

Both Duff and Tadros here raise a very broad and much-contested issue within ethics, which is this: when moral considerations exist pro and con regarding doing some action A, when do these "pro" considerations amount to a prima facie or pro tanto duty to A and when do they simply disappear when they are outweighed or precluded by the countervailing considerations? My own read of only some of the very considerable literature on this question since W. D. Ross in the 1930's,[26] is that there are two very different readings of prima facie/pro tanto duties that give quite different answers to our question.

One reading is epistemic. Reasons giving prima facie/pro tanto duties in this sense are parts of optimal decision procedures. They are where we are best advised to start if we wish to make a good decision. They mark epistemic breathing stations in the sense

[21] Antony Duff, "Legal Moralism and Public Wrongs," this volume.

[22] Tadros, "The Wrong and the Free."

[23] Tadros, "The Wrong and the Free,"79.

[24] Duff, "Legal Moralism and Public Wrongs," 99.

[25] Tadros, "The Wrong and the Free," 87.

[26] W. D. Ross, *The Right and the Good* (Oxford: Oxford University Press, 1935).

that they tell us where we should pause in our deliberations before we move on to other considerations.

The second reading is not epistemic but substantive. When a reason for action constitutes a prima facie/pro tanto duty in this sense, there are real consequences that do not disappear just because the consideration(s) behind that prima facie duty are outweighed or precluded by even weightier considerations. In a classic illustration, one has a pro tanto duty to the proverbial workman trapped on the trolley line not to turn the trolley onto his line (thereby killing him) even if that pro tanto duty is replaced by a conflicting duty to turn the trolley to save five workmen on another track who would otherwise be struck and killed by the trolley. Such a substantively pro tanto duty is then cashed out in terms of moral consequences: some "agent-regret" should be felt; some apology should be made; some compensation should be paid; etc.

As I understand him, Duff seems to view prima facie/pro tanto duties in the epistemic sense. For his objection to my theory—that the fact that behavior is morally wrong is always a prima facie reason to prohibit it with the criminal law—is that it *starts* in the wrong place. Duff tells us that "we must start not with wrongs but with the idea of the public."[27] Or again: "we must begin not with wrongs . . . but with the idea of the public realm . . . ."[28] Of a piece with this is Duff's imagining of a committee to draft a code of professional ethics for some profession; what they need, Duff tells us, is "the logical ordering of the committee's deliberation . . . [such that] when the committee does come to discuss the proper content and scope of the code of ethics, it will not begin with the whole realm of moral wrongdoing as its canvas."[29]

I don't see how any of this gives Duff any reason—even a prima facie or pro tanto reason—either to fault my theory of legislation or to promote his own, "public wrongdoing" theory of legislation. For even on his own theory, a public wrong, at the end of the day, still has to be a wrong as well as public to be prohibitable. Of what relevance is it if there are many cases where we find it expedient to suspend the wrongness question because we are pretty sure that the behavior in question is "private" in the relevant sense (and thus under Duff's theory, not prohibitable even if it is morally wrong). Duff urges us to put the "public" leg of the pants on first. Maybe this is good advice in applying his own theory but that doesn't make the other pants leg disappear. The behavior being not wrong is still a reason against prohibition, just as the behavior being wrong is a reason in favor of prohibition.

I used to think that Duff could evade this kind of response by me by treating "public wrong" as a fused idiom.[30] Just as an "intellectual dwarf" or a "mental midget" is not a person who is both small and smart, so Duff might urge that a "public wrong" is not an act that is both wrong and public. I thought that Duff could take this escape route because of Duff's seeming insistence that what is a public wrong depended on how a community regarded some action. If they regarded it as central to their sense of identity as a community, then it was a public wrong (irrespective of whether the behavior was really wrong or not). But now Duff tells us that it doesn't matter what contemporary

[27] Duff, "Legal Moralism and Public Wrongs," 103.
[28] Duff, "Legal Moralism and Public Wrongs," 103.
[29] Duff, "Legal Moralism and Public Wrongs," 105.
[30] On fused idioms, see W. V. O. Quine, *Word and Object* (Cambridge, Mass.: MIT Press, 1960), 132.

Nigerians (or Ugandans) think—no matter how central to their sense of self-identity it may be to ban homosexuality, homosexuality is not a public wrong.[31] So I guess public wrongs do need to be wrongs too, in Duff's mind as well as my own. In which case wrongness as such is a reason for prohibition for Duff as much as for me.

Tadros objects that the fact that an act is a *trivial* wrong gives no reason, not even a prima facie one, for prohibition. At least when arguing against me, Tadros's trigger for criminal prohibition is thus degree of wrongdoing—non-triviality—rather than its public quality, as is the case for Duff. Yet part of the worry here for Tadros is the same as it is for Duff, and it is subject to the same rejoinder. For Tadros too (in part) seems to think that pro tanto/prima facie is an epistemic matter. If a consideration amounts to a pro tanto duty for Tadros, then a deliberator must give weight to it in his practical reasoning.[32] Moreover, "he ought not to rule out [such pro tanto consideration] in advance of considering the reasons to violate his duty ...."[33] A pro tanto consideration is one that stays in contention as the actor decides what to do. And Tadros thinks wrongdoing as such does not remain in contention as a consideration because triviality can rule it out.

Yet as with Duff, this epistemic reading is by-the-by to the point at issue here. Even if it is sometimes efficient or expedient to consider triviality first and to rule out consideration of whether an action is wrong (on the grounds that even if it is, it is obviously trivial), still wrongness remains as a reason for prohibition. For this epistemic reading of Tadros too, then, if an act is morally wrong prima facie it ought to be prohibited by the criminal law.

Tadros has in correspondence denied that he gives the prima facie line an epistemic reading, even in part. Yet this is hard to square with the great lengths to which he goes to draw out what I think can only be an epistemic point here. He urges that the suffering caused by state-imposed punishments will always be excessively disproportionate for trivial wrongdoing; that therefore such trivial wrongdoing should always not be prohibited by the criminal law; and that the triviality of the wrongdoing is clearer than the question of whether the behavior actually is wrongdoing at all. Therefore, one should always decide the triviality question first, and needn't get to the question of wrongdoing. And therefore, in the epistemic sense wrongdoing does not give rise to pro tanto duty to prohibit because it can be ruled out in advance by its triviality.

Yet this elaborate elaboration by Tadros goes no distance towards showing that wrongdoing gives no reason (or prima facie duty) to prohibit. It only shows that consideration of such reason is not always apt if one can easily see that some other consideration will trump this reason. It is still, after all, a reason to prohibit, even if it gets demoted in the order of its consideration.

Unlike Duff, Tadros also gives a substantive reading to the pro tanto notion, and he intends this as his primary sense of "prima facie/pro tanto." As Tadros puts it "for a person who has a *pro tanto* duty . . . secondary duties typically arise . . . [such as] the duty to apologize and the duty to pay compensation."[34] Finding that the state has no such

[31] Duff, "Legal Moralism and Public Wrongs," 109.

[32] Tadros, "The Wrong and the Free," 89.

[33] Tadros, "The Wrong and the Free," 89.

[34] Tadros, "The Wrong and the Free," 89.

secondary duties in cases where trivial wrongdoing goes both unprohibited and unpunished, Tadros concludes that wrongdoing does not give rise to any substantive pro tanto duty on the part of legislators to criminalize it.

Tadros is surely right that a pro tanto duty (in the substantive sense) has moral implications even in cases where such duty is outweighed or precluded by other countervailing considerations. Substantively pro tanto duties do not disappear in such circumstances. Yet Tadros is too narrow in what he expects those consequences to be. Secondary deontic duties (such as duties of apology or repair) are one possibility; but surely these are not apt for many duties such as *tout court* duties (duties owed to no one). With pro tanto versions of such free-standing duties that are not owed to anyone, there is no one to be compensated nor is there anyone to whom an apology could be appropriate. Sometimes surely the moral consequence of a reason being a pro tanto duty is only that of feeling a certain way or having a certain belief. And state actors may well be rightly blamed morally because they lack such feelings or beliefs in situations where minor wrongs are done by them, even when those wrongs give rise to no other secondary duties of apology, repair, or punishment.

The most important difference between Duff and Tadros on one hand, and me on the other, lies not in these nuances of whether wrongdoing gives rise to prima facie or pro tanto reasons to criminalize. That difference lies rather in the content of the principle that precludes criminalization of certain wrongs. I think the content of that principle is best described and justified in terms of the value of *liberty*. Duff thinks the limitation of that principle should be drawn in terms of *private* wrongdoing. I have elsewhere criticized the Duff public/private wrongdoing line, and I leave it to the reader to ascertain whether Duff has better articulated a defensible principle in these terms.

Tadros appears to have limited sympathy for Duff's privacy limitation on criminal legislation, but instead of promoting his own formulation of these limits Tadros goes after my way of drawing out the principle in terms of liberty. Broadly speaking, there are two sorts of arguments Tadros advances: first, that negative liberty to do any action whatsoever is not even prima facie good; and second that attaching criminal sanctions to behaviors does not retard liberty (even if the liberty to do such behaviors were prima facie good).

As to the first of these, Tadros runs a bit roughshod over my five-part taxonomy of reasons showing negative liberty (freedom from coercion) to be of instrumental value to persons. To begin with, Tadros truncates my list from five to four, and in doing so leaves out the most important item on that list, Millian autonomy. Tadros sees the value of Millian autonomy: "People have reason to value making decisions for themselves."[35] His mistake is to think that I don't think the same thing. Second, Tadros mistakes what he calls my "argument from opportunity." Tadros would stick me (and Rawls, on whom I rely here) with the utilitarian view "that it is good that people get what they want, whatever it is that they may happen to want."[36] Tadros has little difficulty in torching off this utilitarian strawman: "The fact that D wants to torture babies is not a reason for D to torture babies ...."[37] Yet the actual point Rawls was making (and that I adopt for these purposes) was this: even when one doesn't know what it is one wants (say, from

[35] Tadros, "The Wrong and the Free," 84.
[36] Tadros, "The Wrong and the Free," 81.
[37] Tadros, "The Wrong and the Free," 81.

"behind a veil of ignorance"), one will value negative liberty as a necessary means to having autonomy in its more basic, Humean sense, viz. being able to conform the world to one's ends through one's actions.

These interpretive corrections aside, the cogency of many of Tadros's spate of objections about liberty can be tested by his intended reductio on rape. Tadros regards it as absurd that one might repeal legal prohibition (or legal enforcement or victim self-help if the laws remain on the books) of rape in order to give would-be rapists the opportunity to freely decide not to rape for moral reasons rather than for merely prudential reasons. Yet doesn't the absurdity lie in the assumption that such repeal would expose women to greater risk of rape? Suppose, contrary to fact, repeal (etc.) would have no impact on the number or the identity of rapes. Suppose, that is, the exact same rapes would take place in the world we are imagining as in our present world with its legal prohibition, enforcement, and self-help about rape. Now is it absurd to think that the repeal world is better because the refraining from rape is both freely chosen and done for the more virtuous reasons?

Recall what it is that it is my burden to establish with regard to a mere presumption in favor of liberty. Not that, all things considered, the value of free-choice processes and right reasons trumps the value of better behavior; only that, all else equal (such as the same level of moral behavior), it is better if, pace Mill, people choose that behavior though their own free choice processes, and, pace Kant, they are motivated to their behavior by worthy rather than by unworthy motives. Millian and Kantian autonomy need only give prima facie reasons to stay the state's hand, meaning that such reasons can get trumped by other values like the value of there being fewer rapes.

Not only are Millian and Kantian autonomy of value when it costs us nothing in the way of worse behavior, but surely these kinds of autonomy are of sufficient value that sometimes they will outweigh the value of better behavior. The evolutionary biologist Thomas Huxley once opined that "if some great power would agree to make me always think what was true and do what is right, on condition of being some sort of a clock wound up every morning before I got out of bed, I would close instantly with the offer."[38] If the kind of clockwork referred to here eliminates both the presence of intelligent choice and the adoption of reasons for that choice, is Huxley's valuation plausible? B. F. Skinner thought so,[39] but then Skinner notoriously gave no value to either Millian or Kantian autonomy. Perhaps Tadros is comfortable with Skinner's position "beyond freedom and dignity," and if so then issue is joined.

The second sort of argument Tadros advances against me here is one urging that criminalizing behavior, with its inevitable threatening and then delivering of punishment, does not take away liberty. As Tadros puts it, "if we are neutral about the quality of the opportunities that one has, being threatened with punishment... neither increases or decreases one's opportunities."[40] (This, because while such threats eliminate the opportunity to do some action, A, without penalty, such threats create the

[38] T. H. Huxley, "On Descartes' *Discourse on Method*," Chapter 4 of Huxley's *Methods and Results* (New York: Macmillan, 1893).

[39] B. F. Skinner, *Beyond Freedom and Dignity* (New York: Knopf and Co., 1971), 62.

[40] Tadros, "The Wrong and the Free," 81.

opportunity to do A and receive the penalty.) And, Tadros adds, even if "threats plausibly interfere with liberty," still *warnings* by the state do not.[41]

Neither of these last points by Tadros is very plausible. The "I am not threatening you, I am warning you" distinction trades on the distinction between an intention and a predictive belief. Relying on that distinction in this context is about as plausible as relying on the (again, true enough) distinction between a threat and a promise (as in the familiar if childish saying, "that is not a threat but a promise"). In all three cases—of promissory undertaking, expression of intention, or statement of belief—the state has created aversive consequences attached to certain behaviors and these are but three different ways of drawing a would-be actor's attention to those consequences. One's choice set is restricted, no matter with which speech-act such restrictions are announced.

Tadros's first point here is no better—indeed, one suspects it is a bit tongue-in-cheek. It would be a poor notion of liberty that regarded the attachment of, say, the death penalty to some act such as going to the circus as not impeding liberty (because what, now one has the substitute opportunity of going to the circus and dying?). Any opportunity-set notion of liberty has to have the resources to classify some "opportunities" as so costly that they are not opportunities.

In the last main section of his chapter, Tadros raises the kind of external, all-things-considered kind of judgment that I discussed earlier with respect to Husak. For Tadros rebels against my limitation of criminal legislation to the prohibition of moral wrongs with the same kind of argument. Even if the function of the criminal law is to punish those who deserve it, Tadros tells us, and even if this function demands that, prima facie, all and only moral wrongdoing be prohibited in the criminal codes—even so, other values may intrude to justify criminal prohibition of non-wrongful actions on other grounds. As Tadros says, "real-world expansion of criminal law often arises due to political pressures. ..."[42] and "It is best not to ignore these processes in a theory of criminal law."[43] Tadros gives the example of a country threatened with invasion by a powerful aggressor unless it criminalizes some morally innocent behavior such as homosexuality.

Yet I can easily and harmlessly concede all of this because it touches nothing I care about. A theory of criminal legislation (such as legal moralism purports to be) need not catalogue all the values external to the value served by criminal law (*ex hypothesi*, giving just deserts) that *could*, in some conceivable circumstance, justify using criminal law for non-just-deserts ends. Mousetraps can be used as paperweights if the need arises, yet the theory of a good mousetrap need not include how well it does in holding down papers in a high wind. Such external considerations are no more relevant here than were Husak's three "drawbacks of punishment" relevant to what the proper ends of punishment are.

IV. Double Jeopardy and Proportional Punishment

The two most general questions often asked about criminal law are, first, "*Why* is there a system of law whose distinctive feature is that it punishes people?" And second, "*What* is it within such a system that should be prohibited so that it can be punished?"

[41] Tadros, "The Wrong and the Free," 84.
[42] Tadros, "The Wrong and the Free," 90.
[43] Tadros, "The Wrong and the Free," 90.

I turn now from the five chapters that consider these "why punish?" and "what to punish?" questions, to a third general question. Gideon Yaffe's chapter[44] considers an aspect of this third general question, which is: "How much should an offender be punished?" This is often called the proportionality question in criminal law.

In the last three chapters of my *Act and Crime* I analyze one of the doctrines that in Anglo-American law is used to promote proportionality of punishment. This is the doctrine forbidding the state from twice putting anyone in jeopardy of criminal trial or punishment for committing the same offense. Yaffe ventures two criticisms of my treatment of double jeopardy. The first is to question whether indeed double-jeopardy doctrines are best seen as protecting against disproportional punishment, or whether they shouldn't rather be seen as protecting some other values.

Yaffe recognizes that he presents my views on this matter in terms different than those I myself used to present my theory originally:[45] Yaffe nonetheless hopes that I recognize my theory in his different presentation of it. And I do. One of the pleasures of having commentators as gifted as Yaffe and others in this volume lies in seeing one's own views in a new light.

My linking of double-jeopardy doctrines to the value of proportional punishment, was a simple one.[46] To be punished twice or more for the same thing is to be punished too much—assuming, as Yaffe too acknowledges, that the punishment for each offense is not set too low initially. Yaffe contrasts this goal for double-jeopardy law with a different goal: this is the goal of preventing the state from stacking the odds in its favor in criminal trials, by doing the trials over (and over) again until it gets a verdict that it likes. This would not only be unfair, but it also makes verdicts less likely to reflect the truth of the matters such verdicts are about.

It is in fact pretty standard in the legal literature on double jeopardy to articulate a series of goals served by the double-jeopardy prohibition.[47] These certainly include my concern; no over-punishment beyond desert. Also included is a pair of secondary concerns that Yaffe rightly attributes to me; first, the concern that duplicative trials cause unnecessary harm and trauma to those accused of crimes, and second, the concern that finality is needed for criminal proceedings no less than for civil proceedings under the analogous civil law doctrines of *res judicata*. And Yaffe's preferred value, protecting against one-sided repetition that is both unfair and inaccurate, is also prominently mentioned in that literature.[48]

Given this list of plausible values served by the doctrines of double jeopardy, how do Yaffe and I argue for one of these values being the main or dominant point of the institution? Part of our common mode of argument here lies in the fit of the doctrines to the values: if the doctrines would be those that a rational person would believe would produce certain valuable states of affairs and not others, then those values are the values served by such doctrines.

In this regard Yaffe brings up two aspects of the doctrines of double jeopardy as it is practiced in America. One is the dual-sovereign rule: double jeopardy is not

[44] Gideon Yaffe, "Moore in Jeopardy, Again," this volume.
[45] Gideon Yaffe, "Moore in Jeopardy, Again," 112, n. 2.
[46] Moore, 1993c, ch. 12. [47] Moore, 1993c, ch. 12. [48] Moore, 1993c, ch. 12, 313.

prohibited if different sovereigns (different states, or one state and the federal government) are placing the accused in jeopardy for the same offense. Yaffe recognizes that my proportional punishment rationale should oppose this doctrine, whereas his "no unfair and inaccurate do-over" rationale need not. Yaffe is perspicuous on both counts. Yet the dual-sovereign doctrine itself is a much-criticized doctrine. It is an artifact of federalism, does not exist in non-federal systems, and ought to be rejected even in ours. One isolated, lousy legal doctrine is a poor basis for touting advantages for one's view as to the values the entire system of doctrines should be seen to serve.

Moreover, any view, mine included, can justify the dual-sovereign exception to double jeopardy. All that is needed is to supplement one's dominant rationale—say, my proportional punishment rationale—with another value, that of the autonomy of sovereigns in trying and punishing crimes over which they have jurisdiction. Surely protecting this last value is in fact the motivation for the dual-sovereignty exception. In any case, if one weighs this value heavily, that will rationalize the dual-sovereignty exception without diminishing at all my point, which is that the general rationale for the double-jeopardy prohibition is the keeping of punishments proportional to desert.

Yaffe has better shot selection (as they say in basketball) with a second set of double-jeopardy doctrines. Yaffe raises a query about *double* jeopardy—why not a ban only on *triple* jeopardy, or on *quadruple* jeopardy? Here he recognizes my theory does its work properly: while three and four times the normal punishment for an offense is disproportional, so too is two times. Still, Yaffe seeks at least parity of fit for his theory. Do-overs (where the choice to do over is asymmetrically vested in the state) give those motivated by concerns other than accuracy the ability to tilt the odds in their favor.

Yet I am not sure that Yaffe's theory achieves parity of fit with my own in justifying this bit of double-jeopardy doctrine. After all, why wouldn't Yaffe's theory favor *no* multiple-jeopardy limitations at all, so long as the power to do over was symmetrically vested (and where any disparity of resources between the state and the accused is remedied)? On the assumption that do-overs increase accuracy (think of Yaffe's retotaling of receipts in bookkeeping), why shouldn't the only jeopardy limitation in service of Yaffe's value be one where the diminishing returns of retrial in terms of accuracy are exceeded by the costs?

I turn to Yaffe's second criticism. This focuses on my analysis of when there is a "sameness of offense" for purposes of the double-jeopardy prohibition. Yaffe recognizes that my analysis has two parts to it, corresponding, first, to the sameness of wrong-type—what Yaffe calls "norms"—and, second, to sameness of wrong-tokens—what Yaffe just calls "wrongs." I will use Yaffe's terminology instead of mine to keep our discussions in this volume more easily tracking of one another.

Sameness of offense can fail in one of two ways under my analysis. First, even when there is but a single act-token done by the defendant, that act-token may instantiate two or more norms. A grabbing of a purse can be both a battery and a theft, for example, and one can be separately tried and punished for each without offending double jeopardy. Second, even when there is only one norm involved—say the norm against armed robbery—a defendant can do this on two or more occasions, such as robbing one bank on Monday and another bank on Tuesday. In either case there is no bar to separate trials and separate punishments, because there is no "sameness of offense," the trigger for the double-jeopardy prohibition.

I devote a separate chapter of my *Act and Crime* to each of these two parts of my sameness-of-offense analysis.[49] Yaffe focuses only on the second part, explicitly recognizing nonetheless that sameness of offense requires both sameness of norms and sameness of wrongs instantiating those norms.[50]

As to the sameness-of-wrongs part of the analysis, Yaffe first describes my theory and then proposes an amendment to it that he favors. Yaffe in his description of my theory describes me as "flinching" from my usual steadfastness in applying metaphysics to aid in the solution of moral and legal problems.[51] Specifically, he sees me as here putting aside entirely the metaphysics of act-token individuation and using instead a policy-justified, "wrong-relative" mode of individuation. As he puts it, "Michael is committed here to . . . wrongs . . . [being] individuated differently from . . . acts . . . ."[52] This leads Yaffe to formally state my view of sameness of offense as existing when but only when, for two putatively distinct act-tokens AT1 and AT2:

(1) the norms that made AT1 and AT2 wrong are identical (numerically "the same"); and
(2) the moral property P that makes AT1 and AT2 wrong is also the same.[53]

Yaffe motivates (2) for my view by adverting to the "one defendant, two-shots each causally contributing to the death of one victim" case: although there are two act-tokens in such a case, there is only one norm being violated (the one prohibiting killing) and only one property (causing the death of the victim) making each of these act-tokens wrong; so only one offense, not two, and double jeopardy prohibits successive trials or punishments.

Yaffe then applies my view to the "two defendants, two shots each causally contributing to the death of one victim" case. Both common moral intuition (including Yaffe's and mine) and the settled law regards this as two instances of wrongdoing, not one, and so double jeopardy does not prohibit two trials and punishment for homicide even though there is only one dead victim.

Yaffe sees that I argue for this result[54] by individuating the norms that are violated not only by act-types (such as, "killing a human being") but also by the identities of the agents who do them and the victims to whom they are done. Morality, on this view, is structured in Hohfeldian terms: morality's norms are seen as agent and victim relative, so their content is "Jones ought not to kill Smith," rather than the Biblical "Don't kill." Yaffe then demurs:

> [W]e could have reached the same result with an importantly different theory of wrong individuation. We might have thought that a wrong is not just a token act that violates a norm but is, instead, a token act *by an agent* that violates a norm.[55]

[49] Moore, 1993c, ch. 12, chs. 13–14.

[50] Yaffe concedes, at least *arguendo*, my theory in Chapter 13 of *Act and Crime* of the individuation of norms. Yaffe, "Moore in Jeopardy, Again," 118, n. 12.

[51] Yaffe, "Moore in Jeopardy, Again," 111, 112.

[52] Yaffe, "Moore in Jeopardy, Again," 113.

[53] Yaffe, "Moore in Jeopardy, Again," 119.

[54] Moore, 1993c, 356–65.

[55] Yaffe, "Moore in Jeopardy, Again," 120–1 (emphasis in original).

This then yields Yaffe's "Agent-, Norm, and Wrong-Relative Theory" of sameness of offense, one where the identity of the agent is a third and separate requirement (in addition to sameness of norm and sameness of wrong-making property).[56]

This may strike many readers as a small difference between my theory and Yaffe's amended version; indeed, so small a difference as to make no difference. Both theories decide the cases the same way; both theories rely on sameness in the identity of agents who do wrongs; the only difference is that my theory (as Yaffe sees it) only asks the agent-identity question as an aspect of norm-individuation (wrong-*type* individuation), whereas his asks it as part of wrong-individuation (wrong-*token* individuation).

Now I want to argue that even this small difference does not exist, because Yaffe has misunderstood (slightly) my theory. Start with Yaffe's amused description of me as "flinching" from legal use of the metaphysics of act-token individuation.[57] I may indeed flinch here, but it is not a full flinch because I do in fact make use of the relevant metaphysics. This fact is important here because with that metaphysics I place Yaffe's agent-identity question squarely within my theory of wrong individuation, whereas Yaffe says that only his amended theory can so place it.

The second conjunct of my overall theory of sameness of offense aims to capture where it is or is not the case that a defendant has violated the same norm *more than once*. Yaffe gives me a univocal test here, in terms of identity of the wrong-making property possessed by two putatively distinct act-tokens. In fact I have a much more complicated, three-part disjunctive test here, of which property identity is only one part of one disjunct.

Start with the most straightforward disjunct, where the two putative act-tokens AT1 and AT2 are in fact one and the same act token. For example, the norm prohibits killing human beings; suppose it is true that defendant D on Monday at 10:28 am: shot victim V to death; killed V; did a terrible thing to V; moved his finger on the trigger of a gun; etc. On the "coarse-grained" theory of act-token individuation that Yaffe and I both accept,[58] these are but different ways of describing one and the same act. Because there is only one act-token, there is only one wrong-token of one norm (killing) and thus a sameness of offense that bars double jeopardy.

On any plausible metaphysics of acts,[59] they, like other events and states, are constituted as the acts they are by three variables: (1) the person who does them (or more generally in the case of non-actional events, the object involved); (2) the properties they exemplify; and (3) the temporal location (a duration, not a point) at which they exist. If there is sameness of agent, sameness of properties, and sameness of time, then there is sameness of act-token.

This much of the metaphysics of act-token individuation I do not flinch from but endorse for use in my theory of double jeopardy. The "flinching" comes with the next two disjuncts—for while act-token identity is sufficient under my theory for wrong

[56] Yaffe, "Moore in Jeopardy, Again," 121.

[57] Yaffe apparently pictures me as the Stonewall Jackson of metaphysical legal theorists. You remember: Jackson never flinched but stood like a stone wall in the face of advancing Union armies.

[58] I discuss the coarse-grained theory of act and event individuation in Moore, 1993c, 280–92, 369–71. See also Moore, 2009d, ch. 14.

[59] Moore, 1993c, 369.

identity, it is not necessary, so that wrong identity might exist even when act-token identity does not.

The second disjunct focuses on the possibility that Yaffe identifies. In cases like that of "one defendant but two act-tokens jointly causing the death of a single victim," there is sameness of wrong despite lack of identity between the act-tokens constituted by the two separate shots. What makes the two shootings be two separate act-tokens is both difference of temporal location and difference in properties. What makes them nonetheless the same for wrong-individuation purposes is two things: same *wrong-making* property (even if not same properties in total), and same *agent*.

The third disjunct is one I discuss[60] but which is not adverted to by Yaffe. These are cases where again there is sameness of agent; there may or may not be sameness of wrong-making property; and there is not sameness of temporal location but there is *closeness* of temporal location. My example in *Act and Crime* was the squeezing off of five shots in quick succession into an unoccupied building; under current law this counts as but one wrong despite the lack of both act-token identity and wrong-making property. (I call this in *Act and Crime* the "volume discount" for rapidly sequenced, qualitatively similar actions.)

Now notice: for all three disjuncts of my theory of wrong individuation, agent identity is crucial. For if the two putatively distinct act-tokens AT1 and AT2 are done by different agents, then in all three cases there can be no identity of wrongs (and therefore no sameness of offense). It is true that I also individuate norms (and not just wrongs) by the agents who violate them. This I find independently plausible. But that does not preclude agent-identity from entering into wrong-individuation, for my theory no less than Yaffe's.

Now consider Yaffe's elaboration of the *Russell* case[61] (the three shooters in a gun battle with each other, one of whose bullets kills an innocent bystander). Understanding that my theory of wrong-individuation depends on agent identity robs Yaffe of his objection that I need "the Three Norm Theory to be true if [I am] to explain why D3's double jeopardy argument should be rejected."[62] I don't *need* the agent-relative mode of norm individuation to be true (even though on independent grounds I believe it to be true). So I can match Yaffe step for step in rejecting each defendant's claim of sameness of offense by saying, like Yaffe, that D3's wrong-token is different from D2's, and different yet again from D1's, even if (contrary to fact) each of them violated the same norm.

Interestingly Yaffe and I probably disagree about how certain versions of the facts of *Russell* should be decided, even though our theories of wrong-individuation do not here differ. For Yaffe is sure in his own mind that all three shooters in *Russell* should be punished as depraved-heart murderers even though only one of them actually shot and killed the innocent bystander. (It is this certainty that he touts for his theory of wrong-individuation over the theory he attributes to me.)

There are certainly versions of the facts of *Russell* where I would agree with Yaffe that all three shooters are guilty of depraved-heart murder. When each shooter by his participation in the gun battle substantially encourages the other two to shoot back, then

[60] Moore, 1993c, 390 n. 1; Moore, 2009d, 559.
[61] *People v. Russell*, 91 N.Y.2d 280, 693 N. E.2d 193 (1998).
[62] Yaffe, "Moore in Jeopardy, Again," 121.

each is a cause of the death of the innocent bystander; when each is also "depraved-heart reckless," each is then guilty of his own depraved-heart murder.

Yet Yaffe posits a version where the two whose bullets did not kill the victim, are only *de minimus* causal contributors to the victim's death, and where each knows that fact so that the probability of killing each consciously entertains is less than is required for depraved-heart recklessness. It is supposed to be an advantage for a theory, Yaffe thinks, if it can nonetheless convict all three of depraved-heart murder. On the contrary, as Yaffe anticipates, I find such a conclusion to be a cost of any theory that generates it, not a benefit. As I argue at length,[63] we should each be judged by what our actions contribute to some wrong or harm, and by the culpability with which we each made that contribution. To increase our blame by what others do or the culpability with which they do it is a form of vicarious liability that violates the principle of proportional punishment.

Yaffe anticipates that I will "bite the bullet" in this way; yet despite his admission that if I do he has "little to say,"[64] he in fact goes on to say quite a lot. Yaffe posits the somewhat recherché, 1,000-cylinder gun case (where each defendant without prior preconcert puts in one of the 1,000 bullets in the gun that kills the victim, and where Yaffe stipulates that 1-in-1,000 odds are too low for the recklessness required for the crime of reckless endangerment). Given those facts, my response here is the same as in *Russell*: no one of these 1,000 defendants is guilty, and any theory that says that they are is a bad theory.

This is particularly evident in the glaringly fictional route Yaffe uses to reach this result. Like the court in *Russell* itself (which talked about one gun battle rather than separate acts of shooting by three separate shooters), Yaffe imagines "a single joint act here—filling the gun with bullets—that is violative of the very norm to which the endangerment statute gives legal force."[65] Now who is running roughshod over the metaphysical facts? This isn't flinching from metaphysical steadfastness—this is full-scale retreat! By any plausible theory of act-token individuation, there were as many acts of bullet placements as there were agents doing them—in this case, one thousand. Because my theory of wrong-individuation is built on the correct metaphysics of act-token individuation, I can reach the correct conclusion about this case: there were 1,000 tokens of wrongdoing, none of which were accompanied by the requisite level of culpability.

In any case, recall that all of this latter talk is a bit by-the-by. For my actual theory of wrong-individuation *could* reach Yaffe's conclusions as well as does his theory, for both theories are equally sensitive to the identity of agents. Fortunately, my theory doesn't require me to reach all of Yaffe's conclusions, for some of them are quite counterintuitive.

V. The Need for Accomplice Liability

This last discussion with Gideon Yaffe (about multiple-defendant gun battles and thousand-cylinder guns) dovetails nicely with the topic that interests Leo Katz in his

[63] Moore, 2009d, 319–23. [64] Yaffe, "Moore in Jeopardy, Again," 122.
[65] Yaffe, "Moore in Jeopardy, Again," 123.

contribution to this volume.[66] Katz explores my thesis that accomplice liability should be eliminated. That thesis of mine was defended on the grounds that the relations of causation and counterfactual dependence, when properly construed, capture all and only the cases where there should be liability for a completed crime; that therefore the present accomplice liability doctrines of Anglo-American criminal law either sweep too wide in creating a too-extensive liability for completed crimes, or they are redundant to liability as a principal for completed crimes.[67] Katz's general strategy is to present cases where liability for a completed crime seems intuitively correct yet where (even my reconstrued) notions of causation and of counterfactual dependence are insufficient to justify such liability—ergo, the need for some other basis of liability, viz. the *sui generis* accomplice liability that I reject.

Homing in on the precise demarcation of the kind of cases he needs is tricky for Katz. His lead example proves to be an unfortunate one to select for his purposes. This is the example of two defendants, D1 and D2, each of whom shoot a bullet into victim V, killing him. Each bullet was sufficient to kill V then and there by itself; and they were simultaneous. Katz thus starts with a classic example of a concurrent overdetermination case[68] where there is causation of V's death by each D1 and D2 even though there is no counterfactual dependence of V's death upon D1's act or upon D2's act, considered individually.

The reason this example ill suits Katz's purposes is because there *is* causation by D1 and D2 in such cases, both under my theory and under settled law.[69] So there is no need for recourse to some non-causal basis ("acting in concert") to impose liability here. Katz thus modifies the example to add in a balance of evils (or "necessity") defense. There are two variations of this necessity defense story. In the first, D1 and D2 each know that the other is going to shoot and kill V, and each has a good moral reason to shoot V himself because that will relieve a relative of a painful condition. Katz concedes that this reason would not be good enough for either D1 or D2 to kill V on his own, but thinks that it would be a good enough reason to shoot at someone (V) who is, after all, going to die anyway. In the second variation, a third party, T, apprises D1 and D2 of each other's existence and plans and tells them that if they make their simultaneous shots at V, he (T) will enable each of them (via payment of money) to save a relative of theirs from a painful disease. Katz: both D1 and D2 would have a necessity defense in the first variation but not the second; further, it is each shooter knowingly co-ordinating with the other that makes the difference between the two variations; and this "difference is entirely non-causal."[70]

Unpacking this complicated example, first ask yourself why D1 and D2 would have the necessity defense in the first variation when their simultaneous shots are not done in the coordinated fashion instigated by T. The defense exists because of an oddity I have noted before about necessity: one may be able to justify causing harm in overdetermination cases (where the harm does not counterfactually depend on any

66 Leo Katz, "Do We Need a Doctrine of Complicity?," this volume.

67 Moore, 2007c; Moore, 2009d, ch. 13.

68 See Moore, 2009d, 114–18, 410–25, for a description and analysis of the various kinds of overdetermination cases.

69 Moore, 2009d, 115–16.

70 Katz, "Do We Need a Doctrine of Complicity?," 136.

defendant's individual action), even though one could not justify causing that same harm for that same reason in non-overdetermination cases.[71] Thus, if one shoots too late, so that V is already dead; or if one shoots too early, so that one's bullet kills V before the second bullet arrives;[72] or if one shoots on time, so that V dies from both bullets—in all variations, that the harm was going to happen (or had happened, or was happening) anyway matters for purposes of justifying the act.

Why that is so is a puzzle, but it is not the puzzle Katz wants to raise. He finds it troublesome for my theory that there *is* liability in the second variation, and urges a recognition of acting-in-concert accomplice liability as the solution. Yet the second variation just isn't a problem for me: both D1 and D2 were substantial causers of V's death, neither had sufficient reason to be such causers, and therefore they may well be liable as principals, just as Katz says.[73] The oddity is why they are *not* liable in the uncoordinated case. Until we know this we cannot see what role coordination plays in removing a defense they would otherwise have had.

Katz does better with his other examples. Although he does not do so, we would do well to separate them into two classes. The first is constituted by certain prevention, failure-to-prevent ("omission"), and double-prevention cases. Katz cites one of the most famous, James McLaughlin's prospector in the desert case.[74] In Katz's variation of this much-used case, D1 poisons the water V will need to survive in the desert, but D2 drills a hole draining the poisoned water out; and V dies of thirst in the desert.

This example has the structure Katz needs. For on my analysis of this overdetermination-by-double-prevention case,[75] neither D1 nor D2 caused the death of V (because the *absence* of something (such as potable water) can neither be an effect of their acts nor a cause of V's death). Given the sufficiency of what each did to guarantee V's death, neither act was individually necessary for that death. Thus, there is no counterfactual dependence of V's death on either of the defendant's actions. There being no causation and no counterfactual dependence, D1 and D2 are each not liable for the death of V. (They each are liable as attempters, but inchoate liability is not Katz's concern.) Katz agrees with this conclusion in McLaughlin's version of the case, when D1 and D2 do not know of each other; but urges there should be liability in cases where each knows of the other's plans and coordinates his activity in light of this. Ergo, Katz thinks, a need for accomplice liability to ground this last conclusion.

Katz should extend this analysis to what I call overdetermination-by-prevention and to overdetermination-by-omission cases, too.[76] For in these cases I also acknowledge that there is no causation and no counterfactual dependence; so if Katz can make liability intuitive in the cooperative versions of these cases, that would be grist for his mill, too. Take a famous overdetermination-by-omission case, the one where D1 (the mechanic) fails to fix the brakes he was duty-bound to fix, and D2 (the driver) fails to apply the brakes when needed to avoid a collision. Most judges affirm my theory here:

[71] Moore, 2009d, 66–8.

[72] These I call the acceleration cases. Moore, 2009d, 66–8.

[73] I am conceding Katz his conclusion in these cases only *arguendo*. It is not clear to me that the cooperative nature of the second pair of shootings removes the necessity defense.

[74] James McLaughlin, "Proximate Cause," 39 *Harvard Law Review* 149–99 (1925), 155 n. 25.

[75] Moore, 2009d, 466–7.

[76] Moore, 2009d, 457–9, 449–51.

no causation, no counterfactual dependence, no liability.[77] But if the mechanic and the driver knew of each other's plan, and coordinated their own inactions accordingly, then according to Katz there should be liability for the collision, and this must be because of the cooperative nature of their inactivities.

Katz also includes the well-known *Tally* case[78] as one of his examples, a case that I would classify as being still in the first class of examples. Judge Tally's act of sending the telegram (that countermanded an earlier warning telegram) did not cause the victim's death, nor was that death counterfactually dependent on the judge's act. My own conclusion is therefore that Tally is guilty only of the inchoate crimes of attempt and/or risk creation, but he is not guilty of any form of homicide. Katz agrees, but again Katz would convict Tally of homicide if Tally coordinated his activity with the activities of the actual killers of the victim.

The second class of cases on which Katz relies are those of *de minimis* causation where there is no counterfactual dependence. *Wilcox*[79] and *Hicks*[80] are his examples, but he could as well have used Yaffe's gun battle and 1,000-cylinder gun cases as well. In all such cases, each defendant makes a *de minimis* causal contribution to some bad outcome—death of a victim, illegal jazz performance, polluted lake, or whatever. The bad outcome would have occurred just the same (or only *de minimis*ly different) without each defendant's action. Yet, per Katz, if the defendants coordinated their tiny contributions in light of other contributions they knew others were also making, then each is liable for the bad outcome.

A common reaction to both of these classes of cases is to think that all defendants are liable for all outcomes. Often this result is reached by a Yaffe-like clumping: ask not what each individual contributed to the outcome, but ask rather what the activity of all individuals summed together contributed (which in each case, is a lot). Yet this is too undiscriminating for Katz. He needs to accept my view of these cases (which is: no liability for the outcome, only for the trying or the risking) so that he can then distinguish the coordination version of such cases, find liability, and base that new liability on the cooperative nature of the interaction.

Consider Katz's two classes of cases one at a time, taking the overdetermination class first. Katz has difficulty picturing a plausible motivation for these coordinating actors. After all, each is doing (or omitting to do) something that he knows will be by itself sufficient to obtain the result he intends. Such actors don't need others' help to get what they want. The one plausible thing they could wish to achieve by cooperation is to insulate themselves from liability. That is, they might calculate this way: each defendant knows that his causal contribution will be non-existent in the eyes of the law; each also knows that his contribution will not be necessary for the bad outcomes either; each also knows what the others plan to do; each also knows the law and its underlying morality well enough that he knows that neither he nor any of the others can be liable for the outcome because of this absence of causation and of counterfactual dependence; he knows that the others know this too; so each does his act which is sufficient to allow the bad result he intends; everyone else does too; and the bad outcome ensues.

[77] Moore, 2009d, 450 n.53.

[78] *State ex rel. Attorney General v. Tally*, 15 So. 727 (Ala. 1894).

[79] *Wilcox v. Jefferey*, [1951]-1 All Eng. Rep. 464.

[80] *Hicks v. United States*, 150 US 442 (1893).

Such contriving defendants are too clever by half. They are like many of the Jesuitical types that populate Katz's books,[81] in that they think they can skirt around the conditions of moral and legal liability while still getting what they want. If morality and the law are so wooden-headed that they cannot cut them off, they could literally get away with murder. So they need to be held liable. But how? In most of this first class of cases the motivations of the contriving cooperators are such that now, with the contriving state of mind, each of their actions becomes necessary for the bad outcome. Take the two would-be killers of the prospector in the desert. If neither of them would do what they did unless they were assured of not being liable for the death of V, then the action of each is necessary for that assurance, which assurance is itself necessary for them to act as they did. It now takes both of them acting to motivate either of them to act; each action is now necessary for the death of the victim.

Yet under other assumptions about the motivations in these cases, this won't be true. D1 and D2 in the prospector case, for example, might be willing to go ahead without any assurance that they won't be liable—they might each rely on not getting caught, for example. But if this is true, then don't we lose the sense that each should be liable for the completed crime of murder? After all, each contriving defendant (where absence of liability is not a crucial part of the motivation) differs not at all from the solo defendant (where absence of liability is not a crucial part of the motivation) who "lucks out" in finding his intended victim helpless before some natural force. If natural bad luck had poisoned or drained the water out of the prospector's barrel before D2 drilled his holes, nature would be a sufficient causer or double-preventer of the prospector's death, in which event D2 "lucked out"—he tried to be a factor in the prospector's death but he wasn't. The same should be true if it wasn't nature but another person poisoning or draining the water.

The temptation is to make a unit out of the two defendants in cases like the prospector in a way that it is not tempting to "unify" one person and nature. Yet this temptation is to be resisted because it results in a vicarious liability—holding one person liable because of what another did. With express agreements and literal agency, as Katz recognizes, liability is OK because it is not vicarious—once one rids oneself of any notion of "intervening causation," procuring accomplices are typically themselves substantial causers. It is true vicarious liability (where there is no express agency) that is anathema to proportional punishment.

Katz's second class of cases require a different analysis. Here, recall, each defendant's act is either not necessary at all or to any degree for the criminally prohibited state of affairs, or it is necessary only to a *de minimis* degree; likewise each defendant is only a *de minimis* cause of the bad state of affairs. Yet collectively, all of these defendants' acts do substantially cause the harm; and collectively they are also necessary for the harm to occur. Katz (and Yaffe too) intuits that there should be liability for the completed crime in such cases even though the Moorean pillars for such liability (causation or counterfactual dependence) are absent.

These cases are troublesome but that is because Katz and Yaffe stipulate something into their examples that we will need to retract. Take Yaffe's gun battle example,

[81] Leo Katz, *Ill-Gotten Gains* (Chicago: University of Chicago Press, 1996).

modified to make more plausible the crucial stipulation. Suppose it is a gun battle between three rival gangs (not three individuals, as in the actual case); each gang has a thousand members each of whom fires one shot in the gun battle; one of the bullets strikes and kills an innocent bystander. Katz and Yaffe would concede that the one who fired the shot that struck and killed the bystander was a substantial cause of that death; yet the 2,999 others' causal contribution is only by way of the encouragement each shot fired gives to others to keep firing; and we are to stipulate that these 2,999 causal contributors are all *de minimis*, considered individually. Katz and Yaffe challenge me to find a way to hold all for some form of the completed crime of homicide.

Yet I decline the challenge. Each shooter's shot was only a *de minimis* causal contribution; and it was not necessary to the victim's death. Each non-lethal shooter is liable for some form of inchoate crime only, either reckless endangerment or attempted murder. It is only when one ups the causal contribution of each so as to make it not *de minimis*—as in Yaffe's three-shooter case—that there should be liability for the completed crime.

Does this crisp response become problematic if we change a feature of these cases, namely, suppose that there is no one of the causal contributors who is not merely a *de minimis* cause? Several thousand polluters, for example, each of whom individually contributes a tiny amount while knowing (or even cooperatively intending) that thousands of others are as well. Now there is no one liable despite a criminally prohibited state of affairs being intentionally brought about by human agency. Should there be liability in such cases, despite the absence of (individual) causation and of (individual) counterfactual dependence? To my mind the answer is no, so I needn't scramble around to find some non-causal, non-counterfactual basis for liability. But even if the answer were yes, I am not sure how this would advance Katz's thesis about the retention of accomplice liability for cooperative activity. After all, unlike the 1000 cylindered gun and gun battle examples, here there is no guilty principal with which all others can be accomplices. So Katz and I would equally seem to be in trouble if liability is needed in such cases.

VI. Negligence

Some of the chapters in this volume attend to the elements of responsibility rather than to the more general criminal law topics of punishment, legislation or proportionality. One of these elements is negligence, to which Ken Simons devotes his chapter.[82] Simons does an admirable job in tracing the various and changing things that I have written about negligence over the years. And he is fair in his assessment of my current resting place on negligence: my views are "squishy," something of a "hodge-podge," pluralistic in their conception of when liability rightly attaches under the present doctrines of negligence, and skeptical of there being a punishable culpability of negligence when negligence is taken to be truly inadvertent creation of an unreasonable risk.[83]

[82] Kenneth Simons, "Reluctant Pluralist: Moore on Negligence," *this volume*.
[83] Simons, "Reluctant Pluralist," 139.

There is a bit of a tension (that Simons does not comment upon) between being both a pluralist and a skeptic about negligence. For a pluralist believes that negligence is not one thing but is rather several (say eight?) different things, whereas a skeptic seemingly denies that negligence is anything at all. The tension is relieved by attending to the difference between a positive (or descriptive) theory of negligence law and a normative (or reform) theory of that law. As to the first, I and my co-author, Heidi Hurd, are indeed pluralists: we can account for much but not all of what is called by the courts negligence liability by our "archipelago" of eight different bases for blame. As to the second, we are skeptics: there should be no liability for cases where the actor truly did not advert to the relevant risks because no one is morally blamable for true inadvertence; this, despite the fact that there is liability for such cases under present law.

Simons raises several points of possible or actual disagreement as he describes our account, so I shall respond briefly to some of these seriatim as they occur in his chapter. The first of these concerns the place of negligence along the culpability/wrongdoing divide. Is negligence a measure of wrongful action, viz., action that risks more loss than gain? Or is negligence a measure of culpability, viz., if one has done some act A made wrong by A having property P, to be negligent is to unreasonably risk P being present? Or should we be eclectic and say that in torts where the norm is, "Don't act unreasonably," negligence measures wrongdoing, whereas in criminal law (and the law of intentional torts) where norms prohibit actions like "don't kill" or "don't rape," negligence measures the culpability of risking (that death might ensue from one's acts or that sex might be without consent of the victim)?

I should I suppose confess that I haven't had the courage to revisit what I said on this topic in the scattered writings of the past to which Simons refers. Since he has read those writings more recently than have I, I am confident he gets what I said right. But irrespective of what I may have elsewhere said, what I now think is this: negligence always and everywhere only measures culpability. This follows from what I have always held to be true, which is that wrongdoing is a matter of harms (and benefits) *caused* and not harms (and benefits) *risked*. Therefore unreasonable risk never is about wrongdoing; unreasonably risking actions are wrongful only insofar as the risks making them unreasonable are realized, i.e., the harms risked are *caused*. A miss really is as good as a mile, as far as wrongdoing is concerned.

This crisp (not "squishy") conclusion is not a matter of idiomatic speech using the words "wrong" and "wrongdoing," for I recognize that there are idiomatic usages of these words along lines contrary to my stipulations. Rather, it is a matter of theoretical consistency and thus of stipulative meaning to these terms. The conclusion follows from the objective theory of wrongdoing I have always defended. Take an act A by D causing the death of V. Suppose, in scenario 1, that A posed a low risk of death of V, but promised a high likelihood of saving many lives of other innocent persons. As it turned out, in fact, A did cause the death of V and saved no lives. Or suppose, in scenario 2, that A posed a high risk of V's death and that there was no offsetting benefit foreseeable to D as he acted. Yet as it turned out, although V was killed, many innocent lives were saved by D doing A.

By my lights, D did wrong in scenario 1 but not in scenario 2, for the good consequences actually justified the taking of V's life in the latter case but not the former. Of course, D in the second scenario might well be culpable if he consciously chose to do A knowing of these risks and ignorant of these benefits; and D in the first scenario is not culpable because under the facts as he reasonably believed them to be he was saving life at reasonable cost. But wrongdoing (on the objective theory of it) is purely objective; only killings that *actually* save lives are justified and thus not wrong. Killings that don't may be non-culpable through being excused, but they were still the wrong thing to do.

Simons agrees with none of this, but resolution of this large issue will have to await another occasion (if not another life). Simons's second worry has to do with the drawability of lines measuring degrees of negligence. Hurd and I urge that criminal recklessness should be distinguished from criminal negligence in part by the degree of imbalance that exists between the downside and the upside risks of any given action. Simons objects that criminal negligence already is distinguished from civil negligence by being "gross," and thus that our proposal requires a finding of "gross, gross" risk to find recklessness. (Even worse, Simons thinks, is that for depraved-heart recklessness, we would need a finding of gross, gross, gross risk-taking!)

This objection sounds better than it is. To begin with, Simons worries about how juries will react to these "gross" discriminations; but it is always a mistake to judge a criterion of law by how it will play in jury instructions. Jury instructions are a matter of decisional heuristics, itself a branch of cognitive psychology. Good instructions are what produce accurate jury verdicts, even if what they instruct jurors to do is errant nonsense. Holistic judgments of degrees of negligence in my experience do quite well (in terms of accuracy and consistency) despite our inability to give juries any meaningful guides about how to measure degrees of negligence. Indeed, judgments of negligence generally are commonly thought to resist meaningful guides, which is why there is so little "law of negligence" of the sort that Holmes mistakenly envisioned ("stop, look, and listen," etc.).

A third item of disagreement that Simons raises lies in my rejection, as he sees it, of H. L. A. Hart's incapacity basis for negligence culpability. In truth, for many years I thought Hart was persuasive when he argued:

1. True negligence exists when: (a) one fails to advert to risks one *could* have adverted to, given one's individual capacities; and (b) when one *should* (ought to) have adverted to a risk given its magnitude and the value of the interest risked.
2. Whenever one *should* do something that one *can* do, one is culpable if one doesn't do it. Therefore:
3. Negligence is culpable.

This seems rather plausible, does it not? If we ought to have done something, and we didn't do it even when we could have done it, we are blameworthy, are we not? The intended conclusion is that there is a culpability of unexercised capacity, as Hart called it.

Simons finds our rejection of Hart "unconvincing."[84] But that is because he construes our conclusion to be "that the capacity judgment is irrelevant to culpability."[85] Not so! Rather, our claim is that capacity judgments in this context presuppose that other desert determiners are or are not present, and once we see that context-sensitivity point, we will see that morally relevant capacities/incapacities depend wholly on these

[84] Simons, "Reluctant Pluralist," 147. [85] Simons, "Reluctant Pluralist," 147.

other desert determiners. We don't throw away capacity judgments; we interpret them to be non-basic.

Compare intentional wrongdoing. By my analyses,[86] the culpability of choice depends on two counterfactuals being true: when D does some wrongful act A, (1) D would have *not* done A if he had chosen not to do it, and (2) D would have chosen not to do A if he had wanted very badly not to do A. True enough, these counterfactuals depend on the morally salient conditions of choice and desire. Even so, these counterfactuals do give the content of the capacities required for intentional wrongdoing. For intentional wrongdoing as for negligence, we don't discard capacity judgments in responsibility contexts; we rather interpret them.

With the true negligence of inadvertent risk-creation, the relevant capacities are cognitive, not volitional as with intentional wrongdoing. "He could have adverted to risk R" is translated into "He would have adverted to R if X." We query what X can be in this context; it cannot be choice; nor can it be wanting, or even trying. It looks like the only thing that could be "X" in this context would be morally salient character. As in "he would have adverted to R if he cared about others as much as he cares about himself." And we then argue that character is no proper basis for a punishable moral blame.

This doesn't eliminate capacity judgments in the context of negligence; it rather reduces such judgments to what matters to their truth, which seemingly is character. So this is really where issue should be joined for Simons. He thinks persons are blamable for bad character (when it issues in bad actions) whereas I and Hurd do not. This is indeed Simons's fourth point of disagreement.

Simons thinks that it is acceptable to filter capacity judgments through character ("D would have adverted to the risk if he cared more about V," for example) because he, unlike me, is willing to blame for bad character. Not just blame in the aretaic sense that we don't invite persons with bad character to dinner, we shun their company, we disapprove of their lives in the biographies we write about them, etc.; rather, in the more robust sense that they deserve to be punished—to be made to suffer—for who they are. We liberals find this anathema, and so here issue is indeed joined.

VII. Negligence as Culpability, and Culpability as a Proximate Cause Test

Some of the themes of Ken Simons's chapter are also addressed by the friendly but hard-hitting chapter by John Oberdiek.[87] Oberdiek's topic is nominally distinct from Simons's: the harm-within-the-risk test for proximate causation in negligence cases. Yet some themes, notably the wrongdoing/culpability distinction as applied to negligence, recur.

Oberdiek examines three questions in his chapter. In the order in which he presents them: (1) What is the harm-within-the-risk test in tort law and do I (and my partner in crime here, Heidi Hurd) get it right in our description of that legal test? (2) Is the harm-within-the-risk test conceptually incoherent, as we claim? And (3), is the

[86] Moore, 2014b; Moore, 2014d; Moore, 2014e.

[87] John Oberdiek, "Putting (and Keeping) Proximate Cause in its Place," this volume.

harm-within-the-risk test normatively undesirable? Oberdiek focuses most of his attention on (2), but let me briefly respond to his concerns in (1) and (3) before turning to the main show.

As to (1), Hurd and I are criticized for treating the harm-within-the-risk test as an aspect of culpability, not of responsibility—and "negligence liability . . . [in fact] tracks a defendant's responsibility, not culpability."[88] I am more than a little unclear what meaning Oberdiek intends for either "responsibility" or "culpability." Apparently for Oberdiek, responsibility in torts is focused on objective facts like the fact that the defendant's actions caused the plaintiff's injuries,[89] whereas culpability apparently is focused on subjective facts like the fact that the defendant possessed one of the mental states of intention or belief that make up what the criminal law calls *mens rea* or "guilty mind."[90] I find both of Oberdiek's stipulated senses peculiar, and thus his criticism wide of the mark.

As to "responsibility," Oberdiek joins Simons in thinking that negligence measures wrongdoing. For negligence for Oberdiek consists of "faulty conduct"[91] in the sense of an action unreasonably risking the causing of harm to someone. Unlike Simons, Oberdiek thinks that such objective wrongdoing excludes negligence from also being a form of culpability. By this Oberdiek does *not* mean what some tort theorists would mean in saying this. When Richard Epstein and George Fletcher urged that tort law does and should exclude considerations of culpability and focus on causation[92] or asymmetrical risk imposition,[93] they were making a quite different point to the one Oberdiek intends. Unlike Epstein or Fletcher, Oberdiek wishes to include *unreasonable* risk-taking in his conception of negligence, but nonetheless thinks that unreasonable risk imposition does not measure culpability.

Oberdiek is working with too narrow a notion of culpability. It is true (as Hurd and I examine in the work that Simons revisits in his chapter in this volume)[94] that *how* negligence measures culpability is a matter of some dispute. Indeed, Hurd and I argue that inadvertent negligence never gives rise to a culpability properly punishable by criminal law. But no one anywhere in this debate thinks that negligence in torts is not a measure of some kind of culpability, one that can be called "fault."

The standard view is that inadvertent negligence involves the culpability of unexercised capacity. Even though some harm-causer *could* have adverted to a risk, and even though he *should* have adverted to that risk because it was an unreasonable risk to take in light of the reasons for taking it, he nonetheless acted in a way that realized that risk. In short, he should have done something he could have done and for not doing so he is culpable.

88 Oberdiek, "Putting (and Keeping) Proximate Cause in its Place," 157.
89 Oberdiek, "Putting (and Keeping) Proximate Cause in its Place," 158.
90 Oberdiek, "Putting (and Keeping) Proximate Cause in its Place," 157.
91 Oberdiek, "Putting (and Keeping) Proximate Cause in its Place," 158.
92 Richard Epstein, "A Theory of Strict Liability," 2 *Journal of Legal Studies* 151–204 (1973).
93 George Fletcher, "Fairness and Utility in Tort Theory," 85 *Harvard Law Review* 537–73 (1972).
94 Moore, 2011d; Moore, 2011e.

With that brush cleared, now see that as a description of existing tort law it is hardly misguided (let alone "fundamentally misguided")[95] to describe the harm-within-the-risk test as being part of the analysis of the kind of *culpability* required for tort liability. As Hurd and I presented in detail in our history of the doctrine,[96] to ask whether the harm that in fact happened is an instance of the type of harm the risk of which made the defendant negligent, is to ask the second (or "fit") question of culpability. The thought was that, just as a harm-token has to be an instance of the type of harm intended for intentional torts, so a harm-token has to be an instance of the type of harm unreasonably risked for negligent torts. These are both culpability enquiries, even if Oberdiek wishes to stipulate a meaning to "culpability" making them otherwise labeled in his private lexicon.

As to (3), Hurd and I adopted Judge Friendly's view in *Kinsman Transit*: there is "no reason why an actor engaging in conduct which entails a large risk of small damage and a small risk of other and greater damage . . . should be relieved of responsibility for the latter simply because the chance of its occurrence, if viewed alone, may not have been large enough to require the exercise of care."[97] In our own language, if a defendant is doing something he should not do because it unreasonably imposes risk R1, and that act causes a harm not an instance of R1, why should he escape liability and leave the loss on an entirely faultless (i.e., not *culpable*) party?

Here tort law (and the corrective justice ideal behind it) does differ from criminal law (and the retributive justice ideal behind it). Harms caused by culpable actors, even when such harms were outside the risk making the actor culpable, should be compensated, even if such harms should not be part of the calculus of desert appropriate for punishment. The same is true for intentionally imposed harms. Criminal law rightly completes its culpability analysis by asking whether the harm in fact caused by the defendant's action is an instance of the type of harm he intended when he did that action, assigning the culpability of *intentional* crimes only if the answer to this "fit question" is affirmative. Yet by our and Friendly's normative argument, tort law should not ask this fit question, even for intentional torts. The intentional tortfeasor is doing what he should not be doing, and even if the harm that action caused is different than the type of harm intended, he should be liable. (This is a considerable expansion of the tort law doctrine of transferred intent, but ours is here a normative argument, not a descriptive or interpretive one.)

Oberdiek sidesteps giving any answer to the Friendly–Moore–Hurd normative argument. He instead contents himself with the observation that on our view mere knowability of a risk is sufficient to make an actor liable for any realization of that risk, and he criticizes us for not requiring a degree of knowability that it would be unreasonable for the actor to ignore. As I argue below, Oberdiek's criticism would have bite anywhere but in the class of cases at issue for the harm-within-the-risk test, namely cases where the actor is already unreasonable in not adverting to larger risks that happened not to materialize. But in any case, no amount of quibbling about the degree of knowability required here is in point: the Friendly argument goes through for this class of cases even if the small risk was completely unknowable to the defendant when he acted.

[95] Oberdiek, "Putting (and Keeping) Proximate Cause in its Place," 157.

[96] Moore, 2002a. [97] Judge Friendly is quoted in Moore, 2009d, 199.

Turning now to (2): Oberdiek's main query is our conceptual argument against the harm-within-the-risk test. We and Oberdiek separate "the" conceptual argument into two strands, although these two strands are related. One strand is what we variously call the "typing" or the "description" problem. Any harm-token can be multiply described because any such token instantiates multiple types of harms. Yet whether a risk of some type of harm occurring is large enough for it to be unreasonable to overlook it when one acts depends mightily on how finely grained the type of harm chosen is. A risk of any and all kinds of *property damage* posed by winding a clock too tightly, for example, is likely much larger than is the risk of a denting-one's-car kind of property damage posed by the winding of the clock.[98]

This radical indeterminacy of the harm-within-the-risk test could be reduced if there were some agreed-upon, commonly used, or authoritative way to fix the breadth of the types of harms one is to use in assessing the risk. Indeed, in an earlier article I go through what I regarded as an exhaustive list of the possibilities here.[99] One of those ways is seized upon by Oberdiek. He confidently proclaims that "it is a brute fact that people characterize risks similarly," we all share a "roughly similar conceptual scheme"; there is therefore a "level of generalization that ordinary persons typically bring to bear in describing or categorizing relevant event-types ...."[100]

If saying it could make it so, this confident, unhedged assertion would surely do it. But even when accompanied by clicking his heels together three times, such confident pronouncements by Oberdiek—and to be fair, by Steven Shavell, Herbert Hart, and Tony Honoré[101] before him—are false. And it is an empirical question, testable and tested by social science. But if we are going to do this from the armchair, does Oberdiek really think there is some narrow range of typings and descriptions that ordinary folk will agree to about, for example, a plaintiff's broken window caused to be broken by a defendant's cricket ball? Plaintiff suffered: a broken window; damage to her house; harm; breaking of a window in her house; breaking of a new picture window in the house; breaking of a plexi-glass, reinforced, supposedly "unbreakable" window in her house; breaking of the most expensive window in her house; breaking of her sitting-room window; breaking of a window into a million pieces; breaking of a window with 4,036 lines of fracture; etc., etc.

Until one of us does the social science on this empirical issue, I guess that Oberdiek and I will have to simply voice our disagreement, and move on. Oberdiek, however, tries to buttress his "brute facts" of conventional categorization in a couple of odd ways. One is to head off into game theory, and to note that coordination games often have determinate solutions when there is some salient convention known to parties who wish to coordinate their behavior.[102] Presumably the point is to illustrate the "brute fact" that there are, sometimes at least, salient conventions around which parties'

[98] The example is more fully spelled out in Moore, 2002c.

[99] Moore, 1993a. This earlier article dealt with the typing (or "description") problem in the context of the foreseeability test of proximate causation, not the harm-within-the-risk test, but the problem is the same in both contexts.

[100] Oberdiek, "Putting (and Keeping) Proximate Cause in its Place," 161.

[101] I deal with Hart and Honoré's (and Steve Shavell's) recourse to conventional convergence of category usage in Moore, 1997b, 392–5.

[102] Oberdiek, "Putting (and Keeping) Proximate Cause in its Place," 161.

expectations can crystallize. To solve the famous Schelling problem (of where to meet in Manhattan), they might indeed meet in Grand Central Station. But what if the salience needed was a *description* of Grand Central Station? Is there a salience to: "42nd street's biggest attraction"; "New York City's last train station"; "the former home of the New York Central"; "New York prostitutes' favorite haunt"; "the site of a famous takings case involving Penn Central"; etc., etc.?

Another odd move for Oberdiek is his attempted use of the "ordinary person's capacity to foresee harm" as the appropriate benchmark for typing harms. Oberdiek tells us that there is a "common knowledge that can be expected to be available to ordinary persons regarding the probability of those event-types."[103] Yet surely this common sense about probabilities can be brought to bear only if there is first a fixing of the relevant event-type, and that is the question.

I think that what has misled Oberdiek here is his justifiable confidence that ordinary people make predictions all the time, and often they make similar predictions. Yet this humdrum fact, while true enough, cuts no ice here. For predictions in everyday life are made with the relevant type already fixed by the description used in the question asked. So if the prediction is that the Rutgers football team will lose their next game (again!), the type is fixed—any kind of *loss* will verify the prediction; any kind of *win* will falsify it. It is true that after the event occurs, we might ask, "how likely was it that they would suffer *that loss*?" If "that loss" refers to the loss-token actually suffered, then there is a typing problem and radical indeterminacy looms. But we all understand that with such past-tense expressions we are usually to paraphrase them into "how likely was it that Rutgers would lose again?"—that is, suffer *some* instance of the type, losing. That everyday predictive practice is as successful and as shared as it is thus helps Oberdiek's case not at all.

In my early essay on problems in the typing of events risked, I raised a separate problem.[104] This was the moral arbitrariness of conventionally shared modes of categorization, even assuming (*arguendo*) that such modes existed. Oberdiek takes this argument by me seriously so that he engages at length in trying to find a "moralized conception of risk imposition,"[105] one that can isolate a level of event-categorization that is "somehow anchored in a cogent characterization of risk ...."[106]

To see the point that Oberdiek and I are making here against critics like Stephen Perry, suppose in the window-breaking example that the plaintiff leads a very boring life and everyone knows this. So boring, in fact, that her window being broken by the cricket ball was the most exciting thing that happened to her all week. Suppose further that everyone thus settles on this as the salient description of the event. Surely, even with this supposition, we should not frame the risk as a risk of exciting this person when we ask whether the harm that happened was within the risk. This, because risking the enlivenment of the plaintiff's existence was not a risk making the defendant negligent.

[103] Oberdiek, "Putting (and Keeping) Proximate Cause in its Place," 162.
[104] Moore, 1993a, 393–5.
[105] Oberdiek, "Putting (and Keeping) Proximate Cause in its Place," 163.
[106] Oberdiek, "Putting (and Keeping) Proximate Cause in its Place," 162.

So one restriction on the event typology for use in the harm-within-the risk-test is that the event types used must be limited to those that are morally relevant in this context. And in the context of assessing culpability for imposing unreasonable risk, the morally relevant event-types will be *harm*-types. Yet this restriction in fact lessens very little the indeterminacy of the test. For a window breaking can still be characterized as a harm event, a property-damage event, a damage-to-window event, a broken-picture-window event, etc.

Further lessening of the indeterminacy here might be sought in the hope that within this morally relevant type of event-types (harms), there will be one common type most people will pick out when they ask the culpability question, "what risk made this defendant culpable?" Again, this is an empirical question, and again, my armchair bets are in the negative. But Oberdiek appears not to rest his case for determinacy only on the supposed brute facts of convergent typing of harm-events in this context; he also appears to think that an artificial (or hypothetical) convergence can be constructed. The constructed convergence will be "that characterization of risk that can be morally justified to both defendant and plaintiff as a matter of mutual moral accountability."[107] I find this last constructivist bit very puzzling. Corrective justice is not a matter of plaintiffs and defendants making a deal or reaching some mutually acceptable accommodation. What should be "morally justifiable" to them is what should be morally justifiable to all of us, viz. a typing of risks such that admittedly culpable (negligent) defendants pay only for the harms within the risks that made them culpable. Yet what risks are these? The indeterminacy in picking the types of harms risked still looms undiminished.

Oberdiek also believes he has an answer to the second indeterminacy Hurd and I directed against the harm-within-the-risk rule. This second indeterminacy stems from the *multiple* risks that must be taken into account as one applies the test. Even assuming one has ready to hand some solution for the typing questions about each harm-token, there remains the problem that any action risks many harms besides the one it causes.[108] The hitting of the cricket ball that breaks the window, for example, may also have risked: the hitting of the plaintiff's person; the frightening of the plaintiff; the death of the plaintiff's parakeet; a denting of the plaintiff's car; etc., etc. All such risks are risks making the actor negligent.

The worry for the harm-within-the-risk test is not that we don't know which risk to pick as we decide whether the harm that happened was within "the" risk that made the actor negligent. For the simple answer to that worry is that the defendant is liable if the harm that happened was within *any* of the risks the imposition of which made him negligent. Rather, the worry is that any harm that is in fact caused by a defendant's action, no matter how remote, bizarre, unlikely, or unforeseeable that harm may be, had to have some likelihood of happening; thus, some risk; thus, one of the risks going into the package of risks making the defendant negligent. This makes the harm-within-the-risk test no limit at all on liability unless such risks are artificially eliminated from use in the test; and no non-arbitrary way is given as to how to do that.

107 Oberdiek, "Putting (and Keeping) Proximate Cause in its Place," 164.

108 Moore, 2002a.

Hurd and I recognized when we made this argument that one rejoinder would be to urge a *de minimis* limitation on risk such that a *de minimis* risk, "if (miraculously) it does materialize in harm, that harm falls outside the risks considered in the HWR test."[109] In Oberdiek's hands *de minimis* is construed as, "unreasonable to expect a defendant to advert to."

The first thing to notice about such *de minimis* responses is that they are hostage to there being some answer to the first, the typing problem, about risk. For any seemingly *de minimis* risk can be made substantial and thus non-*de minimis* by increasing the generality of the description of the harm risked.

The second thing to notice is that, at most, Oberdiek's version of this response only lessens indeterminacy but does not eliminate it. Suppose that some harms, when narrowly typed, are so unlikely that their possibility is not within the ambit of duty of a reasonable person to discover. Even so, that leaves many minor risks (that are not *de minimis* in Oberdiek's sense) in the package of risks that make one negligent; and thus those harms are within the risk, contrary to the classic examples given to defend the doctrine. That a heavy can might drop on another's foot and injure it if the can is clumsily handled, for example, may well be a minor risk compared to the explosion more likely because the can is filled with nitroglycerin. Yet this minor risk is hardly one that the reasonable person should not foresee and take into account as he carries the can. Such minor harms remain "within the risk," even with Oberdiek's limitation working as he sees it working.

The third thing to notice about Oberdiek's version of the *de minimis* response is that it ignores the special class of cases of negligence with which it must deal. For, remember, in the cases relevant to test the harm-within-the-risk test, the defendant's act already is a negligent thing to do because of other, larger risks (that happened not to be realized as things turned out). So when Oberdiek asks what precautionary calculations we can fairly demand of this class of defendants with respect to the bizarre, remote, or unlikely harm that actually happened, he forgets that these are defendants who have no justification whatsoever for their actions. For such defendants' "burdens of adequate precautions" (or other reasons for forgoing the action) have already been found wanting compared to the larger, unrealized risks their actions posed. Therefore, contrary to Oberdiek's assertion, anything that is possible is knowable to them and they have a duty to know it. All harms that are caused by such defendants' actions were possible; therefore knowable; therefore part of the package of risks making such defendants negligent; and therefore "within the risk," no matter how rare, unlikely, bizarre, and freakish.

Oberdiek concludes to his own satisfaction that "the risk rule . . . is on a secure conceptual foundation, after all."[110] Not so. Each of our original two conceptual objections thus retains its force versus the harm-within-the-risk test, despite Oberdiek's heroic rescue efforts for the test. Either problem is deadly for the test; the two together overdetermine the uselessness of the test. The two problems together, after all, show the test to be "conceptually bankrupt" and "conceptually incoherent"; they make the case for abandonment of the test "conclusive."[111]

109 Moore, 2009d, 193.

110 Oberdiek, "Putting (and Keeping) Proximate Causation in its Place," 168.

111 Moore, 2009d, 197, 225.

VIII. Omissions, Absences, Negative Facts, and their Truth-Makers: Wright, Spector, and Fumerton as Three "Nattering Nabobs of Negativity"

If I say nothing about this subject, according to Richard Wright my omission could easily *cause* various things, such as insult, disappointment, etc.;[112] according to Horacio Spector, my silence, while not a cause, might be a "causally sufficient condition of a negative causal factor" contributing to such states of affairs of insult, disappointment, etc.;[113] according to Richard Fumerton, omissions and other absences have a robust enough existence that they can serve as the truth-makers in statements containing negative facts (like the fact that I didn't say anything).[114] So plainly I need to say something (in a positive way of course) about these three "nattering nabobs of negativity."[115]

Before I do so, let me acknowledge that Richard Wright in his chapter raises numerous issues besides those surrounding omissions and other absences. Yet these other issues all have to do with the continued defense Wright wishes to mount for his NESS conception of causation. And I see little enhancement of the light thrown on these issues by Wright's contribution here beyond what has been said before, pro and con[116] (although there seems to be an appreciable increase in the heat). So I shall let the existing exchanges between Wright and myself speak for themselves on how NESS fares as a theory of causation.

Turning to the negative, let us start with an issue that must be addressed by all who would argue about the existence, moral salience, or causal potency of omissions, and that is the conceptual issue of just what omissions are.[117] I and Spector both take omissions to be a species within a larger genus, so let me approach the genus first. At bottom, the problem of negativity is *absence*. Something is absent when it is *not* present.

Even saying something this obvious immediately gets one to conundrums like those Richard Fumerton addresses: for a negative proposition like, "it is not the case that James saved Smith" to be true, mustn't there be something existent in the world that makes the proposition true? Let us defer this most basic question about negative "things" (negative propositions, negative facts, negative properties, negative states of affairs, negative events, negative causes, negative duties, etc.).

Start with absences as if they were unproblematic, and build from there. Spector has his own taxonomy of morally relevant negative items in mind, but I still prefer my own, more discriminating taxonomy,[118] which goes like this:

[112] Richard Wright, "Causation: Metaphysics or Intuition?" this volume.

[113] Horacio Spector, "The Moral Asymmetry Between Acts and Omissions," this volume.

[114] Richard Fumerton, "Moore and the Metaphysics of Causation," this volume.

[115] Then Vice-President Spiro Agnew's well-known and alliterative appellation for certain political opponents.

[116] See particularly the exchange between Wright and myself in Benedikt Kahmen and Markus Stepanians (eds.), *Critical Essays on "Causation and Responsibility"* (Berlin: de Gruyter, 2013). Wright's contribution is, "The NESS Account of Natural Causation: A Response to Criticisms," *Critical Essays on "Causation and Responsibility"* 13–66. Mine is Moore, 2013b, 334–48. We each cite earlier versions in this exchange in these articles.

[117] An issue I have addressed several times in my work. See Moore, 1993c, 22–31; Moore, 1997b, 262–77; Moore, 2009d, 52–5, 436–44.

[118] Moore, 2009d, chs. 3, 18.

1. *Preventions* are (seemingly—I retract this later) actions that cause an absence. When Jones prevents Smith from dying, he causes an absence of a death of Smith.
2. The *omissions* we care about morally and legally are (seemingly again) absences of preventative actions that cause the harm that would have been prevented.
3. *Double (or "pre-emptive") preventions* are preventative actions that prevent a preventer from preventing a harm or other state of affairs. My old example: you tie up a life-guard and prevent him from preventing Smith from drowning.[119] Seemingly an action causes an absence which in turn causes an ill-effect. Absences thus serve here as causal intermediaries, that is, as both causes and effects.
4. *Allowings* are doubly-preventative actions where what is removed by the allowing act is some barrier to the occurrence of some state of affairs to which the actor was morally entitled to return.
5. *Doings* are voluntary acts that cause some state of affairs. When Jones *kills* Smith, Jones by some action causes Smith's death.

Spector recognizes items 2, 3, and 5 on this list; but fails to separate single preventions, 1, from double preventions, 3; fails to distinguish allowings as a subspecies of double preventions; and adds a counterfactual element to omissions, so that an omission becomes an absence of prevention *that the actor had the ability to prevent.*

Once we are clear of what we are talking about when we talk about the negative in moral contexts, the next obvious question is the moral one that is at the center of Spector's chapter: is omitting to prevent some harm h morally worse than, better than, or on a par with, doing some action that causes h? (One of the benefits of the richer taxonomy of negative things given above is that it allows you to see there are *four* moral questions here, not one, as I explore in my work; yet for brevity let us stick with Spector's question, which is certainly a central one of the four.)

Spector agrees with me in thinking that there is a moral difference between acts causing a harm and omissions failing to prevent that very same harm: holding all else equal so as to isolate the respective contributions of active causings versus passive omittings, omitters are less blameworthy than causers. This moral difference means that, in a naturalistic meta-ethics, there must be some natural property difference underlying the moral difference—for if moral properties like blameworthiness supervene on natural properties (as Spector and I both think they do), any difference in moral properties must be accompanied by some natural difference. (Spector quibbles with me that I call for a metaphysical rather than a factual difference;[120] in truth "metaphysical" in my usage is just "factual" at a high level of abstraction.)

The third question that naturally follows is, on what natural property(ies) does this moral difference depend? Here again Spector agrees with me in thinking that the natural properties are those of causation and of counterfactual dependence: the more blameworthy *doing* requires causation, whereas the less blameworthy *omitting* requires only counterfactual dependence.

[119] Moore, 1993c, 278 n. 42.
[120] Spector, "The Moral Asymmetry Between Acts and Omissions," 188.

This answer to the third question quickly leads to the fourth and fifth questions to ask here: fourth, why should causing make this moral difference? And, fifth, why can't omissions also be causes of the harms they fail to prevent? As to the fourth question, Spector expounds at length on what he calls his "transcendental argument" for there being such a moral difference.[121] The Kantian label is due to Spector's modesty: his argument "perhaps does not show that the moral asymmetry view is true in an external, objectivist sense. But it shows that its dismissal is not a practical option ...."[122] This, because moral responsibility itself presupposes *individual* responsibility, and that is possible, Spector argues, only if we can separate our agency from the agency of others, itself dependent on an agent-relative (i.e., deontological) understanding of moral obligation such that what we *do* marks the boundary of (at least "primary") agency.

My own argument for why there is a moral difference is somewhat similar to Spector's (although not being a transcendental idealist, I cast the argument in moral realist terms). Agent-neutral (or "consequentialist") views of moral obligation, if not side-constrained by agent-relative obligations and permissions, make us responsible for both too much as well as too little. Needed are the restrictions and permissions of deontology,[123] and needed for those restrictions and permissions not to become hopelessly contradictory in their commands and licenses, is that deontological obligation is by-and-large restricted to *actions* we should not do, not actions we should not *omit* to do.[124]

At the end of the day I am not sure that either Spector's argument or my own amount to much more than a display of our common intuition that agency is more bound up with *doing* and thereby *causing* some harm than it is bound up with doing nothing and having that harm's occurrence counterfactually depend on our passivity. Still, that is a pretty robust intuition on its own, and at our age (when the argument chains get shorter and shorter), that is not such a bad place to rest.

The fifth question is a big one—are omissions themselves but a kind of cause? Rightly generalized, the question really is, can *absences* be the relata of singular causal relations, either as causes or as effects? It might seem that answering this causal question depends on a prior answer to the sixth and most basic question here, which is the question I alluded to before with reference to Richard Fumerton: do omissions and other absences exist in their own mode of existence so that their "presences" can be the truth-makers for negative statements like, "Jones's failure to water the plants caused the plants' deaths?"

We have reason to hold this sixth and most basic question in abeyance, however. On certain theories of the causal relation absences needn't be truth-makers in order for causal statements with negative conditions in them to be true. I refer to what I and Fumerton call *generalist* theories of causation, theories according to which singular causal relations are not parts of our basic ontology; rather, causal *laws* are basic, and singular causal statements are to be reduced to such laws (together with space/time locators for the particulars instantiating the laws). This view of the causal relation dispenses with any need for absences as particulars. My omission to water a plant is not an existent

[121] Spector, "The Moral Asymmetry Between Acts and Omissions," 198.
[122] Spector, "The Moral Asymmetry Between Acts and Omissions," 202.
[123] Moore, 2009d, 36–41. [124] Moore, 2012e.

particular, as my watering of the plant would be. Rather, I omit to water the plant at some time t whenever the type of action, plant watering, is uninstantiated by any act-token at t. And it is plausible to think, as did Mill, that there can be lawful connections between uninstantiated types as well as between types that are instantiated on the occasion in question.

Wright and Spector both hold a version of Mill's generalist theory of causation. Yet interestingly Wright (like Mill himself, at least most of the time) plumps for causation of and by absences, while Spector does not. Wright's line of argument is a familiar one, as he acknowledges in his extensive reliance on my former ANU colleague and regular critic, Jonathan Schaffer.[125] Wright too sees that his generalist theory of causation can accommodate omissions (preventions, double-preventions, allowings) as causes or effects without his having to pay any heavy ontological price: "No implausible ontology is required; no ghostly entities are involved."[126] Quite so. As I argue elsewhere,[127] generalists about causation need not commit to the existence of negative entities, properties, or states of affairs.

Yet Wright's enthusiastic embrace of this happy prospect should be tempered by the undesirability of treating absences as causes. If omitting to prevent a death is just another way of causing that death, why is there that difference in moral blameworthiness of acts versus omissions that Spector and I think plainly exists?[128] If it is not causation that is the natural property underlying this moral difference, what is that property or properties? Schaffer, on whom Wright here relies, at least takes a stab at answering these queries,[129] but Wright says nothing (which, by his own ontology, is a true absence).

Again, an embrace of negative conditions as causes seems less than happy once one considers how this exacerbates what I call the promiscuity worry about generalist theories.[130] Fumerton sees this in his article in this volume:

> [L]awful connections extend indefinitely into the past and the future. My stabbing you with my knife is . . . [a] condition of your dying, but so is your failure to stop me, and Obama's failure to stop me, and your failure to carry a loaded gun that you would have used to stop me, and my mother's giving birth to me, and so on. . . . [C]onditions are all over the place and we will need to rely heavily on pragmatic and evaluative considerations to select from among the lawfully sufficient conditions those for which we hold a person responsible.[131]

To be sure, there are costs the other way if one refuses causal relata status to absences, as Schaffer ably demonstrates.[132] Still, I have elsewhere answered how these costs can be

125 Jonathan Schaffer, "Causes Need not be Physically Connected to their Effects: The Case for Negative Causation," in C. Hitchcock (ed.), *Contemporary Debates in the Philosophy of Causation* (Oxford: Blackwell, 2004); Schaffer, "Contrastive Causation in the Law," 16 *Legal Theory* 259–97 (2010); Schaffer, "Disconnection and Responsibility," 18 *Legal Theory* 399–435 (2012).

126 Wright, "Causation: Metaphysics or Intuition?" 179.

127 Moore, 2009d, 478–80.

128 Moore, 2009d, 447–9.

129 Schaffer, "Disconnection and Responsibility," 429–31, 432–44. Why these "stabs" are mere pinpricks is laid out by me in Moore, 2012a, at 506–9.

130 Moore, 1993c, 268–9; Moore, 2009d, 396–9, 477–8.

131 Fumerton, "Moore on the Metaphysics of Causation," 217.

132 Schaffer, "Disconnection and Responsibility."

minimized, and once minimized, paid,[133] so repeating the answers to Wright's repetition of Schaffer would not be fruitful.

Spector, like myself, thinks the balance of these costs and benefits clearly tips in favor of not regarding omissions and other absences as causes. He thus adjusts his version of a generalist theory of causation so that "omissions are not logically equivalent to the negative (or positive) causal conditions they fail to prevent."[134] While I sympathize with Spector's desire to adjust the generalist theory of causation as to deny any place for omissions as antecedent conditions in causal laws, I am quite unsure how he justifies the adjustment. Much of the justification seems to lie in his certainty that negative conditions have no truth-makers in the absences to which they putatively refer. Peculiarly, Spector is *not* being ontologically abstemious here ("no negative entities," etc.); rather, his is a multiple realizability worry:

> Though the set of causal conditions of the lady's being robbed must include the negative condition that the lady was not aided, the pedestrian's omission does not guarantee that negative causal condition. In effect, we can hypothesize that another pedestrian or the police aided the lady, or could have aided the lady....Therefore, non-preventative omissions are not logically equivalent to the negative (or positive) causal conditions they fail to prevent.[135]

Yet if one has no ontological objection to absences being truth-makers of negative propositions, why couldn't one combine the absences of the pedestrian and of everyone else into the truth-maker for the negative predicate, "not aided?"

In any case, however generalists settle between themselves whether their theory of causation does or does not countenance omissions and other absences as causes, there remain the nagging problems besetting the generalist theory itself. Richard Fumerton nicely summarizes these problems.[136] Fumerton starts with the same perspective as do I in my causation book,[137] noting that there are three plausible building blocks we all have to work with: causal laws, singular causal relations, and counterfactual dependence. My book defends the singularist view: causal relations are basic, and causal laws are derived from these relations, counterfactual dependence being derived from the laws. Generalists like Wright and Spector regard the laws as basic, and derive both singular causal relations and counterfactual dependence from the laws. Fumerton then shows how difficult it is to start with either laws or counterfactual dependence and derive singular causal relations from either. The problem, of course, is circularity, that is, keeping the items being defined out of the definition defining them.

Wright thinks that circularity is a charge uniquely directed to his version of a generalist theory. But in truth the circularity danger looms for any non-primitivist theory of causation. Wright's theory does suffer from pretty overt circularity, although he emphatically denies it. Yet just because Wright avoids using the words, "cause" or

[133] Moore, 2012a.

[134] Spector, "The Moral Asymmetry Between Acts and Omissions," 190.

[135] Spector, "The Moral Asymmetry Between Acts and Omissions," 190–1.

[136] Fumerton, "Moore on the Metaphysics of Causation," 204–7.

[137] I devote separate chapters of *Causation and Responsibility* (Moore, 2009d) to each of these three building blocks: to counterfactual dependency, Chapters 16–18; to nomic sufficiency, Chapter 19; and to singular causation, Chapter 20.

"counterfactual dependence" when he defines causal laws, this does not mean that those notions are not implicit within his definition.[138] His "regardless..." and "would not be entailed..." clauses are plainly counterfactual. His "successional relation" is plainly a cause-based stipulation of asymmetry and temporal ordering in no way built into the supposedly basic notion of lawful sufficiency. "Distinctness" is plainly added to further restrict lawful sufficiency so as to rule out counterexamples. And "immediacy" is construed so as to bring in causal process ideas that enable him to rule out pre-emptive overdetermination counterexamples.

Wright proudly lumps all of these restrictions together to announce the discovery of a new form of sufficiency, "causal sufficiency."[139] Yet causal sufficiency is so constructed that it is just another name for causation. The whole process is like a "proof" that a square is a circle that goes like this: take a circle and add four right-angled pieces to its circumference of just the right size and shape; call the resulting lumpy mixture, a kind of circle, namely a "squared circle"—and identify squares as a kind of circle.

If we reject the generalist theory of causation, whether in Wright's hands or in the hands of others, then we need to answer the sixth question earlier distinguished: are there negative states of affairs, negative events, negative properties, that can serve as the truth-makers for negative propositions like "it was the failure to water the plants that caused the plants to die."

Notice that this is not the question of whether there are negative propositions, nor the question of whether there are *true* negative propositions, nor the question whether there are negative truths. That, as Fumerton rightly says, is unproblematic, so that "if facts *were* truths... we would have no principled reason to reject the view that omissions or failures to act can be causes."[140] Yet Fumerton joins me in denying that truths—true propositions—can be causes.[141] Truths are about the world; they are not in the world to do any causing.

So the ontological question of relevance here is not about the existence of negative truths. Rather, it is the question of whether truth-makers of negative truths exist. Is there a state of affairs (or "fact")[142] that corresponds with and makes true the negative proposition that Fumerton does not believe in the generalist theory of causation? Fumerton, remarkably enough, argues for an affirmative answer.

Fumerton bases this conclusion on two arguments. The first I shall call the back-door argument because it proceeds by eliminating any other truth-maker for true

[138] Wright repeats his definition of causal laws in his "Causation: Metaphysics or Intuition," 172.

[139] Wright *says* that he uses "the phrase, 'causal sufficiency' to refer to the requirement... that all of the conditions in the antecedent of the causal law must be instantiated on the particular occasion." Wright, "Causation: Metaphysics or Intuition?" 172. Yet this counterfactual requirement—of each condition being necessary for the sufficiency of the set—is built into any plausible account of causal laws starting with regular succession; as Fumerton shows, this much you need for *lawful* sufficiency. "Causal sufficiency" for Wright in reality names the lumpy mixture of all the things essential for singular causal relations. Thus my charge: cause is equated with causal sufficiency is equated with cause.

[140] Fumerton, "Moore on the Metaphysics of Causation," 214.

[141] Fumerton, "Moore on the Metaphysics of Causation," 209; Moore, 2009d, 353, 445.

[142] I am, in this chapter, adopting Fumerton's terminology even though it differs from the terminology I employ in *Causation and Responsibility*. "Facts," as Fumerton uses the term, embrace what I call states of affairs; what I call "facts" in *Causation and Responsibility*, Fumerton calls, "truths." There is nothing of substantive significance going on in our differing choice of labels because Fumerton and I agree entirely on the nature of the things so labelled.

negative proportions and then seizes upon negative facts as the last possibility not eliminated. And in fact, the alternative possibilities for truth-makers for negative truths are neither numerous nor appealing. The one that comes to mind is the one Fumerton considers, what I call elsewhere the "hole in the donut" strategy:[143] if we inventory all of Fumerton's beliefs and find that none of those beliefs has as its object that the generality theory of causation is true, then this complete list of beliefs is the truth-maker for the negative truth in question. The donut is the truth-maker for the negative propositions about an absence of donut in the middle (i.e., a hole).

Fumerton objects to this strategy because of its circular use of a negative fact to complete the description of the "donut." This fact allegedly is that there are *no* more beliefs than these on the inventory. If one were to avoid explicit words of negation, saying perhaps "these are *all* the beliefs he has," Fumerton would no doubt reply that "all" implies "*not* some other." Yet whether this last reply is good is quite a technical matter of modern logic that I cannot pretend to know how to answer. In the standard quantified predicate logic that we all teach, "for all x, x is F" does imply "it is *not* the case that there is some x such that x is *not* F." Yet there are alternative logics that have material implication and universality as primitives, so that no use of negation is required to give meaning to "all." So perhaps one can complete the list of actual beliefs by use of an "all" that is non-committing to negation. The issue being beyond my expertise, I leave it.[144]

Fumerton sees that one might sidestep his argument by denying "that we need a distinct fact as the truth-maker for every distinct true proposition."[145] For then there could be true negative propositions even if there were no negative facts making them true. Fumerton gives as an example a true disjunctive proposition where one of the disjuncts is false: "Either the moon is made of green cheese or Chicago is in Illinois."[146] Now the truth-maker is an unproblematically positive fact, viz. Chicago really is in Illinois. But Fumerton excludes negative propositions from this sidestep maneuver because negative propositions have no such positive states of affairs making them true.

I should have thought Fumerton's sidestep maneuver for disjunctive propositions would rather go like this. A disjunctive proposition is just a truth functional combination of two propositions, just as are conjunctive propositions, equivalence propositions, or material implication propositions. The truth-makers for all of them is just the truth-maker for each of their component propositions, plus the truth-tabular definition of the logical connectives. There is no place and no need for some larger truth-maker (unless one thinks there is some semantics to the logical connectives beyond the truth tables usually assigned as such semantics). Once one appreciates that negation is just another logical connective, then it would seem we could treat negative propositions in the same way. Their truth-makers are the falsity of the corresponding positive proposition. The truth-makers for "Jones failed to water the plants yesterday" are all the ways in which "Jones watered the plants yesterday" is false.

143 Moore, 2009d, 437–9.

144 See the summary of the alternative logics of Nicod, Pearce, and Russell, in A. N. Prior, "Negation," in Paul Edwards (ed.), *Encyclopedia of Philosophy*, Vol. 5 (New York: Macmillan, 1967), 458–63, at 462–3.

145 Fumerton, "Moore on the Metaphysics of Causation," 214.

146 Fumerton, "Moore on the Metaphysics of Causation," 214.

Treating negation as simply a formal, truth-tabular operation invites a like treatment for statements of equivalence when both sides of the biconditional are false. The truth-maker for such true equivalence statements just is the falsity of each of the two component propositions. A like treatment is seemingly appropriate for statements of material implication where the antecedent is false.

Furthermore, with doubly negated statements, Fumerton would seem committed to layers of negative facts: the truth-maker for "it is not the case that there are no bananas" would be the negative fact that there was no negative fact about bananas. Whereas, on the view advocated here, the truth-tabular definition of negation makes possible the two operations by virtue of which the falsity of a falsehood is true; the welcome upshot of this is that the truth-maker of the quoted banana statement is the positive fact that there are some bananas.

So it seems to me that Fumerton's anticipated sidestepping of his back-door argument applies more broadly than he thinks it does. Another avenue some would be inclined to explore would be Fumerton's theory of truth. Such exploration could lead to an even broader evasion of Fumerton's argument here, by denying generally the whole correspondence truth machinery of truth-makers, truth-bearers, and correspondence between them. That response, however, does not tempt me.[147]

Fumerton's second argument is based on his claimed direct awareness of absences. This depends on Fumerton's controversial view that "phenomenological awareness is the ultimate ground of *all* ontological commitment."[148] It also depends on the also controversial view that one can be directly aware of the absence of elephants as well as one can be directly aware of one's own pain.

What Fumerton doesn't address is the main argument on the other side of the question of whether there are negative facts. That argument is that negative facts are mysterious and spooky. They are not mysterious and spooky in the way that Fumerton (following P. L. Heath) describes as that of the "know-nothings": the know-nothings believe that our familiar "holes and gaps, lacks and losses, absences, silences . . . voids and vacancies . . . " are "but perceived fragments of nothingness . . . ."[149] True nothingness *is* mysterious, particularly since modern physics teaches us that empty space is not nothing. Absences can make sense without partaking of some more comprehensive nothingness.

Even so, it is more than a little difficult to say anything very informative about the nature of negative facts. An absent elephant is no kind of elephant at all, not even a ghostly one. Yet if the absence of elephants on some particular occasion is a particular, what is it? Fumerton rightly scorns a Meinongian elephant as something that "has being but doesn't exist."[150] But are Fumerton's negative facts any better described?

If there were negative facts, that would change things for me considerably. Then it would be much more difficult to resist the conclusion that omissions could be causes,

[147] See my reliance on Fumerton's correspondence theory of truth to fend off some metaphysical objections to truth-makers by Markus Stepanians, in Moore, 2013b, 371–3.

[148] Fumerton, "Moore on the Metaphysics of Causation," 215.

[149] P. L. Heath, "Nothing," in Paul Edwards (ed.), *The Encyclopedia of Philosophy*, Vol. 5 (New York: Macmillan, 1967), 524.

[150] Fumerton, "Moore on the Metaphysics of Causation," 209.

and that, more generally, absences could be causes or effects. Then it would be challenging to urge that it is causation that underlies the moral difference between acts and omissions. But fortunately, it is a fact that there are no negative facts.[151] Really.

IX. Ferzan's Construction (and Rebuttal) of Moore on Self-Defense

Causation, negligence, and harm-within-the-risk all have to do with the prima facie case of liability in Anglo-American tort and criminal law systems. But, as is well-known, the culpability and the wrongdoing that can be attributed when these requirements are satisfied, is prima facie only. For, at the end of the day, prima facie wrongdoing might not actually be wrongdoing—it might be *justified* by considerations beyond those involved in judging voluntariness of action or causation of bad states of affairs. Similarly, the prima facie culpability might turn out at the end of the day not to be a real culpability—the actor's wrongful choice might have been made because of *excusing conditions* such as non-culpable ignorance, mistake, duress, or other forms of incapacity.

Kim Ferzan focuses her chapter on what is usually classified as one of these justifying circumstances; that going under the rubric of self-defense. Stephen Morse focuses a part of his chapter on what is conventionally classified as being one of these excusing circumstances; that related to mental defect, immaturity, or disease. In this section I consider Ferzan's comments on self-defense, and in the one that follows I briefly discuss Morse's conception of mental illness as providing a kind of excuse.

The lovely tone of Ferzan's chapter on self-defense[152] could lull one into not to rising to one's own defense. Yet the interesting and challenging content of what she says makes that a dangerous thing to do. One of the intriguing aspects of her chapter is that she by and large has to construct her target—the views I should have on self-defense—before she criticizes them. For, as she notes, I have paid scant attention to self-defense, referring to it in scattered writings but never systematically "conquering" the topic. Ferzan opines that perhaps this lack of attention is due to some belief on my part that the topic is easy. I don't think I have ever thought that. The explanation for the paucity of my attention here is more mundane: one can only write about so many things. Ferzan does an admirable job in working with the limited material she has to construct a view that, now that I have seen it, I am happy to claim as my own. She raises four criticisms of that view. I shall consider each below, although not quite in the order in which she presents them.

First, she accurately sees that my general view of the rationale of self-defense is laid out in terms made familiar by Phillip Montague:[153] when a culpable aggressor causes the necessity that either he or his intended victim be killed, his culpable causation of the need for that choice justifies him suffering the hard end of it. Ferzan rightly sees this as a kind fairness-in-the-distribution-of-an-inevitable-harm kind of rationale, and

[151] In order to avoid contradicting myself, what sense of "fact" must I be using here, mine or Fumerton's?
[152] Kimberly Kessler Ferzan, "Self Defense: Tell Me Moore," this volume.
[153] Phillip Montague, "Self Defense and Choosing Between Lives," 40 *Philosophical Studies*, 207–19 (1981).

questions whether this "is the most perspicuous way to see" the justifiability of self-defense.[154]

I see Ferzan as here raising two doubts. One stems from the fact that in self-defense situations harm to someone is not inevitable, for the "culpable aggressor could just change his mind ...."[155] Yet I am at a loss as to why Ferzan thinks that "there is something important about [that] fact ...."[156] From the point of view of the person who has to make the choice in the use of defensive force—the victim and those willing to aid him—the aggressor's threatening action is just like a force of nature. If the killing is truly necessary, then chatting, seducing, pleading, etc. with the aggressor will be no more availing that it would be to an avalanche. *Given* the threat (the withdrawal of which the victim of the aggression does not control), death to someone is inevitable. This I take to be the intended takeaway of Montague saying that defensive force applied by victims of culpable aggression and by those who aid them is "a matter of justice in the distribution of harms that are unavoidable *from their standpoints*."[157] Ferzan is correct that I don't subjectivize justifications to the beliefs and perspectives of actors; but that is not what I would mean by the Montague statement.

Montague does unfortunately lump intervening defenders of others with self-defenders. While Anglo-American criminal law does tend to do this too (with its "stand in the shoes" doctrine), there are some subtle differences between the two classes of defenders that sometimes matter. These turn on the fact that self-defense is an agent-relative justification (in the sense I will describe shortly) whereas defense of others is, usually, an agent-neutral (or "consequentialist") justification.[158] The difference is that the self-defense privilege does not depend on the maximizing of good consequences, but the defense-of-others privilege—like that of balance of evils—does.

This renders somewhat curious the example Ferzan uses to raise her second doubt here. The example is of a proposed defense of another, Desdemona, by a third-party intervenor.[159] In Ferzan's version of Shakespeare's tale there are three candidates for the human shield needed to save Desdemona: Othello, the culpable aggressor who set up the threat; Iago, the provocateur who egged Othello on with misinformation; and a generally evil person, Claudius, who had nothing to do with creating the threat to Desdemona. Ferzan challenges "Moore's simple justice" to answer what she regards as a complex question of distribution.[160] Let's see.

If Desdemona were awake and had the means to do so, she could plainly exercise her agent-relative privilege to use Iago or Othello, or both, to take the hit for her. She returns their own bullets to them—what could be a more fitting instance of divine justice? Claudius is not a threat; she would have only a balance-of-evils justification to use

[154] Ferzan, "Self-Defense: Tell Me Moore," 228.

[155] Ferzan, "Self-Defense: Tell Me Moore," 228.

[156] Ferzan, "Self-Defense: Tell Me Moore," 228.

[157] Phillip Montague, "Self-Defense, Culpability, and Distributive Justice," 29 *Law and Philosophy* 75 (2009), 84, quoted, with emphasis added, in Ferzan, "Self-Defense: Tell Me Moore," 228.

[158] The hedge because some duties of protection, such as those owing by parents to their own children, are agent-relative.

[159] Ferzan, "Self-Defense: Tell Me Moore," 228.

[160] Ferzan, "Self-Defense: Tell Me Moore," 229.

him as a shield. And unless Claudius's generally evil nature reduces him to a kind of human garbage, intentionally killing him in this way is forbidden to Desdemona.[161]

As to using Claudius as the needed shield, the third-party intervener is also forbidden to balance evils in this way. Iago and Othello, on the other hand, are each culpable causers of Desdemona's peril; someone must die because of what they have done and either may be killed as a matter of "Moore's simple justice." Which one, if it only requires one? The most culpable one who is also the most substantial cause of the peril. Ferzan thinks that is Iago,[162] as do I; those more Humean in their blaming might pick Othello, because for them Othello's nasty temper is part of his bad character and is therefore inculpatory and not exculpatory. There is nothing hard here, is there?

Ferzan's first and third points are conveniently discussed together. The first is to question whether I can extend my "divine justice" account of defending against *culpable* aggressors, to also use it as an account of why one may defend against *innocent* aggressors. Montague himself does not extend his account to innocent-aggression cases, so why (and how) do I? Ferzan just doesn't "get it."[163]

Ferzan sees that I think in innocent-aggressor cases, "without culpability... causation and necessity... is enough."[164] But she doesn't find that morally intelligible. Yet think of rescue situations where legally one generally has no duty to rescue. If, however, one has innocently caused the condition of peril, then one has a legal duty to intervene to save the victim from that peril. The motto might be, "let he who has disturbed (i.e., caused to be worse) the status quo restore that status quo if she can." In innocent-aggressor cases, typically the innocent aggressor acts in a way that threatens the defendant—the former causes the peril to the latter. If he could do so, surely such an aggressor should end the peril to defendant his action poses. But he can't. The defendant, however, can do it for him, and when he does so, he is justified.

It is true, as Ferzan notes, that at one point I put this in terms of ownership of risks.[165] The innocent creator of a peril to another "owns" the risk he has created and has a duty to prevent the risk's realization if he can. Innocent aggressors too could be seen as owning the risks they have created or are a part of (such as the terrorist's shield case Ferzan mentions), and because of this must accept as their own the hard end of that risk's realization. I now think that the "ownership of risks" metaphor can lead us astray, as in the ducking cases where one doesn't own the risk naturally coming at one so that one is not permitted to duck.[166]

What of Nozick's famous *Falling Large Man* kind of examples where the innocent aggressor does not even *act* so as to put the defendant in peril?[167] In such cases it is the "innocent aggressor's" moving body that threatens the victim, not the person himself. Without action, it is difficult to say that the innocent "aggressor" is causing the peril or, indeed, that he is aggressing at all. These are either cases of excuse, or, more likely, instances of the kind of agent-relative justification that Ferzan too allows, based on each

161 Using Claudius in other, less robust ways (such as ducking to allow the bullet to hit him) is not forbidden. Nor is some kind of full or partial *excuse* ruled out in this case.

162 Ferzan, "Self-Defense: Tell Me Moore," 229, n. 53.

163 Ferzan, "Self-Defense: Tell Me Moore," 226.

164 Ferzan, "Self-Defense: Tell Me Moore," 226.

165 Moore, 1997b, 714.

166 Moore, 2009d, 61–5.

167 Robert Nozick, *Anarchy, State and Utopia* (New York: Oxford University Press, 1974), 34–5.

individual's greater interest in his or her own life and welfare.[168] When no one is even causally responsible for the fact that one of us must die, we each are still entitled to prefer ourselves. From Cicero onwards, when two come to a plank that will only support one, one may justifiably throw the other off.[169]

Ferzan wonders what I think I "would lose by abandoning the strong-permission approach in favor of an agent-relative permission."[170] The first thing to do here is to converge on a common vocabulary. A strong permission, as I define it, is an agent-relative permission. A strong permission to A not only constitutes an absence of agent-relative obligation not to A (which is what weak permissions do), but it also permits A to be done even when bad net consequences follow. What Ferzan means to be contrasting is the "return a harm to he who caused the threat of such harm to exist" kind of permission, from the "you may favor yourself and your near and dear as you distribute upside benefits and downside harms" kind of permission. Both of these are strong permissions and both are agent-relative permissions. But that doesn't mean they are not different permissions, nonetheless.

As can be seen from my treatment of the last example considered, *Falling Large Man*, I, like Ferzan, think that there are permissions based in self-favoritism, and that this is one of them. Unlike her, I think true innocent-aggressor cases are based on the "divine justice" rationale, not the self-favoritism rationale. Ask yourself what difference it makes, and we can see an important difference between Ferzan and myself that bears on her third criticism.

Change the facts of Nozick's *Falling Large Man* in two ways. First, suppose again, as in the original, that if Victor (the man in the bottom of the well) shoots his ray gun, Tony (the falling fat guy) will die but Victor will live; but now suppose that Tony has a ray gun too, one that if he uses will defeat Victor's ray gun, allowing Tony to live but Victor to die. If Victor uses his gun, may Tony also use his?

Second, suppose a third party, Harry, is there, and he has an anti-ray gun. He could negate Victor's rays, in which event Victor dies and Tony lives; or he could negate Tony's rays, in which event Tony dies and Victor lives; or he could negate both rays, in which event Victor again dies and Tony again lives. Which shot should he take: one or the other? Neither? Both?

If one thinks that Tony's privilege in the original version of the hypothetical is based on self-favoritism, then in the first variation there will be what Heidi Hurd calls "moral combat."[171] For Tony too has this privilege and each is therefore privileged to shoot his gun. Victor dies. Further, on the self-favoritism view, Harry has no basis to prefer one to the other; he should holster his ray gun. Again, Victor dies.

Whereas if (contrary to what Ferzan and I actually think about this case) Victor's privilege in the initial version of the hypothetical is based on a divine justice view, there

[168] This kind of agent-relative reason—where one is entitled to favor oneself and the near and dear—Tom Nagel calls "reasons of autonomy." Nagel, *The View From Nowhere* (New York: Oxford University Press, 1985).

[169] Aside from her objection of moral unintelligibility here, Ferzan throws in a dose of causal skepticism, citing Coase for the proposition that "causation is reciprocal." Coase was indeed a causal skeptic, but as I show in Moore, 2009d, 92–5, what is correct in Coase is not the skepticism whereby causation becomes reciprocal, but rather the irrelevance of causation to liability rules that achieve efficient resource allocation.

[170] Ferzan, "Self-Defense: Tell Me Moore," 227.

[171] Heidi Hurd, *Moral Combat* (Cambridge: Cambridge University Press, 1999).

will be no symmetrical privileges between Victor and Tony. Victor may use his ray gun but Tony may not because (*ex hypothesi*) he was the threatening aggressor. Tony dies. And in the second variation, Harry does have a basis to choose between Victor and Tony, and he should choose against the innocent aggressor, Tony. So Harry fires against Tony's ray, and Tony dies.

When Bob Nozick raised these variations on the original ray gun story, he didn't resolve them, saying only he would "tiptoe around these incredibly difficult issues ...."[172] Yet notice what clear implications each rationale has for defending against self-defense (the first variation) and third-party aid (the second variation). With one of these theories or the other, we need do no tiptoeing.

More pertinent here, notice also that Ferzan's generally preferred answer (in terms of self-favoritism) generates moral combat, whereas my preferred answer for true cases of innocent aggression does not. Moral combat is an undesirable characteristic of moral or legal systems of norms. It is not as bad as outright contradiction between the obligations that bind us all—what Kant (with his usual penchant for hyperbole) called "inconceivable." Yet it is pretty bad, because, as Hurd says, it makes us moral gladiators, where the success of one can only be purchased via another's failure.[173] If Tony were *obligated* to defend himself, and Victor is likewise *obligated* to defend himself, then we have moral combat. If Tony has merely a Hohfeldian privilege to defend himself, unaccompanied by any claim-right to non-interference with his privileged action, and if Victor has the same, then we have moral combat in a secondary sense: morality licenses actual combat in that what morality permits you to do others can still rightfully stop you from doing.[174]

My objection to Ferzan's rights-forfeiture (or "liability") view of self-defense is not some general objection to there being normative powers that change moral relations.[175] There surely are such, and just as surely culpable aggression is an act having such moral consequences. My objection is that Ferzan's shifts of normative relations in the innocent-aggressor cases are only half-hearted and half-way. One can do the right thing in resisting innocent aggression,[176] on her view, and yet: (1) it can also be true that the innocent aggressor is right in resisting the victim's resistance; and (2) the victim herself would have no right to the aid of third parties in doing the "right thing" she is supposedly doing in resisting the aggression. Ferzan's view creates a "sort of right thing" appraisal of actions, half-way between "forbidden" and "really right."

Sometimes, as in Cicero's two men on a plank and in Nozick's falling fat man, this "sort of right thing" view is thrust upon us. Yet for true innocent-aggressor cases, it is not. The defendant is right to defend herself against an innocent aggressor, the aggressor is wrong to resist that defense, and third parties are wrong to aid such resistance but right to aid such defense.

Ferzan's fourth and last set of worries constitute what she knows will be a *reductio ad absurdum* kind of argument. She urges that my view (about fairness in returning harm to its sender) may result in a deterrence-like argument for punishing culpable

172 Nozick, *Anarchy, State, and Utopia*, at 35.

173 Hurd, *Moral Combat*, at 10.

174 Hurd, *Moral Combat*, 279–81.

175 As Ferzan construes my reluctance, "Self-Defense: Tell Me Moore," 229–30.

176 Or in turning a trolley onto a track where it will kill one non-aggressing workman.

wrongdoers and even a deterrence-justified punishment of innocents. The essential premise to get the *reductio* off the ground is the supposition that not punishing some (culpable or innocent) wrongdoer makes it *more likely* that either that wrongdoer or someone else like her will do like wrongs to the victim in the future. Such a wrongdoer is thus the (culpable or innocent) cause of the victim's *peril*. One can thus prevent the peril's realization by visiting a like harm on him via punishment.

The first thing to do with this *reductio* is to cleanse it of its epistemic features. We need to transform risk assessments and probability into objective inevitability and certainty. This, because in Ferzan's own view of things, risks and probability assessments are epistemic; objectively, macro-sized items either will happen or they won't. An omniscient God never calculates the odds. So transform "more likely" into "will certainly bring about"; and transform "peril" into "will certainly happen." Then the question is, if V certainly will be wronged by D or by those like D unless V hurts D now, and if V hurting D now will certainly eliminate V getting wronged by D or others in the future, may V hurt (i.e., "punish") D if some wrongful act of D's was the substantial cause of the certainty that more of the same lies in wait for V in the future? Suppose there is a "wrong-requital" machine in some society. If D wrongs V, the machine infallibly reads that that wrongdoing will substantially cause future wrongs against V by D or by others. Further, if V presses the "punishment" button on the machine, D and others like him will be prevented from again hurting V, although the means of prevention will be painful for D. Would V be right to press the button?

I think the answer is, "of course." D, by his wrongful action, culpably or innocently, will cause V to suffer more such wrongs in the future, unless D prevents them by suffering harsh treatment. D has a duty to prevent the harm he will otherwise cause if he can, and (thanks to the wrong-requital machine) he can.

Yet this isn't a theory of *punishment*. This is a preventative system (at the moment only imaginable in a science fiction world). But it is imaginable, and once imagined it is indeed just by the principle of self-defense I defend. There is no inconsistency in having both a backwards-looking retributive punishment system and a forward-looking preventative system. Both could be just systems. The only hard question is whether prevention-justified hard treatment, when it has been received first, counts as a credit against retributive-justified hard treatment. Does being quarantined for some disease count against punishment for that disease in an Erewhonian society?[177] If retributivism is the "jealous mistress" that I have said it is in the past,[178] the answer should be no.

X. Moore on Morse on Metaphysics of Mind

Like others in this volume, Stephen Morse wishes to discuss our disagreements more than our agreements. This is of course as it should be, but Stephen faces tough sledding because (as he notes) he and I agree on so much relating to mind, action, and responsibility that significant points of disagreement are few and far between. Yet despite our

177 Samuel Butler, *Erewhon* (London: Butler/Trubner and Co., 1872).

178 Moore, 1997b, 28 ("To the extent that someone is punished for reasons other than that he deserved to be punished, retributive justice is not achieved.")

being joined at the hip on many subjects, Morse manages to find five issues on which he and I might not fully agree.

These five issues are: first, the relevance of metaphysics to law; second, the particular relevance of the metaphysics of action to solve seemingly borderline cases of responsible action such as sleep-walking, habitual behavior, etc.; third, whether severe mental illness excuses *carte blanche* for those in that status or whether it excuses only to the extent that it causes or instantiates some more traditional kind of excusing condition; fourth, whether one such "other excusing condition" could be a "control" (as opposed to a "cognitive") incapacity condition; and fifth, how much we may reasonably expect neuroscience to contribute to law.

I shall focus on only the first of these items. I omit discussion of the fifth because Morse and I have no significant disagreements here. As to the second, I long ago had my say both on why the metaphysics of action is the right place to look for answers about seemingly borderline cases, and on what that answer is.[179] On the fourth issue, Morse and I do disagree on whether there is a viable, separable excuse of volitional impairment, but our disagreement here is somewhat academic in two pejorative senses of the word. One sense is due to the fact that verifying lack of control is beyond the present abilities of psychiatry and of neuroscience so that the existence of such as excuse is, in insanity contexts, largely without practical effect. The second way our disagreement is academic is due to the semantic nature of our disagreement: Morse calls the excusing condition that I call, "volitional impairment," with his own label, "irrationality"; while I find this usage of Morse's peculiarly broad, it is a harmless enough stipulation if it in fact covers the same conditions as my own label.

There is a live debate between Morse and myself on the third issue, that as to whether or not insanity is a status excuse. Like most criminal law theorists, but unlike me, Morse does not believe that insanity marks a general criterion of personhood, an exemption rather than an excuse; rather for Morse insanity operates as what I call a true excuse,[180] a situation where ignorance, mistake, or compulsion exists about the very act of which the defendant is accused. Those who hold Morse's view have the burden of saying what excusing condition exists when mental disease excuses—is it ignorance/mistake, compulsion, the combination that Morse calls lack of rationality, or something else? Morse and his many allies here also have the burden of saying what the connection must be between mental disease and the crime of which the mentally ill person is accused in order for mental illness to constitute a true excuse. That mental illness must *cause* the criminal behavior is an old favorite, but one now encrusted with well-charted difficulties.[181] That mental illness must *incapacitate* the defendant from doing other than the crime he did is another possibility, but Morse has no truck with loss of control as a form of excuse. So Morse plumps for lack of rationality; not in general, but on the occasion on which the crime is done. I think that Morse's view is the most plausible alternative to my own view of why, when, and how mental disease excuses. Still (out of insight hopefully more than stubbornness) I stick to my lifelong view that the moral relevance of the severe forms of mental disease we call "craziness," "lunacy," or legal insanity are rooted

[179] Moore, 1994c. [180] Moore, 1985c. [181] Moore, 2014f.

in more fundamental features of personhood than those captured by the usual excusing conditions of ignorance, mistake, or compulsion.

The remainder of this response to Morse is focused on the first of the differences between us that Morse addresses. I focus on this difference because it is here that Morse calls into question something quite general and quite central to much of my work. This is the relevance of metaphysics to law. It has been my lifelong penchant for finding metaphysics—whether it is the metaphysics of mind, action, events, freedom, possible worlds, moral qualities, religion, etc.—legally relevant. Morse refuses to honor this penchant of mine, giving two reasons. First, "country lawyers" (which Morse charmingly here pretends to be) cannot resolve such metaphysical issues. They lack the expertise to resolve them themselves, and they cannot rely on some accepted consensus of metaphysicians on such issues because there is no such consensus. Morse's second reason is that law is a practical discipline in the sense that academic law has a legal system (Morse's "railroad") to run, and for this practical business Morse finds the search for such metaphysical understanding as might be available to be "in large measure a distraction."

Morse is dissembling in giving both of these reasons. As to the supposed insolubility of metaphysical questions, Morse himself has solved some big ones to his own satisfaction. Some examples are: (1) Morse rejects both eliminative materialism and metaphysical dualism about mental substances and he accepts some non-skeptical form of physicalism, either reductionist or, more likely, non-reductionist; (2) Morse rejects both libertarianism and hard determinism and accepts some form of soft-determinism (or "compatibilism"); (3) Morse accepts the causal theory of action and rejects any form of *sui generis* agent-causation; and (4) Morse accepts a counterfactual understanding of ability. Morse adopts these metaphysical conclusions because he (like me) thinks that they are *correct*; he does not accept them because there is some philosophical consensus about them, because in truth no such consensus exists (this is true even about dualism, about which there has now been considerable philosophical retrenchment).

True enough, Morse draws back from taking sides on more particular variations of the metaphysical positions to which he subscribes. Thus, he is not sure: (1) whether his is a reductionist or non-reductionist physicalism about the mind; (2) about which version of compatibilism to adopt—a source-compatibilism (like Jay Wallace's) or a classically conditionalist compatibilism (like Kadri Vivehlin's); (3) about which version of the causal theory of action to hold—one that accepts intentions and volitions as causal intermediaries between belief/desire sets and actions, or one that does not; (4) about whether to accept the going Lewis–Stalnaker view of the truth-makers for counterfactuals in terms of close possible worlds, or whether the older, Goodman-style view (in terms of law-projected states of affairs) might not be correct. Yet these are qualifications to the details of Morse's metaphysical views; they do not weaken or eliminate his holding of such views in the least.

Such qualifications can only reduce Morse's first point, then, to the true but harmless homily: go as far as you can into the depths of metaphysics, and then rely on the work of others that you are hopeful will take you the rest of the way. Indeed, none of us can go it alone to the ultimate depth of all of the deep metaphysical issues relevant to legal and moral responsibility; this too I am happy to confess. So the difference between us comes down merely to a difference in how much each of us judges it possible to travel by one's own lights and to discern where the likely truth lies in the views of others who have gone further. I undoubtedly am more of an optimist here than is Morse.

At this point Morse no doubt would like to pull the second arrow from his quiver, the one proclaiming that the "country lawyer" *need not* (as opposed to cannot) delve deep into these metaphysical issues. Morse appears to believe that the details at such depths are legally irrelevant. Yet Morse can ill afford to believe this. As he recognizes, his entire body of work on responsibility rests on some forms of compatibilism, physicalism, and the causal theory of action all being true. And Morse is also correct that there are plausible variations in each of these positions that he holds and that he only needs one such variation of each to be true, it not mattering for his purposes which version that is. Yet Morse can have no confidence that *any* one of these versions is true unless and until he has confidence that *one* of these (mutually exclusive) variations is itself true. My confidence that the exclusive disjunction, "p or q or r," is true can be no greater than my confidence in the truth of the most promising disjunct.

Of course we all have to get on with life, "run railroads," as Morse says, adjudicate law cases, etc.; and of course we must engage in these practical activities with less than perfect knowledge. Yet this inevitable fact of life goes no distance towards establishing the irrelevance of better and better answers to metaphysical questions; after all, the practical reality of there being limited time and other resources with which to make decisions applies to all decisions and to all relevant inputs into all decisions. This inevitable fact of life cuts no ice, particularly in favor of short-changing metaphysical questions in law.

I have hitherto been speaking about the relevance of metaphysics to foundational issues on responsibility, issues foundational in the sense that they call into question the sense of anyone ever being responsible and blameworthy for anything. But there are much more discrete, non-foundational issues to which such metaphysics is also relevant.[182] I refer to legal issues such as: How many occurrences of insured event-types were there when the Twin Towers were destroyed? Does one legally cause a harm when one's act is a necessary condition for that harm's occurrence, or must the *aspect* of that act that made it culpable also be necessary? If one intends to shoot a stump, and that "stump" is in reality a person, does one intend to shoot a person? If one knows that shooting the person will alert the savages from whom one is hiding, when one shoots anyway does one do so with the intention of alerting the savages? If the defendant pulled the trigger in one state, the bullet stuck the victim in another state, and the victim died in a third state, in what state and when did the act of killing take place?

These questions, and thousands like them, are raised internal to our moral and legal blaming practices. (They are "internal" in the sense that they do not call into question our blaming practices; rather, they call for interpretations of those practices.) And metaphysics can help in answering such questions. Such help is sometimes needed because sometimes our practices call for answers to questions about the nature of things like the causal relation, the sizing, the temporal or spatial location of events, the nature of causal relata, the individuations of mental content, and the like. True enough, one cannot automatically assume that when legal or moral rules locate actions, individuate

[182] Moore, 2014a.

mental content, etc., the best interpretation of those rules is given by the correct metaphysics. Rather the best interpretation of those rules is to be found by paying attention to the values ("purpose," "spirit") served by such rules. But often those values dictate that the best legal and moral interpretation just is the correct metaphysical interpretation. We hold someone responsible for *causing* a certain harm such as death, for example, only when that person's acts really did cause that death in the correct metaphysical sense of "caused"; likewise we hold someone responsible for causing another's *death* only when that other is really and truly dead. In such cases, there is no help for moralists and lawyers—even "country lawyers"—to delve into the metaphysics enough to yield the legally relevant (and indeed, legally determinative) answers.

XI. Deontology for Alexander and for Moore: A Tale of Two Theories

It is moderately amusing that Larry Alexander and I have jointly written the entry for "Deontological Ethics" in the *Stanford Encyclopedia of Philosophy*,[183] for in truth we disagree about much in deontology. Still, the exercise was possible because we organized the article into agent-centered versus patient-centered deontologies—one for Moore, and one for Alexander. The current article by Alexander,[184] and this response, present us with the opportunity to display our differences rather than submerge them in one (supposedly) univocal article.

We do agree on some basics. We both divide substantive (as opposed to meta-) ethics into deontic and aretaic parts. Moreover, we regard these parts as independent: we do not reduce the ethics of virtuous character to some deontic duties, nor do we reduce deontic duties to being mere proxies for bad character. Second, within deontic ethics, we are both deontologists, that is, people who believe that persons are not always obligated to maximize intrinsically good states of affairs in their actions and institutions, and who also believe that sometimes persons are obligated to do things that do not maximize such good states of affairs. Beyond that, and thirdly, Alexander appears to agree with my "three layer cake"[185] view of deontic ethics. At the first layer, there is some consequentialist principle, C, a principle that makes an action or institution right if it is productive of more intrinsically good states of affairs than any available alternative. In truth, neither of us have worked out what we believe in detail C to hold; one can profitably leave that to consequentialists who after all have more at stake in this issue than do either of us.

The second layer consists of those obligations that constrain (i.e., forbid) the fulfillment of C in certain circumstances. This layer also consists of those prerogatives that permit C not to be fulfilled in certain circumstances. And the third layer consists in the "return of the repressed," namely the return of the normative force of good and bad states of affairs even in circumstances to which either deontological constraints or prerogatives would otherwise apply. There are cases over some "threshold" of awful

183 Moore, 2007d; Moore, 2012c.

184 Larry Alexander, "The Means Principle," this volume.

185 Moore, 2009d, 36–41. Notice that Phillip Montague, considered next, rejects the "side-constraint" view of deontology of both of us.

consequences where the awfulness of the states of affairs constitutes an overriding reason to act so as to avoid them.[186]

It is the second layer of this "cake" where Alexander's and my differences emerge. To contrast our two deontological theories, it is first necessary to clarify what they are. Let me start with my own theory. Mine is a pluralist theory about both restraints and prerogatives. There are lots of them, way too many to fit on one stone tablet, even if you are some kind of god. And there is no overarching, single principle that has all of these as its instantiations or implications. (Well, pace Aquinas[187] maybe this one: "Do good and avoid evil.")

Despite their multiplicity, restraints have common "scope" limitations. In my agent-centered view of deontology, these scope limitations all have to do with the *agency* we are not to contaminate. Such agency is maximally implicated when we:

(1) act, rather than:
  (a) merely omit to prevent;[188]
  (b) merely possess or are in some state, character trait, or status;[189]
  (c) merely mentally act without that act causing bodily movements;[190]
  (d) merely have bodily movements that are not willed.[191]
(2) intend to cause some bad state of affairs by such action, rather than:
  (a) merely acting while being ignorant or mistaken about the wrong-making characteristics of one's act;[192]
  (b) merely acting in such a way as to unreasonably risk that one's action will have wrong-making characteristics;[193]
  (c) merely believing that one's action will or might have wrong-making characteristics.[194]
(3) substantially cause a bad state of affairs, as opposed to:
  (a) merely failing to prevent (omissions);[195]
  (b) merely allowing (in a non-omissive sense);[196]
  (c) merely redirecting an already existing force;[197]

[186] Although Alexander has closely questioned threshold deontology (Alexander, "Deontology at the Threshold," 37 *San Diego Law Review*, 893 (2000) (festschrift on Moore's *Placing Blame*), he also knows that deontology has to defuse in some way the otherwise devastating counterexamples of moral catastrophes demanded by an unregimented deontology. See Moore, 2012e, for the limited list of unappealing alternatives to threshold deontology.

[187] Aquinas, *Summa Theologica* I-II q. 94 a. 2 (The first precept of the natural law is to do good and avoid evil).

[188] Moore, 1993c, 22–34, 54–9; Moore, 1997b, 277–86; Moore, 2009d, 51–9.

[189] Moore, 1993c, 19–22, 49–54; Moore, 1997b, ch. 13.

[190] Moore, 1993c, ch. 6.

[191] Moore, 1993c, 17–19, 95–112.

[192] Moore, 2011b.

[193] Moore, 2011d; Moore, 2011e.

[194] Moore, 1997b, ch. 9.

[195] Moore, 2009d, 51–9.

[196] Moore, 2009d, 61–5.

[197] Moore, 2009d, 75–6.

(d) merely accelerating a harm about to happen anyway;[198]
(e) merely enabling another person to substantially cause;[199]
(f) merely enabling a natural event to substantially cause;[200]
(g) being in some other way a *de minimis* cause.[201]

(4) Substantially cause a harm that matches closely the type of harm one intended to cause by so acting.[202]

Thus, in the famous *transplant* hypothetical that Alexander too mentions, the surgeon may not maximize the saving of life by cutting out the organs of a perfectly healthy patient because his agency is strongly implicated in all of these dimensions.

Alexander characterizes my agent-relative view of deontology as being "quite an orthodox one."[203] (He really knows how to hurt a guy—and I thought when I first articulated this comprehensive view of agency in the '80s I was quite original!) But the intended slight is without sting because he misconstrues my view as "intention-focused."[204] A glance at the above list of agency-determiners shows that it is not. As I explicitly say about this list, it is causation that "is the big dog in this pack," the "major desert-determiner within deontological morality,"[205] not intention. But notice that because of this misconstrual by Alexander, every one of his intended counterexamples does not challenge my actual theory (as opposed to the orthodox theory Alexander reads me as holding).

Alexander poses five intended counterexamples to the "intention-focused" theory: ill-motivated trolley switchmen, executioner, CIA operative, euthanasia doctor, and terror bomber subbing in for strategic bomber.[206] All of these have the following structure: the actions are permissible absent the bad intention of the actor, and his bad intention is not sufficient to make them impermissible. Yet only a strongly "intention-focused" theory would hold that intention alone is sufficient for impermissibility. As I say explicitly, the presence of a bad intention is not sufficient for impermissibility, and neither is the absence of such intention sufficient for permissibility.[207] Bad intentions constitute an agency-*enhancing* factor, but they are not *criterial* of the agency on which agent-centered restrictions focus.[208]

Alexander might have added counterexamples (to the "intention-focused" view that he wishes to attack) that are the converse of the five he does use. The one I give in my work is the doctor who saves five patients by use of a machine that necessarily pumps

[198] Moore, 2009d, 65–8. As I note, acceleration cases use the absence of substantial counterfactual dependence to qualify otherwise substantial causation, raising some unique puzzles that I mentioned earlier with respect to Katz.

[199] Moore, 2009d, 68–73.

[200] Moore, 2009d, 74.

[201] Moore, 2009d.

[202] Moore, 2009d, 43–51, 158–9, 208–10; Moore, 2012d.

[203] Alexander, "The Means Principle," 264.

[204] Alexander, "The Means Principle," 264.

[205] Moore, 2009d, 77.

[206] Alexander, "The Means Principle," 259–60.

[207] Moore, 2009d, 50–1.

[208] Not to belabor the obvious, but notice that it is redirection and acceleration that make trolley-turning and euthanasia permissible, respectively; it is the role-relative permission that makes executions and spying OK; and it is the permissible-strategic intention of the strategic bomber (who programs the bombing run beforehand) that makes the bombing permissible, despite the terror bomber's later, terroristic intention as he sits dumbly carrying out a pre-programmed bombing run.

poisonous exhaust gas into another patient's room, thereby killing him.[209] If an intention to kill were *necessary* for impermissibility, this should be permissible; but intuitively it is not, making intention no more *necessary* for impermissibility than it is sufficient.

Alexander does give other intended counterexamples to the "intention-focused" theory. One of these is about good intentions, rather than bad ones. Alexander tells us that good intentions "cannot render a morally impermissible act permissible";[210] this is often true, but it is irrelevant. No theory using intentions to mark the border of permissibility uses them in such a way. And Alexander's three-tracked-trolley case[211] is even further afield, being decided by considerations having nothing to do with deontology at all.[212]

To my own satisfaction at least, my agent-relative version of deontology emerges unscathed by Alexander's attack on some strongly "intention-focused" view. Let us then turn to his own patient-centered version of deontology, and test its defenses with some slings and arrows of our own. The first question, again, is clarificatory: just what does this version say?

Alexander is an ambitious monist about both deontological restraints and prerogatives. He thinks that there is one principle (and a "corollary") that, by and large, covers them both. That principle is the "Means Principle," or MP. With regard to deontological obligations, the MP asserts:

> An act required or permitted by C is nonetheless forbidden if the good consequences that are the bases of its endorsement by C are produced by the unconsented-to use of persons' bodies, labor, or talents. In other words, the MP enjoins the appropriation of another's body, labor, or talent without that person's consent where appropriation is the causal path by which otherwise good consequences are produced.[213]

With regard to the permissions of deontology, Alexander thinks that they all are captured by a single "corollary" of the MP, which is that persons "are not to be compelled" (by the state or by anyone else) to positively act so as to bring about the good consequences required by C.[214] Although Alexander hedges his bets slightly, he is pretty sure he has captured all of deontology—both permissions and obligations—with the MP and its corollary. One stone tablet will be fine for this view—indeed, Moses could make do with a small piece of slate.

"Means Principle" is an odd choice for a label for Alexander's view of deontology. For "means" and "ends" are intention-drenched notions, and yet Alexander plainly intends (means?) not to use "means" in any way implicating intention. Some state of affairs is a means to some other state of affairs, for Alexander, not because some actor *intends* the first to be the means by which he attains the second; rather, because the first is a causal

[209] Moore, 2009d, 50. [210] Alexander, "The Means Principle," 260.

[211] Alexander, "The Means Principle," 260.

[212] A decent consequentialist principle C would forbid the use of the track with one workman if another track with no workmen on it is available for the diversion. (This remains true even if the badly motivated switchman will not direct the train at all unless he can direct it so as to kill the one; my version of C obligates him to turn it from the five workman track, and he has no agent-centered prerogative not to do so.) Being outside of deontology (by redirection) and thus in the land where good and bad consequences determine rightness of action, is no guarantee that one is outside the strong obligations punishable by the criminal law.

[213] Alexander, "The Means Principle," 252. [214] Alexander, "The Means Principle," 256.

intermediary between the defendant's action and the further state of affairs that C recommends as good. This is what Alexander means when he says that "the best interpretation of the MP is a causal one."[215]

Alexander builds his notion of *using* from this causal path idea. Unfortunately Alexander never tells us what he means by *causing*, and this omission handicaps our ability to understand what Alexander's idiosyncratic notion of *using* comes to. We don't know specifically whether Alexander builds counterfactual notions into causation, so that a cause of some harm must be a necessary condition of that harm's occurrence. Perhaps we can finesse this lapse in the following way. Suppose Alexander agrees with me that a cause of H need not be a necessary condition of H. Then Alexander should be construed as saying that using involves more than causing harm to the one used; it also requires that the harm to the other must be *necessary* for the occurrence of some good state of affairs for another that is the further effect of the harm. For example, in the original *trolley* scenario, Alexander tells us that the one trapped workman's death is not necessary to save the other five trapped workmen—turning the trolley would save the five whether or not the one is on the diversion track. Whereas in *fat man* where Alexander tells us that "pushing the fat man onto the track is the only way to prevent the trolley from killing the five workers," harm to the fat worker is needed because it is his bulk that stops the trolley and saves the five; without harm to fat man, the five cannot be saved.

As I read Alexander, this causal-path-plus-counterfactual notion of using[216] displaces any other, more idiomatic senses of the word. So displaced is not only the sense dependent upon intended means to intended ends, but also displaced is any unjust enrichment sense of using (because there is no requirement that there be any benefit to the actor or to anyone he cares about). And also a consumption sense of "using," whereby one uses up another's body, talents, resources, etc., in the sense of ingesting or otherwise destroying them. Yet such displacements rob Alexander's thesis of much of its intuitive power. Indeed, I suspect that he intentionally trades on the connotations of these more idiomatic senses of "using" to make his conclusions sound more plausible than they in fact are.

In any case, Alexander's spare sense of using seems both under- and over-inclusive. As to the former, imagine a variation of *trolley* I shall call *fat man with boulder behind*. The defendant in this scenario drops the fat fellow in front of the trolley and again his bulk stops the trolley (thus his body is consumed in the stopping and he dies). But there is a large boulder behind fat man and in front of the five trapped workmen. So the "use" of fat man wasn't necessary. In the causation-plus-counterfactual-dependence sense of

[215] Alexander, "The Means Principle," (quote in original Alexander draft).

[216] I am here assuming that these two criteria of using—causal path, and counterfactual dependence—always point in the same direction. In fact they do not. In some epiphenomenal cases, where the harm to the victim is a co-effect with some good consequences, the common cause being defendant's action, there can be counterfactual dependence of the good consequences on the harm to the victim, yet there is no causal path from the defendant's action to those good consequences that has the harm to the victim as a causal intermediary. For example, in regular *trolley* the act of diverting the trolley kills the one and it saves the five. But add Alexander's supposition, that the switchman would not have diverted the trolley unless the one trapped workman was there (the latter was his most hated enemy, e.g.). Then the saving of the five counterfactually depends on the death of the one, yet the death is not on the causal path to that saving from the defendant's switching.

using, there was no using of the fat man and so, in Alexander's view, no deontological prohibition on dropping him onto the tracks just for the hell of it. Alexander may wish to deny this, but how can he if using requires that the harm caused to the one used was necessary to some benefit to others?

Indeed, such pre-emptive overdetermination cases are the tip of a very large iceberg threatening Alexander's ship of means. For such cases reveal a point long conceded by Alexander, which is that there is no using of another in unmotivated, gratuitous but intentional killing of an innocent. For in such cases there is no benefit or other good state of affairs to which the death of the victim killed was either necessary or a causal intermediary. Surely this is an embarrassment for Alexander's view of deontology. If the intentional killing of an innocent human being—or make it a huge gaggle of Ferzan's innocent babies—does not lie within one's inventory of deontologically prohibited actions, one has a deficient inventory.[217] Alexander's deontology seems counterintuitively under-inclusive.

But Alexander's MP is also over-inclusive. By the causal path/necessary criterion of using, do not many actions we do amount to "usings?" After all, all actions have effects, some good, some bad, many indifferent. Where the bad effects do not so outweigh the good effects as to make such actions prohibited by C, such actions are "required or permitted by C"; where the good effects are further effects of the bad effects, and are thus on the right "causal path"; and where the happening of the bad effects is necessary for the happening of the good effects; then we have an Alexanderian *using*, prohibited by deontology. So: I buy a new sleeveless vest and the fabric in the vest causes my dance-partner to get a skin rash (she is allergic). Her rash (given its need for treatment) causes a doctor (whose practice was financially precarious) to stay in business. Had she not had the rash, the doctor would have had to cease his practice, a bad thing given the need for his services in the community. Therefore, the heavy machinery of deontological obligation categorically forbid me to buy that vest! Indeed, since such examples are common as dirt, I don't see how any of us are ever free to get out of bed in the morning and do much of anything.

The obvious way to remedy this over extension of "using" is by adding the knowledge and intentions of the actor to the story. Once I intend to save the doctor's practice by causing a rash on my dance partner, I might more idiomatically be said to have *used* her. But Alexander will have none of this, for he rightly sees that this leads him back to some "intention-focused" deontology.

A last but basic worry about Alexander's deontology is its motivation. Once one strips "using" of its usual connotations (of intended means to an end, of unjust enrichment, of consumption), what makes it morally intelligible to think that using is bad? Some good state of affairs for one person is produced through some bad state of affairs for another (when the bad is necessary for there to be good), and this is supposed to be wrong. Whereas if the causal path is such that the good and the bad states of affairs are epiphenomenal of one another—that is, where the bad to one person is not a causal

[217] I raise this objection (with Alexander's concurrence that it is a problem) in our "Deontological Ethics." Moore, 2007d; Moore, 2012e. If killing babies for fun is problematic as a deontologically prohibited action, I should think one's deontology is in serious trouble.

intermediary on the path from one's act to the good to the other person—everything is OK.

I have long urged Alexander (and his hardy band of fellow-travelers here, Ferzan, Morse, Kadish, etc.) to think that causation matters to degrees of blameworthiness.[218] I meant, of course, that Alexander et al. should take seriously the result-luck that makes us more blamable if we succeed in causing what we try to cause than if we only try and fail. Alexander's version of using makes causation matter, only not in the result-luck way but in a manner I find bizarre and difficult to motivate.

It might be that with enough ingenuity Alexander can use his notion of "using" to connect all the dots—that is, to yield the intuitively right result in the now standard examples in this part of ethical philosophy. He touts his interpretation of deontology as best because it does "account for our intuitions about certain stock cases."[219] But he needs more than this to defend his interpretation. Contrast the "intention-focused" versions of deontology that he sees as his opponents. They also claim to be able to connect all the dots. But in addition they can say something about why this way of connecting the dots has independently intuitive attraction: with Aquinas, they can say that it infects one's agency to "set your will towards evil, either as means or as ends."[220] Alexander at one point sees that he needs to take up this task. But what he tells us is only that "the causal path *is* what is significant."[221] But why? It cannot be what he next says here, viz. if one's act "satisfied C only by using someone's body, labor, or talents as a resource without the person's consent ...,"[222] because *using* is itself defined in terms of causal path. "Causal path is morally significant because causal path is morally significant," is true but not very helpful.[223]

XII. Moral Pluralism, Conflicts, and the Shape of Moral Principles

Philip Montague thinks he disagrees with me more than in fact he does.[224] To see that, let me start where he himself begins, with some things about which we do in fact agree (and about which we even agree that we agree).

Montague is interested, as I am, in the general shape of deontological constraints—or, as he puts it, in the "logical form of moral principles" and in the "logic of principle based moral inference.[225] Montague agrees with me that the "royal road" to exploring that shape is through moral dilemmas when we face at least an apparent clash

[218] Moore, 1997b; Moore, 2009d. [219] Alexander, "The Means Principle," 252.

[220] Moore, 1997b, 409 ("We are the authors of evil when we aim to achieve it in a way that we are not if we merely anticipate that evil coming about as a result of our actions.") The tie of agency to intention is at least as old as Aquinas, who speaks of one "setting oneself towards evil" when one intends, either as ends or means, a prohibited state of affairs. Aquinas, *Summa Theologica*, I-II, q 94 a 7.

[221] Alexander, "The Means Principle," (quote in original Alexander draft).

[222] Alexander, "The Means Principle," 254.

[223] I do no better with what Alexander elsewhere says about the moral intelligibility of the MP: "The core idea is that we are not resources for others' benefit without our consent.... Enforceable morality has no jurisdiction over us as resources for its ends." Notice the anthropomorphizing of morality to make more compelling an intentionalist sense of "using."

[224] Richard Montague, "Moral Dilemmas and Moral Theory: Toward a Viable Deontology," this volume.

[225] Montague, "Moral Dilemmas and Moral Theory," 265.

of such moral principles.[226] As he approvingly quotes and paraphrases me, there is a two-way street here: we can fruitfully use moral dilemmas to infer the general shape of deontology, and we can use deontology's general shape to help resolve particular moral dilemmas.[227]

Montague also agrees with me on a distinction over which I too have long labored, that between two kinds of reasons.[228] There are subjective reasons that explain why some historical person did what he did. These are to be distinguished from the reasons of interest here, objective reasons that do not have as their business the explanation of historical actions; rather, their business is to evaluate (justify or condemn) such actions. The objective reasons of morality are thus "not in the head" whereas subjective, explanatory reasons are. Montague and I further agree that these two kinds of reasons can generate two kinds of moral dilemmas, subjective ones and objective ones. Only the latter can constitute the "royal road" to deontology's general shape, so only these are what he and I both discuss.

Montague and I further agree that it is an unacceptable view of morality that holds that objective moral dilemmas present us with contradictory obligations. While such contradictory obligations may not be "inconceivable," as Kant put it (with his penchant for overstatement),[229] it would be an unfair morality that guaranteed us moral failure no matter what we did when we confronted an objective moral dilemma. Such a morality would be a kind of joke on the human race, played by some malevolent Greek god toying with us for his own cruel pleasure. Montague and I agree that such a view of morality is to be avoided if at all possible.

So, terrific—Montague and I are comrades in arms, locked shoulder to shoulder, singing Kumbaya together! Things only get interesting when we get to issues where Montague at least thinks we disagree.

For present purposes I would distinguish two kinds of objective moral dilemmas. The first would be the kind of moral dilemmas created by pluralistic deontological theories. Larry Alexander, last discussed, is an example of a monistic deontological theorist, for Alexander's deontological obligations all purport to stem from a single principle, the "Means Principle."[230] My own views are, by contrast, pluralistic: morality confronts us with a large number of agent-relative obligations, such as "Don't kill," "Don't deceive," etc. The first kind of objective moral dilemma arises because of possible conflicts between the distinct moral obligations that exist in my pluralistic view of the matter. I shall call this kind of objective moral dilemma the "internal" kind, because the conflict is solely between deontological reasons and thus is internal to deontology.

By contrast, external moral dilemmas are created by conflicts between deontological obligations and consequentialist obligations. These are the second kind of objective moral dilemmas that I shall discuss. They are also Montague's major focus in his criticism of my views.

[226] The "royal road" phraseology is my own. I adapt it from Freud's saying that dreams were the "royal road to the unconscious."

[227] Montague, "Moral Dilemmas and Moral Theory," 265.

[228] Moore, 2000a, 141–42.

[229] I. Kant, *The Metaphysical Elements of Justice*, John Ladd, trans., (Indianapolis: Bobbs-Merrill, 1965), 25.

[230] Alexander, "The Means Principle."

Let me first focus on the second kind of objective moral dilemmas, because (Montague to the contrary notwithstanding) this one is easy for my view to deal with. To begin with, Montague thinks that I have overlooked his distinction between a consequentialist *property* and a consequentialist *obligation*. As he correctly notes, a consequentialist property can easily be accommodated within some deontological obligation. Causing death, for example, is a consequentialist property of some actions; but it can figure in a deontological obligation, such as "Don't kill." Whereas a consequentialist obligation is distinct from any deontological obligation; in views such as mine, such obligations give agent-neutral reasons for action, whereas deontological obligations gives agent-relative reasons for action.

Because Montague thinks I overlook this distinction, he interprets me as appealing to consequentialist obligations when I have no need to do so; "nothing Moore says about consequentialist reasons and obligations requires that his theory contains consequentialism as a component."[231] Not true! Take my example, discussed also by Montague;[232] our positive obligation to rescue strangers from drowning. True enough, failing to prevent a preventable death is a consequentialist *property* of such actions. Yet I make it perfectly plain that what makes our obligations here consequentialist is *not* that they rely on this consequentialist property; it is rather the ease with which such obligations can be overcome by the obtaining of other good consequences should this rescue be omitted. Deontological obligations "patrol the borders of permissible consequentialist justification," as I have long put it.[233] Such obligations are consequentialist because of their openness to consequentialist (agent-neutral) justification, not because they rely on consequentialist properties.

The main focus of Montague's critique of my "three-level," or "side-constrained," view of deontic ethics is that in objective moral dilemma each of my first two levels will singly dictate an obligation, and that these obligations will then contradict one another. Yet this criticism is surely based on an unsympathetic interpretation of my three-level view of ethics.[234] Montague treats each layer as if the other layers did not exist. That is how he gets the first layer, the consequentialist one, to dictate an obligation to do some action A, and then the second layer, the deontological one, to generate an obligation not to do A.[235] Yet the layers of course are not isolated but related. They say:

(1) maximize intrinsic value; *unless*

(2) doing so violates a deontological obligation; *unless*

(3) following that obligation produces horrendous consequences (beyond some threshold of moral horror).

Now there is no contradiction in examples like Montague's, because the first and consequentialist principle does *not* obligate one to do A in cases where deontological principles say one should not.

[231] Montague, "Moral Dilemmas," 272. [232] Montague, "Moral Dilemmas," 271.

[233] Moore, 2008a.

[234] Laid out in Moore, 2009d, 36–41, and applied in Moore, 1989h, 280–344, and in Moore, 2012b, 434–66.

[235] Montague, "Moral Dilemmas," 272–3.

Anticipating this response, Montague then complains that it "provides no basis for drawing conclusions about the moral status of [A]."[236] Yet implicit in the lexical ordering of these three layers is the guidance Montague seeks: "maximize good consequences, unless doing so violates a deontological obligation, *in which case do what the latter obligation demands*."

I conclude that on any fair reading of my three-level view, there simply is no contradiction here. Nor is there a vacuum of moral guidance.

Montague is more interesting if we direct his criticism towards moral dilemmas of the first kind, those internal to a pluralist deontology such as mine. For with these kinds of conflicts of obligation, neither I nor other deontologists have lexical priorities that we can plausibly assert to exist, and that renders such conflicts apparent only. Here contradiction (conflict of obligations) truly looms.

To my knowledge there are only two general strategies for defusing the looming contradictions, both of which I have alluded to in my earlier work.[237] Montague also explores both of these strategies, and adopts one of them as his own. The first is what Montague (and many others) call the strategy of "specification." Short and snappy moral injunctions of the kind that can be fit on one stone tablet (like "Don't kill") are taken to be elliptical references to much more fully specified principles that contain many exceptions, such as "Don't kill, *unless* necessary to protect one's family from the aggression of the one you kill, *unless* in a just war and the victim is a combatant, etc., etc." The specificationist thesis is that a fully specified morality will contain no contradictory injunctions because of these exceptionally complicated, moral principles all fitting together like some large mosaic.

The second strategy, and the one that Montague favors, focuses on the *force* of deontological principles, not their *content*. Unlike the specificationist strategy, this strategy leaves the content of moral principles short and snappy. But now, the force of such principles is reduced from "all-out" to "presumptive" (or "prima facie") only. The force of such principles, in Montague's language, becomes "non-deductive" in the sense that one cannot deduce what one is obligated to do from any one such principle. It is only the weight of all such principles that determines one's obligation in a given case. This feature of the second strategy thus gives Montague his desired conclusion about objective moral dilemmas: "pluralistic moral theories that incorporate presumptive principles can accommodate objective moral dilemmas without generating contradictions."[238]

Montague accurately sees that I rely on both strategies in my work. To see why and how I combine these two strategies, it is helpful to see why Montague "sets aside"[239] the specificationist strategy. Montague does this on epistemic grounds. Moral principles, for him, are by their nature action-guiding in the sense that moral agents are to find them useful in reasoning about what to do in particular situations. His objection to a

[236] Montague, "Moral Dilemmas," 273.

[237] Moore, 2000a, 143–5. It might seem that the earlier discussion of substantively pro tanto or prima facie duties with regard to Tadros offers a third possibility. Yet the substantively pro tanto duties of Tadros are all-out duties in terms of their force, not presumptive only. They differ from Tadros's non pro tanto duties only in the secondary duties that they imply. They thus do not present any genuinely third alternative here.

[238] Montague, "Moral Dilemmas," 276.

[239] His language. Montague, "Moral Dilemmas," 274.

fully specified description of morality (as the specificationists see the content of that morality) is that it would be so complicated that it wouldn't be useful to such reasoning. As Montague puts this point explicitly: "the specifying principle plays no useful role in . . . reasoning about what . . . to do."[240] Or again: "the principles that result from employing . . . specification can't provide bases for drawing conclusions about the moral status of actions to which more than one principle applies . . . ."[241]

If one thinks of moral principles only as action-guiding principles, it is easy to agree with Montague's objection to specification. Fully specified principles are indeed too complicated (in their interlocking structure) for us to grasp and use them in the service of this action-guiding function. Fully specified principles are epistemic failures as guides to decisions. Yet moral principles also have as their function true descriptions of our obligations, for such principles are the determiners of what makes actions right and wrong. Put differently, such principles are metaphysical principles as much or more than they are merely epistemic principles. And for this function of moral principles, full specification with all-out (other than merely presumptive or prima facie) force will be needed.

So, at the end of the day, Montague and I appear to disagree only about whether moral principles have more than a merely epistemic, action-guiding function. For if they do—if they have as their alternative function the true description of right and wrong action—nothing in Montague's epistemic objections to specificationism would prevent him from being, like me, a specificationist in his moral metaphysics.

XIII. The Explanationist Defense of a Morally Realist Meta-Ethics

I have a fond spot in my heart touched by Jeremy Waldron's chapter[242] critiquing my morally realist meta-ethics. As Waldron recounts, he and I were pretty much the "jurisprudence" part of the Jurisprudence and Social Policy Program in the late '80s at UC Berkeley. The course in jurisprudence required of all first year JSP graduate students that we co-taught had as its centerpiece the formal debate on meta-ethics that Waldron and I engaged in for the benefit of those students. It was such an enjoyable interchange that we not only repeated it at Berkeley but also took it on the road, to the annual meeting of the Society for Realism and Anti-realism at one of the Eastern Division's American Philosophical Association meetings.

I have to confess that the edge is now off this old debate for me. Part of the reason for this is that I am less certain than I was then that it matters so much to either personal or professional concerns how the debate comes out.[243] I have long thought that the realist/conventionalist debate in meta-ethics mattered greatly to issues about legal reasoning.[244] But I am less sure that the realist/non-cognitivist debate has the same

240 Montague, "Moral Dilemmas," 276, n. 29.

241 Montague, "Moral Dilemmas," 273.

242 Jeremy Waldron, "Just No Damned Good," this volume.

243 My recounting of why the debate matters to both personal and professional concerns is in Moore, 1992b, 2442–91. Waldron and I have apparently exchanged places a bit on this issue, since he at one point remarked to me that the enthusiasm for rights in his early work in substantive ethics on rights has become a bit blunted by his meta-ethical skepticism.

244 Moore, 1985b.

implications. That is because the non-cognitivist (of the Simon Blackburn/Jeremy Waldron type) claims at least to be able to duplicate the realist in disdaining the obeisance to social convention that is the hallmark of moral relativists and other conventionalist approaches to meta-ethics. And it is this obeisance to convention (even when it is only a pretense, as it often is) that badly warps legal reasoning.[245]

Another reason why this debate has been a bit blunted for me is that the meta-ethical views Waldron and I each espoused in the late '80s were then fresh and full of promise. Blackburn was still developing his quasi-realist version of non-cognitivism, and the "Cornell realists" were busy producing versions of the explanationist defense of moral realism. But, almost thirty years later, these positions are encrusted by a rich secondary literature that dates some of our past concerns.

Mostly, however, the edge of the debate is somewhat blunted for me because neither side penetrated far enough into the explanationist approach to ontology generally to confidently apply that approach in the defense of moral realism specifically. I still share the basic motivation for the explanationist approach: everything, no matter how ordinary or extraordinary it may seem to one's intuitive ontology, has to earn its place in that ontology by being part of one's best explanations of various features of the one natural world in which we live. Numbers, electrons, intentions, and moral rights all have to be shown to exist by this same, naturalistic criterion.

The linchpin for such an approach to ontology lies in the notions of "explanation," of "best explanation," and of "explanatory competition." As to the first, "explanation" needs considerable regimentation from its ordinary, idiomatic usage to do the ontological work demanded of it by the explanationist approach to ontology. I suspect, for example, that if I were to begin such regimentation I would do so by divorcing explanation from any notions of human understanding. I would also sever it from any tie to the antecedent information base or the subsequent uptake of any particular audience. Further, I would limit the relevant explanations to those using the natural relations of causation, counterfactual dependence, and raises in conditional possibility, and the laws built on these.[246] But even so it would be a daunting task to so limit the notion of explanation that it could be sufficiently objective to carry the load of being our one test for ontological commitment.

Waldron correctly points out that the explanationist defense of moral realism requires more than the kind of crisp, objective notion of explanation just mentioned. As much it needs a scale of evaluation for explanations, criteria of goodness in explanation that allow us to pronounce some as better than others and perhaps even one as "the best." Some of what makes an explanation best will already be included in one's regimented notion of explanation—fitting the data, for example, meaning (in a deductive account of explanation) having that data's occurrence as the deductive implications of one's explanatory theory. But given the underdetermination of theory by any finite set of data—the Duhemian thesis so revived by Quine—supplementary criteria of goodness of explanation are needed; criteria like simplicity, consilience, scope, etc.

245 I charted this warping of legal reasoning early on in Moore, 1982a, 1061–71.

246 For an example of the kind of regimentation I have in mind, see Wesley Salmon, *Scientific Explanation and the Causal Structure of the World* (Princeton: Princeton University Press, 1984); Michael Strevens, *Depth: An Account of Scientific Explanation* (Cambridge, Mass.: Harvard University Press, 2008).

Third, it is a thorny issue of when explanations of some given data actually compete with (as opposed to complement) one another. Genetic explanations of belief, for example, often do not compete with realist explanations. One can explain my belief that a proton caused a vapor trail in a cloud chamber by the historical genesis of such a belief (who taught me, what was taught, receptivity and mental set, etc.); yet usually this is not thought to compete with a realist explanation of such a belief (my belief about vapor trails is caused by the fact that there is a proton in the cloud chamber causing the vapor trail). Such a criterion for competitive (as opposed to complementary) explanations is obviously crucial for the explanationist defense of moral realism; but it is also badly in need of systematization.

These three notions—explanation, best explanation, and explanatory competition—are all crucial to any sophisticated use of the explanationist argument for ontological commitment. It required 600-plus pages of often dense writing for me to penetrate very far into the complex metaphysics of the causal relation in my most recent book.[247] It occurred to me as I was writing that book that it would require at least as much effort to systemize the three explanatory notions I have just referred to. In the absence of such systematization, I now find it hard to see my former explanationist defense of moral realism as much more than a kind of dabbling at the surface.

That said, let me engage Waldron in a little dabbling on the surfaces he visits. Start with Waldron's three necessary conditions for a valid inference about ontology on explanationist grounds. His second criterion, which I would put first, is that the words used in the statements constituting the explanation actually refer to the entities whose existence the explanation is being used to defend. Waldron reminds us of one of Quine's criteria for "referential position" here, that of penetrating the surface grammar of an expression to see what the real unit of semantic significance might be.[248] It is a mistake, Quine told us, to look for dints, sakes, and troths because these terms occur only in fused idioms where the phrase ("by dint of," "for the sake of," "pledged her troth"), not the word, is the smallest unit of semantic significance.

Quine and Waldron are surely right here: some true explanation using some term "x" does not support the existence of x, s if "x" is not used referentially in the explanation. Yet Waldron tries to make a less modest point with this initial criterion. He seeks to show that the Cornell realists cannot limit the explanandum—that is, *what* they explain—to moral beliefs, on the supposed ground that this is an insufficient variety of contexts so that terms like "goodness" or "rights" would then not be used referentially. Waldron has his finger on a real worry here, the worry Brian Leiter calls the "problem of explanatory narrowness."[249] Yet this is a problem in its own right (that I shall discuss shortly); it is in no way dependent on some fusion of moral terms like "rights," etc., a fusion supposedly occurring because of highly limited contexts of use.[250]

[247] Moore, 2009d.

[248] W. V. O. Quine, *Word and Object* (Cambridge, Mass.: MIT Press, 1960), 103, 132.

[249] Brian Leiter, "Moral Facts and Best Explanations," 18 *Social Philosophy and Policy* 79 (2001).

[250] Waldron's argument here is reminiscent of Dan Dennett's early attempt to put Quine's insight about "fused idioms" to a like use. See Daniel Dennett, *Content and Consciousness* (London: Routledge and Kegan-Paul, 1969), ch. 1. Dennett uses what he calls "the fusion strategy" in an attempt to show that mental-state terms are not used referentially. The common problem for Dennett and Waldron is a simple one: the contexts of usage for moral terms (Waldron) or mental-state terms (Dennett) is not nearly so limited as is the contexts of Quine's dints, sakes, and troths.

Waldron's first criterion, indispensability, is also plausible if limited properly. Explanationist defenses of certain ontological commitments do require that the entities in question be *needed* in the best explanations of other phenomena. Yet Waldron's notion of "indispensability" can be no sharper than the three notions of explanation, best explanation, and explanatory competition just discussed. When for example there are complementary explanations, not competing explanations, the entities in question need have no place in certain of such explanations.

Waldron's third criterion is a tricky one. Waldron is certainly right that non-commital (or inverted-comma) use of moral terms in explanation is not relevant to the existence of moral entities. For such use is about the sociology of belief, not about moral facts. Needed, Waldron tells us, is the committed, first-person use where speakers perform the illocutionary act of prescription as well as description. In Mackie's striking phrase, moral qualities have to be referred to in ways that preserve their "have-to-be-doneness" (or we might say, "their reason-giving qualities").[251]

If I were Waldron, I think that I would make this third criterion even stronger. It is not enough, this criterion would say, that a moral quality has a necessary place in the best explanation of some natural phenomena. It is not enough, for example, that the virtue of courage best explains why someone did some courageous action. Rather, what the stronger criterion demands is that the moral fact *that courage is virtuous* have a necessary place in such explanation. It is the fact that courage is virtuous (good) that must have a necessary place in the explanation of behavior, not just courage itself.[252]

If Waldron's third criterion is amended in this way, then notice how restricted are the plausible uses of the explanationist argument to defend moral realism. Such uses are seemingly restricted to a particular kind of naturalistic moral realism that I have long called, "human nature naturalism" (or "HNN").[253] HNN is the view that the abstract norms of morality not only exist in the objective world, giving us objective reasons for action and for belief. Correlates of such norms also exists in our "nature"—in our dispositions to believe certain moral truths and in our dispositions to act in conformity to such norms, even if such dispositions are weak and paired with opposing dispositions. For seemingly only HNN makes plausible how Waldron's third criterion (construed in the extended way that I have just stated) can be satisfied. Because of the link HNN supposes to exist between the objective reasons given by morality and the subjective reasons that actually motivate ("move") us to action, it is plausible to think that the reason-giving nature of moral qualities is part of the best explanation for certain human behaviors. Without HNN, it is hard to make out how this causal link is supposed to work.

The next thing Waldron explores is what the natural phenomena are that are (arguably) best explained by the existence of moral entities, qualities, and states of affairs. Waldron first chides me for my rather naked desperation to find something, anything, that can best be explained by the existence of moral things. Yet (as I am sure Waldron would acknowledge) factors that *justify* one's beliefs need not be the same factors as

[251] J. L. Mackie, *Ethics: Inventing Right and Wrong* (New York: Penguin Books, 1977), ch. 1.

[252] Gilbert Harman goes this route in his "Moral Explanations of Naturalist Fact—Can Moral Claims Be Tested Against Moral Reality?," 24 *Southern Journal of Philosophy* (Supp.) 57 (1986), 63.

[253] Moore, 2000a, 297.

those that *motivate* one to those beliefs. My eagerness to find an explanation of the right kind should not thus be held against acceptance of such explanation, if indeed I do find one of the right kind.

Waldron also puts aside my emphasis on moral *beliefs* as the principal thing to be explained by moral entities, qualities, and states of affairs. One of Waldron's three grounds for this I have already dealt with. That is the alleged fact that we need more than explanations of moral beliefs in which moral things figure, on pain of there being insufficient contexts for words naming moral things to function in referential positions.

Waldron's second reason here is also deficient. He worries that the pragmatic connection between saying "I believe P" and saying "P" will confuse things. It will not, however, the moment one sees this condition of pragmatically appropriate utterance for what it is and sees that such pragmatic connection has nothing to do with any causal connection between the states of affairs, respectively described by "P" and by "I believe P." And it is only the latter, causal connection to moral belief that the explanationist defense of moral realism needs.

Waldron's third objection also fares poorly. It is that we beg the question about moral realism by supposing that moral beliefs are really *beliefs*—representational states of cognition. Yet it is easy not to beg any questions here in framing explanatory competitions: call our moral reactions by some dummy term, "attitudes," "responses," "reactions," "X," whatever. Then, if they are indeed best explained by the existence of moral entities, etc., we can conclude that these reactions were truly *beliefs*. Pants on one leg at a time is fine here.

Waldron does better in chiding me for one of my reasons for preferring beliefs as the explananda of moral explanations. This was my "solve two problems at once" rationale. Whether or not I can kill "two philosophical birds with one stone,"[254] efficiency in exposition is not much of a reason for picking explananda. A better reason is this one. Most of the phenomena that moral explanationists (like Nick Sturgeon, David Brink, Geoff Sayre-McCord, Bill Lycan, Joshua Cohen, Peter Railton, Richard Boyd, and myself) use as explananda are what Bernard Williams once called "belief-dependent" phenomena—beliefs themselves and the actions, historical trends, and the like, done because of certain beliefs.[255] What Williams meant was that if moral entities, etc., were to cause such phenomena to exist, it would only be through the beliefs of certain actors. So if the injustice of slavery is part of the best explanation for historical movements to abolish it, that will most plausibly be through the beliefs (that slavery is unjust) of those constituting such movements.

If this is right—and I believe it is—then it becomes crucial for the explanationist defense of moral realism to explain moral beliefs by moral facts. Otherwise the moral fact explanations of historical trends, etc., will have to compete with (rather than complement) subjective explanations of those trends in terms of the moral beliefs of the historical actors. And that, as Brian Leiter shows, is a difficult competition to know how to adjudicate.[256]

[254] Waldron, "'No Damned Good,'" 283.

[255] Said by Williams in November, 1988, at yet another UC Berkeley discussion of my side of this debate, at an organization then calling itself "BAGPIPE" (Bay Area Group for Philosophy, Politics, and Economics).

[256] Leiter, "Moral Facts and Best Explanations."

In any case, however much the explanationist strategy needs to explain moral beliefs by moral facts, Waldron and I agree that the explanationist needs to explain *more than* moral beliefs with moral facts. In my earlier work I distinguish four sorts of items for which moral realism might provide the best explanation.[257] Waldron focuses on one of these, the behaviors and behavioral trends that are the stuff of history.

In assessing these explanations, Waldron puts his finger on what I have long regarded as a central issue for naturalist-realists such as myself. Naturalist-realists about morality are committed to there being some intimate relation between moral properties such as goodness and natural properties such as generosity or satisfaction of desire. Exactly what this intimate relation might be makes some difference in this context, but to see the difference it makes let us first pursue the issue Waldron wishes to raise. Waldron's question is: why isn't the best explanation of the historical behaviors in question framed in terms of the natural properties (on which the moral properties in some sense depend) rather than in terms of the moral properties themselves?

Although the question is a good one, it is not clear that Waldron's examples raise it very well. Waldron chides me for explaining Hitler's behavior as due to Hitler's moral depravity, and Waldron chides Nick Sturgeon for his explaining Passed Midshipman Woodworth's failure to rescue the Donner party by reference to Woodsworth being "no damned good." Waldron rejects both of these as not being "satisfying accounts" because "surely... we would ask, 'No damned good—*how*?' ... 'No damned good' ... is too general to be the best explanation."[258]

Waldron's response here is handicapped by his omission to tell us what is a moral property as opposed to what is a non-moral, natural property. He appears to think that Hitler's having racist attitudes, for example, is a natural property, while depravity is not; he also appears to think that Woodworth's cowardice, vanity, timidity, and lack of discipline are natural properties, whereas Woodworth's badness (i.e., "no damned good") is a moral property. But surely it is open to think that all of these are moral properties; indeed, that the way Hitler was depraved was to be racist, that the ways Woodworth was no damned good were to be cowardly, vain, timid, and undisciplined.

So construed, then Waldon's complaint about generality amounts to no more than an objection based on Gricean pragmatics, viz. in some or perhaps even in most contexts we expect more detailed specification of the moral properties that best explain the behaviors in question. Such a Grice-like objection of course cuts no meta-ethical ice. If a more conventionally appropriate explanation is one that mentions more specific moral properties, that should be fine with Sturgeon, myself, and other naturalist-realists. The best explanation still involves reference to moral properties.

Waldon might respond in one of three ways here. The first is to deny that being racist, cowardly, vain, timid, or undisciplined are moral properties. Yet now Waldron needs an account of why that is so in terms of some theory about the natural/moral divide. Is the theory one of conventional illocutionary force? That is, that saying "x is racist" or "x is cowardly" is always less often or less severely condemnatory than saying "x is depraved" or "x is no damned good?" One problem with this view is that it is far

[257] Moore, 1992b, 2506–11. [258] Waldron, "'No Damned Good,'" 287.

from clear that the more specific description is always less evaluative than the more general. Compare the customary condemnatory force attached to "you are a murderer" with that attached to "you are a wrongdoer."

But the main worry here is that customary evaluative force seems a poor criterion of hiving off the moral from the natural. If I were Waldron, I would thus turn to a second response. I would try to shift the burden of distinguishing natural from moral properties to the naturalist-realist: it is Moore and his crowd that need the distinction because of their meta-ethical stance; by my own meta-ethics (non-cognitivism), Waldron might say, there are no moral properties and so no distinction that I need draw. Thus, if the examples of Hitler and Woodworth don't get us to natural properties, revise the example to get to whatever naturalist-realists like Moore think are natural properties, and the same point can then be made (about the best explanation being in terms of the underlying natural properties rather than in terms of the overlying moral properties).

There are two problems with this imagined response by Waldron. One is that it is not clear that the revised examples will retain the plausibility of Waldron's actual examples. Suppose cowardice, for example, is taken to be the moral property, and "feels too much fear" and/or "yields too easily to fear" are taken to be the natural properties on which cowardice depends. Is it intuitively plausible that Woodworth's disappointing behavior is better explained by the amount of fear he felt and/or by his inability to face fear, than by his cowardice?

Second, and more fundamentally, if non-cognitivists get to use their end-of-the-day meta-ethics to disclaim distinguishing moral properties from natural ones, so too can those with differing end-of-the-day meta-ethics. Naturalist-realists too can disclaim the distinction in light of *their* commitment to some form of identity thesis, according to which moral properties just *are* natural properties, and all the natural properties on which moral properties depend just are moral properties. In such a view, explanations couched in terms of "felt too much fear," "was a coward," and "was no damned good" will differ in their generality but will not differ in the degree to which they invoke natural as opposed to moral properties.

If I were Waldron, I would eschew either of the two responses I have just suggested for him. I would instead pursue the line introduced earlier. On this line of attack, it is not enough that moral/natural properties like cowardice/no damned good best explain behaviors like Woodworth's. Needed (the claim is) is that the fact that being a coward is morally bad must enter into the best explanation of Woodworth's behavior. Put in other words, the claim is that it must be the condemnatory force of cowardice—its being morally condemnable—that enters into the best explanation, and not just cowardice itself.

I earlier said that if this is a legitimate demand, then the only plausible way for a naturalist-realist to meet it would be by becoming a human-nature naturalist (that is, someone who thinks that objective reasons for action are things to which human beings are subjectively inclined). Not myself subscribing to human-nature naturalism, my own answer is to reject the legitimacy of the demand. For the demand hives off something only a non-cognitivist can hive off as "ethics," namely the condemnatory/commendatory force of various expressions. If goodness is just the staining of the world by projecting our attitudes upon it, one can treat such commendatory force as constituting the moral. But naturalist-realists do not regard the moral this way, and to demand that they do (as a kind of entry-ticket to legitimate explanatory competition) is just to assume that such realism is false from the start.

In the penultimate section of his chapter Waldron raises supervenience, as though the supervenience of moral properties upon natural properties (a supervenience claimed to exist by naturalist-realists like myself) raises special problems for use of the explanationist argument. I am puzzled by this. "Supervenience" has been a much overused word in both ethics and the philosophy of mind. In its core sense, it simply means asymmetrical co-variance, namely: if the supervening property varies, then so must some of the properties supervened upon (the "base properties"); but if some base property varies, then no variation in the supervening property need take place, although it might.

Such asymmetrical co-variance between sets of properties is partly explained by a multiple realizability thesis: the supervening property may be alternatively "realized" by different base properties on different occasions. That is why difference in base properties need not betoken any difference in supervening properties. Such supervenience is also explained by what is misleadingly called a "token-identity" claim: each supervening property as it is instantiated on any given occasion is identical to some base property(ies), even though such base property(ies) can differ from occasion to occasion. That is why any change in the supervening property must be accompanied by some change in base properties.[259]

As applied to the naturalist-realism that I defend, the wrongness sometimes possessed by human actions supervenes on the consequentialist property of causing harm to others. But apart from this consequentialist base property, the moral property of wrongness also supervenes on other natural properties, such as offensive to others, or enhancing of one's own self-loathing, or contributing to human misery, etc.

The objection coming out of all of this that Waldron confesses to have at one time accepted is that the base properties always will furnish better explanations than will supervening properties. Waldron now rejects this conclusion in cases where laws emerge only at the level of supervening properties and not at the level of base properties. Yet I do not see what tempted Waldron to the general view to begin with. Good explanations are where you find them and I see no basis for a blanket preference for base over supervening properties. For one thing, such a blanket preference for base properties probably leads one eventually to the view that micro-physics provides the best explanation of everything—biological survival as well as quantum weirdness, envious intentions as well as gravitational force, etc. For another, if items like consilience mark quality of explanation, then seemingly the more general explanations involved in use of supervening properties should be preferred.

Yet without any presumption in favor of base-property explanations over supervening-property explanations, we seem to be back at the same issue as we were discussing before; on a case-by-case basis, are moral property explanations better than natural property explanations, or are they worse?

[259] This last on the assumption that no natural property realizes two or more moral properties.

XIV. Judicial Interpretation of Legal Texts

One of my long-term interests in the area of jurisprudence has been in legal interpretation. Three of this volume's present authors focus on differing aspects of my writings on this topic. Michael Shapiro raises some general concerns about my natural law theory of interpretation,[260] while Brian Bix focuses on one well-known aspect of that theory of interpretation, its reliance on K-P (or "realist") semantics.[261] Les Green critically discusses the tie that I think to exist between what judges should do in interpreting texts, on one hand, and what judges are obligated by their role as judges to do, on the other.[262] I shall consider each of these topics, the first two more or less together, and then the third separately.

In broad terms both Bix and Shapiro appear to agree with me on what a theory of legal interpretation is, about how such a theory is made up of a conglomerate of different ingredients, and how this conglomerate echoes the ingredients that go into a theory of normal (i.e., not legal) communication. As to the first of these points, all three of us think that "legal interpretation" names the activity that judges do in applying the general standards that are authoritative law to the particular facts of disputed law cases, so as to yield those concrete propositions of law (such as, "this contract is valid") decisive of those particular law cases. A *theory* of legal interpretation, accordingly, is a recipe whose primary function is to describe the right-making characteristics of a good ("correct," "valid," "true") legal interpretation, and that may have as its secondary function the guidance of judges as to how they are to do their interpretive tasks as they judge.

Bix, Shapiro, and I similarly agree on the conglomerate nature of plausible theories of legal interpretation. Indeed, this is one of Shapiro's criticisms of Justice Scalia's originalist/traditionalist theory of constitutional interpretation, viz. such a one- or two-ingredient theory is woefully incomplete in its ability to decide very many cases. We three also agree on how a theory of legal interpretation should bear some resemblance to a theory of ordinary, non-legal communication. After all, legal texts are produced by lawmakers who both mean something by them and mean to achieve something by uttering them (including the securing of uptake by the audiences (citizens and judges) to whom they are directed).

Shapiro thus includes in legal interpretation three items familiar from the theory of communication: authorial intentions, linguistic meaning, and audience belief. In my writings I do the same, although I subdivide "linguistic meaning" into logic, syntax, semantics, and pragmatics.[263] Shapiro then adds two other ingredients, a Moorean "'all-things-considered' value judgment about the best result in this case," and a Scalian trajectory to a developing consensus. By contrast I actually think there are six or seven other ingredients that might plausibly be added to form an overall theory of legal interpretation.[264]

[260] Michael Shapiro, "Conceptual Breakage and Reconstruction: Michael S. Moore's Natural Law Theory of Interpretation," this volume.

[261] Brian Bix, "Metaphysical Realism and Legal Reasoning," this volume.

[262] Leslie Green, "Law and the Role of a Judge," this volume.

[263] Moore, 1985b, 288–91.

[264] I summarize my overview of ten possible ingredients in an overall theory of legal interpretation in the Symposium on Law and Linguistics, 73 *Washington University Law Quarterly* 884–99 (1995).

Much of Bix's commentary in sections II and III of his chapter consists of a reminder that no one ingredient in an overall theory of interpretation should predominate. As earlier mentioned, this is also Shapiro's criticism of Scalia's originalist theory of interpretation. Bix makes it sound like this is a criticism of my theory as well, with the overemphasis of my theory supposedly being on the ordinary semantics in English of words used in legal texts. Yet I can fully agree with Bix when he urges that

> in the understanding and application of legal norms, one should be cautious in applying conventional ideas about semantics, pragmatics, and reference when speaking about the language of legal norms, seeing that sort of analysis as being only *a part* of the overall process of legal reasoning—perhaps a *major* part, and the *starting point* of analysis, but with an important supplement still to be added.[265]

I can also agree with Bix and Shapiro as to what (among other things) that "important supplement" includes: the value (or "purpose" in a non-mentalistic, functional sense) of the rule in which the word appears (Bix), and the all-things-considered safety-valve question of general justice (Shapiro). At most there is here only a disagreement in emphasis between Bix and myself, not of substance.

Both Bix and Shapiro focus specifically on one possible ingredient in an overall theory of legal interpretation, and that is authorial intention. Both Bix and Shapiro appear to believe that authorial intention has a legitimate place in legal interpretation. As Shapiro puts it, "looking to what authors had in mind is an instinctive course for ascertaining meaning."[266] Bix adds, more specifically: "the role of those (judges and others) who apply legal norms should be focused on recovering the choice made by [official] decision-makers... [and this] encourages a focus on lawmakers' intentions ...."[267] Shapiro's main complaint about Scalia's reliance on the intentions of the Framers of the Constitution is incompleteness, yet while this is a valid complaint, the more radical complaint is Bix's: there is good reason to look to such authorial intention only if the Framers themselves were authoritative for succeeding generations on what the Constitution should be taken to mean.

The truth is that legal texts vary enormously as to the importance of authorial intention. With regard to the US Constitution, there is very little reason to pay attention to what the Framers thought about what punishments are cruel, what process is due, when protection of law is equal, etc. It is true that I have myself in this context based interpretive conclusions on Framers' intentions; but this was conditional and *arguendo: if* one were to rely on the intentions of Madison, Hamilton, and Bingham, then one should rely on the dominant intentions that these natural rights theorists actually had. As natural rights theorists they would have had only what I have called "spare semantic intentions" when they drafted the texts in question, which are intentions to name real moral entities and qualities whose nature was to guide meaning.[268] Such nature of moral

265 Bix, "Metaphysical Realism and Legal Reasoning," 315, (italics in original).

266 Shapiro, "Conceptual Breakage and Reconstruction," 299.

267 Bix, "Metaphysical Realism and Legal Reasoning," 316.

268 My coinage of "spare semantic intentions" first appeared in Moore, 1985b. I applied this analysis of authorial intentions to the Framers of the Constitution in Moore, 1989g. I qualify even this reliance on the spare semantic intentions of the Framers in Moore, 2001b.

entities and qualities may as easily contradict the Framers' particular thoughts about what punishments are cruel, etc., as they might agree with them.

At the other pole of the continuum (on the relevance of authorial intention to legal interpretations) are texts like wills and contracts. In such contexts we have good reason to care what testators intended to do with their property and with what obligations contractors intended to be bound. Our normative theories make these authors masters of their fates in these dimensions, so legal interpreters should care very much what these authors meant by what they said. Statutes are somewhere in between these poles, although I think authorial intentions for such texts are much closer to their level of (ir)relevance for constitutional texts than to their level of relevance for contractual and testamentary texts. One stunning problem for statutes, of which I was an early expositor,[269] is the lack of any very determinate author for statutory texts.

In addition to authorial intention, Bix has also focused on another of the ingredients in an overall theory of legal interpretation, the semantics of words and sentences in a natural language such as English. His main criticism of my realist semantics he here puts aside. (The criticism put aside is the Gertrude Stein-like objection that, as to metaphysical essences, "there is no there there.") Bix contents himself here with a lesser objection, raising a kind of relevance worry: even when legal interpretation should turn on the ordinary English semantics of some word appearing in a legal text, and even when there is some metaphysical essence that could be taken to be the reference of that word, the correct semantics is not to look to that essence to fix the word's legal meaning. Even if tomatoes are not really vegetables, and even if whales are not really fish, in some legal contexts the desirability of rule-of-law notice and of furthering the purpose of some statutes might dictate an ordinary usage, behavioral semantics over the realist semantics I often prefer.

Here, too, Bix and I can at most have a disagreement of emphasis. In my own work I have urged that sometimes the right semantics for use in legal interpretation will not be the realist semantics. For example, in the "unborn widow" cases under the rule against perpetuities, when the testator devises Blackacre to "A's widow for life, then to their children and their heirs who shall attain the age of 21," the phrase "A's widow" can be taken in one of two ways: either as (a) referring to Mary, A's wife at the time the will was written, or (b) to any woman who is married to A when A dies, who could be someone other than Mary (and so young as not to be a life-in-being at the time the conveyance takes effect). The prevailing legal construal of this phrase is attributive and not referential and this seems plausible enough, even though it goes against my general semantic recommendations.[270]

The main theme of Shapiro's chapter is one of the main themes of his lifetime of work. This is the challenge to our conventional understanding of the world presented by technological change. J. L. Austin once quipped how "fact is richer than diction,"[271]

[269] Moore, 1981.

[270] I discuss this and other examples of legal interpretation not using a realist semantics, in Moore, 2014a.

[271] J. L. Austin, "A Plea for Excuses," 56 *Proceedings of the Aristotelian Society* 1 (1956).

and Shapiro's examples show us how our own inventiveness can make that true. Shapiro documents how personal identity, human reproduction, death, etc., as traditionally conceived by us, can be and are challenged by our own creation of cloning abilities and other technological advances.

As Shapiro and Bix both realize, allowing judges to deal with such novel cases in a determinate way was one of my motives for urging adoption of realist semantics in legal contexts. We run out of conventions in such novel cases because conventions are developed only about situations that have arisen before. They thus do not cover the abnormal and the unforeseen. Both Bix and Shapiro recognize that the metaphysical nature of kinds will run out less quickly and less often than will the conventional understanding of such kinds. They nonetheless question whether nature itself can be fully determinate in these technologically produced, novel cases. Bix doubts, for example, whether our best theory about the nature of death can univocally resolve all the variations of "near-death" experiences that technology can now produce. Bix urges that legal decision-makers might have to settle for "different types or levels of death."[272]

Part of Bix's point is a reiteration of the point of his that I earlier addressed, viz. that sometimes the value or purpose behind a certain rule dictates a different meaning be given to a word that also appears in other legal rules with different purposes. For "death," this would be the point that the legal death that triggers legitimate organ donation is different than the legal death that triggers testamentary dispositions, is different yet again from the death that triggers a prosecution for murder rather than for attempted murder, etc. Again, my response to this point of Bix's is to agree in principle that sometimes this is so, but to disagree that it is so with respect to this example. I think that the purpose of each of these rules using death as a trigger for different legal consequences is both univocal and realist: organs should be taken, property transferred, and murders prosecuted, only when someone is really dead.

A second aspect of Bix's point here is the latent conventionalism in it. Bix worries that "the *concept* 'death' may be too simple" to deal with the variations in natural conditions technology now makes possible.[273] Bix thinks that classifying these conditions as dead/not-dead requires "right answers to the difficult moral and policy questions we face" in these sorts of decisions.[274] Yet Bix cannot saddle realist semantics with the limitations of a *concept* of death, for concepts are simply conventions of a certain sort (either lists of properties as in definitions, or similarity relations to paradigm examples). The nature of death is not a concept, nor is it bounded by a concept. Moreover, discovering that nature is also an exercise that is not limited to any existing concept of death, no matter how widely shared; rather, that nature is given by the insights of advancing scientific knowledge, even ones that go beyond our existing concept of death. As Shapiro recognizes, death involves the cessation of personhood, and while that partly involves cessation of certain bodily functions, it also involves judgments about the essential attributes of personhood and their cessation. The nature of death is thus far less convention-dependent, and far more (moral- as well as scientific-) theory-dependent, than Bix here allows.

[272] Bix, "Metaphysical Realism and Legal Reasoning," 313.
[273] Bix, "Metaphysical Realism and Legal Reasoning," 313 (emphasis added).
[274] Bix, "Metaphysical Realism and Legal Reasoning," 313.

There is a third aspect to Bix's point here that survives my rejoinders above to the first two aspects. It is this: technology now makes possible a smoothly graded continuum in the diminution of those properties our best theory of death stipulates determine when someone is dead. Surely, Bix might say (joined here I think by Shapiro), some judgment is required as to where to draw the line on these continua. The law for its own reasons famously lumps the world into exclusive categories; someone is either dead or not-dead. She cannot legally be "sort-of dead," "almost dead," "partly dead," etc. The Bix/Shapiro worry here is that nature does not match the law in bivalently dividing reality.[275]

The point I take to be a serious one. The worry is that even if the world is full of natural kinds—kinds whose deep nature far outstrips our conventional indications of kind-ness in its determinateness—even so, that nature too can be indeterminate, at least in some of its dimensions. There can be, in other words, fuzzy-bordered natural kinds. Put differently, vagueness about such kinds need not always be an indeterminateness in conventional indicators of kind-ness, but may rather betoken an irreducible sort of ontological vagueness. Even if helium is a natural kind whose nature is given by its atomic number, there are "helium" isotopes with different atomic numbers; even if tigers are a natural kind whose nature is given in part by inter-reproducibility, there are "tigons" and "ligers" (offspring of one tiger and one lion) that cannot themselves reproduce; etc.

Some theorists of vagueness dispute that there is such a thing as ontological vagueness.[276] Somewhat reluctantly, I suppose, I find it difficult to agree with them. Yet notice that for some kinds like death, this is not as defeating a concession as it might seem. For as I stated before, death involves the cessation of personhood as much as it involves cessation of human species-hood, and this requires a moral theory of personhood. So perhaps morally infused kinds like death do not suffer from ontological vagueness, even if helium, animal species, and the like do. Shapiro indicates his doubts that even this is the case. Moral reality, he suggests, runs out in the face of technological innovation no less than does physical reality.

I have long thought this last question to be an interesting one. Some moral realists, such as Aquinas (and his contemporary reincarnation, John Finnis), appear to believe that moral reality is "gappy." There is no morally preferable way, Aquinas tells us, of arranging the details of bailments of personal property. Human law just has to coordinate about such matters to resolve them one way or the other, since, morally speaking, any of a variety of ways is as good as another.[277] My own morally realist meta-ethics has never accepted this gappy view of moral reality. For one thing, such a gappy view does not square very well with the phenomenology of our moral experience. No matter how hard the moral dilemma, we never reach the sense that it doesn't matter what we do. This is true even on matters as trivial as what kind of notice of recall we need to give to those to whom we bail our personal property. (We may be *at liberty* to do such things in

[275] Billy Crystal in the Rob Reiner film, *The Princess Bride*, apparently views nature differently: "There is a big difference," Billy tells us, "between 'almost dead' and 'all dead.'"

[276] See, e.g., Roy Sorenson, *Vagueness and Contradiction* (Oxford: Oxford University Press, 2001).

[277] Aquinas, *Summa Theologica*.

a number of different ways, but that is different from thinking there is no better or worse way of doing them.)

The upshot is that death may not be fuzzy-bordered even if there are fuzzy-bordered natural kinds. In any event, such fuzziness, where and when it exists, only decreases the advantage in determinateness held by a realist semantics over its conventionalist competitors; it does not eliminate it.

In the fourth section of his chapter Bix gently raises Andrei Marmor's objection to use of a realist semantics in law. Marmor's objection is to one implication of realist semantics, namely under such a semantics there is the possibility that most people could be radically wrong about what the law is or requires. Bix quotes Marmor for the proposition that such "an extensive misidentification of the law would seem profoundly mysterious."[278]

Bix himself largely defuses this worry nicely on my behalf. My usual example of such radical and global error is the popularly passed Proposition in California in the 1980s that rejected the Model Penal Code's definition of insanity as an excuse for criminal liability and sought to return legal insanity to the conception of it that has prevailed in England since the *M'Naghten* decision of 1843. The Proposition defined legal insanity as "a defect of reason, due to disease of the mind, such that the accused does not know the nature and quality of his action *and* does not know that such actions are wrong."[279] Almost all readers of the Proposition may well have thought that the "and" that is emphasized meant conjunction, as it normally does. If so, they were wrong: "and," as here used, means "or." This is because, in a realist semantics, "insanity" referred to something (the *M'Naghten* test) whose nature differed from the definition of it given in the Proposition. As the California Supreme Court reasoned,[280] if the spare semantic intention of those who voted for the Proposition was to "return to *M'Naghten*," then construing "and" to mean "or" was the way to do so because that disjunctive test was the true nature of the *M'Naghten* conception of legal insanity.

What one can concede to Marmor is this much: when notice to citizens of what the law requires is quite important, then that ingredient which maximally serves such notice (audience belief) can trump the semantics of the expressions used in one's overall theory of interpretation. In such cases, indeed, the conventional understanding will be the right understanding, and there will be no global error possible. Two points, however: first, in many cases notice to citizens is not that important. This is true about the law of excuses such as insanity; it is also true of Bix's example, the amount or kind of punishment attached to various degrees of homicide. In these cases, there is no trumping of realist semantics by audience belief to be done, and global error becomes possible. Second, even when a realist semantics is trumped within one's overall theory of interpretation by something else such as audience belief, that does not constitute an argument against use of a realist semantics. My argument for use of such semantics in legal interpretation was always conditional: *insofar as the ordinary semantics of English should govern*, realist semantics should presumptively be used.

278 Andrei Marmor, *Interpretation and Legal Theory* (Oxford: Oxford University Press, 1992), 97, quoted in Bix, "Metaphysical Realism and Legal Reasoning," 319.

279 Quoted in *People v. Skinner*, 39 Cal 3rd 765 (1985) (emphasis added).

280 *People v. Skinner*, 39 Cal 3rd 765 (1985).

Section V of the discussion in Bix's chapter considers my suggestion that a realist semantics should be applied to the question that has long dominated general jurisprudence, which is the "What is law?" question. In the article of mine that Bix discusses,[281] I outline how such a semantics would be applied to an artifactual term such as "law," urging that one would have to find law to be an instrumental good (or "functional kind"), that is, a kind whose essential nature was given by the functions (or goods) that it served and not by the structural means by which it served those functions. My article was speculative, provisional, and interpretive of the works of others such as Fuller, Finnis, and Dworkin. I myself remained non-committal, and I still do. So does Bix, apparently, although he has his "skeptical doubts" about there being unique functions served by law that give it its essential nature.

I have not been similarly non-committal about one aspect of law's essential nature when law is viewed in particular (rather than general) jurisprudence. When the question of internal jurisprudence, "What is the law?," is asked by a participant within some particular legal system, I have urged that law, whatever else it is, is something that obligates judges (in their role as judges) to follow it in their decisions. Les Green's chapter in this volume wishes to dispute this.

Green presents his arguments as three in number, but I think they are more fruitfully packaged as a twosome and I will so treat them. His first argument is that "some standards that a judge is morally obligated to apply are not law."[282] Green proffers the principles of arithmetic, the semantics and syntax of natural languages such as English, and certain moral principles as three examples of standards that judges are sometimes obligated to apply in their role as judges but that are not part of the law.

To assess this argument of Green's first requires that we be clear on what the thesis that Green believes himself to be attacking is. One possibility is the thesis he explicitly quotes from me as his target: (1) "if a standard does not give a judge an obligation it is not part of the law."[283] By contraposition, (1) is equivalently rendered as: if a standard is part of the law, it obligates judges in their role as judges. Yet (1) is not contravened by Green's first argument. Thesis (1) does not address whether judges are obligated by non-legal standards. So Green must have in mind the converse of (1) as the thesis he wishes to attack. The converse is: (2) If a standard obligates a judge in her role as a judge, such standard is part of the law.

In fact, in my prior writings I have defended both (1) and (2). Their conjunction of course yields: (3) A standard is part of the law if and only if it obligates judges in their role as judges. Despite this, it is important to separate the two conjuncts of (3) into (1) and (2) because only the second of these is addressed by Green's arguments. I gather he finds (1) as intuitive as do I. Laws necessarily obligate judges in their role as judges, at least prima facie and pro tanto.

It is also important to separate (1) from (2) because the systemic implications of these theses differ. Thesis (1) is important in the natural-law/legal-positivist debate, because if law necessarily obligates judicial obedience, and if the only thing that can obligate anyone ultimately is morality, then law seemingly must have some connection to morality, (a natural law thesis). Thesis (2), by contrast, has no such implications for the

[281] Moore, 1992a. [282] Green, "Law and the Role of a Judge," 325.
[283] Green, "Law and the Role of a Judge," 323, 332.

natural-law/legal-positivist debate. Rather, thesis (2) bears on what I shall call the *richness* of law. When judges decide disputed cases, are they always, in all parts of their reasonings, doing something properly called, "applying the law?" Or are they doing other things as they decide such cases, such as resolving disputes, making new law, changing old law, etc.?

So I am not unconcerned about Green's critique, even if it fails to touch on the natural-law argument just sketched with respect to thesis (1). Returning then to Green's first argument, notice how narrowly he interprets the phase, "applying the law." The three items Green excludes from this phrase—arithmetic, semantics, moral principles—I would include in it, in the following way. Applying the law in my analysis has always included four activities: (a) finding and stating authoritative, general legal standards ("the law" in a narrow sense); (b) finding the facts of any given case; (c) connecting the general standards of law to true descriptions of particular facts via interpretive conclusions; and (4) applying deductive logic to the legal, factual, and interpretive premises to yield a concrete legal proposition decisive of the case in question.[284]

Now, let's consider Green's supposed counterexamples. Principles of arithmetic I take to be matters of fact. Finding that some plaintiff suffered $100 in medical costs, $100 in travel costs, $100 in lost future earnings, and $100 in pain and suffering damages, are all findings of fact. But so is the arithmetical conclusion that plaintiff suffered a total of $400 in damages. Green can have his conclusion that these truths of "arithmetic are not laws of England";[285] but surely these truths are part and parcel of *applying* the laws of England to the facts of particular law cases. True enough, such truths of arithmetic are not proved at trial; they are judicially noticed. But surely that makes no difference. They are a part of applying law to *facts*, nonetheless.

Similarly, the syntactic, semantic, and pragmatic principles of natural languages, along with the moral principles needed to decide law cases, are also part and parcel of a judge applying the law to the facts of a particular case. For judges need to connect their factual findings to general statements of authoritative law via interpretive premises that they construct out of just these kinds of ingredients. As I summarized in my earlier discussion of Shapiro and Bix, a theory of legal interpretation, if it is at all plausible, must include all of these items (and more). One cannot interpret law without paying attention to these standards of language and of morals. Since interpreting law is part of the process of applying law, these too cannot be the counterexamples Green hoped to find.

Green's second argument is a more subtle one. It is like his first in that it urges that the obligations constitutive of the judicial role include more than the obligation to apply the law. The first argument proceeds by pointing to standards that are supposed to be the judge's obligation to apply that are not *law*. The second argument purports to broaden the judicial role even further. According to this argument, the obligations constitutive of the judicial role include obligations to do things other than *apply* standards of any kind, legal or otherwise. As Green sees it, judges have law-improving obligations and law-protecting obligations in addition to their law-applying obligations. These are "important creative powers" of the judicial role. And while they are "anchored in the principles of the rule of law," they "do not arise from principles of law."

[284] Moore, 1981; Moore, 1985b. [285] Green, "Law and the Role of a Judge," 325.

To keep the discussion manageable, let us exclude Green's "law-protecting" obligations and focus on his "law-improving powers" of a judge. Green here has in mind powers such as the following powers of judges to:

(a) overrule precedent decisions;
(b) overrule the plain meaning of a statute;
(c) narrow the holding of a precedent case by:
  (i) distinguishing it; or
  (ii) confining its holding to its exact facts;
(d) narrow the plain meaning of a statute:
  (i) to less than it would otherwise cover, or
  (ii) to just those instances where the legislature explicitly intended it to apply;
(e) create new law in situations where:
  (i) there is no precedent decision at all on point; or
  (ii) there is precedent on both sides of the question; or
  (iii) there is precedent that is "not on all fours" but that can be extended by analogy to cover the present case;
(f) create new law in situations where:
  (i) there is no statute covering the situation one way or the other; or
  (ii) statutes conflict in what they require in the situation at hand; or
  (iii) there is a statute in the vicinity but its language is vague, ambiguous, or in some other way unclear in its application to this case.

Judges in the Anglo-American legal tradition in which Green and I have both grown up do in fact exercise all of these powers. Moreover, we both agree with most legal theorists that it is right that judges have and exercise these powers, as much as we may disagree about matters of extent or about particular exercises of these powers. So the live question is how to think of what judges are doing when they exercise these powers.

As Green recognizes, it is my view that judges in all instances (a)–(f) above are doing nothing more and nothing different than *applying the law*. In all cases the law as they declare it to be is the law that was so before they declared it so. This is even true of the overruling powers (a) and (b); when judges overrule common-law precedent or statutory plain meaning, they are not changing the law—they are changing what is said about the law, but not the law itself. As Blackstone said, judicial pronouncements may be *evidence* of the law but they are not the law itself.

Green regards this as "overkill." On his view, judges are changing the law when they overrule; changing the law when they distinguish or narrow plain meaning; creating new law when they make novel decisions, extend by analogy old precedents, clarify vagueness and ambiguity, or resolve conflicts in legal standards. That is why Green regards these as "creative powers" rather than law-applying powers. It is why he thinks of them as improving the existing law rather than merely applying that existing law.

Notice that the real issue here between myself and Green thus devolves into what we mean by *law*. Green has the typical positivist view that law is constituted by precedent cases and plain meanings as historical facts.[286] That is why exercise of any of the six powers above either creates new law where none previously existed or it changes law that did exist. By contrast, I think the law is much broader than this historical-facts view of law can or will admit. The law on my view includes those principles and values that determine the rightful exercise of these powers. It includes the furtherance of such rule-of-law values as protecting reliance, minimizing surprise, furthering equality, and the like; it also includes the substantive values that nonetheless can properly motivate a judge to overrule, distinguish, clarify, narrow, etc. There is a law, for example, on overruling.[287] It includes factors rendering prior decisions vulnerable to overruling; and it includes factors inclining one against overruling, such as the importance of notice to criminal defendants. The balance of these factors is the law, not the precedent overruled.

An outsider to this familiar debate in jurisprudence might well enquire about just what kind of a debate Green and I are having about the proper reach of "law?" One possibility is that this is a debate about the most accurate description of our concept of law. The question so construed then is: which way of regarding these law-improving obligations of judges is most enshrined in our legal practices? Such legal practices include, but are not limited to, our linguistic practices in our ordinary usage of "law" and its cognates. And by my armchair sociology, my sense is that most speakers regard, for example, the US Supreme Court as *changing* the law when it overrules one of its Constitution-interpreting precedents. But our non-linguistic legal practices cut the other way. Two such practices are here salient. One is the practice so noted by Ronald Dworkin; the treatment of hard cases as nonetheless having right answers in terms of litigants having pre-existing legal rights and duties to win or lose such cases. This practice requires law to already include what Green would say was created by judicial action. The second practice is that of retroactive overruling of both common-law precedents and statutory plain meaning. No matter how different or surprising the new decision might be, our uniform practice is to treat the law announced for the first time in an overruling decision as to have always been the law, and as such, as fully applicable to facts occurring prior to the overruling decision.[288] Green recognizes that this latter practice goes against his interpretation of law, but urges that in so practicing overruling we "compromise one aspect of the rule of law, namely the principle that laws should be prospective in force."[289] Yet our practice in this respect does not contravene this rule-of-law principle—so long as one has my richer notion of *law* rather than Green's spare notion.

So as a matter of teasing out a concept of law from how we in fact practice law the verdict is, while mixed, slanted against Green's spare, positivist notion of law. Still, Green might urge that the debate is not one of descriptive jurisprudence but is rather one of a

[286] Thus Herbert Hart, like Green, thought that a statutory or common law rule's "hard core of settled meaning is law in some centrally important sense ...." Hart, "Positivism and the Separation of Law and Morals," 71 *Harvard Law Review* 593–629 (1958).

[287] As Justice O'Connor recognized as her opinion in *Planned Parenthood of Southeastern Pennsylvania v. Casey*, 505 US 833 (1992).

[288] The only exception in the US is the US Supreme Court's occasional prospective overruling in certain constitutional criminal procedure cases.

[289] Green, "Law and the Role of a Judge," 336.

normative jurisprudence. The question so construed then becomes which concept of law, if adopted by legal actors within the legal system, will produce the best results (i.e., the best judging for judges, the best law-making for legislators, the best level of obedience for citizens)? Green focuses on judges and queries "what value would there be in charging judges to work with the rule, 'Apply the law and only the law,'" when the law they are charged to apply is "Moore's capacious idea of 'law' . . ."?[290]

The arguments on my side of the fence here are familiar. They include the thought that judges do better judging if they never say to themselves in hard cases, "well, now I have run out of law and I am free to make it up as I please." They do better because they search harder for persuasive analysis, hidden principles, non-obvious statutory purposes, and the like; items that if found make for better judging. A similar, and similarly familiar, thought concerns the practice of overruling. The thought is that judges do better in exercising this power if they see themselves as never free from the "law of overruling." Such felt constraint makes them think more carefully about the rule-of-law costs to overruling, costs that vary from area of law to area of law and even from case to case. Such felt constraint also constrains the "enthusiasm for 'moral realism'" that Green worries I have too much of; activist judges might otherwise give license to their own values as motivating too many overrulings.

A different kind of normative argument here is one that does not appeal to the good or bad consequences that will ensue if legal actors adopt one or other concept of law. Rather, this form of normative argument concerns the coherence of our own view as external theoreticians of the law. One ground for urging rejection of a concept of law is that it leads to incoherence and absurdity within one's own theory of judicial obligation.

Such I have urged to be the case with Green's narrow view of law. For on Green's narrow view, when judges exercise their law-improving powers, two things are true: first, they are not applying existing law but are rather creating new law or changing old law; and two, in doing such creative and reformative tasks, they are not bound by any law (even if they are guided by rule-of-law principles, which are not law, Green assures us). These two features combine to yield a conclusion I find absurd: that, on Green's view, judges are sometimes obligated—obligated by their role as judges—to go against the law in their decisions.

Green apparently agrees with me that "to think of these [law-improving] activities as proper and as going against the law would be absurd."[291] Yet he gives us no hint as to how he avoids this absurd implication of his view with regard to overrulings. Nor can I see any way for him to avoid this conclusion. A judicial obligation to change the law, where the act of change is not itself guided by some law of change, is necessarily an obligation to go against the law, is it not?

Green rejoins with his own intended *reductio* of my view of law. He urges that my "expansive" notion of law is so expansive that the judicial obligation to apply the law will be no other and no different than the obligation of each of us to do the right thing. If this is so, Green continues, then there can be no such thing as a judge stepping outside of the judicial role on occasion, because all relevant considerations are already

[290] Green, "Law and the Role of a Judge," 341.

[291] Green, "Law and the Role of a Judge," 336.

before him *within* the role. And "if it is not possible to step outside it," then "there is no judicial role."[292] And this, Green thinks, is absurd.

Whether Green's conclusion here is absurd is a matter of some contention. Heidi Hurd's important book, *Moral Combat*, urges generally that there is no such thing as a role-relative morality; she urges more specifically that judges must take into account the consequences of their decisions for how citizens must make their decisions, and citizens must take into account the consequences of their decisions for how judges must make their decisions. For her, the conclusion that there should be no gap between what is right for judges and what is right for citizens is not absurd at all.[293]

While I am sympathetic to Hurd's view here, I am not committed to it. To see this, consider Green's argument to the contrary. Green correctly attributes to me the belief that "every valid reason that could be relevant to a judicial decision applies in virtue of the fact that the person is a judge; none of them applies only in out-of-role, off-duty circumstances." Yet unnoticed by Green is that he needs to be able to attribute the converse belief to me to get his "absurd" conclusion. For Green, I need to believe that no valid reason that could be relevant to a judicial decision applies only in in-the-role, on-duty circumstances.[294] And this belief I might well deny. The judicial role is plausibly construed to give judges special (or especially heavily weighted) concerns for the values going under the name of the rule of law. It is plausible (Hurd to the contrary notwithstanding) to think that citizens do not. The upshot is that the balance of reasons for judges can sometimes be different than it is for citizens. Stepping out of role then becomes quite possible for judges—it means discounting the weighting that judges especially owe to the rule-of-law values, reducing that weight down to the weight they have for non-judicial-role-occupying citizens.

So on normative grounds, too, I think the case is strong for my "capacious" view of law in preference to Green's stingier view. And again, with such a capacious view of law, it becomes much more plausible to urge the thesis of mine that Green here attacks, viz. that the obligation of judges is to apply the law and only the law in their decisions of disputed cases.

Green also chides me for thinking that I can change something as basic as our concept of law. He urges that that would take "more than philosophical argument"—such change requires that we "change the way we normally talk and think, and, probably, the way we live."[295] But that criticism presupposes that Green has won the descriptive debate earlier discussed. And by my lights, he has not. The concept of law that we "live" by is the one presupposed by our legal practices. And those, as I earlier summarized, by and large presuppose the capacious concept of law that Green rejects. Conservatism about conceptual change can be a double-edged sword, and here it cuts the one who would wield it.

292 Green, "Law and the Role of a Judge," 337–8.

293 Hurd, *Moral Combat*.

294 Green, "Law and the Role of a Judge," 337.

295 Green, "Law and the Role of a Judge," 341.

XV. Coda

No one has ever accused me of not enjoying a good argument. So this has been fun. All of the contributors to this volume have crossed swords with me, or stood shoulder to shoulder as we crossed swords with others, on far too many issues and too many occasions to count. But this occasion is a special one for me. I am quite touched that the occasion of my finally reaching middle age should motivate my friends and colleagues to once again joust with me on issues we all care about. Nothing could be a more welcome and a more fitting tribute, and I deeply appreciate it.

My friend Alan Schwartz once remarked that our scholarly lives are essentially solitary forms of existence. While I have always thought that that was basically true, on occasions such as the present one we get to put a social face on this otherwise solo struggle with ideas. This social face makes the work so much more sustaining, enjoyable, and rewarding.

I am particularly touched by the dedicated effort of my best colleague, friend, co-author, and omnipresent discussant, who also happens to be my wife, Heidi Hurd. In her contribution to this volume she has managed to restate, reorganize, and make what sense can be made of the entire corpus of my writings. Just reading that amount of material is a daunting enterprise, let alone digesting it in the elegant form she has produced. I am grateful for what can only be (yet another) act of love.

Finally, the efforts of those who conceived of this volume, organized both it and the conference from which it sprang, are deeply appreciated. I refer to the editors of the volume, Kim Ferzan and Stephen Morse, who along with Heidi made this project go. I can think of no better act of friendship than what they have done here, and I hope I am worthy of it.

Bibliography of the Works of Michael S. Moore

Moore, Michael S. 1965. "The Right to Counsel for Indigents in Oregon." *Oregon Law Review* 44: pp. 255–300.

Moore, Michael S. 1968. "Criminal Discovery." *Hastings Law Journal* 19: pp. 865–917.

Moore, Michael S. 1975a. "Some Myths About 'Mental Illness.'" *Inquiry* 18: pp. 233–65.

Moore, Michael S. 1975b. "Some Myths About 'Mental Illness.'" Revised and expanded, *Archives of General Psychiatry* 32: pp. 1483–97.

Moore, Michael S. 1975c. "Mental Illness and Responsibility," *Bulletin of the Menninger Clinic* 39: pp. 308–28, summarized in 1976. *Psychiatry Digest* (May): p. 40.

Moore, Michael S. 1978a. "Definition of Mental Illness." In *Critical Issues in Psychiatric Diagnosis*, edited by Robert Spitzer and Donald Klein. New York: Raven Press.

Moore, Michael S. 1978b. "The Briggs Amendment: It Discriminates Against Homosexuals." Editorial debate with Senator John Briggs. *Los Angeles Herald Examiner*. September 14.

Moore, Michael S. 1979a. "Legal Conceptions of Mental Illness." In *Mental Illness: Law and Public Policy*, edited by Baruch A. Brody and Hugo Tristram Engelhardt. The Netherlands: D. Reidel Publishing Co.

Moore, Michael S. 1979b. "Responsibility for Unconsciously Motivated Action." *International Journal of Law and Psychiatry* 2: pp. 323–47.

Moore, Michael S. 1980a. "The Nature of Psychoanalytic Explanation." *Psychoanalysis and Contemporary Thought* 3: pp. 459–543.

Moore, Michael S. 1980b. "Responsibility and the Unconscious." *Southern California Law Review* 53: pp. 1563–663.

Moore, Michael S. 1981. "The Semantics of Judging." *Southern California Law Review* 54: pp. 151–295.

Moore, Michael S. 1982a. "Moral Reality." *Wisconsin Law Review* (1982): pp. 1061–156.

Moore, Michael S. 1982b. "What's Wrong with the Laws that Acquitted John Hinckley?" Lead editorial, *San Diego Union*, July 4. Reprinted in *Los Angeles Daily Journal*, July 10.

Moore, Michael S. 1982c. "Closet Retributivism." *USC Cites* (Spring–Summer): pp. 9–16.

Moore, Michael S. 1983a. "Drunk-Driving Law: Precise is Vague?" *Los Angeles Times*, June 8.

Moore, Michael S. 1983b. "Rebalancing the Scales of Justice: Gravity of the Punishment Must Fit the Offense." *Los Angeles Times*, July 3.

Moore, Michael S. 1983c. "The Relevance of Philosophy to Law and Psychiatry." *Int'l J. of Law and Psychiatry* 6: pp. 177–92.

Moore, Michael S. 1983d. "The Unity of Self." In *Nature Animated*, edited by Michael Ruse. The Netherlands: D. Reidel Publishing Co. (Western Ontario Series in the Philosophy of Science).

Moore, Michael S. 1983e. "The Nature of Psychoanalytic Explanation." Revised and expanded. In *Mind and Medicine: Explanation and Evaluation in Psychiatry and the Biomedical Sciences*, edited by Lawrence Laudan. Los Angeles: University of California Press. (Pittsburgh Series in the Philosophy of Science).

Moore, Michael S. 1984a. "The Contributions of Lawyers to the American Legislative Process, and Their Education for that Role." *Seoul Law Journal* 25: pp. 8–38.

Moore, Michael S. 1984b. "The Need for a Theory of Legal Theories: Assessing Pragmatic Instrumentalism." *Cornell Law Review* 69: pp. 988–1013.

Moore, Michael S. 1984c. "The Limits of Legislation." *USC Cites* (Fall): pp. 23–32.

Moore, Michael S. 1984d. *Law and Psychiatry: Rethinking the Relationship*. Cambridge: Cambridge University Press.

Moore, Michael S. 1985a. "The Moral and Metaphysical Sources of the Criminal Law." In *NOMOS xxvii: Criminal Justice*, Annual Volume of the American Society for Political and Legal Philosophy, edited by John Chapman and Ronald Pennock. New York: New York University Press.
Moore, Michael S. 1985b. "A Natural Law Theory of Interpretation." *Southern California Law Review* 58: pp. 277–398.
Moore, Michael S. 1985c. "Causation and the Excuses." *California Law Review* 73: pp. 1091–149. Reprinted in *Justification and Excuse: Comparative Perspectives*, Vol. II, edited by Albin Eser and George Fletcher, Freiburg, Germany: Max Planck Institute.
Moore, Michael S. 1985d. "Politics Is Not the Basis for Judging the Judges." *Los Angeles Times*, July 29.
Moore, Michael S. 1985e. "Justices' Personal Values Must at Times Give Way." *Los Angeles Times*, July 30.
Moore, Michael S. 1985f. "Rose Bird Should Go." *Los Angeles Times*, July 31.
Moore, Michael S. 1985g. "The Determinist Theory of Excuses." (Review of Norval Morris, *Madness and the Criminal Law*). *Ethics* 95: pp. 909–19.
Moore, Michael S. 1986a. "Activist Judging and Retention Elections." *USC Law* (Fall–Winter): pp. 24–7.
Moore, Michael S. 1986b. "An Invitation to Senseless AIDS Bias." *Los Angeles Times*, June 29.
Moore, Michael S. 1986c. "How Much Credence to Give to Fear Itself?" *Los Angeles Times*, July 17.
Moore, Michael S. 1986d. "A Judicial Balance of Power vs. Duty." *Los Angeles Times*, October 7.
Moore, Michael S. 1986e. "Returning the Court to Greatness." *Los Angeles Times*, November 6.
Moore, Michael S. 1987a. "Metaphysics, Epistemology, and Legal Theory." *Southern California Law Review* 60: pp. 453–506.
Moore, Michael S. 1987b. "Thomson's Preliminaries About Causation and Rights." *Chicago-Kent Law Review* 63: pp. 497–521.
Moore, Michael S. 1987c. "Intentions and Mens Rea." In *Issues in Contemporary Legal Philosophy: The Influence of H. L. A. Hart*, edited by Ruth Gavison. Oxford: Clarendon Press.
Moore, Michael S. 1987d. "Precedent, Induction, and Ethical Generalization." In *Precedent in Law*, edited by Laurence Goldstein. Oxford: Oxford University Press.
Moore, Michael S. 1987e. "The Moral Worth of Retribution." In *Character, Responsibility, and the Emotions*, edited by Ferdinand Schoeman. Cambridge: Cambridge University Press. Reprinted in *Philosophy of Law*, edited by Joel Feinberg and Hyman Gross, 4th edn. (1990), 5th edn. 1995; in *Philosophy of Law*, edited by Joel Feinberg and Jules Coleman, 6th edn. 2000; and in *Punishment and Rehabilitation*, edited by Jeffrie Murphy, 3rd edn. 1995. Belmont: Wadsworth.
Moore, Michael S. 1987f. "Judge Bork, a Contradiction in Terms." *Los Angeles Times*, September 18.
Moore, Michael S. 1987g. "State Supreme Court Lets the Law Have Its Day." *Los Angeles Times*, October 26.
Moore, Michael S. 1988a. "Ed Meese: If He Can't Respect Office, Why Stay?" *Los Angeles Times*, March 31.
Moore, Michael S. 1988b. "Mind, Brain and Unconscious." In *Mind, Psychoanalysis, and Science*, edited by Peter Clark and Crispin Wright. Oxford: Basil Blackwell, Ltd.
Moore, Michael S. 1988c. "Originalist Theories of Constitutional Interpretation." *Cornell Law Review* 73: pp. 364–70.
Moore, Michael S. 1988d. "The Exportability of the Madisonian Compromise." *USC Law* (Fall–Winter). Reprinted in *The Influence of the U.S. Constitution on Pacific Nations*, edited by F. E. Cameron, Hawaii: Kapalua Pacific Center.
Moore, Michael S. 1989a. "The Constitution as Hard Law." *Constitutional Commentary* 6: pp. 51–67.
Moore, Michael S. 1989b. "The Written Constitution and Interpretivism." *Harvard Journal of Law and Public Policy* 12: pp. 3–14.
Moore, Michael S. 1989c. "Review of Fingarette, *Heavy Drinking*." *Ethics* 99: pp. 660–61.
Moore, Michael S. 1989d. "Roe v. Wade Was No Misstep." *Los Angeles Times*, April 24.

Moore, Michael S. 1989e. "Law, Authority, and Razian Reasons." *Southern California Law Review* 62: pp. 827–96.
Moore, Michael S. 1989f. "The Interpretive Turn in Modern Theory: A Turn for the Worse?" *Stanford Law Review* 41: pp. 871–957.
Moore, Michael S. 1989g. "Do We Have an Unwritten Constitution?" *Southern California Law Review* 63: pp. 107–39.
Moore, Michael S. 1989h. "Torture and the Balance of Evils." *Israel Law Review* 23: pp. 280–344.
Moore, Michael S. 1989i. "Sandelian Anti-Liberalism." *California Law Review* 77: pp. 539–51. Reprinted (in Italian translation) in *Comunitarismoe Liberalismo*, edited by Alessandro Ferrara, Rome: Editori Riuniti. 1992.
Moore, Michael S. 1990a. "Choice, Character, and Excuse." *Social Philosophy and Policy* 7: pp. 219–48. Reprinted in *Crime, Culpability, and Remedy*, edited by Ellen Frankel-Paul, Oxford: Basil Blackwell, Ltd.
Moore, Michael S. 1990b. "A Theory of Criminal Law Theories." In *Tel Aviv University Studies in Law*, Vol. 10, edited by Dan Friedmann. Tel Aviv: Tel Aviv University Press.
Moore, Michael S. 1990c. "Introduction" to the American edition of H. L. A. Hart's *The Concept of Law*. Birmingham: Gryphon Classics.
Moore, Michael S. 1991a. "Three Concepts of Rules." *Harvard Journal of Law and Public Policy* 14: pp. 771–95.
Moore, Michael S. 1991b. "Unnatural Brawl over Natural Law." *Los Angeles Times*, September 3.
Moore, Michael S. 1991c. "Sanford Kadish." *California Law Review* 79: pp. 1401–7.
Moore, Michael S. 1992a. "Law as a Functional Kind." In *Natural Law Theories*, edited by Robert George. Oxford: Oxford University Press.
Moore, Michael S. 1992b. "Moral Reality Revisited." *Michigan Law Review* 90: pp. 2424–533.
Moore, Michael S. 1993a. "Foreseeing Harm Opaquely." In *Action and Value in Criminal Law*, edited by John Gardner, Jeremy Horder, and Stephen Shute. Oxford: Oxford University Press.
Moore, Michael S. 1993b. "Justifying Retributivism." *Israel Law Review* 24: pp. 15–49.
Moore, Michael S. 1993c. *Act and Crime: The Philosophy of Action and Its Implications for Criminal Law*. Oxford: Oxford University Press, Clarendon Law Series. Paperback edition, OUP, 2010.
Moore, Michael S. 1994a. "Interpreting Interpretation." (In Hebrew). *Tel Aviv University Law Review* 18: pp. 359–86. Reprinted (in English) in *Interpretation and Law*, edited by Andrei Marmor, Oxford: Oxford University Press.
Moore, Michael S. 1994b. "The Independent Moral Significance of Wrongdoing." *Journal of Contemporary Legal Issues* 1: pp. 1–45.
Moore, Michael S. 1994c. "More on Act and Crime." *University of Pennsylvania Law Review* 142: pp. 1749–840.
Moore, Michael S. 1995a. "Good Without God." In *Natural Law, Liberalism, and Morality*, edited by Robert George. Oxford: Oxford University Press.
Moore, Michael S. 1995b. "Prima Facie Moral Culpability." *Boston University Law Review* 75: pp. 319–33.
Moore, Michael S. 1995c. "Plain Meaning and Linguistics—A Case Study." *Washington University Law Quarterly* 73: pp. 1253–62.
Moore, Michael S. 1995d. "Joel Feinberg." *Arizona Law Review* 37: pp. 7–9.
Moore, Michael S. 1995e. "Judicial Logic—A Contradiction in Terms?" *Penn Law Journal* XXX, No. 1.
Moore, Michael S. 1996. "The Dead Hand of Constitutional Tradition." *Harvard Journal of Law and Public Policy* 19: pp. 263–74.
Moore, Michael S. 1997a. "Legal Principles Revisited." *Iowa Law Review* 82: pp. 867–91.
Moore, Michael S. 1997b. *Placing Blame: A General Theory of the Criminal Law*. Oxford: Oxford University Press. Paperback edition, OUP, 2010.
Moore, Michael S. 1998a. "Liberty and Drugs." In *Morality, Legality and Drugs*, edited by Pablo De Greiff. Ithaca: Cornell University Press.

Moore, Michael S. 1998b. "Liberty and Supererogation." *Jahrbuch für Recht und Ethik* 6: pp 111–43. (*Yearbook for Law and Ethics*).
Moore, Michael S. 1998c. "Hart's Concluding Scientific Postscript." *Legal Theory* 4: pp. 301–27.
Moore, Michael S. 1998d. "Causation and Responsibility." *Social Philosophy and Policy* 16: pp. 1–51. Reprinted in *Responsibility*, edited by Ellen Frankel Paul, Fred D. Miller, and Jeffrey Paul, Cambridge: Cambridge University Press.
Moore, Michael S. 1999a. "Victims and Retribution: A Reply to Professor Fletcher." *Buffalo Criminal Law Review* 3: pp. 101–25. Reprinted (in German translation) in *Die Stellung des Opfers im Strafrechtssystem*, edited by Bernd Schunemann and Markus D. Dubber, Berlin: Carl Heymanns Verlag.
Moore, Michael S. 1999b. *Foundations of Criminal Law*, co-edited with Leo Katz and Stephen Morse, Oxford Interdisciplinary Readers in Law Series, New York: Oxford University Press. Reprinted by Foundation Press, Mineola, NY, 2000.
Moore, Michael S. 2000a. *Educating Oneself in Public: Critical Essays in Jurisprudence*. Oxford: Oxford University Press.
Moore, Michael S. 2000b. "The Metaphysics of Causal Intervention." *California Law Review* 88: pp. 827–77.
Moore, Michael S. 2000c. "Theories of Areas of Law." *San Diego Law Review* 37: pp. 731–41.
Moore, Michael S. 2000d. "Remembrance of Things Past." *Southern California Law Review* 74: pp. 239–50.
Moore, Michael S. 2001a. "Law as Justice," *Social Philosophy and Policy* 18: pp. 115–45. Reprinted in *Natural Law and Modern Moral Philosophy*, edited by Ellen Frankel Paul, Fred D. Miller, and Jeffrey Paul, Cambridge: Cambridge University Press.
Moore, Michael S. 2001b. "Justifying the Natural Law Theory of Constitutional Interpretation." *Fordham Law Review* 69: pp. 2087–117. Translated into Spanish as "Una Justification de la Teoria Iusnaturalista de la Interpretacion Constitutional," *Annuario Da Facultada de Pereito da Universidad da Coruna* (Coruna, Spain, 2005).
Moore, Michael S. 2001c. "Natural Rights, Judicial Review, and Constitutional Interpretation." In *Legal Interpretation, Judicial Powers, and Democracy*, edited by Jeffrey Goldsworthy and Tom Campbell. Aldershot, UK: Ashgate Publishing Ltd.
Moore, Michael S., and Heidi Hurd. 2002a. "Negligence in the Air." In *Negligence in the Law, Theoretical Inquiries in Law*, Vol. 3, edited by Ariel Porat. Jerusalem: Graphit Press.
Moore, Michael S. 2002b. "Legal Reality: A Naturalist Approach to Legal Ontology." *Law and Philosophy* 21: pp. 619–705.
Moore, Michael S. 2002c. "Actus Reus." In *Encyclopedia of Crime and Justice*, edited by Joshua Dressler, 2nd edn. New York: Macmillan.
Moore, Michael S. 2002d. "Causation." In *Encyclopedia of Crime and Justice*, edited by Joshua Dressler, 2nd edn. New York: Macmillan.
Moore, Michael S. 2002e. "Retributivism." In *Encyclopedia of Crime and Justice*, edited by Joshua Dressler, 2nd edn. New York: Macmillan.
Moore, Michael S. 2003a. "The Plain Truth About Legal Truth." *Harvard Journal of Law and Public Policy* 26: pp. 23–47.
Moore, Michael S. 2003b. "For What Must We Pay? Causation and Counterfactual Baselines." *San Diego Law Review* 40: pp. 1181–272.
Moore, Michael S. 2004a. "The Destruction of the World Trade Center and the Law on Event-Identity." *Proceedings of The Royal Institute of Philosophy (Philosophia Supplementary Volume)*. In *Action and Agency*, edited by John Hyman and Helen Steward. Cambridge: Cambridge University Press.
Moore, Michael S., and Heidi Hurd. 2004b. "Punishing Hatred and Prejudice." *Stanford Law Review* 56: pp. 1081–146.
Moore, Michael S. 2004c. *Objectivity in Law and Ethics: Essays in Moral and Legal Ontology*. Aldershot: Ashgate Publishing Ltd and Rutland: Dartmouth Press.

Moore, Michael S. 2005a. "Causal Relata." In *Philosophia Practica Universalis: Festschrift for Joachim Hruschka*, edited by Sharon Byrd and Jan C. Joerden, *Annual Review of Law and Ethics* 13: pp. 589–641.

Moore, Michael S. 2005b. "Freedom." *Harvard Journal of Law and Public Policy* 29: pp. 9–26.

Moore, Michael S. 2007a. "Can Objectivity Be Grounded in Semantics?" *Social, Political, and Legal Philosophy* 2: pp. 235–60.

Moore, Michael S. 2007b. "Four Reflections on Law and Morality." *William and Mary Law Review* 48: pp. 1523–69.

Moore, Michael S. 2007c. "Causing, Aiding, and the Superfluity of Accomplice Liability." *University of Pennsylvania Law Review* 156: pp. 395–452.

Moore, Michael S and Larry Alexander 2007d. "Deontological Ethics." In the *Stanford Encyclopedia of Philosophy*. June 15. Online at <http://plato.stanford.edu/entries/ethics-deontological/>.

Moore, Michael S. 2008a. "Patrolling the Borders of Consequentialist Justification." *Law and Philosophy* 27: pp. 35–96.

Moore, Michael S. 2008b. "Morality in Eighth Amendment Jurisprudence." *Harvard Journal of Law and Public Policy* 31: pp. 47–65.

Moore, Michael S. 2009a. "Editor's Introduction: The Nature of Singularist Theories of Causation." *The Monist* 92: pp. 3–22.

Moore, Michael S. 2009b. "Counterfactual Dependence as a Non-Causal Desert-Determiner." *Australian Journal of Legal Philosophy* 34: pp. 1–52.

Moore, Michael S. 2009c. "A Tale of Two Theories." *Criminal Justice Ethics* 28: pp. 27–48.

Moore, Michael S. 2009d. *Causation and Responsibility: An Essay in Law, Morals, and Metaphysics*. Oxford: Oxford University Press. Paperback edition, OUP, 2010. Spanish edition, Madrid: Marcel Pons, 2011.

Moore, Michael S. 2010. "Renewed Questions About the Causal Theory of Action." In *Causing Human Action: New Perspectives on the Causal Theory of Action*, edited by Jesus H. Aguilar and Andrei A. Buckareff. Cambridge: MIT Press, a Bradford Book.

Moore, Michael S. 2011a. "Libet's Challenge(s) to Responsible Agency." In *Conscious Will and Responsibility: A Tribute to Benjamin Libet*, edited by Walter Sinnott-Armstrong and Lynn Nadel. Oxford: Oxford University Press.

Moore, Michael S. 2011b. "Intention as a Marker of Moral Responsibility and Legal Punishability." In *The Philosophical Foundations of Criminal Law*, edited by Antony Duff and Stuart Green. Oxford: Oxford University Press.

Moore, Michael S. 2011c. "Causation in the Law." In *The Oxford Handbook for Philosophy and the Criminal Law*, edited by John Deigh and David Dolinko. Oxford: Oxford University Press.

Moore, Michael S., and Heidi Hurd. 2011d. "Punishing the Awkward, the Stupid, the Weak, and the Selfish: The Culpability of Negligence." *Criminal Law and Philosophy* 5: pp. 147–98.

Moore, Michael S., and Heidi Hurd. 2011e. "The Culpability of Negligence." In *Crime, Punishment, and Responsibility*, edited by Rowan Cruft, Matt Kramer, and Mark Reiff, pp. 311–48. Oxford: Oxford University Press.

Moore, Michael S. 2011f. "Causation Revisited." *Rutgers Law Review* 42: pp. 451–509. (Symposium issue on Michael Moore's *Causation and Responsibility*).

Moore, Michael S. 2012a. "Four Friendly Critics: A Response." *Legal Theory* 18: pp. 491–542. (Symposium issue on Michael Moore's *Causation and Responsibility*).

Moore, Michael S. 2012b. "Targeted Killings and the Morality of Hard Choices." In *Targeted Killings: Law and Morality in an Asymmetrical World*, edited by Andrew Altman, Claire Finkelstein, and Jens David Ohlin, pp. 434–66. Oxford: Oxford University Press.

Moore, Michael S. 2012c. "The Various Relations Between Law and Morality in Contemporary Legal Philosophy." *Ratio Juris* 25: pp. 435–71. (Symposium issue on Michael Moore's Perspective on the Relation Between Law and Morality).

Moore, Michael S. 2012d. "Moore's Truths About Causation and Responsibility: A Reply to Alexander and Ferzan." *Criminal Law and Philosophy* 6: pp. 445–62.

Moore, Michael S., and Larry Alexander. 2012e."Deontological Ethics." In *Stanford Encyclopedia of Philosophy*, edited by Edward N. Zalta, 2nd edn.

Moore, Michael S. 2012f. "The Specialness of the General Part of the Criminal Law." In *The Sanctity of Life and the Criminal Law: Essays in Honour of Glanville Williams*, edited by Dennis Baker. Cambridge: Cambridge University Press.

Moore, Michael S. 2012g. "Responsible Choices, Desert-Based Legal Institutions, and the Challenges of Contemporary Neuroscience." *Social Philosophy and Policy* 29: pp. 233–79.

Moore, Michael S. 2013a. "Author's Reply." (Response to Helen Beebee, Phil Dowe, and Stephen Mumford). *Jurisprudence* 4: pp. 121–37. (Symposium issue on Michael Moore's *Causation and Responsibility*).

Moore, Michael S. 2013b. "Further Thoughts on Causation (And Related Topics) Prompted by Fifteen Critics." In *Critical Essays on Causation and Responsibility*, edited by Benedikt Kahmen and Markus Stepanians, pp. 333–416. Berlin, Germany: D. Gruyter Gmbh.

Moore, Michael S. 2013c. "Yaffe's Attempts." *Legal Theory* 19: pp. 136–77.

Moore, Michael S. 2014a. "Truth-makers for Propositions of Law and for Propositions About Law." In Spanish in *Law and Truth*, edited by Jorge Cordio and German Sucar, Madrid: Marcial Pons. Reprinted in English in *Vagueness and the Law*, edited by Geert Keil and Ralf Poscher. Oxford: Oxford University Press.

Moore, Michael S. 2014b. "Compatibilism(s) for Neuroscientists." In *Law and the Philosophy of Action*, edited by Enrique Villanueva, pp. 1-59, Rodopi Philosophical Studies.

Moore, Michael S. 2014c. "Liberty's Constraints on What Should Be Criminalized." In *Criminalization: The Political Morality of the Criminal Law*, edited by A. Duff et al., pp. 182-212, Oxford: Oxford University Press.

Moore, Michael S. 2014d. "The Neuroscience of Volitional Incapacity." In *Law and Neuroscience*: State of the Art, edited by Dennis Patterson. Oxford: Oxford University Press.

Moore, Michael S. 2014e. "Stephen Morse on the Fundamental Psycho-Legal Error." *Criminal Law and Philosophy* forthcoming.

Moore, Michael S. 2014f. "The Quest for a Responsible Responsibility Test: Norwegian Insanity Law After Breivik." Report to the Norwegian Parliamentary Commission on Revision of the Laws of Norway on Insanity, *Criminal Law and Philosophy*, 9: pp. 645-93.

Moore, Michael S., and Heidi Hurd. 2015a. "The Mens Rea of Accomplice Liability." *Social Policy and Philosophy* 32 (forthcoming).

Moore, Michael S. 2015b. "Responses and Appreciations." This volume.

Moore, Michael S. 2015c. "Liberty and the Constitution," Duke Law Journal, forthcoming.

Moore, Michael S. 2015d. "Nothing but a Pack of Neurons." In Neurolaw, edited by Bebhinn Donnelly, Cambridge: Cambridge University Press.

Name Index

Please note that page references to footnotes will be followed by the letter 'n.'

Subject Index

Please note that "MSM" refers to Michael S. Moore. Page references to footnotes will be followed by the letter 'n.'